THE
HOLY BIBLE

International Standard Version

NEW TESTAMENT

DAVIDSON PRESS

23621 La Palma Ave., H-460
Yorba Linda, CA 92887-5536

THE
HOLY BIBLE

International Standard Version

NEW TESTAMENT

The Holy Bible: International Standard Version®
U.S. English Imprint
The New Testament with CD-ROM
Copyright © 1999 Davidson Press, Inc.
ALL RIGHTS RESERVED INTERNATIONALLY.

Final Release Edition 1.00
Version Number: 1.00
Build Number: 1
Build Date: 15 February 1999

Reference Number: NT 1.00
Release Date: 15 May 1999
CAM Format: Logos, PDF, SGML, STEP, XML
Document Format: MSWord 7; Quark Xpress

Old Testament citations in the ISV New Testament conform to *Old Testament Quotations in the New Testament: A Complete Survey*, Archer, Gleason L. and Chirichigno, Gregory C., eds., (Chicago: Moody Press, 1983). Printed in the USA and published by Davidson Press, Inc., 23621 La Palma Avenue, #H-460, Yorba Linda, CA 92887-5536. Please direct comments, critiques, and/or notices of errata to Davidson Press, Inc., at the above address. Visit our web site at http://davidsonpress.com.

Library of Congress Catalog Card Number: 98-88364
ISBN 1-891833-11-1 Casebound (Bible Explorer CD) US $29.95
ISBN 1-891833-13-8 Casebound (Logos Library CD) US $29.95
ISBN 1-891833-12-X Bonded Leather US $49.95

23621 La Palma Avenue, #H-460,
Yorba Linda, CA 92887-5536
email: info@davidsonpress.com

Special thanks to: the Ernesto and Jessie Belante Family Trust, Robert J. Cannone, Dan Garner, Douglas E. Hartman, the Ellen F. Woods Trust, and the Joshua Davidson Charitable Remainder Annuity Trust. Their generous support made the production of this work possible. Cover Design: Larry Vilott (copyright © 1999 Davidson Press, Inc.). Cover Photo: Sunset over Earth © 1993 Corel Corporation. Layout: Auto-Graphics, Inc., Pomona, CA.

A portion of the sale of this copy of the ISV New Testament benefits the Learn Foundation and its efforts to bring up-to-date tools for biblical study and research to a new generation.

Table of Contents

(Abridged)

Abbreviations Used in the ISV New Testament

Aram.	Aramaic language	LXX	Septuagint, Greek version of the OT
c.	*circa*, about		
cf.	*confer*, compare	ms., mss.	manuscript(s)
ch., chs.	chapter(s)	MT	The Hebrew pointed Masoretic Text of the OT
e.g.	*exempli gratia*, for example		
ff.	following (verses, pages)	NT	New Testament
Gk.	Greek language of the NT	OT	Old Testament
Heb.	Hebrew languages, usually of the Masoretic Text of the OT	Or	An alternate rendering
		p., pp.	page(s)
		pl.	plural
I.e.	*Id est*, that is	sing.	singular
Lit.	Literally	v., vv.	verse(s)

Book Abbreviations for the ISV Bible

Genesis	Gen	Nahum	Nah
Exodus	Exod	Habakkuk	Hab
Leviticus	Lev	Zephaniah	Zeph
Numbers	Num	Haggai	Hag
Deuteronomy	Deut	Zechariah	Zech
Joshua	Josh	Malachi	Mal
Judges	Judg	Matthew	Matt
Ruth	Ruth	Mark	Mark
1 Samuel	1Sam	Luke	Luke
2 Samuel	2Sam	John	John
1 Kings	1Kings	Acts	Acts
2 Kings	2Kings	Romans	Rom
1 Chronicles	1Chr	1 Corinthians	1Cor
2 Chronicles	2Chr	2 Corinthians	2Cor
Ezra	Ezra	Galatians	Gal
Nehemiah	Neh	Ephesians	Eph
Esther	Esth	Philippians	Phil
Job	Job	Colossians	Col
Psalms	Ps	1 Thessalonians	1Thes
Proverbs	Prov	2 Thessalonians	2Thes
Ecclesiastes	Eccl	1 Timothy	1Tim
Song of Solomon	Song	2 Timothy	2Tim
Isaiah	Isa	Titus	Titus
Jeremiah	Jer	Philemon	Phlm
Lamentations	Lam	Hebrews	Heb
Ezekiel	Ezek	James	James
Daniel	Dan	1 Peter	1Peter
Hosea	Hos	2 Peter	2Peter
Joel	Joel	1 John	1John
Amos	Amos	2 John	2John
Obadiah	Obad	3 John	3John
Jonah	Jonah	Jude	Jude
Micah	Mic	Revelation	Rev

Table of Contents
(Expanded)

Matthew

Matthew

Matthew

Mark

Luke

John

John

Publisher's Preface
to the
International Standard Version
New Testament

 The Bible isn't just one book. Perhaps we should include a subtitle ("The Encyclopedia of Divine Wisdom") because the Bible is actually composed of 66 separate works written by over 40 authors over a period of about two thousand years. It displays a remarkable harmony of thought, historical content, intent and expression.

For the last three millennia, the Bible has exercised an unparalleled influence on the lives of individuals and nations. People of faith throughout the centuries have recorded the revelation of God pertaining to the affairs of daily life. The experiences of prophets, kings, and common people have been communicated through the written text of Scripture.

Jewish and Christian scholars have been concerned to make sure that the Hebrew, Aramaic, and Greek texts would be communicated to each new generation. Even though governments and rulers have attempted to prevent the distribution of the translated Bible in many periods of history, faithful scholars such as John Wycliffe and William Tyndale gave their very lives to translate and distribute the books of the Bible. In every period of revival and renewal in the church, the Bible was central.

And now for a new millennium, this major English language translation of the Bible embodies the best results of modern scholarship as to the meaning of Scripture, and it expresses this meaning in clear and natural English. The International Standard Version® (ISV®), produced for the twenty-first century by The Learn Foundation of Yorba Linda, California, offers an exciting opportunity to read and study the Scriptures in a fresh, new way.

The ISV is "international" in that slang and regionalisms are avoided, and "standard" in that it is designed for public worship, for church school curricula, for religious publishing, and for both personal and group study. And with the ISV text, study tools, and software readily available to the public via the Internet, the ISV provides new opportunities for in-depth study of God's Word anywhere in the world, by anyone, and at any time.

The New Testament you hold in your hands is the first portion of the complete ISV Bible to be made available in print. A combined Old and New Testament edition will be released in the year 2000. As the Old Testament books are completed, they can be found on the Davidson Press website at http://davidsonpress.com.

Charles Welty, Publisher
Davidson Press, Inc.
Yorba Linda, CA

The Uniqueness of the ISV

With so many English language Bible translations available today, the reader is faced with an important question: "What distinguishes the ISV from other English language translations?" The ISV offers five features that distinguish it from other recent English language translations:

1. The ISV Is a New Translation, Not a Revision

The ISV is a totally new work translated directly from the original languages of Scripture and derived from no other English translation. The ISV was produced by Bible scholars who believe that "All Scripture is inspired by God and is useful for teaching, for reproof, for correction, and for training in righteousness" (2 Timothy 3:16 ISV). The ISV takes advantage not only of the most ancient manuscripts available, but also of the most recent archaeological discoveries. The translators of the ISV have selected the English equivalent that most closely reflects the meaning of the original Hebrew, Aramaic, and Greek texts.

2. The ISV Is a Computer-Friendly Translation

The ISV is the first English Bible conceived, designed, translated, and formatted primarily for a computer-literate generation. It is being produced entirely in a computer aided media (CAM) format. In its electronic format, the ISV will be the first Bible translation ever published with version numbers. English language Bible readers who have access to the Internet's World Wide Web will be able to read the ISV under the Learn Foundation's tradename *International Standard Version (Internet)*® (ISVi®) at the Learn Foundation's web site at http://isv.org. The latest electronic version of the ISVi will also be available in compressed formats compatible with many contemporary Bible research software programs. Printed copies of the ISV also contain version numbers. (See the reverse of the title page for the version number of this edition.)

3. The ISV Is Sensitive to Poetic Forms in the Original Text

The ISV treats subtle nuances of the original texts with special care. For example, several passages of the Bible appear to have been rendered in poetic form when first penned by their authors. The ISV has meticulously crafted these original passages as true poems—thus communicating a sense of their original literary form as well as translating the original intent of the author. As a result, passages that would have been read as poetry by first century readers actually appear in poetic form in the ISV. For example, see Christ's complaint to the Pharisees recorded in Luke 7:32 and 35 (page 152), the Christ Hymn of Philippians 2:6-11 (pages 139-140), the Apostle Paul's description of love in 1 Corinthians 13 (page 388), the Common Confession of 1 Timothy 3:16 (page 465), Paul's Hymn to Christ in Titus 3:4-7 (page 479), Paul's witty quote of the ancient Greek poet Epimenides in Titus 1:12 (page 478), and the "trustworthy sayings" of Paul in 1 Timothy 1:15 (page 463), 1 Timothy 3:1 (page 464), 1 Timothy 4:8 (page 466), and 2 Timothy 2:11 (page 473).

4. The ISV is Sensitive to Literary Forms in the Original Text

The ISV treats synoptic parallels with special sensitivity. Historical narratives in the Gospels of Matthew, Mark, and Luke were carefully examined in the original Greek text in order to compare each occurrence in the text where the narratives appeared to describe similar instances. Unlike all other English language translations available today, the ISV translates each separate synoptic instance with exact translational parity in each textual occurrence. In those parallel passages where the Greek text occurs with word-for-word synoptic identity, readers will discover that the ISV translates these passages into word-for-word English equivalents. In those parallel passages where the Greek text in the parallel passages approaches, but does not reach, a word-for-word identity, the ISV has adjusted the English language translation to reflect the similar, but not exact, nature of the parallel passages. To the best of our knowledge and belief, this level of translational accuracy *has rarely been attained* in any English language translation produced to date.

The reader will notice—particularly in the four Gospels and in the Book of Acts—that the ISV usually shifts its style of English composition in order to utilize contractions when translating quoted words of a speaker, even though the ISV generally avoids the use of contractions when rendering historical narratives or written correspondence. The Committee intended that a sense of the informal be communicated when people are speaking and that a sense of the formal be communicated when people are writing.

5. The ISV Is a Literal-Idiomatic Translation

The translation theory behind the ISV is different from theories employed in previous Bible translations. Traditionally, two basic methods of Bible translation have been used. The older method (and for many centuries practically the only method used) has been labeled "literal" or "formal equivalent."

This type of translation allows readers to identify as fully as possible with the source languages of Scripture and to understand as much as they can of the Bible's customs, manners of thought, and means of expression.

The other method is termed "idiomatic" or "functional equivalent." The goal of an idiomatic translation is to achieve the closest natural equivalent in modern language to match the ideas of the original text. Idiomatic translations have little or no concern for maintaining the grammatical forms, sentence structure, and consistency of word usage of the source languages.

All major translations of the Bible fall somewhere on a scale between complete formal equivalence and complete functional equivalence. Some of these translations are quite literal (e.g., the King James Version [KJV], the New King James Version [NKJV®], the American Standard Version of 1901 [ASV], the New American Standard Bible [NASB®], the Revised Standard Version [RSV®], and the New Revised Standard Version [NRSV®]). Other translations lean toward the idiomatic end of the spectrum (e.g., the New International Version [NIV®], the New English Bible [NEB®], the Revised English Bible [REB®], the Good News Bible [GNB®], the New Living Translation [NLT®], and the Contemporary English Version [CEV®]).

It is clear that each of these methods of Bible translation has its weaknesses. Competent Bible translators have always recognized that a strictly literal translation of the words of Scripture can be misleading. For example, "the wicked will not stand in the judgment" might be interpreted as proving that evil people actually would not be judged. Hence literalness is not always equivalent to accuracy.

On the other hand, the limitations of idiomatic translations are also obvious. Such translations frequently tend to cast the words of Scripture into new molds that convey the ideas in a significantly different spirit or emphasis. Idiomatic translations have, in a sense, a commentary built into them; they represent a choice made by the translators as to what the *translators* think a passage means. For that reason, an idiomatic translation is easier to read but less reliable for careful study.

A good translation will steer a careful course between word-for-word translation and interpretation under the guise of translating. In other words, a good translation will be both *reliable* and *readable*. The best translation, then, is one that is both accurate and idiomatic at the same time. It will make every effort to reproduce the culture and exact meaning of the text without sacrificing readability. The Learn Foundation calls this type of translation "literal-idiomatic."

Of these three basic types of translation—literal, literal-idiomatic, and idiomatic—the translators of the ISV have, without hesitation, opted for the second. This is not because it happens to be the middle option, simply avoiding extremes, but because the literal-idiomatic translation is the only choice that avoids the dangers of over-literalness and of over-interpretation discussed above. Teaching biblical truth demands extreme fidelity to the original text of Scripture. However, a translation of the Bible need not sacrifice English clarity in order to maintain a close correspondence to the source languages. The goal of the ISV, therefore, has been both accuracy and excellence in communication.

How the ISV Is Being Produced

The Foundation has provided for the actual work of translating by appointing:

a.   A *Committee on Translation*, which is overseeing the work of translation from beginning to end, including the supervision of all consultants. These individuals have been selected for their competence in biblical studies and on the basis of an inter-denominational representation of the worldwide Christian community.

b.   A *General Editor*, who is responsible for organizing and directing the work of the Committee on Translation. The General Editor continually evaluates the project in terms of the quality of the translation and the efficiency with which the work is being pursued.

c.   *Associate Editors* for the Old and New Testaments, who are especially capable in the biblical languages and exegesis. Associate Editors coordinate all Committee procedures related to their areas of expertise.

After the Committee on Translation produces draft translations of the books of the Bible, a select group of *Contributing Scholars* carefully reviews the drafts and offers suggestions for their improvement. At the same time, *English Review Scholars* check the translation for adherence to modern literary and communication standards and suggest stylistic improvements for the consideration of the Committee on Translation.

Finally, a *Board of Reference* reviews the translation in terms of its usefulness in preaching, teaching, evangelism, and educational materials. The Board of Reference is comprised of individuals from national Christian organizations, administrative officers from institutions of higher education, and individuals who have rendered significant Christian service on regional, national, or international levels.

Principles of Translation Used in the ISV

The following 25 principles of translation are being followed in producing the ISV.

1. For the Old Testament, the Masoretic text as published in the latest edition of the *Biblia Hebraica Stuttgartensia* is used as the base text, in consultation with other ancient Hebrew texts (such as the Dead Sea Scrolls and the Samaritan Pentateuch) and ancient versions (the Septuagint, the Vulgate, the Syriac Peshitta, and the Targums). Restraint is exercised in the use of conjectural emendations from the Masoretic Hebrew text. All significant departures from *Stuttgartensia*, as well as all significant textual variants, are indicated in footnotes.

2. For the New Testament, the 27th edition of the Nestle-Aland *Novum Testamentum Graece* and the fourth corrected edition of the United Bible Societies' *Greek New Testament* are the base text. All significant textual variants are indicated in footnotes.

3. The ISV uses literary English, avoiding idioms that come and go, and is as traditional as necessary. Terms such as "justification," "redemption," and "atonement" have been retained. Where the Committee on Translation determines that a word-for-word translation is unacceptable, a change can be made in the direction of a more current language idiom. In these instances, the more literal rendering is indicated in a footnote.

4. When the text can be understood in different ways, an attempt is made either to provide a rendering in which the same ambiguity appears in English, or to decide the more likely sense and translate accordingly. In the latter case, a footnote indicates the alternative understanding of the text. In general, the ISV attempts to preserve the relative ambiguity of the text rather than to make positive statements that depend on the translators' judgment or that might reflect theological bias.

5. Whenever possible, a short sentence is translated by a short sentence. However, a very long sentence may be translated in two or more sentences, provided the original intent of the text is accurately reflected.

6. Regarding the Greek tenses, the ISV is guided by observing the grammatical nuances of the Greek in conjunction with the language rules of contemporary English. The policy of distinguishing the Greek imperfect tense from the aorist indicative is followed when the dis-

tinction is grammatically significant and stylistically acceptable. For example, in addition to the progressive imperfect (e.g., "he was proclaiming"), other possible renderings of the imperfect tense include the inceptive imperfect ("he began to proclaim"), the iterative imperfect ("he used to proclaim"), and the customary imperfect ("he would proclaim"). Where the context indicates that no distinction is being made between the imperfect and the aorist, the aoristic imperfect ("he proclaimed") is used.

7. Special attention is given to the translation of Hebrew, Aramaic, and Greek conjunctions. They are rendered in ways that best fit the immediate context or omitted in translation without a footnote when deemed pleonastic.

8. In the Old Testament, the traditional "LORD" is used for *Yahweh*. Where the Hebrew *Adonai Yahweh* occurs, the rendering "Lord GOD" is used. Most titles of God are translated in the text, with the original title placed in a footnote.

9. A noun may be substituted for a pronoun when it is needed for clarity. In these cases, the literal rendering is placed in a footnote.

10. Characteristic features of the original languages, such as order of words and the structure of phrases and clauses, are to be reproduced in translation wherever possible without sacrificing English style.

11. The use of inclusive language is limited to where the meaning of the original text is inclusive of both sexes, and then only without compromising scholarly integrity or good English style. Specifically:

    a. The generic use of "he," "him," "his," "himself," etc. may be used to translate generic third person masculine singular pronouns in Hebrew, Aramaic, and Greek. Person and number are retained: Generally, singulars are not changed to plurals, and third person statements are not changed to second person or first person statements.

    b. Substantival participles such as *ho pisteuon* may be rendered inclusively: "the one who believes," "the person who believes," etc.

    c. "Man," "mankind," "humankind," "humanity," "people," "human beings," etc. may be used to designate the human race or human beings in general.

   d. Hebrew *zaqar* and Greek *aner* are usually translated "man" or "men."

   e. The Greek plural noun *anthropoi* may be translated "people" or "persons" instead of "men." The singular *anthropos* may be translated "person" or "man" when it refers to a male human being.

   f. The Greek indefinite pronoun *tis* may be rendered "anyone," "someone," "a person," "a man," etc.

   g. Pronouns such as the Greek *oudeis* may be rendered "no one," "no person," etc.

   h. When used substantivally, the Hebrew *kol* and the Greek *pas* may be rendered "everyone," "every man," or (in the plural) "all people."

   i. "Son of Man" as a traditional reference to Christ is retained.

   j. Masculine references to God are retained. Because the original languages of Scripture provide no special indication (other than grammatical context, of course) to identify pronouns or predicate nominatives that refer to deity, predicate nominatives and pronouns whose antecedent is God the Father, Jesus, or the Holy Spirit are rarely capitalized.

   k. Descriptive adjectives or titles referring to Satan are not capitalized (e.g., the "devil", the "ruler of the demons, etc.").

   l. The Greek plural noun *adelphoi* is normally rendered "brothers" but may be changed to such expressions as "fellow believers" or "dear friends" in appropriate contexts.

   m. Hebrew *ben* and Greek *huios* may be rendered "child" or "children" and "son" or "sons."

   n. Hebrew *ab* and Greek *pater* may be rendered "parent" or "parents," "ancestor" or "ancestors," "fathers" or "forefathers."

12. The serial comma is used before the last item in a series of persons, places, or things.

13. The relative pronoun "which" is used (1) after a comma, (2) in the expression "that which," and (3) in a question. Otherwise, the pronoun "that" is used.

14. For the future tense, the auxiliary verb "will" is used in the New Testament in place of "shall." In the Old Testament, "shall" may be

used in contexts where the language is imperatival (e.g., "you shall not murder"). With the simple future, "will" is used.

15. The Hebrew and Greek words traditionally translated "Behold!" are rendered in ways that best fit the immediate context and that best represent contemporary English usage (e.g., "Look," "See," "Suddenly," "Here," "Indeed," etc.).

16. Because the Hebrew and Greek equivalents to the English "It came to pass…" are often only transitional words marking the beginning of a new episode, they are sometimes not reproduced. In other instances, the translator may use a more natural English equivalent (e.g., "It was so," "And then," "Later," etc.).

17. In parallel texts such as the Synoptic Gospels, 1 & 2 Samuel, 1 & 2 Kings, and 1 & 2 Chronicles, consistency of rendering is carefully observed.

18. The Hebrew and Greek counterpart for "saying," when pleonastic, may be omitted in translation without a footnote.

19. Marginal notes may include literal renderings (Lit.), alternate renderings (Or), explanatory words or phrases (I.e.), notes on significant textual variants, and other explanatory comments. With textual variants, language such as "the earliest and best manuscripts omit…" or "most manuscripts add…" is avoided. Instead, the following language is used: "other manuscripts lack…," "other manuscripts read…," etc.

20. When the New Testament quotes from the Old Testament, quotation marks surround the quote and a reference to the source of the quotation is footnoted. The sources of New Testament quotations from literature other than the Old Testament are also referenced in footnotes, when known.

21. Italics are not used to indicate words that have been supplied in translation. If additional words are necessary for the sense of the translation, the literal rendering is set forth in a footnote. Alternatively, an explanatory footnote may be added indicating that the original text lacks the additional wording.

22. Subheads are used to identify flow of thought and themes. Parallel passages, where they exist, are cited in subheads.

23. Parentheses may be used in the text whenever called for by the sense of the passage. The ISV does not use brackets to indicate disputed verses. Instead, footnotes indicate the absence of such verses in some manuscripts.

24. Poetic passages in both the Old and New Testaments are printed in poetic form. Certain New Testament hymns and sayings are rendered in free verse (e.g., 2 Timothy 2:11-13).

25. Quoted statements of speakers may be rendered into English using contractions (e.g., "can't," "won't," "don't," etc.) in order to communicate a sense of natural spoken informality. The use of English language contractions will usually be avoided when translating historical narratives or apostolic correspondence in order to communicate a sense of formal literary composition. The use of English language contractions is usually avoided in commands.

About the Learn Foundation Triglyph

The ISV logo is a triglyph of three historic symbols: The upper symbol is the *Menorah*. The center symbol is the *Magen David* ("Star of David"). The lower symbol, the *Ichthus*, is that of a fish. The *Menorah* is the traditional symbol of Judaism. The *Magen David* appears to have become identified with Judaism during the medieval period. Today, it is the official symbol of the State of Israel and appears on its national flag. The *Ichthus* was used by the early Christians as an identifying mark between believers. In the Greek language, the word "fish" (ΙΧΘΥΣ) is an acrostic that spells out the words "Jesus Christ Son of God Savior."

The ISV triglyph is a combination of all three historic images, thus symbolizing the historic roots from which the Church emerged. The original triglyph from which the ISV logo is derived was discovered by a Greek Orthodox monk on Mount Zion, Jerusalem, in an informal archaeological dig. The original triglyph was inscribed on at least five different stones that may have their origin in the Byzantine period, fourth to sixth centuries, A.D. If this claim is accurate, the existence of this triglyph means that the *Magen David* has existed as a symbol of dispersed Israel from the early Christian centuries.

The Learn Foundation claims the image of the triglyph as it appears on the cover of this volume as a trademark to indicate the foundation's exclusive rights to utilize it for use in Bible translations and Bible study tools. These tools include volumes produced by various ministry subsidiaries of the Learn Foundation. Davidson Press uses the triglyph with the consent of the Learn Foundation.

ISV Research and Translation Team

The International Standard Version is being developed by a team of biblical scholars, consisting of the Committee on Translation, Contributing Scholars, and English Review Scholars. The following are the ISV team members at press time:

Committee on Translation

George Giacumakis, Jr., Ph.D. — General Editor
  Professor of History and Director, Mission Viejo Campus
  California State University, Fullerton
Edward M. Curtis, Ph.D. — Associate Editor, Old Testament
  Professor of Old Testament
  Talbot School of Theology, Biola University
David Alan Black, D.Theol. — Associate Editor, New Testament
  Professor of New Testament and Greek
  Southeastern Baptist Theological Seminary
Ronald D. Rietveld, Ph.D. — Translation Language Stylist
  Professor of History
  California State University, Fullerton
William P. Welty, M.Div. — Member
  Director, The Learn Foundation

Contributing Scholars

Gleason L. Archer, Ph.D., Trinity Evangelical Divinity School, Emeritus
Craig L. Blomberg, Ph.D., Denver Seminary
James A. Brooks, D.Phil., Bethel Theological Seminary
Gary M. Burge, Ph.D., Wheaton College
Richard J. Erickson, Ph.D., Fuller Theological Seminary
Craig A. Evans, Ph.D., Trinity Western University, Langley, British Columbia
Harold W. Hoehner, Ph.D., Dallas Theological Seminary
Dennis F. Kinlaw, Ph.D., Asbury College, Emeritus
Arthur H. Lewis, Ph.D., Bethel College, Emeritus
Malcolm F. Lowe, Ph.D., Ecumenical Theological Research Fraternity, Jerusalem
Scott E. McClelland, Ph.D., Evangelical Free Church, Yorba Linda, California
Douglas J. Moo, Ph.D., Trinity Evangelical Divinity School
Robert A. Morey, D.Min., California Institute of Apologetics, Anaheim, California
Halvor Ronning, Ph.D. candidate, Jerusalem House of Bible Translators, Israel
J. Robert Vannoy, Ph.D., Biblical Theological Seminary

English Review Committee

John J. Brugaletta, Ph.D., California State University, Fullerton
Robert D. Carpenter, M.D., The Learn Foundation
Ted Curtis Smythe, Ph.D., California State University, Fullerton, Emeritus
Efrem Zimbalist, Jr.

THE
NEW TESTAMENT

International Standard Version

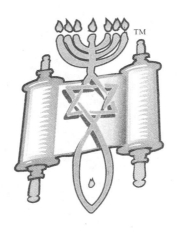

THE GOSPEL ACCORDING TO
MATTHEW

1:1
a Gen12:3; 22:18;
Ps132:11;
Isa 11:1; Jer23:5;
Matt22:42;
Lk3:23;
John7:42;
Acts2:30; 13:23;
Rom1:3; Gal3:16

The Ancestry of Jesus Christ
(Luke 3:23–28)

1 [1]This is a record[a] of the birth of Jesus Christ,[b] the son of David, the son of Abraham.[a]
[2]Abraham fathered Isaac, Isaac fathered Jacob, and Jacob fathered Judah and his brothers.[b] [3]Judah fathered Perez and Zerah by Tamar, Perez fathered Hezron, Hezron

1:2
b Gen21:2-3;
25:26; 29:35

fathered Aram,[c] [4]Aram fathered Aminidab, Aminidab fathered Nahshon, and Nahshon fathered Salmon. [5]Salmon fathered Boaz by Rahab, Boaz fathered Obed by Ruth, Obed fathered Jesse, [6]and Jesse fathered King David.[d]

1:3
c Gen38:27;
Ruth4:18;
1Chr2:5,9

David fathered Solomon by the wife of Uriah, [7]Solomon fathered Rehoboam, Rehoboam fathered Abijah, Abijah fathered Asaph,[ce] [8]Asaph[c] fathered Jehoshaphat, Jehoshaphat fathered Joram, Joram fathered Uzziah, [9]Uzziah fathered Jotham, Jotham fathered Ahaz, Ahaz fathered Hezekiah,

1:6
d 1Sam16:1;
17:12;
2Sam12:24

[10]Hezekiah fathered Manasseh, Manasseh fathered Amos,[d] and Amos[d] fathered Josiah.[f] [11]Josiah fathered Jechoniah and his brothers at the time of the deportation to Babylon.[g]

1:7
e 1Chr3:10

[12]After the deportation to Babylon Jechoniah fathered Salathiel, Salathiel fathered Zerubbabel,[h] [13]Zerubbabel fathered Abiud, Abiud fathered Eliakim, Eliakim fathered Azor, [14]Azor fathered Zadok, Zadok fathered Achim,

1:10
f 2Kings20:21;
1Chr3:13

Achim fathered Eliud, [15]Eliud fathered Eleazar, Eleazar fathered Matthan, and Matthan fathered Jacob. [16]Jacob fathered Joseph, the husband of Mary, who was the mother of Jesus,[e] who is called the Christ.[b]

1:11
g 2Kings24:14-16;
25:11;
1Chr3:15-16;
2Chr36:10,20;
Jer27:20; 39:9;
52:11,15,28-30;
Dan1:2

[17]So all the generations from Abraham to David were fourteen[f] generations, and from David to the deportation to Babylon were fourteen generations, and from the deportation to Babylon to the Christ[b] were fourteen generations.

1:12
h 1Chr3:17,19;
Ezra3:2; 5:2;
Neh12:1; Hag1:1

---

a *1:1* Lit. *A record* b *1:1,1:16,1:17* I.e. the Messiah c *1:7,1:8* Other mss. read *Asa* d *1:10* Other mss. read *Amon* e *1:16* Lit. *of whom Jesus was born* f *1:17* The numerical value of the name David in Heb. is fourteen.

The Virgin Birth of Jesus Christ
(Luke 2:1–7)

¹⁸Now the birth of Jesus Christ[a] happened in this way. When his mother Mary was engaged[b] to Joseph, before they lived together she was discovered to be pregnant by the Holy Spirit.[a] ¹⁹But her husband Joseph, being a righteous man and unwilling to disgrace her, decided to divorce her secretly.[b]

²⁰After he had thought about it, an angel of the Lord appeared to him in a dream and said, "Joseph, son of David, don't be afraid to take Mary as your wife, for what has been conceived in her is from the Holy Spirit.[c] ²¹She will give birth to a son, and you are to name him Jesus,[c] because he is the one who will save his people from their sins."[d]

²²Now all this happened to fulfill what was declared by the Lord through the prophet when he said,

²³"See, a virgin will become pregnant[e]
and give birth to a son,
and they will name him Immanuel,"[d]

which means, "God with us." ²⁴When Joseph got up from his sleep, he did as the angel of the Lord had commanded him and took Mary as his wife.[e] ²⁵He didn't have marital relations with her[f] until she had given birth to a son.[g] Then he named him Jesus.[f]

The Visit of the Wise Men

¹After Jesus had been born in Bethlehem of Judea in the days of King Herod, wise men[h] from the east arrived in Jerusalem[g] ²and asked, "Where is the one who was born king of the Jews? We saw his star in the east[i] and have come to worship him."[h]

³When King Herod heard this he was troubled, and all the people of Jerusalem[j] with him. ⁴He called together all the high priests and scribes of the people and asked them

a*1:18* I.e. the Messiah b*1:18* Engagement involved a legally binding promise of marriage. c*1:21 Jesus* is the Gk. for *Joshua*, meaning *The Lord saves* d*1:23* Isa 7:14 e*1:24* Lit. *took his wife* f*1:25* Lit. *didn't know her* g*1:25* Other mss. read *to her firstborn son* h*2:1* Or *astrologers*; Gk. *magi* i*2:2* Or *at its rising* j*2:3* Lit. *and all Jerusalem*

2

2:4
a 2Chr34:13;
36:14; Mal2:7

where the Christ**a** was to be born.*a* **5**They told him, "In Bethlehem of Judea. For that's what was written by the prophet:

> **6**'O Bethlehem in the land of Judah,*b*
>   you are by no means least among the rulers
>   of Judah.
> For from you will come a ruler
>   who will shepherd**b** my people Israel.' "**c**

2:6
b Mic5:2;
John7:42;
Rev2:27

7Then Herod secretly called together the wise men**d** and found out from them the time the star had appeared. **8**Then he sent them to Bethlehem, saying, "As you go, search carefully for the child. When you find him, tell me so that I, too, may go and worship him."

9After listening to the king, they set out. The star they had seen in the east**e** went ahead of them until it came and stopped over the place where the child was. **10**When they saw the star, they were ecstatic with joy. **11**After they went into the house and saw the child with his mother Mary, they fell down and worshiped him. Then they opened their treasure sacks and offered him gifts of gold, frankincense, and myrrh.*c* **12**Then, having been warned in a dream not to go back to Herod, they left for their own country by a different road.*d*

2:11
c Ps72:10;
Isa60:6

The Escape to Egypt

13After they had gone, an angel of the Lord appeared to Joseph in a dream and said, "Get up, take the child and his mother, and flee to Egypt. Stay there until I tell you, because Herod intends to search for the child and kill him." **14**So Joseph**f** got up and took the child and his mother and left at night for Egypt. **15**He stayed there until Herod's death in order to fulfill what was declared by the Lord through the prophet when he said, "Out of Egypt I called my Son."**g***e*

2:12
d Matt1:20

The Massacre of the Infants

16When Herod saw that he'd been tricked by the wise

2:15
e Hos 11:1

---

a*2:4* I.e. the Messiah   **b***2:6* Or *govern*   **c***2:6* Mic 5:2; 2 Sam 5:2
d*2:7* Or *astrologers*; Gk. *magi*   **e***2:9* Or *at its rising*   **f***2:14* Lit. *he*
g*2:15* Hos 11:1

men,[a] he became absolutely furious. He ordered the killing of all the male children in Bethlehem and all its neighboring regions who were two years old and younger, according to the time that he had determined from the wise men.[a] [17]Then what was declared by the prophet Jeremiah was fulfilled when he said,[a]

> [18]"A voice was heard in Ramah:
>   wailing and great mourning.
> Rachel was crying for her children.
>   She refused to be comforted,
>   because they no longer existed."[b]

The Return from Egypt

[19]But after Herod died, an angel of the Lord appeared in a dream to Joseph in Egypt [20]and said, "Get up, take the child and his mother, and go to the land of Israel. For those who were trying to kill the child are dead."

[21]So Joseph[c] got up and took the child and his mother and went into the land of Israel. [22]But when he heard that Archelaus was ruling over Judea in place of his father Herod, he was afraid to go there. Having been warned in a dream, he left for the region of Galilee.[b] [23]He came and settled in a town called Nazareth in order to fulfill what was said by the prophets: "He will be called a Nazarene."[d][c]

John the Baptist Prepares the Way for Jesus

(Mark 1:1–8; Luke 3:1–9, 15–17; John 1:19–28)

3 [1]In those days John the Baptist appeared. He kept preaching in the wilderness of Judea[d] [2]and saying, "Repent, for the kingdom of heaven is near!"[e] [3]He was the one the prophet Isaiah was referring to when he said,[f]

> "He is a voice calling out in the wilderness:
>   'Prepare the way for the Lord!
>   Make his paths straight!' "[e]

---

a 2:16 Or *astrologers*; Gk. *magi*   b 2:18 Jer 31:15   c 2:21 Lit. *he*
d 2:23 The Gk. *Nazoraios* may be a word play between Heb. *netser*, meaning *branch* (see Isa 11:1), and the name *Nazareth*.   e 3:3 Isa 40:3

2:17
a Jer 31:15

2:22
b Matt3:13; Lk2:39

2:23
c Jdg13:5; 1Sam1:11; John1:45

3:1
d Josh14:10; Mark1:4,15; Lk3:2-3; John1:28

3:2
e Dan2:44; Matt4:17; 10:7

3:3
f Isa40:3; Mark1:3; Lk1:76; 3:4; John1:23

4

3:4
a Lev 11:22;
1Sam14:25-26;
2Kings1:8;
Zech13:4;
Mark1:6

3:5
b Mark1:5; Lk3:7

3:6
c Acts19:4,18

3:7
d Matt12:34;
23:33; Lk3:7-9;
Rom5:9;
1Thes1:10

3:9
e John8:33,39;
Acts13:26;
Rom4:1,11,16

3:10
f Matt7:19;
Lk13:7,9;
John15:6

3:11
g Isa4:4; 44:3;
Mal3:2; Mark1:8;
Lk3:16;
John1:15,26,33;
Acts1:5; 2:3-4;
11:16; 19:4;
1Cor12:13

3:12
h Mal3:3; 4:1;
Matt13:30

3:13
i Matt2:22;
Mark1:9; Lk3:21

3:16
j Isa 11:2; 42:1;
Mark1:10;
Lk3:22;
John1:32-33

3:17
k Ps2:7; Isa42:1;
Matt12:18; 17:5;
Mark1:11;
Lk9:35;
John12:28;
Eph1:6; Col1:13;
2Peter1:17

4John had clothing made out of camel's hair and wore[a] a leather belt around his waist. His diet consisted of locusts and wild honey.[a] 5Then the people of Jerusalem[b] and all Judea and all the region along the Jordan began to go out to him.[b] 6They were being baptized by him in the Jordan river while they confessed their sins.[c]

7But when John[c] saw many Pharisees and Sadduccees coming to where he was baptizing,[d] he said to them, "You children of serpents! Who warned you to flee from the coming wrath?[d] 8Produce fruit that is consistent with repentance! 9Don't think you can say to yourselves, 'We have Abraham for our forefather.' For I tell you that God can raise up descendants for Abraham from these stones![e] 10The ax already lies against the roots of the trees. So every tree not producing good fruit will be cut down and thrown into the fire.[f] 11I am baptizing you with[e] water as a token of repentance.[f] But the one who is coming after me is stronger than I am, and I am not worthy to carry his sandals. It is he who will baptize you with[e] the Holy Spirit and fire.[g] 12His winnowing fork is in his hand. He will clean up his threshing floor and gather his grain into the barn, but he will burn the chaff with inextinguishable fire."[h]

John Baptizes Jesus
(Mark 1:9–11; Luke 3:21–22)

13Then Jesus came from Galilee to the Jordan to be baptized by John.[i] 14But John tried to stop him, saying, "I need to be baptized by you, and are you coming to me?" 15But Jesus answered him, "Let it be this way for now, for this is the proper way for us to fulfill all righteousness." Then John[c] let him.

16When Jesus had been baptized, he immediately came up out of the water. Suddenly the heavens opened up for him, and he saw the Spirit of God coming down like a dove and landing on him.[j] 17Then a voice from heaven said, "This is my Son, whom I love. I am pleased with him!"[k]

---

a *3:4* The Gk. lacks *wore*   **b** *3:5* Lit. *Then Jerusalem*   **c** *3:7,3:15* Lit. *he*   **d** *3:7* Lit. *to his baptism*   **e** *3:11* Or *in*   **f** *3:11* Lit. *for repentance*

Jesus Is Tempted by Satan
(Mark 1:12–13; Luke 4:1–13)

4 [1]Then Jesus was led by the Spirit into the wilderness to be tempted by the devil.*a* [2]After fasting for forty days and forty nights, he finally became hungry.

[3]Then the tempter came and said to him, "Since*a* you are the Son of God, tell these stones to become loaves of bread." [4]But he answered, "It is written,*b*

> 'Aperson must not live on bread alone,
>   but on every word coming
>   out of the mouth of God.' "**b**

[5]Then the devil took him to the Holy City*c* and had him stand on the highest point of the Temple.*c* [6]He said to Jesus,**d** "If you are the Son of God, throw yourself down. For it is written,*d*

> 'God*e* will put his angels in charge of you,'

and

> 'With their hands they will hold you up,
>   so that you will never hit your foot against a
>   rock.' "**f**

[7]Jesus said to him, "It is also written,*e*

> 'You must not tempt the Lord your God.' "**g**

[8]Once more the devil took him to a very high mountain and showed him all the kingdoms of the world and their splendor. [9]He said to Jesus,**d** "I will give you all of these things if you will bow down and worship me!" [10]Then Jesus said to him, "Go away,**h** Satan! For it is written*f*

> 'You must worship the Lord your God
>   and serve only him.' "**i**

[11]Then the devil left him, and angels came and began caring for him.*g*

---

a*4:3* Or *If*　　b*4:4* Deut 8:3　　c*4:5* I.e. Jerusalem　　d*4:6,4:9* Lit. *to him*
e*4:6* Lit. *He*　　f*4:6* Ps 91:11-12　　g*4:7* Deut 6:16　　h*4:10* Other mss. read
Get behind me　　i*4:10* Deut 6:13

4:1
*a*1Kings18:12;
Ezek3:14; 8:3;
11:1,24; 40:2;
43:5; Mark1:12;
Lk4:1; Acts8:39

4:4
*b*Deut8:3

4:5
*c*Neh 11:1,18;
Isa48:2; 52:1;
Matt27:53;
Rev 11:2

4:6
*d*Ps91:11-12

4:7
*e*Deut6:16

4:10
*f*Deut6:13; 10:20;
Josh24:14;
1Sam7:3

4:11
*g*Heb1:14

4:12
a Mark1:14;
Lk3:30; 4:14,31;
John4:43

Jesus Begins His Ministry in Galilee

(Mark 1:14–15; Luke 4:14–15)

¹²Now when Jesus[a] heard that John had been arrested, he went back to Galilee.[a] ¹³He left Nazareth and came and settled in Capernaum by the sea, in the regions of Zebulun and Naphtali, ¹⁴in order to fulfill what was declared by the prophet Isaiah when he said,

4:15
b Isa9:1-2

¹⁵"O Land of Zebulun and land of Naphtali,[b]
on the road to the sea, across the Jordan,
Galilee of the Gentiles!

4:16
c Isa42:7; Lk2:32

¹⁶The people living[b] in darkness have seen a great light,[c]
and for those living[b] in the land and shadow of death,
a light has risen."[c]

4:17
d Matt3:2; 10:7;
Mark1:14-15

¹⁷From then on, Jesus began to preach and to say, "Repent, for the kingdom of heaven is near!"[d]

4:18
e Mark1:16-18;
Lk5:2; John1:42

Jesus Calls Four Fishermen

(Mark 1:16–20; Luke 5:1–11)

¹⁸While Jesus[a] was walking beside the Sea of Galilee, he saw two brothers—Simon, who is called Peter, and his brother Andrew. They were throwing a net into the sea because they were fishermen.[e] ¹⁹He said to them, "Follow me, and I'll make you fish for people!"[d][f] ²⁰So at once they left their nets and followed him.[g] ²¹Going on from there he saw two other brothers—James, the son of Zebedee, and his brother John. They were in a boat with their father Zebedee repairing their nets. When he called them,[h] ²²they immediately left the boat and their father and followed him.

4:19
f Lk5:10-11

4:20
g Mark10:28;
Lk18:28

4:21
h Mark1:19-20;
Lk5:10

Jesus Ministers to Many People

(Luke 6:17–19)

²³Then he went throughout Galilee, teaching in their synagogues, proclaiming the gospel of the kingdom, and healing every disease and every illness among the people.[i]

4:23
i Matt9:35; 24:14;
Mark1:14,21,34,
39; Lk4:15,44

---

a 4:12,4:18 Lit. *he*   **b** 4:16 Lit. *sitting*   **c** 4:16 Isa 9:1-2   **d** 4:19 Lit. *make you fishermen of people*

[4:25] [a]Mark3:7

²⁴His fame spread throughout Syria, and people^a brought to him all who were sick—those afflicted with various diseases and pains, the demon-possessed, the epileptics, and the paralyzed—and he healed them. ²⁵Large crowds followed him from Galilee, the Decapolis,^b Jerusalem, Judea, and from across the Jordan.^a

[5:1] [b]Mark3:13,20

Jesus Teaches about the Kingdom

[5:3] [c]Ps51:17; Prov16:19; 29:23; Isa57:15; 66:2; Lk6:20

5 ¹When Jesus^c saw the crowds, he went up on a hillside and sat down. His disciples came to him,^b ²and he opened his mouth and began to teach them, saying,

The Blessed Attitudes
(Luke 6:20–23)

[5:4] [d]Isa61:2-3; Lk6:21; John16:20; 2Cor1:7; Rev21:4

³"How blessed are those who are destitute in spirit,^c
for the kingdom of heaven belongs to them!
⁴"How blessed are those who mourn,^d
for it is they who will be comforted!
⁵"How blessed are those who are humble,^{de}
for it is they who will inherit the earth!
⁶"How blessed are those who are hungry and
thirsty for righteousness,^{ef}
for it is they who will be satisfied!
⁷"How blessed are those who are merciful,^g
for it is they who will receive mercy!
⁸"How blessed are those who are pure in heart,^h
for it is they who will see God!
⁹"How blessed are those who make peace,
for it is they who will be called God's
children!
¹⁰"How blessed are those who are persecuted for
righteousness' sake,ⁱ
for the kingdom of heaven belongs to them!

[5:5] [e]Ps37:11; Rom4:13

[5:6] [f]Isa55:1; 65:13

[5:7] [g]Ps41:1; Matt6:14; Mark 11:25; 2Tim1:16; Heb6:10; James2:13

[5:8] [h]Ps15:2; 24:4; 1Cor13:12; Heb12:14; 1John3:2-3

¹¹"How blessed are you whenever people^a insult you, persecute you, and say all sorts of evil things against you

---

^a4:24,5:11 Lit. *they*   ^b4:25 Lit. *the Ten Cities*, a loose federation of ten cities strongly influenced by Greek culture   ^c5:1 Lit. *He*   ^d5:5 Or *gentle*   ^e5:6 Or *justice*

[5:10] [i]2Cor4:17; 2Tim2:12; 1Peter3:14

5:11
a Lk6:22;
1Peter4:14

5:12
b 2Chr36:16;
Neh9:26;
Matt23:34,37;
Lk6:23;
Acts5:41; 7:52;
Rom5:3;
1Thes2:15;
James1:2;
1Peter4:13

5:13
c Mark9:50;
Lk14:34-35

5:14
d Prov4:18;
Phil2:15

5:15
e Mark4:21;
Lk8:16; 11:33

5:16
f John15:8;
1Cor14:25;
1Peter2:12

5:17
g Rom3:31; 10:4;
Gal3:24

5:18
h Lk16:17

5:19
i James2:10

5:20
j Rom9:31; 10:3

5:21
k Exod20:13;
Deut5:17

falsely[a] because of me![a] [12]Rejoice and be extremely glad, because your reward in heaven is great! For that's how they persecuted the prophets who came before you."[b]

Salt and Light in the World
(Mark 9:50; Luke 14:34–35)

[13]"You are the salt of the world. But if the salt should lose its taste, how can it be made salty again? It's good for nothing but to be thrown outside and trampled on by people.[c] [14]You are the light of the world. A city located on a hill can't be hidden.[d] [15]People[b] don't light a lamp and put it under a basket but on a lampstand, and it gives light to everyone in the house.[e] [16]In the same way, let your light shine before people in such a way that they'll see your good works and glorify your Father in heaven."[f]

Jesus Fulfills the Law and the Prophets

[17]"Don't think that I came to destroy the Law or the Prophets. I didn't come to destroy them, but to fulfill them.[g] [18]For truly I tell you, until heaven and earth disappear, not one letter[c] or one stroke of a letter will disappear from the Law until everything has been accomplished.[h] [19]So whoever sets aside[d] one of the least of these commandments and teaches others to do the same will be called least in the kingdom of heaven. But whoever does them and teaches them will be called great in the kingdom of heaven.[i] [20]For I tell you, unless your righteousness greatly exceeds that of the scribes and Pharisees, you'll never get into the kingdom of heaven!"[j]

Teaching about Anger

[21]"You've heard that it was said to those who lived long ago, 'You must not murder,'[e] and 'Whoever murders will be subject to punishment.'[fk] [22]But I say to you, anyone who is angry with his brother without a cause[g] will be subject to punishment. And whoever says to his brother 'Raka!'[h] will

---

a5:11 Other mss. lack *falsely*   b5:15 Lit. *They*   c5:18 Lit. *one iota*   d5:19 Or *breaks*   e5:21 Exod 20:13; Deut 5:17   f5:21 Exod 21:12; Lev 24:17   g5:22 Other mss. lack *without a cause*   h5:22 Raka is Aram. for *You worthless one*

be subject to the Council.[a] And whoever says 'You fool!' will be subject to hell[b] fire.[a]

23"So if you're presenting your gift at the altar and remember there that your brother has something against you,[b] 24leave your gift there before the altar and first go and be reconciled to your brother. Then come and offer your gift.[c] 25Come to terms quickly with your opponent while you're on the way to court,[c] or your opponent may hand you over to the judge, and the judge to the guard, and you'll be thrown into prison.[d] 26Truly I tell you, you will not get out of there until you pay back the last penny!"

Teaching about Adultery

27"You've heard that it was said, 'You must not commit adultery.'[d][e] 28But I say to you, anyone who looks at a woman with lust for her has already committed adultery with her in his heart.[f] 29So if your right eye causes you to sin, tear it out and throw it away. It's better for you to lose one of your members than to have your whole body thrown into hell.[e][g] 30And if your right hand causes you to sin, cut it off and throw it away from you. It's better for you to lose one of your members than to have your whole body go into hell."[e]

Teaching about Divorce
(Matthew 19:9; Mark 10:11–12; Luke 16:18)

31"It was also said, 'Whoever divorces his wife must give her a written notice of divorce.'[f][h] 32But I say to you, any man who divorces his wife, except for sexual immorality, causes her to commit adultery. And whoever marries a divorced woman commits adultery."[i]

Teaching about Oaths

33"Again, you've heard that it was said to those who lived long ago, 'You must not swear an oath falsely,' but 'You must fulfill your oaths to the Lord.'[g][j] 34But I tell you

---

a5:22 Or Sanhedrin   b5:22 Lit. the fire of Gehenna; Gehenna is a Gk. transliteration of the Heb. for "Valley of Hinnom"   c5:25 Lit. while you're with him on the way   d5:27 Exod 20:14; Deut 5:18   e5:29,5:30 Gk. Gehenna   f5:31 Deut 24:1,3   g5:33 Lev 19:12; Num 30:2; Deut 23:21-23

5:22
[a] James 2:20;
1 John 3:15

5:23
[b] Matt 8:4; 23:19

5:24
[c] Job 42:8;
Matt 18:19;
1 Tim 2:8;
1 Peter 3:7

5:25
[d] Ps 32:6;
Prov 25:8;
Isa 55:6;
Lk 12:58-59

5:27
[e] Exod 20:14;
Deut 5:18

5:28
[f] Gen 34:2;
2 Sam 11:2;
Job 31:1;
Prov 6:25

5:29
[g] Matt 18:8-9;
19:12;
Mark 9:43-47;
Rom 8:13;
1 Cor 9:27; Col 3:5

5:31
[h] Deut 24:1;
Jer 3:1; Matt 19:3;
Mark 10:2

5:32
[i] Matt 19:9;
Lk 16:18;
Rom 7:3;
1 Cor 7:10-11

5:33
[j] Exod 20:7;
Lev 19:12;
Num 30:2;
Deut 5:11; 23:23;
Matt 23:16

5:34
*a*Isa66:1;
Matt23:16,18,22;
James5:12

5:35
*b*Ps48:2; 87:3

5:37
*c*Col4:6;
James5:12

5:38
*d*Exod21:24;
Lev24:20;
Deut19:21

5:39
*e*Prov20:22;
24:29; Isa50:6;
Lam3:30;
Lk6:29;
Rom12:17,19;
1Cor6:7;
1Thes5:15;
1Peter3:9

5:41
*f*Matt27:32;
Mark15:21

5:42
*g*Deut15:8,10;
Lk6:30,35

5:43
*h*Lev19:18;
Deut23:6;
Ps41:10

5:44
*i*Lk6:27,35;
23:34; Acts7:60;
Rom12:14,20;
1Cor4:12-13;
1Peter2:23; 3:9

5:45
*j*Job25:3

5:46
*k*Lk6:32

5:48
*l*Gen17:1;
Lev 11:44; 19:2;
Lk6:36; Eph5:1;
Col1:28;
4:12James1:4;
1Peter1:15-16

not to swear at all, neither by heaven, because it's God's throne,*a* ³⁵nor by the earth, because it's his footstool, nor by Jerusalem, because it's the city of the Great King.*b* ³⁶Nor should you swear by your head, because you can't make one hair white or black. ³⁷Instead, let your word be 'Yes' for 'Yes' and 'No' for 'No.' Anything more than that comes from the evil one."*c*

Teaching about Retaliation
(Luke 6:29–30)

³⁸"You've heard that it was said, 'An eye for an eye and a tooth for a tooth.'*a d* ³⁹But I tell you not to resist an evildoer. On the contrary, whoever slaps you on the right cheek, turn the other to him as well.*e* ⁴⁰If anyone wants to sue you and take your shirt, let him have your coat as well. ⁴¹And if anyone forces you to go one mile, go two with him.*f* ⁴²Give to the person who asks you for something, and don't turn away from the person who wants to borrow something from you."*g*

Teaching about Love for Enemies
(Luke 6:27–28, 32–36)

⁴³"You've heard that it was said, 'You must love your neighbor'*b* and hate your enemy.*h* ⁴⁴But I say to you, love your enemies, and pray for those who persecute you,*i* ⁴⁵so that you'll become children of your Father in heaven. For he makes his sun rise on the evil and the good, and he lets rain fall on the righteous and the unrighteous.*j* ⁴⁶For if you love those who love you, what reward will you have? Even the tax collectors do the same, don't they?*k* ⁴⁷And if you greet only your brothers, what great thing are you doing? Even the Gentiles*c* do the same, don't they? ⁴⁸So be perfect,**d** as your heavenly Father is perfect."**d***l*

---

a5:38 Exod 21:24; Lev 24:20; Deut 19:21   **b**5:43 Lev 19:18   **c**5:47 Other mss. read *tax collectors*   **d**5:48 Or *mature*

Teaching about Giving Money to the Poor

6 [1]"Be careful not to practice your righteousness in front of people in order to be noticed by them. If you do, you'll have no reward from your Father in heaven. [2]So whenever you give to the poor, don't blow a trumpet before you like the hypocrites do in the synagogues and in the streets so that they will be praised by people. Truly I tell you, they have their full reward![a] [3]But when you give to the poor, don't let your left hand know what your right hand is doing, [4]so that your giving may be done in secret. And your Father who sees in secret will reward you."[ab]

Teaching about Prayer
(Luke 11:2–4)

[5]"And whenever you pray, don't be like the hypocrites who love to stand in the synagogues and on the street corners so that they will be seen by people. Truly I tell you, they have their full reward! [6]But whenever you pray, go into your room, close the door, and pray to your Father who is in secret. And your Father who sees in secret will reward you.[ac]

[7]"When you're praying, don't say meaningless words like the Gentiles do, for they think they'll be heard because of their wordiness.[d] [8]Don't be like them, because your Father knows what you need before you ask him.

[9]"Therefore, this is how you should pray:[e]

'Our Father in heaven,
    may your name be kept holy.
[10]May your kingdom come.[f]
    May your will be done,
        on earth as it is in heaven.
[11]Give us today our daily bread,[bg]
[12]and forgive us our sins,[ch]
        as we have forgiven those who have sinned
            against us.[d]

---

a 6:4,6:6 Other mss. read *reward you openly*   b 6:11 Or *our bread from above*   c 6:12 Or *debts*   d 6:12 Or *our debtors*

Side references:

6:2
[a] Rom 12:8

6:4
[b] Lk 14:14

6:6
[c] 2 Kings 4:33

6:7
[d] 1 Kings 18:26,29; Eccl 5:2

6:9
[e] Lk 11:2

6:10
[f] Ps 103:20-21; Matt 26:39,42; Acts 21:14

6:11
[g] Job 23:12; Prov 30:8

6:12
[h] Matt 18:21

6:13
a 1Chr29:11;
Matt26:41;
Lk22:40,46;
John17:15;
1Cor10:13;
2Peter2:9;
Rev3:10

[13]And never bring us into temptation,[a]
but deliver us from the evil one.'[a]

[14]For if you forgive people their offenses, your heavenly Father will also forgive you. [b] [15]But if you don't forgive people their offenses,[b] your Father will not forgive your offenses."[c]

6:14
b Mark 11:25-26;
Eph4:32;
Col3:13

Teaching about Fasting

[16]"Whenever you fast, don't be gloomy like the hypocrites. They put on sad faces to show others they're fasting. Truly I tell you, they have their full reward![d] [17]But when you fast, put oil on[c] your head and wash your face,[e] [18]so that your fasting will not be noticed by others but by your Father who sees in secret. And your Father who is in secret will reward you."[d]

6:15
c Matt18:35;
James2:13

Teaching about Treasures
(Luke 12:33–34)

[19]"Stop storing up treasures for yourselves on earth, where moths and rust destroy and where thieves break in and steal.[f] [20]But keep on storing up treasures for yourselves in heaven, where moths and rust do not destroy and where thieves do not break in and steal.[g] [21]For where your treasure is, there your heart will be also."

6:16
d Isa58:5

6:17
e Ruth3:3;
Dan10:3

The Lamp of the Body
(Luke 11:34–36)

[22]"The eye is the lamp of the body. So if your eye is healthy, your whole body will be full of light.[h] [23]But if your eye is evil, your whole body will be full of darkness. So if the light in you is darkness, how great is that darkness!"

6:19
f Prov23:4;
1Tim6:17;
Heb13:5;
James5:1

6:20
g Matt19:21;
Lk12:33-34;
18:22; 1Tim6:19;
1Peter1:4

God and Riches
(Luke 16:13)

[24]"No one can serve two masters. For either he will hate one and love the other, or be loyal to one and despise the other. You cannot serve God and riches!"[e][i]

6:22
h Lk 11:34,36

6:24
i Lk16:13;
Gal1:10;
1Tim6:17;
James4:4;
1John2:15

---

a 6:13 Other mss. read *evil one. For yours is the kingdom and the power and the glory forever. Amen.*   **b** 6:15 Other mss. lack *their offenses*   **c** 6:17 Or *anoint*   **d** 6:18 Other mss. read *reward you openly*   **e** 6:24 Lit. *mammon,* an Aram. term meaning *wealth*

Stop Worrying
(Luke 12:22–34)

25"That's why I'm telling you to stop worrying about your life—what you will eat or what you will drink[a]—or about your body—what you will wear. Life is more than food, and the body more than clothing, aren't they?[a] 26Look at the birds in the sky. They don't plant or harvest or gather food into barns, and yet your heavenly Father feeds them. You're more valuable than they are, aren't you?[b] 27Can any of you add a single hour to your span of life[b] by worrying? 28And why do you worry about clothes? Consider the lilies in the field and how they grow. They don't work or spin yarn, 29but I tell you that not even Solomon in all his splendor was clothed like one of them. 30Now if that's the way God clothes the grass in the field, which is alive today and thrown into an oven tomorrow, won't he clothe you much better—you who have little faith?

31"So don't ever worry by saying, 'What are we going to eat?' or 'What are we going to drink?' or 'What are we going to wear?' 32For it is the Gentiles who are eager for all those things. Surely your heavenly Father knows that you need all of them! 33But first be concerned about God's kingdom and his righteousness,[c] and all of these things will be provided for you as well.[c] 34So never worry about tomorrow, for tomorrow will worry about itself. Each day has enough trouble of its own."

Judging Others
(Luke 6:37–38, 41–42)

7 1"Stop judging, so that you won't be judged.[d] 2For with the judgment you use,[d] you will be judged. And with the measure you use,[e] you will be measured.[e] 3"Why do you see the speck in your brother's eye but fail to notice the beam in your own eye?[f] 4Or how can you say to your brother, 'Let me take the speck out of your eye,' when the beam is in your own eye? 5You hypocrite! First

---

a 6:25 Other mss. lack *or what you will drink*   b 6:27 Or *add one cubit to your height*   c 6:33 Other mss. read *his kingdom and righteousness*
d 7:2 Lit. *judge*   e 7:2 Lit. *measure*

6:25
a Ps55:22;
Lk12:22-23;
Phil4:6;
1Peter5:7

6:26
b Job38:41;
Ps147:9; Lk12:24

6:33
c 1Kings3:13;
Ps37:25;
Mark10:30;
Lk12:31;
1Tim4:8

7:1
d Lk6:37;
Rom2:1; 14:3-4,
10,13; 1Cor4:3,5;
James4:11-12

7:2
e Mark4:24;
Lk6:38

7:3
f Lk6:41-42

7:6
*a*Prov9:7-8; 23:9;
Acts13:45-46

remove the beam from your own eye, and then you'll see clearly enough to remove the speck from your brother's eye."

Despising the Holy

7:7
*b*Matt21:22;
Mark 11:24;
Lk 11:9-10;
18:1John14:13;
15:7; 16:23-24;
James1:5-6;
1John3:22;
5:14-15

6"Never give what is holy to dogs or throw your pearls before pigs. Otherwise, they'll trample them with their feet and then turn around and attack you."*a*

Ask, Search, Knock
(Luke 11:9–13)

7:8
*c*Prov8:17;
Jer29:12-13

7"Keep asking, and it will be given to you. Keep searching, and you will find. Keep knocking, and the door**a** will be opened for you.*b* 8For everyone who keeps asking will receive, and the person who keeps searching will find, and the person who keeps knocking will have the door**a** opened."*c*

7:9
*d*Lk 11:11-13

9"There isn't a person among you who would give his son a stone if he asked for bread, is there?*d* 10Or if he asks for a fish, he wouldn't give him a snake, would he? 11So if you

7:11
*e*Gen6:5; 8:21

who are evil know how to give good gifts to your children, how much more will your Father in heaven give good things to those who keep on asking him!*e* 12Therefore, whatever you want people to do for you, do the same for them, for this is the Law and the Prophets."*f*

7:12
*f*Lev19:18;
Matt22:40;
Lk6:31;
Rom13:8-10;
Gal5:14;
1Tim1:5

The Narrow Gate
(Luke 13:24)

13"Go in through the narrow gate. For the gate is wide and the road is spacious that leads to destruction, and many people are going in by it.*g* 14How narrow is the gate and how constricted is the road that leads to life, and few are the people who find it!"

7:13
*g*Lk13:24

A Tree Is Known by Its Fruit
(Luke 6:43–44)

7:15
*h*Deut13:3;
Jer23:16; Mic3:5;
Matt24:4-5,11,
24; Mark13:22;
Acts20:29-30;
Rom16:17-18;
Eph5:6; Col2:8;
2Tim3:5;
2Peter2:1-3;
1John4:1

15"Beware of false prophets who come to you in sheeps' clothing but inwardly are savage wolves.*h* 16By their fruit

a 7:7,7:8 Lit. *it*

you will know them. Grapes aren't gathered from thorns, or figs from thistles, are they?*a* ¹⁷In the same way, every good tree produces good fruit, but a rotten tree produces bad fruit.*b* ¹⁸A good tree can't produce bad fruit, and a rotten tree can't produce good fruit. ¹⁹Every tree not producing good fruit will be cut down and thrown into a fire.*c* ²⁰So by their fruit you will know them."

I Never Knew You
(Luke 6:46; 13:25–27)

²¹"Not everyone who keeps saying to me, 'Lord, Lord,' will get into the kingdom of heaven, but only the person who keeps doing the will of my Father in heaven.*d* ²²Many will say to me on that day, 'Lord, Lord, we prophesied in your name, drive out demons in your name, and performed many miracles in your name, didn't we?'*e* ²³Then I'll tell them plainly, 'I never knew you. Get away from me, you evildoers!' "*af*

The Two Foundations
(Luke 6:47–49)

²⁴"Therefore, everyone who hears these words of mine and obeys them is like a wise man who built his house on a rock.*g* ²⁵The rain fell, the floods came, and the winds blew and beat against that house, but it didn't collapse because its foundation was on the rock.

²⁶"Everyone who hears these words of mine and doesn't obey them is like a foolish man who built his house on sand. ²⁷The rain fell, the floods came, and the winds blew and battered that house, and it collapsed, and its collapse was total."*b*

²⁸When Jesus had finished saying all these things,*c* the crowds were utterly amazed at his teaching.*h* ²⁹For he was teaching them like a person who had authority, and not like their scribes.*i*

---

a 7:23 Ps 6:8   **b** 7:27 Lit. *great*   **c** 7:28 Lit. *finished all these sayings*

7:16
a Matt7:20; 12:33;
Lk6:43-44

7:17
b Jer 11:19;
Matt12:33

7:19
c Matt3:10;
Lk3:9;
John15:2, 6

7:21
d Hos8:2;
Matt25:11-12;
Lk6:46; 13:25;
Acts19:13;
Rom2:13;
James1:22

7:22
e Num24:4;
John 11:51;
1Cor13:2

7:23
f Ps5:5; 6:8;
Matt25:12,41;
Lk13:25,27;
2Tim2:19

7:24
g Lk6:47

7:28
h Matt13:54;
Mark1:22; 6:2;
Lk4:32

7:29
i John7:46

8:2
ᵃMark1:40;
Lk5:12

8:4
ᵇLev14:3-4,10;
Matt9:30;
Mark5:43;
Lk5:14

8:5
ᶜLk7:1

8:8
ᵈPs107:20;
Lk15:19,21

8:11
ᵉGen12:3;
Isa2:2-3; 11:10;
Mal1:11;
Lk13:29;
Acts10:45; 11:18;
14:27; Rom15:9;
Eph3:6

8:12
ᶠMatt13:42,50;
21:43; 22:13;
24:51; 25:30;
Lk13:28;
2Peter2:17;
Jude1:13

Jesus Cleanses a Leper

(Mark 1:40–45; Luke 5:12–16)

8 ¹When Jesusᵃ came down from the hillside, large crowds followed him. ²Suddenly a leperᵇ came up to him, fell down before him, and said, "Sir,ᶜ if you want to, you can make me clean."ᵃ ³So Jesusᵈ reached out his hand, touched him, and said, "I do want to. Be made clean!" And instantly his leprosy was made clean. ⁴Then Jesus said to him, "See to it that you don't speak to anyone. Instead, go and show yourself to the priest, and then offer the sacrifice that Moses commanded as proof to the authorities."ᵉᵇ

Jesus Heals a Centurion's Servant

(Luke 7:1–10; John 4:43–54)

⁵When Jesusᵃ returned to Capernaum, a centurionᶠ came up to him and kept begging him,ᶜ ⁶"Sir,ᶜ my servant is lying at home paralyzed and in terrible pain." ⁷Jesusᵈ said to him, "I will come and heal him." ⁸The centurion replied, "Sir,ᶜ I'm not worthy to have you come into my house.ᵍ But just say the word, and my servant will be healed.ᵈ ⁹For I, too, am a man under authority and have soldiers under me. I say to one 'Go' and he goes, to another 'Come' and he comes, and to my servant 'Do this' and he does it."

¹⁰When Jesus heard this, he was amazed and said to those who were following him, "Truly I tell you, not evenʰ in Israel have I found this kind of faith! ¹¹I tell you, many will come from east and west and will feast with Abraham, Isaac, and Jacob in the kingdom of heaven.ᵉ ¹²But the citizensⁱ of that kingdom will be thrown into the outer darkness. In that place there will be wailing and gnashing of teeth."ʲᶠ

¹³Then Jesus said to the centurion, "Go. It will be done for you just as you have believed." And his servant was healed that very hour.

ᵃ8:1,8:5 Lit. *he*   ᵇ8:2 I.e. a man with a serious skin disease   ᶜ8:2,8:6,8:8 Or *Lord*   ᵈ8:3,8:7 Lit. *He*   ᵉ8:4 Lit. *to them*   ᶠ8:5 I.e. a commander of about 100 soldiers   ᵍ8:8 Lit. *under my roof*   ʰ8:10 Other mss. read *in no one*   ⁱ8:12 Lit. *sons*   ʲ8:12 I.e. extreme pain

17

Jesus Heals Many People
(Mark 1:29–34; Luke 4:38–41)

14When Jesus went into Peter's house, he saw Peter's^a mother-in-law lying in bed, sick with a fever.^a 15He touched her hand, and the fever left her. Then she got up and began serving him.

16When evening came, people^b brought to him many who were possessed by demons. He drove out the spirits with a word and healed all those who were sick.^b 17This was to fulfill what was declared by the prophet Isaiah when he said,^c

> "It was he who took our illnesses away
>   and removed our diseases."^c

The Would-Be Followers of Jesus
(Luke 9:57–62)

18When Jesus saw the large crowds around him, he gave orders to cross to the other side.^d

19Then a scribe came up and said to him, "Teacher, I will follow you wherever you go."^d 20Jesus told him,

> *"Foxes have holes and birds^e have nests,*
>   *But the Son of Man has no place to rest."^f*

21Then another of his disciples said to him, "Lord,^g first let me go and bury my father."^e 22But Jesus told him, "Follow me, and let the dead bury their own dead."

Jesus Calms the Sea
(Mark 4:35–41; Luke 8:22–25)

23When Jesus^h got into the boat, his disciples went with him. 24Suddenly a violent storm came up on the sea, so that the boat began to be swamped by the waves. Yet Jesus^h kept sleeping.^f 25Theyⁱ went to him and woke him up, saying, "Lord, save us! We're going to die!" 26He said to them, "Why are you afraid, you who have little faith?" Then he got up

---

8:14 [a]Mark1:29-31; Lk4:38-39; 1Cor9:5

8:16 [b]Mark1:32; Lk4:40-41

8:17 [c]Isa53:4; 1Peter2:24

8:19 [d]Lk9:57-58

8:21 [e]1Kings19:20; Lk9:59-60

8:24 [f]Mark4:37; Lk8:23

---

a*8:14* Lit. *his*   b*8:16* Lit. *they*   c*8:17* Isa 53:4   d*8:18* I.e. to the other side of the Sea of Galilee   e*8:20* Lit. *birds in the sky*   f*8:20* Lit. *no place to lay his head*   g*8:21* Or *Sir*   h*8:23,8:24* Lit. *he*   i*8:25* Other mss. read *The disciples*

8:26
*a*Ps65:7; 89:9;
107:29

8:28
*b*Mark5:1;
Lk8:26

8:34
*c*Deut5:25;
1Kings17:18;
Lk5:8; Acts16:39

9:1
*d*Matt4:13

9:2
*e*Matt8:10;
Mark2:3; Lk5:18

9:4
*f*Ps139:2;
Matt12:25;
Mark12:15;
Lk5:22; 6:8; 9:47;
11:17

and reprimanded the winds and the sea, and there was a great calm.*a* 27The men were amazed and said, "What kind of man is this? Even the winds and the sea obey him!"

Jesus Heals Two Demon-Possessed Men
(Mark 5:1–20; Luke 8:26–39)

28When Jesus*a* arrived on the other side in the region of the Gerasenes,*b* two demon-possessed men met him as they were coming out of the tombs. They were so violent that no one could travel on that road.*b* 29Suddenly they screamed, "What do you want with us, Son of God? Did you come here to torture us before the proper time?"

30Now a large herd of pigs was grazing some distance away from them. 31So the demons began to plead with Jesus,*c* saying, "If you drive us out, send us into that herd of pigs." 32He said to them, "Go," and they came out and went into the pigs. Suddenly, the whole herd rushed down the cliff into the sea and died in the water.

33Then those who had taken care of the pigs ran away. When they came into the city they announced everything, especially what had happened to the demon-possessed men. 34Then the whole city went out to meet Jesus, and as soon as they saw him, they begged him to leave their region.*c*

Jesus Heals a Paralyzed Man
(Mark 2:1–12; Luke 5:17–26)

9 1After getting into a boat, Jesus*a* crossed to the other side and came to his own city.*d* 2All at once some people*d* began bringing to him a paralyzed man lying on a stretcher. When Jesus saw their faith, he said to the paralyzed man, "Be courageous, son! Your sins are forgiven."*e*

3Then some of the scribes said to themselves, "This fellow is blaspheming!" 4But Jesus knew*e* their thoughts and said, "Why do you have such evil thoughts in your hearts?*f* 5For which is easier: to say 'Your sins are forgiven,' or to

---

a8:28,9:1 Lit. *he*   **b**8:28 Other mss. read *Gergesenes*; still other mss. read *Gadarenes*   **c**8:31 Lit. *with him*   **d**9:2 Lit. *they*   **e**9:4 Lit. *saw*

say, 'Get up and walk'? [6]But I want you to know[a] that the Son of Man has authority on earth to forgive sins." Then he said to the paralyzed man, "Get up, pick up your stretcher, and go home!"

[7]So the man[b] got up and went home. [8]When the crowds saw this, they became frightened,[c] and they glorified God for giving such authority to humans.

Jesus Calls Matthew
(Mark 2:13–17; Luke 5:27–32)

[9]As Jesus went on from there, he saw a man named Matthew sitting at the tax collector's desk and said to him, "Follow me." So he got up and followed him.[a]

[10]While he was having dinner at Matthew's[d] home, many tax collectors and notorious[e] sinners arrived and began eating with Jesus and his disciples.[b] [11]The Pharisees saw this and said to his disciples, "Why does your teacher eat with tax collectors and notorious[f] sinners?"[c] [12]When Jesus[b] heard that, he said, "Healthy people don't need a physician, but sick people do. [13]Go and learn what this means: 'I want mercy and not sacrifice.'[g] For I didn't come to call righteous people, but sinners."[d]

A Question about Fasting
(Mark 2:18–22; Luke 5:33–39)

[14]Then John's disciples came to Jesus[h] and asked, "Why do we and the Pharisees fast often,[i] but your disciples don't fast?"[e] [15]Jesus said to them, "The wedding guests can't mourn as long as the groom is with them, can they? But the days will come when the groom will be taken away from them, and then they will fast.[f]

The Unshrunk Cloth
(Mark 2:21; Luke 5:36)

[16]"No one puts a piece of unshrunk cloth on an old garment. For the patch pulls away from the garment, and a

---

a 9:6 Lit. *So that you'll know* b 9:7,9:12 Lit. *he* c 9:8 Other mss. read *they were amazed* d 9:10 Lit. *the* e 9:10 The Gk. lacks *notorious* f 9:11 The Gk. lacks *notorious* g 9:13 Hos 6:6 h 9:14 Lit. *to him* i 9:14 Other mss. lack *often*

Cross-refs: 9:9 a Mark2:14; Lk5:27 | 9:10 b Mark2:15; Lk5:29 | 9:11 c Matt 11:19; Lk5:30; 15:2; Gal2:15 | 9:13 d Hos6:6; Mic6:6-8; Matt12:7; 1Tim1:15 | 9:14 e Mark2:18; Lk5:33; 18:12 | 9:15 f John3:29; Acts13:2-3; 14:23; 1Cor7:5

9:18
*a*Mark5:22;
Lk8:41

worse tear results. [17]Nor do people[a] pour new wine into old wineskins. If they do, the skins will burst, the wine will spill out, and the skins will be ruined. Instead, they pour new wine into fresh wineskins, and both are preserved."

9:20
*b*Mark5:25;
Lk8:43

Jesus Heals an Official's Daughter and a Woman with Chronic Bleeding
(Mark 5:21–43; Luke 8:40–56)

9:22
*c*Lk7:50; 8:48;
17:19; 18:42

[18]While Jesus[b] was telling them these things, an official came up, fell down before him, and said, "My daughter has just died. But come and lay your hand on her, and she will live."[a] [19]So Jesus got up and followed him, along with his disciples.

[20]Just then a woman who had been suffering from chronic bleeding for twelve years came up behind him and touched the fringe of his robe.[b] [21]For she had been saying to herself, "If I just touch his robe, I will get well." [22]When Jesus turned and saw her, he said, "Be courageous, daughter! Your faith has made you well." And from that very hour the woman was well.[c]

9:23
*d*2Chr35:25;
Mark5:38;
Lk8:51

[23]When Jesus came to the official's house and saw the flute players and the crowd making a commotion,[d] [24]he said, "Go away! The girl hasn't died but is sleeping." They laughed and laughed at him.[e] [25]But when the crowd had been driven outside, he went in and took the girl by the hand, and she got up. [26]The news of this spread throughout that land.

9:24
*e*Acts20:10

Jesus Heals Two Blind Men

9:27
*f*Matt15:22;
20:30-31;
Mark10:47-48;
Lk18:38-39

[27]As Jesus was traveling on from there, two blind men followed him, shouting, "Have mercy on us, Son of David!"[f] [28]When he had gone into the house, the blind men came to him. Jesus asked them, "Do you believe I can do this?" They said to him, "Yes, Lord!"[c] [29]Then he touched their eyes and said, "According to your faith, let it be done for you!" [30]And their eyes were opened. Then Jesus sternly told them, "See to it that nobody knows about this."[g] [31]But they went out and spread the news about him throughout that land.[h]

9:30
*g*Matt8:4; 12:16;
17:9; Lk5:14

9:31
*h*Mark7:36

---

a *9:17* Lit. *they*   **b** *9:18* Lit. *he*   **c** *9:28* Or *Sir*

Jesus Heals a Man Who Couldn't Talk

³²As they were going out, a man who couldn't talk because he was demon-possessed was brought to him.*a* ³³As soon as the demon had been driven out, the man**a** began to speak. The crowds were amazed and said, "Nothing like this has ever been seen in Israel!" ³⁴But the Pharisees kept saying, "He drives out demons by the ruler of demons."**b**b

The Compassion of Jesus

³⁵Then Jesus began traveling through all the cities and villages, teaching in their synagogues, proclaiming the gospel of the kingdom, and healing every disease and every illness.*c* ³⁶When he saw the crowds, he was deeply moved with compassion for them, because they were troubled and helpless, like sheep without a shepherd.*d* ³⁷Then he said to his disciples, "The harvest is vast, but the workers are few.*e* ³⁸So ask the Lord of the harvest to send out workers into his harvest."*f*

Jesus Appoints Twelve Apostles
(Mark 3:13–19; Luke 6:12–16)

10 ¹Then Jesus**c** called his twelve disciples to him and gave them authority over unclean spirits, so that they could drive them out and heal every disease and every illness.*g* ²These are the names of the twelve apostles: first, Simon (who is called Peter) and his brother Andrew; James, the son of Zebedee, and his brother John;*h* ³Philip and Bartholomew; Thomas and Matthew the tax collector; James, the son of Alphaeus, and Thaddaeus;**d** ⁴Simon the Cananaean**e** and Judas Iscariot, who later**f** betrayed Jesus.**g***i*

Jesus Sends Out the Twelve
(Mark 6:7–13; Luke 9:1–6)

⁵These were the twelve whom Jesus sent out, charging them with the words, "Don't turn off into the road that leads to the Gentiles, and don't enter a town of the Samaritans.*j*

---

a *9:33* Lit. *the man who couldn't talk*   b *9:34* Other mss. lack this verse
c *10:1* Lit. *he*   d *10:3* Other mss. read *Lebbaeus called Thaddaeus*
e *10:4* Cananaean is Aram. for *Zealot*   f *10:4* Lit. *also*   g *10:4* Lit. *him*

9:32
a Matt 12:22;
Lk 11:14

9:34
b Matt 12:24;
Mark 3:22;
Lk 11:15

9:35
c Matt 4:23;
Mark 6:6;
Lk 13:22

9:36
d Num 27:17;
1 Kings 22:17;
Ezek 34:5;
Zech 10:2;
Mark 6:34

9:37
e Lk 10:2;
John 4:35

9:38
f 2 Thes 3:1

10:1
g Mark 3:13-14;
6:7; Lk 6:13; 9:1

10:2
h John 1:42

10:4
i Lk 6:15;
John 13:26;
Acts 1:13

10:5
j 2 Kings 17:24;
Matt 4:15;
John 4:9,20

10:6
*a*Isa53:6;
Jer50:6,17;
Ezek34:5-6,16;
Matt15:24;
Acts13:46;
1Peter2:25

10:7
*b*Matt3:2; 4:17;
Lk9:2; 10:9

10:8
*c*Acts8:18,20

10:9
*d*1Sam9:7;
Mark6:8; Lk9:3;
10:4; 22:35

10:10
*e*Lk10:7;
1Cor9:7;
1Tim5:18

10:11
*f*Lk10:8

10:13
*g*Ps35:13;
Lk10:5

10:14
*h*Neh5:13;
Mark6:11; Lk9:5;
10:10-11;
Acts13:51; 18:6

10:15
*i*Matt 11:22,24

10:16
*j*Lk10:3;
Rom16:19;
1Cor14:20;
Eph5:15;
Phil2:15

10:17
*k*Matt24:9;
Mark13:9;
Lk12:11; 21:12;
Acts5:40

10:18
*l*Acts12:1; 24:10;
25:7,23;
2Tim4:16

10:19
*m*Exod4:12;
Jer1:7;
Mark13:11-13;
Lk12:11;
21:14-15

10:20
*n*2Sam23:2;
Acts4:8; 6:10;
2Tim4:17

10:21
*o*Mic7:6;
Matt10:35-36;
Lk21:16

10:22
*p*Dan12:12-13;
Matt24:13;
Mark13:13;
Lk21:17

⁶Go, instead, to the lost sheep of the nation*a* of Israel.*a* ⁷As you go, keep on proclaiming, 'The kingdom of heaven is near!'*b* ⁸Heal the sick, raise the dead, cleanse lepers, drive out demons. Without payment you have received. Without payment you are to give.*c* ⁹Don't take any gold, silver, or copper in your moneybags,*d* ¹⁰or a traveling bag for the trip, or an extra shirt,*b* or sandals, or a walking stick. For the worker deserves his food.*e*

¹¹"Whatever town or village you enter, find out who is worthy in it and stay there until you leave.*f* ¹²As you enter the house, greet it. ¹³If the house is receptive,*c* let your blessing of peace come on it. But if it isn't receptive,*c* let your blessing of peace return to you.*g* ¹⁴If no one welcomes you or listens to your words, as you leave that house or town, shake its dust off your feet.*h* ¹⁵Truly I tell you, it will be more bearable for the land of Sodom and Gomorrah on the day of judgment than for that town!"*i*

Coming Persecutions
(Mark 13:9–13; Luke 21:12–17)

¹⁶"See, I'm sending you out like sheep among wolves. So be as cunning as serpents and as innocent as doves.*j* ¹⁷Watch out for people, for they will hand you over to the local councils and whip you in their synagogues.*k* ¹⁸Because of me you will be brought before governors and kings to testify to them and the Gentiles.*l* ¹⁹When they hand you over, don't worry about how you are to speak or what you are to say,*d* for in that hour what you are to say will be given to you.*m* ²⁰For it won't be you speaking, but the Spirit of your Father speaking through*e* you.*n*

²¹"Brother will hand brother over to death, and a father his child. Children will rebel against parents and have them put to death.*o* ²²You will be hated by everyone because of my name. But the person who endures to the end will be saved.*p* ²³So when they persecute you in one town, flee to the next. For truly I tell you, you certainly will not have

---

a*10:6* Lit. *house*   **b***10:10* Lit. *two shirts*   **c***10:13* Lit. *worthy*   **d***10:19* Lit. *about how or what you are to say*   **e***10:20* Or *in*

gone through the towns of Israel before the Son of Man comes.[a]

24"A disciple is not above his teacher, and a slave is not above his master.[b] 25It's enough for a disciple to be like his teacher and a slave to be like his master. If they have called the head of the house Beelzebul, how much more will they do the same to those[a] of his household!"[c]

Fear God
(Luke 12:2–7)

26"So never be afraid of them. For there is nothing covered that will not be exposed, and nothing secret that will not be made known.[d] 27What I tell you in darkness you must speak in the daylight, and what is whispered[b] in your ear you must shout from the housetops. 28Stop being[c] afraid of those who kill the body but can't kill the soul. Instead, be afraid of the one who can destroy both body and soul in hell.[d][e]

29"Two sparrows are sold for a penny, aren't they? Yet not one of them will fall to the ground without your Father's permission.[e] 30Indeed, even the hairs on your head have all been counted![f] 31So stop being[f] afraid. You are worth more than a bunch of sparrows."

Acknowledging Christ
(Luke 12:8–9)

32"Therefore, everyone who acknowledges me before people I, too, will acknowledge before my Father in heaven.[g] 33But whoever denies me before people I, too, will deny before my Father in heaven."[h]

Not Peace, but a Sword
(Luke 12:51–53; 14:26–27)

34"Don't think that I came to bring peace on earth. I didn't come to bring peace but a sword![g][i] 35For I came to turn[j]

---

a 10:25 Lit. how much more those   b 10:27 Lit. what you hear   c 10:28 Or Don't be   d 10:28 Gk. Gehenna   e 10:29 Lit. apart from your Father f 10:31 Or don't be   g 10:34 I.e. conflict

10:23 a Matt2:13; 4:12; 12:15; 16:28; Acts8:1; 9:25; 14:6

10:24 b Lk6:40; John13:16; 15:20

10:25 c Matt12:24; Mark3:22; Lk 11:15; John8:48,52

10:26 d Mark4:22; Lk8:17; 12:2-3

10:28 e Isa8:12-13; Lk12:4; 1Peter3:14

10:30 f 1Sam14:45; 2Sam14:11; Lk21:18; Acts27:34

10:32 g Lk12:8; Rom10:9-10; Rev3:5

10:33 h Mark8:38; Lk9:26; 2Tim2:12

10:34 i Lk12:49,51-53

10:35 j Mic7:6

10:36
ᵃPs41:9; 55:13;
Mic7:6;
John13:18

'a man against his father,
a daughter against her mother,
and a daughter-in-law against her mother-in-law.
³⁶A person's enemies will be members of his own
family.'ᵃᵃ

10:37
ᵇLk14:26

³⁷"The person who loves his father or mother more than me isn't worthy of me, and the person who loves a son or daughter more than me isn't worthy of me.ᵇ ³⁸The person who doesn't take up his cross and follow me isn't worthy of me.ᶜ ³⁹The person who finds his life will lose it, and the person who loses his life because of me will find it."ᵈ

10:38
ᶜMatt16:24;
Mark8:34;
Lk9:23; 14:27

Rewards
(Mark 9:41)

⁴⁰"The person who receives you receives me, and the person who receives me receives the one who sent me.ᵉ ⁴¹The person who receives a prophet asᵇ a prophet will receive a prophet's reward, and the person who receives a righteous person asᵇ a righteous person will receive a righteous person's reward.ᶠ ⁴²Truly I tell you, whoever gives even a cup of cold water to one of these little ones because he'sᵇ a disciple will never lose his reward."ᵍ

10:39
ᵈMatt16:25;
Lk17:33;
John12:25

10:40
ᵉMatt8:5;
Lk9:48; 10:16;
John12:44; 13:20;
Gal4:14

10:41
ᶠ1Kings17:10;
18:4; 2Kings4:8

John the Baptist Sends Messengers to Jesus
(Luke 7:18–35)

11 ¹When Jesus had finished instructing his twelve disciples, he left there to teach and preach in their cities.

²Now when John in prison heard about the activities of Christ,ᶜ he sent a messageᵈ by his disciplesʰ ³and asked him, "Are you the Coming One, or should we wait for someone else?"ⁱ

10:42
ᵍMatt8:5-6;
25:40; Mark9:41;
Heb6:10

⁴Jesus answered them, "Go and tell John what you hear and see: ⁵the blind see, the lame walk, lepers are cleansed, the deaf hear, the dead are raised, and the destitute hear the

11:2
ʰMatt14:3;
Lk7:18-19

11:3
ⁱGen49:10;
Num24:17;
Dan9:24;
John6:14

a 10:36 Mic 7:6   b 10:41,10:42 Lit. *in the name of*   c 11:2 I.e. the Messiah
d 11:2 Lit. *he sent*

good news.[a] [6]How blessed is anyone who is not offended by me!"[b]

[7]As they were leaving, Jesus began to speak to the crowds about John. "What did you go out into the wilderness to see? A reed shaken by the wind?[c] [8]Really, what did you go out to see? A man dressed in fancy clothes? See, those who wear fancy clothes live in kings' houses. [9]Really, what did you go out to see? A prophet? Yes, I tell you, and even more than a prophet![d] [10]This is the man about whom it is written,[e]

> 'See, I'm sending my messenger ahead of you,
>   who will prepare your way before you.'[a]

[11]Truly I tell you, among those born of women no one has appeared who is greater than John the Baptist. Yet even the least important person in the kingdom of heaven is greater than he.

[12]"From the days of John the Baptist until the present, the kingdom of heaven has been forcefully advancing,[b] and violent people have been attacking it.[f] [13]For all the prophets and the Law prophesied up to the time of John,[g] [14]and if you're willing to accept it, he is Elijah who is to come.[c][h] [15]Let the person who has ears[d] listen![i]

[16]"To what can I compare this generation? It's like little children who sit in the marketplaces and shout to each other,[j]

> [17]'A wedding song we played for you,
>   The dance you did but scorn.
> A woeful dirge we chanted, too,
>   But then you would not mourn.'

[18]For John didn't come eating or drinking, yet people[e] say, 'He has a demon!' [19]The Son of Man came eating and drinking, and they say, 'Look, a glutton and a drunk, a friend of tax collectors and notorious[f] sinners!'[k]

---

a 11:10 Mal 3:1   **b** 11:12 Or *has been under violent attack*   **c** 11:14 Or *is about to come*   **d** 11:15 Other mss. read *ears to hear*   **e** 11:18 Lit. *they*   **f** 11:19 The Gk. lacks *notorious*

11:5
[a]Ps22:26;
Isa29:18; 35:4-6;
42:7; 61:1;
Lk4:18;
John2:23; 3:2;
5:36; 10:25,38;
14:11; James2:5

11:6
[b]Isa8:14-15;
Matt13:57; 24:10;
26:31;
Rom9:32-33;
1Cor1:23; 2:14;
Gal5:11;
1Peter2:8

11:7
[c]Lk7:24;
Eph4:14

11:9
[d]Matt14:5;
21:26; Lk1:76;
7:26

11:10
[e]Mal3:1;
Mark1:2; Lk1:76;
7:27

11:12
[f]Lk16:16

11:13
[g]Mal4:6

11:14
[h]Mal4:5;
Matt17:12;
Lk1:17

11:15
[i]Matt13:9; Lk8:8;
Rev2:7,11,17,29;
3:6,13,22

11:16
[j]Lk7:31

11:19
[k]Matt9:10;
Lk7:35

11:20
aLk10:13

Absolved from every act of sin,
Is wisdom by her kith and kin."[a]

Jesus Denounces Unrepentant Cities
(Luke 10:13–15)

11:21
bJonah3:7-8

11:22
cMatt10:15,24

20Then Jesus[b] began to denounce the cities in which most of his miracles had taken place, because they didn't repent.[a] 21"How terrible it will be for you, Chorazin! How terrible it will be for you, Bethsaida! For if the miracles that happened in you had taken place in Tyre and Sidon, they would have repented long ago in sackcloth and ashes.[b] 22Indeed I tell you, it will be more bearable for Tyre and Sidon on the day of judgment than for you![c] 23And you, Capernaum! You won't be lifted up to heaven, will you? You'll go down to the grave![c] For if the miracles that happened in you had taken place in Sodom, it would have remained to this day.[d] 24Indeed I tell you, it will be bearable for the land of Sodom on the day of judgment than for you!"[e]

11:23
dIsa14:13;
Lam2:1

11:24
eMatt10:15

Jesus Praises the Father and Invites the Disciples to Come to Him
(Luke 10:21–22)

11:25
fPs8:2;
Matt16:17;
Lk10:21;
1Cor1:19,27; 2:8;
2Cor3:14

25At that time Jesus said, "I praise you, Father, Lord of heaven and earth, because you have hidden these things from wise and intelligent people and have revealed them to infants.[f] 26Yes, Father, for this is what was pleasing to you. 27All things have been entrusted to me by my Father. No one fully knows the Son except the Father, and no one fully knows the Father except the Son and the person to whom the Son chooses to reveal him.[g]

11:27
gMatt28:18;
Lk10:22;
John1:18; 3:35;
6:46; 10:15; 13:3;
17:2; 1Cor15:27

28"Come to me, all of you who are weary and loaded down with burdens, and I will give you rest. 29Place my yoke on you and learn from me, for I am gentle and humble in heart, and you will find rest for your souls.[h] 30For my yoke is pleasant,[d] and my burden is light."[i]

11:29
hJer6:16;
Zech9:9;
John13:15;
Phil2:5,7-8;
1Peter2:21;
1John2:6

---

a 11:19 Lit. *by all her children*; other mss. read *by her actions*   b 11:20 Lit. *he*   c 11:23 Gk. *Hades*, a reference to the realm of the dead   d 11:30 Or *kind*; i.e., a yoke that has been custom-fitted

11:30
i1John5:3

Jesus Is Lord of the Sabbath
(Mark 2:23–28; Luke 6:1–5)

12 ¹At that time Jesus walked through the grainfields on the Sabbath. His disciples became hungry and began picking heads of grain to eat.*ᵃ* ²When the Pharisees saw this, they said to him, "Look! Your disciples are doing what is not lawful to do on the Sabbath!"

³But he said to them, "Haven't you read what David did when he and his companions were hungry?*ᵇ* ⁴How is it that he went into the house of God and ate the Bread of the Presence, which was not lawful for him and his companions to eat but was reserved*ᵃ* for the priests?*ᶜ* ⁵Or haven't you read in the Law that on the Sabbath the priests in the Temple violate the Sabbath and yet are innocent?*ᵈ* ⁶But I tell you, something greater than the Temple is here!*ᵉ* ⁷If you had known what 'I want mercy and not sacrifice'*ᵇ* means, you wouldn't have condemned the innocent.*ᶠ* ⁸For the Son of Man is Lord of the Sabbath."

Jesus Heals a Man with a Paralyzed Hand
(Mark 3:1–6; Luke 6:6–11)

⁹Moving on from there, Jesus*ᶜ* went into their synagogue.*ᵍ* ¹⁰Suddenly a man with a paralyzed hand appeared. The people*ᵈ* asked Jesus*ᵉ* if it was lawful to heal on the Sabbath, intending to accuse him of doing something wrong.*ʰ*

¹¹But he said to them, "Is there a man among you who, if he had one sheep and it fell into a ditch on the Sabbath, wouldn't take hold of it and pull it out?*ⁱ* ¹²How much more is a human being worth than a sheep! So it is lawful to do good on the Sabbath."

¹³Then he said to the man, "Hold out your hand." He held it out and it became normal, as healthy as the other. ¹⁴The Pharisees, however, went out and plotted against Jesus*ᵉ* to kill him.*ʲ*

---

a *12:4* Lit. *but only*   **b** *12:7* Hos 6:6   **c** *12:9* Lit. *he*   **d** *12:10* Lit. *They*
e *12:10,12:14* Lit. *him*

Side references:

12:1
*ᵃ*Deut23:25;
Mark2:23; Lk6:1

12:3
*ᵇ*1Sam21:6

12:4
*ᶜ*Exod25:30;
29:32-33;
Lev8:31; 24:5,9

12:5
*ᵈ*Num28:9;
John7:22

12:6
*ᵉ*2Chr6:18;
Mal3:1

12:7
*ᶠ*Hos6:6;
Mic6:8;
Matt9:13

12:9
*ᵍ*Mark3:1; Lk6:6

12:10
*ʰ*Lk13:14;
14:3John9:16

12:11
*ⁱ*Exod23:4-5;
Deut22:4

12:14
*ʲ*Matt27:1;
Mark3:6; Lk6:11;
John5:18; 10:39;
11:53

28

12:15
aMatt10:23; 19:2;
Mark3:7

Jesus, God's Chosen Servant

15When Jesus became aware of this, he left that place. Many crowds[a] followed him, and he healed all of them,[a] 16ordering them not to make him known.[b] 17This was to fulfill what was declared by the prophet Isaiah when he said,

12:16
bMatt9:30

> 18"Here is my Servant whom I have chosen,[c]
>   whom I love, and with whom my soul is pleased!
> I will put my Spirit on him,
>   and he will proclaim justice[b] to the Gentiles.[c]
> 19He will not quarrel or shout,
>   and no one will hear his voice in the streets.
> 20He will not snap off a broken reed
>   or snuff out a smoldering wick
>   until he brings justice[b] to victory.
> 21And in his name the Gentiles[c] will hope."[d]

12:18
cIsa42:1;
Matt3:17; 17:5

Jesus Is Accused of Working with Beelzebul
(Mark 3:20–30; Luke 11:14–23; 12:10)

22Then a demon-possessed man who was blind and unable to talk was brought to him. Jesus[e] healed him so that the man[f] could speak and see.[d] 23All the crowds were amazed and kept saying, "This man isn't the Son of David, is he?" 24But when the Pharisees heard this, they said, "This man drives out demons only by Beelzebul, the ruler of the demons."[e]

12:22
dMatt9:32;
Mark3:11;
Lk 11:14

12:24
eMatt9:34;
Mark3:22;
Lk 11:15

25He knew what they were thinking and said to them, "Every kingdom divided against itself is destroyed, and every city or household divided against itself will not stand.[f] 26So if Satan drives out Satan, he's divided against himself. How, then, can his kingdom stand? 27If I drive out demons by Beelzebul, by whom do your own followers[g] drive them out? That's why they will be your judges! 28But if I drive out demons by the Spirit of God, then the kingdom of God has come to you.[g] 29How can someone go into a strong man's

12:25
fMatt9:4;
John2:25;
Rev2:23

12:28
gDan2:44; 7:14;
Lk1:33; 11:20;
17:20-21

a 12:15 Other mss. lack *crowds*   b 12:18,12:20 Or *judgment*   c 12:18,12:21 Or *nations*   d 12:21 Isa 42:1-4   e 12:22 Lit. *He*   f 12:22 Lit. *the man who was unable to talk*   g 12:27 Lit. *sons*

house and carry off his possessions without first tying up the strong man? Then he can ransack his house.*a*

30"The person who isn't with me is against me, and the person who doesn't gather with me scatters. 31So I tell you, every sin and blasphemy will be forgiven,**a** but blasphemy against the Spirit will not be forgiven.*b* 32Whoever speaks a word against the Son of Man will be forgiven, but whoever speaks against the Holy Spirit will not be forgiven, either in this age or in the one to come."*c*

A Tree Is Known by Its Fruit
(Luke 6:43–45)

33"Either make the tree good and its fruit good, or make the tree rotten and its fruit rotten. For a tree is known by its fruit.*d* 34You children of serpents! How can you say anything good when you are evil? For the mouth speaks out of the abundance of the heart.*e* 35A good person brings good things out of a good treasure, and an evil person brings evil things out of an evil treasure. 36I tell you, on the day of judgment people will give an account for every thoughtless**b** word they utter. 37For by your words you'll be acquitted, and by your words you'll be condemned."

The Sign of Jonah
(Mark 8:11–12; Luke 11:29–32)

38Then some of the scribes and Pharisees said to Jesus,**c** "Teacher, we want to see a sign from you."*f* 39But he replied to them, "An evil and adulterous generation craves a sign. Yet no sign will be given to it except the sign of the prophet Jonah.*g* 40For just as Jonah was in the stomach of the sea creature for three days and three nights,**d** so the Son of Man will be in the heart of the earth for three days and three nights.*h* 41The men of Nineveh will stand up with this generation at the judgment and will condemn it, because they repented at the preaching of Jonah. But look—something greater than Jonah is here!*i* 42The queen of the south will stand up with this generation at the judgment and will

---

a 12:31 Lit. *will be forgiven to people*　**b** 12:36 Or *worthless*　**c** 12:38 Lit. *to him*　**d** 12:40 Jonah 1:17

12:29
a Isa49:24;
Lk 11:21-23

12:31
b Mark3:28;
Lk12:10;
Acts7:51;
Heb6:4; 10:26,
29; 1John5:16

12:32
c Matt 11:19;
13:55; John7:12,
52; 1Tim1:13

12:33
d Matt7:17;
Lk6:43-44

12:34
e Matt3:7; 23:33;
Lk6:45

12:38
f Matt16:1;
Mark8:11;
Lk 11:16,29;
John2:18;
1Cor1:22

12:39
g Isa57:3;
Matt16:4;
Mark8:38;
John4:48

12:40
h Jonah1:17

12:41
i Jer3:11;
Ezek16:51-52;
Jonah3:5;
Lk 11:32;
Rom2:27

12:42
a 1Kings10:1;
2Chr9:1;
Lk 11:31

condemn it, because she came from the ends of the earth to hear the wisdom of Solomon. But look—something greater than Solomon is here!"*a*

The Return of the Unclean Spirit
(Luke 11:24–26)

12:43
b Job1:7;
Lk 11:24;
1Peter5:8

⁴³"Whenever an unclean spirit goes out of a person, it wanders through waterless places looking for a place to rest but finds none.*b* ⁴⁴Then it says, 'I'll go back to the home*a* I left.' When it arrives, it finds it empty, swept clean, and put in order. ⁴⁵Then it goes and brings with it seven other spirits more evil than itself, and they go in and settle there. And so the final condition of that person becomes worse than the first. That's just what will happen to this evil generation!"*c*

12:45
c Heb6:4; 10:26;
2Peter2:20-22

The True Family of Jesus
(Mark 3:31–35; Luke 8:19–21)

12:46
d Matt13:55;
Mark3:31; 6:3;
Lk8:19-21;
John2:12; 7:3,5;
Acts1:14;
1Cor9:5;
Gal1:19

⁴⁶While Jesus*b* was still speaking to the crowds, his mother and brothers were standing outside, wanting to speak to him.*d* ⁴⁷Someone told him, "Look! Your mother and your brothers are standing outside asking to speak to you."*c* ⁴⁸He asked the man who told him, "Who is my mother, and who are my brothers?" ⁴⁹Then pointing with his hand at his disciples, he said, "Here are my mother and my brothers! ⁵⁰For whoever does the will of my Father in heaven is my brother and sister and mother."*e*

12:50
e John15:14;
Gal5:6; 6:15;
Col3:11;
Heb2:11

The Parable about a Sower
(Mark 4:1–9; Luke 8:4–8)

13:1
f Mark4:1

13 ¹That day Jesus left the house and sat down beside the sea.*f* ²Such large crowds gathered around him that he got into a boat and sat down, while the entire crowd stood on the shore.*g* ³Then he began to tell them many things in parables. He said, "Listen! A sower went out to sow.*h* ⁴As he was sowing, some seeds fell along the path, and birds came and ate them up. ⁵Other seeds fell on stony ground, where they didn't have a lot of soil. They sprouted at once because the soil wasn't deep.

13:2
g Lk5:3; 8:4

13:3
h Lk8:5

a 12:44 Lit. *my home*   b 12:46 Lit. *he*   c 12:47 Other mss. lack this verse

⁶But when the sun came up, they were scorched. Since they didn't have any roots, they dried up. ⁷Other seeds fell among thornbushes, and the thornbushes came up and choked them. ⁸But other seeds fell on good soil and produced a crop, some a hundred, some sixty, and some thirty times[b] what was sown.[a][a] ⁹Let the person who has ears[b] listen!"[b]

The Purpose of the Parables
(Mark 4:10–12; Luke 8:9–10)

¹⁰Then the disciples came and said to Jesus,[c] "Why do you speak to people[d] in parables?" ¹¹He answered them, "You have been given knowledge about the secrets of the kingdom of heaven, but it hasn't been given to them.[c] ¹²For to anyone who has, more will be given, and he will have more than enough. But from the one who doesn't have anything, even what he has will be taken away from him.[d] ¹³That's why I speak to them in parables, because

> 'they look but don't see,
> and they listen but don't hear or
> understand.'

¹⁴With them the prophecy of Isaiah is being fulfilled, which says:[e]

> 'You will listen and listen but never understand.
> You will look and look but never comprehend.
> ¹⁵For this people's heart has become dull,[f]
> and their ears are hard of hearing.[e]
> They have shut their eyes
> so that they might not see with their eyes,
> and hear with their ears,
> and understand with their heart and turn,
> and I would heal them.'[f]

¹⁶"How blessed are your eyes because they see, and your ears because they hear![g] ¹⁷For truly I tell you, many

---

a 13:8 Lit. *thirty times*   b 13:9 Other mss. read *ears to hear*   c 13:10 Lit. *to him*   d 13:10 Lit. *to them*   e 13:15 Lit. *they hear with ears of heaviness*   f 13:15 Isa 6:9-10

32

13:8
a Gen26:12

13:9
b Matt 11:15;
Mark4:9

13:11
c Matt 11:25;
16:17; Mark4:11;
1Cor2:10;
1John2:27

13:12
d Matt25:29;
Mark4:25;
Lk8:18; 19:26

13:14
e Isa6:9;
Ezek12:2;
Mark4:12;
Lk8:10;
John12:40;
Acts28:26-27;
Rom 11:8;
2Cor3:14-15

13:15
f Heb5:11

13:16
g Matt16:17;
Lk10:23-24;
John20:29

13:17
a Heb 11:13;
1Peter1:10-11

prophets and righteous people longed to see the things you see but didn't see them, and to hear the things you hear but didn't hear them."[a]

Jesus Explains the Parable about the Sower
(Mark 4:13–20; Luke 8:11–15)

13:18
b Mark4:14;
Lk8:11

[18]"Listen, then, to the parable about the sower.[b] [19]When anyone hears the word about the kingdom yet doesn't understand it, the evil one comes and snatches away what was sown in his heart. This is what was sown along the path.[c]

13:19
c Matt4:23

[20]As for what was sown on the stony ground, this is the person who hears the word and accepts it at once with joy.[d] [21]But since he doesn't have any root in himself, he lasts for only a short time. When trouble or persecution comes along because of the word, he immediately falls away.[e] [22]As for what was sown among the thornbushes, this is the person who hears the word, but the worries of life and the deceitful pleasures of wealth choke the word so that it can't produce a crop.[f] [23]But as for what was sown on good soil, this is the person who hears the word, understands it, and produces a crop that yields a hundred, sixty, or thirty times what was sown."[a]

13:20
d Isa58:2;
Ezek33:31-32;
John5:35

The Parable about the Weeds among the Wheat

[24]He presented another parable to them, saying, "The kingdom of heaven may be compared to a man who sowed good seed in his field. [25]While people were sleeping, his enemy came and sowed weeds among the wheat and went away. [26]When the crop came up and bore grain, the weeds appeared, too. [27]The owner's servants came and said to him, 'Master, you sowed good seed in your field, didn't you? Then where did these weeds come from?' [28]He told them, 'An enemy did this!' The servants said to him, 'Then do you want us to go and pull them out?' [29]He said, 'No, for if you pull out the weeds, you might pull out the wheat with them. [30]Let both grow together until the harvest, and at harvest time I will tell the reapers, "Gather the weeds first and tie

13:21
e Matt 11:6;
2Tim1:15

13:22
f Jer4:3;
Matt19:23;
Mark10:23;
Lk18:24;
1Tim6:9;
2Tim4:10

---

a *13:23* The Gk. lacks *what was sown*

them in bundles for burning, but bring the wheat into my barn." "'[a]

The Parables about a Mustard Seed and Yeast
(Mark 4:30–32; Luke 13:18–21)

[31]He presented another parable to them, saying, "The kingdom of heaven is like a mustard seed that a man took and planted in his field.[b] [32]Although it's the smallest of[a] all seeds, when it's fully grown it's larger than the garden plants and becomes a tree, and the birds in the sky come and nest in its branches."

[33]He told them another parable: "The kingdom of heaven is like yeast that a woman took and mixed with[b] three measures of flour until all of it was leavened."[c]

Why Jesus Used Parables
(Mark 4:33–34)

[34]Jesus told the crowds all these things in parables. He didn't them tell anything without using a parable.[c][d] [35]This was to fulfill what was declared by the prophet[d] when he said,[e]

"I will open my mouth to speak in parables.[e]
I will declare what has been hidden
　　from the foundation of the world."[f]

Jesus Explains the Parable about the Weeds

[36]Then Jesus[g] left the crowds and went into the house. His disciples came to him and said, "Explain to us the parable about the weeds in the field." [37]He answered, "The person who sowed good seed is the Son of Man, [38]while the field is the world. The good seed are those who belong to[h] the kingdom, while the weeds are those who belong to[h] the evil one.[f] [39]The enemy who sowed them is the devil, the harvest is the end of the age, and the reapers are the angels.[g] [40]Just as weeds are gathered and burned with fire, so it will be at end of the[i] age. [41]The Son of Man will send his angels,

---

a13:32 Or *it's smaller than*　b13:33 Lit. *hid in*　c13:34 Lit. *without a parable*　d13:35 Other mss. read *Isaiah the prophet*　e13:35 Lit. *my mouth in parables*　f13:35 Ps 78:2　g13:36 Lit. *he*　h13:38 Lit. *the sons of*　i13:40 Other mss. read *this*

Cross-reference column:

13:30
a Matt3:12

13:31
b Isa2:2-3;
Mic4:1;
Mark4:30;
Lk13:18-19

13:33
c Lk13:20

13:34
d Mark4:33-34

13:35
e Ps78:2;
Rom16:25-26;
1Cor2:7; Eph3:9;
Col1:26

13:38
f Gen3:13;
Matt24:14; 28:19;
Mark16:15,20;
Lk24:47;
John8:44;
Acts13:10;
Rom10:18;
Col1:6; 1John3:8

13:39
g Joel3:13;
Rev14:15

13:41
*a*Matt18:7;
2Peter2:1-2

and they'll gather from his kingdom everything that causes others to sin and those who practice lawlessness,*a* 42and they'll throw them into a blazing furnace. In that place there will be wailing and gnashing of teeth.*ab* 43Then the righteous will shine like the sun in their Father's kingdom. Let the person who has ears*b* listen!"*c*

13:42
*b*Matt3:12; 13:12,
50; Rev19:20;
20:10

The Parable about a Hidden Treasure

44"The kingdom of heaven is like treasure hidden in a field that a man found and hid. In his joy he went and sold everything he had and bought that field."*d*

13:43
*c*Dan12:3;
Matt15:9;
1Cor15:42-43,58

The Parable about a Valuable Pearl

45"Again, the kingdom of heaven is like a merchant searching for fine pearls. 46When he found a very valuable pearl, he went and sold everything he had and bought it."*e*

13:44
*d*Isa55:1;
Phil3:7-8;
Rev3:18

The Parable about a Net

47"Again, the kingdom of heaven is like a large net thrown into the sea that gathered all kinds of fish.*f* 48When it was full, the fishermen*c* hauled it ashore. Then they sat down, sorted the good fish into containers, and threw the bad ones away. 49That's how it will be at the end of the age. The angels will go out and separate the evil from the righteous*g* 50and will throw them into a blazing furnace. In that place there will be wailing and gnashing of teeth."*ah*

13:46
*e*Prov2:4;
3:14-15; 8:10,19

13:47
*f*Matt22:10

New and Old Treasures

51"Do you understand all these things?" They said to him, "Yes." 52Then he told them, "That's why every scribe who has been trained for the kingdom of heaven is like the master of a household who brings both new and old things out of his treasure chest."*i*

13:49
*g*Matt25:32

Jesus Is Rejected at Nazareth
(Mark 6:1–6; Luke 4:16–30)

53When Jesus had finished these parables, he left that place. 54He went to his hometown and began teaching the

13:50
*h*Matt13:42

13:52
*i*Song7:13

a 13:42,13:50 I.e. extreme pain   **b** 13:43 Other mss. read *ears to hear*   **c** 13:48 Lit. *they*

people[a] in their synagogue in such a way that they were amazed and said, "Where did this man get this wisdom and these miracles?[a] 55This is the builder's[b] son, isn't it? His mother is named Mary, isn't she? His brothers are James, Joseph, Simon, and Judas, aren't they?[b] 56And his sisters are all with us, aren't they? So where did this man get all these things?" 57And they were offended by him. But Jesus told them, "A prophet is without honor only in his hometown and in his own home."[c] 58He didn't perform many miracles there because of their unbelief.[d]

Jesus Recalls the Death of John the Baptist
(Mark 6:14–29; Luke 9:7–9)

14 1At that time Herod the tetrarch,[c] hearing about the fame of Jesus,[e] 2said to his servants, "This is John the Baptist! He has been raised from the dead, and that's why these miracles are at work in him."

3For Herod had arrested John, bound him with chains, and put him in prison on account of Herodias, his brother Philip's wife.[d][f] 4For John had been telling him, "It's not lawful for you to have her."[g] 5Although Herod[e] wanted to kill him, he was afraid of the crowd, since they regarded John[f] as a prophet.[h]

6But when Herod's birthday celebration was held, the daughter of Herodias danced before the guests.[g] She pleased Herod 7so much that he promised with an oath to give her whatever she asked for. 8Prompted by her mother, she said, "Give me, right here on a platter, the head of John the Baptist." 9Though the king was saddened at this, because of his oaths and his guests he ordered it to be given. 10So he sent word[h] and had John beheaded in prison. 11His head was brought on a platter and given to the girl, and she took it to her mother. 12When John's[i] disciples came, they carried off the body and buried it. Then they went and told Jesus.

---

a 13:54 Lit. *them*　　b 13:55 Or *carpenter's*　　c 14:1 I.e. Herod Antipas, a son of King Herod and ruler over one of four districts in and around Palestine　　d 14:3 Other mss. read *his brother's*　　e 14:5 Lit. *he*　　f 14:5 Lit. *him*　　g 14:6 Lit. *in the middle*　　h 14:10 The Gk. lacks *word*　　i 14:12 Lit. *his*

Marginal cross-references

13:54
a Matt 2:23; Mark 6:1; Lk 4:16, 23

13:55
b Isa 49:7; Matt 12:46; Mark 6:3; 15:40; Lk 3:23; John 6:42

13:57
c Matt 11:6; Mark 6:3-4; Lk 4:24; John 4:44

13:58
d Mark 6:5-6

14:1
e Mark 6:14; Lk 9:7

14:3
f Mark 6:17; Lk 3:19-20

14:4
g Lev 18:16; 20:21

14:5
h Matt 21:26; Lk 20:6

14:13
a Matt10:23;
12:15; Mark6:32;
Lk9:19;
John6:1-2

Jesus Feeds More Than Five Thousand People

(Mark 6:30–44; Luke 9:10–17; John 6:1–14)

¹³When Jesus heard this, he left that place and went by boat[a] to a deserted place by himself. The crowds heard of it and followed him on foot from the towns.[a] ¹⁴As Jesus got out of the boat,[b] he saw a large crowd. He had compassion for them and healed their sick.[b]

¹⁵Now when evening came, the disciples went to him and said, "This is a deserted place, and it's already late. Send the crowds away so that they can go into the villages and buy food for themselves."[c] ¹⁶But Jesus said to them, "They don't need to go away. You give them something to eat." ¹⁷They told him, "We don't have anything here except five loaves of bread and two fish." ¹⁸He said, "Bring them here to me." ¹⁹Then he ordered the crowds to sit down on the grass. Taking the five loaves and the two fish, he looked up to heaven and blessed them. Then he broke the loaves in pieces and gave them to his disciples, and the disciples gave them to the crowds.[c][d] ²⁰All of them ate and were filled. Then the disciples[d] picked up what was left of the broken pieces, twelve baskets full. ²¹Now those who had eaten were about five thousand men, besides women and children.

14:14
b Matt9:36;
Mark6:34

14:15
c Mark6:35;
Lk9:12; John6:5

Jesus Walks on the Sea

(Mark 6:45–52; John 6:15–21)

²²Jesus[e] immediately made the disciples get into a boat and cross to the other side ahead of him, while he sent the crowds away. ²³After sending the crowds away, he went up on a hillside by himself to pray. When evening came, he was there alone.[e]

²⁴By this time the boat was in the middle of the sea[f] and was being battered by the waves, for the wind was against them. ²⁵Shortly before dawn[g] he came to them, walking on the sea. ²⁶When the disciples saw him walking on the sea,

14:19
d Matt15:36

14:23
e Mark6:46;
John6:16

---

a 14:13 Lit. *left that place by boat*   b 14:14 Lit. *he got out*   c 14:19 Lit. *the disciples to the crowds*   d 14:20 Lit. *they*   e 14:22 Lit. *He*   f 14:24 Other mss. read *many furlongs from the land*   g 14:25 Lit. *In the fourth watch of the night*

they were terrified and said, "It's a ghost!" They screamed in terror.*a*

27Immediately Jesus said to them, "Be courageous! It is I. Stop being afraid!" 28Peter answered him, "Lord, if it's you, order me to come to you on the water." 29Jesus*a* said, "Come on!" So Peter got down out of the boat and started walking on the water and came*b* to Jesus. 30But when he noticed the strong*c* wind, he was frightened. As he began to sink, he shouted, "Lord, save me!"

31At once Jesus reached out his hand, caught him, and said to him, "You who have little faith, why did you doubt?" 32When they got into the boat, the wind stopped blowing. 33Then the men in the boat began to worship Jesus,*d* saying, "You certainly are the Son of God!"*b*

Jesus Heals the Sick in Gennesaret
(Mark 6:53–56)

34They crossed over and came to shore at Gennesaret.*c* 35When the men of that place recognized Jesus,*d* they sent word*e* throughout that region, and they brought to him all who were sick. 36They kept begging him to let them touch just the fringe of his robe, and all who touched it were completely healed.*d*

Jesus Challenges the Tradition of the Elders
(Mark 7:1–23)

15 1Then some Pharisees and scribes came from Jerusalem to Jesus and said,*e* 2"Why do your disciples disregard the tradition of the elders? For they don't wash their hands when they eat."*f f*

3But he answered them, "Why do you also disregard the commandment of God because of your tradition? 4For God said,*g* 'Honor your father and your mother,'*h* and 'Whoever curses father or mother must certainly be put to death.'*i g*

---

a14:29 Lit. *He*   b14:29 Other mss. read *to go*   c14:30 Other mss. lack *strong*   d14:33,14:35 Lit. *him*   e14:35 The Gk. lacks *word*   f15:2 Lit. *eat bread*   g15:4 Other mss. read *commanded, saying*   h15:4 Exod 20:12; Deut 5:16   i15:4 Exod 21:17; Lev 20:9

14:26
*a*Job9:8

14:33
*b*Ps2:7;
Matt16:16; 26:63;
Mark1:1; Lk4:41;
John1:49; 6:69;
11:27; Acts8:37;
Rom1:4

14:34
*c*Mark6:53

14:36
*d*Matt9:20;
Mark3:10;
Lk6:19;
Acts19:12

15:1
*e*Mark7:1

15:2
*f*Mark7:5; Col2:8

15:4
*g*Exod20:12;
21:17; Lev19:3;
20:9; Deut5:16;
27:16; Prov20:20;
23:22; 30:17;
Eph6:2

15:5
a Mark7:11-12

15:7
b Mark7:6

15:8
c Isa29:13;
Ezek33:31

15:9
d Isa29:13;
Col2:18-22;
Titus1:14

15:10
e Mark7:14

15:11
f Acts10:15;
Rom14:14,17,20;
1Tim4:4;
Titus1:15

15:13
g John15:2;
1Cor3:12

15:14
h Isa9:16;
Mal2:8;
Matt23:16;
Lk6:39

15:15
i Mark7:17

15:16
j Matt16:9;
Mark7:18

15:17
k 1Cor6:13

15:18
l James3:6

15:19
m Gen6:5;
9:21Prov6:14;
Jer17:9;
Mark7:21

[5]But you say 'Whoever tells his father or his mother, "Whatever support you might have received from me has been given to God," '[aa] [6]does not have to honor his father.[b] Because of your tradition, then, you have revoked the authority of God's word.[c] [7]You hypocrites! How well did Isaiah prophesy of you when he said,[b]

[8]'These people honor me with their lips,[c]
> but their hearts are far from me.
[9]Their worship of me is empty,[d]
> because they teach human rules as
> doctrines.' "[d]

[10]Then he called the crowd and said to them, "Listen and understand![e] [11]It's not what goes into the mouth that makes a person unclean. It's what comes out of the mouth that makes a person unclean."[f]

[12]Then the disciples came and said to him, "Do you realize that the Pharisees were offended when they heard this statement?" [13]He replied, "Every plant that my heavenly Father did not plant will be pulled up by the roots.[g] [14]Leave them alone. They are blind guides of the blind.[e] If one blind person leads another blind person, both will fall into a ditch."[h]

[15]Then Peter said to him, "Explain to us this[f] parable."[i] [16]Jesus[g] said, "Are you still so ignorant?[j] [17]Don't you know that everything that goes into the mouth passes into the stomach and then goes out into a toilet?[k] [18]But the things that come out of the mouth come from the heart, and it is those things that make a person unclean.[l] [19]For it is out of the heart that evil thoughts come, as well as murder, adultery, sexual immorality, stealing, false testimony, and slander.[hm] [20]These are the things that make a person unclean. But eating with unwashed hands doesn't make a person unclean."

---

a 15:5 Lit. *is a gift*   **b** 15:6 Other mss. read *his father or his mother*
c 15:6 Other mss. read *Law*; still other mss. read *commandment*
d 15:9 Isa 29:13   **e** 15:14 Other mss. lack *of the blind*   **f** 15:15 Other mss. read *the*   **g** 15:16 Lit. *He*   **h** 15:19 Or *blasphemy*

A Canaanite Woman's Faith
(Mark 7:24–30)

²¹Then Jesus left that place and went to the region of Tyre and Sidon.*ᵃ* ²²Suddenly a Canaanite woman from that territory came near and began to shout, "Have mercy on me, Lord, Son of David! My daughter is severely demon-possessed!"

²³But he didn't answer her at all.*ᵃ* Then his disciples came up and kept urging him, "Send her away, for she keeps on screaming after us." ²⁴But he replied, "I was sent only to the lost sheep of the nation*ᵇ* of Israel."*ᵇ*

²⁵Then she came and fell down before him, saying, "Lord, help me!" ²⁶He replied, "It's not right*ᶜ* to take the children's bread and throw it to the puppies."*ᶜ* ²⁷She said, "Yes, Lord. But even the puppies eat the crumbs that fall from their masters' tables." ²⁸Then Jesus answered her, "O Woman, your faith is great! Let it be done for you as you want." That very hour her daughter was healed.

Jesus Heals Many People

²⁹Jesus left there and went along the Sea of Galilee. Then he went up on a hillside and sat down there.*ᵈ* ³⁰Large crowds came to him, bringing with them the lame, the blind, the crippled, those unable to talk, and many others. They placed them at his feet, and he healed them.*ᵉ* ³¹As a result, the crowd was amazed to see those who were unable to talk speaking, the crippled healed, the lame walking, and the blind seeing. So they praised the God of Israel.

Jesus Feeds More Than Four Thousand People
(Mark 8:1–10)

³²Then Jesus called his disciples and said, "I have compassion for the crowd because they've already been with me for three days and have nothing to eat. I don't want to send them away without food, or they may faint on the road."*ᶠ* ³³The disciples asked him, "Where in the wilderness are we to get enough bread to feed such a crowd?"*ᵍ* ³⁴Jesus said to

---

15:21
*ᵃ*Mark7:24

15:24
*ᵇ*Matt10:5-6;
Acts8:25-26;
13:46; Rom15:8

15:26
*ᶜ*Matt7:6; Phil3:2

15:29
*ᵈ*Matt4:18;
Mark7:31

15:30
*ᵉ*Isa35:5-6;
Matt 11:5; Lk7:22

15:32
*ᶠ*Mark8:1

15:33
*ᵍ*2Kings4:43

---

a15:23 Lit. *a word*   **b**15:24 Lit. *house*   **c**15:26 Other mss. read *lawful*

15:36
a 1Sam9:13;
Matt14:19;
Lk22:19

them, "How many loaves of bread do you have?" They said, "Seven, and a few small fish."

³⁵Ordering the crowd to sit down on the ground, ³⁶he took the seven loaves and the fish and gave thanks. Then he broke them in pieces and kept giving them to his disciples, and the disciples gave them**ᵃ** to the crowds.*a* ³⁷All of them ate and were filled. Then the disciples**ᵇ** picked up what was left of the broken pieces, seven baskets full.

15:39
b Mark8:10

³⁸Now those who had eaten were four thousand men, besides women and children. ³⁹After he sent the crowds away, he got into a boat and went to the region of Magadan.**ᶜ***b*

The Demand for a Sign from Heaven
(Mark 8:11–13; Luke 12:54–56)

16:1
c Matt12:38;
Mark8:11;
Lk 11:16;
12:54-56;
1Cor1:22

16 ¹When the Pharisees and Sadducees arrived, as a test they asked Jesus**ᵈ** to show them a sign from heaven.*c* ²He replied to them, "You say,

> 'Red sky at night, what a delight.
> ³Red sky in the morning, cloudy and storming.'

You know how to interpret the appearance of the sky, yet you can't interpret the signs of the times?**ᵉ** ⁴An evil and adulterous generation craves a sign, but no sign will be given to it except the sign of Jonah." Then he left them and went away.*d*

16:4
d Matt12:39

The Yeast of the Pharisees and Sadducees
(Mark 8:14–21)

⁵When his disciples reached the other side, they had forgotten to take any bread along.*e* ⁶Jesus said to them, "Watch out! Beware of the yeast of the Pharisees and Sadducees!"*f* ⁷They began to discuss this among themselves and said, "We didn't take any bread." ⁸Knowing this, Jesus said, "You who have little faith, why are you discussing among

16:5
e Mark8:14

16:6
f Lk12:1

---

a 15:36 The Gk. lacks *gave them*   **b** 15:37 Lit. *they*   **c** 15:39 Other mss. read *Magdala*   **d** 16:1 Lit. *him*   **e** 16:3 Other mss. lack *You say. . . the signs of the times?*

yourselves the fact that you don't have any bread? [9]Don't you understand yet? Don't you remember the five loaves for the five thousand and how many baskets you collected,[a] [10]or the seven loaves for the four thousand and how many baskets you collected?[b] [11]How can you fail to understand that I wasn't talking to you about bread? Beware of the yeast of the Pharisees and Sadducees!" [12]Then they understood that he didn't say to beware of the yeast in the loaves of bread,[a] but of the teaching of the Pharisees and Sadducees.

Peter Declares His Faith in Jesus
(Mark 8:27–30; Luke 9:18–21)

[13]When Jesus had come to the region of Caesarea Philippi, he asked his disciples, "Who do people say the Son of Man is?"[c] [14]They said, "Some say[b] John the Baptist, others Elijah, and still others Jeremiah or one of the prophets.[d] [15]He said to them, "But who do you say I am?" [16]Simon Peter answered, "You are the Christ,[c] the Son of the living God!"[e] [17]Then Jesus said to him, "How blessed are you, Simon, son of John![d] For flesh and blood has not revealed this to you, but my Father in heaven has.[f] [18]I tell you that you are Peter,[e] and it is on this rock[f] that I will build my church, and the forces of hell[g] will not overpower it.[g] [19]I will give you the keys to the kingdom of heaven. Whatever you prohibit on earth will have been prohibited[h] in heaven, and whatever you permit on earth will have been permitted[i] in heaven."[h] [20]Then he strictly ordered the disciples not to tell anyone that he was the Christ.[c][i]

Jesus Predicts His Death and Resurrection
(Mark 8:31–9:1; Luke 9:22–27)

[21]From that time on, Jesus began to show his disciples that he would have to go to Jerusalem and suffer a great deal because of the elders, the high priests, and the scribes. Then he would be killed, but on the third day he would be raised.[j] [22]But Peter took him aside and began to reprimand

---

a 16:12 Other mss. read *the loaf of bread*   b 16:14 Lit. *Some*
c 16:16,16:20 I.e. the Messiah   d 16:17 Gk. *Bariona*   e 16:18 Gk. *Petros*
f 16:18 Gk. *petra*   g 16:18 Lit. *gates of Hades*, a reference to the realm of the dead   h 16:19 Or *will be prohibited*   i 16:19 Or *will be permitted*

16:9
a Matt14:17;
John6:9

16:10
b Matt15:34

16:13
c Mark8:27;
Lk9:18

16:14
d Matt14:2;
Lk9:7-9

16:16
e Matt14:33;
Mark8:29;
Lk9:20;
John6:69; 11:27;
Acts8:37; 9:20;
Heb1:2,5;
1John4:15; 5:5

16:17
f 1Cor2:10;
Gal1:16; Eph2:8

16:18
g Job38:17;
Ps9:13; 107:18;
Isa38:10;
John1:42;
Eph2:20;
Rev21:14

16:19
h Matt18:18;
John20:23

16:20
i Matt17:9;
Mark8:30;
Lk9:21

16:21
j Matt20:17;
Mark8:31; 9:31;
10:33; Lk9:22;
18:31; 24:6-7

16:23
a 2Sam19:22;
Rom8:7

16:24
b Matt10:38;
Mark8:34;
Lk9:23; 14:27;
Acts14:22;
1Thes3:3;
2Tim3:12

16:25
c Lk17:33;
John12:25

16:26
d Ps49:7-8

16:27
e Job34:11;
Ps62:12;
Prov24:12;
Jer17:10; 32:19;
Dan7:10;
Zech14:5;
Matt25:31; 26:64;
Mark8:38;
Lk9:26; Rom2:6;
1Cor3:8;
2Cor5:10;
1Peter1:17;
Jude1:14;
Rev2:23; 22:12

16:28
f Mark9:1; Lk9:27

17:1
g Mark9:2;
Lk9:28

17:5
h Deut18:15,19;
Isa42:1;
Matt3:17;
Mark1:11;
Lk3:22;
Acts3:22-23;
2Peter1:17

17:6
i 2Peter1:18

17:7
j Dan8:18; 9:21;
10:10,18

17:9
k Matt16:20;
Mark8:30; 9:9

him, saying, "God be merciful to you, Lord! This must never happen to you!" [23]But Jesus[a] turned around and said to Peter, "Get behind me, Satan! You're an offense[b] to me, for you are not thinking God's thoughts but human thoughts!"[a]

[24]Then Jesus said to his disciples, "If anyone wants to follow me, he must deny himself, pick up his cross, and keep on following me.[b] [25]For whoever wants to save his life will lose it, but whoever loses his life for me will find it.[c] [26]For what profit will a person have if he gains the whole world and forfeits his own life? Or what can a person give in exchange for his life?[d] [27]The Son of Man is going to come with his angels in his Father's glory, and then he will repay everyone according to what he has done.[e] [28]Truly I tell you, some people standing here will not experience[c] death before they see the Son of Man coming in his kingdom."[f]

Jesus' Appearance Is Changed
(Mark 9:2–13; Luke 9:28–36)

17 [1]Six days later, Jesus took Peter, James, and his brother John and led them up a high mountain by themselves.[g] [2]His appearance was changed in front of them, his face shone like the sun, and his clothes became as white as light. [3]Suddenly, Moses and Elijah appeared to them, talking with Jesus.[d]

[4]Then Peter said to Jesus, "Lord, it's good that we're here! If you want, I will set up three shelters[e]—one for you, one for Moses, and one for Elijah." [5]He was still speaking when a bright cloud suddenly overshadowed them. A voice from the cloud said, "This is my Son, whom I love. I am pleased with him. Keep on listening to him!"[h]

[6]When the disciples heard this, they fell on their faces and were terrified.[i] [7]But Jesus came up to them and touched them, saying, "Get up, and stop being afraid."[j] [8]When they raised their eyes, they saw no one but Jesus all by himself.

[9]On their way down the mountain, Jesus ordered them, "Don't tell anyone about this vision until the Son of Man has been raised from the dead."[k] [10]So the disciples asked him,

---

a 16:23 Lit. *he*   **b** 16:23 Or *a hindrance*   **c** 16:28 Lit. *taste*   **d** 17:3 Lit. *with him*   **e** 17:4 Or *tents*

"Why, then, do the scribes say that Elijah must come first?"[a][a] [11]He answered them, "Elijah is indeed coming and will restore all things.[b] [12]But I tell you that Elijah has already come, yet people[b] didn't recognize him and treated him just as they pleased. In the same way, the Son of Man is going to suffer at their hands."[c] [13]Then the disciples understood that he had been speaking to them about John the Baptist.[d]

Jesus Heals a Boy with a Demon
(Mark 9:14–29; Luke 9:37–42)

[14]When they came to the crowd, a man came up to Jesus,[c] knelt down in front of him,[e] [15]and said, "Sir,[d] have mercy on my son, for he is an epileptic and suffers terribly. Often he falls into fire and often into water. [16]I brought him to your disciples, but they couldn't heal him."

[17]Jesus replied, "You unbelieving and perverted generation! How long must I be with you? How long must I put up with you? Bring him here to me!" [18]Then Jesus reprimanded the demon, and it came out of him, and the boy was healed that very hour.

[19]Then the disciples came to Jesus privately and said, "Why couldn't we drive it out?" [20]He told them, "Because of your lack of faith.[e] For truly I tell you, if you have faith like a grain of mustard seed, you can say to this mountain, 'Move from here to there,' and it will move, and nothing will be impossible for you."[f][f]

Jesus Again Predicts His Death and Resurrection
(Mark 9:30–32; Luke 9:43–45)

[22]While they were gathering together[g] in Galilee, Jesus told them, "The Son of Man is going to be betrayed into human hands.[g] [23]They will kill him, but he will be raised on the third day." Then they were filled with grief.

Questions about the Temple Tax
[24]When they came to Capernaum, the collectors of the

---

a17:10 Mal 4:5   b17:12 Lit. *they*   c17:14 Lit. *to him*   d17:15 Or *Lord*
e17:20 Other mss. read *your little faith*   f17:20 Other mss. read *for you.*
[21]*But this kind does not come out except by prayer and fasting.*
g17:22 Other mss. read *staying*

17:10
aMal4:5;
Matt 11:14;
Mark9:11

17:11
bMal4:6;
Lk1:16-17;
Acts3:21

17:12
cMatt 11:14; 14:3,
10; 16:21;
Mark9:12-13

17:13
dMatt 11:14

17:14
eMark9:14;
Lk9:37

17:20
fMatt21:21;
Mark 11:23;
Lk17:6;
1Cor12:9; 13:2

17:22
gMatt16:21;
20:17; Mark8:31;
9:30-31; 10:33;
Lk9:22,44; 18:31;
24:6-7

17:24
a Mark9:33

18:1
b Mark9:33;
Lk9:46; 22:24

18:3
c Ps131:2;
Matt19:14;
Mark10:14;
Lk18:16;
1Cor14:20;
1Peter2:2

18:4
d Matt20:27;
23:11

18:5
e Matt10:42;
Lk9:48

18:6
f Mark9:42;
Lk17:1-2

18:7
g Matt26:24;
Lk17:1;
1Cor 11:19

18:8
h Matt5:29-30;
Mark9:43,45

temple tax[a] came up to Peter and said, "Your teacher pays the temple tax,[a] doesn't he?" [a] 25He answered, "Yes." When Peter[b] came home,[c] Jesus spoke to him first, saying, "What do you think, Simon? From whom do kings on the earth collect tolls or tributes? From their subjects,[d] or from others?" 26When he said, "From others," Jesus said to him, "In that case, the subjects[d] are exempt. 27However, so that we don't offend them, go to the sea and throw in a hook. Take the first fish that comes up and open its mouth, and you will find a coin.[e] Take it and give it to them for me and you."

True Greatness

(Mark 9:33–37; Luke 9:46–48)

18 1At that time the disciples came to Jesus and said, "So who is the greatest in the kingdom of heaven?"[b] 2Calling a little child forward, he had him stand among them. 3Then he said, "Truly I tell you, unless you change[f] and become like little children, you will never get into the kingdom of heaven.[c] 4Therefore, whoever humbles himself like this little child is the greatest in the kingdom of heaven,[d] 5and whoever receives a little child like this in my name receives me."[e]

Causing Others to Sin

(Mark 9:42–48; Luke 17:1–2)

6"If anyone causes one of these little ones who believe in me to sin, it would be better for him if a large millstone were hung around his neck and he were drowned in the bottom of the sea.[f] 7How terrible it will be for the world because it causes people to sin! Temptations to sin are bound to happen, but how terrible it will be for that person who causes someone to sin![g]

8"So if your hand or your foot causes you to sin, cut it off and throw it away. It's better for you to enter life injured or crippled than to have two hands or two feet and be thrown into eternal fire.[h] 9And if your eye causes you to sin, tear it out and throw it away. It's better for you to enter life with

---

a 17:24 Gk. *didrachma* b 17:25 Lit. *he* c 17:25 Or *went into the house* d 17:25,17:26 Lit. *sons* e 17:27 Gk. *stater*, a coin worth two didrachmas f 18:3 Lit. *turn*

one eye than to have two eyes and be thrown into hell fire.^a

¹⁰"See to it that you do not despise one of these little ones. For I tell you, their angels in heaven always see the face of^b my Father in heaven."^c^a

The Parable about a Lost Sheep
(Luke 15:3–7)

¹²"What do you think? If a man has a hundred sheep and one of them strays, he leaves the ninety-nine in the hills and goes to look for the one that has strayed, doesn't he?^b ¹³If he finds it, truly I tell you that he rejoices over it more than over the ninety-nine that haven't strayed. ¹⁴In the same way, it is not the will of your^d Father in heaven that one of these little ones should be lost."

Dealing with a Brother Who Sins
(Luke 17:3)

¹⁵"If your brother sins against you,^e go and confront him while the two of you are alone. If he listens to you, you have won back your brother.^c ¹⁶But if he doesn't listen, take one or two others with you so that 'every word may be confirmed by the testimony^f of two or three witnesses.'^g^d ¹⁷If, however, he ignores them, tell it to the congregation.^h If he also ignores the congregation,^h regard him as a Gentile and a tax collector.^e

¹⁸"Truly I tell you, whatever you prohibit on earth will have been prohibitedⁱ in heaven, and whatever you permit on earth will have been permitted^j in heaven.^f ¹⁹Furthermore, truly I tell you that if two of you agree on earth about anything you request, it will be done for you by my Father in heaven.^g ²⁰For where two or three have come together in my name, I am there among them."

---

a*18:9* Lit. *the Gehenna of fire* b*18:10* I.e. have access to c*18:10* Other mss. read *in heaven*. ¹¹*For the Son of Man came to save the lost.* d*18:14* Other mss. read *our*; still other mss. read *my* e*18:15* Other mss. lack *against you* f*18:16* Lit. *mouth* g*18:16* Deut 19:15 h*18:17* Or *church* i*18:18* Or *will be prohibited* j*18:18* Or *will be permitted*

18:10
a Esth 1:14;
Ps 34:7;
Zech 13:7;
Lk 1:19; Heb 1:14

18:12
b Lk 15:4

18:15
c Lev 19:17;
Lk 17:3;
James 5:20;
1 Peter 3:1

18:16
d Deut 17:6;
19:15; John 8:17;
2 Cor 13:1;
Heb 10:28

18:17
e Rom 16:17;
1 Cor 5:9;
2 Thes 3:6,14;
2 John 1:10

18:18
f Matt 16:19;
John 20:23;
1 Cor 5:4

18:19
g Matt 5:24;
1 John 3:22; 5:14

18:21
a Lk17:4

The Parable about an Unforgiving Servant

²¹Then Peter came up and asked him, "Lord, how many times may my brother sin against me and I have to forgive him? Seven times?" *a* ²²Jesus said to him, "I tell you, not just seven times, but seventy-seven times!*ab*

²³"That's why the kingdom of heaven may be compared to a king who wanted to settle accounts with his servants. ²⁴When he had begun to settle the accounts, a person who owed him ten thousand talents*b* was brought to him. ²⁵Because he couldn't pay, his master ordered him, his wife, his children, and all that he had to be sold so that payment could be made.*c* ²⁶Then the servant fell down and bowed low before him, saying, 'Be patient*c* with me, and I will repay you everything!' ²⁷The master of that servant had compassion and released him, canceling his debt.

²⁸"But when that servant went away, he found one of his fellow servants who owed him a hundred denarii.*d* He grabbed him, seized him by the throat, and said, 'Pay what you owe!' ²⁹Then his fellow servant fell down and began begging him, 'Be patient with me and I will repay you!' ³⁰But he refused and went and had him thrown into prison until he would repay the debt.

³¹"When his fellow servants saw what had happened, they were very disturbed and went and reported to their master all that had happened. ³²Then his master sent for him and said to him, 'You evil servant! I canceled that entire debt for you because you begged me. ³³Shouldn't you have had mercy on your fellow servant, just as I had mercy on you?' ³⁴In anger his master handed him over to the torturers*e* until he could repay the entire debt. ³⁵This is how my heavenly Father will treat each one of you unless you forgive your brother from your hearts."*d*

18:22
b Matt6:14;
Mark 11:25;
Col3:13

18:25
c 2Kings4:1;
Neh5:8

18:35
d Prov21:13;
Matt6:12;
Mark 11:26;
James2:13

---

a *18:22* Or *seventy times seven*   b *18:24* A talent was worth a lifetime of wages for an average laborer.   c *18:26* Other mss. read *Master, be patient*   d *18:28* The denarius was the usual day's wage for a laborer.   e *18:34* Or *jailers*

Teaching about Divorce
(Mark 10:1–12)

19 ¹When Jesus had finished saying these things,ᵃ he left Galilee and went to the territory of Judea on the other sideᵇ of the Jordan.ᵃ ²Large crowds followed him, and he healed them there.ᵇ

³Some Pharisees came to him in order to test him. They asked, "Is it lawful for a manᶜ to divorce his wife for any reason?" ⁴He answered them, "Haven't you read that the one who madeᵈ them at the beginning 'made them male and female'ᵉᶜ ⁵and said, 'That's why a man will leave his father and mother and will be united with his wife, and the two will become one flesh'?ᶠᵈ ⁶So they are no longer two, but one flesh. Therefore, what God has joined together, man must stop separating."

⁷They asked him, "Why, then, did Moses order us 'to give a certificate of divorce and divorce her'?"ᵍᵉ ⁸He said to them, "It was because you were hard-hearted that Moses allowed you to divorce your wives! But from the beginning it was not this way. ⁹I tell you that whoever divorces his wife, except for sexual immorality, and marries another woman commits adultery."ʰᶠ

¹⁰His disciples said to him, "If that is the relationship of a man with his wife, it's not worth getting married!"ᵍ ¹¹But he said to them, "Not everyone can accept this saying, except those to whom celibacyⁱ has been granted.ʰ ¹²For some men are celibate from birth,ʲ while others are celibate because they have been made that way by others. Still others are celibate because they have made themselves that way for the sake of the kingdom of heaven. Let anyone accept this who can."ⁱ

Jesus Blesses the Little Children
(Mark 10:13–16; Luke 18:15–17)

¹³Then some little children were brought to him so that

---

a *19:1* Lit. *finished these sayings*　b *19:1* I.e., the east side　c *19:3* Other mss. lack *for a man*　d *19:4* Other mss. read *created*　e *19:4* Gen 1:27; 5:2
f *19:5* Gen 2:24　g *19:7* Deut 24:1, 3　h *19:9* Other mss. read *adultery, and the man who marries a divorced woman commits adultery*　i *19:11* Lit. *it*
j *19:12* Lit. *from the mother's womb*

19:1
ᵃMark10:1;
John10:40

19:2
ᵇMatt12:15

19:4
ᶜGen1:27; 5:2;
Mal2:15

19:5
ᵈGen2:24;
Mark10:5-9;
1Cor6:16; 7:2;
Eph5:31

19:7
ᵉDeut24:1;
Matt5:31

19:9
ᶠMatt5:32;
Mark10:11;
Lk16:18;
1Cor7:10-11

19:10
ᵍProv21:19

19:11
ʰ1Cor7:2,7,9,17

19:12
ⁱ1Cor7:32,34;
9:5,15

19:13
a Mark10:13;
Lk18:15

he might lay his hands on them and pray. But the disciples reprimanded those who brought them.^a^a ¹⁴Jesus, however, said, "Let the little children come to me, and stop keeping them away. For the kingdom of heaven belongs to people like these."^b ¹⁵When he had laid his hands on them, he went on from there.

19:14
b Matt18:3

A Rich Young Man Comes to Jesus
(Mark 10:17–22; Luke 18:18–23)

¹⁶Just then a man came up to Jesus^b and said, "Teacher,^c what good deed should I do to have eternal life?"^c ¹⁷Jesus^d said to him, "Why ask me about what is good? There is only one who is good.^e If you want to get into that life, you must keep the commandments."

19:16
c Mark10:17;
Lk10:25; 18:18

¹⁸The young man^d said to him, "Which ones?" Jesus said, "'You must not murder,^f you must not commit adultery,^g you must not steal,^h you must not give false testimony,ⁱ^d ¹⁹honor your father and mother,'ⁱ and 'you must love your neighbor as yourself.' "^k^e ²⁰The young man said to him, "I have kept all of these.^l What do I still lack?" ²¹Jesus said to him, "If you want to be perfect, go and sell what you own and give the money^m to the destitute, and you will have treasure in heaven. Then come back and follow me."^f ²²But when the young man heard this statement he went away sad, because he had many possessions.

19:18
d Exod20:13;
Deut5:17

19:19
e Lev19:18;
Matt15:4; 22:39;
Rom13:9;
Gal5:14;
James2:8

Salvation and Reward
(Mark 10:23–31; Luke 18:24–30)

²³Then Jesus said to his disciples, "Truly I tell you, it will be hard for a rich person to get into the kingdom of heaven.^g ²⁴Again I tell you, it is easier for a camel to squeeze through the eye of a needle than for a rich person to get into the kingdom of God." ²⁵When the disciples heard this, they were completely astonished and said, "Who, then, can be

19:21
f Matt6:20;
Lk12:33; 16:9;
Acts2:45;
4:34-35;
1Tim6:18-19

---

a *19:13* Lit. *reprimanded them*   **b** *19:16* Lit. *to him*   **c** *19:16* Other mss. read *Good Teacher*   **d** *19:17,19:18* Lit. *He*   **e** *19:17* Other mss. read *Why do you call me good? No one is good except for one—God*   **f** *19:18* Exod 20:13; Deut 5:17   **g** *19:18* Exod 20:14; Deut 5:18   **h** *19:18* Exod 20:15; Deut 5:19   **i** *19:18* Exod 20:16; Deut 5:20   **j** *19:19* Exod 20:12; Deut 5:16   **k** *19:19* Lev 19:18   **l** *19:20* Other mss. read *kept all of these since I was a young man*   **m** *19:21* The Gk. lacks *the money*

19:23
g Matt13:22;
Mark10:24;
1Cor1:26;
1Tim6:9-10

saved?" 26Jesus looked at them intently and said, "For humans this is impossible, but for God all things are possible."*a*

27Then Peter said to him, "See, we've left everything and followed you. So what will we get?"*b* 28Jesus said to them, "Truly I tell you, when the Son of Man sits on his glorious throne in the renewed creation, you who have followed me will also sit on twelve thrones, governing the twelve tribes of Israel.*c* 29In fact, everyone who has left his homes, brothers, sisters, father, mother, children, or fields because of my name will receive a hundred times as much*a* and will inherit eternal life.*d* 30But many who are first will be last, and the last will be first."*e*

The Workers in the Vineyard

20 1"For the kingdom of heaven is like a landowner who went out early in the morning to hire workers for his vineyard. 2After agreeing with the workers for one denarius*b* a day, he sent them into his vineyard. 3When he went out about nine o'clock,*c* he saw others standing in the marketplace without work. 4He said to them, 'You go into the vineyard, too, and I will pay you whatever is right.' 5So off they went. He went out again about noon*d* and about three o'clock*e* and did the same thing. 6About five o'clock*f* he went out and found some others standing around. He said to them, 'Why are you standing here all day long without work?' 7They told him, 'Because no one has hired us.' He said to them, 'You go into the vineyard as well.'

8"When evening came, the owner of the vineyard said to his manager, 'Call the workers and give them their wages, beginning with the last and ending with*g* the first.' 9Those who were hired at five o'clock*f* came, and each received a denarius. 10When the first came, they thought they would receive more, but each received a denarius as well. 11When they received it, they began to complain to the landowner,

---

a*19:29* Other mss. read *many times as much*   b*20:2 The* denarius was the usual day's wage for a laborer.   c*20:3* Lit. *the third hour*   d*20:5* Lit. *the sixth hour*   e*20:5* Lit. *the ninth hour*   f*20:6,20:9* Lit. *the eleventh hour*   g*20:8* Lit. *and up to*

20:15
*a*Deut15:9;
Prov23:6;
Matt6:23;
Rom9:21

¹²saying, 'These last fellows worked only one hour, yet you've made them equal to us who have endured the burden of the day and the scorching heat!' ¹³But he said to one of them, 'Friend, I'm not treating you unfairly. You did agree with me for a denarius, didn't you? ¹⁴Take what's

20:16
*b*Matt19:30;
22:14

yours and go. I want to give this last man as much as I gave you.ᵃ ¹⁵I'm allowed to do what I want with my own money,ᵇ am I not? Or is your eye evilᶜ because I am good?'ᵃ ¹⁶In the same way, the last will be first, and the first will be last. For many are called, but few are chosen."ᵈᵇ

20:17
*c*Mark10:32;
Lk18:31;
John12:12

Jesus Predicts His Death and Resurrection a Third Time
(Mark 10:32–34; Luke 18:31–34)

¹⁷When Jesus was going up to Jerusalem, he took the twelve disciplesᵉ aside and said to them on the way,ᶜ ¹⁸"See,

20:18
*d*Matt16:21

we're going up to Jerusalem, and the Son of Man will be handed over to the high priests and scribes, and they will condemn him to death.ᵈ ¹⁹Then they will hand him over to

20:19
*e*Matt27:2;
Mark15:1,16;
Lk23:1;
John18:28;
Acts3:13

the Gentiles to be mocked, whipped, and crucified, but on the third day he will be raised."ᵉ

The Request of the Mother of James and John
(Mark 10:35–45)

²⁰Then the mother of Zebedee's sons came to Jesusᶠ with

20:20
*f*Matt4:21;
Mark10:35

her sons. She bowed down in front of him to ask him for a favor.ᶠ ²¹He asked her, "What do you want?" She said to him, "Promiseᵍ that these two sons of mine will sit, one at your right and one at your left, in your kingdom."ᵍ ²²Jesus

20:21
*g*Matt19:28

replied, "You don't realize what you're asking. Can you drink the cup that I'm going to drink?"ʰ They told him, "We can."ʰ ²³He said to them, "You will indeed drink my cup. But it's not my business to grant you a seat at my right hand

20:22
*h*Matt26:39,42;
Mark14:36;
Lk12:50; 22:42;
John18:11

or at my left. These positions have already been prepared for others by my Father."ⁱ

²⁴When the ten heard this, they became furious with the

---

a 20:14 Lit. *to this last man as also to you*   b 20:15 Lit. *things*   c 20:15 I.e. envious   d 20:16 Other mss. lack *For many are called, but few are chosen*   e 20:17 Other mss. lack *disciples*   f 20:20 Lit. *to him*   g 20:21 Lit. *Say*   h 20:22 Other mss. read *to drink, or be baptized with the baptism with which I'm going to be baptized?*

20:23
*i*Matt25:34;
Acts12:2;
Rom8:17;
2Cor1:7; Rev1:9

two brothers.[a] [25]But Jesus called the disciples[a] and said, "You know that the rulers of the Gentiles lord it over them and their superiors act like tyrants over them. [26]That's not the way it should be among you. Instead, whoever wants to be great among you must be your servant,[b] [27]and whoever wants to be first among you must be your slave.[c] [28]That's the way it is with the Son of Man. He didn't come to be served, but to serve and to give his life as a ransom for many people."[d]

Jesus Heals Two Blind Men
(Mark 10:46–52; Luke 18:35–43)

[29]As they were leaving Jericho, a large crowd followed Jesus.[b][e] [30]When two blind men who were sitting by the roadside heard that Jesus was passing by, they shouted, "Have mercy on us, Lord,[c] Son of David!"[f] [31]The crowd sternly told them to be silent, but they shouted even louder, "Have mercy on us, Lord, Son of David!"

[32]Jesus stopped and called them, saying, "What do you want me to do for you?" [33]They told him, "Lord, let our eyes be opened!" [34]Then Jesus, deeply moved with compassion, touched their eyes and at once they could see again. So they followed him.

The King Enters Jerusalem
(Mark 11:1–11; Luke 19:28–38; John 12:12–19)

21 [1]When they came near Jerusalem and had reached Bethphage on the Mount of Olives, Jesus sent two disciples on ahead and[g] [2]said to them, "Go into the village ahead of you. At once you will find a donkey tied up and a colt with it. Untie them, and bring them to me. [3]If anyone says anything to you, tell him, 'The Lord needs them,' and that person will send them at once."

[4]Now this happened to fulfill what had been spoken through the prophet when he said,

> [5]"Tell the people[d] of Zion,[h]
>   'Look, your king is coming to you![e]

---

a 20:25 Lit. *them*　b 20:29 Lit. *him*　c 20:30 Other mss. read *Jesus*
d 21:5 Lit. *daughter*　e 21:5 Isa 62:11

20:24
*a*Mark10:41;
Lk22:24-25

20:26
*b*Matt23:11;
Mark9:35; 10:43;
1Peter5:3

20:27
*c*Matt18:4

20:28
*d*Isa53:10-11;
Dan9:24,26;
Matt26:28;
Lk22:27;
John 11:51-52;
13:4,14;
Rom5:15,19;
Phil2:7; 1Tim2:6;
Titus2:14;
Heb9:28;
1Peter1:19

20:29
*e*Mark10:46;
Lk18:35

20:30
*f*Matt9:27

21:1
*g*Zech14:4;
Mark 11:1;
Lk19:29

21:5
*h*Isa62:11;
Zech9:9;
John12:15

21:6
a Mark 11:4

He is humble and mounted on a donkey,
  even on a colt of a donkey.' "*a*

21:7
b 2Kings9:13

⁶So the disciples went and did as Jesus had directed them.*a* ⁷They brought the donkey and the colt and put their coats on them, and he sat on them.*b* ⁸Many people in the crowd spread their own coats on the road, while others began cutting down branches from the trees and spreading them on the road.*c* ⁹Both the crowds that went ahead of him and those that followed him kept shouting,*d*

21:8
c Lev23:40;
John12:13

"Hosanna**b** to the Son of David!
How blessed is the one who comes
  in the name of the Lord!
Hosanna in the highest heaven!"**c**

21:9
d Ps 118:25-26;
Matt23:39

¹⁰When he came into Jerusalem, the whole city was trembling with excitement. The people**d** were asking, "Who is this?"*e* ¹¹The crowds kept saying, "This is the prophet Jesus, the man from Nazareth in Galilee."*f*

21:10
e Mark 11:15;
Lk19:45;
John2:13,15

Jesus Throws Merchants and Moneychangers out of the Temple

(Mark 11:15–19; Luke 19:45–48; John 2:13–22)

21:11
f Matt2:23;
Lk7:16;
John6:14; 7:40;
9:17

¹²Then Jesus went into the Temple,**e** threw out all who were selling and buying in the Temple, and overturned the moneychangers' tables and the chairs of those who sold doves.*g* ¹³He told them, "It is written, 'My house is to be called a house of prayer,'**f** but you are turning it into a hideout**g** for bandits!"*h*

21:12
g Deut14:25;
Mark 11:11;
Lk19:45;
John2:15

¹⁴Blind and lame people came to him in the Temple, and he healed them. ¹⁵But when the high priests and the scribes saw the amazing things that he had done and the children shouting in the Temple, "Hosanna**b** to the Son of David," they became furious ¹⁶and asked him, "Do you hear what these people are saying?" Jesus said to them, "Yes! Haven't you ever read, 'From the mouths of infants and nursing babies you have created praise'?"**h***i*

21:13
h Isa56:7;
Jer7:11;
Mark 11:17;
Lk19:46

21:16
i Ps8:2

---

a 21:5 Zech 9:9   **b** 21:9,21:15 Hosanna is Heb. for *Please save* or *Praise*.
c 21:9 Ps 118:25-26; Ps 148:1   **d** 21:10 Lit. *They*   **e** 21:12 Other mss. read *temple of God*   **f** 21:13 Isa 56:7; Jer 7:11   **g** 21:13 Lit. *cave*   **h** 21:16 Ps 8:2

17Then he left them and went out of the city to Bethany and spent the night there.*a*

Jesus Curses a Fig Tree
(Mark 11:12–14, 20–24)

18In the morning, while Jesus*a* was returning to the city, he became hungry.*b* 19Seeing a fig tree by the roadside, he went up to it and found nothing on it but leaves. He said to it, "May fruit never come from you again!" And immediately the fig tree dried up.*c*

20When the disciples saw this, they were amazed and said, "How did the fig tree dry up so quickly?"*d* 21Jesus answered them, "Truly I tell you, if you have faith and do not doubt, not only will you be able to do what has been done to the fig tree, but you will also say to this mountain, 'Be lifted up and thrown into the sea,' and it will happen.*e* 22You will receive whatever you ask for in prayer, if you believe."*f*

Jesus' Authority Is Challenged
(Mark 11:27–33; Luke 20:1–8)

23Then Jesus*a* went into the Temple. While he was teaching, the high priests and the elders of the people came to him and asked, "By what authority are you doing these things, and who gave you this authority?"*g* 24Jesus answered them, "I, too, will ask you one question.*b* If you answer it for me, I will also tell you by what authority I am doing these things. 25Where did John's authority to baptize*c* come from? From heaven or from humans?" They began discussing this among themselves, saying, "If we say, 'From heaven,' he will say to us, 'Then why didn't you believe him?' 26But if we say, 'From humans,' we're afraid of the crowd, for all regard John as a prophet."*h* 27So they said to Jesus, "We don't know." He in turn told them, "Then I won't tell you by what authority I am doing these things."

The Parable about Two Sons

28"But what do you think? A man had two sons. He went to the first and said, 'Son, go and work in the vineyard

---

a 21:18,21:23 Lit. *he*   *b* 21:24 Lit. *one word*   *c* 21:25 Lit. *John's baptism*

21:17
a Mark 11:11;
John 11:18

21:18
b Mark 11:12

21:19
c Mark 11:13

21:20
d Mark 11:20

21:21
e Matt17:20;
Lk17:6;
1Cor13:2;
James1:6

21:22
f Matt7:7;
Mark 11:24;
Lk 11:9;
James5:16;
1John3:22; 5:14

21:23
g Exod2:14;
Mark 11:27;
Lk20:1; Acts4:7;
7:27

21:26
h Matt14:5;
Mark6:20;
Lk20:6

21:31
a Lk7:29,50

21:32
b Matt3:1;
Lk3:12-13

21:33
c Ps80:9;
Song8:11; Isa5:1;
Jer2:21;
Matt25:14-15;
Mark12:1;
Lk20:9

21:34
d Song8:11-12

21:35
e 2Chr24:21;
36:16; Neh9:26;
Matt5:12; 23:34,
37; Acts7:52;
1Thes2:15;
Heb 11:36-37

21:38
f Ps2:2,8;
Matt26:3;
27:1John 11:53;
Acts4:27;
Heb1:2

21:39
g Matt26:50;
Mark14:46;
Lk22:54;
John18:12;
Acts2:23

21:41
h Lk20:16; 21:24;
Acts13:46; 15:7;
18:6; 28:28;
Rom9:1-33;
10:1-21; 11:1-36;
Heb2:3

21:42
i Ps 118:22;
Isa28:16;
Mark12:10;
Lk20:17;
Acts4:11;
Eph2:20;
1Peter2:6-7

today.' [29]His son[a] replied, 'I don't want to,' but later he changed his mind and went. [30]Then the father[b] went to the other son[c] and told him the same thing. He replied, 'I will,[d] sir,' but he didn't go. [31]Which of the two did the father's will?" They answered, "The first." Jesus said to them, "Truly I tell you, tax collectors and prostitutes will get into God's kingdom ahead of you.[a] [32]For John came to you showing you the way[e] of righteousness, but you didn't believe him. The tax collectors and prostitutes believed him. But even when you saw that, you didn't change your minds[f] at last and believe him."[b]

The Parable about the Tenant Farmers
(Mark 12:1–12; Luke 20:9–19)

[33]"Listen to another parable. There was a landowner who planted a vineyard, put a wall around it, dug a wine press in it, and built a watchtower. Then he leased it to tenant farmers and went abroad.[c] [34]When harvest time approached, he sent his servants to the tenant farmers to collect his produce.[d] [35]But the farmers took his servants and beat one, killed another, and attacked another with stones.[e] [36]Again, he sent other servants to them, a greater number than the first, but the tenant farmers[g] treated them the same way. [37]Finally, he sent his son to them, thinking, 'They will respect my son.' [38]But when the tenant farmers saw his son, they said to one another, 'This is the heir. Come on, let's kill him and get his inheritance!'[f] [39]So they grabbed him, threw him out of the vineyard, and killed him.[g] [40]Now when the owner of the vineyard returns, what will he do to those farmers?" [41]They said to him, "He will put those horrible men to a horrible death. Then he will lease the vineyard to other farmers who will give him his produce at harvest time."[h]

[42]Jesus said to them, "Have you never read in the Scriptures,[i]

'The stone that the builders rejected

---

a 21:29 Lit. *He*   b 21:30 Lit. *he*   c 21:30 Lit. *the other*   d 21:30 Lit. *I*
e 21:32 Lit. *came to you in the way*   f 21:32 Or *repent*   g 21:36 Lit. *they*

> has become the cornerstone.^a
> This was the Lord's doing,
>   and it is amazing in our eyes'?^b

⁴³That's why I tell you that the kingdom of God will be taken away from you and given to a people who will produce fruit for it.^a ⁴⁴The person who falls over this stone will be broken to pieces, but it will crush anyone on whom it falls."^{cb}

⁴⁵When the high priests and the Pharisees heard his parables, they knew that he was talking about them. ⁴⁶Although they wanted to arrest him, they were afraid of the crowds, for they considered him a prophet.^c

The Parable about a Wedding Banquet
(Luke 14:15–24)

22 ¹Again Jesus spoke to them in parables. He said,^d ²"The kingdom of heaven may be compared to a king who gave a wedding banquet for his son. ³He sent his servants to call those who had been invited to the wedding, but they refused to come. ⁴So^d he sent other servants, saying, 'Tell those who have been invited, "Look, I've prepared my dinner. My oxen and fattened calves have been slaughtered. Everything is ready. Come to the wedding!"'^e ⁵But they paid no attention to this and went away, one to his farm, another to his business. ⁶The rest grabbed the king's^e servants, treated them brutally, and then killed them. ⁷Then the king became outraged. He sent his troops, and they destroyed those murderers and burned their city.^f

⁸"Then he said to his servants, 'The wedding is ready, but those who were invited were not worthy.^g ⁹So go into the roads leading out of town and invite as many people as you can find to the wedding.' ¹⁰Those servants went out into the streets and brought in all the people they found, evil and good alike, and the wedding hall was packed with guests.^h

¹¹"When the king came in to see the guests, he noticed a

---

a *21:42* Or *capstone*   b *21:42* Ps 118:22-23   c *21:44* Other mss. lack this verse   d *22:4* Lit. *Again*   e *22:6* Lit. *his*

Cross-references (margin):

21:43
a Matt8:12

21:44
b Isa8:14-15; 60:12; Dan2:44; Zech12:3; Lk20:18; Rom9:33; 1Peter2:8

21:46
c Matt21:11; Lk7:16; John7:40

22:1
d Lk14:16; Rev19:7,9

22:4
e Prov9:2

22:7
f Dan9:26; Lk19:27

22:8
g Matt10:11,13; Acts13:46

22:10
h Matt13:38,47

22:11
a 2Cor5:3;
Eph4:24;
Col3:10,12;
Rev3:4; 16:15;
19:8

man there who was not wearing wedding clothes.*a* [12]He said to him, 'Friend, how did you get in here without wedding clothes?' But the man*a* was speechless. [13]Then the king told his servants, 'Tie his hands and feet, and throw him into the outer darkness! In that place there will be weeping and gnashing of teeth.'*b b* [14]For many are invited, but few are chosen."*c*

22:13
b Matt8:12

A Question about Paying Taxes
(Mark 12:13–17; Luke 20:20–26)

[15]Then the Pharisees went and planned how to trap Jesus*c* in conversation.*d* [16]They sent their disciples to him along with the Herodians.*d* They said, "Teacher, we know that you are sincere and that you teach the way of God

22:14
c Matt20:16

truthfully. You don't favor any individual, for you pay no attention to external appearance. [17]So tell us what you think. Is it lawful to pay taxes to Caesar or not?"

[18]But Jesus recognized their wickedness and said, "Why are you testing me, you hypocrites? [19]Show me the coin used for the tax." They brought him a denarius.*e* [20]Then he

22:15
d Mark12:13;
Lk20:20

asked them, "Whose face and name is this?" [21]They said to him, "Caesar's." So he said to them, "Then give back to Caesar the things that are Caesar's, and to God the things that are God's."*e*

[22]When they heard this, they were amazed. Then they left him and went away.

22:21
e Matt17:25;
Rom13:7

A Question about the Resurrection
(Mark 12:18–27; Luke 20:27–40)

[23]That same day some Sadducees, who say there is no resurrection, came to Jesus*f* and asked him,*f* [24]"Teacher, Moses said, 'If a man dies having no children, his brother must marry the widow and have children for his brother.'*g g*

22:23
f Mark12:18;
Lk20:27;
Acts23:8

[25]Now there were seven brothers among us. The first one married and died, and since he had no children, he left his widow to his brother. [26]The same thing happened with the second brother, and then the third, and finally with the rest

22:24
g Deut25:5

---

a 22:12 Lit. *he*   *b* 22:13 I.e. extreme pain   *c* 22:15 Lit. *him*   *d* 22:16 I.e. Roman sympathizers   *e* 22:19 The denarius was the usual day's wage for a laborer.   *f* 22:23 Lit. *to him*   *g* 22:24 Deut 25:5-6

of the brothers.ᵃ ²⁷Finally, the woman died, too. ²⁸Now in the resurrection, whose wife of the seven will she be, since all of them had married her?"ᵇ

²⁹Jesus answered them, "You are mistaken because you don't know the Scriptures or God's power.ᵃ ³⁰For in the resurrection, peopleᶜ neither marry nor are given in marriage but are like the angelsᵈ in heaven. ᵇ ³¹As for the resurrection from the dead, haven't you read what was spoken to you by God when he said, ³²'I am the God of Abraham, the God of Isaac, and the God of Jacob'?ᵉ Heᶠ is not the God of the dead, but of the living."ᶜ

³³When the crowds heard this, they were amazed at his teaching.ᵈ

The Greatest Commandment
(Mark 12:28–34; Luke 10:25–28)

³⁴When the Pharisees had heard that Jesusᵍ had silenced the Sadducees, they got together in the same place.ᵉ ³⁵One of them, an expert in the Law, tested him by asking,ᶠ ³⁶"Teacher, which is the greatest commandment in the Law?" ³⁷Jesusᵍ said to him, "'You must love the Lord your God with all your heart, with all your soul, and with all your mind.'ʰᵍ ³⁸This is the greatest and most importantⁱ commandment. ³⁹The second is like it: 'You must love your neighbor as yourself.'ⁱʰ ⁴⁰All the Law and the Prophets depend on these two commandments."ⁱ

A Question about David's Son
(Mark 12:35–37; Luke 20:41–44)

⁴¹While the Pharisees were still gathered,ᵏ Jesus asked them,ʲ ⁴²"What do you think about the Christ?ˡ Whose son is he?" They told him, "David's." ⁴³He asked them, "Then how can David by the Spirit call him 'Lord' when he says,

⁴⁴'The Lord said to my Lord,ᵏ

---

a22:26 Lit. *with the seven*   b22:28 Lit. *had her*   c22:30 Lit. *they*
d22:30 Other mss. read *God's angels*   e22:32 Exod 3:6   f22:32 Other
mss. read *God*   g22:34,22:37 Lit. *he*   h22:37 Deut 6:5   i22:38 Or *first*
j22:39 Lev 19:18   k22:41 Lit. *were gathered*   l22:42 I.e. the Messiah

Cross references
22:29 aJohn20:9

22:30 b1John3:2

22:32 cExod3:6,16; Mark12:26; Lk20:37; Acts7:32; Heb 11:16

22:33 dMatt7:28

22:34 eMark12:28

22:35 fLk10:25

22:37 gDeut6:5; 10:12; 30:6; Lk10:27

22:39 hLev19:18; Matt19:19; Mark12:31; Lk10:27; Rom13:9; Gal5:14; James2:8

22:40 iMatt7:12; 1Tim1:5

22:41 jMark12:35; Lk20:41

22:44 kPs 110:1; Acts2:34; 1Cor15:25; Heb1:13; 10:12-13

22:46
a Mark12:34;
Lk14:6; 20:40

23:2
b Neh8:4,8;
Mal2:7;
Mark12:38;
Lk20:45

23:3
c Rom2:19

23:4
d Lk 11:46;
Acts15:10;
Gal6:13

23:5
e Num15:38;
Deut6:8; 22:12;
Prov3:3;
Matt6:1-2,5,16

23:6
f Mark12:38-39;
Lk 11:43; 20:46;
3John1:9

23:8
g 2Cor1:24;
James3:1;
1Peter5:3

23:9
h Mal1:6

23:11
i Matt20:26-27

23:12
j Job22:29;
Prov15:33; 29:23;
Lk14:11; 18:14;
James4:6;
1Peter5:5

23:13
k Mark12:40;
Lk20:47;
2Tim3:6;
Titus1:11

"Sit at my right hand,
until I put your enemies under your feet" '?[a]

[45]If David calls him Lord, how can he be his son?"
[46]No one could answer him at all,[b] and from that day on no one dared to ask him another question.[a]

Jesus Denounces the Scribes and the Pharisees
(Mark 12:38–40; Luke 11:37–52; 20:45–47)

23 [1]Then Jesus said to the crowds and to his disciples, [2]"The scribes and the Pharisees sit in Moses' seat.[cb] [3]So do whatever they tell you and follow it, but stop doing what they do, because they don't do what they say.[c] [4]They tie up burdens that are heavy and unbearable and lay them on people's shoulders, but they refuse to lift a finger to remove them.[d]

[5]"They do all their actions to be seen by people. They increase the size of their phylacteries[d] and lengthen the tassels of their garments.[e] [6]They love to have the places of honor at feasts, the best seats in the synagogues,[f] [7]to be greeted in the marketplaces, and to be called 'Rabbi'[e] by people.

[8]"But you are not to be called 'Rabbi,' for you have only one teacher, and all of you are brothers.[g] [9]And don't call anyone on earth 'Father,' for you have only one Father, the one in heaven.[h] [10]Nor are you to be called 'Teachers,' for you have only one teacher, the Christ![f] [11]The person who is greatest among you must be your servant.[i] [12]Whoever exalts himself will be humbled, and whoever humbles himself will be exalted.[j]

[13]"How terrible it will be for you, scribes and Pharisees, you hypocrites! You shut the door to the kingdom of heaven in people's faces. You don't go in yourselves, and you don't allow those who are trying to enter to go in.[gk]

---

a *22:44* Ps 110:1   **b** *22:46* Lit. *a word*   **c** *23:2* I.e. speak with Moses' authority   **d** *23:5* I.e. leather cases containing Scripture texts   **e** *23:7* Rabbi is Aram. for *Teacher* or *Master*   **f** *23:10* I.e. the Messiah   **g** *23:13* Other mss. read *to go in. [14]How terrible it will be for you, scribes and Pharisees, you hypocrites! You devour widows' houses and say long prayers to cover it up. Therefore, you will receive greater condemnation!*

¹⁵"How terrible it will be for you, scribes and Pharisees, you hypocrites! You travel over sea and land to make a single convert, and when this happens, you make him twice as fit for hell[a] as you are.

¹⁶"How terrible it will be for you, blind guides! You say, 'Whoever swears an oath by the Sanctuary is excused,[b] but whoever swears an oath by the gold of the Sanctuary must keep his oath.'[c][a] ¹⁷You blind fools! What is more important, the gold or the Sanctuary that made the gold holy?[b] ¹⁸Again you say,[d] 'Whoever swears an oath by the altar is excused,[b] but whoever swears by the gift that is on it must keep his oath.'[c] ¹⁹You blind men![e] Which is more important, the gift or the altar that makes the gift holy?[c] ²⁰So the one who swears an oath by the altar swears by it and by everything on it. ²¹The one who swears an oath by the Sanctuary swears by it and by the one who lives there.[d] ²²And the one who swears an oath by heaven swears by God's throne and by the one who sits on it.[e]

²³"How terrible it will be for you, scribes and Pharisees, you hypocrites! For you give a tenth of your mint, dill, and cummin, but have neglected the more important matters of the Law: justice, mercy, and faithfulness.[f] These are the things you should have practiced, without neglecting the others.[f] ²⁴You blind guides! You filter out a gnat, yet swallow a camel!

²⁵"How terrible it will be for you, scribes and Pharisees, you hypocrites! You clean the outside of the cup and the plate, but inside they are full of greed and self-indulgence.[g] ²⁶You blind Pharisee! First clean the inside of the cup,[g] so that its outside may also be clean.

²⁷"How terrible it will be for you, scribes and Pharisees, you hypocrites! You are like whitewashed tombs that look

---

a23:15 Lit. *twice as much a son of Gehenna*   b23:16,23:18 Lit. *is nothing*
c23:16,23:18 Lit. *owes a debt*   d23:18 Lit. *And*   e23:19 Other mss. read
blind and foolish men   f23:23 Or *faith*   g23:26 Other mss. read *the cup
and the plate*

23:16
[a]Matt5:33-34;
15:14,24

23:17
[b]Exod30:29

23:19
[c]Exod29:37

23:21
[d]1Kings8:13;
2Chr6:2; Ps26:8;
132:14

23:22
[e]Ps 11:4;
Matt5:34;
Acts7:49

23:23
[f]1Sam15:22;
Hos6:6; Mic6:8;
Matt9:13; 12:7;
Lk 11:42

23:25
[g]Mark7:4;
Lk 11:39

23:27
a Lk 11:44;
Acts23:3

23:29
b Lk 11:47

23:31
c Acts7:51-52;
1Thes2:15

23:32
d Gen15:16;
1Thes2:16

23:33
e Matt3:7; 12:34

23:34
f Matt10:17;
21:34-35;
Lk 11:49;
Acts5:40;
7:58-59; 22:19;
2Cor 11:24-25

23:35
g Gen4:8;
2Chr24:20-21;
1John3:12;
Rev18:24

23:37
h Deut32:11-12;
2Chr24:21;
Ps17:8; 91:4;
Lk13:34

23:39
i Ps 118:26;
Matt21:9

beautiful on the outside but inside are full of dead people's bones and every kind of impurity.*a* [28]In the same way, on the outside you look righteous to people, but inside you are full of hypocrisy and lawlessness.

[29]"How terrible it will be for you, scribes and Pharisees, you hypocrites! You build tombs for the prophets and decorate the monuments of the righteous.*b* [30]Then you say, 'If we had been living in the days of our ancestors, we would have had no part with them in shedding the blood*a* of the prophets.' [31]So you testify against yourselves that you are descendants of those who murdered the prophets.*c* [32]Then finish what your ancestors tried to do!*bd* [33]You snakes, you children of serpents! How can you escape being condemned to hell?*ce*

[34]"That's why I'm sending you prophets, wise men, and scribes. Some of them you will kill and crucify, and some of them you will whip in your synagogues and persecute from town to town.*f* [35]As a result, you will be held accountable for*d* all the righteous blood shed on earth, from the blood of the righteous Abel to the blood of Zechariah, the son of Berechiah, whom you murdered between the Sanctuary and the altar.*g* [36]Truly I tell you, all these things will happen to this generation."

Jesus Mourns over Jerusalem
(Luke 13:34–35)

[37]"O Jerusalem, Jerusalem, who kills the prophets and stones to death those who have been sent to her! How often I wanted to gather your children together the way a hen gathers her chicks under her wings, but you didn't want to!*h* [38]Look! Your house is left to you deserted! [39]For I tell you, you will not see me again until you say, 'How blessed is the one who comes in the name of the Lord!' "*ei*

---

a 23:30 Lit. *in the blood*   **b** 23:32 Lit. *Fill up the measure of your ancestors*   **c** 23:33 Gk. *Gehenna*   **d** 23:35 Lit. *on you will come*   **e** 23:39 Ps 118:26

Jesus Predicts the Destruction of the Temple
(Mark 13:1–2; Luke 21:5–6)

24
¹As Jesus left the Temple and was walking away, his disciples came up to him to point out to him the temple buildings.*ᵃ* ²But he said to them, "You see all these things, don't you? Truly I tell you, not one stone here will be left on another that will not be torn down."*ᵇ*

The Coming Persecution
(Mark 13:3–13; Luke 21:7–19)

³While Jesus**ᵃ** was sitting on the Mount of Olives, the disciples came to him privately and said, "Tell us, when will these things take place, and what will be the sign of your coming and of the end of the age?"*ᶜ*

⁴Jesus answered them, "See to it that no one deceives you.*ᵈ* ⁵For many will come in my name and say, 'I am the Christ,'**ᵇ** and they will deceive many people.*ᵉ* ⁶You are going to hear of wars and rumors of wars. See to it that you are not alarmed. These things must take place, but the end hasn't come yet. ⁷For nation will rise up in arms against nation, and kingdom against kingdom. There will be famines and earthquakes in various places.*ᶠ* ⁸But all these things are only the beginning of the birth pains.

⁹"Then they will hand you over to punishment**ᶜ** and will kill you, and you will be hated by all the nations**ᵈ** because of my name.*ᵍ* ¹⁰Then many people will fall by the way and will betray one another and hate one another.*ʰ* ¹¹Many false prophets will appear and deceive many people,*ⁱ* ¹²and because lawlessness will increase, the love of many people will grow cold. ¹³But the person who endures to the end will be saved.*ʲ* ¹⁴And this gospel of the kingdom will be proclaimed throughout the world as a testimony to all nations,**ᵈ** and then the end will come."*ᵏ*

Signs of the End
(Mark 13:14–23; Luke 21:20–24)

¹⁵"So when you see the destructive desecration, men-

---

a 24:3 Lit. *he*   **b** 24:5 I.e. the Messiah   **c** 24:9 Or *tribulation*
d 24:9,24:14 Or *Gentiles*

24:1
ᵃMark13:1;
Lk21:5

24:2
ᵇ1Kings9:7;
Jer26:18;
Mic3:12;
Lk19:44

24:3
ᶜMark13:3;
1Thes5:1

24:4
ᵈEph5:6; Col2:8,
18; 2Thes2:3;
1John4:1

24:5
ᵉJer14:14;
23:24-25;
Matt5:11; 23:24;
John5:43

24:7
ᶠ2Chr15:6;
Isa19:2;
Hag2:22;
Zech14:13

24:9
ᵍMatt10:17;
Mark13:9;
Lk21:12;
John15:20; 16:2;
Acts4:2-3; 7:59;
12:1; 1Peter4:16;
Rev2:10,13

24:10
ʰMatt 11:6;
13:57; 2Tim1:15;
4:10,16

24:11
ⁱMatt4:5,24;
7:15; Acts20:29;
1Tim4:1;
2Peter2:1

24:13
ʲMatt10:22;
Mark13:13;
Heb3:6,14;
Rev2:10

24:14
ᵏMatt4:23; 9:35;
Rom10:18;
Col1:6,23

24:15
*a*Dan9:23,25,27;
12:11;
Mark13:14;
Lk21:20

24:19
*b*Lk23:29

24:21
*c*Dan9:26;
12:1Joel2:2

24:22
*d*Isa65:8-9;
Zech14:2-3

24:23
*e*Mark13:21;
Lk17:23; 21:8

24:24
*f*Deut13:1;
Matt13:5,11;
John6:37;
10:28-29;
Rom8:28-30;
2Thes2:9-11;
2Tim2:19;
Rev13:13

24:27
*g*Lk17:24

24:28
*h*Job39:30;
Lk17:37

24:29
*i*Isa13:10;
Ezek32:7;
Dan7:11-12;
Joel2:10,31; 3:15;
Amos5:20; 8:9;
Mark13:24;
Lk21:25;
Acts2:20;
Rev6:12

tioned by the prophet Daniel, standing in the Holy Place (let the reader take note),[a][a] [16]then those who are in Judea must flee to the mountains. [17]The person who is on the housetop must not come down to get what is in his house, [18]and the person who is in the field must not turn back to get his coat.

[19]"How terrible it will be for women who are pregnant or who are nursing babies in those days![b] [20]Pray that it may not be in winter or on a Sabbath when you flee. [21]For at that time there will be great suffering,[b] the kind that has not happened from the beginning of the world until now and certainly will never happen again.[c] [22]If those days had not been limited, no life would be saved. But for the sake of the elect, those days will be limited.[d]

[23]"At that time, if anyone says to you, 'Look! Here is the Christ!'[c] or 'There he is!', don't believe it.[e] [24]For false christs and false prophets will appear and display great signs and wonders to deceive, if possible, even the elect.[f] [25]Remember, I've told you this beforehand. [26]So if they say to you, 'Look! He's in the wilderness,' don't go out looking for him.[d] And if they say, 'Look! He's in the storeroom,' don't believe it. [27]For just as the lightning comes from the east and flashes as far as the west, so will be the coming of the Son of Man.[g] [28]Wherever there's a dead body, there the vultures will gather."[h]

The Coming of the Son of Man
(Mark 13:24–27; Luke 21:25–28)

[29]"Immediately after the suffering[b] of those days,[i]

'The sun will be darkened,
    the moon will not give its light,
the stars will fall from the sky,
    and the powers of heaven will be shaken loose.'[e]

[30]Then the sign of the Son of Man will appear in the sky, and all the nations[f] of the earth will mourn when they see 'the Son of Man coming on the clouds of heaven'[g] with power

---

a *24:15* Dan 9:27; 11:31; 12:11   **b** *24:21,24,29* Or *tribulation*   **c** *24:23* I.e. the Messiah   **d** *24:26* Lit. *don't go out*   **e** *24:29* Isa 13:10; 34:4; Joel 2:10   **f** *24:30* Lit. *tribes*   **g** *24:30* Dan 7:13

and great glory.*a* 31He will send out his angels with a loud trumpet blast, and they will gather his elect from the four winds, from one end of heaven to another."*b*

The Lesson from the Fig Tree
(Mark 13:28–31; Luke 21:29–33)

32"Now learn a lesson*a* from the fig tree. When its branches become tender and it produces leaves, you know that summer is near.*c* 33In the same way, when you see all these things, you will know that he is near, right at the door.*d*

34"Truly I tell you, this generation will not disappear until these things happen.*e* 35Heaven and earth will disappear, but my words will never disappear."*f*

The Unknown Day and Hour of Christ's Return
(Mark 13:32–37; Luke 17:26–30, 34–36)

36"No one knows when that day or hour will come*b*—not the angels in heaven, not the Son,*c* but only the Father.*g* 37For just as it was in the days of Noah, so it will be when the Son of Man comes. 38In those days before the flood, people*d* were eating and drinking, marrying and giving in marriage right up to the day when Noah went into the ark.*h* 39They were unaware of what was happening*e* until the flood came and swept all of them away. That's how it will be when the Son of Man comes. 40At that time two people will be in the field. One will be taken, and the other will be left behind.*i* 41Two women will be grinding grain at the mill. One will be taken, and the other will be left behind.

42"So keep on watching, because you don't know on what day your Lord is coming.*j* 43But be sure of this: if the owner of the house had known at what watch of the night the thief was coming, he would have stayed awake and not allowed his house to be broken into.*k* 44So you, too, must be ready, because at an hour you are not expecting him the Son of Man will come."*l*

---

a 24:32 Or *parable*   b 24:36 Lit. *about that day and hour*   c 24:36 Other mss. lack *not the Son*   d 24:38 Lit. *they*   e 24:39 The Gk. lacks *of what was happening*

24:30
a Dan7:13;
Zech12:12;
Matt16:27;
Mark13:26;
Rev1:7

24:31
b Matt13:41;
1Cor15:52;
1Thes4:16

24:32
c Lk21:29

24:33
d James5:9

24:34
e Matt16:28;
23:36;
Mark13:30;
Lk21:32

24:35
f Ps102:26;
Isa51:6;
Jer31:35-36;
Matt5:18;
Mark13:31;
Lk21:33;
Heb1:11

24:36
g Zech14:7;
Mark13:32;
Acts1:7;
1Thes5:2;
2Peter3:10

24:38
h Gen6:3-5; 7:5;
Lk17:26;
1Peter3:20

24:40
i Lk17:34

24:42
j Mark13:33;
Lk21:36

24:43
k Lk12:39;
1Thes5:2;
2Peter3:10;
Rev3:3; 16:15

24:44
l Matt25:13;
1Thes5:6

24:45
*a*Lk12:42;
Acts20:28;
1Cor4:2; Heb3:5

24:46
*b*Rev16:15

24:47
*c*Matt25:21,23;
Lk22:29

24:51
*d*Matt8:12; 25:30

25:1
*e*Eph5:29-30;
Rev19:7; 21:2,9

25:2
*f*Matt13:47;
22:10

25:5
*g*1Thes5:6

25:6
*h*Matt24:31;
1Thes4:16

25:7
*i*Lk12:35

25:10
*j*Lk13:25

25:11
*k*Matt7:21-23

The Faithful or the Wicked Servant
(Luke 12:41–48)

45"Who, then, is the faithful and wise servant whom his master has put in charge of his household to give the others[a] their food at the right time?[a] 46How blessed is that servant whom his master finds doing this when he comes![b] 47Truly I tell you, he will put him in charge of all his property.[c]

48"But if that wicked servant says to himself,[b] 'My master has been delayed,' 49and begins to beat his fellow servants and eat and drink with the drunks, 50the master of that servant will come on a day when he doesn't expect him and at an hour that he doesn't know. 51Then his master[c] will punish him[d] severely and assign him a place with the hypocrites. In that place there will be weeping and gnashing of teeth."[e][d]

The Parable about the Ten Bridesmaids

25 1"At that time, the kingdom of heaven will be compared to ten bridesmaids[f] who took their oil lamps and went out to meet the groom.[g][e] 2Now five of them were foolish, and five were wise.[f] 3For when the foolish ones took their lamps, they didn't take any oil with them. 4But the wise ones took flasks of oil with their lamps. 5Since the groom was late, all of them became sleepy and lay down.[g]

6"But at midnight there came a shout: 'The groom is here! Come out to meet him!'[h] 7Then all the bridesmaids[f] woke up and got their lamps ready.[i] 8But the foolish ones said to the wise ones, 'Give us some of your oil, for our lamps are going out!' 9But the wise ones replied, 'No! There will never be enough for us and for you. Better go to the dealers and buy some for yourselves.'

10"While they were away buying it, the groom arrived. Those who were ready went with him into the wedding banquet, and the door was closed.[j] 11Later the other bridesmaids[f] arrived and said, 'Lord, lord, open up for us!'[k] 12But

---

a24:45 Lit. *them*   **b**24:48 Lit. *in his heart*   **c**24:51 Lit. *he*   **d**24:51 Lit. *cut him in pieces*   **e**24:51 I.e. extreme pain   **f**25:1,25:7,25:11 Lit. *virgins*   **g**25:1 Other mss. read *the groom and the bride*

he replied, 'Truly I tell you, I don't know you!'[a] [13]So keep on watching, because you don't know the day or the hour.'[ab]

The Parable about the Talents
(Luke 19:11–27)

[14]"For it's like a man going on a trip who called his servants and turned his money over to them.[c] [15]To one man he gave five talents,[b] to another two, and to another one, based on their ability. Then he went on his trip.[d]

[16]"The one who received five talents went out at once and invested them and earned five more. [17]In the same way, the one who had two talents earned two more. [18]But the one who received one talent went off, dug a hole in the ground, and hid his master's money.

[19]"After a long time the master of those servants returned and settled accounts with them. [20]The one who had received five talents came up and brought five more talents, saying, 'Master, you gave me five talents. See, I've earned five more talents.' [21]His master said to him, 'Well done, good and trustworthy servant! Since you have been trustworthy with a small amount, I will put you in charge of a large amount. Come and share your master's joy!'[e]

[22]"The one with two talents also came forward and said, 'Master, you gave me two talents. See, I've earned two more talents.' [23]His master said to him, 'Well done, good and trustworthy servant! Since you have been trustworthy with a small amount, I will put you in charge of a large amount. Come and share your master's joy!'[f]

[24]"Then the one who had received one talent came forward and said, 'Master, I knew that you were a hard man, harvesting where you haven't planted and gathering where you haven't scattered any seed. [25]Being afraid, I went off and hid your talent in the ground. Here, take what's yours!'

[26]"His master answered him, 'You evil and lazy servant! So you knew that I harvested where I haven't planted and gathered where I haven't scattered any seed? [27]Then you should have invested my money with the bankers. When I

---

a 25:13 Other mss. read *the hour when the Son of Man will come*
b 25:15 A talent was worth a lifetime of wages for an average laborer.

25:12
*a*Ps5:5; Hab1:13; John9:31

25:13
*b*Matt24:42,44; Mark13:33,35; Lk21:36; 1Cor16:13; 1Thes5:6; 1Peter5:8; Rev16:15

25:14
*c*Matt21:33; Lk19:12

25:15
*d*Rom12:6; 1Cor12:7,11,29; Eph4:11

25:21
*e*Matt24:34, 46-47; Lk12:44; 22:29-30; 2Tim2:12; Heb12:2; 1Peter1:8

25:23
*f*Matt25:21

25:29
*a*Matt13:12;
Mark4:25;
Lk8:18; 19:26;
John15:2

25:30
*b*Matt8:12; 24:51

25:31
*c*Zech14:5;
Matt16:27; 19:28;
Mark8:38;
Acts1:11;
1Thes4:16;
2Thes1:7;
Jude1:14; Rev1:7

25:32
*d*Ezek20:38;
34:17,20;
Matt13:49;
Rom14:10;
2Cor5:10;
Rev20:12

25:34
*e*Matt20:23;
Mark10:40;
Rom8:17;
1Cor2:9;
Heb 11:16;
1Peter1:4,9; 3:9;
Rev21:7

25:35
*f*Isa58:7;
Ezek18:7;
Heb13:2;
James1:27;
3John1:5

25:36
*g*2Tim1:16;
James2:15-16

25:40
*h*Prov14:31;
19:17; Matt10:42;
Mark9:41;
Heb6:10

25:41
*i*Ps6:8; Matt7:23;
13:40,42;
Lk13:27;
2Peter2:4;
Jude1:6

returned, I would have received my money back with interest. [28]Take the talent from him and give it to the man who has the ten talents. [29]For to everyone who has, more will be given, and he will have more than enough. But from the person who has nothing, even what he has will be taken away from him. *a* [30]Throw this useless servant into the outer darkness! In that place there will be weeping and gnashing of teeth.' "*ab*

The Judgment of the Nations

[31]"When the Son of Man comes in his glory and all the angels are with him, he will sit on his glorious throne.*c* [32]All the nations will be assembled in front of him, and he will separate them from each other like a shepherd separates the sheep from the goats.*d* [33]He will put the sheep on his right but the goats on his left.

[34]"Then the king will say to those on his right, 'Come, you who have been blessed by my Father, inherit the kingdom prepared for you from the foundation of the world.*e* [35]For I was hungry, and you gave me something to eat. I was thirsty, and you gave me something to drink. I was a stranger, and you welcomed me.*f* [36]I was naked, and you clothed me. I was sick, and you took care of me. I was in prison, and you visited me.'*g*

[37]"Then the righteous will say to him, 'Lord, when did we see you hungry and give you something to eat, or thirsty and give you something to drink? [38]When did we see you as a stranger and welcome you, or naked and clothe you? [39]When did we see you sick or in prison and visit you?' [40]The king will answer them, 'Truly I tell you, in that you did it for one of the least important of these my brothers, you did it for me.'*h*

[41]"Then he will say to those on his left, 'Get away from me, you who are accursed, into the eternal fire that has been prepared for the devil and his angels!*i* [42]For I was hungry, and you gave me nothing to eat. I was thirsty, and you gave me nothing to drink. [43]I was a stranger, and you didn't

---

a *25:30* I.e. extreme pain

welcome me. I was naked, and you didn't clothe me. I was sick and in prison, and you didn't visit me.'

25:45
*a*Prov14:31; 17:5;
Zech2:8; Acts9:5

44"Then they will reply, 'Lord, when did we see you hungry or thirsty or as a stranger or naked or sick or in prison and didn't help you?' 45Then he will say to them, 'Truly I tell you, in that you did not do it for one of the least important of these, you did not do it for me.'*a* 46These people will go away into eternal punishment, but the righteous will go into*a* eternal life."*b*

25:46
*b*Dan12:2;
John5:29;
Rom2:7

The Plot to Kill Jesus
(Mark 14:1–2; Luke 22:1–2; John 11:45–53)

26 1When Jesus had finished saying all these things,*b* he told his disciples, 2"You know that the Passover will take place in two days, and the Son of Man will be handed over to be crucified."*c*

26:2
*c*Mark14:1;
Lk22:1; John12:1

3Then the high priests and the elders of the people assembled in the courtyard of the high priest, who was named Caiaphas.*d* 4They conspired to arrest Jesus by treachery and to kill him. 5But they kept saying, "This must not happen during the festival, so that there may not be a riot among the people."

26:3
*d*Ps2:2;
John 11:47;
Acts4:25

A Woman Prepares Jesus' Body for Burial
(Mark 14:3–9; John 12:1–8)

6While Jesus was in Bethany at the home of Simon the leper,*e* 7a woman came to him with an alabaster jar of very expensive perfume and poured it on his head while he sat at the table. 8But when the disciples saw this they became irritated and said, "Why this waste?*f* 9Surely this perfume could have been sold for a high price and the money given*c* to the destitute."

26:6
*e*Matt21:17;
Mark14:3;
John 11:1-2; 12:3

10Jesus, knowing what was going on,*d* said to them, "Why are you bothering the woman? She has done a beautiful thing for me. 11For you will always have the destitute with you, but you will not always have me.*g* 12When she poured this perfume on my body, she was preparing me for

26:8
*f*John12:4

26:11
*g*Deut15:11;
Matt18:20; 28:20;
John12:8; 13:33;
14:19; 16:5,28;
17:11

---

a25:46 Lit. *the righteous into*   b26:1 Lit. *finished all these sayings*
c26:9 Lit. *and given*   d26:10 Lit. *knowing*

26:14
a Matt10:4;
Mark14:10;
Lk22:3;
John13:2,30

burial. ¹³Truly I tell you, wherever this gospel is proclaimed in the whole world, what she has done will also be told as a memorial to her."

Judas Agrees to Betray Jesus
(Mark 14:10–11; Luke 22:3–6)

26:15
b Zech 11:12;
Matt27:3

¹⁴Then one of the twelve, who was called Judas Iscariot, went to the high priests*a* ¹⁵and said, "What are you willing to give me if I betray him to you?" They placed before him thirty pieces of silver,*b* ¹⁶and from then on he began to look for an opportunity to betray Jesus.**a**

The Passover with the Disciples
(Mark 14:12–21; Luke 22:7–14, 21–23; John 12:21–30)

26:17
c Exod12:6,18;
Mark14:12;
Lk22:7

¹⁷On the first day of the Festival**b** of Unleavened Bread, the disciples went to Jesus and said, "Where do you want us to make preparations for you to eat the Passover meal?"*c* ¹⁸He said, "Go to a certain man in the city and say to him, 'The Teacher says, "My time is near. I will celebrate the Passover with my disciples at your house." '"*c* ¹⁹So the disciples did as Jesus had directed them, and they prepared the Passover meal.

26:20
d Mark14:17-21;
Lk22:14;
John13:21

²⁰When evening came, Jesus**d** was sitting at the table with the twelve.**e***d* ²¹While they were eating, he said, "Truly I tell you, one of you is going to betray me."

²²Feeling deeply distressed, each one began to say to him, "Surely I am not the one, Lord?" ²³He replied, "The man

26:23
e Ps41:9;
Lk22:21;
John13:18

who has dipped his hand into the bowl with me will betray me.*e* ²⁴The Son of Man is going away, just as it has been written about him, but how terrible it will be for that man by whom the Son of Man is betrayed! It would have been better for him if he had never been born."*f*

²⁵Then Judas, who was going to betray him, said, "Rabbi,**f** I'm not the one, am I?" Jesus**g** said to him, "You have

26:24
f Ps22:1-31;
Isa53:1-12;
Dan9:26;
Mark9:12;
Lk24:25-26,46;
John17:12;
Acts17:2-3;
26:22-23;
1Cor15:3

said so."

---

a 26:16 Lit. *him*   **b** 26:17 The Gk. lacks *day of the Festival*   **c** 26:18 Lit. *with you*   **d** 26:20 Lit. *he*   **e** 26:20 Other mss. read *the twelve disciples*   **f** 26:25 Rabbi is Aram. for *Teacher* or *Master*   **g** 26:25 Lit. *He*

The Lord's Supper
(Mark 14:22–26; Luke 22:15–20; 1 Corinthians 11:23–25)

26While they were eating, Jesus took a loaf of bread and blessed it. Then he broke it in pieces and gave it to the disciples, saying, "Take this and eat it. This is my body."[a] 27Then he took a cup, gave thanks, and gave it to them, saying, "Drink from it, all of you.[b] 28For this is my blood of the new[a] covenant that is being poured out for many people for the forgiveness of sins.[c] 29I tell you, I will never again drink the product of the vine until that day when I drink new wine[b] with you in my Father's kingdom."[d] 30After singing a hymn, they went out to the Mount of Olives.[e]

Jesus Predicts Peter's Denial
(Mark 14:27–31; Luke 22:31–34; John 13:36–38)

31Then Jesus said to them, "All of you will turn against me this very night. For it is written[f]

'I will strike the shepherd,
  and the sheep of the flock will be scattered.'[c]

32But after I have been raised, I will go to Galilee ahead of you."[g] 33But Peter said to him, "Even if everyone else turns against you, I certainly won't!" 34Jesus said to him, "Truly I tell you, this very night, before a rooster crows, you will deny me three times."[h] 35Peter told him, "Even if I have to die with you, I will never deny you!" And all the disciples said the same thing.

Jesus Prays in the Garden of Gethsemane
(Mark 14:32–42; Luke 22:39–46)

36Then Jesus went with them to a place called Gethsemane. He said to the disciples, "Sit down here while I go over there and pray."[i] 37Taking Peter and the two sons of Zebedee with him, he began to be grieved and troubled.[j] 38Then he said to them, "My soul is deeply grieved, even to the point of death. Wait here and stay awake with me."[k]

---

a 26:28 Other mss. lack *new*   b 26:29 Lit. *drink it new*   c 26:31 Zech 13:7

Cross references:

26:26
a Mark14:22;
Lk22:19;
1Cor10:16;
11:23-25

26:27
b Mark14:23

26:28
c Exod24:8;
Lev17:11;
Jer31:31;
Matt20:28;
Rom5:15;
Heb9:22

26:29
d Mark14:25;
Lk22:18;
Acts10:41

26:30
e Mark14:26

26:31
f Zech13:7;
Matt 11:6;
Mark14:27;
John16:32

26:32
g Matt28:7,10,16;
Mark14:28; 16:7

26:34
h Mark14:30;
Lk22:34;
John13:38

26:36
i Mark14:32-35;
Lk22:39;
John18:1

26:37
j Matt4:21

26:38
k John12:27

26:39
a Matt20:22;
Mark14:36;
Lk22:42;
John5:30; 6:38;
12:27; Phil2:8;
Heb5:7

³⁹Going on a little farther, he fell on his face and prayed, "O my Father, if it's possible let this cup pass from me. Yet not what I want but what you want!"*a*

⁴⁰When he went back to the disciples, he found them asleep. He said to Peter, "So, you men**a** couldn't stay awake with me for one hour, could you? ⁴¹All of you**a** must stay awake and pray that you won't come into temptation. The spirit is indeed willing, but the flesh is weak."*b*

26:41
b Mark13:33;
14:38; Lk22:40,
46; Eph6:18

⁴²He went away a second time and prayed, "My Father, if this cannot go away unless I drink it, let your will be done." ⁴³Once again he came back and found them asleep, for their eyes were very heavy. ⁴⁴After leaving them again, he went away and prayed again for the third time, saying the same thing. ⁴⁵Then he came back to the disciples and said to them, "You might as well keep on sleeping and rest-ing.**b** Look! The time is near for the Son of Man to be be-trayed into the hands of sinners. ⁴⁶Get up! Let's go! See, the one who is betraying me is near!"

26:47
c Mark14:43;
Lk22:47;
John18:3;
Acts1:16

Jesus Is Arrested

(Mark 14:43–50; Luke 22:47–53; John 18:3–12)

⁴⁷Just then, while Jesus*c* was still speaking, Judas, one of the twelve, arrived. A large crowd armed with swords and clubs was with him. They were from the high priests and elders of the people.*c* ⁴⁸Now the betrayer personally had given them a signal, saying, "The one I kiss**d** is the man. Arrest him."

26:49
d 2Sam20:9

⁴⁹So Judas*c* immediately went up to Jesus and said, "Hello, Rabbi!", and kissed him tenderly.*d* ⁵⁰Jesus said to him, "Friend, why are you here?"**e** Then the other men**f** came forward, took hold of Jesus, and arrested him.*e*

26:50
e Ps41:9; 55:13

⁵¹Suddenly, one of the men with Jesus reached out his hand, drew his sword, and struck the high priest's servant, cutting off his ear.*f* ⁵²Jesus said to him, "Put your sword back in its place! For all who use a sword will be killed by a

---

a 26:40,26:41 Lit. *you* (plural)   **b** 26:45 Or *Are you still sleeping and resting?*   **c** 26:47,26:49 Lit. *he*   **d** 26:48 Disciples customarily greeted their Rabbi with a kiss.   **e** 26:50 Or *do what you came for*   **f** 26:50 Lit. *they*

26:51
f John18:10

sword.*a* 53Don't you think that I could call on my Father, and he would send me more than twelve legions of angels now?*b* 54How, then, would the Scriptures be fulfilled that say this must happen?"*c*

55At this point*a* Jesus said to the crowds, "Have you come out with swords and clubs to arrest me as if I were a revolutionary?*b* Day after day I sat teaching in the Temple, yet you didn't arrest me. 56But all of this has happened so that the writings of the prophets might be fulfilled." Then all the disciples deserted him and ran away.*d*

Jesus Is Tried before the High Priest
(Mark 14:53–65; Luke 22:54–55, 63–71; John 18:13–14, 19–24)

57Those who had arrested Jesus took him to Caiaphas, the high priest, where the scribes and the elders had assembled.*e* 58Peter, however, followed him at a distance as far as the high priest's courtyard. He went inside and sat down with the servants to see how this would end.

59Meanwhile, the high priests and the whole Council*c* were looking for false testimony against Jesus in order to have him put to death. 60But they couldn't find any, even though many false witnesses had come forward. At last two men came forward*f* 61and stated, "This man said, 'I can destroy the Sanctuary of God and rebuild it in three days.' "*g*

62At this, the high priest stood up and said to Jesus,*d* "Don't you have any answer to what these men are testifying against you?"*h* 63But Jesus was silent. Then the high priest said to him, "I command you by the living God to tell us if you are the Christ,*e* the Son of God!"*i* 64Jesus said to him, "You have said so. Nevertheless I tell you,*j*

> From now on you will see 'the Son of Man
> seated at the right hand of Power'
> and 'coming on the clouds of heaven.' "*f*

65Then the high priest tore his robes and said, "He has blasphemed! Why do we still need witnesses? Look, you

---

a26:55 Lit. *In that hour*　b26:55 Or *bandit*　c26:59 Or *Sanhedrin*
d26:62 Lit. *to him*　e26:63 I.e. the Messiah　f26:64 Ps 110:1; Dan 7:13

26:52
*a*Gen9:6;
Rev13:10

26:53
*b*2Kings6:17;
Dan7:10

26:54
*c*Isa53:7,24;
Lk24:25,44,46

26:56
*d*Lam4:20;
Matt26:54;
John18:15

26:57
*e*Mark14:53;
Lk22:54;
John18:12-13,24

26:60
*f*Deut19:15;
Ps27:12; 35:11;
Mark14:55;
Acts6:13

26:61
*g*Matt27:40;
John2:19

26:62
*h*Mark14:60

26:63
*i*Lev5:1;
1Sam14:24,26;
Isa53:7;
Matt27:12,14

26:64
*j*Ps 110:1;
Dan7:13;
Matt16:27; 24:30;
Lk21:27; 26:31;
John1:51;
Acts7:55;
Rom14:10;
1Thes4:16;
Rev1:7

26:65
a 2Kings18:37;
19:1

yourselves have just heard the blasphemy!*a* 66What is your verdict?" They replied, "He deserves to die!"*b*

26:66
bLev24:16;
John19:7

67Then they spit in his face and hit him. Some slapped him,*c* 68saying, "Prophesy to us, you Christ!*a* Who is the one who hit you?"*d*

Peter Denies Jesus

(Mark 14:66–72; Luke 22:56–62; John 18:15–18, 25–27)

26:67
cIsa50:6; 53:3;
Matt27:30;
Lk22:63;
John19:3

69Now Peter was sitting outside in the courtyard when a servant girl came up to him and said, "You, too, were with Jesus the Galilean."*e* 70But he denied it in front of them all, saying, "I don't know what you're talking about."

26:68
dMark14:65;
Lk22:64

71As he went out to the gateway, another woman saw him and said to those who were there, "This man was with Jesus from Nazareth."*b* 72Again he denied it and swore with an oath, "I don't know the man!"

26:69
eMark14:66;
Lk22:55;
John18:16-17,25

73After a little while the people who were standing there came up and said to Peter, "Obviously you're also one of them, because your accent gives you away."*f*

26:73
fLk22:59

74Then he began to invoke a divine curse and to swear with an oath, "I don't know the man!" Just then a rooster crowed.*g* 75Peter remembered the words of Jesus when he said, "Before a rooster crows, you will deny me three times." Then Peter*c* went outside and cried bitterly.*h*

26:74
gMark14:71

Jesus Is Taken to Pilate

(Mark 15:1; Luke 23:1–2; John 18:28–32)

26:75
hMatt26:34;
Mark14:30;
Lk22:61-62;
John13:38

27 1When morning came, all the high priests and the elders of the people conspired against Jesus to put him to death.*i* 2They bound him with chains, led him away, and handed him over to Pontius*d* Pilate, the governor.*j*

The Death of Judas

(Acts 1:18–19)

27:1
iPs2:2;
Mark15:1;
Lk22:66;
23:1John18:28

3Then Judas, who had betrayed him, regretted what had

27:2
jMatt20:19;
Acts3:13

a *26:68* I.e. Messiah   b *26:71* Or *Jesus the Nazarene;* the Gk. *Nazoraios* may be a word play between Heb. *netser,* meaning *branch* (see Isa 11:1), and the name *Nazareth.*   c *26:75* Lit. *he*   d *27:2* Other mss. lack *Pontius*

happened when he saw that Jesus[a] was condemned. He brought the thirty pieces of silver back to the high priests and elders,[a] [4]saying, "I have sinned by betraying innocent[b] blood." But they said, "What do we care? See to that yourself." [5]So he flung the pieces of silver into the Sanctuary and went outside. Then he went away and hanged himself.[b]

[6]The high priests picked up the pieces of silver and said, "It's not lawful to put this into the Temple treasury, because it's blood money." [7]So they decided to use the money to buy the potter's field as a burial ground for foreigners. [8]That's why that field has been called the Field of Blood to this day.[c] [9]Then what had been declared through the prophet Jeremiah was fulfilled when he said,[d]

> "They[c] took the thirty pieces of silver,
>   the price of the man on whom a price had
>   been set by the Israelites,[d]
> [10]and they[e] gave them for the potter's field,
>   as the Lord commanded me."[f]

Pilate Questions Jesus
(Mark 15:2–5; Luke 23:3–5; John 18:33–38)

[11]Meanwhile, Jesus was made to stand in front of the governor. The governor asked him, "Are you the king of the Jews?" Jesus said, "You say so."[e] [12]While Jesus[a] was being accused by the high priests and elders, he made no reply.[f] [13]Then Pilate said to him, "Don't you hear how many charges they're bringing against you?"[g] [14]But Jesus[a] did not reply at all; as a result, the governor was very surprised.

Jesus Is Sentenced to Death
(Mark 15:6–15; Luke 23:13–25; John 18:39–19:16)

[15]At every festival[g] the governor had a custom of releasing to the crowd any prisoner whom they wanted.[h] [16]At that time they were holding a notorious prisoner named Barabbas.[h] [17]So when the people[i] had gathered, Pilate asked

Cross references (margin):

27:3 [a]Matt26:14-15

27:5 [b]2Sam17:23; Acts1:18

27:8 [c]Acts1:19

27:9 [d]Zech 11:12-13

27:11 [e]Mark15:2; Lk23:3; John18:33,37; 1Tim6:13

27:12 [f]Matt26:63; John19:9

27:13 [g]Matt26:62; John19:10

27:15 [h]Mark15:6; Lk23:17; John18:39

27:20
a Mark15:11;
Lk23:18;
John18:40;
Acts3:14

them, "Which man do you want me to release for you—Barabbas,[a] or Jesus who is called the Christ?"[b] [18]For he knew that they had handed Jesus[c] over because of jealousy.

[19]While he was sitting on the judge's seat, his wife sent him a message.[d] It said, "Have nothing to do with that righteous man, for today I have suffered terribly because of a dream about him." [20]But the high priests and elders persuaded the crowds to ask for Barabbas and to demand that Jesus be put to death.[a] [21]So the governor said to them, "Which of the two men do you want me to release for you?" They said, "Barabbas!" [22]Pilate said to them, "Then what should I do with Jesus, who is called the Christ?"[b] They all said, "Let him be crucified!" [23]He asked, "What has he done wrong?" But they kept shouting louder and louder, "Let him be crucified!"

27:24
b Deut21:6

27:25
c Deut19:10;
Josh2:19;
2Sam1:16;
1Kings2:32;
Acts5:28

[24]Pilate saw that he was getting nowhere, but that a riot was about to break out instead. So he took some water and washed his hands in front of the crowd, saying, "I am innocent of this man's[e] blood. You must see to that yourselves."[b] [25]All the people answered, "Let his blood be on us and our children!"[c] [26]Then he released Barabbas for them, but he had Jesus whipped and handed over to be crucified.[d]

27:26
d Isa53:5;
Mark15:15;
Lk23:16,24-25;
John19:1,16

The Soldiers Make Fun of Jesus
(Mark 15:16–20; John 19:2–3)

27:27
e Mark15:15;
John19:2

[27]Then the governor's soldiers took Jesus into the imperial headquarters[f] and gathered the whole company of soldiers around him.[e] [28]They stripped[g] him and put a scarlet robe on him.[f] [29]Twisting some thorns into a crown, they placed it on his head and put[h] a stick in his right hand. They knelt down in front of him and began making fun of him, saying, "Long live the king of the Jews!"[g] [30]Then they spit on him and took the stick and kept hitting him on his head.[h]

27:28
f Lk23:11

27:29
g Ps69:19;
Isa53:3

[31]When they had finished making fun of him, they

27:30
h Isa50:6;
Matt26:67

---

a 27:17 Other mss. read *Jesus Barabbas*　b 27:17,27:22 I.e. the Messiah　c 27:18 Lit. *him*　d 27:19 Lit. *sent to him*　e 27:24 Other mss. read *this righteous man's*　f 27:27 Lit. *praetorium*　g 27:28 Other mss. read *clothed*　h 27:29 The Gk. lacks *put*

stripped him of the robe, put his own clothes back on him, and led him away to crucify him.[a]

Jesus Is Crucified
(Mark 15:21–32; Luke 23:26–43; John 19:17–27)

[32]As they were leaving, they found a man from Cyrene named Simon, whom they forced to carry Jesus'[a] cross.[b] [33]When they came to a place called Golgotha (which means Skull Place),[c] [34]they offered him a drink of wine mixed with gall. But when he tasted it, he refused to drink it.[d] [35]After they had crucified him, they divided his clothes by throwing dice.[e] [36]Then they sat down there and continued guarding him.[f] [37]Above his head they placed the charge against him. It read, "This is Jesus, the king of the Jews."[g]

[38]At that time two revolutionaries[b] were crucified with him, one on his right and the other on his left.[h] [39]Those who passed by kept insulting[c] him, shaking their heads,[i] [40]and saying, "You who were going to destroy the Sanctuary and rebuild it in three days—save yourself! If you're the Son of God, come down from the cross!"[j]

[41]In the same way the high priests, along with the scribes and elders, were also making fun of him. They kept saying, [42]"He saved others but can't save himself! He is the king of Israel. Let him[d] come down from the cross now, and we'll believe in him. [43]He trusts in God. Let God[e] rescue him now if he cares for him. After all, he said, 'I am the Son of God.' "[k] [44]Even the revolutionaries[b] who were crucified with him kept insulting him in the same way.[l]

Jesus Dies on the Cross
(Mark 15:33–41; Luke 23:44–49; John 19:28–30)

[45]Now from noon[f] on, darkness came over the whole land[g] until three in the afternoon.[h][m] [46]About three o'clock[h] Jesus cried out with a loud voice, "Eli, Eli, lema sabachthani?", which means, "My God, my God, why have you forsaken me?"[i][n] [47]When some of the people standing there

---

a27:32 Lit. his   b27:38,27:44 Or bandits   c27:39 Or blaspheming
d27:42 Other mss. read If he is the king of Israel, let him   e27:43 Lit. him
f27:45 Lit. the sixth hour   g27:45 Or earth   h27:45,27:46 Lit. the ninth
hour   i27:46 Ps 22:1

27:31
aIsa53:7

27:32
bNum15:35;
1Kings21:13;
Mark15:21;
Lk23:26;
Acts7:58;
Heb13:12

27:33
cMark15:22;
Lk23:33;
John19:17

27:34
dPs69:21;
Matt27:48

27:35
ePs22:18;
Mark15:24;
Lk23:34;
John19:24

27:36
fMatt27:54

27:37
gMark15:26;
Lk23:38;
John19:19

27:38
hIsa53:12;
Mark15:27;
Lk23:32-33;
John19:18

27:39
iPs22:7; 109:25;
Mark15:29;
Lk23:35

27:40
jMatt26:61,63;
John2:19

27:43
kPs22:8

27:44
lMark15:32;
Lk23:39

27:45
mAmos8:9;
Mark15:33;
Lk23:44

27:46
nPs22:1; Heb5:7

27:48
*a*Ps69:21;
Mark15:36;
Lk23:36;
John19:29

27:50
*b*Mark15:37;
Lk23:46

27:51
*c*Exod26:31;
2Chr3:14;
Mark15:38;
Lk23:45

27:54
*d*Matt27:36;
Mark15:39;
Lk23:47

27:55
*e*Lk8:2-3

27:56
*f*Mark15:40

27:57
*g*Mark15:42;
Lk23:50;
John19:38

27:60
*h*Isa53:9

heard this, they said, "He's calling for Elijah."[a] [48]So one of the men at once ran off, took a sponge, and soaked it in some sour wine. Then he put it on a stick and offered Jesus[b] a drink.[a] [49]But the others kept saying, "Wait! Let's see if Elijah will come and save him."[c]

[50]Then Jesus cried out with a loud voice again and gave up his spirit.[b] [51]Suddenly the curtain[d] in the Sanctuary was torn in two from top to bottom, the earth shook, the rocks were split open,[c] [52]the tombs were opened, and the bodies of many saints who had died[e] were raised. [53]After his resurrection, they came out of their tombs and went into the Holy City[f] and appeared to many people. [54]When the centurion[g] and those guarding Jesus with him saw the earthquake and the other things that were taking place, they were terrified and said, "This man certainly was the Son of God!"[d]

[55]Now many women were also there, watching from a distance. They had accompanied Jesus from Galilee and had ministered[h] to him.[e] [56]Among them were Mary Magdalene, Mary the mother of James and Joseph, and the mother of Zebedee's sons.[f]

Jesus Is Buried
(Mark 15:42–47; Luke 23:50–56; John 19:38–42)

[57]When evening came, a rich man arrived from Arimathea. His name was Joseph, and he had become a disciple of Jesus.[g] [58]He went to Pilate and asked for the body of Jesus, and Pilate ordered it to be handed over.

[59]So Joseph took the body and wrapped it in a clean linen cloth. [60]Then he placed it in his own new tomb, which he had cut out of the rock. After rolling a large stone across the door of the tomb, he went away.[h] [61]But Mary Magdalene and the other Mary remained there, sitting in front of the tomb.

---

a *27:47* Elijah in Heb. sounds like *Eli* **b** *27:48* Lit. *him* **c** *27:49* Other mss. read *save him." And another took a spear and pierced his side, and water and blood came out.* **d** *27:51* This curtain separated the Holy Place from the Most Holy Place. **e** *27:52* Lit. *fallen asleep* **f** *27:53* I.e. Jerusalem **g** *27:54* A Roman centurion commanded about 100 men. **h** *27:55* Or *provided for*

The Tomb Is Secured

⁶²The next day (which is after the Day of Preparation), the high priests and Pharisees gathered before Pilate ⁶³and said, "Sir, we remember how that impostor said while he was still alive, 'After three days I will be raised.'ᵃ ⁶⁴Therefore, order the tomb to be secured until the third day, or his disciples may go and steal him and then tell the people, 'He has been raised from the dead.' Then the last deception would be worse than the first one."

⁶⁵Pilate told them, "You haveᵃ a military guard. Go and make the tombᵇ as secure as you know how." ⁶⁶So they went and secured the tomb by putting a seal on the stone in the presence of the guards.ᵇ

Jesus Is Raised from the Dead
(Mark 16:1–8; Luke 24:1–12; John 20:1–10)

28 ¹After the Sabbath, around dawn on the first day of the week, Mary Magdalene and the other Mary went to take a look at the tomb.ᶜ ²Suddenly there was a powerful earthquake. For an angel of the Lord had come down from heaven, stepped forward, rolled the stone away, and was sitting on it.ᵈ ³His appearance was like lightning, and his clothes were as white as snow.ᵉ ⁴Because they were so afraid of him, the guards shook and became like dead men.

⁵But the angel said to the women, "Stop being afraid! For I know you're looking for Jesus, who was crucified. ⁶He's not here. He has been raised, just as he said. Come and see the place where heᶜ was lying.ᶠ ⁷Then go quickly and tell his disciples that he's risen from the dead. He's going ahead of you into Galilee, and you'll see him there. Remember, I've told you!"ᵍ

⁸So they quickly left the tomb with awe and great joy and ran to tell his disciples. ⁹Suddenly Jesus met them and said, "Greetings!" They went up to him, took hold of his feet, and worshiped him.ʰ ¹⁰Then Jesus said to them, "Stop being afraid! Go and tell my brothers to go to Galilee, and there they will see me."ⁱ

---

a27:65 Or *Take*   b27:65 Lit. *it*   c28:6 Other mss. read *the Lord*

27:63
aMatt16:21;
17:23; 20:19;
26:61; Mark8:31;
10:34; Lk9:22;
18:33; 24:6-7;
John2:19

27:66
bDan6:17

28:1
cMatt27:56;
Mark16:1;
Lk24:1; John20:1

28:2
dMark16:5;
Lk24:4;
John20:12

28:3
eDan10:6

28:6
fMatt12:40;
16:21; 17:23;
20:19

28:7
gMatt26:32;
Mark16:7

28:9
hMark16:9;
John20:14

28:10
iJohn20:17;
Rom8:29;
Heb2:11

28:16
a Matt26:7,32

28:18
b Dan7:13-14;
Matt 11:27; 16:28;
Lk1:32;
10:22John3:35;
5:22; 13:3; 17:2;
Acts2:36;
Rom14:9;
1Cor15:27;
Eph1:10,21;
Phil2:9-10;
Heb1:2; 2:8;
1Peter3:22;
Rev17:14

28:19
c Isa52:10;
Mark16:15;
Lk24:47;
Acts2:38-39;
Rom10:18;
Col1:23

28:20
d Acts2:42

The Guards Report to the High Priests

[11]While the women were on their way, some of the guards went into the city and told the high priests all that had happened. [12]So they met with the elders and agreed on a plan to give the soldiers a large[a] amount of money. [13]They said, "Say that his disciples came at night and stole him while you were sleeping. [14]If this is reported to the governor, we'll satisfy him and keep you out of trouble."[b] [15]So the soldiers[c] took the money and did as they were instructed. This story has been spread among the Jews to this day.

Jesus Commissions His Disciples

(Mark 16:14–18; Luke 24:36–49; John 20:19–23; Acts 1:6–8)

[16]The eleven disciples went into Galilee to the hillside to which Jesus had directed them.[a] [17]When they saw him they worshiped him, though some had doubts.

[18]Then Jesus came up and said to them, "All authority in heaven and on earth has been given to me.[b] [19]Therefore, as you go, make disciples of all nations, baptizing them in the name of the Father, and of the Son, and of the Holy Spirit,[c] [20]teaching them to obey all that I have commanded you. And remember, I am with you every day[d] until the end of the age."[ed]

---

a 28:12 Or *sufficient*   b 28:14 Lit. *from worry*   c 28:15 Lit. *they*
d 28:20 Lit. *all the days*   e 28:20 Other mss. read *age. Amen*

THE GOSPEL ACCORDING TO
MARK

John the Baptist Prepares the Way for Jesus
(Matthew 3:1–12; Luke 3:1–9, 15–17; John 1:19–28)

1 ¹This is the beginning[a] of the gospel of Jesus Christ, the Son of God.[b][a] ²As it is written in the prophet Isaiah,[b]

> "See! I'm sending my messenger ahead of you,
>   who will prepare your way.[c]
> ³He is a voice calling out in the wilderness:[c]
>   'Prepare the way for the Lord!
>   Make his paths straight!' "[d]

⁴John was baptizing in the wilderness, proclaiming a baptism of repentance for the forgiveness of sins.[d] ⁵People from the whole Judean countryside[e] and all the people of Jerusalem were going out to him. They were being baptized by him while they confessed their sins.[e] ⁶Now John was dressed in camel's hair with[f] a leather belt around his waist. He ate locusts and wild honey.[f] ⁷He kept proclaiming, "The one who is coming after me is stronger than I am. I'm not worthy to bend down and untie his sandal straps.[g] ⁸I baptized you with[g] water, but it is he who will baptize you with[g] the Holy Spirit."[h]

John Baptizes Jesus
(Matthew 3:13–17; Luke 3:21–22)

⁹In those days Jesus came from Nazareth in Galilee and was baptized by John in the Jordan.[i] ¹⁰Just as he was coming up out of the water, he saw the heavens split open and the Spirit coming down like a dove on him.[j] ¹¹Then a voice came from heaven: "You are my Son, whom I love. I am pleased with you!"[k]

---

a1:1 Lit. *The beginning*   **b**1:1 Other mss. lack *the Son of God*   **c**1:2 Mal 3:1   **d**1:3 Isa 40:3   **e**1:5 Lit. *The whole Judean countryside*   **f**1:6 Lit. *and*   **g**1:8 Or *in*

1:1
[a]Matt14:33; Lk1:35; John1:34

1:2
[b]Mal3:1; Matt 11:10; Lk7:27

1:3
[c]Isa40:3; Matt3:3; Lk3:4; John1:15

1:4
[d]Matt3:1; Lk3:3; John3:23

1:5
[e]Matt3:5

1:6
[f]Lev 11:22; Matt3:4

1:7
[g]Matt3:11; John1:27; Acts13:25

1:8
[h]Isa44:3; Joel2:28; Acts1:5; 2:4; 10:45; 11:15-16; 19:4; 1Cor12:13

1:9
[i]Matt3:13; Lk3:21

1:10
[j]Matt3:16; John1:32

1:11
[k]Ps2:7; Matt3:17; Mark9:7

80

1:12
*a*Matt4:1; Lk4:1

Jesus Is Tempted by Satan
(Matthew 4:1–11; Luke 4:1–13)

[12]At once the Spirit drove him into the wilderness. [a] [13]He

1:13
*b*Matt4:11

was in the wilderness for forty days being tempted by Satan. He was with the wild animals, and the angels were caring for him.[b]

1:14
*c*Matt4:12,23

Jesus Begins His Ministry in Galilee
(Matthew 4:12–17; Luke 4:14–15)

[14]Now after John had been arrested, Jesus went to Galilee and proclaimed the gospel about the kingdom[a] of God. [c]

1:15
*d*Dan9:25;
Matt3:2; 4:17;
Gal4:4; Eph1:10

[15]He said, "The time is fulfilled, and the kingdom of God is near! Repent, and keep believing in the gospel!"[d]

Jesus Calls Four Fishermen
(Matthew 4:18–22; Luke 5:1–11)

1:16
*e*Matt4:18; Lk5:4

[16]While Jesus[b] was walking beside the Sea of Galilee, he saw Simon and his brother Andrew. They were throwing a net into the sea because they were fishermen.[e] [17]Jesus said to them, "Follow me, and I'll make you fish for people!"[c] [18]So

1:18
*f*Matt19:27;
Lk5:11

immediately they left their nets and followed him.[f] [19]Going on a little farther he saw James, the son of Zebedee, and his brother John. They were in a boat repairing their nets.[g] [20]He

1:19
*g*Matt4:21

immediately called them, and they left their father Zebedee in the boat with the hired men and followed him.

Jesus Heals a Man with an Unclean Spirit
(Luke 4:31–37)

1:21
*h*Matt4:13;
Lk4:31

[21]Then they went to Capernaum. As soon as it was the Sabbath, Jesus[b] went into the synagogue and began to teach.[h] [22]The people[d] were utterly amazed at his teaching, for he was teaching them like one with authority and not

1:22
*i*Matt7:28

like their scribes. [i] [23]Suddenly[e] there was a man in their synagogue who had an unclean spirit. He screamed,[j] [24]"What do you want with us, Jesus of Nazareth? Have you come to

1:23
*j*Lk4:33

destroy us? I know who you are—the Holy One of God!"[k] [25]But Jesus reprimanded him, saying, "Be quiet, and come

---

1:24
*k*Matt8:29

a1:14 Other mss. lack *about the kingdom*   **b**1:16,1:21 Lit. *he*   **c**1:17 Lit. *make you fishermen of people*   **d**1:22 Lit. *They*   **e**1:23 Lit. *Immediately*

81

out of him!"*a* ²⁶At this, the unclean spirit shook the man,ᵃ cried out with a loud voice, and came out of him.*b* ²⁷All the people were so stunned that they kept saying to each other, "What is this? A new teaching with authority! He tells even the unclean spirits what to do, and they obey him!" ²⁸At once his fame began to spread throughout the surrounding region of Galilee.

1:25
*a*Mark1:34

1:26
*b*Mark9:20

Jesus Heals Many People
(Matthew 8:14–17; Luke 4:38–41)

²⁹After they left the synagogue, they went directly to the house of Simon and Andrew, along with James and John.*c* ³⁰Now Simon's mother-in-law was lying in bed, sick with a fever, so they told Jesusᵃ about her at once. ³¹He went up to her, took her by the hand, and helped her up. The fever left her, and she began serving them.

1:29
*c*Matt8:14;
Lk4:38

³²When evening came, after the sun had set, peopleᵇ started bringing to him all those who were sick or possessed by demons.*d* ³³In fact, the whole city gathered at the door. ³⁴He healed many who were sick with various diseases, and he drove out many demons. However, he wouldn't allow the demons to speak because they knew who he was.*e*

1:32
*d*Matt8:16;
Lk4:40

Jesus Goes on a Preaching Tour
(Luke 4:42–44)

1:34
*e*Mark3:12;
Lk4:41;
Acts16:17-18

³⁵In the morning, while it was still very dark, Jesusᶜ got up and went to a deserted place and prayed there.*f* ³⁶Simon and his companions searched diligently for him. ³⁷When they found him, they told him, "Everyone's looking for you." ³⁸He said to them, "Let's go to the neighboring towns so that I can preach there, too. For that's why I came out here."*dg* ³⁹So he went throughout Galilee, preaching in their synagogues and driving out demons.*h*

1:35
*f*Lk4:42

Jesus Cleanses a Leper
(Matthew 8:1–4; Luke 5:12–16)

1:38
*g*Isa61:1; Lk4:43;
John16:28; 17:4

⁴⁰Then a leperᵉ came to Jesusᶠ and began pleading with him. He fell on his knees and said to him, "If you want to,

---

ᵃ1:26,1:30 Lit. *him* ᵇ1:32 Lit. *they* ᶜ1:35 Lit. *he* ᵈ1:38 Lit. *came out*
ᵉ1:40 I.e. a man with a serious skin disease ᶠ1:40 Lit. *to him*

1:39
*h*Matt4:23;
Lk4:44

1:40
*a*Matt8:2; Lk5:12

you can make me clean."[a] [41]Moved with compassion, Jesus[a] reached out his hand, touched him, and said to him, "I do want to. Be made clean!" [42]Instantly the leprosy left him, and he was clean.

[43]Then Jesus[b] sternly warned him and drove him away at once, [44]saying to him, "See to it that you don't say anything to anyone. Instead, go and show yourself to the priest, and then offer for your cleansing what Moses commanded as proof to the authorities."[c][b] [45]But when the man[a] left, he began to proclaim it freely. He spread the word so widely that Jesus[a] could no longer enter a town openly, but had to stay out in deserted places. Still, people[d] kept coming to him from everywhere.[c]

1:44
*b*Lev14:3-4,10;
Lk5:14

1:45
*c*Mark2:13;
Lk5:15

Jesus Heals a Paralyzed Man
(Matthew 9:1–8; Luke 5:17–26)

2 [1]Several days later Jesus[a] returned to Capernaum, and it was reported that he was at home.[d] [2]So many crowds had gathered that there wasn't any room left for them, even in front of the door. Jesus[b] was speaking the word to them [3]when some people[d] came and brought to him a paralyzed man being carried by four men. [4]Since they couldn't bring him to Jesus because of the crowd, they made an opening in the roof over the place where he was. They dug through it and let down the cot on which the paralyzed man was lying. [5]When Jesus saw their faith, he said to the paralyzed man, "Son, your sins are forgiven."

2:1
*d*Matt9:1; Lk5:18

2:7
*e*Job14:4;
Isa43:25

[6]Some scribes were sitting there, arguing among themselves,[e] [7]"Why does this man talk this way? He is blaspheming! Who can forgive sins but God alone?"[e] [8]At once, Jesus knew in his spirit what they were saying to themselves. He said to them, "Why are you arguing about such things among yourselves?[f] [9]Which is easier: to say to the paralyzed man, 'Your sins are forgiven,' or to say, 'Get up, pick up your cot, and walk'?[g] [10]But I want you to know[g] that the Son of Man has authority on earth to forgive sins." Then

2:8
*f*Matt9:4

2:9
*g*Matt9:5

---

a1:41,1:45,2:1 Lit. *he*   **b**1:43,2:2 Lit. *He*   **c**1:44 Lit. *to them*   **d**1:45,2:3 Lit. *they*   **e**2:6 Lit. *in their hearts*   **f**2:8 Lit. *in your hearts*   **g**2:10 Lit. *So that you'll know* he said to the paralyzed man, [11]"I say to you, get up, pick up your cot, and go home!" [12]So the man[a] got up, immediately picked up his cot, and went out before all of them. The result was that all of the people were amazed and began to glorify God, saying, "We have never seen anything like this!"

Jesus Calls Matthew
(Matthew 9:9–13; Luke 5:27–32)

[13]Jesus[b] went out again beside the sea. The whole crowd kept coming to him, and he kept teaching them.[a] [14]As he was walking along, he saw Levi, the son of Alphaeus, sitting at the tax collector's desk. Jesus[b] said to him, "Follow me!" So Levi[a] got up and followed him.[b]

[15]Later he was having dinner at Levi's[c] house. Many tax collectors and notorious[d] sinners were also eating with Jesus and his disciples, for there were many who were following him.[c] [16]When the scribes and the Pharisees saw him eating with notorious[d] sinners and tax collectors, they said to his disciples, "Why does he eat and drink[e] with tax collectors and notorious[d] sinners?" [17]When Jesus heard that, he said to them, "Healthy people don't need a physician, but sick people do. I didn't come to call righteous people, but sinners."[d]

A Question about Fasting
(Matthew 9:14–17; Luke 5:33–39)

[18]Now John's disciples and the Pharisees would fast regularly. Some people[f] came and asked Jesus,[g] "Why do John's disciples and the Pharisees' disciples fast, but your disciples don't fast?"[e] [19]Jesus said to them, "The wedding guests can't fast while the groom is with them, can they? As long as they have the groom with them, they can't fast. [20]But the days will come when the groom will be taken away from them, and then they will fast on that day.

The Unshrunk Cloth
(Matthew 9:16; Luke 5:36)

[21]"No one sews a piece of unshrunk cloth on an old

---

a 2:12,2:14 Lit. *he*   b 2:13,2:14 Lit. *He*   c 2:15 Lit. *his*
d 2:15,2:16,2:17 The Gk. lacks *notorious*   e 2:16 Other mss. lack *and drink*
f 2:18 Lit. *They*   g 2:18 Lit. *him*

2:13
a Matt9:9

2:14
b Matt9:9; Lk5:27

2:15
c Matt9:10

2:17
d Matt9:12-13;
18:11; Lk5:31-32;
19:10; 1Tim1:15

2:18
e Matt9:14;
Lk5:33

2:23
*a*Deut23:25;
Matt12:1; Lk6:1

garment. If he does, the patch pulls away from it—the new from the old—and a worse tear is made. 22And no one pours new wine into old wineskins. If he does, the wine will make the skins burst, and both the wine and the skins will be ruined. Instead, new wine is poured into*a* fresh wineskins."

Jesus Is Lord of the Sabbath
(Matthew 12:1–8; Luke 6:1–5)

2:25
*b*1Sam21:6

23Jesus*b* happened to be going through the grainfields on the Sabbath. As they made their way, his disciples began picking the heads of grain.*a* 24The Pharisees said to him, "Look! Why are they doing what is not lawful on the Sabbath?" 25He said to them, "Haven't you read what David did when he and his companions were hungry and in need?*b*

2:26
*c*Exod29:32-33;
Lev24:9

26How was it that he went into the House of God when Abiathar was high priest and ate the Bread of the Presence, which was not lawful for anyone but the priests to eat, and gave some of it to his companions?"*c* 27Then he said to them, "The Sabbath was made for people, not people for the Sabbath. 28Therefore, the Son of Man is Lord even of the Sabbath."*d*

Jesus Heals a Man with a Paralyzed Hand
(Matthew 12:9–14; Luke 6:6–11)

2:28
*d*Matt12:8

3 1Jesus*b* went into the synagogue again, and a man with a paralyzed hand was there.*e* 2The people*c* watched Jesus*d* closely to see whether he would heal the man*d* on the Sabbath, intending to accuse him of doing something wrong. 3He said to the man with the paralyzed hand, "Come forward."*e* 4Then he asked them, "Is it lawful to do good or to do evil on the Sabbath, to save a life or to kill

3:1
*e*Matt12:9; Lk6:6

it?" But they were silent. 5Jesus*b* looked around at them with anger, for he was deeply hurt because of their hardness of heart. Then he said to the man, "Hold out your hand." The man*b* held it out, and his hand was restored to health. 6Immediately the Pharisees, along with the Herodians,*f* went out and began to plot against him to kill him.*f*

3:6
*f*Matt12:14;
22:16

---

a2:22 Lit. *new wine into*   **b**2:23,3:1,3:5 Lit. *He*   **c**3:2 Lit. *They*
d3:2 Lit. *him*   **e**3:3 Lit. *into the middle*   **f**3:6 I.e. Roman sympathizers

Jesus Encounters a Large Crowd

[7]So Jesus retired with his disciples to the sea. A large crowd from Galilee, Judea,[a] [8]Jerusalem, Idumea, from across the Jordan, and from the region around Tyre and Sidon followed him. They came to him because they kept hearing about everything he was doing. [9]Jesus[a] told his disciples to have a boat ready for him so that the crowd wouldn't crush him. [10]For he had healed so many people that all who had diseases kept crowding up against him in order to touch him. [11]Whenever the unclean spirits saw him, they would fall down in front of him and scream, "You are the Son of God!"[b] [12]But he sternly ordered them again and again not to tell people who he was.[c]

Jesus Appoints Twelve Apostles

(Matthew 10:1–4; Luke 6:12–16)

[13]Then Jesus[b] went up on a hillside and called to him those whom he wanted and they came to him.[d] [14]He appointed twelve whom he called apostles to accompany him, to send them out to preach, [15]and to have the authority to drive out demons. [16]He appointed these twelve:[c] Simon (to whom he gave the name Peter);[e] [17]James, the son of Zebedee; John, the brother of James (to whom he gave the name Boanerges, that is, Sons of Thunder); [18]Andrew; Philip; Bartholomew; Matthew; Thomas; James, the son of Alphaeus; Thaddeus;[d] Simon the Cananaean;[e] [19]and Judas Iscariot, who later[f] betrayed him.

Jesus Is Accused of Working with Beelzebul

(Matthew 12:22–32; Luke 11:14–23; 12:10)

[20]Then he went home. The crowd came together again, so that Jesus and his disciples[g] couldn't even eat.[f] [21]When his family heard about it, they went to restrain him. For they kept saying, "He's out of his mind!"[g]

[22]The scribes who had come down from Jerusalem kept repeating, "He has Beelzebul," and "He drives out demons

---

a[3:9] Lit. *He*   b[3:13] Lit. *he*   c[3:16] Other mss. lack *He appointed these twelve*   d[3:18] Other mss. read *Lebbaeus*   e[3:18] Cananaean is Aram. for *Zealot.*   f[3:19] Lit. *also*   g[3:20] Lit. *so that they*

3:7
a Lk6:17

3:11
b Matt14:33;
Mark1:1,23-24;
Lk4:41

3:12
c Matt12:16;
Mark1:25,34

3:13
d Matt10:1;
Lk6:12; 9:1

3:16
e John1:42

3:20
f Mark6:31

3:21
g John7:5; 10:20

3:22
a Matt9:34; 10:25;
Lk 11:15;
John7:20; 8:48,
52; 10:22

by the ruler of demons."*a* [23]So Jesus*a* called them together and began to speak to them in parables. "How can Satan drive out Satan?*b* [24]If a kingdom is divided against itself, that kingdom cannot stand. [25]And if a household is divided against itself, that household will not stand. [26]So if Satan rebels against himself and is divided, he cannot stand. Indeed, his end has come. [27]No one can go into a strong man's house and carry off his possessions without first tying up the strong man. Then he can ransack his house.*c* [28]Truly I tell you, people will be forgiven their sins and whatever blasphemies they utter.*bd* [29]But whoever blasphemes against the Holy Spirit can never have forgiveness, but is guilty of an eternal sin." [30]For they had been saying, "He has an unclean spirit."

3:23
b Matt12:25

3:27
c Isa49:24;
Matt12:29

The True Family of Jesus
(Matthew 12:46–50; Luke 8:19–21)

[31]Then his mother and his brothers arrived. They stood outside and sent word*c* to him and called for him.*e* [32]A crowd was sitting around him. They said to him, "Look! Your mother and your brothers*d* are outside asking for you." [33]He answered them, "Who are my mother and my brothers?" [34]Then looking at the people sitting around him, he said, "Here are my mother and my brothers! [35]Whoever does the will of God is my brother and sister and mother."

3:28
d Matt12:31;
Lk12:10;
1John5:16

The Parable about a Sower
(Matthew 13:1–9; Luke 8:4–8)

3:31
e Matt12:46;
Lk8:19

4 [1]Then Jesus*a* began to teach again beside the sea. Such a large crowd gathered around him that he got into a boat and sat in it,*e* while the entire crowd remained beside the sea on the shore.*f* [2]He began teaching them many things in parables. While he was teaching them he said,*g* [3]"Listen! A sower went out to sow. [4]As he was sowing, some seeds fell along the path, and birds came and ate them up. [5]Others fell on stony ground, where they didn't have a lot of soil. They sprouted at once because the soil wasn't

4:1
f Matt13:1; Lk8:4

4:2
g Mark12:38

---

a 3:23,4:1 Lit. *he*   **b** 3:28 Lit. *they blaspheme*   **c** 3:31 Lit. *sent*
d 3:32 Other mss. read *your brothers and sisters*   **e** 4:1 Lit. *on the sea*

deep. ⁶But when the sun came up, they were scorched. Since they didn't have any roots, they dried up. ⁷Others fell among thornbushes, and the thornbushes came up and choked them, and they didn't produce anything. ⁸But others fell on good soil and produced a crop. They grew up, increased in size, and produced thirty, sixty, or one hundred times what was sown."ᵃᵃ ⁹He added, "Let the person who has ears to hear listen!"

The Purpose of the Parables
(Matthew 13:10–17; Luke 8:9–10)

¹⁰When he was alone with his followersᵇ and the twelve, they began to ask him about the parables.ᵇ ¹¹He said to them, "The secret about the kingdom of God has been given to you. But to those on the outside, everything comes in parablesᶜ ¹²so thatᵈ

> 'they may see clearly but not perceive,
> and they may hear clearly but not understand,
> otherwise they might turn around and be forgiven.' "ᶜ

Jesus Explains the Parable about the Sower
(Matthew 13:18–23; Luke 8:11–15)

¹³Then he said to them, "You don't understand this parable, so how can you understand any of the parables? ¹⁴The sower sows the word.ᵉ ¹⁵Some people are like the seedsᵈ along the path, where the word is sown. When they hear it, Satan immediately comes and takes away the word that was sown in them. ¹⁶Others are like the seedsᵈ sown on the stony ground. When they hear the word, they accept it at once with joy. ¹⁷But since they don't have any roots in themselves, they last for only a short time. When trouble or persecution comes along because of the word, they immediately fall away. ¹⁸Still others are like the seedsᵉ sown among the thornbushes. These are the people who hear the word, ¹⁹but the worries of life, the deceitful pleasures of wealth,

---

a4:8 Lit. *one hundred times*   b4:10 Lit. *with those around him*   c4:12 Isa 6:9-10   d4:15,4:16 Lit. *These are the ones*   e4:18 Lit. *are those*

4:8
ᵃJohn15:5;
Col1:6

4:10
ᵇMatt13:10;
Lk8:9

4:11
ᶜ1Cor5:12;
Col4:5;
1Thes4:12;
1Tim3:7

4:12
ᵈIsa6:9;
Matt13:14;
Lk8:10;
John12:40;
Acts28:26;
Rom 11:8

4:14
ᵉMatt13:19

4:19
*a*1Tim6:9,17

4:21
*b*Matt5:15;
Lk8:16; 11:33

4:22
*c*Matt10:26;
Lk12:2

4:23
*d*Matt 11:15;
Mark 11:9

4:24
*e*Matt7:2; Lk6:38

4:25
*f*Matt13:12;
25:29; Lk8:18;
19:26

4:26
*g*Matt13:24

4:29
*h*Rev14:15

4:30
*i*Matt13:31;
Lk13:18;
Acts2:41; 4:4;
5:14; 19:20

and the desires for other things come in and choke the word so that it can't produce a crop.*a* ²⁰Others are like the seeds*a* sown on good soil. They hear the word, accept it, and produce crops—thirty, sixty, or one hundred times what was sown."*b*

A Light under a Basket
(Luke 8:16–18)

²¹Then Jesus*c* said to them, "A lamp isn't brought indoors to be put under a basket or under a bed, is it? It's to be put on a lampstand, isn't it?*b* ²²For nothing is hidden except for the purpose of having it revealed, and nothing is secret except for the purpose of having it come to light.*c* ²³If anyone has ears to hear, let him listen!"*d*

²⁴He went on to say to them, "Pay attention to what you're listening to! With the measure you use,*d* you will be measured, and still more will be given to you.*e* ²⁵For whoever has, will have more given to him. But whoever has nothing, even what he has will be taken away."*f*

The Parable about a Growing Seed

²⁶He was also saying, "The kingdom of God is like a man who scatters seeds on the ground.*g* ²⁷He sleeps and gets up night and day while the seeds sprout and grow, although he doesn't know how. ²⁸The ground produces grain by itself, first the stalk, then the head, then the full grain in the head. ²⁹But when the grain is ripe, he immediately swings his sickle because the harvest time has come."*h*

The Parable about a Mustard Seed
(Matthew 13:31–32; Luke 13:18–19)

³⁰He was also saying, "How can we show what the kingdom of God is like, or what parable can we use to describe it?*i* ³¹It is like a mustard seed planted in the ground. Although it's the smallest of*e* all the seeds on earth, ³²when it's planted it comes up and becomes larger than all the garden plants. It grows such large branches that the birds in the sky can nest in its shade."

---

a4:20 Lit. *are those* **b**4:20 The Gk. lacks *what was sown* **c**4:21 Lit. *he*
d4:24 Lit. *measure* **e**4:31 Or *smaller than*

Why Jesus Used Parables
(Matthew 13:34–35)

4:33
a Matt13:34;
John16:12

33With many other parables like these, Jesus[a] kept speaking the word to them according to their ability to understand them.[a] 34He didn't tell them anything without using a parable,[b] though he explained everything to his disciples in private.

Jesus Calms the Sea
(Matthew 8:23–27; Luke 8:22–25)

35That day, when evening had come, he said to them, "Let's cross to the other side."[b] 36So they left the crowd and took him along in the boat just as he was.[c] Other boats were with him. 37A violent windstorm came up, and the waves began breaking into the boat, so that the boat was rapidly[d] being swamped. 38But Jesus[a] was in the back of the boat, asleep on a cushion. So they woke him up and said to him, "Teacher, don't you care that we're going to die?" 39Then he got up, reprimanded the wind, and said to the sea, "Hush! Be still!" Then the wind stopped blowing, and there was a great calm. 40He said to them, "Why are you such cowards? Don't you have any faith yet?" 41They were overcome with fear and kept saying to one another, "Who is this man? Even the wind and the sea obey him!"

4:35
b Matt8:18,23;
Lk8:22

Jesus Heals a Demon-Possessed Man
(Matthew 8:28–34; Luke 8:26–39)

5 1They arrived at the other side of the sea in the territory of the Gerasenes.[e c] 2Just as Jesus[a] stepped out of the boat, a man with an unclean spirit came out of the tombs and met him. 3He lived among the tombs, and no one could restrain him any longer, not even with a chain. 4He had often been restrained with shackles and chains but had snapped the chains apart and broken the shackles in pieces. No one could tame him. 5Night and day he kept screaming

---

a4:33,4:38,5:2 Lit. *he* b4:34 Lit. *without a parable* c4:36 I.e. without making any special preparations d4:37 Lit. *already* e5:1 Other mss. read *Gergesenes*; still other mss. read *Gadarenes*

5:1
c Matt8:28;
Lk8:26

5:17
ᵃMatt8:34;
Acts16:39

among the tombs and on the mountainsides and kept cutting himself with stones.

⁶When he saw Jesus from a distance, he ran and fell down in front of him, ⁷screaming in a loud voice, "What do you want with me, Jesus, Son of the Most High God? I command you in the name of God not to torture me!" ⁸For Jesusᵃ had been saying to him, "Come out of the man, you unclean spirit!" ⁹Then Jesusᵃ asked him, "What's your name?" He said to him, "My name is Legion,ᵇ because there are many of us." ¹⁰He kept pleading with Jesusᶜ not to send them out of the territory.

¹¹Now a large herd of pigs was grazing on a hillside nearby. ¹²So the demonsᵈ begged him, "Send us among the pigs, so that we can go into them!" ¹³So he let them do this. The unclean spirits came out of the manᵉ and went into the pigs, and the herd of about 2,000 rushed down the cliff into the sea and drowned there.ᶠ

¹⁴Then those who had taken care of the pigs ran away. In the city and countryside they told what had happened.ᵍ So the peopleᵈ went to see what had happened. ¹⁵When they came to Jesus and saw the man who had been possessed by the legion of demons, sitting there dressed and in his right mind, they were frightened. ¹⁶The people who had seen it told them what had happened to the demon-possessed man and the pigs. ¹⁷So they began to beg Jesusᶜ to leave their territory.ᵃ

¹⁸As he was getting into the boat, the man who had been demon-possessed kept begging him to let him go with him.ᵇ ¹⁹But Jesusᵃ wouldn't let him. Instead, he told him, "Go home to your family, and tell them how much the Lord has done for you and how merciful he has been to you." ²⁰So the manᵃ left and began proclaiming in the Decapolisʰ how much Jesus had done for him. And everyone was utterly amazed.

ᵃ5:8,5:9,5:19,5:20 Lit. *he*   ᵇ5:9 A Roman legion consisted of about 6,000 men.   ᶜ5:10,5:17 Lit. *him*   ᵈ5:12,5:14 Lit. *they*   ᵉ5:13 Lit. *came out* ᶠ5:13 Lit. *drowned in the sea*   ᵍ5:14 Lit. *they told it*   ʰ5:20 Lit. *the Ten Cities*, a loose federation of ten cities strongly influenced by Greek culture.

5:18
ᵇLk8:38

91

Jesus Heals Jairus' Daughter and a Woman with Chronic Bleeding

(Matthew 9:18–26; Luke 8:40–56)

²¹When Jesus again had crossed to the other side in a boat,ᵃ a large crowd gathered around him by the seashore.ᵃ ²²Then a synagogue leader named Jairus arrived. When he saw Jesus,ᵇ he fell at his feetᵇ ²³and begged him repeatedly, "My little daughter is dying. Come and lay your hands on her so that she may get well and live." ²⁴So Jesusᶜ went with him. A huge crowd kept following him and jostling him.

²⁵Now there was a woman who had been suffering from chronic bleeding for twelve years.ᶜ ²⁶Although she had endured a great deal under the care of many doctors and had spent all of her money, she had not been helped at all but rather grew worse. ²⁷Since she had heard about Jesus, she came up behind him in the crowd and touched his robe. ²⁸For she had been saying, "If I can just touch his robe, I will get well." ²⁹Her bleeding stopped at once, and she felt in her body that she was healed from her illness.

³⁰Immediately Jesus became aware that power had gone out of him. So he turned around in the crowd and asked, "Who touched my clothes?"ᵈ ³¹His disciples said to him, "You see the crowd jostling you, and yet you ask, 'Who touched me?'" ³²But he kept looking around to see the woman who had done this. ³³So the woman, knowing what had happened to her, came in fear and trembling, fell down before him, and told him the whole truth. ³⁴He told her, "Daughter, your faith has made you well. Go in peace and be healed from your illness."ᵉ

³⁵While he was still speaking, some peopleᵈ came from the synagogue leader's homeᵉ and said, "Your daughter is dead. Why bother the Teacher anymore?"ᶠ ³⁶But when Jesus heardᶠ what they said, he told the synagogue leader, "Stop being be afraid! Just keep on believing." ³⁷Jesusᵍ allowed no one to go with him except Peter, James, and John, the brother of James. ³⁸When they came to the home of the

---

ᵃ5:21 Other mss. lack *in a boat*   ᵇ5:22 Lit. *him*   ᶜ5:24 Lit. *he*
ᵈ5:35 Lit. *they*   ᵉ5:35 Lit. *from the synagogue leader*   ᶠ5:36 Other mss. read *overheard*   ᵍ5:37 Lit. *He*

5:21
ᵃMatt9:1; Lk8:40

5:22
ᵇMatt9:18; Lk8:41

5:25
ᶜLev15:25; Matt9:20

5:30
ᵈLk6:19; 8:46

5:34
ᵉMatt9:22; Mark10:52; Acts14:9

5:35
ᶠLk8:49

5:39
a John 11:11

5:40
b Acts 9:40

5:43
c Matt 8:4; 9:30;
12:16; 17:9;
Mark 3:12;
Lk 5:14

6:1
d Matt 13:54;
Lk 4:16

6:2
e John 6:42

6:3
f Matt 11:6; 12:46;
Gal 1:19

6:4
g Matt 13:57;
John 4:44

6:5
h Gen 19:22;
32:25; Matt 13:58;
Mark 9:23

6:6
i Isa 59:16;
Matt 9:35;
Lk 13:22

6:7
j Matt 10:1;
Mark 3:13-14;
Lk 9:1

synagogue leader, Jesus[a] saw mass confusion. People[b] were crying and sobbing loudly. 39He went into the house[c] and said to them, "Why all this confusion and crying? The child isn't dead but is sleeping."[a] 40They laughed and laughed at him. But he forced all of them outside. Then he took the child's father and mother, along with the men who were with him, and went into the room where[d] the child was.[b] 41He took her by the hand and said to her, "Talitha koum,"[e] which means, "Little girl, I tell you, get up!" 42The little girl got up at once and started to walk, for she was twelve years old. Instantly they were overcome with astonishment. 43But Jesus[a] strictly ordered them not to let anyone know about this. He also told them to give her something to eat.[c]

Jesus Is Rejected at Nazareth
(Matthew 13:53–58; Luke 4:16–30)

6 1Jesus[f] left that place and went back to his hometown,[g] and his disciples followed him.[d] 2When the Sabbath came, he began to teach in the synagogue, and many who heard him were utterly amazed. They said, "Where did this man get all these things? What is this wisdom that has been given to him? What great miracles are being done by his hands![e] 3This is the builder,[h] the son of Mary, and the brother of James, Joseph, Judas, and Simon, isn't it? His sisters are here with us, aren't they?" And they were offended by him.[f] 4And Jesus was telling them, "A prophet is without honor only in his hometown, among his relatives, and in his own home."[g] 5He couldn't work a miracle there except to lay his hands on a few sick people and heal them.[h] 6He was utterly amazed at their unbelief. Then he went around to the villages and continued teaching.[i]

Jesus Sends Out the Twelve
(Matthew 10:1, 5–15; Luke 9:1–6)

7He called the twelve and began to send them out two by two, giving them authority over unclean spirits.[j] 8He instructed them to take nothing along on the trip except a

---

a 5:38,5:43 Lit. *he*   b 5:38 Lit. *They*   c 5:39 Lit. *He went in*   d 5:40 Lit. *went to where*   e 5:41 *This* expression is Heb/.Aram.   f 6:1 Lit. *He*   g 6:1 I.e. Nazareth   h 6:3 Or *carpenter*

walking stick—no bread, no traveling bag, nothing in their moneybag. [9]They could wear sandals but not take along an extra shirt.[a][a] [10]He kept telling them, "Whenever you go into a home, stay there until you leave that place.[b] [11]If any place will not welcome you and the people[b] refuse to listen to you, when you leave, shake its dust off your feet as a testimony against them."[c]

[12]So they went and preached that people[b] should repent. [13]They also kept driving out many demons; and they kept pouring oil on many who were sick and healing them.[d]

Jesus Recalls the Death of John the Baptist
(Matthew 14:1–12; Luke 9:7–9)

[14]King Herod heard about this, because Jesus'[c] name had become well-known. He was[d] saying, "John the Baptist has been raised from the dead! That's why these miracles are at work in him."[e] [15]Others were saying, "He is Elijah." Still others were saying, "He is a prophet like one of the other[e] prophets."[f] [16]But when Herod heard about it, he said, "John, whom I beheaded, has been raised!"[g] [17]For Herod himself had sent men who arrested[f] John, bound him with chains, and put him in prison on account of Herodias, his brother Philip's wife. For Herod[g] had married her. [18]John had been telling Herod, "It's not lawful for you to have your brother's wife."[h] [19]So Herodias held a grudge against John[h] and wanted to kill him. But she couldn't do it [20]because Herod was afraid of John. He knew that John[g] was a righteous and holy man, and so he protected him. When he listened to John,[i] he did much of what he said.[j] In fact, he liked listening to him.[i]

[21]An opportunity came during Herod's birthday celebration, when he gave a banquet for his top officials, military officers, and the most important people of Galilee.[j] [22]When the daughter of Herodias[k] came in and danced, she pleased Herod and his guests. So the king told the girl, "Ask

---

a 6:9 Lit. *two shirts*   b 6:11,6:12 Lit. *they*   c 6:14 Lit. *his*   d 6:14 Other mss. read *They were*   e 6:15 Lit. *one of the*   f 6:17 Lit. *sent and arrested* g 6:17,6:20 Lit. *he*   h 6:19 Lit. *against him*   i 6:20 Lit. *to him*   j 6:20 Lit. *did many things*; other mss. read *he became very disturbed*   k 6:22 Other mss. read *his daughter by Herodias*

6:9
a Acts12:8

6:10
b Matt10:11;
Lk9:4; 10:7-8

6:11
c Matt10:14;
Lk10:10;
Acts13:51; 18:6

6:13
d James5:14

6:14
e Matt14:1; Lk9:7

6:15
f Matt16:14;
Mark8:28

6:16
g Matt14:2;
Lk3:19

6:18
h Lev18:16; 20:21

6:20
i Matt14:5; 21:6

6:21
j Gen40:20;
Matt14:6

6:23
a Esth5:3,6; 7:2

me for anything you want, and I'll give it to you." ²³He swore with an oath to her, "I'll give you anything you ask for, up to half of my kingdom."*a* ²⁴So she went out and asked her mother, "What should I ask for?" Her mother*a* replied, "The head of John the Baptist." ²⁵Immediately the girl*b* hurried back to the king with her request, "I want you to give me right now the head of John the Baptist on a platter." ²⁶The king was deeply saddened, yet because of his oaths and his guests he didn't want to refuse her.*b* ²⁷So the king at once sent a soldier and ordered him to bring John's*c* head. The soldier*d* went and beheaded him in prison. ²⁸Then he brought John's*c* head on a platter and gave it to the girl, and the girl gave it to her mother. ²⁹When John's*c* disciples heard about this, they came and carried off his body and laid it in a tomb.

6:26
b Matt14:9

6:30
c Lk9:10

Jesus Feeds More Than Five Thousand People
(Matthew 14:13–21; Luke 9:10–17; John 6:1–14)

6:31
d Matt14:13;
Mark3:20

³⁰The apostles gathered around Jesus and told him everything they had done and taught.*c* ³¹He said to them, "Come away to a deserted place all by yourselves and rest for a while." For so many people were coming and going that Jesus and the apostles*e* didn't even have time to eat.*d* ³²So they went away in a boat to a deserted place by themselves.*e*

6:32
e Matt14:13

³³But many people saw them leave and recognized them. So they hurried there on foot from all the towns and arrived ahead of them. ³⁴When Jesus got out of the boat,*f* he saw a large crowd. He had compassion for them, because they were like sheep without a shepherd, and he began to teach them many things.*f*

6:34
f Matt9:36; 14:14;
Lk9:11

³⁵When it was quite late, his disciples came to him and said, "This is a deserted place, and it's already late.*g* ³⁶Send the crowds*g* away so that they can go to the neighboring farms and villages and buy themselves something to eat." ³⁷But he answered them, "You give them something to eat." They said to him, "Should we go and buy two hundred

6:35
g Matt14:15;
Lk9:12

---

a6:24 Lit. *She*   b6:25 Lit. *she*   c6:27,6:28,6:29 Lit. *his*   d6:27 Lit. *He*
e6:31 Lit. *and they*   f6:34 Lit. *When he got out*   g6:36 Lit. *them*

denarii[a] worth of bread and give it to them to eat?"[a] 38He asked them, "How many loaves of bread do you have? Go and see." They found out and told him, "Five loaves of bread[b] and two fish."[b]

39Then he ordered them to have all the people sit down in groups on the green grass. 40So they sat down in groups of hundreds and fifties. 41Taking the five loaves and the two fish, he looked up to heaven and blessed them. Then he broke the loaves in pieces and kept giving them to his disciples to set before the people.[c] He also divided the two fish among them all.[c] 42All of them ate and were filled. 43Then the disciples[d] picked up twelve baskets full of leftover bread and fish. 44There were five thousand men who had eaten the loaves.

Jesus Walks on the Sea
(Matthew 14:22–33; John 6:15–21)

45Jesus[e] immediately made his disciples get into a boat and cross to Bethsaida ahead of him, while he sent the crowd away.[d] 46After saying goodbye to them, he went up on a hillside to pray.

47When evening had come, the boat was in the middle of the sea, while he was alone on the land.[e] 48He saw that they were straining at the oars, because the wind was against them. Shortly before dawn[f] he came to them, walking on the sea. He intended to go up right beside them.[f] 49But when they saw him walking on the sea, they thought it was a ghost and began to scream. 50All of them saw him and were terrified. Immediately Jesus[g] said to them, "Have courage! It is I. Stop being afraid!" 51Then he got into the boat with them, and the wind stopped blowing. The disciples[h] were utterly astounded, 52for they didn't understand the significance of the loaves. Instead, their hearts were hardened.[g]

---

a6:37 The denarius was the usual day's wage for a laborer.   b6:38 The Gk. lacks *loaves of bread*   c6:41 Lit. *before them*   d6:43 Lit. *they*   e6:45 Lit. *He*   f6:48 Lit. *In the fourth watch of the night*   g6:50 Lit. *he*   h6:51 Lit. *They*

6:37
aNum 11:13,22;
2Kings4:43

6:38
bMatt14:17;
15:34; Mark8:5;
Lk9:13; John6:9

6:41
c1Sam9:13;
Matt26:26

6:45
dMatt14:22;
John6:17

6:47
eMatt14:23;
John6:16-17

6:48
fLk24:28

6:52
gMark3:5;
8:17-18; 16:14

6:53
a Matt14:34

Jesus Heals the Sick in Gennesaret
(Matthew 14:34–36)

[53]When they had crossed over, they came to shore at Gennesaret and anchored the boat.[a] [54]As soon as they got out of the boat, the people recognized Jesus.[a] [55]They ran all over the countryside and began to carry the sick on their cots to any place where they heard he was. [56]Wherever he went, whether into villages, towns, or farms, people[b] would put their sick in the marketplaces and beg him to let them touch even the fringe of his robe. And all who touched it were healed.[b]

6:56
b Matt9:20;
Mark5:27-28;
Acts19:12

Jesus Challenges the Tradition of the Elders
(Matthew 15:1–20)

7 [1]The Pharisees and some of the scribes who had come from Jerusalem gathered around Jesus.[cc] [2]They noticed that some of his disciples were eating[d] with unclean hands, that is, without washing them. [3](For the Pharisees and indeed all the Jewish people don't eat unless they wash their hands properly,[e] following the tradition of their elders. [4]They don't eat anything from the marketplace unless they dip it in water. They also observe many other traditions, such as the washing of cups, jars, brass pots, and dinner tables.)[f]

7:1
c Matt15:1

[5]So the Pharisees and the scribes asked Jesus,[a] "Why don't your disciples live according to the tradition of the elders? Instead, they eat[g] with unclean hands."[d] [6]He told them, "Isaiah was right when he prophesied about you hypocrites. As it is written,[e]

7:5
d Matt15:2

> 'These people honor me with their lips,
>   but their hearts are far from me.
> [7]Their worship of me is empty,
>   because they teach human rules as
>   doctrines.'[h]

[8]You abandon the commandment of God and hold to

7:6
e Isa29:13;
Matt15:8

---

a 6:54,7:5 Lit. *him*   b 6:56 Lit. *they*   c 7:1 Lit. *around him*   d 7:2 Lit. *eating bread*   e 7:3 Lit. *with a fist*   f 7:4 Other mss. lack *and dinner tables*   g 7:5 Lit. *eat bread*   h 7:7 Isa 29:13

human tradition." [9]Then he said to them, "You have a fine way of rejecting the commandment of God in order to keep your own tradition! [10]For Moses said, 'Honor your father and your mother,'[a] and 'Whoever curses his father or mother must certainly be put to death.'[ba] [11]But you say, 'If anyone tells his father or mother, "Whatever support you might have received from me is Corban" (that is, an offering to God),[b] [12]you no longer let him do anything for his father or mother.' [13]You are destroying the word of God through the[c] tradition you have handed down. And you do many other things like that."

[14]Then he called the crowd again and said to them, "Listen to me, all of you, and understand![c] [15]Nothing that goes into a person from the outside can make him unclean. It's what comes out of a person that makes a person unclean. [16]If anyone has ears to hear, let him listen!"[dd]

[17]When he had left the crowd and gone home, his disciples began asking him about the parable.[e] [18]He said to them, "Are you so ignorant? Don't you know that nothing that goes into a person from the outside can make him unclean? [19]For it doesn't go into his heart but into his stomach, and then goes out into a toilet." (By saying this, he declared all foods clean.)[e] [20]He continued, "It's what comes out of a person that makes a person unclean. [21]For it is from within, from the human heart, that evil thoughts come, as well as sexual immorality, stealing, murder,[f] [22]adultery, greed, wickedness, cheating, shameless lust, envy, slander,[f] arrogance, and foolishness. [23]All these things come from within and make a person unclean."

The Faith of a Woman from Syria
(Matthew 15:21–28)

[24]Jesus[g] left that place and went to the territory of Tyre and Sidon.[h] He went into a house and didn't want anyone to know he was there. However, it couldn't be kept a secret.[g] [25]In fact, a woman whose little daughter had an unclean

Side notes:

7:10 [a]Exod20:12; 21:17; Lev20:9; Deut5:16; Prov20:20; Matt15:4

7:11 [b]Matt15:5; 23:18

7:14 [c]Matt15:10

7:16 [d]Matt 11:15

7:17 [e]Matt15:15

7:21 [f]Gen6:5; 8:21; Matt15:19

7:24 [g]Matt15:21

---

[a]7:10 Exod 20:12; Deut 5:16   [b]7:10 Exod 21:17; Lev 20:9   [c]7:13 Lit. *your*   [d]7:16 Other mss. lack this verse.   [e]7:19 Lit. *He cleansed all foods*   [f]7:22 Or *blasphemy*   [g]7:24 Lit. *He*   [h]7:24 Other mss. lack *and Sidon*

7:31
a Matt15:29

7:32
b Matt9:32;
Lk 11:14

7:33
c Mark8:23;
John9:6

7:34
d Mark6:41;
John 11:33,38,41;
17:1

7:35
e Isa35:5-6;
Matt 11:5

7:36
f Mark5:43

8:1
g Matt15:32

spirit immediately heard about him and came and fell down at his feet. 26Now the woman happened to be a Greek, born in Phoenicia in Syria. She kept asking him to drive the demon out of her daughter. 27But he kept telling her, "First let the children be filled. It's not right to take the children's bread and throw it to the puppies." 28But she answered him, "Yes,a Lord. Yet even the puppies under the table eat some of the children's crumbs." 29Then he said to her, "Because you have said this, go! The demon has left your daughter." 30So she went home and found the child lying in bed, and the demon was gone.

Jesus Heals a Deaf Man with a Speech Impediment

31Then Jesusb left the territory of Tyre and went through Sidon towards the Sea of Galilee, in the territory of the Decapolis.ca 32Some peopled brought to him a deaf man who also had a speech impediment. They begged Jesuse to lay his hand on him.b 33Jesusf took him away from the crowd to be alone with him. Putting his fingers into the man'sg ears, he touched his tongue with saliva.c 34Then he looked up to heaven, sighed, and said to him, "Ephphatha,"h that is, "Be opened!"d 35At once the man'sg ears were opened and his tongue was released, and he began to talk normally.e 36Then Jesusb ordered the peoplei not to tell anyone. But the more he kept ordering them, the more they kept spreading the news.f 37They were startled beyond measure, saying, "He does everything well! He even makes deaf people hear and mute people talk!"

Jesus Feeds More Than Four Thousand People
(Matthew 15:32–39)

8 1In those days, when a large crowd again had gathered with nothing to eat, Jesusb called his disciples and said to them,g 2"I have compassion for the crowd because they've already been with me for three days and have nothing to eat. 3If I send them away to their homes

---

a 7:28 Other mss. lack Yes   b 7:31,7:36,8:1 Lit. he   c 7:31 Lit. the Ten Cities, a loose federation of ten cities strongly influenced by Greek culture   d 7:32 Lit. They   e 7:32 Lit. him   f 7:33 Lit. He   g 7:33,7:35 Lit. his   h 7:34 This expression is Heb./Aram.   i 7:36 Lit. them

hungry, they will faint on the road. Some of them have come a long distance." [4]His disciples answered him, "Where could get anyone get enough bread to feed these people out here in the wilderness?" [5]He asked them, "How many loaves of bread do you have?" They said, "Seven."[a] [6]So he ordered the crowd to sit down on the ground. Then he took the seven loaves and gave thanks. He broke them in pieces and kept giving them to his disciples to distribute. So they served them to the crowd. [7]They also had a few small fish. He blessed them and said that the fish[a] should also be distributed.[b] [8]The people[b] ate and were filled. Then the disciples[c] picked up the leftover pieces—seven large baskets full. [9]Now about four thousand men were there. Then he sent them on their way. [10]Immediately he got into a boat with his disciples and went to the region of Dalmanutha.[d][c]

The Demand for a Sign from Heaven
(Matthew 16:1–4)

[11]The Pharisees came and began arguing with Jesus.[e] They tested him by demanding from him a sign from heaven.[d] [12]He sighed deeply in his spirit and said, "Why does this generation demand a sign? Truly I tell you, no sign will be given to this generation." [13]Then he left them. He got into a boat again and crossed to the other side.

The Yeast of the Pharisees and Sadducees
(Matthew 16:5–12)

[14]Now the disciples[c] had forgotten to take any bread along and had only one loaf with them in the boat.[e] [15]Jesus[f] had been warning them, "Watch out! Beware of the yeast of the Pharisees and the yeast of Herod!"[g][f]

[16]So they were discussing with one another the fact that they didn't have any bread.[g] [17]Knowing this, Jesus[h] said to them, "Why are you discussing the fact that you don't have any bread? Don't you understand or perceive yet? Are your hearts hardened?[h] [18]Do you have eyes but fail to see? Do

Side notes:
8:5 [a]Matt15:34; Mark6:38
8:7 [b]Matt14:19; Mark6:41
8:10 [c]Matt15:39
8:11 [d]Matt12:38; 16:1John6:30
8:14 [e]Matt16:5
8:15 [f]Matt16:6; Lk12:1
8:16 [g]Matt16:7
8:17 [h]Mark6:52

---

a 8:7 Lit. these   b 8:8 Lit. They   c 8:3,8:14 Lit. they   d 8:10 Other mss. read Mageda; still other mss. read Magdala   e 8:11 Lit. with him   f 8:15 Lit. He   g 8:15 Other mss. read of the Herodians   h 8:17 Lit. he

8:19
a Matt14:20;
Mark6:43;
Lk9:17; John6:13

you have ears but fail to hear?[a] Don't you remember? [19]When I broke the five loaves for the five thousand, how many baskets did you fill with leftover pieces?" They told him, "Twelve."[a] [20]"When I broke the seven loaves[b] for the four thousand, how many large baskets did you fill with the leftover pieces?" They told him, "Seven."[b] [21]Then he said to them, "Don't you perceive yet?"[c]

8:20
b Matt15:37;
Mark15:8

Jesus Heals a Blind Man in Bethsaida

8:21
c Mark6:17,52

[22]As they came to Bethsaida, some people[c] brought a blind man to Jesus[d] and begged him to touch the man.[e] [23]Jesus[f] took the blind man by the hand and led him out of the village. He spit into his eyes, placed his hands on him, and asked him, "Do you see anything?"[d] [24]The man[f] looked up and said, "I see people, but they look like trees walking around." [25]Then Jesus[g] placed his hands on the man's[h] eyes again, and he saw clearly. His sight was restored, and he saw everything perfectly even from a distance. [26]Then Jesus[g] sent him home, saying, "Don't go into the village or tell anyone in the village."[i][e]

8:23
d Mark7:33

8:26
e Matt8:4;
Mark5:43

Peter Declares His Faith in Jesus
(Matthew 16:13–20; Luke 9:18–21)

8:27
f Matt16:13;
Lk9:18

[27]Then Jesus and his disciples went to the villages around Caesarea Philippi. On the way he was asking his disciples, "Who do people say I am?"[f] [28]They answered him, "Some say[j] John the Baptist, others Elijah, and still others one of the prophets."[g] [29]Then he began to ask them, "But who do you say I am?" Peter answered him, "You are the Christ!"[k][h] [30]Jesus[f] sternly ordered them not to tell anyone about him.[i]

8:28
g Matt14:2

Jesus Predicts His Death and Resurrection
(Matthew 16:21–28; Luke 9:22–27)

8:29
h Matt16:6;
John6:69; 11:27

[31]Then he began to teach them that the Son of Man would have to suffer a great deal and be rejected by the

---

a *8:18* Jer 5:21 b *8:20* Lit. *When the seven* c *8:22* Lit. *they* d *8:22* Lit. *to him* e *8:22* Lit. *him* f *8:23,8:24,8:30* Lit. *He* g *8:25,8:26* Lit. *he* h *8:25* Lit. *his* i *8:26* Other mss. lack *or tell anyone in the village* j *8:28* The Gk. lacks *Some say* k *8:29* I.e. the Messiah

8:30
i Matt16:20

elders, the high priests, and the scribes. Then he would be killed, but after three days he would rise again.*a* 32He was speaking about this matter quite openly. But then Peter took him aside and began to reprimand him. 33But turning and looking at his disciples, Jesus*a* reprimanded Peter, saying, "Get behind me, Satan! For you are not thinking God's thoughts but human thoughts!"

34Then Jesus*a* called the crowd to himself along with his disciples and said to them, "If anyone wants to follow me, he must deny himself, pick up his cross, and then keep on following me.*b* 35For whoever wants to save his life will lose it, but whoever loses his life for me and for the gospel will save it.*c* 36For what profit will a person have if he gains the whole world and forfeits his own life? 37Indeed, what can a person give in exchange for his life? 38If anyone is ashamed of me and my words in this adulterous and sinful generation, the Son of Man will be ashamed of him when he comes with the holy angels in his Father's glory."*d*

9 1Then he said to them, "Truly I tell you, some people standing here will not experience*b* death until they see the kingdom of God arrive with power."*e*

Jesus' Appearance Is Changed
(Matthew 17:1–13; Luke 9:28–36)

2Six days later, Jesus took Peter, James, and John and led them up a high mountain to be alone with him. His appearance was changed in front of them,*f* 3and his clothes became dazzling white, whiter than anyone*c* on earth could bleach them.*g* 4Then Elijah appeared to them, accompanied by Moses, and they were talking with Jesus.

5Then Peter said to Jesus, "Rabbi, it's good that we're here! Let's set up three shelters*d*—one for you, one for Moses, and one for Elijah." 6(Peter*e* didn't know how to respond, for they were terrified.) 7Then a cloud came and overshadowed them. A voice came out of the cloud and said,*f* "This is my Son, whom I love. Keep on listening to

---

a8:33,8:34 Lit. *he*   b9:1 Lit. *taste*   c9:3 Lit. *anyone who cleans*   d9:5 Or *tents*   e9:6 Lit. *He*   f9:7 The Gk lacks *and said*

8:31 a Matt16:21; 17:22; Lk9:22
8:34 b Matt10:38; 16:24; Lk9:23; 14:27
8:35 c John12:25
8:38 d Matt10:33; Lk9:26; 12:9; Rom1:16; 2Tim1:8; 2:12
9:1 e Matt16:28; 24:30; 25:31; Lk9:27; 22:18
9:2 f Matt17:1; Lk9:28
9:3 g Dan7:9; Matt28:3

9:9
aMatt17:9

9:11
bMal4:5;
Matt17:10

9:12
cPs22:6; Isa53:2;
Dan9:26;
Lk23:11; Phil2:7

9:13
dMatt 11:14;
17:12; Lk1:17

9:14
eMatt17:14;
Lk9:37

9:17
fMatt17:14;
Lk9:38

9:20
gMark1:26;
Lk9:42

him!" [8]Suddenly, as they looked around, they saw no one with them but Jesus all by himself.

[9]On their way down the mountain, he ordered them not to tell anyone what they had seen until the Son of Man had risen from the dead.[a] [10]They kept the matter to themselves but argued about what "rising from the dead" meant. [11]So they asked him, "Don't the scribes say that Elijah must come first?"[b] [12]He told them, "Elijah is indeed coming first and will restore all things. Why, then, is it written that the Son of Man must suffer a great deal and be treated shamefully?[c] [13]But I tell you that Elijah has come, yet people[a] treated him just as they pleased, as it is written about him."[d]

Jesus Heals a Boy with a Demon
(Matthew 17:14–20; Luke 9:37–43a)

[14]When they came to the other[b] disciples, they saw a large crowd around them and some scribes arguing with them.[e] [15]The whole crowd was very surprised to see Jesus[c] and ran to welcome him. [16]He asked the scribes,[d] "What are you arguing about with them?" [17]A man in the crowd answered him, "Teacher, I brought my son to you. He has a spirit that won't let him talk.[f] [18]Whenever it brings on a seizure, it throws him to the ground. Then he foams at the mouth, grinds his teeth, and becomes stiff. So I asked your disciples to drive the spirit[e] out, but they didn't have the power."

[19]Jesus[f] said to them, "You unbelieving generation! How long must I be with you? How long must I put up with you? Bring him to me!" [20]They brought the boy[c] to him. When the spirit saw Jesus,[c] it immediately threw the boy[c] into convulsions. He fell on the ground and kept rolling around and foaming at the mouth.[g] [21]Then Jesus[g] asked his father, "How long has this been happening to him?" He said, "Since he was a child. [22]The spirit[h] has often thrown him into fire and into water to destroy him. But if you are able to do anything, have pity on us and help us!" [23]Jesus said to him, "'If you are

a9:13 Lit. *they* b9:14 The Gk. lacks *other* c9:15,9:20 Lit. *him* d9:16 Lit. *them* e9:18 Lit. *it* f9:19 Lit. *He* g9:21 Lit. *he* h9:22 Lit. *It*

able?' Everything is possible for the person who believes!"[a] [9:23 a Matt17:20; Mark 11:23; Lk17:6; John 11:40]
24With tears flowing,[a] the child's father at once cried out, "I do believe! Help my unbelief!"

25When Jesus saw that a crowd was running to the scene, he reprimanded the unclean spirit, saying to it, "You spirit that won't let him talk or hear—I command you to come out of him and never enter him again!" 26The spirit[b] screamed, shook the child[c] violently, and came out. The boy was like a corpse, and many said that he was dead. 27But [9:28 b Matt17:19] Jesus took his hand and helped him up, and he stood up.

28When Jesus[d] had come home, his disciples asked him privately, "Why couldn't we drive it out?"[b] 29He told them, "This kind can come out only by prayer and fasting."[e]

Jesus Again Predicts His Death and Resurrection
(Matthew 17:22–23; Luke 9:43b–45)

30Then they left that place and were making a trip [9:31 c Matt17:22; Lk9:44] through Galilee. Jesus[f] didn't want anyone to know it, 31for he was teaching his disciples and saying to them, "The Son of Man will be betrayed into human hands. They will kill him, but after being dead for three days he will be raised."[c] 32They didn't understand what this statement meant, and they were afraid to ask him.

True Greatness
(Matthew 18:1–5; Luke 9:46–48)

33Then they came to Capernaum. While Jesus[d] was at [9:33 d Matt18:1; Lk9:46; 22:24] home, he asked the disciples,[g] "What were you arguing about on the road?"[d] 34But they kept silent, for on the road they had argued with one another about who was the [9:35 e Matt20:26-27; Mark10:43] greatest.

35So he sat down and called the twelve. He told them, "If anyone wants to be first he must be last of all and servant of all."[e] 36Then he took a little child and had him stand among them. He took him in his arms and said to them,[f]

---

a 9:24 Other mss. lack *With tears flowing*   b 9:26 Lit. *It*   c 9:26 The Gk. lacks *the child*   d 9:28,9:33 Lit. *he*   e 9:29 Other mss. lack *and fasting* [9:36 f Matt18:2; Mark10:16] f 9:30 Lit. *He*   g 9:33 Lit. *them*

9:37
a Matt10:40;
Lk9:48

9:38
b Num 11:28;
Lk9:49

9:39
c 1Cor12:3

9:40
d Matt12:30

9:41
e Matt10:42

9:42
f Matt18:6;
Lk17:1

9:43
g Deut13:6;
Matt5:29; 18:8

9:44
h Isa66:24

9:49
i Lev2:13;
Ezek43:24

9:50
j Matt5:13;
Lk14:34;
Rom12:18;
14:19;
2Cor13:11;
Eph4:29; Col4:6;
Heb12:14

[37]"Whoever welcomes a child like this in my name welcomes me, and whoever welcomes me welcomes not me but the one who sent me."[a]

The True Follower of Jesus
(Luke 9:49–50)

[38]John said to Jesus,[a] "Teacher, we saw someone driving out demons in your name. We tried to stop him, because he wasn't a follower like us."[b] [39]But Jesus said, "Don't stop him! For no one who works a miracle in my name can slander me soon afterwards.[c] [40]For whoever is not against us is for us.[d] [41]Truly I tell you, whoever gives you a cup of water to drink because you belong to Christ[b] will never lose his reward."[e]

Causing Others to Sin
(Matthew 18:6–9; Luke 17:1–2)

[42]"If anyone causes one of these little ones who believe in me to sin, it would be better for him if a large millstone were hung around his neck and he were thrown into the sea.[f] [43]So if your hand causes you to sin, cut it off. It is better for you to enter life injured than to have two hands and go to hell,[c] to the fire that cannot be put out.[g] [44]In that place, worms never die, and the fire is never put out.[d][h] [45]And if your foot causes you to sin, cut it off. It is better for you to enter life crippled than to have two feet and be thrown into hell.[c] [46]In that place, worms never die, and the fire is never put out.[d] [47]And if your eye causes you to sin, tear it out. It is better for you to enter the kingdom of God with one eye than to have two eyes and be thrown into hell.[c] [48]In that place, worms never die, and the fire is never put out. [49]For everyone will be salted with fire, and every sacrifice will be salted with salt.[e][i] [50]Salt is good. But if salt loses its taste, how can you restore its flavor? Keep on having salt among yourselves, and live in peace with one another."[j]

---

a 9:38 Lit. *to him*   b 9:41 I.e. the Messiah   c 9:43,9:45,9:47 Gk. *Gehenna*
d 9:44,9:46 Other mss. lack this verse   e 9:49 Other mss. lack *and every sacrifice will be salted with salt*

Teaching about Divorce
(Matthew 19:1–12)

10 ¹Then Jesus[a] left that place and went into the territory of Judea on the other side of the Jordan. Crowds gathered around him again, and he began to teach them again as was his custom.[a] ²Some Pharisees came to test him. They asked, "Is it lawful for a man to divorce his wife?"[b] ³He answered them, "What did Moses command you?" ⁴They said, "Moses allowed a man to write a certificate of divorce and to divorce her."[bc] ⁵But Jesus said to them, "It was because of your hardness of heart that he wrote this command for you. ⁶But from the beginning of creation, 'God[c] made them male and female.'[dd] ⁷'That's why a man will leave his father and mother and will be united with his wife,[e] ⁸and the two will become one flesh.'[e] So they are no longer two, but one flesh. ⁹Therefore, what God has joined together, man must stop separating."

¹⁰Back in the house, the disciples asked him about this again. ¹¹So he said to them, "Whoever divorces his wife and marries another woman commits adultery against her.[f] ¹²And if a woman[f] divorces her husband and marries another man, she commits adultery."

Jesus Blesses the Little Children
(Matthew 19:13–15; Luke 18:15–17)

¹³Some people[g] were bringing little children to Jesus[h] to have him touch them. But the disciples reprimanded those who brought them.[ig] ¹⁴When Jesus saw this, he became furious and told them, "Let the little children come to me, and stop keeping them away. For the kingdom of God belongs to people like these.[h] ¹⁵Truly I tell you, whoever doesn't receive the kingdom of God as a little child will never get into it at all."[i] ¹⁶Then he picked them up in his arms, laid his hands on them, and tenderly blessed them.

---

a 10:1 Lit. *he*   b 10:4 Deut 24:1,3   c 10:6 Other mss. read *He*
d 10:6 Gen 1:27; 5:2   e 10:8 Gen 2:24   f 10:12 Lit. *she*   g 10:13 Lit. *They*
h 10:13 Lit. *to him*   i 10:13 Lit. *reprimanded them*

10:1 a Matt19:1; John10:40; 11:7

10:2 b Matt19:3

10:4 c Deut24:1; Matt5:31; 19:7

10:6 d Gen1:27; 5:2

10:7 e Gen2:24; 1Cor6:16; Eph5:31

10:11 f Matt5:32; 19:9; Lk16:18; Rom7:3; 1Cor7:10-11

10:13 g Matt19:13; Lk18:15

10:14 h 1Cor14:20; 1Peter2:2

10:15 i Matt18:3

10:17
ᵃMatt19:16;
Lk18:18

A Rich Man Comes to Jesus
(Matthew 19:16–30; Luke 18:18–30)

¹⁷As Jesusᵃ was setting out on a journey, a man ran up to him, knelt down in front of him, and asked him, "Good Teacher, what must I do to inherit eternal life?"ᵃ ¹⁸Jesus said to him, "Why do you call me good? No one is good except for one—God. ¹⁹You know the commandments: 'Never murder.'ᵇ 'Never commit adultery.'ᶜ 'Never steal.'ᵈ 'Never give false testimony.'ᵉ 'Never cheat.' 'Honor your father and mother.'"ᶠᵇ ²⁰The manᵍ replied to him, "Teacher, I have kept all of these since I was a young man." ²¹Jesus looked at him and loved him. He told him, "You're missing one thing. Go and sell everything you own, give the moneyʰ to the destitute, and you will have treasure in heaven. Then come back and follow me."ᶜ ²²But the manᵃ was shocked at this statement and went away sad, because he had many possessions.

²³Then Jesus looked around and said to his disciples, "How hard it will be for those who have wealth to get into the kingdom of God!"ᵈ ²⁴The disciples were startled by these words. But Jesus said to them again, "Children, how hard it is for those who trust in their wealthⁱ to get into the kingdom of God!ᵉ ²⁵It is easier for a camel to squeeze through the eye of a needle than for a rich person to get into the kingdom of God." ²⁶They were utterly amazed and said to one another,ʲ "Then who can be saved?" ²⁷Jesus looked at them intently and said, "For humans it is impossible, but not for God. All things are possible for God."ᶠ

²⁸Then Peter began to say to him, "See, we've left everything and followed you."ᵍ ²⁹Jesus said, "Truly I tell you, there is no one who has left his home, brothers, sisters, mother, father, children, or fields because of me and the gospel ³⁰who will not receive a hundred times as much here in this world—homes, brothers, sisters, mothers, children, and fields, along with persecutions—as well as eternal life in

10:19
ᵇExod20:1-26;
Rom13:9

10:21
ᶜMatt6:19-20;
19:21; Lk12:33;
16:9

10:23
ᵈMatt19:23;
Lk18:24

10:24
ᵉJob31:24;
Ps52:7; 62:10;
1Tim6:17

10:27
ᶠJer32:17;
Matt19:26;
Lk1:37

10:28
ᵍMatt19:27;
Lk18:28

ᵃ*10:17,10:22* Lit. *he*   ᵇ*10:19* Exod 20:13; Deut 5:17   ᶜ*10:19* Exod 20:14; Deut 5:18   ᵈ*10:19* Exod 20:15; Deut 5:19   ᵉ*10:19* Exod 20:16; Deut 5:20   ᶠ*10:19* Exod 20:12; Deut 5:16   ᵍ*10:20* Lit. *He*   ʰ*10:21* The Gk. lacks *the money*   ⁱ*10:24* Other mss. lack *for those who trust in their wealth*   ʲ*10:26* Other mss. read *to him*

the age to come.*a* 31But many who are first will be last, and the last will be first."*b*

Jesus Predicts His Death and Resurrection a Third Time
(Matthew 20:17–19; Luke 18:31–34)

32Jesus and his disciples**a** were on the road going up to Jerusalem, and Jesus was walking ahead of them. They were utterly amazed, and the others who followed were afraid. Once again, he took the twelve aside and began to tell them what was going to happen to him.*c* 33"See, we're going up to Jerusalem. The Son of Man will be handed over to the high priests and the scribes, and they will condemn him to death. Then they will hand him over to the Gentiles, 34and they will make fun of him, spit on him, whip him, and kill him. But after three days he will be raised."

The Request of James and John
(Matthew 20:20–28)

35James and John, the sons of Zebedee, went to Jesus**b** and said to him, "Teacher, we want you to do for us whatever we ask you."*d* 36He asked them, "What do you want me to do for you?" 37They said to him, "Let us sit in your glory, one at your right and one at your left." 38But Jesus told them, "You don't realize what you're asking. Can you drink the cup that I'm going to drink or be baptized with the baptism with which I'm going to be baptized?" 39They told him, "We can." Jesus said to them, "You will drink the cup that I'm going to drink and be baptized with the baptism with which I'm going to be baptized. 40But it's not my business to grant you a seat at my right or my left. Those positions have already been prepared for others."

41When the ten heard this, they began to be furious with James and John.*e* 42Then Jesus called the disciples**c** and said to them, "You know that those who are recognized as rulers among the Gentiles lord it over them, and their superiors act like tyrants over them.*f* 43That's not the way it should be among you. Instead, whoever wants to become great among you must be your servant,*g* 44and whoever wants to be first

---

a10:32 Lit. *They*   **b**10:35 Lit. *to him*   **c**10:42 Lit. *them*

10:30
*a*2Chr25:9;
Lk18:30

10:31
*b*Matt19:30;
20:16; Lk13:30

10:32
*c*Matt20:17;
Mark8:31; 9:31;
Lk9:22; 18:31

10:35
*d*Matt20:20

10:41
*e*Matt20:24

10:42
*f*Lk22:25

10:43
*g*Matt20:26,28;
Mark9:35;
Lk9:48

10:45
a Matt20:28;
John13:14;
Phil2:7; 1Tim2:6;
Titus2:14

among you must be a slave to everyone. ⁴⁵For even the Son of Man didn't come to be served, but to serve and to give his life as a ransom for many people."*a*

Jesus Heals Blind Bartimaeus
(Matthew 20:29–34; Luke 18:35–43)

⁴⁶Then they came to Jericho. As Jesus,*a* his disciples, and a large crowd were leaving Jericho, a blind beggar named Bartimaeus, the son of Timaeus, was sitting by the road.*b* ⁴⁷When he heard that it was Jesus of Nazareth, he began to shout, "Jesus, Son of David, have mercy on me!" ⁴⁸Many people sternly told him to be quiet, but he kept shouting even louder, "Son of David, have mercy on me!" ⁴⁹So Jesus stopped and said, "Call him!" So they called the blind man and told him, "Have courage! Get up. He's calling you." ⁵⁰The blind man*b* threw off his coat, jumped up, and went to Jesus. ⁵¹Then Jesus asked him, "What do you want me to do for you?" The blind man said to him, "Rabbouni,*c* I want to see again." ⁵²Jesus told him, "Go. Your faith has made you well." At once the man*a* could see again, and he began to follow Jesus*d* on down the road.*c*

10:46
b Matt20:29;
Lk18:35

10:52
c Matt9:22;
Mark5:34

The King Enters Jerusalem
(Matthew 21:1–11; Luke 19:28–40; John 12:12–19)

11 ¹When they came near Jerusalem, at Bethphage and Bethany, near the Mount of Olives, Jesus*a* sent two of his disciples on ahead*d* ²and said to them, "Go into the village ahead of you. As soon as you go into it, you will find a colt tied up that no one has ever ridden.*e* Untie it, and bring it. ³If anyone asks you, 'Why are you doing this?,' say, 'The Lord needs it,' and he will send it back here at once."

⁴So they went and found the colt outside in the street tied up next to a doorway. While they were untying it, ⁵some men standing there asked them, "What are you doing untying that colt?" ⁶The disciples*f* told them what Jesus had said, and the men*g* let them go.

11:1
d Matt21:1;
Lk19:29;
John12:14

---

a 10:46,10:52,11:1 Lit. *he*   b 10:50 Lit. *He*   c 10:51 Rabbouni is Heb./Aram. for *My Teacher*   d 10:52 Lit. *him*   e 11:2 Lit. *has ever sat on*   f 11:6 Lit. *They*   g 11:6 Lit. *they*

[7]They brought the colt to Jesus and threw their coats on it, and he sat on it. [8]Many people spread their coats on the road, while others spread leafy branches that they had cut in the fields.[a] [9]Those who went ahead and those who followed him were shouting,[b]

"Hosanna![a]
How blessed is the one who comes
　in the name of the Lord!
[10]How blessed is the coming kingdom[c]
　of our forefather David!
Hosanna in the highest heaven!"[b]

[11]Then Jesus went into Jerusalem and into the Temple and looked around at everything. Since it was already late, he went out with the twelve to Bethany.[d]

Jesus Curses a Fig Tree
(Matthew 21:18–19)

[12]The next day, while they were leaving Bethany, Jesus[c] became hungry.[e] [13]In the distance he saw a fig tree covered with leaves. He went to see if he could find anything on it. When he came to it, he found nothing but leaves because it wasn't the season for figs.[f] [14]So he said to it, "May no one ever eat fruit from you again!" Now his disciples were listening to this.

Jesus Throws Merchants and Moneychangers out of the Temple
(Matthew 21:12–17; Luke 19:45–48; John 2:13–22)

[15]When they came to Jerusalem, he went into the Temple and began to throw out those who were selling and those who were buying in the Temple. He overturned the money-changers' tables and the chairs of those who sold doves.[g] [16]He wouldn't even let anyone carry a vessel through the Temple. [17]Then he began to teach them, saying, "It is written, is it not, 'My house is to be called a house of prayer for all

11:8
a Matt 21:8

11:9
b Ps 118:26

11:10
c Ps 148:1

11:11
d Matt 21:12

11:12
e Matt 21:18

11:13
f Matt 21:19

11:15
g Matt 21:12;
Lk 19:45;
John 2:14

---

a *11:9* Hosanna is Heb. for *Please save* or *Praise*.　b *11:10* Ps 118:25-26; Ps 148:1　c *11:12* Lit. *he*

11:17
a Isa56:7; Jer7:11

nations'?**a** But you have turned it into a hideout**b** for bandits!"*a* [18]When the high priests and elders heard this, they began to look for a way to kill him. For they were afraid of him, because the whole crowd was amazed at his teaching.*b* [19]When evening came, Jesus and his disciples**c** would leave the city.

11:18
b Matt7:28;
21:45-46;
Mark1:22;
Lk4:32; 19:47

The Lesson from the Dried Up Fig Tree
(Matthew 21:20–22)

11:20
c Matt21:19

[20]While they were walking along early in the morning, they saw the fig tree dried up to its roots.*c* [21]Peter remembered and said to him, "Rabbi, look! The fig tree you cursed has dried up!" [22]Jesus said to them, "Have faith in God! [23]Truly I tell you, if anyone says to this mountain, 'Be lifted up and thrown into the sea,' and if he doesn't doubt in his heart but believes that what he says will happen, it will be done for him.*d* [24]That's why I tell you, whatever you ask for in prayer, believe that you have received**d** it and it will be yours.*e*

11:23
d Matt17:20;
21:21; Lk17:6

[25]"Whenever you stand up to pray, forgive whatever you have against anyone, so that your Father in heaven will forgive your sins.*f* [26]But if you don't forgive, your Father in heaven will not forgive your sins."*e**g*

11:24
e Matt7:7;
Lk 11:9;
John14:13; 15:7;
16:24;
James1:5-6

Jesus' Authority Is Challenged
(Matthew 21:23–27; Luke 20:1–8)

[27]Then again they went into Jerusalem. While Jesus**f** was walking in the Temple, the high priests, the scribes, and the elders came to him*h* [28]and asked him, "By what authority are you doing these things, and who gave you this authority to do them?" [29]Jesus said to them, "I'll ask you one question.**g** Answer me, and then I'll tell you by what authority I am doing these things. [30]Was John's authority to baptize**h** from heaven or from humans? Answer me."

11:25
f Matt6:14;
Col3:13

[31]They began discussing this among themselves. "If we say, 'From heaven,' he will say, 'Then why didn't you

11:26
g Matt18:35

---

a*11:17* Isa 56:7; Jer 7:11   b*11:17* Lit. *cave*   c*11:19* Lit. *When evening came, they*   d*11:24* Other mss. read *are receiving;* still other mss. read *will receive*   e*11:26* Other mss. lack this verse   f*11:27* Lit. *he*   g*11:29* Lit. *one word*   h*11:30* Lit. *John's baptism*

11:27
h Matt21:23;
Lk20:1

believe him?' ³²But if we say, 'From humans. . .'?" For they were afraid of the crowd, because everyone really thought John was a prophet.ᵃ ³³So they answered Jesus, "We don't know." Then Jesus told them, "Then I won't tell you by what authority I am doing these things."

The Parable about the Tenant Farmers
(Matthew 21:33–46; Luke 20:9–19)

12 ¹Then Jesusᵃ began to speak to them in parables. "A man planted a vineyard. He put a wall around it, dug a pit for the wine press, and built a watchtower. Then he leased it to tenant farmers and went abroad.ᵇ ²At the right time he sent a servant to the farmers to collect from them a share of the produce from the vineyard. ³But the farmersᵇ grabbed the servant,ᶜ beat him, and sent him back empty-handed. ⁴Again, the manᵃ sent another servant to them. They beat the servantᶜ over the head and treated him shamefully. ⁵Then the manᵃ sent another, and that one they killed. So it was with many other servants.ᵈ Some of these they beat, and others they killed. ⁶He still had one more person to send,ᵉ a son whom he loved. Finally, he sent him to them, saying, 'They will respect my son.' ⁷But those farmers said to one another, 'This is the heir. Come on, let's kill him, and the inheritance will be ours!' ⁸So they grabbed him, killed him, and threw him out of the vineyard.

⁹"Now what will the owner of the vineyard do? He will come and destroy the farmers and give the vineyard to others. ¹⁰Haven't you ever read this Scripture:ᶜ

> 'The stone that the builders rejected
>   has become the cornerstone.ᶠ
> ¹¹This was the Lord's doing,
>   and it is amazing in our eyes'?"ᵍ

¹²They were trying to arrest him but were afraid of the

11:32
ᵃMatt3:5; 14:5;
Mark6:20

12:1
ᵇMatt21:33;
Lk22:9

12:10
ᶜPs 118:22

ᵃ12:1,12:4,12:5 Lit. *he*   ᵇ12:3 Lit. *they*   ᶜ12:3,12:4 Lit. *him*   ᵈ12:5 Lit. *with many others*   ᵉ12:6 Lit. *He still had one*   ᶠ12:10 Or *capstone*
ᵍ12:11 Ps 118:22-23

12:12
a Matt21:45-46;
Mark 11:18;
John7:25,30,44

crowd. Realizing that he had spoken this parable against them, they left him alone and went away.*a*

A Question about Paying Taxes
(Matthew 22:15–22; Luke 20:20–26)

[13]Then the leaders*a* sent some Pharisees and some Herodians*b* to him, intending to trap him in what he said.*b* [14]They came and said to him, "Teacher, we know that you are sincere. You don't favor any individual, for you pay no attention to external appearance. Rather, you teach the way of God truthfully. Is it lawful to pay taxes to Caesar or not? Should we pay them or should we not?" [15]But Jesus*c* recognized their hypocrisy and said to them, "Why are you testing me? Bring me a denarius and let me see it." [16]So they brought one. Then he asked them, "Whose face and name is this?" They said to him, "Caesar's." [17]So Jesus said to them, "Give back to Caesar the things that are Caesar's, and to God the things that are God's." And they were utterly amazed at him.

12:13
b Matt22:15;
Lk20:20

A Question about the Resurrection
(Matthew 22:23–33; Luke 20:27–40)

12:18
c Matt22:23;
Lk20:27;
Acts23:8

[18]Then some Sadducees, who say there is no resurrection, came to Jesus*d* and asked him,*c* [19]"Teacher, Moses wrote for us that if a man's brother dies and leaves a wife but no child, he should marry the widow and have children for his brother.*ed* [20]There were seven brothers. The first one married and died without having children. [21]Then the second married her and died without having children, and so did the third. [22]None of the seven left any children. Last of all, the woman died, too. [23]In the resurrection, whose wife will she be, since the seven had married her?"

12:19
d Deut25:5

[24]Jesus said to them, "Aren't you mistaken because you don't know the Scriptures or God's power? [25]For when people*a* rise from the dead, they neither marry nor are given in marriage but are like the angels in heaven.*e* [26]As for the dead being raised, haven't you read in the book of Moses, in

12:25
e 1Cor15:42,49,
52

a 12:13,12:25 Lit. *they*   *b* 12:13 I.e. Roman sympathizers   *c* 12:15 Lit. *he*
d 12:18 Lit. *to him*   *e* 12:19 Deut 25:5-6

the story about the bush, how God said, 'I am the God of Abraham, the God of Isaac, and the God of Jacob'?[a] [a] 27He is not the God of the dead, but of the living. You are badly mistaken!"

The Greatest Commandment
(Matthew 22:34–40; Luke 10:25–28)

28Then one of the scribes came near and heard them arguing with one another. He saw how well Jesus[b] answered them, so he asked him, "Which commandment is the most important of them all?"[b] 29Jesus answered, "The most important is, 'Hear, O Israel, the Lord our God is one Lord,[c] 30and you must love the Lord your God with all your heart, with all your soul, with all your mind, and with all your strength.'[c] 31The second is this: 'You must love your neighbor as yourself.'[d] No other commandment is greater than these."[d]

32Then the scribe said to him, "Well said,[e] Teacher! You have told the truth that 'God[b] is one, and there is no other besides him.'[f][e] 33To love him with all your heart, with all your understanding, and with all your strength, and to love your neighbor as yourself is more important than all the burnt offerings and sacrifices."[f] 34When Jesus saw how wisely the man[b] answered, he told him, "You are not far from the kingdom of God." After that, no one dared to ask him another question.[g]

A Question about David's Son
(Matthew 22:41–46; Luke 20:41–44)

35While Jesus was teaching in the Temple, he said, "How can the scribes say that the Christ[g] is David's son?[h] 36David himself said in the Holy Spirit,[i]

> 'The Lord said to my Lord,
>   "Sit at my right hand,
>   until I put your enemies under your feet." '[h]

---

a12:26 Exod 3:6   b12:28,12:32,12:34 Lit. *he*   c12:30 Deut 6:4-5
d12:31 Lev 19:18   e12:32 Lit. *Well*   f12:32 Deut 6:4   g12:35 I.e. the Messiah   h12:36 Ps 110:1; other mss read *until I make your enemies a footstool for your feet." '*

12:26
*a*Exod3:6

12:28
*b*Matt22:35

12:29
*c*Deut6:4;
Lk10:27

12:31
*d*Lev19:18;
Matt22:39;
Rom13:9;
Gal5:14;
James2:8

12:32
*e*Deut4:39;
Isa45:6,14; 46:9

12:33
*f*1Sam15:22;
Hos6:6;
Mic6:6-8

12:34
*g*Matt22:46

12:35
*h*Matt22:41;
Lk20:41

12:36
*i*2Sam23:2;
Ps 110:1

12:38
*a*Matt23:1;
Mark4:2;
Lk 11:43; 20:46

12:40
*b*Matt23:14

12:41
*c*2Kings12:9;
Lk21:1

12:43
*d*2Cor8:12

12:44
*e*Deut24:6;
1John3:17

13:1
*f*Matt24:1;
Lk21:5

13:2
*g*Lk19:44

³⁷David himself calls him Lord. Then how can he be his son?" The large crowd kept listening to him with delight.

Jesus Denounces the Scribes
(Matthew 23:1–36; Luke 20:45–47)

³⁸As he taught, he said, "Beware of the scribes! They like to walk around in long robes, to be greeted in the market-places,*a* ³⁹and to have the best seats in the synagogues and the places of honor at banquets. ⁴⁰They devour widows' houses*a* and say long prayers to cover it up. They will receive greater condemnation!"*b*

The Widow's Offering
(Luke 21:1–4)

⁴¹As Jesus*b* sat facing the offering box, he watched how the crowd was dropping their money into it.*c* Many rich people were dropping in large amounts.*c* ⁴²Then a destitute widow came and dropped in two small copper coins, worth about a cent. ⁴³He called his disciples and said to them, "Truly I tell you, this destitute widow has dropped in more than all of those who are contributing to the offering box.*d* ⁴⁴For all of them contributed out of their surplus, but she, in her poverty, has dropped in everything she had to live on."*e*

Jesus Predicts the Destruction of the Temple
(Matthew 24:1–2; Luke 21:5–6)

13 ¹As Jesus*b* was leaving the Temple, one of his disciples said to him, "Look, Teacher, what large stones and what beautiful buildings!"*f* ²Jesus said to him, "Do you see these large buildings? Not one stone will be left on another here that will not be torn down."*g*

The Coming Persecution
(Matthew 24:3–14; Luke 21:7–19)

³As Jesus*b* was sitting on the Mount of Olives facing the Temple, Peter, James, John, and Andrew were asking him privately, ⁴"Tell us, when will these things take place, and

---

a12:40 I.e. rob widows by taking their houses   b12:41,13:1,13:3 Lit. *he*
c12:41 Lit. *into the offering box*

what will be the sign when these things will be put into effect?"[a]

[5]Jesus began to say to them, "See to it that no one deceives you.[b] [6]Many will come in my name and say, 'I am he,' and they will deceive many people. [7]But when you hear of wars and rumors of wars, stop being alarmed. These things must take place, but the end hasn't come yet. [8]For nation will rise up in arms against nation, and kingdom against kingdom. There will be earthquakes and famines in various places. These things are only the beginning of the birth pains.[c]

[9]"As for yourselves, be on your guard! People[a] will hand you over to local councils, and you will be beaten in their synagogues. You will stand before governors and kings to testify to them because of me.[d] [10]But first, the gospel must be proclaimed to all nations.[e]

[11]"When they take you away and hand you over for trial, don't worry ahead of time about what you will say. Instead, say whatever is given to you in that hour, for it won't be you speaking, but the Holy Spirit.[f] [12]Brother will betray brother to death, and a father his child. Children will rebel against their parents and have them put to death.[g] [13]You will be hated continuously by everyone because of my name. But the person who endures to the end will be saved."[h]

Signs of the End
(Matthew 24:15–28; Luke 21:20–24)

[14]"So when you see the destructive desecration standing where it should not be (let the reader take note),[b] then those who are in Judea must flee to the mountains.[i] [15]The person who is on his housetop must not come down and go into his house to take anything out of it, [16]and the person who is in the field must not turn back to get his coat.

[17]"How terrible it will be for women who are pregnant or who are nursing babies in those days![j] [18]Pray that it may not be in winter. [19]For those days will be a time of suffering,[c] a kind that has not happened from the beginning of the creation that God made until now and certainly will never

---

a *13:9* Lit. *They*   b *13:14* Dan 9:27; 11:31; 12:11   c *13:19* Or *tribulation*

13:4
a Matt24:3;
Lk21:7

13:5
b Jer29:8; Eph5:6;
1Thes2:3

13:8
c Matt24:8

13:9
d Matt10:17-18;
24:9; Rev2:10

13:10
e Matt24:14

13:11
f Matt10:19;
Lk12:11; 21:14;
Acts2:4; 4:8,31

13:12
g Mic7:6;
Matt10:21; 24:10;
Lk21:16

13:13
h Dan12:12;
Matt10:22; 24:9,
13; Lk21:17;
Rev2:10

13:14
i Dan9:27;
Matt24:15;
Lk21:21

13:17
j Lk21:23; 23:29

13:19
a Dan9:26;
12:1Joel2:2;
Matt24:21

13:21
b Matt24:23;
Lk17:23; 21:8

13:23
c 2Peter3:17

13:24
d Dan7:10;
Zeph1:15;
Matt24:29;
Lk21:25

13:26
e Dan7:13-14;
Matt16:27; 24:30;
Mark14:62;
Acts1:11;
1Thes4:16;
2Thes1:7,10;
Rev1:7

13:28
f Matt24:32;
Lk21:29

13:31
g Isa40:8

happen again.*a* 20If the Lord did not limit those days, no one would be saved. But for the sake of the elect whom he has chosen, he has limited those days.

21"At that time, if anyone says to you, 'Look! Here is the Christ!',*a* or, 'Look! There he is!', don't believe it.*b* 22For false christs and false prophets will appear and produce signs and omens to deceive, if possible, the elect. 23So be on your guard! I've told you everything before it happens."*c*

The Coming of the Son of Man
(Matthew 24:29–31; Luke 21:25–28)

24"But after the suffering of those days,*d*

'The sun will be darkened,
the moon will not give its light,
25the stars will fall from the sky,
and the powers of heaven will be shaken loose.'*b*

26Then people*c* will see 'the Son of Man coming in clouds'*d* with great power and glory.*e* 27He will send out his angels and gather his elect from the four winds, from the ends of the earth to the ends of heaven."

The Lesson from the Fig Tree
(Matthew 24:32–35; Luke 21:29–33)

28"Now learn a lesson*e* from the fig tree. When its branches become tender and it produces leaves, you know that summer is near.*f* 29In the same way, when you see these things taking place, you will know that he is near, right at the door. 30Truly I tell you, this generation will not disappear until all these things take place. 31Heaven and earth will disappear, but my words will never disappear."*g*

The Unknown Day and Hour of Christ's Return
(Matthew 24:36–44)

32"No one knows when that day or hour will come*f*—not

---

a 13:21 I.e. the Messiah   *b* 13:25 Isa 13:10; 34:4; Joel 2:10   *c* 13:26 Lit. *they*   *d* 13:26 Dan 7:13   *e* 13:28 Or *parable*   *f* 13:32 Lit. *about that day and hour*

the angels in heaven, not the Son, but only the Father. [33]Be careful! Watch out! For you don't know when the time will come.[a]

[34]"It's like a man who went on a trip. As he left home, he put his servants in charge, each with his own work, and he ordered the doorkeeper to be alert.[b] [35]So keep on watching, because you don't know when the master of the house is coming—whether in the evening, at three o'clock in the morning,[a] or at dawn.[c] [36]Otherwise, he may come suddenly and find you asleep. [37]I'm telling you what I'm telling everyone: Be alert!"

The Plot to Kill Jesus
(Matthew 26:1–5; Luke 22:1–2; John 11:45–53)

14

[1]Now it was two days before the Passover and the Festival of Unleavened Bread. So the high priests and the scribes were looking for a way to arrest Jesus secretly and to have him put to death.[d] [2]For they kept saying, "This must not happen during the festival, or else there will be a riot among the people."

A Woman Anoints Jesus' Body for Burial
(Matthew 26:6–13; John 12:1–8)

[3]While Jesus[b] was in Bethany at the home of Simon the leper, and sitting at the table, a woman arrived with an alabaster jar of very expensive perfume made from pure nard. She broke open the jar and poured the perfume on his head.[e] [4]Some who were there said to one another in irritation, "Why was the perfume wasted like this? [5]This perfume could have been sold for more than three hundred denarii[c] and the money given to the destitute." So they got extremely angry with her.

[6]But Jesus said, "Leave her alone. Why are you bothering her? She has done a beautiful thing for me. [7]For you will always have the destitute with you and can help them whenever you want, but you will not always have me.[f] [8]She has done what she could. She poured perfume on my body

---

a 13:35 Lit. at cock crow   b 14:3 Lit. he   c 14:5 A denarius was the average day's wage for a laborer.

13:33
a Matt24:42;
25:13; Lk12:40;
21:34;
Rom13:11;
1Thes5:6

13:34
b Matt24:45;
25:14

13:35
c Matt24:42,44

14:1
d Matt26:2;
Lk22:1;
John 11:55; 13:1

14:3
e Matt26:6;
Lk7:37;
John12:1,3

14:7
f Deut15:11

14:10
a Matt26:14;
Lk22:3-4

in preparation for my burial. ⁹Truly I tell you, wherever the gospel is proclaimed in the whole world, what she has done will also be told as a memorial to her."

Judas Agrees to Betray Jesus
(Matthew 26:14–16; Luke 22:3–6)

¹⁰Then Judas Iscariot, one of the twelve, went to the high priests to betray Jesus**ᵃ** to them.**ᵃ** ¹¹When they heard this, they were delighted and promised to give him money. So he began to look for a good opportunity to betray him.

The Passover with the Disciples
(Matthew 26:17–25; Luke 22:7–14, 21–23; John 13:21–30)

14:12
b Matt26:17;
Lk22:7

¹²On the first day of the Festival**ᵇ** of Unleavened Bread, when the Passover lamb is sacrificed, Jesus'**ᶜ** disciples asked him, "Where do you want us to go and make preparations for you to eat the Passover meal?"**ᵇ** ¹³He sent two of his disciples and told them, "Go into the city, and you will meet a man carrying a jug of water. Follow him. ¹⁴When he goes into a house,**ᵈ** say to its owner that the Teacher asks, 'Where is my room where I can eat the Passover meal with my disciples?' ¹⁵Then he will show you a large upstairs room that is furnished and ready. Get everything ready for us there." ¹⁶So the disciples left and went into the city. They found everything just as Jesus**ᵉ** had told them, and they prepared the Passover meal.

14:17
c Matt26:20

¹⁷When evening came, Jesus**ᵉ** arrived with the twelve.**ᶜ** ¹⁸While they were at the table eating, Jesus said, "Truly I tell you, one of you is going to betray me, one who is eating with me." ¹⁹They began to get very sad. They said to him one after another, "Surely I am not the one, am I?" ²⁰He said to them, "It's one of you twelve, the one who is dipping his bread into the bowl with me. ²¹For the Son of Man is going away, just as it has been written about him, but how terrible it will be for that man by whom the Son of Man is betrayed! It would have been better for him if he had never been born."**ᵈ**

14:21
d Matt26:24;
Lk22:22

---

a 14:10 Lit. him   **b** 14:12 The Gk. lacks of the Festival   **c** 14:12 Lit. his
d 14:14 Lit. Wherever he enters   **e** 14:16,14:17 Lit. he

The Lord's Supper
(Matthew 26:26–30; Luke 22:15–20; 1 Corinthians 11:23–25)

22While they were eating, Jesus[a] took a loaf of bread and blessed it. Then he broke it in pieces and gave it to them, saying, "Take some. This is my body."[a] 23Then he took a cup, gave thanks, and gave it to them, and they all drank from it. 24He said to them, "This is my blood of the covenant that is being poured out for many people. 25Truly I tell you, I will never again drink the product of the vine until that day when I drink new wine[b] in the kingdom of God." 26After singing a hymn, they went out to the Mount of Olives.[b]

Jesus Predicts Peter's Denial
(Matthew 26:31–35; Luke 22:31–34; John 13:36–38)

27Then Jesus said to them, "All of you will turn against me. For it is written,[c]

> 'I will strike the shepherd,
>   and the sheep will be scattered.'[c]

28But after I have been raised, I will go to Galilee ahead of you."[d] 29But Peter said to him, "Even if everyone else turns against you, I certainly won't."[e] 30Jesus said to him, "Truly I tell you, today, this very night, before a rooster crows twice, you will deny me three times." 31But Peter[a] kept saying emphatically, "Even if I have to die with you, I will never deny you!" And all the others kept saying the same thing.

Jesus Prays in the Garden of Gethsemane
(Matthew 26:36–46; Luke 22:39–46)

32Then they came to a place called Gethsemane, and he said to his disciples, "Sit down here while I pray."[f] 33He took Peter, James, and John along with him, and he began to be distressed and troubled. 34So he said to them, "I am deeply grieved, even to the point of death. Wait here and stay awake."[g] 35Going on a little farther, he fell to the ground and kept praying that if it were possible the hour might pass from

---

a 14:22,14:31 Lit. *he*   b 14:25 Lit. *drink it new*   c 14:27 Zech 13:7

14:22
a Matt26:26;
Lk22:19;
1Cor 11:23

14:26
b Matt26:30

14:27
c Zech13:7;
Matt26:31

14:28
d Mark16:7

14:29
e Matt26:33-34;
Lk22:33-34;
John13:37-38

14:32
f Matt26:36;
Lk22:39;
John18:1

14:34
g John12:27

14:36
a John5:30; 6:38;
Rom8:15;
Gal4:6; Heb5:7

him. ³⁶He kept repeating, "Abba!ᵃ Father! All things are possible for you. Take this cup away from me. Yet not what I want but what you want!"ᵃ

³⁷When he went back, he found them asleep. He said to Peter, "Simon, are you asleep? You couldn't stay awake for one hour, could you? ³⁸All of youᵇ must stay awake and pray that you won't come into temptation. The spirit is indeed willing, but the flesh is weak."ᵇ

14:38
b Rom7:23;
Gal5:17

³⁹He went away again and prayed the same prayer as before.ᶜ ⁴⁰Once again he came back and found them asleep, for their eyes were very heavy. They didn't even know what they should say to him.

⁴¹He came back a third time and said to them, "You might as well keep on sleeping and resting.ᵈ Enough of that! The time has come. Look! The Son of Man is being betrayed into the hands of sinners.ᶜ ⁴²Get up! Let's go! See, the one who is betraying me is near!"ᵈ

14:41
c John13:1

Jesus Is Arrested
(Matthew 26:47–56; Luke 22:47–53; John 18:3–12)

⁴³Just then, while Jesusᵉ was still speaking, Judas, one of the twelve, arrived. A crowd armed with swords and clubs was with him. They were from the high priests, the scribes, and the elders.ᵉ ⁴⁴Now the betrayer personally had given them a signal, saying, "The one I kissᶠ is the man. Arrest him, and lead him safely away." ⁴⁵So Judasᵉ immediately went up to Jesusᵍ and said, "Rabbi,"ʰ and kissed him tenderly.

14:42
d Matt26:46;
John18:1-2

⁴⁶Then the menⁱ took hold of Jesusʲ and arrested him. ⁴⁷But one of those standing there drew his sword and struck the high priest's servant, cutting off his ear. ⁴⁸Jesus said to them, "Have you come out with swords and clubs to arrest me as if I were a revolutionary?ᵏᶠ ⁴⁹Day after day I was with you in the Temple teaching, yet you didn't arrest me. But

14:43
e Matt26:47;
Lk22:47;
John18:3

---

a 14:36 Abba is Heb./Aram. for *Father*   **b** 14:38 Lit. *You* (plural)
c 14:39 Lit. *the same word*   **d** 14:41 Or *Are you still sleeping and resting?*
e 14:43,14:45 Lit. *he*   **f** 14:44 Disciples customarily greeted their Rabbi with a kiss.   **g** 14:45 Lit. *to him*   **h** 14:45 Other mss. read *Rabbi, Rabbi.*
i 14:46 Lit. *they*   **j** 14:46 Lit. *of him*   **k** 14:48 Or *bandit*

14:48
f Matt26:55;
Lk22:52

the Scriptures must be fulfilled."*a* 50Then all the disciples**a**
deserted him and ran away.*b*

The Young Man Who Ran Away

51A certain young man was following Jesus.**b** He was
wearing nothing but a linen sheet. They grabbed him, 52but
he left the linen sheet behind and ran away naked.

Jesus Is Tried before the High Priest
(Matthew 26:57–68; Luke 22:54–55; John 18:13–14, 19–24)

53Then the men**c** took Jesus to the high priest. All the
high priests, elders, and scribes had gathered together.*c*
54Peter followed him at a distance as far as the high priest's
courtyard. He was sitting with the servants and warming
himself at the fire.

55Meanwhile, the high priests and the whole Council**d**
were looking for some testimony against Jesus in order to
have him put to death, but they couldn't find any.*d* 56Al-
though many people gave false testimony against him, their
testimony didn't agree.

57Then some men stood up and gave false testimony
against him, saying, 58"We ourselves heard him say, 'I will
destroy this Sanctuary made by human**e** hands, and in three
days I will build another one not made by human**e** hands.' "*e*
59But even on this point their testimony didn't agree.

60Then the high priest stood up before them**f** and asked
Jesus, "Don't you have any answer to what these men are
testifying against you?"*f* 61But he kept silent and didn't answer at all. The high priest asked him again, "Are you the
Christ,**g** the Son of the Blessed One?"*g* 62Jesus said, "I am.*h*

> And 'you will see the Son of Man
> seated at the right hand of the Power'
> and 'coming with the clouds of
> heaven.' "*h*

63Then the high priest tore his clothes and said, "Why do

14:49
*a*Ps22:6; Isa53:7;
Lk22:37; 24:44

14:50
*b*Ps88:8;
Mark14:27

14:53
*c*Matt26:57;
Lk22:54;
John18:13

14:55
*d*Matt26:59

14:58
*e*Mark15:29;
John2:19

14:60
*f*Matt26:62

14:61
*g*Isa53:7;
Matt26:63

14:62
*h*Matt24:30;
26:64; Lk22:69

---

a14:50 Lit. *all of them*   **b**14:51 Lit. *him*   **c**14:53 Lit. *They*   **d**14:55 Or
Sanhedrin   **e**14:58 The Gk. lacks *human*   **f**14:60 Lit. *in the middle*
g14:60 I.e. the Messiah   **h**14:62 Ps 110:1; Dan 7:13

14:66
a Matt26:58,69;
Lk22:55;
John18:16

we still need witnesses? ⁶⁴You have heard his blasphemy! What is your verdict?" All of them condemned him as deserving death. ⁶⁵Some of them began to spit on him. They blindfolded him and kept hitting him with their fists. They kept telling him, "Prophesy!" Even the servants took him and slapped him around.

Peter Denies Jesus
(Matthew 26:69–75; Luke 22:56–62; John 18:15–18, 25–27)

14:69
b Matt26:71;
Lk22:58;
John18:25

⁶⁶While Peter was down in the courtyard, one of the high priest's servant girls came by.*ᵃ* ⁶⁷When she saw Peter warming himself, she glared at him and said, "You, too, were with Jesus from Nazareth." ⁶⁸But he denied it, saying, "I don't know or understand what you're talking about." Then he went out into the entryway. Just then a rooster crowed.**ᵃ** ⁶⁹The servant girl saw him and again said to those

14:70
c Matt26:73;
Lk22:59;
John18:26;
Acts2:7

who were standing around, "This man is one of them!"*ᵇ* ⁷⁰Again he denied it. After a little while the people who were standing there began to say to Peter again, "Obviously you're one of them, because you are a Galilean!"*ᶜ* ⁷¹Then he began to invoke a divine curse and to swear with an oath, "I don't know this man you're talking about!" ⁷²Just then a rooster crowed a second time. Peter remembered that Jesus

14:72
d Matt26:75

said to him, "Before a rooster crows twice, you will deny me three times." Then Peter**ᵇ** broke down and cried.*ᵈ*

Jesus Is Taken to Pilate
(Matthew 27:1–2, 11–14; Luke 23:1–5; John 18:28–38)

15:1
e Ps2:2;
Matt27:1;
Lk22:66;
23:1 John18:28;
Acts3:13; 4:26

15 ¹As soon as it was morning, the high priests convened a meeting with the elders and scribes and the whole Council.*ᶜ* They bound Jesus with chains, led him away, and handed him over to Pilate.*ᵉ* ²Pilate asked him, "Are you the king of the Jews?" Jesus**ᵈ** answered him, "You say so."*ᶠ* ³The high priests kept accusing him of many things. ⁴So Pilate asked him again, "Don't you have any answer? Look how many accusations they're

---

15:2
f Matt27:11

a14:68 Other mss. lack *Just then a rooster crowed*   **b**14:72 Lit. *he*
c15:1 Or *Sanhedrin*   **d**15:2 Lit. *He*

bringing against you!"[a] [5]But Jesus no longer answered anything, so that Pilate was astonished.[b]

Jesus Is Sentenced to Death
(Matthew 27:15–26; Luke 23:13–25; John 18:39–19:16)

[6]At every festival[a] Pilate[b] would release any one prisoner whom the people[c] requested.[c] [7]Now there was a man in prison named Barabbas. He was with the insurgents who had committed murder during the rebellion. [8]So the crowd came and began to ask Pilate[d] to do for them what he always did. [9]Pilate answered them, "Do you want me to release the king of the Jews for you?" [10]For he knew that the high priests had handed Jesus[e] over because of jealousy. [11]But the high priests stirred up the crowd to get him to release Barabbas for them instead.[d] [12]So Pilate said to them again, "Then what should I do with the man you call[f] the king of the Jews?" [13]They shouted back, "Crucify him!" [14]Pilate asked them, "Why? What has he done wrong?" But they shouted even louder, "Crucify him!" [15]So Pilate, wanting to satisfy the crowd, released Barabbas for them, but he had Jesus whipped and handed over to be crucified.[e]

The Soldiers Make Fun of Jesus
(Matthew 27:27–31; John 19:2–3)

[16]The soldiers led Jesus[e] into the courtyard of the palace (that is, the governor's headquarters)[g] and called out the whole guard.[f] [17]They dressed him in a purple robe, twisted some thorns into a crown, and placed it on his head.[h] [18]They began to greet him, "Long live the king of the Jews!" [19]They kept hitting him on the head with a stick, spitting on him, kneeling in front of him, and worshiping him. [20]When they had finished making fun of him, they stripped him of the purple robe, put his own clothes back on him, and led him away to crucify him.

---

a[15:6] I.e. Passover   b[15:6] Lit. *he*   c[15:6] Lit. *they*   d[15:8] The Gk. lacks *Pilate*   e[15:10,15:16] Lit. *him*   f[15:12] Other mss. lack *the man you call*   g[15:16] Lit. *praetorium*   h[15:17] Lit. *on him*

Margin notes:
15:4
a Matt27:13

15:5
b Isa53:7;
John19:9

15:6
c Matt27:15;
Lk23:17;
John18:39

15:11
d Matt27:20;
Acts3:14

15:15
e Matt27:26;
John19:1,16

15:16
f Matt27:27

15:21
a Matt27:32;
Lk23:26

15:22
b Matt27:33;
Lk23:33;
John19:17

15:23
c Matt27:34

15:24
d Ps22:18;
Lk23:34;
John19:23

15:25
e Matt27:45;
Lk23:44;
John19:14

15:26
f Matt27:37;
John19:19

15:27
g Isa53:12;
Matt27:38;
Lk22:37

15:29
h Ps22:7;
Mark14:58;
John2:19

15:32
i Matt27:44;
Lk23:39

15:33
j Matt27:45;
Lk23:44

15:34
k Ps21:1;
Matt27:46

Jesus Is Crucified

(Matthew 27:32–44; Luke 23:26–43; John 19:17–27)

21They forced a certain passer-by who was coming in from the country to carry Jesus'[a] cross. He was Simon of Cyrene, the father of Alexander and Rufus.[a] 22They took Jesus[b] to a place called Golgotha, which means Skull Place.[b] 23They tried to give him wine mixed with myrrh, but he wouldn't take it.[c]

24Then they crucified him. They divided his clothes among themselves by throwing dice to see what each one would get.[d] 25It was nine in the morning[c] when they crucified him.[e] 26The written notice of the charge against him read, "The king of the Jews."[f] 27They crucified two revolutionaries[d] with him, one on his right and the other on his left.[e][g] 29Those who passed by kept insulting[f] him, shaking their heads, and saying, "Ha! You who were going to destroy the Sanctuary and rebuild it in three days[h]—30save yourself and come down from the cross!"

31In the same way the high priests, along with the scribes, were also making fun of him among themselves. They kept saying, "He saved others but can't save himself! 32Let the Christ,[g] the king of Israel, come down from the cross now so that we may see it and believe." Even the men who were crucified with him kept insulting him.[i]

Jesus Dies on the Cross

(Matthew 27:45–56; Luke 23:44–49; John 19:28–30)

33At twelve noon,[h] darkness came over the whole land[i] until three in the afternoon.[j][j] 34At three o'clock[j] Jesus cried out with a loud voice, "Eloi, eloi, lema sabachthani?", which means, "My God, my God, why have you forsaken me?"[k][k] 35When some of the people standing there heard this, they said, "Listen! He's calling for Elijah!" 36So someone ran and soaked a sponge in some sour wine. Then he put it on a stick

---

a 15:21 Lit. *his*   **b** 15:22 Lit. *him*   **c** 15:25 Lit. *the third hour*   **d** 15:27 Or *bandits*   **e** 15:27 Other mss. read *on his left.* 28*Then the Scripture was fulfilled that says, "He was counted with criminals."*   **f** 15:29 Or *blaspheming*   **g** 15:32 I.e. the Messiah   **h** 15:33 Lit. *the sixth hour*   **i** 15:33 Or *earth*   **j** 15:33,15:34 Lit. *the ninth hour*   **k** 15:34 Ps 22:1

and offered Jesus[a] a drink, saying, "Wait! Let's see if Elijah comes to take him down!"[a]

37Then Jesus gave a loud cry and breathed his last.[b] 38The curtain[b] in the Sanctuary was torn in two from top to bottom.[c] 39When the centurion[c] who stood facing Jesus[a] saw how he had cried out and breathed his last,[d] he said, "This man certainly was the Son of God!"[d]

40Now there were women watching from a distance. Among them were Mary Magdalene, Mary the mother of young James and Joseph, and Salome.[e] 41They used to accompany him and care for him while he was in Galilee. Many other women who had come up to Jerusalem with him were there, too.[f]

Jesus Is Buried
(Matthew 27:57–61; Luke 23:50–56; John 19:38–42)

42It was the Day of Preparation, that is, the day before the Sabbath. Since it was already evening,[g] 43Joseph of Arimathea, a highly respected member of the Council,[e] who was waiting for the kingdom of God, went boldly to Pilate and asked for the body of Jesus.[h] 44Pilate wondered if Jesus[f] had already died. So he summoned the centurion to ask him if he was in fact dead. 45When he learned from the centurion that he was dead, he let Joseph have the corpse. 46Joseph[g] bought some linen cloth, took the body[h] down, and wrapped it in the cloth. Then he laid it in a tomb that had been cut out of the rock and rolled a stone against the door of the tomb.[i] 47Now Mary Magdalene and Mary the mother of Joseph saw where he was laid.

Jesus Is Raised from the Dead
(Matthew 28:1–8; Luke 24:1–12; John 20:1–10)

16 1When the Sabbath was over, Mary Magdalene, Mary the mother of James, and Salome bought spices to go and anoint Jesus.[a][j] 2Very early on the first day of the week, when the sun had just come up,

---

a 15:36,15:39,16:1 Lit. *him*   b 15:38 This curtain separated the Holy Place from the Most Holy Place.   c 15:39 A Roman centurion commanded about 100 men.   d 15:39 Other mss. read *saw how he had breathed his last* e 15:43 Or *Sanhedrin* f 15:44 Lit. *he* g 15:46 Lit. *He* h 15:46 Lit. *it*

15:36
a Ps69:21;
Matt27:48;
John19:29

15:37
b Matt27:50;
Lk23:45;
John19:30

15:38
c Matt27:51;
Lk23:45

15:39
d Matt27:54;
Lk23:46

15:40
e Ps38:11;
Matt27:55;
Lk23:49

15:41
f Lk8:2-3

15:42
g Matt27:57;
Lk23:50;
John19:38

15:43
h Lk2:25,38

15:46
i Matt27:59-60;
Lk23:53;
John19:40

16:1
j Matt28:1;
Lk23:56; 24:1;
John20:1

16:2
*a*Lk24:1;
John20:1

16:5
*b*Lk24:3;
John20:11-12

16:6
*c*Matt28:5-7

16:7
*d*Matt26:32;
Mark14:28

16:8
*e*Matt28:8;
Lk24:9

16:9
*f*Lk8:2;
John20:14

16:10
*g*Lk24:10;
John20:18

16:11
*h*Lk24:11

16:12
*i*Lk24:13

they were going to the tomb.*a* ³They kept saying to one another, "Who will roll away the stone for us from the entrance to the tomb?" ⁴Then they looked up and saw that the stone had been rolled away. (For it was a very large stone.)

⁵As they went into the tomb, they saw a young man dressed in a white robe sitting on the right side. They were utterly astonished.*b* ⁶But he said to them, "Stop being astonished! You're looking for Jesus of Nazareth, who was crucified. He has been raised. He's not here. Look at the place where they laid him.*c* ⁷But go and tell his disciples, especially Peter, that he's going ahead of you into Galilee. There you will see him, just as he told you."*d*

⁸So they left the tomb and ran away, for shock and astonishment had overwhelmed them. They didn't say a thing to anyone, because they were afraid.*ae*

Jesus Appears to Mary Magdalene
(Matthew 28:9–10; John 20:11–18)

⁹After Jesus*b* rose early on the first day of the week, he appeared first to Mary Magdalene, from whom he had driven out seven demons.*f* ¹⁰She went and told those who had been with him and who now were grieving and crying.*g* ¹¹When they heard that he was alive and that he had been seen by her, they wouldn't believe it.*h*

Jesus Appears to Two Disciples
(Luke 24:13–35)

¹²After this he appeared in a different form to two disciples*c* as they were walking into the country.*i* ¹³They went back and told the others, who didn't believe them either.

Jesus Commissions His Disciples
(Matthew 28:16–20; Luke 24:36–49; John 20:19–23; Acts 1:6–8)

¹⁴Finally he appeared to the eleven disciples*d* while they

---

a16:8 Some mss. end Mark here; others include verses 9-20. Some mss. conclude the book with the following shorter ending (others include the shorter ending and then continue with verses 9-20): *They reported to those who were with Peter everything they had been commanded. After this, Jesus sent out through them, from east to west, the sacred and indestructible message of eternal salvation. Amen.*   b16:9 Lit. *he*   c16:12 Lit. *two of them*   d16:14 Lit. *to the eleven themselves*

were eating. He reprimanded them for their unbelief and stubbornness, because they had not believed those who had seen him after he had risen.*ᵃ* ¹⁵Then he said to them, "Go into all the world and proclaim the gospel to the whole creation.*ᵇ* ¹⁶The one who believes and is baptized will be saved, but the one who doesn't believe will be condemned.*ᶜ*

¹⁷"These are the signs that will accompany those who believe: In my name they will drive out demons; they will speak in new tongues;*ᵈ* ¹⁸they will pick up snakes in their hands;**ᵃ** even if they drink any deadly poison it will not hurt them; and they will place their hands on the sick, and they will recover."*ᵉ*

Jesus Is Taken Up to Heaven
(Luke 24:50–53; Acts 1:9–11)

¹⁹So the Lord Jesus,**ᵇ** after talking with them, was taken up to heaven and sat down at the right hand of God.*ᶠ* ²⁰The disciples**ᶜ** went out and preached everywhere, while the Lord kept working with them and confirming the message by the signs that accompanied it.*ᵍ*

---

a16:17 Other mss. lack *in their hands*   **b**16:19 Other mss. lack *Jesus*   **c**16:20 Lit. *They*

16:14
ᵃLk24:36;
John20:19;
1Cor15:5

16:15
ᵇMatt28:19;
John15:16;
Col1:23

16:16
ᶜJohn3:18,36;
12:48; Acts2:38;
16:30-32;
Rom10:9;
1Peter3:21

16:17
ᵈLk10:17;
Acts2:4; 5:16;
8:7; 10:46; 16:18;
19:6,12;
1Cor12:10,28

16:18
ᵉLk10:19;
Acts5:15-16;
9:17; 28:5,8;
James5:14-15

16:19
ᶠPs 110:1;
Lk24:51;
Acts1:2-3; 7:55

16:20
ᵍActs5:12; 14:3;
1Cor2:4-5;
Heb2:4

THE GOSPEL ACCORDING TO
LUKE

1:2
a Mark 1:1;
John 15:27;
Heb 2:3;
1 Peter 5:1;
2 Peter 1:16;
1 John 1:1

1:3
b Acts 1:1; 11:4;
15:19,25,28;
1 Cor 7:40

1:4
c John 20:31

1:5
d 1 Chr 24:10,19;
Neh 12:4,17;
Matt 2:1

1:6
e Gen 7:1; 17:1;
1 Kings 9:4;
2 Kings 20:3;
Job 1:1; Acts 23:1;
24:16; Phil 3:6

1:8
f 1 Chr 24:19;
2 Chr 8:14; 31:2

1:9
g Exod 30:7-8;
1 Sam 2:28;
1 Chr 23:13;
2 Chr 29:11

1:10
h Lev 16:17;
Rev 8:3-4

1:11
i Exod 30:1

1:12
j Jdg 6:22; 13:22;
Dan 10:8; Lk 2:9;
10:29; Acts 10:4;
Rev 1:17

1:13
k Lk 1:60,63

1:14
l Lk 1:58

Luke's Dedication to Theophilus

1 ¹Since many people have attempted to write an orderly account of the events that have been fulfilled among us, ²just as they were passed down to us by those who had been eyewitnesses and servants of the word from the beginning,*a* ³I, too, have carefully investigated everything from the beginning and have decided to write an orderly account for you, most excellent Theophilus,*b* ⁴so that you may know the certainty about the things you have been taught.*c*

The Birth of John the Baptist Is Foretold

⁵In the days of King Herod of Judea, there was a priest named Zechariah, who belonged to the priestly order of Abijah. His wife was a descendant of Aaron, and her name was Elizabeth.*d* ⁶Both of them were righteous in the sight of God, and they lived blamelessly according to all of the commandments and regulations of the Lord.*e* ⁷They had no children because Elizabeth was barren and because both of them were getting on in years.ᵃ

⁸When Zechariah**ᵇ** was serving with his division of priests in God's presence,*f* ⁹he was chosen by lot to go into the Sanctuary of the Lord and burn incense, according to the custom of the priests.*g* ¹⁰The entire congregation of people was praying outside at the time when the incense was burned.*h*

¹¹An angel of the Lord appeared to him, standing at the right side of the incense altar.*i* ¹²When Zechariah saw him, he was shaken, and fear overwhelmed him.*j* ¹³But the angel said to him, "Stop being afraid, Zechariah, because your prayer has been heard. Your wife Elizabeth will bear you a son, and you are to name him John.*k* ¹⁴You will have joy and gladness, and many people will rejoice at his birth.*l* ¹⁵For he

---

a *1:7* Lit. *in their days*   **b** *1:8* Lit. *he*

will be great in the sight of the Lord. He will never drink wine or any strong drink, and he will be filled with the Holy Spirit even before he is born.*a* 16He will bring many of Israel's descendants back to the Lord their God.*b* 17He is the one who will go before the Lord**a** with the spirit and power of Elijah to turn the hearts of parents to their children and the disobedient to the wisdom of the righteous, and to prepare the people to be ready for the Lord."*c*

18Then Zechariah said to the angel, "How can I know this is so? For I'm an old man, and my wife is getting on in years."**b***d* 19The angel answered him, "I am Gabriel! I stand in the very presence of God. I have been sent to speak to you and to tell you this good news.*e* 20But because you didn't believe my words, which will be fulfilled at the proper time,**c** you will become silent and unable to speak until the day this happens."*f*

21Meanwhile, the people kept waiting for Zechariah and wondering why he stayed in the Sanctuary so long. 22But when he did come out, he was unable to speak to them. Then they realized that he had seen a vision in the Sanctuary. He kept motioning to them but remained unable to speak. 23When the days of his service were over, he went home.*g*

24After this,**d** his wife Elizabeth became pregnant and remained in seclusion for five months. She said, 25"This is what the Lord did for me when he looked favorably on me and took away my public disgrace."*h*

The Birth of Jesus Is Foretold

26In the sixth month of her pregnancy,**e** the angel Gabriel was sent by God to a city in Galilee called Nazareth, 27to a virgin engaged to a man named Joseph, a descendant**f** of David. The virgin's name was Mary.*i* 28The angel**g** came to her and said, "Greetings, you who are highly favored! The Lord is with you!"**h***j* 29She was startled by his statement and

---

a1:17 Lit. *before him*   **b**1:18 Lit. *in her days*   **c**1:20 Lit. *in their times*   **d**1:24 Lit. *After those days*   **e**1:26 Lit. *In the sixth month*   **f**1:27 Lit. *of the house*   **g**1:28 Lit. *He*   **h**1:28 Other mss. read *is with you! How blessed are you among women!*

1:15
a Num 6:3;
Jdg 13:4; Jer 1:5;
Lk 7:33; Gal 1:15

1:16
b Mal 4:5-6

1:17
c Mal 4:5;
Matt 11:14;
Mark 9:12

1:18
d Gen 17:17

1:19
e Dan 8:16;
9:21-23;
Matt 18:10;
Heb 1:14

1:20
f Ezek 3:26; 24:27

1:23
g 2Kings 11:5;
1Chr 9:25

1:25
h Gen 30:23;
Isa 4:1; 54:1,4

1:27
i Matt 1:18;
Lk 2:4-5

1:28
j Jdg 6:12;
Dan 9:23; 1C:19

1:29
a Lk 1:12

1:31
b Isa 7:14;
Matt 1:21; Lk 2:21

1:32
c 2Sam 7:11-12;
Ps 132:11;
Isa 9:6-7; 16:5;
Jer 23:5; Mark 5:7;
Rev 3:7

1:33
d Dan 2:44; 7:14,
27; Obad 1:21;
Mic 4:7;
John 12:34;
Heb 1:8

1:35
e Matt 1:20; 14:33;
26:63-64;
Mark 1:1;
John 1:34; 20:31;
Acts 8:37;
Rom 1:4

1:37
f Gen 18:14;
Jer 32:17;
Zech 8:6;
Matt 19:26;
Mark 10:27;
Lk 18:27;
Rom 4:21

1:39
g Josh 21:9-11

1:42
h Jdg 5:24; Lk 1:28

1:46
i 1Sam 2:1;
Ps 34:2-3; 35:9;
Hab 3:18

tried to figure out what his greeting meant.*a* ³⁰Then the angel told her, "Stop being afraid, Mary, for you have found favor with God. ³¹Listen! You will become pregnant and give birth to a son, and you are to name him Jesus.*b* ³²He will be great and will be called the Son of the Most High, and the Lord God will give him the throne of his forefather David.*c* ³³He will rule over the house of Jacob forever, and his kingdom will never end."*d*

³⁴Mary asked the angel, "How can this be, since I have not had relations with a man?"*a* ³⁵The angel answered her, "The Holy Spirit will come over you, and the power of the Most High will cover you. Therefore, the child will be holy and will be called the Son of God.*e* ³⁶And listen! Elizabeth, your relative, has herself conceived a son in her old age. This is the sixth month for the woman who was said to be barren. ³⁷For nothing is impossible for God."*f* ³⁸Then Mary said, "Truly I am the Lord's servant. Let everything you have said happen to me." Then the angel left her.

Mary Visits Elizabeth

³⁹At this time*b* Mary set out and hurried to a Judean city in the hill country.*g* ⁴⁰She went into Zechariah's home and greeted Elizabeth. ⁴¹When Elizabeth heard Mary's greeting, the baby jumped in her womb. Elizabeth was filled with the Holy Spirit ⁴²and exclaimed with a loud cry, "How blessed are you among women, and how blessed is the fruit of your womb!*h* ⁴³Why should this happen to me, to have the mother of my Lord visit me! ⁴⁴For as soon as the sound of your greeting reached my ears, the baby in my womb jumped for joy. ⁴⁵How blessed is this woman for believing that what was spoken to her by the Lord would be fulfilled!"

Mary's Song of Praise

⁴⁶Then Mary said,*i*

"My soul praises the greatness of the Lord!
⁴⁷ *My spirit exults in God, my Savior,*

---

a 1:34 Lit. *I have not known a man*   b 1:39 Lit. *In those days*

48　　　　　*for he has looked favorably on his humble*
　　　　　　　servant.^a

From now on, all generations will call me blessed,

49　　　*because the Almighty has done great things*
　　　　　　　for me.^b
　　　　His name is holy.

⁵⁰*His mercy lasts from generation to generation*^c
　　　for those who fear him.

⁵¹*He displayed his mighty power with his arm.*^d
　　　He scattered people who were proud in mind and
　　　　　heart.^a

⁵²*He pulled powerful rulers from their thrones*^e
　　　and lifted up humble people.

⁵³*He filled hungry people with good things*^f
　　　and sent rich people away with nothing.

⁵⁴*He helped his servant Israel,*^g
　　　remembering to be merciful,

⁵⁵*according to the promise he made* **b** *to our ancestors*^h —
　　　to Abraham and his descendants forever."

⁵⁶Now Mary stayed with Elizabeth^c about three months and then went back home.

The Birth of John the Baptist

⁵⁷When the time came for Elizabeth to have her child, she gave birth to a son. ⁵⁸Her neighbors and relatives heard that the Lord had shown his great mercy to her, and they rejoiced with her.ⁱ

⁵⁹On the eighth day they went to the Temple^d to circumcise the child. They were going to name him Zechariah after his father,^j ⁶⁰but his mother said, "Absolutely not! He must be named John."^k ⁶¹Their friends^e said to her, "None of your relatives has that name." ⁶²So they motioned to the baby's^f father to see what he wanted to name him. ⁶³He asked for a writing tablet and wrote, "His name is John." And everyone was amazed.^l

⁶⁴Suddenly, Zechariah's^g mouth was opened and his

---

a 1:51 Lit. *in the mind of their heart*　**b** 1:55 Lit. *just as he spoke*　**c** 1:56 Lit. *with her*　**d** 1:59 Lit. *they went*　**e** 1:61 Lit. *They*　**f** 1:62 Lit. *to his*　**g** 1:64 Lit. *his*

1:48
a 1Sam 1:11;
Ps 138:6;
Mal 3:12;
Lk 11:27

1:49
b Ps 71:19; 111:9;
126:2-3

1:50
c Gen 17:7;
Exod 20:6;
Ps 103:17-18

1:51
d Ps 33:10; 98:1;
118:15; Isa 40:10;
51:9; 52:10;
1Peter 5:5

1:52
e 1Sam 2:6;
Job 5:11; Ps 113:6

1:53
f 1Sam 2:5;
Ps 34:10

1:54
g Ps 98:3; Jer 31:3,
20

1:55
h Gen 17:19;
Ps 132:11;
Rom 11:28;
Gal 3:16

1:58
i Lk 1:14

1:59
j Gen 17:12;
Lev 12:3

1:60
k Lk 1:13

1:63
l Lk 1:13

1:64
a Lk 1:20

1:65
b Lk 1:39

1:66
c Gen 39:2;
Ps 80:17; 89:21;
Lk 2:19,51;
Acts 11:21

1:67
d Joel 2:28

1:68
e Exod 3:16; 4:31;
1Kings 1:48;
Ps 41:13; 72:18;
106:48; 111:9;
Lk 7:16

1:69
f Ps 132:17

1:70
g Jer 23:5-6;
30:10; Dan 9:24;
Acts 3:21;
Rom 1:2

1:72
h Lev 26:42;
Ps 98:3; 105:8-9;
106:45;
Ezek 16:60;
Lk 1:54

1:73
i Gen 12:3; 17:4;
22:16-17;
Heb 6:13,17

1:74
j Rom 6:18,22;
Heb 9:14

1:75
k Jer 32:39-40;
Eph 4:24;
2Thes 2:13;
2Tim 1:9;
Titus 2:12;
1Peter 1:15;
2Peter 1:4

1:76
l Isa 40:3; Mal 3:1;
4:5; Matt 11:10;
Lk 11:17

1:77
m Mark 1:4; Lk 3:3

1:79
n Isa 9:2; 42:7;
49:9; Matt 4:16;
Acts 26:18

tongue was set free, and he began to speak and praise God.*a* [65]Fear came over all their neighbors, and all over the hill country of Judea all these things were being discussed.*b* [66]All the people who heard about it debated in their minds what had happened and said, "What will this child become?" For it was obvious that the hand of the Lord was with him.*c*

The Prophecy of Zechariah

[67]Then his father Zechariah was filled with the Holy Spirit and prophesied:*d*

[68]*"Blessed be the Lord God of Israel!*e*
        He has taken care of his people and has set them free.*
[69]*He has raised up a horn of salvation*a* for us*f*
        from the family of his servant David,*
[70]*just as he promised long ago through*g*
        the mouth of his holy prophets*
[71]*that he would save us from our enemies*
        and from the grip of all who hate us.*
[72]*He has shown mercy to our ancestors*h*
        and remembered his holy covenant,*
[73]   *the oath that he swore to our ancestor*
                *Abraham.*i*
He granted us [74]*deliverance from our enemies' grip*j*
        so that we could serve him without fear
[75]*and be holy and righteous before him all of our days.*k*
[76]   *And you, child, will be called a prophet of the*
                *Most High.*l*
For you will go ahead of the Lord to prepare his ways
[77]   *and to give his people the knowledge of salvation*m*
                through the forgiveness of their sins.
[78]*Because of the tender mercy of our God,*
        *a new day has dawned*b* on us,*
[79]*to shine on those who sit in darkness and in death's*
                *shadow,*n*
        and to guide our feet into the way of peace."

---

a *1:69* I.e. a mighty Savior   **b** *1:78* Lit. *the dawn from on high has broken*

⁸⁰Now the child continued to grow and to become strong in spirit.ᵃ He lived in the wilderness until the day he appeared in Israel.ᵃ

The Birth of Jesus
(Matthew 1:18–25)

2 ¹Now in those days a decree went out from Caesar Augustus that the whole world should be registered. ²This was the first registration taken while Quirinius was governor of Syria.ᵇ ³So all the people went to their hometowns to be registered.

⁴Joseph, too, went up from the city of Nazareth in Galilee to Judea, to the city of David called Bethlehem, because he was a descendant ofᵇ the household and family of David.ᶜ ⁵He went there to be registeredᶜ with Mary, who had been promised to him in marriage and was pregnant.ᵈ

⁶While they were there, the time came for her to have her child, ⁷and she gave birth to her first child, a son. She wrapped him in strips of cloth and laid him in a manger, because there wasn't any room for them in the inn.ᵈᵉ

The Shepherds Visit Jesus

⁸In that region there were shepherds living in the fields, watching their flock during the night. ⁹An angel of the Lord appeared to them, and the glory of the Lord shone around them, and they were terrified.ᶠ ¹⁰Then the angel said to them, "Stop being afraid! Listen! I'm bringing you good news of great joy for all the people.ᵍ ¹¹Today your Savior, Christᵉ the Lord, was born in the city of David.ʰ ¹²This will be a sign for you: You will find a baby wrapped in strips of cloth and lying in a manger."

¹³Suddenly a multitude of the Heavenly Army appeared with the angel, praising God and saying,ⁱ ¹⁴"Glory to God in the highest, and peace on earth to people who enjoy his favor!"ᶠʲ

¹⁵When the angels had left them and gone back to

---

a 1:80 Or *in the Spirit*   **b** 2:4 Lit. *he was of*   **c** 2:5 Lit. *To be registered*   **d** 2:7 Or *in the guest room*   **e** 2:11 I.e. Messiah   **f** 2:14 Other mss. read *peace on earth, and favor to people*

1:80 ᵃMatt 3:1; 11:7; Lk 2:40

2:2 ᵇActs 5:37

2:4 ᶜ1Sam 16:1,4; Matt 1:16; Lk 1:27; John 7:42

2:5 ᵈMatt 1:16; Lk 1:27

2:7 ᵉMatt 1:25

2:9 ᶠLk 1:12

2:10 ᵍGen 12:3; Matt 28:19; Mark 1:15; Lk 1:31-32; 24:47; Col 1:23

2:11 ʰIsa 9:6; Matt 1:16,21; 16:16; Lk 1:43; Acts 2:36; 10:36; Phil 2:11

2:13 ⁱGen 28:12; 32:1-2; Ps 103:20-21; 148:2; Dan 7:10; Heb 1:14; Rev 5:11

2:14 ʲIsa 57:19; Lk 1:79; 19:38; John 3:16; Rom 5:1; Eph 1:6; 2:4,7,17; 3:10, 21 Col 1:20; 2Thes 2:16; 1John 4:9-10; Rev 5:13

2:19
a Gen 37:11;
Lk 1:51,66

2:21
b Gen 17:12;
Lev 12:3;
Matt 1:21,25;
Lk 1:31,59

2:22
c Lev 12:2-4,6

2:23
d Exod 13:2;
22:29; 34:19;
Num 3:13; 8:17;
18:15

2:24
e Lev 12:2,6,8

2:25
f Isa 40:1;
Mark 15:43;
Lk 2:38

2:26
g Ps 89:48;
Heb 11:5

2:27
h Matt 4:1

heaven, the shepherds said to one another, "Let's go to Bethlehem and see what has taken place—what the Lord has told us about." [16]So they went quickly and found Mary and Joseph with the baby, who was lying in the manger. [17]When they saw this, they repeated what they had been told about this child. [18]All who heard it were amazed at what the shepherds told them, [19]but Mary continued to treasure in her heart all these things and to ponder them.[a] [20]Then the shepherds returned to their flock,[a] glorifying and praising God for everything they had heard and seen, just as it had been told to them.

Jesus Is Circumcised

[21]After eight days had passed, the child[b] was circumcised and named Jesus, the name given to him by the angel before he was conceived in the womb.[b]

Jesus Is Presented in the Temple

[22]When the time came for their purification according to the Law of Moses, Joseph and Mary[c] took Jesus[d] up to Jerusalem to present him to the Lord.[c] [23]As it is written in the Law of the Lord, "Every firstborn son is to be designated as holy to the Lord."[e][d] [24]They also offered a sacrifice according to what is specified in the Law of the Lord: "a pair of turtledoves or two young pigeons."[f][e]

[25]Now a man named Simeon was in Jerusalem. This man was righteous and devout. He was waiting for the one who would comfort[g] Israel, and the Holy Spirit rested on him.[f] [26]It had been revealed to him by the Holy Spirit that he would not die[h] until he had seen the Lord's Christ.[i][g]

[27]Moved by the Spirit, he went into the Temple. When the parents brought the child Jesus to do for him what was customary under the Law,[h] [28]Simeon[b] took the child[d] in his arms and praised God, saying,

---

a *2:20* The Gk. lacks *to their flock*   **b** *2:21,2:28* Lit. *he*   **c** *2:22* Lit. *they*
d *2:22,2:28* Lit. *him*   **e** *2:23* Exod 13:2, 12, 15   **f** *2:24* Lev 12:8   **g** *2:25* Lit.
waiting for the comfort of   **h** *2:26* Lit. *see death*   **i** *2:26* I.e. Messiah

29"*Master, now you are allowing your servant to leave*
          in peace[a]
     according to your word.
30*For my eyes have seen your salvation,*[b]
31   *which you prepared for all people to see—*
32*a light that will reveal salvation*[a] *to the Gentiles*[c]
     and bring glory to your people Israel."

33Jesus'[b] father and mother kept wondering at the things being said about him. 34Then Simeon[c] blessed them and said to Mary, his mother, "This child is destined to cause many in Israel to fall or rise. He will be a sign that will be disputed,[d] 35so that the inner thoughts of many people can be revealed. Indeed, a sword will pierce your own soul, too."[e]

36Now Anna, a prophetess, was also there. She was a descendant of Phanuel from the tribe of Asher. She was very old, having lived with her husband for seven years after her marriage, 37and then as a widow for eighty-four years. She never left the Temple, but continued to worship there night and day with times of fasting and prayer.[f] 38Just then she came forward and began to thank God and to speak about the child[d] to all who were waiting for the redemption of Jerusalem.[g]

The Return to Nazareth

39After doing everything required by the Law of the Lord, Joseph and Mary[e] returned to their hometown of Nazareth in Galilee. 40The child continued to grow and to become strong. He was filled with wisdom, and God's favor was with him.[h]

Jesus Visits the Temple

41Every year Jesus'[f] parents would go to Jerusalem for the Passover Festival.[i] 42When he was twelve years old, they went up to the festival as usual. 43When the days of the festival[g] were over, they left for home. The young man Jesus stayed behind in Jerusalem, but his parents didn't know it. 44They thought that he was in the group of travelers. After

---

a 2:32 Lit. *a light for revelation*   b 2:33 Lit. *His*   c 2:34 Lit. *he*   d 2:38 Lit. *about him*   e 2:39 Lit. *they*   f 2:41 Lit. *his*   g 2:43 Lit. *When the days*

2:29
a Gen 46:30;
Phil 1:23

2:30
b Isa 52:10; Lk 3:6

2:32
c Isa 9:2; 42:6;
49:6; 60:1-3;
Matt 4:16;
Acts 13:47; 28:28

2:34
d Isa 8:14;
Hos 14:9;
Matt 21:44;
Acts 28:22;
Rom 9:32-33;
1Cor 1:23-24;
2Cor 2:16;
1Peter 2:7-8

2:35
e Ps 42:10;
John 19:25

2:37
f Acts 26:7;
1Tim 5:5

2:38
g Mark 15:43;
Lk 15:25; 24:21

2:40
h Lk 1:80; 2:52

2:41
i Exod 23:15,17;
34:23; Deut 16:1,
16

2:47
a Matt 7:28;
Mark 1:22;
Lk 4:22,32;
John 7:15,46

traveling for a day, they started to look for him among their relatives and friends. ⁴⁵When they didn't find him, they went back to Jerusalem, anxiously looking for him. ⁴⁶Three days later they found him in the Temple sitting among the teachers, listening to them and asking them questions. ⁴⁷All who heard him were amazed at his intelligence and his answers.ᵃ

2:49
b John 2:16

⁴⁸When his parentsᵃ saw him, they were shocked. His mother asked him, "Son, why have you treated us like this? Your father and I have been worried sick looking for you!" ⁴⁹He said to them, "Why were you looking for me? Didn't you know that I had to be in my Father's house?"ᵇᵇ

2:50
c Lk 9:45; 18:34

⁵⁰But they didn't understand what he said to them.ᶜ ⁵¹Then he went down with them and returned to Nazareth. And he remained in submission to them. His mother continued to treasure all these things in her heart.ᵈ ⁵²Meanwhile, Jesus kept on growing in wisdom and maturity,ᶜ and in favor with God and people.ᵉ

2:51
d Dan 7:28;
Lk 2:19

John the Baptist Prepares the Way for Jesus
(Matthew 3:1–12; Mark 1:1–8; John 1:19–28)

2:52
e 1Sam 2:26;
Lk 2:40

3 ¹Now in the fifteenth year of the reign of Caesar Tiberius, when Pontius Pilate was governor of Judea, Herod was tetrarch of Galilee, his brother Philip was tetrarch of the region of Ituraea and Trachonitis, Lysanias was tetrarch of Abilene, ²and Annas and Caiaphas were high priests, the word of God came to John, the son of Zechariah, in the wilderness.ᶠ

3:2
f John 11:49,51;
18:13; Acts 4:6

³Johnᵈ went into all the region around the Jordan, proclaiming a baptism of repentance for the forgiveness of sins.ᵍ ⁴As it is written in the book of the words of the prophet Isaiah,ʰ

3:3
g Matt 3:1;
Mark 1:4; Lk 1:77

"He is a voice calling out in the wilderness:
'Prepare the way for the Lord! Make his paths straight!
⁵Every valley will be filled,
and every mountain and hill will be leveled.
The crooked ways will be made straight,
and the rough roads will be made smooth.

3:4
h Isa 40:3;
Matt 3:3;
Mark 1:3;
John 1:23

a 2:48 Lit. they   b 2:49 Or about my Father's work   c 2:52 Or height
d 3:3 Lit. He

⁶Everyone^a will see the salvation^a
    that God has provided.' "^b

⁷John would say to the crowds that were coming out to be baptized by him, "You children of serpents! Who warned you to flee from the coming wrath?^b ⁸Produce fruit that is consistent with repentance! Don't begin to say to yourselves, 'We have Abraham for our forefather.' For I tell you that God can raise up descendants for Abraham from these stones! ⁹The ax already lies against the roots of the trees. So every tree not producing good fruit will be cut down and thrown into a fire."^c

¹⁰The crowds kept asking him, "What, then, should we do?"^d ¹¹He answered them, "The person who has two coats must share with the one who doesn't have any, and the person who has food must do the same."^e ¹²Even some tax collectors came to be baptized. They asked him, "Teacher, what should we do?"^f ¹³He told them, "Stop collecting more money than the amount you are told to collect."^g ¹⁴Even some soldiers were asking him, "And what should we do?" He told them, "Never extort money from anyone by threats or blackmail, and be satisfied with your pay."^h

¹⁵Now the people were filled with expectation, and all of them were wondering if John was perhaps the Christ.^c ¹⁶John replied to all of them, "I am baptizing you with^d water. But the one who is more powerful than I is coming. I am not worthy to untie his sandal straps. It is he who will baptize you with^d the Holy Spirit and fire.ⁱ ¹⁷His winnowing fork is in his hand to clean up his threshing floor. He will gather the grain into his barn, but he will burn the chaff with inextinguishable fire."^j

¹⁸With many other exhortations John^e continued to proclaim the good news to the people. ¹⁹Now Herod the tetrarch had been rebuked by John^f because he had married^g his brother's wife Herodias and because of all the evil things Herod had done.^k ²⁰Added to all this, Herod^e locked John up in prison.

---

a *3:6* Lit. *All flesh*   b *3:6* Isa 40:3-5   c *3:15* I.e. the Messiah   d *3:16* Or *in*   e *3:18,3:20* Lit. *he*   f *3:19* Lit. *by him*   g *3:19* Lit. *because of*

3:6
a Ps 98:2;
Isa 52:10; Lk 2:10

3:7
b Matt 3:7

3:9
c Matt 7:19

3:10
d Acts 2:37

3:11
e Lk 11:41;
2Cor 8:14;
James 2:15-16;
1John 3:17; 4:20

3:12
f Matt 21:32;
Lk 7:29

3:13
g Lk 19:8

3:14
h Exod 23:1;
Lev 19:11

3:16
i Matt 3:11

3:17
j Mic 4:12;
Matt 13:30

3:19
k Matt 14:3;
Mark 6:17

3:21
a Matt 3:13;
John 1:32

Jesus Is Baptized
(Matthew 3:13–17; Mark 1:9–11)

[21]When all the people had been baptized, Jesus, too, was baptized. While he was praying, heaven opened,[a] [22]and the Holy Spirit came down to him in bodily form like a dove. Then a voice came from heaven saying,[a] "You are my Son, whom I love. I am pleased with you!"[b]

3:23
b Num 4:3,35,39,
43,47; Matt 13:55;
John 6:42

The Ancestry of Jesus
(Matthew 1:1–17)

[23]Jesus himself was about thirty years old when he began his ministry.[c] He was (so it was thought) the son of Joseph, the son of Heli,[b] [24]the son of Matthat, the son of Levi, the son of Melchi, the son of Jannai, the son of Joseph, [25]the son of Mattathias, the son of Amos, the son of Nahum, the son of Esli, the son of Naggai, [26]the son of Maath, the son of Mattathias, the son of Semein, the son of Josech, the son of Joda, [27]the son of Joanan, the son of Rhesa, the son of Zerubbabel, the son of Shealtiel,[d] the son of Neri, [28]the son of Melchi, the son of Addi, the son of Cosam, the son of Elmadam, the son of Er, [29]the son of Joshua, the son of Eliezer, the son of Jorim, the son of Matthat, the son of Levi, [30]the son of Simeon, the son of Judah, the son of Joseph, the son of Jonam, the son of Eliakim, [31]the son of Melea, the son of Menna, the son of Matattha, the son of Nathan, the son of David,[c] [32]the son of Jesse, the son of Obed, the son of Boaz, the son of Salmon,[e] the son of Nahshon,[d] [33]the son of Amminadab, the son of Admin, the son of Arni, the son of Hezron, the son of Perez, the son of Judah, [34]the son of Jacob, the son of Isaac, the son of Abraham, the son of Terah, the son of Nahor,[e] [35]the son of Serug, the son of Reu, the son of Peleg, the son of Eber, the son of Shelah, [36]the son of Cainan, the son of Arphaxad, the son of Shem, the son of Noah, the son of Lamech,[f] [37]the son of Methuselah, the son of Enoch, the son of Jared, the son of Mahalaleel, the son of

3:31
c 2Sam 5:14;
1Chr 3:5;
Zech 12:12

3:32
d Ruth 4:18;
1Chr 2:10

3:34
e Gen 11:24,26

3:36
f Gen 5:6; 11:10,
12

---

a 3:22 *The* Gk. lacks *saying*   b 3:22 Other mss. read *You are my Son. Today I have become your father.*   c 3:23 The Gk. lacks *his ministry*
d 3:27 Gk. *Salathiel*   e 3:32 Other mss. read *Sala*

Cainan, ³⁸the son of Enos, the son of Seth, the son of Adam, the son of God.ᵃ

Jesus Is Tempted by Satan
(Matthew 4:1–11; Mark 1:12–13)

4 ¹Then Jesus, filled with the Holy Spirit, returned from the Jordan. He was led by the Spirit into the wilderness,ᵇ ²where he was being tempted by the devil for forty days. During those days he ate nothing at all, so when they were over he was hungry.ᶜ

³The devil said to him, "If you are the Son of God, tell this stone to become a loaf of bread." ⁴Jesus answered him, "It is written,ᵈ

> 'A person must not live on bread alone,
> but on every word of God.' "ᵃ

⁵The devilᵇ also took him to a high placeᶜ and showed him all the kingdoms of the world in an instant. ⁶He said to Jesus,ᵈ "I will give you all this authority and the glory of these kingdoms.ᵉ For it has been given to me, and I give it to anyone I please.ᵉ ⁷So if you will worship me, all this will be yours." ⁸But Jesus answered him, "It is written,ᶠ

> 'You must worship the Lord your God
> and serve only him.' "ᶠ

⁹The devilᵇ also took him into Jerusalem and had him stand on the highest point of the Temple. He said to Jesus,ᵈ "Sinceᵍ you are the Son of God, throw yourself down from here.ᵍ ¹⁰For it is written,ʰ

> 'Godᵇ will put his angels in charge of you
> to watch over you carefully.
> ¹¹With their hands they will hold you up,
> so that you will never hit your foot against a
> rock.' "ʰ

---

a 4:4 Deut 8:3; Other mss. lack *but on every word of God*
b 4:5,4:9,4:10 Lit. *He*   c 4:5 Lit. *took him up*   d 4:6,4:9 Lit. *to him*
e 4:6 Lit. *their glory*   f 4:8 Deut 6:13   g 4:9 Or *If*   h 4:11 Ps 91:11-12

3:38
a Gen 5:1-2

4:1
b Matt 4:1;
Mark 1:12;
Lk 1:14; 2:27

4:2
c Exod 34:28;
1 Kings 19:8

4:4
d Deut 8:3

4:6
e John 12:31;
14:30; Rev 13:2,7

4:8
f Deut 6:13; 10:20

4:9
g Matt 4:5

4:10
h Ps 91:11

4:12
a Deut 6:16

¹²Jesus answered him, "It has been said,*a*

'You must not tempt the Lord your God.' "**a**

¹³After the devil had finished tempting Jesus in every possible way, he left him until another time.*b*

Jesus Begins His Ministry in Galilee

4:13
b John 14:30;
Heb 4:15

(Matthew 4:12–17; Mark 1:14–15)

¹⁴Then Jesus returned to Galilee in the power of the Holy Spirit. Meanwhile, the news about him spread throughout the surrounding country.*c* ¹⁵He began to teach in their synagogues and was continuously receiving praise from everyone.

Jesus Is Rejected at Nazareth

4:14
c Matt 4:12;
Lk 4:1; John 4:43;
Acts 10:37

(Matthew 13:53–58; Mark 6:1–6)

¹⁶Then Jesus**b** came to Nazareth, where he had been raised. As was his custom, he went into the synagogue on the Sabbath day. When he stood up to read,*d* ¹⁷the scroll of the prophet Isaiah was handed to him. Unrolling the scroll, he found the place where it was written,

4:16
d Matt 2:23;
13:54; Mark 6:1;
Acts 13:14; 17:2

¹⁸"The Spirit of the Lord is on me,*e*
because he has anointed me to tell
the good news to the poor.
He has sent me to announce release to the prisoners
and recovery of sight to the blind,
to set oppressed people free,
¹⁹and to announce the year of the Lord's favor."**c**

²⁰Then he rolled up the scroll, gave it back to the attendant, and sat down. The eyes of everyone in the synagogue

4:18
e Isa 61:1

were fixed on him. ²¹Then he began to say to them, "Today this Scripture has been fulfilled in your hearing."

²²All the people began to speak well of him and to wonder at the gracious words flowing from his mouth. They said, "This is Joseph's son, isn't it?"*f* ²³So he said to them, "You'll probably quote this proverb to me, 'Doctor, heal

4:22
f Ps 45:2;
Matt 13:54;
Mark 6:2; Lk 2:47;
John 6:42

yourself! Do all the things here in your hometown that we

---

a*4:12* Deut 6:16   **b***4:16* Lit. *he*   **c***4:19* Isa 61:1-2; 58:6

141

hear you did in Capernaum.' "[a] [24]He added, "Truly I tell you, a prophet isn't accepted in his hometown.[b] [25]In truth I tell you that there were many widows in Israel in Elijah's time, when the heaven was closed for three years and six months and there was a severe famine everywhere in the land.[c] [26]Yet Elijah wasn't sent to a single one of them except to a widow at Zarephath in Sidon. [27]There were also many lepers in Israel in the prophet Elisha's time, yet not one of them was cleansed except Naaman the Syrian."[d]

[28]Then all the people in the synagogue became furious when they heard this. [29]They got up, forced Jesus[a] out of the city, and led him to the edge of the hill on which their city was built, intending to throw him off of it. [30]But he walked right through the middle of them and went away.[e]

Jesus Heals a Woman with an Unclean Spirit
(Mark 1:21–28)

[31]Then Jesus[b] went down to Capernaum, a city in Galilee, and kept teaching the people[c] on the Sabbath.[f] [32]They were utterly amazed at his teaching, because his message was spoken[d] with authority.[g]

[33]In the synagogue was a man who had a spirit of an unclean demon. He screamed with a loud voice,[h] [34]"Oh, no! What do you want with us, Jesus of Nazareth? Have you come to destroy us? I know who you are—the Holy One of God!"[i] [35]But Jesus reprimanded him, saying, "Be quiet, and come out of him!" At this, the demon threw the man[a] down in the middle of the synagogue[e] and came out of him without hurting him. [36]Amazement came on all of them, and they kept saying to one another, "What kind of statement is this? For with authority and power he tells the unclean spirits what to do, and they come out!" [37]So news about him spread to every place in the surrounding region.

Jesus Heals Many People
(Matthew 8:14–17; Mark 1:29–34)

[38]Then Jesus[b] got up to leave the synagogue and went

---

a 4:29,4:35 Lit. him   b 4:31,4:38 Lit. he   c 4:31 Lit. them   d 4:32 The Gk. lacks spoken   e 4:35 Lit. in the middle

4:23
[a] Matt 4:13; 11:23; 13:54; Mark 6:1

4:24
[b] Matt 13:57; Mark 6:4; John 4:44

4:25
[c] 1Kings 17:9; 18:1 James 5:17

4:27
[d] 2Kings 5:14

4:30
[e] John 8:59; 10:39

4:31
[f] Matt 4:13; Mark 1:21

4:32
[g] Matt 6:28-29; Titus 2:15

4:33
[h] Mark 1:23

4:34
[i] Ps 16:10; Dan 9:24; Lk 1:35; 4:41

4:38
*a*Matt 8:14;
Mark 1:29

into Simon's house. Now Simon's mother-in-law was sick with a high fever, so they asked Jesus[a] about her.[a] 39He bent over her, reprimanded the fever, and it left her. She got up at once and began serving them.

40When the sun was setting, all those who had any friends[b] suffering from various diseases brought them to him. He began placing his hands on each of them and healing them.[b] 41Even demons came out of many people, screaming, "You are the Son of God!" But Jesus[c] reprimanded them and ordered them not to speak, because they knew he was the Christ.[d][c]

4:40
*b*Matt 8:16;
Mark 1:32

Jesus Goes on a Preaching Tour
(Mark 1:35–39)

4:41
*c*Mark 1:25,34;
3:11; Lk 1:34-35

42At daybreak he left and went to a deserted place, and the crowds kept looking for him. When they came to him, they tried to keep him from leaving them.[d] 43But he said to them, "I have to proclaim the good news about the kingdom of God in the other cities also, for that is what I was sent to do." 44So he continued to preach in the synagogues of Galilee.[e][e]

4:42
*d*Mark 1:35

Jesus Calls His First Disciples
(Matthew 4:18–22; Mark 1:16–20)

5 1One day as the crowd was pressing in on him to listen to God's word, Jesus[c] was standing by the lake of Gennesaret.[f] 2He saw two boats lying on the shore, but the fishermen had stepped out of them and were washing their nets. 3So Jesus[c] got into one of the boats (the one that belonged to Simon) and asked him to push out a little from the shore. Then Jesus[c] sat down and began to teach the crowds from the boat.

4:44
*e*Mark 1:39

4When he had finished speaking, he said to Simon, "Push out into deep water, and lower your nets for a catch."[g] 5Simon answered, "Master, we've worked hard all night and caught nothing. But if you say so, I'll lower the nets." 6After the men[f] had done this, they caught so many fish that the

5:1
*f*Matt 4:18;
Mark 1:16

5:4
*g*John 21:6

a *4:38* Lit. *him*   **b** *4:40* Lit. *people*   **c** *4:41,5:1,5:3* Lit. *he*   **d** *4:41* I.e. the Messiah   **e** *4:44* Other mss. read *of Judea*   **f** *5:6* Lit. *they*

nets began to tear. [7]So they signaled to their partners in the other boat to come and help them. They came and filled both boats until the boats[a] began to sink. [8]When Simon Peter saw this, he fell down at Jesus' knees and said, "Leave me, Lord! I'm a sinful man!"[a] [9]For Simon[b] and all the people who were with him were amazed at the number of fish they had caught, [10]and so were James and John, Zebedee's sons and Simon's partners. Then Jesus said to Simon, "Stop being afraid. From now on you will be catching people."[b] [11]So when they brought the boats to shore, they left everything and followed Jesus.[cc]

Jesus Cleanses a Leper
(Matthew 8:1–4; Mark 1:40–45)

[12]One day while Jesus[b] was in one of the cities, a man covered with leprosy saw Jesus and fell on his face, begging him, "Lord, if you want to, you can make me clean."[d] [13]So Jesus[b] reached out his hand and touched him, saying, "I do want to. Be made clean!" Instantly the leprosy left him. [14]Then Jesus[b] ordered him, "Don't tell anyone. Instead, go and show yourself to the priest and make an offering for your cleansing as Moses commanded as proof to the authorities."[de] [15]But the news about Jesus[e] spread even more, and many crowds began gathering to hear him and to be healed of their diseases.[f] [16]However, he continued his habit of going away to deserted places and praying.[g]

Jesus Heals a Paralyzed Man
(Matthew 9:1–8; Mark 2:1–12)

[17]One day as Jesus[b] was teaching, some Pharisees and teachers of the Law happened to be sitting near by. They had come from every village in Galilee and Judea and from Jerusalem. The power of the Lord was present to heal them.[f] [18]Some men were bringing a paralyzed man on a stretcher. They were trying to take him into the house[g] and put him in front of Jesus.[hh] [19]When they couldn't find a way to get him in because of the crowd, they went up on the roof and let

---

a 5:7 Lit. *they*   b 5:9,5:12,5:13,5:14,5:17 Lit. *he*   c 5:11 Lit. *him*
d 5:14 Lit. *to them*   e 5:15 Lit. *about him*   f 5:17 Other mss. read *was present with him to heal*   g 5:18 Lit. *take him in*   h 5:18 Lit. *in front of him*

Marginal cross-references:

5:8 a 2Sam 6:9; 1Kings 17:18

5:10 b Matt 4:19; Mark 1:17

5:11 c Matt 4:20; 19:27; Mark 1:18; Lk 18:28

5:12 d Matt 8:2; Mark 1:40

5:14 e Lev 14:4,10, 21-22; Matt 8:4

5:15 f Matt 4:25; Mark 3:7; John 6:2

5:16 g Matt 14:23; Mark 6:46

5:18 h Matt 9:2; Mark 2:3

5:21
a Ps 32:5;
Isa 43:25;
Matt 9:3;
Mark 2:6-7

him down on his stretcher through the tiles into the middle of the room,[a] right in front of Jesus. [20]When Jesus[b] saw their faith, he said, "Mister,[c] your sins are forgiven."

[21]The scribes and the Pharisees began to argue among themselves, saying, "Who is this man who is uttering blasphemies? Who can forgive sins but God alone?"[a] [22]Because Jesus knew that they were arguing, he said to them, "Why are you arguing about this among yourselves?[d] [23]Which is easier: to say 'Your sins are forgiven,' or to say 'Get up and walk'? [24]But I want you to know[e] that the Son of Man has authority on earth to forgive sins." Then he said to the paralyzed man, "I say to you: Get up, pick up your stretcher, and go home!" [25]So the man[b] immediately stood up in front of them and picked up what he had been lying on. Then he went home, praising God. [26]Amazement seized all the people, and they began to praise God. They were filled with awe and declared, "We have seen wonderful things today!"

5:27
b Matt 9:9;
Mark 2:13-14

Jesus Calls Levi
(Matthew 9:9–13; Mark 2:13–17)

[27]After that Jesus[b] went out and saw a tax collector named Levi sitting at the tax collector's desk. He said to him, "Follow me!"[b] [28]So Levi[b] left everything behind, got up, and followed him.

[29]Then Levi gave a large banquet at his home for Jesus.[f] A large crowd of tax collectors and others were eating with them.[c] [30]The Pharisees and their scribes were complaining to Jesus's[g] disciples, "Why do you eat and drink with tax collectors and notorious[h] sinners?" [31]But Jesus answered them, "Healthy people don't need a physician, but sick people do. [32]I have not come to call righteous people, but sinners, to repentance."[d]

5:29
c Matt 9:10;
Mark 2:15;
Lk 15:1

A Question about Fasting
(Matthew 9:14–17; Mark 2:18–22)

[33]Then they said to him, "John's disciples frequently fast and pray, and so do the disciples of[i] the Pharisees. But your

5:32
d Matt 9:13;
1 Tim 1:15

---

a 5:19 Lit. *into the middle*   b 5:20,5:25,5:27,5:28 Lit. *he*   c 5:20 Lit. *Man*
d 5:22 Lit. *in your hearts*   e 5:24 Lit. *So that you'll know*   f 5:29 Lit. *for him*   g 5:30 Lit. *his*   h 5:30 The Gk. lacks *notorious*   i 5:33 Lit. *those of*

disciples[a] keep right on eating and drinking."[a] 34But Jesus said to them, "You can't force the wedding guests to fast while the groom is still with them, can you? 35But the days will come when the groom will be taken away from them, and in those days they will fast."

The Unshrunk Cloth
(Matthew 9:16; Mark 2:21)

36Then he told them a parable: "No one tears a piece of cloth from a new garment and sews it on an old garment. If he does, the new will tear, and the piece from the new will not match the old.[b] 37And no one pours new wine into old wineskins. If he does, the new wine will make the skins burst, the wine[b] will be spilled, and the skins will be ruined. 38Rather, new wine is to be poured into fresh wineskins. 39No one who has been drinking old wine wants new wine, for he says, 'The old is excellent!' "[c]

Jesus Is Lord of the Sabbath
(Matthew 12:1–8; Mark 2:23–28)

6 1Once, on the second Sabbath after the first,[d] Jesus[e] was walking through some grainfields. His disciples were picking the heads of grain, rubbing them in their hands, and eating them.[c] 2Some of the Pharisees asked, "Why are you doing what is not lawful on the Sabbath?"[d] 3Jesus answered them, "Haven't you read what David did when he and his companions became hungry?[e] 4How was it that he went into the house of God and took and ate the Bread of the Presence, which was not lawful for anyone but the priests to eat, and gave some of it to his companions?"[f] 5Then he said to them, "The Son of Man is Lord of the Sabbath."

Jesus Heals a Man with a Paralyzed Hand
(Matthew 12:9–14; Mark 3:1–6)

6Once, on another Sabbath, Jesus[e] went into a synagogue and began teaching. A man whose right hand was paralyzed was there.[g] 7The scribes and the Pharisees were

---

5:33
[a] Matt 9:14;
Mark 2:18

5:36
[b] Matt 9:16-17;
Mark 2:21-22

6:1
[c] Matt 12:1;
Mark 2:23

6:2
[d] Exod 20:10

6:3
[e] 1Sam 21:6

6:4
[f] Lev 24:9

6:6
[g] Matt 12:9;
Mark 3:1;
Lk 13:14;
14:3 John 9:16

---

a 5:33 Lit. *yours*   b 5:37 Lit. *it*   c 5:39 Other mss. lack this verse
d 6:1 Other mss. read *on a Sabbath*   e 6:1,6:6 Lit. *he*

6:12
ᵃMatt 14:23

6:13
ᵇMatt 10:1

6:14
ᶜJohn 1:42

6:16
ᵈJude 1:1

6:17
ᵉMatt 4:25;
Mark 3:7

6:19
ᶠMatt 14:36;
Mark 5:30;
Lk 8:46

watching Jesus[a] closely to see[b] whether he would heal on the Sabbath, in order to find a way of accusing him of doing something wrong. ⁸But Jesus[c] knew what they were thinking. So he said to the man with the paralyzed hand, "Get up, and stand in the middle of the synagogue."[d] So he got up and stood there.

⁹Then Jesus said to them, "I ask you, is it lawful to do good or to do evil on the Sabbath, to save a life or to destroy it?" ¹⁰He looked around at all of them and then said to the man,[e] "Hold out your hand." The man[f] did so, and his hand was restored to health. ¹¹The others were filled with fury[g] and began to discuss with each other what they could do to Jesus.

Jesus Appoints Twelve Apostles
(Matthew 10:1–4; Mark 3:13–19)

¹²Now it was in those days that Jesus[c] went to a mountain to pray. He spent the whole night in prayer to God.[a] ¹³When day came, he called his disciples and chose twelve of them, whom he also called apostles:[b] ¹⁴Simon (whom Jesus[c] named Peter), his brother Andrew, James, John, Philip, Bartholemew,[c] ¹⁵Matthew, Thomas, James (the son of Alphaeus), Simon (who was called the Zealot), ¹⁶Judas (the son of James), and Judas Iscariot (who became a traitor).[d]

Jesus Ministers to Many People
(Matthew 4:23–25)

¹⁷Then Jesus[c] came down with them and stood on a level place, along with a huge crowd of his disciples and a large gathering of people from all over Judea, Jerusalem, and the seacoast of Tyre and Sidon.[e] ¹⁸They had come to hear him and to be healed of their diseases. Even those who were being tormented by unclean spirits were being healed. ¹⁹The entire crowd was trying to touch him, because power was coming out from him and healing all of them.[f]

---

a6:7 Lit. *him* b6:7 The Gk. lacks *to see* c6:8,6:12,6:14,6:17 Lit. *he* d6:8 Lit. *in the middle* e6:10 Lit. *to him* f6:10 Lit. *He* g6:11 Or *were stupefied*

Jesus Pronounces Blessings and Judgment
(Matthew 5:1–12)

²⁰Then Jesusᵃ looked at his disciples and said,ᵃ

> "How blessed are you who are poor,
> for the kingdom of God is yours!
> ²¹How blessed are you who are hungry now,ᵇ
> for you will be satisfied!
> How blessed are you who are crying now,
> for you will laugh!

²²How blessed are you whenever people hate you, avoid you, insult you, and slander you because of the Son of Man!ᶜ ²³Rejoice in that day and leap for joy, for your reward in heaven is great! For that's the way their ancestors used to treat the prophets.ᵈ

> ²⁴"But how terrible it will be for you who are rich,ᵉ
> for you have had your comfort!
> ²⁵How terrible it will be for you who are full
> now,ᶠ
> for you will be hungry!
> How terrible it will be for you who are laughing
> now,
> for you will mourn and cry!

²⁶How terrible it will be for you when everyone says nice things about you, for that's the way their ancestors used to treat the false prophets!"ᵍ

Love for Enemies
(Matthew 5:38–48; 7:12a)

²⁷"But I say to you who are listening: Love your enemies. Do good to those who hate you.ʰ ²⁸Bless those who curse you, and pray for those who insult you.ⁱ ²⁹If someone strikes you on the cheek, offer him the other one as well, and if someone takes your coat, don't keep back your shirt either.ʲ ³⁰Keep on giving to everyone who asks you for something, and if anyone takes what is yours, don't insist on

---

ᵃ6:20 Lit. he

6:20
ᵃMatt 5:3; 11:5;
James 2:5

6:21
ᵇIsa 55:1; 61:3;
65:13; Matt 5:4,6

6:22
ᶜMatt 5:11;
John 16:2;
1Peter 2:19; 3:14;
4:14

6:23
ᵈMatt 5:12;
Acts 5:41; 7:51;
Col 1:24;
James 1:2

6:24
ᵉAmos 6:1;
Matt 6:2,5,16;
Lk 12:21; 16:25;
James 5:1

6:25
ᶠProv 14:13;
Isa 65:13

6:26
ᵍJohn 15:19;
1John 4:5

6:27
ʰExod 23:4;
Prov 25:2;
Matt 5:44;
Lk 5:35;
Rom 12:20

6:28
ⁱLk 23:34;
Acts 7:60

6:29
ʲMatt 5:39;
1Cor 6:7

6:30
a Deut 15:7-8,10;
Prov 21:26;
Matt 5:42

6:31
b Matt 7:12

6:32
c Matt 5:46

6:34
d Matt 5:42

6:35
e Ps 37:26,30;
Matt 5:45;
Lk 6:27

6:36
f Matt 5:48

6:37
g Matt 7:1

6:38
h Ps 79:12;
Prov 19:17;
Matt 7:2;
Mark 4:24;
James 2:13

6:39
i Matt 15:14

6:40
j Matt 10:24;
John 13:16; 15:20

6:41
k Matt 7:3

6:42
l Prov 18:17

6:43
m Matt 7:16-17

getting it back.*a* 31Whatever you want people to do for you, do the same for them.*b*

32"If you love those who love you, what thanks do you deserve? Why, even sinners love those who love them.*c* 33If you do good to those who do good to you, what thanks do you deserve? Even sinners do that. 34If you lend anything to those from whom you expect to get something back, what thanks do you deserve? Even sinners lend to sinners to get back what they lend.*d* 35Rather, love your enemies, do good to them, and lend to them, expecting nothing in return. Then your reward will be great, and you will be children of the Most High. For he is kind to ungrateful and evil people.*e* 36Be merciful, just as your Father is merciful."*f*

Judging Others
(Matthew 7:1–5)

37"Stop judging, and you will never be judged. Stop condemning, and you will never be condemned. Forgive, and you will be forgiven.*g* 38Give, and it will be given to you. A large quantity, pressed together, shaken down, and running over will be put into your lap. For with the measure you use,*a* you will be the measured."*h*

39He also told them a parable: "One blind person can't lead another blind person, can he? Both will fall into a ditch, won't they?*i* 40A disciple is not better than his teacher. But everyone who is fully-trained will be like his teacher.*j*

41"Why do you see the speck in your brother's eye but fail to notice the beam in your own eye?*k* 42How can you say to your brother, 'Brother, let me take the speck out of your eye,' when you don't see the beam in your own eye? You hypocrite! First remove the beam from your own eye, and then you'll see clearly enough to remove the speck from your brother's eye."*l*

A Tree Is Known by Its Fruit
(Matthew 7:17–20; 12:34b–35)

43"A good tree doesn't produce rotten fruit, and a rotten tree doesn't produce good fruit.*m* 44For every tree is known

a 6:38 Lit. *measure*

by its own fruit. People[a] don't gather figs from thorny plants or pick grapes from a thorn bush.[a] 45A good person produces good from the good treasure of his heart, and an evil person produces evil from an evil treasure. For it is out of the abundance of the heart that the mouth speaks."[b]

The Two Foundations
(Matthew 7:24–27)

46"Why do you keep calling me 'Lord, Lord,' but don't do what I tell you?[c] 47I will show you what everyone is like who comes to me, hears my words, and acts on them.[d] 48He is like a person building a house, who dug a deep hole to lay the foundation on rock. When a flood came, the floodwaters pushed against that house but couldn't shake it, because it had been founded on the rock.[b] 49But the person who hears what I say[c] but doesn't act on it is like someone who built a house on the ground without any foundation. When the floodwaters pushed against it, that house[d] quickly collapsed, and the ruin of that house was tremendous."

Jesus Heals a Centurion's Servant
(Matthew 8:5–13; John 4:43–54)

7 1After Jesus[e] had finished saying all these things[f] in the hearing of the people, he went to Capernaum.[e] 2There a centurion's servant, whom he valued highly, was sick and about to die. 3When the centurion[e] heard about Jesus, he sent some Jewish elders to him to ask him to come and save his servant's life. 4So they went to Jesus and kept pleading with him, "He deserves to have this done for him, 5because he loves our people and built our synagogue for us."

6So Jesus went with them. He was not far from the house when the centurion sent friends to tell Jesus,[g] "Sir,[h] stop troubling yourself. For I'm not worthy to have you come into my house.[i] 7That's why I didn't presume to come to you. But just say the word, and let my servant be healed. 8For I, too, am a man under authority and have soldiers

---

a 6:44 Lit. They　　b 6:48 Other mss. read had been well built　　c 6:49 The Gk. lacks what I say　　d 6:49 Lit. it　　e 7:1,7:3 Lit. he　　f 7:1 Lit. finished all his sayings　　g 7:6 Lit. him　　h 7:6 Or Lord　　i 7:6 Lit. under my roof

6:44
a Matt 12:33

6:45
b Matt 12:34-35

6:46
c Mal 1:6;
Matt 7:21; 25:11;
Lk 13:25

6:47
d Matt 7:24

7:1
e Matt 8:5

7:14
a John 11:43;
Acts 9:40;
Rom 4:17

under me. I say to one 'Go' and he goes, to another 'Come' and he comes, and to my servant 'Do this' and he does it."

⁹When Jesus heard this, he was amazed at him. Turning to the crowd that was following him, he said, "I tell you, not even in Israel have I found this kind of faith!" ¹⁰Then the men who had been sent returned to the house and found the servant in perfect health.

Jesus Raises a Widow's Son

¹¹Soon afterwards, Jesusª went to a city called Nain. His disciples and a large crowd were going along with him. ¹²As he approached the entrance to the city, a man who had died was being carried out. He was his mother's only son, and she was a widow. A large crowd from the city was with her. ¹³When the Lord saw her, he felt compassion for her. He said to her, "Stop crying." ¹⁴Then he went up and touched the open coffin, and the men who were carrying it stopped. He said, "Young man, I say to you, get up!"ª ¹⁵The dead man sat up and began to speak, and Jesusª gave him back to his

7:16
b Lk 1:65,68;
24:19; John 4:19;
6:14; 9:17

mother. ¹⁶Fear gripped everyone, and they began to praise God, saying, "A great prophet has appeared among us," and "God has helped his people."ᵇ ¹⁷This news about Jesusᵇ spread throughout Judea and all the surrounding countryside.

John the Baptist Sends Messengers to Jesus
(Matthew 11:2–19)

¹⁸John's disciples told him about all these things. So John called two of his disciplesᶜ ¹⁹and sent them to the Lord to ask, "Are you the Coming One, or should we wait for someone else?" ²⁰When the men had come to him, they said, "John the Baptist has sent us to you to ask, 'Are you the Coming One, or should we wait for someone else?' " ²¹At that time Jesusª had healed many people of diseases, plagues, and evil spirits and had given sight to many who were blind. ²²So he answered them, "Go and tell John what you have seen and heard: the blind see, the lame walk, lepers are cleansed, the deaf hear again, the dead are raised,

7:18
c Matt 11:2

---

a *7:11,7:15,7:21* Lit. *he*   **b** *7:17* Lit. *about him*

and the destitute hear the good news.[a] 23How blessed is anyone who is not offended by me!"

24When John's messengers had gone, Jesus[a] began to speak to the crowds about him.[b] "What did you go out into the wilderness to see? A reed shaken by the wind?[b] 25Really, what did you go out to see? A man dressed in fancy clothes? See, those who wear fine clothes and live in luxury are in royal palaces. 26Really, what did you go out to see? A prophet? Yes, I tell you, and even more than a prophet! 27This is the man about whom it is written,[c]

'See, I'm sending my messenger ahead of you,
    who will prepare your way before you.'[c]

28I tell you, among those born of women no one is greater than John. Yet even the least important person in the kingdom of heaven is greater than he."
29All the people who heard this, including the tax collectors, acknowledged that God was right,[d] for they had been baptized with John's baptism.[d] 30But the Pharisees and the experts in the Law rejected God's plan for themselves[e] by refusing to be baptized by him.[e] 31"To what can I compare the people of this generation?[f] 32They are like little children who sit in the marketplace and shout to each other,

'A wedding song we played for you,
    The dance you did but scorn.
A woeful dirge we chanted, too,
    But then you did not mourn.'

33For John the Baptist has come neither eating bread nor drinking wine, yet you say, 'He has a demon!'[g] 34The Son of Man has come eating and drinking, and you say, 'Look, a glutton and a drunk, a friend of tax collectors and notorious[f] sinners!'

35Absolved from every act of sin,[h]
    Is wisdom by her kith and kin."[g]

---

a7:24 Lit. he   b7:24 Lit. about John   c7:27 Mal 3:1; Exod 23:20
d7:29 Or acknowledged God's judgment   e7:30 Or God's decision in their case   f7:34 The Gk. lacks notorious   g7:35 Lit. by all her children; other mss. read by her children

7:22 aIsa 35:5; Matt 11:5; Lk 4:18
7:24 bMatt 11:7
7:27 cMal 3:1
7:29 dMatt 3:5; Lk 3:12
7:30 eActs 20:27
7:31 fMatt 11:16
7:33 gMatt 3:4; Mark 1:6; Lk 1:15
7:35 hMatt 11:19

7:36
a Matt 26:6;
Mark 14:3;
John 11:2

Jesus Forgives a Sinful Woman

36Now one of the Pharisees invited Jesus[a] to eat with him. So he went to the Pharisee's home and took his place at the table.[a] 37There was a woman who was a notorious[b] sinner in that city. When she learned that Jesus[c] was eating at the Pharisee's home, she took an alabaster jar of perfume

7:39
b Lk 15:2

38and knelt at his feet behind him. She was crying and began to wash his feet with her tears and dry them with her hair.[d] Then she kissed his feet over and over again and kept anointing them with the perfume. 39Now the Pharisee who had invited Jesus[a] saw this and said to himself, "If this man were a prophet, he would have known who is touching him and what kind of woman she is. She's a sinner!"[b]

7:46
c Ps 23:5

40Jesus said to him, "Simon, I have something to say to you." "Teacher," he replied, "say it." 41"Two men were in debt to a moneylender. One owed him 500 denarii,[e] and the other 50. 42When they couldn't pay it back, he generously canceled the debts for both of them. Now which of them will love him the most?" 43Simon answered, "I suppose the one

7:47
d 1 Tim 1:14

who had the larger debt canceled." Jesus[f] said to him, "You have answered correctly."

44Then, turning to the woman, he said to Simon, "Do you see this woman? I came into your house. You didn't give me any water for my feet, but this woman has washed my feet

7:48
e Matt 9:2;
Mark 2:5

with her tears and dried them with her hair. 45You didn't give me a kiss, but this woman, from the moment I came in, has not stopped kissing my feet. 46You didn't anoint my head with oil, but this woman has anointed my feet with perfume.[c] 47So I'm telling you that her sins, as many as they are, have been forgiven, and that's why she has shown great love. But the one to whom little is forgiven loves little."[d]

7:49
f Matt 9:3;
Mark 2:7

48Then Jesus[c] said to her, "Your sins are forgiven!"[e] 49Those who were at the table with them began to say among themselves, "Who is this man who even forgives sins?"[f] 50But Jesus[c] said to the woman, "Your faith had saved you. Go in peace."[g]

7:50
g Matt 9:22;
Mark 5:34; 10:52;
Lk 8:48; 18:42

a 7:36,7:39 Lit. *him*   b 7:37 The Gk. lacks *notorious*   c 7:37,7:48,7:50 Lit. *he*   d 7:38 Lit. *the hair of her head*   e 7:41 A denarius was the usual day's wage for a laborer.   f 7:43 Lit. *He*

Some Women Accompany Jesus

8:2
a Matt 27:55-56;
Mark 16:9

8 ¹After this Jesusᵃ traveled from one city and village to another, preaching and spreading the good news about God's kingdom. The twelve were with him, ²as well as some women who had been healed of evil spirits and illnesses: Mary, also called Magdalene, from whom seven demons had gone out;ᵃ ³Joanna, the wife of Herod's household manager Chuza; Susanna; and many other women. These womenᵇ continued to support themᶜ out of their personal resources.

The Parable about a Sower
(Matthew 13:1–9; Mark 4:1–9)

8:4
b Matt 13:2;
Mark 4:1

⁴Now while a large crowd was gathering and people were coming to him from every city, he said in a parable:ᵇ ⁵"A sower went out to sow his seed. As he was sowing, some seeds fell along the path, were trampled on, and the birds of the sky ate them up. ⁶Others fell on stony ground, and as soon as they grew up, they dried up because they had no moisture. ⁷Others fell among thornbushes, and the thornbushes grew with them and choked them. ⁸But others fell on good soil, and when they came up, they produced a hundred times as much as was planted." As he said this, he called out, "Let the person who has ears to hear listen!"

The Purpose of the Parables
(Matthew 13:10–17; Mark 4:10–12)

8:9
c Matt 13:10;
Mark 4:10

⁹Then his disciples began to ask him what this parable meant.ᶜ ¹⁰So he said, "You have been given knowledge about the secrets of the kingdom of God. But to others they are givenᵈ in parables, so thatᵈ

'they look but don't see,
    and they listen but don't understand.' "ᵉ

Jesus Explains the Parable about the Sower
(Matthew 13:18–23; Mark 4:13–20)

¹¹"Now this is what the parable means. The seed is

---

a 8:1 Lit. *he*   b 8:3 Lit. *They*   c 8:3 Other mss. read *him*   d 8:10 The Gk. lacks *they are given*   e 8:10 Isa 6:9-10

8:10
d Isa 6:9;
Mark 4:12

8:11
a Matt 13:18;
Mark 4:14

8:16
b Matt 5:15;
Mark 4:21;
Lk 11:33

8:17
c Matt 10:26;
Lk 12:2

8:18
d Matt 13:12;
25:29; Lk 19:26

8:19
e Matt 12:46;
Mark 3:31

God's word.[a] [12]The ones on the path are the people who listen, but then the devil comes and takes the word away from their hearts, so that they may not believe and be saved. [13]The ones on the stony ground are the people who welcome the word with joy when they hear it. But since they don't have any roots, they believe for a while but in a time of testing fall away. [14]The ones that fell among the thornbushes are the people who listen, but as they go on their way they are choked by the worries, wealth, and pleasures of life, and their fruit doesn't mature. [15]But the ones on the good soil are the people who also hear the word but hold on to it with good and honest hearts and produce a crop through endurance."

A Light under a Bowl
(Mark 4:21–25)

[16]"No one lights a lamp and hides it under a bowl or puts it under a bed. Instead, he puts it on a lampstand so that those who come in will see the light.[b] [17]For there is nothing hidden that will not be revealed, and there is nothing secret that will not become known and come to light.[c] [18]So pay attention to how you listen. For to the one who has, more will be given. However, from the one who doesn't have, even what he thinks he has will be taken away from him."[d]

The True Family of Jesus
(Matthew 12:46–50; Mark 3:31–35)

[19]His mother and his brothers came to him, but they couldn't get near him because of the crowd.[e] [20]He was told, "Your mother and your brothers are standing outside and want to see you." [21]But he answered them, "My mother and my brothers are those who hear the word of God and do it."

Jesus Calms the Sea
(Matthew 8:23–27; Mark 4:35–41)

[22]One day Jesus[a] and his disciples got into a boat. He said to them, "Let's cross to the other side of the lake." So

---

a 8:22 Lit. *he*

they started out.[a] 23Now as they were sailing, Jesus[a] fell asleep. A violent storm swept over the lake, and they were taking on water and were in great danger. 24So they went to him, woke him up, and said, "Master! Master! We're going to die!" He got up and reprimanded the wind and the raging waves. They stopped, and there was calm. 25Then he asked the disciples,[b] "Where is your faith?" Frightened and amazed, they asked one another, "Who is this man? He commands even the winds and the water, and they obey him!"

Jesus Heals a Demon-Possessed Man
(Matthew 8:28–34; Mark 5:1–20)

26They landed in the region of the Gerasenes,[c] which is just across the lake from Galilee.[b] 27When Jesus[a] stepped out on the shore, a certain man from the city met him. The man was controlled by[d] demons and had not worn clothes for a long time. He did not live in a house but in the tombs. 28When he saw Jesus, he screamed, fell down in front of him, and said in a loud voice, "What do you want from me, Jesus, Son of the Most High God? I beg you not to torture me!" 29For Jesus[a] was in the process of ordering the unclean spirit to come out of the man. On many occasions the unclean spirit[e] had seized the man,[f] and though he was kept under guard and bound with chains and shackles, he would break the chains and be driven by the demon into deserted places. 30Jesus asked him, "What's your name?" He answered, "Legion,"[g] for many demons had gone into him. 31Then the demons[h] began begging Jesus[f] not to order them to go into the bottomless pit.[c]

32Now a large herd of pigs was grazing there on the hillside. So the demons[h] begged Jesus[f] to let them go into those pigs, and he let them do this. 33Then the demons came out of the man and went into the pigs, and the herd rushed down the cliff into the lake and drowned.

---

a 8:23,8:27,8:29 Lit. he   b 8:25 Lit. them   c 8:26 Other mss. read
Gadarenes; still other mss. read Gergesenes   d 8:27 Lit. He had   e 8:29 Lit.
it   f 8:29,8:31,8:32 Lit. him   g 8:30 A Roman legion consisted of about
6,000 men.   h 8:31,8:32 Lit. they

8:22
a Matt 8:23;
Mark 4:35

8:26
b Matt 8:28;
Mark 5:1

8:31
c Rev 20:3

8:37
a Matt 8:34;
Acts 16:39

34When those who had taken care of the pigs saw what had happened, they ran away and reported it in the city and in the countryside. 35So the people[a] went out to see what had happened. When they came to Jesus and found the man from whom the demons had gone out sitting at Jesus' feet, dressed and in his right mind, they were frightened. 36The people who had seen it told them how the demon-possessed man had been healed. 37Then all the people from the region surrounding the Gerasenes[b] asked Jesus[c] to leave them, because they were terrified. So he got into a boat and started back.[a]

8:38
b Mark 5:18

38The man from whom the demons had gone out kept begging Jesus[c] to let him go with him. But Jesus[d] sent him away, saying,[b] 39"Go home and declare how much God has done for you." So the man[d] left and kept proclaiming throughout the whole city how much Jesus had done for him.

Jesus Heals Jairus' Daughter and a Woman with Chronic Bleeding
(Matthew 9:18–26; Mark 5:21–43)

40When Jesus came back, the crowd welcomed him, for everyone was expecting him. 41Just then a synagogue leader by the name of Jairus arrived. He fell at Jesus' feet and kept begging him to come to his home,[c] 42because his only daughter, who was about twelve years old, was dying. While Jesus[d] was on his way, the crowds continued to press in on him.

8:41
c Matt 9:18;
Mark 5:22

43In the crowd there was[e] a woman who had been suffering from chronic bleeding for twelve years. Although she had spent all she had on doctors,[f] no one could heal her.[d] 44She came up behind Jesus[g] and touched the fringe of his robe, and her bleeding stopped at once. 45Jesus asked, "Who touched me?" While everyone was denying it, Peter and those who were with him[h] said, "Master, the crowds are

---

a 8:35 Lit. *they*   b 8:37 Other mss. read *Gadarenes*; still other mss. read *Gergesenes*   c 8:37, 8:38 Lit. *him*   d 8:38, 8:39, 8:42 Lit. *he*   e 8:43 Lit. *There was*   f 8:43 Other mss. lack *Though she had spent all she had on doctors*   g 8:44 Lit. *behind him*   h 8:45 Other mss. lack *and those who were with him*

8:43
d Matt 9:20

surrounding you and pressing in on you." ⁴⁶Still Jesus said, "Somebody touched me, for I know that power has gone out of me."ᵃ

⁴⁷When the woman saw that she couldn't hide, she came forward trembling. Bowing down in front of him, she explained in the presence of all the people why she had touched Jesusᵃ and how she had been instantly healed. ⁴⁸He told her, "Daughter, your faith has made you well. Go in peace."

⁴⁹While he was still speaking, someone came from the synagogue leader's homeᵇ and said, "Your daughter is dead. Stop bothering the teacher anymore."ᵇ ⁵⁰But when Jesus heard this, he told the synagogue leader,ᵃ "Stop being afraid! Just believe, and she will get well."

⁵¹When he arrived at the house, he allowed no one to go in with him except Peter, John, James, and the child's father and mother. ⁵²Now everyone was crying and wailing for her. But Jesusᶜ said, "Stop crying! She's not dead but is sleeping."ᶜ ⁵³They laughed and laughed at him, because they knew she was dead. ⁵⁴But he took her hand and called out, "Child, get up!"ᵈ ⁵⁵So her spirit returned, and she got up at once. Then he directed that she be given something to eat. ⁵⁶Her parents were amazed, but he ordered them not to tell anyone what had happened.ᵉ

Jesus Sends Out the Twelve
(Matthew 10:5–15; Mark 6:7–13)

9 ¹Jesusᵈ called the twelve together and gave them power and authority over all the demons and to heal diseases.ᶠ ²Then he sent them to proclaim the kingdom of God and to heal the sick.ᵍ ³He told them, "Don't take anything along on the trip—no walking stick, traveling bag, bread, money, or even an extra shirt.ᵉʰ ⁴When you go into a home, stay there and leave from there.ⁱ ⁵If people don't welcome you, when you leave that city, shake its dust off your feet as a testimony against them."ʲ ⁶So they left and

---

ᵃ8:47,8:50 Lit. *him*   ᵇ8:49 Lit. *from the synagogue leader*   ᶜ8:52 Lit. *he*
ᵈ9:1 Lit. *He*   ᵉ9:3 Lit. *two shirts*

8:46
ᵃMark 5:30;
Lk 6:19

8:49
ᵇMark 5:35

8:52
ᶜJohn 11:11,13

8:54
ᵈLk 7:14;
John 11:43

8:56
ᵉMatt 8:4; 9:30;
Mark 5:43

9:1
ᶠMatt 10:1;
Mark 3:13; 6:7

9:2
ᵍMatt 10:7-8;
Mark 6:12;
Lk 10:1,9

9:3
ʰMatt 10:9;
Mark 6:8; Lk 10:4;
22:35

9:4
ⁱMatt 10:11;
Mark 6:10

9:5
ʲMatt 10:14;
Acts 13:51

9:6
ᵃMark 6:12

went from village to village, spreading the good news and healing diseases everywhere.ᵃ

Herod Tries to See Jesus
(Matthew 14:1–12; Mark 6:14–29)

9:7
ᵇMatt 14:1;
Mark 6:14

7Now Herod the tetrarch heard about everything that was happening. He was puzzled because it was said by some that John had been raised from the dead,ᵇ 8by others that Elijah had appeared, and by still others that one of the ancient prophets had come back to life. 9Herod said, "I beheaded John. But who is this man I'm hearing so much about?" So Herodᵃ kept trying to see Jesus.ᵇᶜ

Jesus Feeds More Than Five Thousand People
(Matthew 14:13–21; Mark 6:30–44; John 6:1–14)

9:9
ᶜLk 23:8

10The apostles came back and told Jesusᵇ everything they had done. Then he took them with him, and they went away by themselves to a city called Bethsaida.ᵈ 11But the crowds found out about this and followed him. He welcomed them and began to speak to them about the kingdom of God and to heal those who needed healing.

9:10
ᵈMatt 14:13;
Mark 6:30

12When the day was drawing to a close, the twelve came to him and said, "Send the crowd away to the neighboring villages and farms so they can rest and get some food, for we are here in a deserted place."ᵉ 13But he said to them, "You give them something to eat." They said, "We have nothing more than five loaves of bread and two fish—unless we go and buy food for all these people." 14Now there were about 5,000 men. So he said to his disciples, "Have them sit in groups of about fifty." 15They did this and got all of them seated. 16Taking the five loaves and the two fish, he looked up to heaven and blessed them. Then he broke the loaves in pieces and kept giving them to the disciples to pass on to the crowd. 17All of them ate and were filled. When they collected the leftover pieces, there were twelve baskets.

9:12
ᵉMatt 14:15;
Mark 6:35;
John 6:1,5

a 9:9 Lit. *he*   b 9:9,9:10 Lit. *him*

159

Peter Declares His Faith in Jesus
(Matthew 16:13–19; Mark 8:27–29)

¹⁸One day while Jesus[a] was praying privately and the disciples were with him, he asked them, "Who do the crowds say I am?"[a] ¹⁹They answered, "Some say[b] John the Baptist, others Elijah, and still others one of the ancient prophets who has come back to life."[b] ²⁰He asked them, "But who do you say I am?" Peter answered, "The Christ[c] of God."[c]

Jesus Predicts His Death and Resurrection
(Matthew 16:20–28; Mark 8:30–9:1)

²¹He strictly ordered and commanded them not to tell this to anyone.[d] ²²He said, "The Son of Man must suffer a great deal and be rejected by the elders, the high priests, and the scribes. Then he must be killed, but on the third day he will be raised."[e]

²³Then he said to all of them, "If anyone wants to come with me, he must deny himself, pick up his cross every day, and keep following me.[f] ²⁴For whoever wants to save his life will lose it, but whoever loses his life for me will save it. ²⁵What profit will a person have if he gains the whole world, but destroys himself or is lost?[g] ²⁶If anyone is ashamed of me and my words, the Son of Man will be ashamed of him when he comes in his glory and the glory of[d] the Father and the holy angels.[h] ²⁷Truly I tell you, some people who are standing here will not experience[e] death until they see the kingdom of God."[i]

Jesus' Appearance Is Changed
(Matthew 17:1–8; Mark 9:2–8)

²⁸Now about eight days after Jesus said this,[f] he took Peter, John, and James with him and went up on a mountain to pray.[j] ²⁹While he was praying, the appearance of his face changed, and his clothes turned dazzling white. ³⁰Suddenly, two men were talking with him. They were Moses and Elijah. ³¹They appeared in glory and were discussing Jesus'

---

a 9:18 Lit. *he*   **b** 9:19 The Gk. lacks *Some say*   **c** 9:20 I.e. The Messiah   **d** 9:26 Lit. *and that of*   **e** 9:27 Lit. *taste*   **f** 9:28 Lit. *after these sayings*

9:18
a Matt 16:13;
Mark 8:27

9:19
b Matt 14:2;
Lk 14:7-8

9:20
c Matt 16:16;
John 6:69

9:21
d Matt 16:20

9:22
e Matt 16:21;
17:22

9:23
f Matt 10:38;
16:24; Mark 8:34;
Lk 14:27

9:25
g Matt 16:26;
Mark 8:36

9:26
h Matt 10:33;
Mark 8:38;
2 Tim 2:12

9:27
i Matt 16:28;
Mark 9:1

9:28
j Matt 17:1;
Mark 9:2

9:32
a Dan 8:18; 10:9

death,**a** which he was about to bring to fulfillment in Jerusalem.

32Now Peter and the men with him had been overcome by sleep. When they woke up, they saw Jesus'**b** glory and the two men standing with him.*a* 33Just as Moses and Elijah**c** were leaving him, Peter said to Jesus, "Master, it's good that we're here! Let's set up three shelters**d**—one for you, one for Moses, and one for Elijah." (Peter**e** didn't know what he was saying.) 34But while he was saying this, a cloud came and overshadowed them, and they were frightened as they went into the cloud. 35Then a voice came out of the cloud and said, "This is my Son, whom I have chosen.**f** Keep listening to him!"*b* 36After the voice had spoken, Jesus was**g** alone. The disciples**h** kept silent and at that time**i** told no one about what they had seen.*c*

9:35
b Matt 3:17;
Acts 3:22

Jesus Heals a Boy with a Demon
(Matthew 17:14–18; Mark 9:14–27)

37The next day, when they had come down from the mountain, a large crowd met Jesus.**j***d* 38Suddenly a man in the crowd shouted, "Teacher, I beg you to look at my son. He's my only child.**k** 39Without warning a spirit takes control of him, and he suddenly screams, goes into convulsions, and foams at the mouth. The spirit**l** mauls him and hates to leave him. 40I begged your disciples to drive it out, but they couldn't."

9:36
c Matt 17:9

41Jesus answered, "You unbelieving and perverted generation! How much longer must I be with you and put up with you? Bring your son here!" 42Even while the boy**m** was coming, the demon knocked him to the ground and threw him into convulsions. But Jesus reprimanded the unclean spirit, healed the boy, and gave him back to his father.

Jesus Again Predicts His Death and Resurrection
(Matthew 17:22–23; Mark 9:30–32)

43So all the people continued to be amazed at the

9:37
d Matt 17:14;
Mark 9:14,17

---

a 9:31 Lit. *his departure*   **b** 9:32 Lit. *his*   **c** 9:33 Lit. *Just as they*   **d** 9:33 Or *tents*   **e** 9:33 Lit. *He*   **f** 9:35 Other mss. read *whom I love*   **g** 9:36 Lit. *was found to be*   **h** 9:36 Lit. *They*   **i** 9:36 Lit. *in those days*   **j** 9:37 Lit. *him*   **k** 9:38 Lit. *only one*; the Gk. lacks *child*   **l** 9:39 Lit. *It*   **m** 9:42 Lit. *he*

greatness of God. Indeed, everyone was astonished at all the things Jesus[a] was doing. So he said to his disciples, [44]"Listen carefully to these words.[b] The Son of Man is going to be betrayed into human hands."[a] [45]But they didn't know what this meant. Indeed, the meaning was hidden from them so that they didn't understand it, and they were afraid to ask him about this statement.[b]

True Greatness
(Matthew 18:1–5; Mark 9:33–37)

[46]Now an argument started among them as to which of them might be the greatest.[c] [47]But Jesus, knowing their inner thoughts, took a little child and had him stand beside him. [48]Then he said to them, "Whoever welcomes this little child in my name welcomes me, and whoever welcomes me welcomes the one who sent me. For the one who is least among all of you is the one who is greatest."[d]

The Person Who Isn't against You Is for You
(Mark 9:38–40)

[49]John said, "Master, we saw someone driving out demons in your name. We tried to stop him, because he wasn't a follower like us."[e] [50]Jesus said to him, "Don't stop him! For whoever is not against you is for you."[f]

A Samaritan Village Refuses to Welcome Jesus
[51]When the days grew closer for Jesus[c] to be taken up to heaven,[d] he was determined to continue his journey to Jerusalem.[g] [52]So he sent messengers on ahead of him. On their way they went into a Samaritan village to get things ready for him. [53]But the people[e] didn't welcome him, because he was determined to go to Jerusalem.[h] [54]When his disciples James and John saw this, they asked, "Lord, do you want us to call fire down from heaven to destroy them, as Elijah did?[f][i] [55]But he turned and reprimanded them. [56]Then they went on to another village.[j]

---

a 9:43 Lit. *he*　　**b** 9:44 Lit. *Put these words into your ears*　　**c** 9:51 Lit. *for him*
d 9:51 Lit. *to be taken up*　　**e** 9:53 Lit. *they*　　**f** 9:54 Other mss. lack *as Elijah did*

Marginal references:

9:44 *a* Matt 17:22

9:45 *b* Mark 9:32; Lk 2:50; 18:34

9:46 *c* Matt 18:1; Mark 9:34

9:48 *d* Matt 10:40; 18:5; 23:11-12; Mark 9:37; John 12:44; 13:20

9:49 *e* Num 11:28; Mark 9:38

9:50 *f* Matt 12:30; Lk 11:23

9:51 *g* Mark 16:19; Acts 1:2

9:53 *h* John 4:4,9

9:54 *i* 2Kings 1:10,12

9:56 *j* John 3:17; 12:47

9:57
a Matt 8:19

9:59
b Matt 8:21

9:61
c 1Kings 19:20

10:1
d Matt 10:1;
Mark 6:7

10:2
e Matt 9:37-38;
John 4:35;
2Thes 3:1

10:3
f Matt 10:16

10:4
g 2Kings 4:29;
Matt 10:9-10;
Mark 6:8; Lk 9:3

10:5
h Matt 10:12

10:7
i Matt 10:10-11;
1Cor 9:4; 10:27;
1Tim 5:18

10:9
j Matt 3:2; 4:17;
10:7; Lk 9:2;
10:11

The Would-Be Followers of Jesus
(Matthew 8:19–22)

57While they were walking along the road, a man said to him, "I will follow you wherever you go."[a] 58Jesus told him,

"Foxes have holes and birds[a] have nests,
But the Son of Man has no place to rest."[b]

59He told another man, "Follow me." But he said, "Lord,[c] first let me go and bury my father."[b] 60But he told him, "Let the dead bury their own dead. But you go and proclaim the kingdom of God."

61Still another man said, "I will follow you, Lord, but first let me say goodbye to those at home."[c] 62Jesus told him, "No one who puts his hand to the plow and looks back is fit for the kingdom of God."

The Mission of the Seventy

10 1After this the Lord appointed seventy[d] other disciples[e] and sent them ahead of him in pairs to every town and place that he intended to go.[d] 2He was telling them, "The harvest is vast, but the workers are few. So ask the Lord of the harvest to send workers out into his harvest.[e] 3Get going! See, I am sending you out like lambs among wolves.[f] 4Don't carry a wallet, a traveling bag, or sandals, and don't greet anyone on the way.[g]

5"Whatever house you go into, first say, 'May there be peace in this house.'[h] 6If a peaceful person lives there, your greeting of peace will remain with him. But if that's not the case, your greeting[f] will come back to you. 7Stay with the same family, eating and drinking whatever they provide, for the worker deserves his pay. Don't move around from house to house.[i]

8"Whenever you go into a town and the people[g] welcome you, eat whatever they serve you, 9heal the sick that are there, and tell them, 'The kingdom of God is near you!'[j] 10But whenever you go into a town and people[g] don't

---

a 9:58 Lit. birds in the sky   b 9:58 Lit. no place to lay his head
c 9:59 Other mss. lack Lord   d 10:1 Other mss. read seventy-two
e 10:1 Lit. others   f 10:6 Lit. it   g 10:8,10:10 Lit. they

welcome you, go out into its streets and say, [11]'We are wiping off your town's dust that clings to our feet in protest against you! But realize this: the kingdom of God is near!'[a] [12]I tell you, on that day it will be easier for Sodom than for that town!'"[b]

Jesus Denounces Unrepentant Cities
(Matthew 11:20–24)

[13]"How terrible it will be for you, Chorazin! How terrible it will be for you, Bethsaida! For if the miracles that happened in you had taken place in Tyre and Sidon, they would have repented long ago, sitting in sackcloth and ashes.[c] [14]It will be easier for Tyre and Sidon at the judgment than for you! [15]And you, Capernaum! You won't be lifted up to heaven, will you? You'll go down to the grave![a][d] [16]The person who listens to you listens to me, and the person who rejects you rejects me. The person who rejects me rejects the one who sent me."[e]

The Return of the Seventy

[17]The seventy[b] came back and joyously reported, "Lord, even the demons are submitting to us in your name!"[f] [18]He said to them, "I was watching Satan fall from heaven like lightning.[g] [19]Look! I have given you the authority to trample snakes and scorpions and to destroy[c] all the enemy's power, and nothing will ever hurt you.[h] [20]However, stop being joyful because the spirits are submitting to you. Rather, be joyful because your names are written in heaven."[i]

Jesus Praises the Father
(Matthew 11:25–27; 13:16–17)

[21]In that hour Jesus[d] was extremely joyful in the Holy Spirit[e] and said, "I praise you, Father, Lord of heaven and earth, because you have hidden these things from wise and intelligent people and have revealed them to infants. Yes, Father, for this is what was pleasing to you.[j] [22]All things have been entrusted to me by my Father. No one knows

---

a 10:15 Gk. *Hades*, a reference to the realm of the dead   b 10:17 Other mss. read *seventy-two*   c 10:19 Lit. *and over*   d 10:21 Lit. *he*   e 10:21 Other mss. read *in the spirit*

10:11
a Matt 10:14;
Lk 9:5;
Acts 13:51; 18:6

10:12
b Matt 10:15;
Mark 6:11

10:13
c Ezek 3:6;
Matt 11:21

10:15
d Gen 11:4;
Deut 1:28;
Isa 14:13;
Jer 51:53;
Ezek 26:20;
32:18; Matt 11:23

10:16
e Matt 10:40;
Mark 9:37;
John 5:23; 13:20;
1 Thes 4:8

10:17
f Lk 10:1

10:18
g John 12:31;
16:11; Rev 9:1;
12:8-9

10:19
h Mark 16:18;
Acts 28:5

10:20
i Exod 32:32;
Ps 69:28; Isa 4:3;
Dan 12:1;
Phil 4:3;
Heb 12:23;
Rev 13:8; 20:12;
21:27

10:21
j Matt 11:25

10:22
a Matt 28:18;
John 1:18; 3:35;
5:27; 6:44,46;
17:2

10:23
b Matt 13:16

10:24
c 1Peter 1:10

10:25
d Matt 19:16;
22:35

10:27
e Lev 19:18;
Deut 6:5

10:28
f Lev 18:5;
Neh 9:29;
Ezek 20:11,13,21;
Rom 10:5

10:29
g Lk 16:15

10:31
h Ps 38:11

10:33
i John 4:9

who the Son is except the Father, and no one knows who[a] the Father is except the Son and the person to whom the Son chooses to reveal him."[a]

23Then he turned to the disciples in private and said to them, "How blessed are the eyes that see what you see![b] 24For I tell you, many prophets and kings wanted to see the things you see but didn't see them, and to hear the things you hear but didn't hear them."[c]

The Good Samaritan

25Just then an expert in the Law stood up to test Jesus.[b] He asked, "Teacher, what must I do to inherit eternal life?"[d] 26Jesus[c] answered him, "What is written in the Law? What do you read there?" 27He answered, "You must love the Lord your God with all your heart, with all your soul, with all your strength, and with all your mind.[d] And you must love[e] your neighbor as yourself."[f][e] 28Jesus[c] told him, "You have answered correctly. Do this, and you will live."[f]

29But the man wanted to justify himself, so he asked Jesus, "And who is my neighbor?"[g] 30After careful consideration, Jesus replied, "A man was going down from Jerusalem to Jericho when he fell into the hands of bandits. They stripped him, beat him, and went away, leaving him half dead. 31By chance, a priest was traveling along that road. When he saw the man,[b] he went by on the other side.[h] 32Similarly, a Levite came to that place. When he saw the man,[b] he also went by on the other side. 33But as he was traveling along, a Samaritan came across the man.[b] When the Samaritan[g] saw him, he was moved with compassion.[i] 34He went to him and bandaged his wounds, pouring oil and wine on them. Then he put him on his own animal, brought him to an inn, and took care of him. 35The next day he took out two denarii[h] and gave them to the innkeeper, saying, 'Take good care of him. If you spend more than that, I'll repay you when I come back.'

---

a 10:22 Lit. *and who*   b 10:25,10:31,10:32,10:33 Lit. *him*   c 10:26,10:28 Lit. *He*   d 10:27 Deut 6:5   e 10:27 The Gk. lacks *you must love*   f 10:27 Lev 19:18   g 10:33 Lit. *he*   h 10:35 A denarius was the usual day's wage for a laborer.

10:38
a John 11:1;
12:2-3

[36]"Of these three men, who do you think was a neighbor to the man who fell into the hands of the bandits?" [37]He said, "The one who showed mercy to him." Jesus told him, "Go and do what he did."

Jesus Visits Mary and Martha

[38]Now as they were traveling along, Jesus[a] went into a village. A woman named Martha welcomed him into her home.[a] [39]She had a sister named Mary, who sat down at the Lord's feet and kept listening to what he was saying.[b] [40]But Martha was worrying about all the things she had to do, so she came to him and asked, "Lord, you do care that my sister has left me to do the work all by myself, don't you? Then tell her to help me." [41]The Lord answered her, "Martha, Martha! You worry and fuss about a lot of things. [42]But there's only[b] one thing you need. Mary has chosen what is better,[c] and it is not to be taken away from her."[c]

10:39
b Lk 8:35;
Acts 22:3;
1Cor 7:32

Teaching about Prayer
(Matthew 6:9–15; 7:7–11)

11 [1]Once Jesus[a] was praying in a certain place. After he had finished, one of his disciples said to him, "Lord, teach us to pray, as John taught his disciples." [2]So he told them, "Whenever you pray you are to say,[d]

> 'Father,[d] may your name be kept holy.
> May your kingdom come.[e]
> [3]Every day, keep giving us our daily bread,[f]
> [4]and forgive us our sins,
>   as we forgive everyone who sins against us.[g]
> And never bring us into temptation.' "[h]

10:42
c Ps 27:4

[5]Then he said to them, "Suppose one of you has a friend, and you go to him at midnight and say to him, 'Friend, let me borrow three loaves of bread. [6]A friend of mine on a trip

---

a 10:38,11:1 Lit. *he* b 10:42 Other mss. read *out of a few things, there's only* c 10:42 Lit. *the better part* d 11:2 Other mss. read *Our Father in heaven* e 11:2 Other mss. read *kingdom come. May your will be done, on earth as it is in heaven* f 11:3 Or *our bread from above* g 11:4 Lit. *is indebted to us* h 11:4 Other mss. read *into temptation, but deliver us from the evil one*

11:2
d Matt 6:9

11:8
a Lk 18:1

has dropped in on me, and I don't have anything to serve him.' 7Suppose he answers from inside, 'Stop bothering me! The door is already locked, and my children are with me in bed. I can't get up and give you anything!' 8I tell you, even though he doesn't want to get up and give him anything because he is his friend, he will get up and give him whatever he needs because of his persistence.a 9So I say to you:

11:9
b Matt 7:7; 21:22;
Mark 11:24;
John 15:7;
James 1:6;
1 John 3:22

Keep asking, and it will be given you. Keep searching, and you will find. Keep knocking, and the doora will be opened for you.b 10For everyone who keeps asking will receive, and the person who keeps searching will find, and the person who keeps knocking will have the doora opened.

11What father among you, if his son asks for bread, would give him a stone, or if he asks for a fish,b would give

11:11
c Matt 7:9

him a snake instead of the fish?c 12Or if he asks for an egg, would he give him a scorpion? 13So if you who are evil know how to give good gifts to your children, how much more will the Father in heaven give the Holy Spirit to those who keep asking him!"

Jesus Is Accused of Working with Beelzebul
(Matthew 12:22–30; Mark 3:20–27)

11:14
d Matt 9:32; 12:22

14Jesusc was driving a demon out of a man who wasd unable to talk. When the demon had gone out, the mane began to speak, and the crowds were amazed.d 15But some of them said, "He drives out demons by Beelzebul, the ruler

11:15
e Matt 9:34; 12:24

of the demons."e 16Others, wanting to test Jesus,f kept asking him for a sign from heaven.f

17Since he knew what they were thinking, he said to them, "Every kingdom divided against itself is devastated, and a divided household collapses.gg 18Now if Satan is divided against himself, how can his kingdom last? For you

11:16
f Matt 12:38; 16:1

say that I drive out demons by Beelzebul. 19And if I drive out demons by Beelzebul, by whom do your own followersh drive them out? That's why they will be your judges! 20But

11:17
g Matt 12:25;
Mark 3:24;
John 2:25

a 11:9,11:10 Lit. it   b 11:11 Other mss. read What father among you, if his son asks for a fish   c 11:14 Lit. He   d 11:14 Lit. driving out a demon that was   e 11:14 Lit. the man who was unable to talk   f 11:16 Lit. him   g 11:17 Lit. and house falls on house   h 11:19 Lit. sons

if I drive out demons by the finger[a] of God, then the kingdom of God has come to you.[a]

21"When a strong man, fully armed, guards his own mansion, his property is safe.[b] 22But when a stronger man than he attacks him and defeats him, he'll take away his armor in which he trusted and divide his plunder.[c] 23The person who isn't with me is against me, and the person who doesn't gather with me scatters."[d]

The Return of the Unclean Spirit
(Matthew 12:43–45)

24"Whenever an unclean spirit goes out of a person, it wanders through dry places looking for a place to rest but doesn't find any. So it says, 'I'll go back to my home that I left.'[e] 25When it arrives, it finds it swept clean and put in order. 26Then it goes and brings with it seven other spirits more evil than itself, and they go in and settle there. And so the final condition of that person is worse than the first."[f]

True Blessedness

27While Jesus[b] was saying this, a woman in the crowd raised her voice and said to him, "How blessed is the womb that gave birth to you and the breasts that nursed you!"[g] 28But he said, "Rather, how blessed are those who hear God's word and obey it!"[h]

The Sign of Jonah
(Matthew 12:38–42; Mark 8:12)

29Now as the crowds continued to throng around Jesus,[c] he began to say, "This generation is an evil generation. It craves a sign, but no sign will be given to it except the sign of Jonah.[i] 30For just as Jonah became a sign[d] to the people of Nineveh, so the Son of Man will be a sign to this generation.[j] 31The queen of the south will stand up at the judgment with the people of this generation and will condemn them, because she came from the ends of the earth to hear the wisdom of Solomon. But look, something greater than Solomon is here![k] 32The men of Nineveh will stand up at the

---

a 11:20 I.e. power   b 11:27 Lit. *he*   c 11:29 Lit. *around him*   d 11:30 The Gk. lacks *a sign*

Margin references
11:20 *a* Exod 8:19
11:21 *b* Matt 12:29; Mark 3:27
11:22 *c* Isa 53:12; Col 2:15
11:23 *d* Matt 12:30
11:24 *e* Matt 12:43
11:26 *f* John 5:14; Heb 6:4; 10:26; 2 Peter 2:20
11:27 *g* Lk 1:28,48
11:28 *h* Matt 7:21; Lk 8:21; James 1:25
11:29 *i* Matt 12:38-39
11:30 *j* Jonah 1:17; 2:10
11:31 *k* 1 Kings 10:1

11:32
a Jonah 3:5

judgment with this generation and will condemn it, because they repented at the preaching of Jonah. But look, something greater than Jonah is here!"*a*

The Lamp of the Body

11:33
b Matt 5:15;
Mark 4:21;
Lk 8:16

(Matthew 5:15; 6:22–23)

33"No one lights a lamp and puts it in a hiding place**a** or under a basket,**b** but on a lampstand, so that those who come in may see its light.*b* 34Your eye is the lamp of your body. When your eye is healthy, your whole body is full of light.

11:34
c Matt 6:22

But when it is evil, your body is full of darkness.*c* 35So be careful that the light in you isn't darkness. 36Now if your whole body is full of light, with no part of it in darkness, it will be as full of light as when a lamp gives you light with

11:38
d Mark 7:3

its rays."

Jesus Denounces the Pharisees and the Experts in the Law

(Matthew 23:1–36; Mark 12:38–40; Luke 20:45–47)

11:39
e Matt 23:25;
Titus 1:15

37After Jesus**c** had said this, a Pharisee invited him to have a meal with him. So Jesus**c** went and took his place at the table. 38The Pharisee was surprised to see that he didn't first wash before the meal.*d* 39But the Lord said to him, "Now you Pharisees clean the outside of the cup and the dish, but inside you are full of greed and evil.*e* 40You fools!

11:41
f Isa 58:7;
Dan 4:27;
Lk 12:33

The one who made the outside made the inside, too, didn't he? 41So give what is inside to the poor, and then everything will be clean for you.*f*

11:42
g Matt 23:23

42"How terrible it will be for you Pharisees! For you give a tenth of your mint, spices, and every kind of herb, but you neglect justice and the love of God. These are the things you should have practiced, without neglecting the others.*g* 43How terrible it will be for you Pharisees! For you love to

11:43
h Matt 23:6;
Mark 12:38-39

have the places of honor in the synagogues and to be greeted in the marketplaces.*h* 44How terrible it will be for you! For you are like unmarked graves, and people walk on them without realizing it."*i*

11:44
i Ps 5:9;
Matt 23:27

a 11:33 Or *cellar*   **b** 11:33 Other mss. lack *or under a basket*   **c** 11:37 Lit. *he*

⁴⁵Then one of the experts in the Law said to him, "Teacher, when you say these things, you insult us, too." ⁴⁶Jesusᵃ said, "How terrible it will be for you experts in the Law, too! For you load people with burdens that are hard to carry, yet you yourselves don't even lift one of your fingers to ease the burdens.ᵃ ⁴⁷How terrible it will be for you! For you build monuments for the prophets, and it was your ancestors who killed them!ᵇ ⁴⁸So you are witnesses and approve of the deeds of your ancestors, because they killed those for whom you are building monuments. ⁴⁹That's why the Wisdom of God said, 'I will send them prophets and apostles. They will kill some of them and persecute others,'ᵇᶜ ⁵⁰so that this generation will be charged with the blood of all the prophets that was shed since the foundation of the world, ⁵¹from the blood of Abel to the blood of Zechariah, who died between the altar and the Sanctuary. Yes, I tell you, it will be charged against this generation!ᵈ ⁵²How terrible it will be for you experts in the Law! For you have taken away the key to knowledge. You didn't go in yourselves, and you kept out those who were trying to go in."ᵉ

⁵³When Jesusᶜ left, the scribes and the Pharisees began to fiercely oppose him and to interrogate him about many things, ⁵⁴watching him closely to trap him in something he might say.ᶠ

A Warning against Hypocrisy

12 ¹Meanwhile, the peopleᵈ had gathered by the thousands and were trampling on one another. Jesusᵃ began to speak first to his disciples. "Watch out for the yeast—that is, the hypocrisy—of the Pharisees!ᵍ ²There is nothing covered that will not be exposed and nothing secret that will not be made known.ʰ ³Accordingly, what you have said in darkness will be heard in the daylight, and what you have whisperedᵉ in private rooms will be shouted from the housetops."

ᵃ11:46,12:1 Lit. *He*   ᵇ11:49 The source of this quotation is unknown.
ᶜ11:53 Lit. *he*   ᵈ12:1 Lit. *crowd*   ᵉ12:3 Lit. *spoken in the ear*

11:46
ᵃMatt 23:4

11:47
ᵇMatt 23:29

11:49
ᶜMatt 23:34

11:51
ᵈGen 4:8;
2Chr 24:20-21

11:52
ᵉMatt 23:13

11:54
ᶠMark 12:13

12:1
ᵍMatt 16:6,12;
Mark 8:15

12:2
ʰMatt 10:26;
Mark 4:22;
Lk 8:17

12:4
a Isa 51:7-8,12-13;
Jer 1:8;
Matt 10:28;
John 15:14-15

Fear God
(Matthew 10:28–31)

4"But I tell you, my friends, never be afraid of those who kill the body and after that can't do anything more.*a* 5I'll show you the one you should be afraid of. Be afraid of the one who has the authority to throw you into hell*a* after killing you. Yes, I tell you, be afraid of him!

12:8
b Matt 10:32;
Mark 8:38;
2Tim 2:12;
1John 2:23

6"Five sparrows are sold for two pennies, aren't they? Yet not one of them is forgotten in God's sight. 7Why, even all the hairs on your head have been counted! Stop being afraid. You are worth more than a bunch of sparrows."

Acknowledging Christ
(Matthew 10:32–33; 12:32; 10:19–20)

8"But I tell you, the Son of Man will acknowledge before God's angels everyone who acknowledges me before people.*b* 9But whoever denies me before people will be denied

12:10
c Matt 12:31-32;
Mark 3:28;
1John 5:16

before God's angels. 10Everyone who speaks a word against the Son of Man will be forgiven, but the person who blasphemes against the Holy Spirit will not be forgiven.*c* 11When people*b* bring you before synagogue leaders,*c* rulers, or authorities, don't worry about how*d* you will defend yourselves or what you will say.*d* 12For in that hour the Holy Spirit will teach you what you are to say."

12:11
d Matt 10:19;
Mark 13:11;
Lk 21:14

The Parable of the Rich Fool

13Then someone in the crowd said to him, "Teacher, tell my brother to divide the family inheritance with me." 14But Jesus*e* said to him, "Mister,*f* who appointed me to be a judge or arbitrator over you people?"*g e* 15Then he said to them, "Be careful to guard yourselves against every kind of greed, for a person's life doesn't consist of the amount of possessions he has."*f*

12:14
e John 18:36

16Then he told them a parable. He said, "The land of a certain rich man produced good crops. 17So he began to think to himself, 'What should I do, since I have no place to

12:15
f 1Tim 6:7

---

a 12:5 Gk. *Gehenna*   b 12:11 Lit. *they*   c 12:11 Lit. *synagogues*
d 12:11 Lit. *about how or what*   e 12:14 Lit. *he*   f 12:14 Lit. *Man*
g 12:14 Lit. *you* (plural)

store my crops?' ¹⁸Then he said, 'This is what I'll do. I'll tear down my barns and build bigger ones, and I'll store all my grain and goods in them. ¹⁹Then I'll say to my soul, "Soul, you've stored up plenty of good things for many years. Take it easy, eat, drink, and enjoy yourself." '*a* ²⁰But God said to him, 'You fool! This very night your life will be demanded from you. Then who will get the things you've accumulated?'*b* ²¹That's how it is with the person who stores up treasures for himself and isn't rich toward God."*c*

Stop Worrying
(Matthew 6:25–34, 19–21)

²²Then Jesus*a* said to his disciples, "That's why I'm telling you to stop worrying about your life—what you will eat—or about your body—what you will wear.*d* ²³For life is more than food, and the body more than clothing. ²⁴Consider the crows.*b* They don't plant or harvest, they don't even have a storeroom or barn, yet God feeds them. How much more valuable are you than birds!*e* ²⁵Can any of you add an hour to your span of life*c* by worrying? ²⁶So if you can't do a small thing like that, why worry about other things? ²⁷Consider how the lilies grow. They don't work or spin yarn, but I tell you that not even Solomon in all his splendor was clothed like one of them. ²⁸Now if that's the way God clothes the grass in the field, which is alive today and thrown into an oven tomorrow, how much more will he clothe you—you who have little faith?

²⁹"So stop concerning yourselves about what you will eat or what you will drink, and stop being distressed. ³⁰For it is the Gentiles who are concerned about all these things. Surely your Father knows that you need them! ³¹Instead, be concerned about his*d* kingdom, and these things will be provided for you as well.*f* ³²Stop being afraid, little flock, for your Father is pleased to give you the kingdom.*g*

³³"Sell your possessions, and give the money to the poor. Make yourselves wallets that don't wear out—a dependable treasure in heaven, where no thief can get close and no moth

---

a 12:22 Lit. *he*   b 12:24 Or *ravens*   c 12:25 Or *add one cubit to your height*
d 12:31 Other mss. read *God's*

172

12:19
a Eccl 11:9;
1 Cor 15:32;
James 5:5

12:20
b Job 20:22; 27:8;
Ps 39:6; 52:7;
Jer 17:11;
James 4:14

12:21
c Matt 6:20;
Lk 6:33;
1 Tim 6:18-19;
James 2:5

12:22
d Matt 6:25

12:24
e Job 38:41;
Ps 147:9

12:31
f Matt 6:33

12:32
g Matt 11:25-26

12:33
a Matt 6:20; 19:21;
Lk 16:9;
Acts 2:45; 4:34;
1 Tim 6:19

can destroy anything.*a* ³⁴For where your treasure is, there your heart will be also."

The Watchful Servants
(Matthew 24:45–51)

12:35
b Matt 25:1;
Eph 6:14;
1 Peter 1:13

³⁵"You must keep your belts fastened and your lamps burning.*b* ³⁶Be like people who are waiting for their master to return from a wedding. As soon as he comes and knocks, they will open the door for him. ³⁷How blessed are those servants whom the master finds watching for him when he comes! Truly I tell you, he will put an apron on, make them sit down at the table, and go around and serve them.*c*

12:37
c Matt 24:46

³⁸How blessed they will be if he comes in the middle of the night or near dawn**a** and finds them awake!**b** ³⁹But be sure of this: if the homeowner had known at what hour the thief was coming, he would have watched and**c** would not have let his house be broken into.*d* ⁴⁰So be ready, because the Son of Man is coming at an hour when you don't expect him."*e*

12:39
d Matt 24:43;
1 Thes 5:2;
2 Peter 3:10;
Rev 3:3; 16:15

12:40
e Matt 24:44;
25:13;
Mark 13:33;
Lk 21:34,36;
1 Thes 5:6;
2 Peter 3:12

⁴¹Peter asked, "Lord, are you telling this parable just for us or for everyone?" ⁴²The Lord said, "Who, then, is the faithful and careful manager whom his master will put in charge of giving all his other servants their share of food at the right time?*f* ⁴³How blessed is that servant whom his master finds doing this when he comes! ⁴⁴Truly I tell you, he will put him in charge of all his property.*g*

12:42
f Matt 24:45;
25:21; 1 Cor 4:2

⁴⁵"But if that servant says to himself,**d** 'My master is taking a long time to come back,' and begins to beat the other servants and to eat, drink, and get drunk,*h* ⁴⁶the master of that servant will come on a day when he doesn't expect him and at an hour that he doesn't know. Then his master**e** will punish him severely**f** and assign him a place with unfaithful people. ⁴⁷That servant who knew what his master wanted but didn't prepare himself or do what was wanted will receive a severe beating.*i* ⁴⁸But the servant**g** who did things that deserved a beating without knowing it will receive a light beating. Much will be required from

12:44
g Matt 24:47

12:45
h Matt 24:48

12:47
i Num 15:30;
Deut 25:2;
John 9:41; 15:22;
Acts 17:30;
James 4:17

---

a 12:38 Lit. *in the second or the third watch*   **b** 12:38 Lit. *finds them so*   **c** 12:39 Other mss. lack *would have watched and*   **d** 12:45 Lit. *in his heart*   **e** 12:46 Lit. *he*   **f** 12:46 Lit. *cut him in pieces*   **g** 12:48 Lit. *the one*

everyone to whom much has been given. But even more will be demanded from the one to whom much has been entrusted."[a]

Not Peace, but Division
(Matthew 10:34–36)

49"I have come to bring fire on earth, and how I wish it were already kindled![b] 50I have a baptism to be baptized with, and what stress I am under until it is completed![c]

51"Do you think that I came to bring peace on earth? Not at all, I tell you, but rather division![d] 52From now on, five people in one household will be divided, three against two and two against three.[e] 53They will be divided father against son, son against father, mother against daughter, daughter against mother, mother-in-law against daughter-in-law, and daughter-in-law against mother-in-law."

Interpreting the Time
(Matthew 16:2–3)

54Then Jesus[a] said to the crowds, "When you see a cloud coming in the west, you immediately say, 'There's going to be a storm,' and that's what happens.[f] 55When you see a south wind blowing, you say, 'It's going to be hot,' and so it is. 56You hypocrites! You know how to interpret the appearance of the earth and the sky, yet you don't know how to interpret the present time?"

Settling with Your Opponent
(Matthew 5:25–26)

57"Why don't you judge for yourselves what is right? 58For example, when you go with your opponent in front of a ruler, do your best to settle with him on the way there. Otherwise, you will be dragged in front of the judge, and the judge will hand you over to an officer, and the officer will throw you into prison.[g] 59I tell you, you will never get out of there until you pay back the last penny!"

---

a 12:54 Lit. he

12:48
a Lev 5:17;
1 Tim 1:13

12:49
b Lk 12:51

12:50
c Matt 20:22;
Mark 10:38

12:51
d Mic 7:6;
Matt 10:34;
Lk 12:49;
John 7:43; 9:16;
10:19

12:52
e Matt 10:35

12:54
f Matt 16:2

12:58
g Ps 32:6;
Prov 25:8;
Isa 55:6;
Matt 5:25

13:6
a Isa 5:2;
Matt 21:19

Repent or Die

13

¹At that time, some people who were there told Jesus[a] about the Galileans whose blood Pilate had mixed with their sacrifices.[b] ²He asked them, "Do you think that these Galileans were more sinful than all the other Galileans because they suffered like this? ³Absolutely not, I tell you! But if you don't repent, then you, too, will all die. ⁴What about those eighteen people who were killed when the tower at Siloam fell on them? Do you think they were worse offenders than all the other people living in Jerusalem? ⁵Absolutely not, I tell you! But if you don't repent, then you, too, will all die."

The Parable about an Unfruitful Fig Tree

⁶Then Jesus[c] told them this parable: "A man had a fig tree that had been planted in his vineyard. He went to look for fruit on it but didn't find any.[a] ⁷So he said to the gardener, 'Look here! For three years I have been coming to look for fruit on this tree but haven't found any. Cut it down! Why should it waste the soil?' ⁸But the gardener[c] replied, 'Sir, leave it alone for one more year, until I dig around it and fertilize it. ⁹Maybe next year it'll bear fruit. If not, then cut it down.' "

13:13
b Mark 16:18;
Acts 9:17

Jesus Heals a Woman on the Sabbath

¹⁰Jesus[d] was teaching in one of the synagogues on the Sabbath. ¹¹A woman was there who had a spirit that had disabled her for eighteen years. She was hunched over and completely unable to stand up straight. ¹²When Jesus saw her, he called to her and said, "Woman, you are free from your illness." ¹³Then he placed his hands on her, and immediately she stood up straight and began praising God.[b]

¹⁴But the synagogue leader, indignant because Jesus had healed on the Sabbath, told the crowd, "There are six days when work is to be done. So come on those days to be healed, and not on the Sabbath day."[c] ¹⁵The Lord replied to him, "You hypocrites! Doesn't each of you on the Sabbath

13:14
c Exod 20:9;
Matt 12:10;
Mark 3:2; Lk 6:7;
14:3

a 13:1 Lit. *him*   b 13:1 I.e. whom Pilate had executed while they were sacrificing animals   c 13:6,13:8 Lit. *he*   d 13:10 Lit. *He*

untie his ox or donkey and lead it out of the stall to give it some water?*[a]* ¹⁶Shouldn't this woman, a descendant of Abraham whom Satan has kept bound for eighteen long years, be set free from this bondage on the Sabbath day?"*[b]* ¹⁷Even while he was saying this, all of his opponents were blushing with shame. But the entire crowd was rejoicing at all the wonderful things he was doing.

The Parables about a Mustard Seed and Yeast
(Matthew 13:31–33; Mark 4:30–32)

¹⁸So Jesus*[a]* went on to say, "What is the kingdom of God like? What can I compare it to?*[c]* ¹⁹It is like a mustard seed that someone took and planted in his garden. It grew and became a tree, and the birds in the sky nest in its branches."

²⁰Again he said, "What can I compare the kingdom of God to? ²¹It is like yeast that a woman took and mixed with*[b]* three measures of flour until all of it was leavened."

The Narrow Door
(Matthew 7:13–14, 21–23)

²²Then Jesus*[a]* taught in one town and village after another as he made his way to Jerusalem.*[d]* ²³Someone asked him, "Lord,*[c]* are only a few people going to be saved?" He said to them, ²⁴"Keep on struggling to get in through the narrow door. For I tell you that many people will try to get in but won't be able to.*[e]* ²⁵After the homeowner gets up and closes the door, you can stand*[d]* outside, knock on the door, and say again and again, 'Lord, open the door for us!' But he will answer you, 'I don't know where you come from.'*[f]* ²⁶Then you will say,*[e]* 'We ate and drank with you, and you taught in our streets.' ²⁷But he will tell you, 'I don't know where you come from. Get away from me, all you evildoers!'*[g]* ²⁸In that place there will be crying and gnashing of teeth*[f]* when you see Abraham, Isaac, Jacob, and all the prophets in the kingdom of God, and you yourselves being driven away on the outside.*[h]* ²⁹People will come from east and west, and from north and south, and will eat in the

---

a 13:18,13:22 Lit. *he*　b 13:21 Lit. *hid in*　c 13:23 Or *Sir*　d 13:25 Lit. *begin to stand*　e 13:26 Lit. *begin to say*　f 13:28 I.e. extreme pain

13:15
a Lk 14:5

13:16
b Lk 19:9

13:18
c Matt 13:31; Mark 4:30

13:22
d Matt 9:35; Mark 6:6

13:24
e Matt 7:13; John 7:34; 8:21; 13:33; Rom 9:31

13:25
f Ps 32:6; Isa 55:6; Matt 7:23; 25:10, 12; Lk 6:46

13:27
g Ps 6:8; Matt 7:23; 25:41; Lk 13:25

13:28
h Matt 8:11-12; 13:42; 24:51

13:30
a Matt 19:30;
20:16; Mark 10:31

kingdom of God. ³⁰You see, some who are last will be first, and some who are first will be last."*ᵃ*

Jesus Mourns over Jerusalem
(Matthew 23:37–39)

³¹At that hour some Pharisees came and told Jesus,ᵃ "Leave and get away from here, for Herod wants to kill you!" ³²He said to them, "Go and tell that fox, 'Listen! I am driving out demons and healing today and tomorrow, and on the third day I will finish my work.*ᵇ* ³³But I must be on my way today, tomorrow, and the next day, for it's not possible for a prophet to be killed outside of Jerusalem.'

³⁴"O Jerusalem, Jerusalem, who kills the prophets and stones to death those who have been sent to her! How often I wanted to gather your children together the way a hen gathers her chicks under her wings, but you didn't want to!ᶜ ³⁵Look! Your house is left to you deserted. I tell you, you will not see me again until you say, 'How blessed is the one who comes in the name of the Lord!' "ᵇᵈ

Jesus Heals a Man on the Sabbath

14 ¹One Sabbath, Jesusᶜ went to the house of a leader of the Pharisees to eat a meal. The guestsᵈ were watching Jesusᵃ closely. ²A man whose body was swollen with fluid suddenly appeared in front of him. ³So Jesus asked the Pharisees and experts in the Law, "Is it lawful to heal on the Sabbath or not?"ᵉ ⁴But they kept silent. So he took hold of the man,ᵉ healed him, and sent him away. ⁵Then he asked them, "If your sonᶠ or ox falls into a well on the Sabbath day, you would pull him out immediately, wouldn't you?"ᶠ ⁶And they couldn't argue with him about this.

A Lesson about Guests

⁷When Jesusᶜ noticed how the guests were choosing the places of honor, he told them a parable. ⁸"When you are invited by someone to a wedding banquet, don't sit down at

13:32
b Heb 2:10

13:34
c Matt 23:37

13:35
d Lev 26:31-32;
Ps 69:25; 118:26;
Isa 1:7; Dan 9:27;
Mic 3:12;
Matt 21:9;
Mark 11:10;
Lk 19:38;
John 12:13

14:3
e Matt 12:10

14:5
f Exod 23:5;
Deut 22:4;
Lk 13:15

the place of honor in case someone more important than you was invited by him. ⁹Then the host who invited both of you would come to you and say, 'Give this person your place.' In disgrace, you would have to take the place of least honor. ¹⁰But when you are invited, go and sit down at the place of least honor. Then, when your host comes, he will tell you, 'Friend, move up higher,' and you will be honored in the presence of all who eat with you.ᵃ ¹¹For everyone who exalts himself will be humbled, but the person who humbles himself will be exalted."ᵇ

¹²Then he told the man who had invited him, "When you give a luncheon or a dinner, stop inviting onlyᵃ your friends, brothers, relatives, or rich neighbors. Otherwise, they may invite you in return and you would be repaid. ¹³Instead, when you give a banquet, make it your habit to invite the poor, the crippled, the lame, and the blind.ᶜ ¹⁴Then you will be blessed because they can't repay you. For you will be repaid at the resurrection of the righteous."

The Parable about a Large Banquet
(Matthew 22:1–10)

¹⁵Now one of those eating with him heard this and said to him, "How blessed is the person who will eatᵇ in the kingdom of God!"ᵈ ¹⁶Jesusᶜ said to him, "A man gave a large banquet and invited many people.ᵉ ¹⁷When it was time for the banquet, he sent his servant to tell those who were invited, 'Come! Everything is now ready.'ᶠ ¹⁸Every single one of them began asking to be excused. The first said to him, 'I bought a field, and I need to go out and see it. Please excuse me.' ¹⁹Another said, 'I bought five pairs of oxen, and I'm on my way to try them out. Please excuse me.' ²⁰Still another said, 'I recently got married, and that's why I can't come.'

²¹"So the servant went back and reported this to his master. Then the master of the house became angry and told his servant, 'Go quickly into the streets and alleys of the town and bring back the poor, the crippled, the blind, and

---

a14:12 Lit. *stop inviting*   b14:15 Lit. *eat bread*   c14:16 Lit. *He*

14:10
ᵃProv 25:6-7

14:11
ᵇJob 22:29;
Ps 18:27;
Prov 29:23;
Matt 23:12;
Lk 18:14;
James 4:6;
1Peter 5:5

14:13
ᶜNeh 8:10,12

14:15
ᵈRev 19:9

14:16
ᵉMatt 22:2

14:17
ᶠProv 9:2,5

14:24
a Matt 21:43; 22:8;
Acts 13:46

the lame.' ²²The servant said, 'Sir, what you ordered has been done, and there is still room.' ²³Then the master told the servant, 'Go out into the streets and the lanes and make the people come in, so that my house may be full. ²⁴For I tell all of you,ᵃ none of those men who were invited will taste anything at my banquet.' "ᵃ

The Cost of Discipleship
(Matthew 10:37–38)

14:26
b Deut 13:6; 33:9;
Matt 10:37;
Rom 9:13;
Rev 12:11

²⁵Now large crowds were traveling with Jesus.ᵇ He turned and said to them, ²⁶"If anyone comes to me and does not hate his father, mother, wife, children, brothers, and sisters, as well as his own life, he can't be my disciple.ᵇ ²⁷Whoever doesn't carry his cross and follow me can't be my disciple.ᶜ

²⁸"Suppose one of you wants to build a tower. He will first sit down and estimate the cost to see whether he has enough money to finish it, won't he?ᵈ ²⁹Otherwise, if he lays a foundation and can't finish the building,ᶜ everyone who

14:27
c Matt 16:24;
Mark 8:34;
Lk 9:23;
2 Tim 3:12

watches will begin to ridicule him ³⁰and say, 'This person started a building but couldn't finish it.'

³¹"Or suppose a king is going to war against another king. He will first sit down and consider whether with 10,000 men he can oppose the one coming against him with 20,000 men, won't he? ³²If he can't, he will send a delegation to ask for terms of peace while the other king isᵈ still far away. ³³In the same way, none of you can be my disciple unless he gives up all his possessions."

14:28
d Prov 24:27

Tasteless Salt
(Matthew 5:13; Mark 9:50)

³⁴"Now, salt is good. But if the salt should lose its taste, how can its flavor be restored?ᵉ ³⁵It is suitable neither for the soil nor for the manure pile. Peopleᵉ throw it away. Let the person who has ears to hear listen!"

14:34
e Matt 5:13;
Mark 9:50

---

a 14:24 Lit. *I tell you* (plural)   **b** 14:25 Lit. *with him*   **c** 14:29 Lit. *can't finish*   **d** 14:32 Lit. *while he is*   **e** 14:35 Lit. *They*

The Parable about God's Love for the Lost

15:1
a Matt 9:10

15 ¹Now all the tax collectors and notorious[a] sinners kept coming to listen to Jesus.[b][a] ²But the Pharisees and the scribes kept complaining, "This man welcomes sinners and eats with them."[b] ³So he told them this parable:

The Story of the Faithful Shepherd
(Matthew 18:12–14)

15:2
b Acts 11:3;
Gal 2:12

⁴"Suppose one of you has a hundred sheep and loses one of them. He leaves the ninety-nine in the wilderness and looks for the one that is lost until he finds it, doesn't he?[c] ⁵When he finds it, he puts it on his shoulders and rejoices. ⁶Then he goes home, calls his friends and neighbors together, and says to them, 'Rejoice with me, for I have found my lost sheep!'[d] ⁷In the same way, I tell you that there will be more joy in heaven over one sinner who repents than over ninety-nine righteous people who need no repentance."[e]

15:4
c Matt 18:12

The Story of the Diligent Housewife

⁸"Or suppose a woman has ten coins and loses one of them.[c] She lights a lamp, sweeps the house, and searches carefully until she finds it, doesn't she? ⁹When she finds it, she calls her friends and neighbors together and says, 'Rejoice with me, for I have found the coin that I lost!' ¹⁰In the same way, I tell you that there is joy in the presence of God's angels over one sinner who repents."

15:6
d 1 Peter 2:10,25

The Story of the Loving Father

¹¹Then Jesus[d] said, "A man had two sons. ¹²The younger son said to his father, 'Father, give me my share of the property.' So the father[d] divided his property between them.[f] ¹³A few days later, the younger son gathered all he had and traveled to a distant country. There he wasted his possessions on wild living. ¹⁴After he had spent everything, a severe famine took place throughout that country, and he

15:7
e Lk 5:32

---

a *15:1 The* Gk. lacks *notorious*   **b** *15:1* Lit. *to him*   **c** *15:8* Lit. *one coin*
d *15:11,15:12* Lit. *he*

15:12
f Mark 12:44

15:20
a Acts 2:39;
Eph 2:13,17

began to be in need. ¹⁵So he went and hired himself out to one of the citizens of that country, who sent him into his fields to feed pigs. ¹⁶He would gladly have filled himself with the husks that the pigs were eating, but no one gave him anything.

¹⁷"Then he came to his senses and said, 'How many of my father's hired men have more food than they can eat, and here I am starving to death! ¹⁸I will get up, go to my father, and say to him, "Father, I have sinned against heaven^a and you. ¹⁹I don't deserve to be called your son anymore. Treat me like one of your hired men." '

²⁰"So he got up and went to his father. While he was still far away, his father saw him and was filled with compassion. He ran to his son,^b put his arms around him, and kissed him affectionately.^a ²¹Then his son said to him, 'Father, I have sinned against heaven^a and you. I don't deserve to be called your son anymore.'^cb ²²But the father said to his servants, 'Hurry! Bring out the best robe and put it on him, and put a ring on his finger and sandals on his feet. ²³Bring the fattened calf and kill it, and let's eat and celebrate! ²⁴For my son was dead and has come back to life. He was lost and has been found.' So they began to celebrate.^c

15:21
b Ps 51:4

²⁵"Now his older son was in the field. As he was coming back to the house, he heard music and dancing. ²⁶So he called to one of the servants and asked what was happening. ²⁷The servant^d told him, 'Your brother has come home, and your father has killed the fattened calf because he got him back safely.'

²⁸"Then the older son^e became angry and wouldn't go into the house.^f So his father came out and began to plead with him. ²⁹But he answered his father, "Listen! All these years I've worked like a slave for you. I've never disobeyed a command of yours. Yet you've never given me so much as a young goat so that I could celebrate with my friends. ³⁰But this son of yours spent your money on prostitutes, and when he came back, you killed the fattened calf for him!'

15:24
c Lk 15:32;
Eph 2:1; 5:14;
Rev 3:1

a 15:18,15:21 I.e. God   b 15:20 Lit. He ran   c 15:21 Other mss. read
anymore. Treat me like one of your hired men.   d 15:27 Lit. He   e 15:28 Lit.
he   f 15:28 Lit. *wouldn't go in*

³¹"His father[a] said to him, 'My child, you are always with me, and everything I have is yours. ³²But we had to celebrate and rejoice, because this brother of yours was dead and has come back to life. He was lost and has been found.' "[a]

The Parable about a Dishonest Manager

16 ¹Now Jesus[b] was saying to the disciples, "A rich man had a business manager who was accused of wasting his property. ²So he called for the manager[c] and asked him, 'What's this I hear about you? Give me a report about your management, because you can't be my manager any longer.'

³"Then the manager said to himself, 'What should I do? My master is taking my position away from me. I'm not strong enough to dig, and I'm ashamed to beg. ⁴I know what I'll do so that people[d] will welcome me into their homes when I'm dismissed from my job.'

⁵"So he called for each of his master's debtors. He asked the first, 'How much do you owe my master?' ⁶The man replied, 'A hundred jars of olive oil.' The manager[a] told him, 'Get your bill. Sit down quickly and write "fifty." ' ⁷Then he asked another debtor,[e] 'How much do you owe?' The man replied, 'A hundred containers of wheat.' The manager[a] told him, 'Get your bill and write "eighty." ' ⁸The master praised the dishonest manager for being so clever. For worldly people[f] are more clever than enlightened people[g] in dealing with their own generation.[b]

⁹"I'm telling you, make friends for yourselves by means of unrighteous riches,[h] so that when they're gone you'll be welcomed[i] into eternal homes.[j][c] ¹⁰Whoever is faithful with very little is also faithful with a lot, and whoever is dishonest with very little is also dishonest with a lot.[d] ¹¹So if you have not been faithful with unrighteous riches,[h] who will trust you with true wealth?[k] ¹²And if you have not been

---

a 15:31,16:6,16:7 Lit. *He*   b 16:1 Lit. *he*   c 16:2 Lit. *for him*   d 16:4 Lit. *they*   e 16:7 The Gk. lacks *debtor*   f 16:8 Lit. *the sons of this age* g 16:8 Lit. *the sons of light*   h 16:9,16:11 Lit. *mammon*, an Aram. term meaning *wealth*   i 16:9 Lit. *they will welcome you*   j 16:9 Lit. *tents* k 16:11 Lit. *with the true*

Margin references:

15:32
a Lk 15:24

16:8
b John 12:36;
Eph 5:8; 1Thes 5:5

16:9
c Dan 4:27;
Matt 6:19; 19:21;
Lk 11:41;
1Tim 6:17-19

16:10
d Matt 25:21;
Lk 19:27

16:13
a Matt 6:24

faithful with what belongs to someone else, who will give you what is your own?

13"No servant can serve two masters. For either he will hate one and love the other, or be loyal to one and despise the other. You can't serve God and riches!"**a***a*

The Law and the Kingdom of God

16:14
b Matt 23:14

(Matthew 11:12–13)

14Now the Pharisees, who love money, had been listening to all this and began to ridicule Jesus.**b***b* 15So he said, to them, "You try to justify yourselves in front of people, but God knows your hearts. For what is highly valued by people is detestable to God.*c*

16:15
c 1Sam 16:7;
Ps 7:9; Lk 10:29

16"The Law and the Prophets were proclaimed until the time of John.*c* Since then, the good news about the kingdom of God has been proclaimed, and everyone is trying to enter it by force.*d* 17However, it is easier for heaven and earth to disappear than for one stroke of a letter in the Law to be dropped.*e* 18Any man who divorces his wife and marries another woman commits adultery, and the man who marries a woman divorced from her husband commits adultery."*f*

16:16
d Matt 4:17;
11:12-13; Lk 7:29

The Rich Man and Lazarus

19"Once there was a rich man who used to dress in purple and fine linen and live in great luxury every day. 20A beggar named Lazarus, who was covered with sores, was brought to his gate. 21He was always craving to satisfy his hunger with what fell**d** from the rich man's table. In fact, even the dogs use to come and lick his sores.

16:17
e Ps 102:21,27;
Isa 40:8; 51:6;
Matt 5:18;
1Peter 1:25

22"One day the beggar died and was carried away by the angels to Abraham's side. The rich man also died and was buried. 23In hell,**e** where he was in constant torture, he looked up and saw Abraham far away and Lazarus by his side. 24So he yelled, 'Father Abraham, have mercy on me! Send Lazarus to dip the tip of his finger in water and to cool

16:18
f Matt 5:32; 19:9;
Mark 10:11;
1Cor 7:10-11

---

a *16:13* Lit. *mammon,* an Aram. term meaning *wealth*   **b** *16:14* Lit. *him*   **c** *16:16* Lit. *were until John*   **d** *16:21* Other mss. read *the scraps that fell*   **e** *16:23* Gk. *Hades,* a reference to the realm of the dead

off my tongue, because I am suffering in this fire.'[a] 25But Abraham said, 'My child, remember that during your lifetime you received blessings,[a] while Lazarus received hardships.[b] But now he is being comforted here, while you suffer.[b] 26Besides all this, a wide chasm has been fixed between us, so that those who want to cross from this side to you can't do so, nor can they cross from your side to us.'

27"The rich man[c] said, 'Then I beg you, father, to send him to my father's house—28for I have five brothers—to warn them, so that they won't come to this place of torture, too.' 29But Abraham said, 'They have Moses and the Prophets. They should listen to them!'[c] 30But the rich man[d] replied, 'No, father Abraham! But if someone from the dead went to them, they would repent.' 31Then Abraham[d] said to him, 'If they do not listen to Moses and the Prophets, they will not be persuaded, even if someone rises from the dead.' "[d]

Jesus Is Sentenced to Death
(Matthew 27:15–31; Mark 15:6–20; Luke 23:13–25)

17 ¹Jesus[c] said to his disciples, "It is inevitable that temptations to sin will come, but how terrible it will be for the person through whom they come![e] ²It would be better for him if a millstone were hung around his neck and he were thrown into the sea than for him to cause one of these little ones to sin.

³"Watch yourselves! If your brother sins, rebuke him, and if he repents, forgive him.[f] ⁴Even if he sins against you seven times in a day and comes back to you seven times and says, 'I repent,' you must forgive him."

Faith and Obedience

⁵Then the apostles said to the Lord, "Give us more faith!" ⁶The Lord replied, "If you have faith the size of a[e] mustard seed, you could say to this mulberry tree, 'Be uprooted and planted in the sea,' and it would obey you![g]

⁷"Suppose a man among you has a servant plowing or

16:24
[a] Isa 66:24;
Zech 14:12;
Mark 9:44

16:25
[b] Job 21:13;
Lk 6:24

16:29
[c] Isa 8:20; 34:16;
John 5:39,45;
Acts 15:21; 17:11

16:31
[d] John 12:10-11

17:1
[e] Matt 18:6-7;
Mark 9:42;
1Cor 11:19

17:3
[f] Lev 19:17;
Prov 17:10;
Matt 18:15,21;
James 5:19

17:6
[g] Matt 17:20;
21:21; Mark 9:23;
11:23

---

[a] 16:25 Lit. *good things*   [b] 16:25 Lit. *and Lazarus in like manner evil things*
[c] 16:27,17:1 Lit. *He*   [d] 16:30,16:31 Lit. *he*   [e] 17:6 Lit. *faith as a*

17:8
a Lk 12:37

watching sheep. Would he say to him when he comes in from the field, 'Come at once and have something to eat'? [8]Of course not. Instead, he would say to him, 'Get dinner ready for me, and put on your apron and wait on me until I eat and drink. Then you can eat and drink.'[a] [9]He doesn't praise the servant for doing what was commanded, does he?

17:10
b Job 22:3; 35:7;
Ps 16:2;
Matt 25:30;
Rom 3:12; 11:35;
1Cor 9:16-17

[10]That's the way it is with you. When you have done everything you were ordered to do, say, 'We are worthless servants. We have done only what we ought to have done.' "[b]

Jesus Cleanses Ten Lepers

[11]One day, Jesus[a] was traveling along the border between Samaria and Galilee on the way to Jerusalem.[c] [12]As

17:11
c Lk 9:51-52;
John 4:4

he was going into a village, ten lepers met him. They stood at a distance[d] [13]and shouted, "Jesus, Master, have mercy on us!"

[14]When he saw them, he told them, "Go and show yourselves to the priests." While they were going, they were made clean.[e] [15]But one of them, when he saw that he was healed, came back and praised God with a loud voice. [16]He

17:12
d Lev 13:46

fell on his face at Jesus'[b] feet and thanked him. Now the man[a] was a Samaritan.

[17]Jesus asked, "Ten men were made clean, weren't they? Where are the other nine? [18]Was none of them found to return and give praise to God except this foreigner?" [19]Then

17:14
e Lev 13:2; 14:2;
Matt 8:4; Lk 5:14

he told the man,[c] "Get up, and go home! Your faith has made you well."[f]

The Coming of the Kingdom
(Matthew 24:23–28, 37–41)

[20]Once Jesus[a] was asked by the Pharisees when the

17:19
f Matt 9:22;
Mark 5:34; 10:52;
Lk 7:50; 8:48;
18:42

kingdom of God would come. He answered them, "The kingdom of God is not coming with a visible display. [21]People[d] won't say, 'Look! Here it is!' or "There it is!' For the kingdom of God is among[e] you."[g]

[22]Then he said to the disciples, "The time will come when you will long to see one of the days of the Son of Man,

17:21
g Lk 17:23;
Rom 14:17

a 17:11, 17:16, 17:20 Lit. *he*   b 17:16 Lit. *his*   c 17:19 Lit. *him*   d 17:21 Lit. *They*   e 17:21 Or *within*

but you will not see it.[a] [23]People[a] will say to you, 'Look! There he is!' or 'Look! Here he is!' Don't go and chase him.[b] [24]For just as lightning flashes and shines from one end of the sky to the other, so will the Son of Man be in his day.[b][c] [25]But first he must suffer a great deal and be rejected by this generation.[d]

[26]"Just as it was in the days of Noah, so it will be in the days of the Son of Man.[e] [27]People[a] were eating, drinking, marrying, and being given in marriage right up to the day when Noah went into the ark. Then the flood came and destroyed all of them. [28]So it was in the days of Lot. People[a] were eating and drinking, buying and selling, planting and building.[f] [29]But on the day when Lot left Sodom, fire and sulfur rained from heaven and destroyed all of them.[g] [30]The day when the Son of Man is revealed will be like that.[h]

[31]"The person who is on the housetop that day must not come down to get the belongings out of his house. The person in the field, too, must not turn back.[i] [32]Remember Lot's wife![j] [33]Whoever tries to save his life[c] will lose it, but whoever loses his life will preserve it.[k] [34]I tell you, two people will be in the same bed that night. One will be taken, and the other will be left behind.[l] [35]Two woman will be grinding grain together. One will be taken, and the other will be left behind."[d]

[37]Then they asked him, "Where, Lord, will this take place?"[e] He told them, "Wherever there's a dead body, there the vultures will gather."[m]

The Parable about the Judge and the Widow

18 [1]Jesus[f] told his disciples[g] a parable about their need to pray all the time and never give up.[n] [2]He said, "In a city there was a judge who didn't fear God or respect people. [3]In that city there was also a widow who kept coming to him and saying, 'Grant me justice against my adversary.' [4]For a while the judge[h] refused. But

---

a 17:23,17:27,17:28 Lit. *They*   b 17:24 Other mss. lack *in his day*
c 17:33 Other mss. read *to make his life secure*   d 17:35 Other mss. read
left behind. [36]*Two people will be in a field. One will be taken, and the other will
be left behind*   e 17:37 Lit. *Where, Lord?*   f 18:1 Lit. *He*   g 18:1 Lit. *them*
h 18:4 Lit. *he*

17:22
a Matt 9:15;
John 17:12

17:23
b Matt 24:23;
Mark 13:21;
Lk 21:8

17:24
c Matt 24:27

17:25
d Mark 8:31; 9:31;
10:33; Lk 9:22

17:26
e Gen 7:1-24;
Matt 24:37

17:28
f Gen 19:1-38

17:29
g Gen 19:16,24

17:30
h 2 Thes 1:7

17:31
i Matt 24:17;
Mark 13:15

17:32
j Gen 19:26

17:33
k Matt 10:39;
16:25; Mark 8:35;
Lk 9:24;
John 12:25

17:34
l Matt 24:40-41;
1 Thes 4:17

17:37
m Job 39:30;
Matt 24:28

18:1
n Lk 11:5; 21:36;
Rom 12:12;
Eph 6:18; Col 4:2;
1 Thes 5:17

18:5
ᵃLk 11:8

later he said to himself, 'I don't fear God or respect people. ⁵Yet because this widow keeps bothering me, I will grant her justice. Otherwise, she will keep coming and wear me out.' "ᵃ

18:7
ᵇRev 6:10

⁶Then the Lord added, "Listen to what the unrighteous judge says. ⁷Won't God grant his chosen people justice when they cry out to him day and night? Is he slow to help them?ᵇ ⁸I tell you, he will give them justice quickly. But when the Son of Man comes, will he find faith on earth?"ᶜ

18:8
ᶜHeb 10:37;
2Peter 3:8-9

The Parable about the Pharisee and the Tax Collector

⁹Jesusᵃ also told this parable to some people who trusted in themselves because they were righteous, but who looked down on everyone else:ᵈ ¹⁰"Two men went up to the Temple to pray. One was a Pharisee, and the other was a tax collector. ¹¹The Pharisee stood by himself and prayed, 'O God, I thank you that I'm not like other people—thieves, dishonest people, adulterers, or even this tax collector.ᵉ ¹²I fast twice a week, and I give a tenth of my entire income.'

18:9
ᵈLk 10:29; 16:15

18:11
ᵉPs 135:2;
Isa 1:15; 58:2;
Rev 3:17

¹³"But the tax collector stood at a distance and would not even look up to heaven. Instead, he continued to beat his chest and said, 'O God, be merciful to me, the sinner that I am!'ᵇ ¹⁴I tell you, this man, rather than the other, went down to his home justified. For everyone who exalts himself will be humbled, but the person who humbles himself will be exalted."ᶠ

18:14
ᶠJob 22:29;
Matt 23:12;
Lk 14:11;
James 4:6;
1Peter 5:5-6

Jesus Blesses the Little Children
(Matthew 19:13–15; Mark 10:13–16)

18:15
ᵍMatt 19:13;
Mark 10:13

¹⁵Now some peopleᶜ even were bringing their infants to Jesusᵈ to have him touch them. But when the disciples saw this, they sternly told the peopleᵉ not to do that.ᵍ ¹⁶Jesus, however, called for them and said, "Let the little children come to me, and stop keeping them away. For the kingdom of God belongs to people like these.ʰ ¹⁷Truly I tell you, whoever doesn't receive the kingdom of God as a little child will never get into it at all."ⁱ

18:16
ʰ1Cor 14:20;
1Peter 2:2

18:17
ⁱMark 10:15

ᵃ18:9 Lit. *He*   ᵇ18:13 The Gk. lacks *that I am*   ᶜ18:15 Lit. *they*
ᵈ18:15 Lit. *to him*   ᵉ18:15 Lit. *them*

An Official Comes to Jesus
(Matthew 19:16–30; Mark 10:17–31)

18Then an official asked Jesus,**a** "Good Teacher, what must I do to inherit eternal life?"*a* 19Jesus said to him, "Why do you call me good? No one is good except for one—God. 20You know the commandments: 'Never commit adultery.**b** Never murder.**c** Never steal.**d** Never give false testimony.**e** Honor your father and mother.' "**f***b* 21The official**g** replied, "I have kept all of these since I was a young man." 22When Jesus heard this, he said to him, "You still need one thing. Sell everything you have and give the money**h** to the destitute, and you will have treasure in heaven. Then come back and follow me."*c* 23But when the official**i** heard this he became sad, because he was very rich.

24So when Jesus saw how sad he was, he**j** said, "How hard it is for rich people to get into the kingdom of God!*d* 25Indeed, it is easier for a camel to squeeze through the eye of a needle than for a rich person to get into the kingdom of God." 26Those who heard him said, "Then who can be saved?" 27Jesus**g** said, "The things that are impossible for people are possible for God."*e*

28Then Peter said, "See, we've left everything we have and followed you."*f* 29Jesus**g** said to them, "Truly I tell you, there is no one who has left his home, wife, brothers, parents, or children because of the kingdom of God**g** 30who will not receive many times as much in this world, as well as eternal life in the age to come."*h*

Jesus Predicts His Death and Resurrection a Third Time
(Matthew 20:17–19; Mark 10:32–34)

31Jesus**g** took the twelve aside and said to them, "See, we're going up to Jerusalem. Everything written by the prophets about the Son of Man will be fulfilled.*i* 32For he will be handed over to the Gentiles and will be mocked, insulted, and spit on.*j* 33After they have whipped him, they

---

a18:18 Lit. *him*   b18:20 Exod 20:14; Deut 5:18   c18:20 Exod 20:13; Deut 5:17   d18:20 Exod 20:15; Deut 5:19   e18:20 Exod 20:16; Deut 5:20   f18:20 Exod 20:12; Deut 5:16   g18:21,18:27,18:29,18:31 Lit. *He*   h18:22 *The* Gk. lacks *the money*   i18:23 Lit. *he*   j18:24 Other mss. read *So Jesus looked at him and*

18:18
*a*Matt 19:16;
Mark 10:17

18:20
*b*Exod 20:12,16;
Deut 5:16-20;
Rom 13:9;
Eph 6:2; Col 3:20

18:22
*c*Matt 6:19-20;
19:21; 1Tim 6:19

18:24
*d*Prov 11:28;
Matt 19:23;
Mark 10:23

18:27
*e*Jer 32:17;
Zech 8:6;
Matt 19:26;
Lk 1:37

18:28
*f*Matt 19:27

18:29
*g*Deut 33:9

18:30
*h*Job 42:10

18:31
*i*Ps 22:1-31;
Isa 53:1-12;
Matt 16:21; 17:22;
20:17; Mark 10:32

18:32
*j*Matt 27:2;
Lk 23:1;
John 18:28;
Acts 3:13

18:34
*a*Mark 9:32;
Lk 2:50; 9:45;
John 10:6; 12:16

will kill him, but on the third day he will rise again." ³⁴But they didn't understand any of this. What he said was hidden from them, and they didn't know what he meant.*a*

Jesus Heals a Blind Man
(Matthew 20:29–34; Mark 10:46–50)

³⁵As Jesus*a* was approaching Jericho, a blind man was sitting by the road begging.*b* ³⁶When he heard the crowd going by, he asked what was happening. ³⁷They told him that Jesus from Nazareth*b* was coming by. ³⁸Then he shouted, "Jesus, Son of David, have mercy on me!" ³⁹The people at the front of the crowd*c* sternly told the blind man*d* to be quiet, but he kept shouting even louder, "Son of David, have mercy on me!"

18:35
*b*Matt 20:29;
Mark 10:46

⁴⁰Then Jesus stopped and ordered the man to be brought to him. When the man*a* came near, Jesus*a* asked him, ⁴¹"What do you want me to do for you?" The blind man*e* said, "Lord, I want to see again!" ⁴²Jesus told him, "Receive your sight! Your faith has made you well."*c* ⁴³Immediately the man*a* could see again and began to follow Jesus,*d* glorifying God. All the people saw this and gave praise to God.*d*

Jesus and Zacchaeus

18:42
*c*Lk 17:19

19 ¹Jesus*e* entered Jericho and was passing through it. ²A man named Zacchaeus was there. He was a leading tax collector, and he was rich. ³He was trying to see who Jesus was, but he couldn't do so because of the crowd. (He was short in height.) ⁴So he ran ahead and climbed a sycamore tree to see Jesus,*d* who was going to pass that way.

⁵When Jesus came to the tree,*f* he looked up and said, "Zacchaeus, hurry and come down! I must stay at your house today." ⁶Zacchaeus*e* came down quickly and was glad to welcome Jesus into his home.*g* ⁷But all the people who saw this began to complain. They said, "He went to be the

18:43
*d*Lk 5:26;
Acts 4:21; 11:18

---

a 18:35,18:40,18:43 Lit. *he*   b 18:37 Or *Jesus the Nazarene*; the Gk. *Nazoraios* may be a word play between Heb. *netser*, meaning *branch* (see Isa 11:1), and the name *Nazareth*.   c 18:39 Lit. *at the front*
d 18:39,18:43,19:4 Lit. *him*   e 18:41,19:1,19:6 Lit. *He*   f 19:5 Lit. *to the place*   g 19:6 Lit. *to welcome him*

guest of a notorious[a] sinner!"[a] [8]Zacchaeus stood up and said to the Lord, "Lord, I'll give half of my possessions to the poor. I'll pay four times as much as I owe[b] if I have cheated anyone in any way."[b] [9]Then Jesus said to him, "Today salvation has come to this home, because he, too, is a descendant of Abraham.[c] [10]For the Son of Man has come to seek and to save the lost."[d]

The Parable about the Coins
(Matthew 25:14–30)

[11]As they were listening to this, Jesus[c] went on to tell a parable. He did so because[d] he was near Jerusalem and because the people[e] thought that the kingdom of God would appear immediately.[e] [12]So he said, "A prince went to a distant country to be appointed king and then to return.[f] [13]He called ten of his servants and gave them ten coins.[f] He said to them, 'Invest this money until I come back.' [14]But the citizens of his country hated him and sent a delegation to follow him, saying, 'We don't want this man to rule over us!'[g]

[15]"After he was appointed king, he came back. He ordered the servants to whom he had given the money to be called so that he could find out what they had made by investing. [16]The first servant[g] came and said, 'Sir, your coin has earned ten more coins.' [17]The king[h] said to him, 'Well done, good servant! Because you have been trustworthy in a very small thing, take charge of ten cities.'[h]

[18]"The second servant[i] came and said, 'Your coin, sir, has earned five coins.' [19]The king[h] said to him, 'You take charge of five cities.'

[20]"Then the other servant[j] came and said, 'Sir, look! Here's your coin. I've kept it in a cloth for safekeeping [21]because I was afraid of you. You are a hard man. You withdraw what you didn't deposit and harvest what you didn't plant.'[i] [22]The king[h] said to him, 'I will judge you by your

---

a[19:7] The Gk. lacks *notorious*   b[19:8] Lit. *four times as much*   c[19:11] Lit. *he*   d[19:11] Lit. *Because*   e[19:11] Lit. *they*   f[19:13] Gk. *minas*. A mina was equivalent to about nine months of wages for a laborer.
g[19:16] Lit. *The first*   h[19:17,19:19,19:22] Lit. *He*   i[19:18] Lit. *The second*
j[19:20] Lit. *the other*

Marginal cross-references:

19:7
a Matt 9:11;
Lk 5:30

19:8
b Exod 22:1;
1Sam 12:3;
2Sam 12:6;
Lk 3:14

19:9
c Lk 13:16;
Rom 4:11-12,16;
Gal 3:7

19:10
d Matt 10:6;
15:24; 18:11

19:11
e Acts 1:6

19:12
f Matt 25:14;
Mark 13:34

19:14
g John 1:11

19:17
h Matt 25:21;
Lk 16:10

19:21
i Matt 25:24

19:22
a 2Sam 1:16;
Job 15:6;
Matt 12:37; 25:26

own words, you evil servant! You knew, did you, that I was a hard man, and that I withdraw what I didn't deposit and harvest what I didn't plant?*a* ²³Then why didn't you put my money in the bank? When I returned, I could have collected it with interest.'

19:26
b Matt 13:12;
25:29; Mark 4:25;
Lk 8:18

²⁴"So the king*a* told those standing nearby, 'Take the coin away from him and give it to the man who has the ten coins.' ²⁵They answered him, 'Sir, he already*b* has ten coins!' ²⁶'I tell you, to everyone who has, more will be given, but from the person who has nothing, even what he has will be taken away.*b* ²⁷But as for these enemies of mine who didn't want me to be their king—bring them here and slaughter them in my presence!' "

19:28
c Mark 10:32

The King Enters Jerusalem
(Matthew 21:1–11; Mark 11:1–11; John 12:12–19)

²⁸After Jesus*a* had said this, he traveled on and went up to Jerusalem.*c* ²⁹When he came near Bethphage and Bethany at the Mount of Olives, he sent two of his disciples on

19:29
d Matt 21:1;
Mark 11:1

ahead*d* ³⁰and said, "Go into the village ahead of you. As you enter, you will find a colt tied up that no one has ever ridden.*c* Untie it, and bring it. ³¹If anyone asks you why you are untying it, say this: "The Lord needs it.' "

³²So those who were sent went off and found it as he had told them. ³³While they were untying the colt, its own-ers asked them, "Why are you untying the colt?" ³⁴The disci-

19:35
e 2Kings 9:13;
Matt 21:7;
Mark 11:7;
John 12:14

ples*d* answered, "The Lord needs it." ³⁵Then they brought the colt to Jesus and put their coats on it, and Jesus sat on it.*e*

³⁶As he was riding along, people*e* kept spreading their coats on the road.*f* ³⁷He was now approaching the descent from the Mount of Olives. The whole crowd of disciples began to rejoice and to praise God with a loud voice for all

19:36
f Matt 21:8

the miracles they had seen. ³⁸They said,*g*

> "How blessed is the king
>   who comes in the name of the Lord!*f*
> Peace in heaven,

19:38
g Ps 118:26;
Lk 2:14; 13:35;
Eph 2:14

---

a 19:24,19:28 Lit. *he*   **b** 19:25 The Gk. lacks *already*   **c** 19:30 Lit. *has ever sat on*   **d** 19:34 Lit. *They*   **e** 19:36 Lit. *they*   **f** 19:38 Ps 118:26

and glory in the highest heaven!"

39Some of the Pharisees in the crowd said to Jesus,ª "Teacher, tell your disciples to be quiet." 40He replied, "I tell you, if they were quiet, the stones would cry out!"ª 41When he came closer and saw the city, he began to cry over it.ᵇ 42He said, "If you had only known today what would bring you peace! But now it is hidden from your eyes. 43For the days will comeᵇ when your enemies will build walls around you, surround you, and close you in on every side.ᶜ 44They will level you to the ground—you and your children within you. They will not leave one stone on another within you, because you didn't recognize the time when God came to help you."ᶜᵈ

Jesus Throws the Merchants out of the Temple
(Matthew 21:12–17; Mark 11:15–19; John 2:13–22)

45Then Jesusᵈ went into the Temple and began to throw out those who were selling things.ᵉ 46He said to them, "It is written, 'My house is to be called a house of prayer,'ᵉ but you turned it into a hideoutᶠ for bandits!"ᶠ

47Jesusᵍ was teaching in the Temple every day. The high priests, the scribes, and the leaders of the people kept looking for a way to kill him,ᵍ 48but they couldn't find a way to do it, because all the people were eager to hear him.

Jesus' Authority Is Challenged
(Matthew 21:23–27; Mark 11:27–33)

20 1One day while he was teaching the people in the Temple and telling them the good news, the high priests and the scribes came with the eldersʰ 2and asked him, "Tell us: By what authority are you doing these things, and who gave you this authority?"ⁱ

3He answered them, "I, too, will ask you a question.ʰ Tell me: 4Was John's authority to baptizeⁱ from heaven or from humans?"

5They discussed this among themselves, saying, "If we

19:40
ªHab 2:11

19:41
ᵇJohn 11:35

19:43
ᶜIsa 29:3-4;
Jer 6:3,6; Lk 21:20

19:44
ᵈ1Kings 9:7-8;
Dan 9:24;
Mic 3:12;
Matt 24:2;
Mark 13:2;
Lk 1:68,78; 21:6;
1Peter 2:12

19:45
ᵉMatt 21:12;
Mark 11:11,15;
John 2:14-15

19:46
ᶠIsa 56:7; Jer 7:11

19:47
ᵍMark 11:18;
John 7:19; 8:37

20:1
ʰMatt 21:23

20:2
ⁱActs 4:7; 7:27

---

a19:39 Lit. *to him*   b19:43 Lit. *come on you*   c19:44 Lit. *the time of your visitation*   d19:45 Lit. *he*   e19:46 Isa 56:7   f19:46 Lit. *cave*   g19:47 Lit. *He*   h20:3 Lit. *a word*   i20:4 Lit. *John's baptism*

20:6
a Matt 14:5; 21:26;
Lk 7:29

say, 'From heaven,' he will ask, 'Then why didn't you believe him?' 6But if we say, 'From humans,' all the people will stone us to death, for they are convinced that John was a prophet."a 7So they answered that they didn't know where it was from. 8Then Jesus told them, "Then I won't tell you by what authority I am doing these things."

The Parable about the Tenant Farmers
(Matthew 21:33–46; Mark 12:1–12)

9Then he began to tell the people this parable: "A man planted a vineyard, leased it to tenant farmers, and went abroad for a long time.b 10At the right time he sent a servant to the farmers in order that they might give him his share of the produce of the vineyard. But the farmers beat him and sent him back empty-handed. 11He sent another servant, and they beat him, too, treated him shamefully, and sent him back empty-handed. 12Then he sent a third, and they wounded him and threw him out, too.

20:9
b Matt 21:33;
Mark 12:1

13"Then the owner of the vineyard said, 'What should I do? I'll send my son whom I love. Maybe they'll respect him.' 14But when the farmers saw him, they talked it over among themselves and said, 'This is the heir. Let's kill him so that the inheritance will be ours!' 15So they threw him out of the vineyard and killed him. Now what will the owner of the vineyard do to them? 16He will come and destroy those farmers and give the vineyard to others." Those who heard him said, "That must never happen!" 17But Jesusa looked at them and said, "What does this text mean:c

20:17
c Ps 118:22;
Matt 21:42

'The stone that the builders rejected
has become the cornerstone'?b

18Everyone who falls on that stone will be broken to pieces, but it will crush anyone on whom it falls."d

19When the scribes and the high priests realized that he had told this parable against them, they wanted to lay their hands on him at that very hour, but they were afraid of the crowd.

20:18
d Dan 2:34-35;
Matt 21:44

a 20:17 Lit. *he*   b 20:17 Or *capstone*; Ps 118:22

A Question about Paying Taxes
(Matthew 22:15–22; Mark 12:13–17)

²⁰So they watched him closely and sent spies who pretended to be honest men in order to trap him in what he would say. They wanted to hand him over to the power and authority of the governor.*ᵃ* ²¹So they asked him, "Teacher, we know that you are right in what you say and teach, and that you don't favor any individual, but teach the way of God truthfully.*ᵇ* ²²Is it lawful for us to pay taxes to Caesar or not?"

²³But he detected their cunning and said to them, ²⁴"Show me a denarius. Whose face and name does it have?" They said, "Caesar's." ²⁵So he said to them, "Then give back to Caesar the things that are Caesar's, and to God the things that are God's."

²⁶So they couldn't catch him before the people in what he said. Amazed at his answer, they became silent.

A Question about the Resurrection
(Matthew 22:23–33; Mark 12:18–27)

²⁷Now some Sadducees, who say there is no resurrection, came to Jesus*ᵃᶜ* ²⁸and asked him, "Teacher, Moses wrote for us that if a man's brother dies and leaves a wife but no child, the man**ᵇ** should marry the widow and have children for his brother.*ᵈ* ²⁹Now there were seven brothers. The first one married and died childless. ³⁰Then the second ³¹and the third married her. In the same way, all seven died and left no children. ³²Finally, the woman died, too. ³³Now in the resurrection, whose wife will the woman be, since the seven had married her?"

³⁴Jesus said to them, "Those who belong to this age marry and are married, ³⁵but those who are considered worthy of a place in that age and in the resurrection from the dead neither marry nor are given in marriage. ³⁶Nor can they die anymore, for they are like the angels and, since they share in the resurrection, are God's children.*ᵉ* ³⁷Even Moses demonstrated in the story about the bush that the dead are raised, when he calls the Lord 'the God of Abraham, the

---

a 20:27 Lit. *to him*   b 20:28 Lit. *the brother*

20:20
ᵃ Matt 22:15

20:21
ᵇ Matt 22:16;
Mark 12:14

20:27
ᶜ Matt 22:23;
Mark 12:18;
Acts 23:6,8

20:28
ᵈ Deut 25:5

20:36
ᵉ Rom 8:23;
1Cor 15:42,49,52;
1John 3:2

20:37
a Exod 3:6

God of Isaac, and the God of Jacob.'ᵃᵃ ³⁸He is not the God of the dead, but of the living, for all people are alive to him."ᵇᵇ

³⁹Then some of the scribes replied, "Teacher, you have given a fine answer." ⁴⁰For they no longer dared to ask him another question.

20:38
b Rom 6:10-11

A Question about David's Son
(Matthew 22:41–46; Mark 12:35–37)

20:41
c Matt 22:42;
Mark 12:35

⁴¹Then he said to them, "How can peopleᶜ say that the Christᵈ is David's son?ᶜ ⁴²For David himself in the book of Psalms says,ᵈ

20:42
d Ps 110:1;
Acts 2:34

'The Lord said to my Lord,
  "Sit at my right hand,
⁴³until I make your enemies a footstool for your
    feet." 'ᵉ

⁴⁴So David calls him Lord. Then how can he be his son?"

Jesus Denounces the Scribes
(Matthew 23:1–36; Mark 12:38–40; Luke 11:37–54)

20:45
e Matt 23:1;
Mark 12:38

⁴⁵While all the people were listening, he said to his disciples,ᵉ ⁴⁶"Beware of the scribes! They like to walk around in long robes and love to be greeted in the marketplaces and to have the best seats in the synagogues and the places of honor at banquets.ᶠ ⁴⁷They devour widows' houses and say long prayers to cover it up. They will receive greater condemnation!"ᵍ

20:46
f Matt 23:5;
Lk 11:43

The Widow's Offering
(Mark 12:41–44)

20:47
g Matt 23:14

21 ¹Now Jesusᶠ looked up and saw rich people dropping their gifts into the offering box.ᵍʰ ²Then he saw a destitute widow drop in two small copper coins. ³He said, "Truly I tell you, this destitute widow has dropped in more than all of them.ⁱ ⁴For all the others contributed to the offeringʰ out of their surplus, but she, in her poverty, dropped in everything she had to live on."

21:1
h Mark 12:41

21:3
i 2Cor 8:12

---

a 20:37 Exod 3:6, 15, 16   b 20:38 Or *all who are with him are alive.*
c 20:41 Lit. *they*   d 20:41 I.e. the Messiah   e 20:43 Ps 110:1   f 21:1 Lit. *he*   g 21:1 Or *treasury*   h 21:4 Other mss. read *to the offering of God*

Jesus Predicts the Destruction of the Temple
(Matthew 24:1–2; Mark 13:1–2)

⁵Now while some people were talking about the Temple—how it was decorated with beautiful stones and gifts dedicated to God—he said,ᵃ ⁶"As for these things that you see, the time will come when not one stone will be left on another that will not be torn down."ᵇ

The Coming Persecution
(Matthew 24:3–14; Mark 13:3–13)

⁷Then they asked him, "Teacher, when will these things be, and what will be the sign that these things are about to take place?" ⁸He said, "Be careful that you are not deceived. For many will come in my name and say, 'I am he' and 'The time is near.' Don't go after them.ᶜ ⁹When you hear of wars and revolutions, never be alarmed. For these things must take place first, but the end won't come right away."

¹⁰Then he went on to say to them, "Nation will rise up in arms against nation, and kingdom against kingdom.ᵈ ¹¹There will be great earthquakes and famines and plagues in various places, and there will be fearful events and awful signs from heaven.

¹²"But before all these things take place, peopleᵃ will arrest you and persecute you. They will hand you over to synagogues and prisons, and you will be brought before kings and governors for my name's sake.ᵉ ¹³It will give you an opportunity to testify.ᶠ ¹⁴So purpose in your hearts not to prepare ahead of time your defense,ᵍ ¹⁵for I will give you such speech and wisdom that none of your opponents will be able to resist or refute it.ʰ

¹⁶"You will be betrayed even by parents, brothers, relatives, and friends, and they will put some of you to death.ⁱ ¹⁷You will be continuously hated by everyone because of my name.ʲ ¹⁸And yet not a hair on your head will be lost.ᵏ ¹⁹By your endurance you will win your souls."

---

a21:12 Lit. *they*

21:5
ᵃMatt 24:1;
Mark 13:1

21:6
ᵇLk 19:44

21:8
ᶜMatt 24:4;
Mark 13:5;
Eph 5:6; 2Thes 2:3

21:10
ᵈMatt 24:7

21:12
ᵉMark 13:9;
Acts 4:3; 5:18;
12:4; 16:24;
25:23;
1Peter 2:13;
Rev 2:10

21:13
ᶠPhil 1:28;
2Thes 1:5

21:14
ᵍMatt 10:19;
Mark 13:11;
Lk 12:11

21:15
ʰActs 6:10

21:16
ⁱMic 7:6;
Mark 13:12;
Acts 7:59; 12:2

21:17
ʲMatt 10:22

21:18
ᵏMatt 10:30

21:20
a Matt 24:15;
Mark 13:14

21:22
b Dan 9:26-27;
Zech 11:1

21:23
c Matt 24:19

21:24
d Dan 9:27; 12:7;
Rom 11:25

21:25
e Matt 24:29;
Mark 13:24;
2Peter 3:10,12

21:26
f Matt 24:29

21:27
g Matt 24:30;
Rev 1:7; 14:14

21:28
h Rom 8:19,23

21:29
i Matt 24:32;
Mark 13:28

21:33
j Matt 24:35

Signs of the End
(Matthew 24:15–21; Mark 13:14–19)

20"When you see Jerusalem surrounded by armies, then understand that its devastation is near.*a* 21Then those in Judea must flee to the mountains, those inside the city must leave it, and those in the countryside must not go into it. 22For these are the days of vengeance when all that is written will be fulfilled.*b*

23"How terrible it will be for those women who are pregnant or who are nursing babies in those days! For there will be great distress in the land*a* and wrath on this people.*c* 24They will fall by the edge of the sword and be carried off as captives among all the nations, and Jerusalem will be trampled on by the Gentiles until the times of the Gentiles are fulfilled."*d*

The Coming of the Son of Man
(Matthew 24:29–31; Mark 13:24–27)

25"There will be signs in the sun, the moon, and the stars, and there will be distress on earth among the nations that are confused by the roaring of the sea and its waves.*e* 26People will faint with fear and apprehension because of the things that are to come on the world, for the powers of heaven will be shaken loose.*f* 27Then they will see 'the Son of Man coming in a cloud'*b* with power and great glory.*g*

28"Now when these things begin to take place, stand up and lift up your heads, for your deliverance is near."*h*

The Lesson from the Fig Tree
(Matthew 24:32–35; Mark 13:28–31)

29Then he told them a parable: "Look at the fig tree and all the trees.*i* 30As soon as they produce leaves, you can see for yourselves and know that summer is already near. 31In the same way, when you see these things taking place, you will know that the kingdom of God is near.

32"Truly I tell you, this generation will not disappear until all these things take place. 33Heaven and earth will disappear, but my words will never disappear."*j*

---

a 21:23 Or *on earth*   b 21:27 Dan 7:13

Be Alert

34"Constantly be on your guard so that your hearts may not be loaded down with self-indulgence, drunkenness, and the worries of this life, or that day will take you by surprise[a] 35like a trap. For it will come on all who live on the face of the earth.[b] 36So be alert at all times, praying that you may have strength to escape all these things that are going to take place and to take your stand in the presence of the Son of Man."[c]

37Now during the day he would teach in the Temple, but at night he would go out and spend the night on what is called the Mount of Olives.[d] 38And all the people would get up early in the morning to listen to him in the Temple.

The Plot to Kill Jesus

(Matthew 26:1–5, 14–16; Mark 14:1–2, 10–11; John 11:45–53)

22 1Now the Festival of Unleavened Bread, which is called the Passover, was near.[e] 2So the high priests and the scribes were looking for a way to put him to death, for they were afraid of the crowd.[f]

3But Satan went into Judas called Iscariot, who belonged to the circle[a] of the twelve.[g] 4So he went off and discussed with the high priests and the temple police how he could betray him to them. 5They were delighted and agreed to give him money.[h] 6He accepted their offer and began to look for a good opportunity to betray him to them when no crowd was present.

The Passover with the Disciples

(Matthew 26:17–25; Mark 14:12–21; John 13:21–30)

7Then the day of the Festival[b] of Unleavened Bread came, on which the Passover lamb had to be sacrificed.[i] 8So Jesus[c] sent Peter and John, saying, "Go and make preparations for us to eat the Passover meal." 9They asked him, "Where do you want us to prepare it?" 10He said to them, "Just after you go into the city, a man carrying a jug of water will meet you. Follow him into the house he enters 11and say to the owner of the house, 'The Teacher asks you,

---

a 22:3 Lit. *number*　　b 22:7 The Gk. lacks *of the Festival*　　c 22:8 Lit. *he*

21:34
a Rom 13:13;
1 Thes 5:6;
1 Peter 4:7

21:35
b 1 Thes 5:2;
2 Peter 3:10;
Rev 3:3; 16:15

21:36
c Ps 1:5;
Matt 24:42; 25:13;
Mark 13:33;
Lk 18:1; Eph 6:13

21:37
d Lk 22:39;
John 8:1-2

22:1
e Matt 26:2;
Mark 14:1

22:2
f Ps 2:2;
John 11:47;
Acts 4:27

22:3
g Matt 26:14;
Mark 14:10;
John 13:2,27

22:5
h Zech 11:12

22:7
i Matt 26:17;
Mark 14:12

22:14
a Matt 26:20;
Mark 14:17

22:16
b Lk 14:15;
Acts 10:41;
Rev 19:9

22:18
c Matt 26:29;
Mark 14:25

22:19
d Matt 26:26;
Mark 14:22;
1Cor 11:24

22:20
e 1Cor 10:16

22:21
f Ps 41:9;
Matt 26:21,23;
Mark 14:18;
John 13:21,26

22:22
g Matt 26:24;
Acts 2:23; 4:28

22:23
h Matt 26:22;
John 13:22,25

22:24
i Mark 9:34;
Lk 9:46

22:25
j Matt 20:25;
Mark 10:42

22:26
k Matt 20:26;
Lk 9:48;
1Peter 5:3

"Where is the room where I can eat the Passover meal with my disciples?" ' 12Then he will show you a large upstairs room that is furnished. Get things ready for us there." 13So they went and found everything just as Jesus[a] had told them, and they prepared the Passover meal.

The Lord's Supper
(Matthew 26:26–30; Mark 14:22–26; 1 Corinthians 11:23–25)

14Now when the hour came, he took his place at the table, along with the apostles.[a] 15He said to them, "I have eagerly desired to eat this Passover meal with you before I suffer. 16For I tell you, I will never again eat one until it finds its fulfillment in the kingdom of God."[b]

17Then he took a cup, gave thanks, and said, "Take this and share it among yourselves. 18For I tell you, from now on I will never drink the product of the vine until the kingdom of God comes."[c]

19Then he took a loaf of bread, gave thanks, broke it in pieces, and gave it to them, saying, "This is my body, which is given for you. Keep on doing this in memory of me."[d]

20He did the same with the cup after supper, saying, "This cup is the new covenant in my blood, poured out for you.[e] 21Yet look! The hand of the man who is betraying me is with me on the table![f] 22For the Son of Man is going away, just as it has been determined, but how terrible it will be for that man by whom he is betrayed!"[g] 23Then they began to discuss among themselves which one of them was going to do this.[h]

An Argument about Greatness

24Now an argument sprang up among them as to which one of them was to be regarded as the greatest.[i] 25But he said to them, "The kings of the Gentiles lord it over them, and those who exercise authority over them are called benefactors.[j] 26But you are not to do so. On the contrary, the greatest among you should become like the youngest, and the one who leads should become like the one who serves.[k] 27For who is greater, the one who sits at the table, or the one

---

a 22:13 Lit. he

who serves? It is the one at the table, isn't it? But I am among you as one who serves.[a]

28"You are the ones who have always stood by me in my trials.[b] 29And I confer on you, just as my Father has conferred on me, a kingdom,[c] 30so that you may eat and drink at my table in my kingdom and sit down on thrones to govern the twelve tribes of Israel."[d]

Jesus Predicts Peter's Denial
(Matthew 26:31–35; Mark 14:27–31; John 13:36–38)

31"Simon, Simon, listen! Satan has asked permission to sift all of you[a] like wheat,[e] 32but I have prayed for you that your own faith may not fail. When you have turned back, you must strengthen your brothers."[f] 33Peter[b] said to him, "Lord, I am ready to go even to prison and to death with you!" 34But Jesus[c] said, "I tell you, Peter, the rooster will not crow today until you deny three times that you know me."[g]

Be Prepared for Trouble

35Then he said to them, "When I sent you out without a wallet, traveling bag, or sandals, you didn't lack anything, did you?" They said, "Nothing at all."[h] 36Then he said to them, "But now the one who has a wallet must take it along, and his traveling bag, too. And the one who has no sword must sell his coat and buy one. 37For I tell you, what has been written about me must be fulfilled: 'He was counted among the criminals.'[d] Indeed, what is written about me must be fulfilled."[i] 38So they said, "Lord, look! Here are two swords." He answered them, "Enough of that!"[e]

Jesus Prays on the Mount of Olives
(Matthew 26:36–46; Mark 14:32–42)

39Then he went out and as usual came to the Mount of Olives. The disciples went with him.[j] 40When he came to the place, he said to them, "Keep on praying that you may not come into temptation."[k] 41Then he withdrew from them about a stone's throw, knelt down, and began to

---

a 22:31 Lit. *to sift you* (plural)   b 22:33 Lit. *He*   c 22:34 Lit. *he*
d 22:37 Isa 53:12   e 22:38 Or *That is enough*

22:27
a Matt 20:28;
Lk 12:37;
John 13:13-14;
Phil 2:7

22:28
b Heb 4:15

22:29
c Matt 24:47;
Lk 12:32;
2Cor 1:7;
2Tim 2:12

22:30
d Ps 49:14;
Matt 8:11; 19:28;
Lk 14:15;
1Cor 6:2;
Rev 3:21; 19:9

22:31
e Amos 9:9;
1Peter 5:8

22:32
f Ps 51:13;
John 17:9,11,15;
21:15-17

22:34
g Matt 26:34;
Mark 14:30;
John 13:38

22:35
h Matt 10:9;
Lk 9:3; 10:4

22:37
i Isa 53:12;
Mark 15:28

22:39
j Matt 26:36;
Mark 14:32;
Lk 21:37;
John 18:1

22:40
k Matt 6:13; 26:41;
Mark 14:38;
Lk 22:46

22:41
ᵃMatt 26:39;
Mark 14:35

pray,ᵃ ⁴²"Father, if you are willing, take this cup away from me. Yet not my will but yours be done!"ᵇ

⁴³Then an angel from heaven appeared to him and gave him strength.ᶜ ⁴⁴In his anguish he prayed more earnestly, and his sweat became like large drops of blood falling on the ground.ᵃᵈ

22:42
ᵇJohn 5:30; 6:38

⁴⁵When he got up from prayer, he went to the disciples and found them asleep from sorrow. ⁴⁶He said to them, "Why are you sleeping? Get up and keep on praying that you may not come into temptation."ᵉ

22:43
ᶜMatt 4:11

Jesus Is Arrested
(Matthew 26:47–56; Mark 14:43–50; John 18:3–11)

22:44
ᵈJohn 12:27;
Heb 5:7

⁴⁷While Jesusᵇ was still speaking, a crowd came up. The man called Judas, one of the twelve, was leading them, and he came close to Jesus to kiss him.ᶠ ⁴⁸But Jesus said to him, "Judas, are you betraying the Son of Man with a kiss?"

22:46
ᵉLk 22:40

⁴⁹When those who were around him saw what was about to take place, they asked, "Lord, should we strike with our swords?" ⁵⁰Then one of them struck the high priest's servant, cutting off his right ear.ᵍ ⁵¹But Jesus said, "No more of this!" So he touched his ear and healed him.

22:47
ᶠMatt 26:47;
Mark 14:43;
John 18:3

⁵²Then Jesus said to the high priests, the temple police, and the elders, who had come for him, "Have you come out with swords and clubs as if I were a revolutionary?ᶜʰ ⁵³While I was with you day after day in the Temple, you didn't lay a hand on me. But this is your hour when darkness reigns!"ᵈⁱ

22:50
ᵍMatt 26:51;
Mark 14:47;
John 18:10

Peter Denies Jesus
(Matthew 26:57–58, 69–75; Mark 14:53–54, 66–72; John 18:12–18, 25–27)

22:52
ʰMatt 26:55;
Mark 14:48

⁵⁴Then they arrested him, led him away, and brought him to the high priest's house. But Peter was following at a distance.ʲ ⁵⁵When they had kindled a fire in the middle of the courtyard and had taken their seats, Peter, too, sat down among them.ᵏ ⁵⁶A servant girl saw him sitting by the fire, stared at him, and said, "This man was with him, too." ⁵⁷But

22:53
ⁱJohn 12:27

22:54
ʲMatt 26:57-58;
John 18:15

22:55
ᵏMatt 26:69;
Mark 14:66;
John 18:17-18

ᵃ22:44 Other mss. lack verses 43 and 44   ᵇ22:47 Lit. *he*   ᶜ22:52 Or *bandit*   ᵈ22:53 Lit. *your hour and the power of darkness*

he denied it, saying, "I don't know him, woman!" [58]A little later a man looked at him and said, "You are one of them, too." But Peter said, "Mister,[a] I am not!"[a] [59]About an hour later another man emphatically asserted, "This man was certainly with him, for he is a Galilean!"[b] [60]But Peter said, "Mister,[a] I don't know what you're talking about!" Just then, while he was still speaking, a rooster crowed.

[61]Then the Lord turned and looked at Peter. Peter remembered the word of the Lord and how he had said to him, "Before a rooster crows today, you will deny me three times."[c] [62]And he went outside and cried bitterly.

Jesus Is Insulted and Beaten
(Matthew 26:67–68; Mark 14:65)

[63]Then the men who were holding Jesus in custody began to make fun of him while they beat him.[d] [64]They blindfolded him and asked him over and over again, "Prophesy! Who is the one who hit you?" [65]And they kept insulting[b] him in many other ways.

[66]As soon as day came, the elders of the people, the high priests, and the scribes assembled and brought him before their Council.[c][e] [67]They said, "If you are the Christ,[d] tell us." But he said to them, "If I tell you, you won't believe me,[f] [68]and if I ask you a question, you won't answer me. [69]But from now on the Son of Man will be seated at the right hand of the mighty God."[e][g] [70]Then they all asked, "Are you, then, the Son of God?" He answered them, "You say that I am."[h] [71]Then they said, "Why do we need any more testimony? We have heard it ourselves from his own mouth!"[i]

Jesus Is Taken to Pilate
(Matthew 27:1–2, 11–14; Mark 15:1–5; John 18:28–38)

23 [1]Then the whole crowd got up and took him to Pilate.[j] [2]They began to accuse him, "We found this man corrupting our nation, forbidding us to pay taxes to Caesar, and saying that he is the Christ,[d] a king."[k] [3]Then Pilate asked him, "Are you the king of the

---

a 22:58,22:60 Lit. Man   b 22:65 Or blaspheming   c 22:66 Or Sanhedrin
d 22:67,23:2 I.e. the Messiah   e 22:69 Or the power of God

Cross references (side column):

22:58
a Matt 26:71;
Mark 14:69;
John 18:25

22:59
b Matt 26:73;
Mark 14:70;
John 18:26

22:61
c Matt 26:34,75;
Mark 14:72;
John 13:38

22:63
d Matt 26:67-68;
Mark 14:65

22:66
e Matt 27:1;
Acts 4:26; 22:5

22:67
f Matt 26:63;
Mark 14:61

22:69
g Matt 26:64;
Mark 14:62;
Heb 1:3; 8:1

22:70
h Matt 26:64;
Mark 14:62

22:71
i Matt 26:65;
Mark 14:62

23:1
j Matt 27:2;
Mark 15:1;
John 18:28

23:2
k Matt 17:27;
22:21;
Mark 12:17;
John 19:12;
Acts 17:7

23:3
a Matt 27:11;
1 Tim 6:13

23:4
b 1 Peter 2:22

23:7
c Lk 3:1

23:8
d Matt 14:1;
Mark 6:14; Lk 9:9

23:11
e Isa 53:3

23:12
f Acts 4:27

23:13
g Matt 27:23;
Mark 15:14;
John 18:38; 19:4

23:14
h Lk 23:1-2,4

23:16
i Matt 27:26;
John 19:1

23:17
j Matt 27:15;
Mark 15:6;
John 18:39

23:18
k Acts 3:14

Jews?" He answered him, "You say so."*a* 4Then Pilate said to the high priests and crowds, "I do not find anything blameworthy in this man."*b* 5But they kept insisting, "He is stirring up the people by teaching all over Judea, beginning in Galilee even to this place."

Jesus Is Sent to Herod

6When Pilate heard this, he asked whether the man was a Galilean. 7When he learned with certainty that Jesus*a* came from Herod's jurisdiction, he sent him off to Herod, for he was in Jerusalem at that time.*c*

8Now Herod was very glad to see Jesus, because he had been wanting to see him for a long time on account of what he had heard about him. He was also hoping to see some sign done by him.*d* 9So he continued to question him for a long time, but Jesus*a* gave him no answer at all.

10Meanwhile, the high priests and the scribes stood by and continued to accuse him vehemently. 11Even*b* Herod and his soldiers treated him with contempt and made fun of him. Then he put a magnificent robe on him and sent him back to Pilate.*e* 12So Herod and Pilate became friends with each other that very day. Before this they had been enemies.*f*

Jesus Is Sentenced to Death
(Matthew 27:15–26; Mark 15:6–15; John 18:39–19:16)

13Then Pilate called the high priests, the other*c* leaders, and the people together*g* 14and said to them, "You brought this man to me as one who turns the people against the government. And here in your presence I have examined him and have not found him guilty of the charges you make against him.*h* 15Nor does Herod, for he sent him back to us. Indeed, he has done nothing to deserve death. 16So I will punish him and let him go."*i* 17Now he was obligated to release someone for them at the festival.*dj*

18But they all shouted out together, "Away with this man! Release Barabbas for us!"*k* 19(This was a man who had

---

a *23:7,23:9* Lit. *he*   **b** *23:11* Other mss. lack *Even*   **c** *23:13* The Gk. lacks *other*   **d** *23:16* Other mss. lack verse 17

been put in prison for a revolt that had taken place in the city and for murder.) [20]But Pilate wanted to let Jesus go, so he appealed to them again, [21]but they continued to shout, "Crucify him! Crucify him!" [22]Then he spoke to them a third time: "What has he done wrong? I have found nothing in him worthy of death. So I will punish him and let him go." [23]But they kept pressing him with loud shouts, demanding that Jesus[a] be crucified, and their shouts began to prevail.

[24]Then Pilate pronounced his sentence that their demand should be carried out.[a] [25]So he released the man who had been put in prison for revolt and murder—the man they continued to demand—but he let them have their way with Jesus.[b]

Jesus Is Crucified
(Matthew 27:32–44; Mark 15:21–32; John 19:17–27)

[26]As they led him away, they took hold of Simon, a man from Cyrene, as he was coming in from the country, and they put the cross on him and made him carry it behind Jesus.[b] [27]A large crowd of people followed him, including some women who kept beating their breasts and wailing for him. [28]But Jesus turned to them and said, "Women[c] of Jerusalem, stop crying for me, but cry for yourselves and for your children. [29]For the days are surely coming when people[d] will say, 'How blessed are the women who couldn't bear children and the wombs that never bore and the breasts that never nursed!'[c] [30]Then they will begin to say to the mountains, 'Fall on us!', and to the hills, 'Cover us up!'[e][d] [31]For if they do this when the wood is green, what will happen when it is dry?"[e]

[32]Two others, who were criminals, were also led away to be executed with him.[f] [33]When they reached the place called The Skull, they crucified him there with the criminals, one on his right and one on his left.[g] [34]Jesus kept saying, "Father, forgive them, for they don't know what they're doing."[f]

---

a 23:23 Lit. he   b 23:25 Lit. he turned Jesus over to their will   c 23:28 Lit. Daughters   d 23:29 Lit. they   e 23:30 Hos 10:8   f 23:34 Other mss. lack Jesus kept saying, "Father, forgive them, for they don't know what they're doing

23:24
a Matt 27:26;
Mark 15:15;
John 19:16

23:26
b Matt 27:32;
Mark 15:21;
John 19:17

23:29
c Matt 24:19;
Lk 21:23

23:30
d Isa 2:19;
Hos 10:8;
Rev 6:16; 9:6

23:31
e Prov 11:31;
Jer 25:29;
Ezek 20:47;
21:3-4;
1Peter 4:17

23:32
f Isa 53:12;
Matt 27:38

23:33
g Matt 27:33;
Mark 15:22;
John 19:17-18

23:34
a Matt 5:44; 27:35;
Mark 15:24;
John 19:23;
Acts 3:17; 7:60;
1Cor 4:12

Then they divided his clothes among them by throwing dice.*a* 35Meanwhile, the people stood looking on. Even the leaders were mocking him and saying, "He saved others. Let him save himself, if he is the Christ*a* of God, whom he has chosen!" *b*

23:35
b Ps 22:17;
Zech 12:10;
Matt 27:39;
Mark 15:29

36The soldiers also made fun of him, coming up and offering him sour wine 37and saying, "If you are the king of the Jews, save yourself!" 38There was also an inscription over him written in Greek, Latin, and Hebrew:*b* "This is the King of the Jews."*c*

39Now one of the criminals hanging there kept insulting*c* him, saying, "You're the Christ,*a* aren't you? Save yourself

23:38
c Matt 27:37;
Mark 15:26;
John 19:19

and us!"*d* 40But the other one reprimanded him, saying, "Aren't you afraid of God, since you are suffering the same penalty? 41We have been condemned justly, for we are getting what we deserve for our deeds, but this man has done nothing wrong." 42Then he went on to say, "Jesus, remember

23:39
d Matt 27:44;
Mark 15:32

me when you come into*d* your kingdom!" 43Jesus*e* said to him, "Truly I tell you, today you will be with me in Paradise."

Jesus Dies on the Cross
(Matthew 27:45–56; Mark 15:33–41; John 19:28–30)

23:44
e Matt 27:45;
Mark 15:33

44It was already about noon,*f* and darkness came over the whole land*g* until three in the afternoon*h e* 45because the sun had stopped shining. And the curtain*i* in the Sanctuary was torn in two.*f* 46Then Jesus cried out with a loud voice and said, "Father, into your hands I entrust my spirit."*j* After he said this, he breathed his last.*g*

23:45
f Matt 27:51;
Mark 15:38

47When the centurion*k* saw what had taken place, he praised God and said, "This man certainly was righteous!"*h* 48When all the crowds who had come together for this spectacle saw what had taken place, they beat their breasts and turned back. 49But all his acquaintances, including the

23:46
g Ps 31:5;
Matt 27:50;
Mark 15:37;
John 19:30;
1Peter 2:23

23:47
h Matt 27:54;
Mark 15:39

---

a 23:35,23:39 I.e. the Messiah   b 23:38 Other mss. lack *written in Greek, Latin, and Hebrew*   c 23:39 Or *blaspheming*   d 23:42 Other mss. read *in* e 23:43 Lit. *He*   f 23:44 Lit. *the sixth hour*   g 23:44 Or *earth*   h 23:44 Lit. *the ninth hour*   i 23:45 This curtain separated the Holy Place from the Most Holy Place.   j 23:46 Ps 31:5   k 23:47 A Roman centurion commanded about 100 men.

women who had followed him from Galilee, were standing at a distance watching these things.*a*

Jesus Is Buried
(Matthew 27:57–61; Mark 15:42–47; John 19:38–42)

50Now there was a man named Joseph, a member of the Council, a good and righteous man,*b* 51who had not voted for their plan and action. He was from the Jewish town of Arimathea, and he was waiting for the kingdom of God.*c* 52He went to Pilate and asked for the body of Jesus. 53Then he took it down, wrapped it in a linen cloth, and laid it in a tomb cut in the rock, in which no one had yet been laid.*d*

54It was the Preparation Day, and the Sabbath was just beginning.*e* 55So the women who had come with Jesus*a* from Galilee, following close behind, saw the tomb and how his body was laid.*f* 56Then they went back and prepared spices and perfumes, and on the Sabbath they rested according to the commandment.*g*

Jesus Is Raised from the Dead
(Matthew 28:1–10; Mark 16:1–8; John 20:1–10)

24 1But on the first day of the week at early dawn they went to the tomb, taking the spices they had prepared.*h* 2They found the stone rolled away from the tomb,*i* 3but when they went in, they didn't find the body of the Lord Jesus.*bj*

4While they were perplexed about this, two men in dazzling robes suddenly stood beside them.*k* 5Because the women were terrified and were bowing their faces to the ground, the men*c* asked them, "Why are you looking among the dead for someone who is living? 6He is not here but has been raised.*d* Remember what he told you while he was still in Galilee,*l* 7'the Son of Man must be handed over to sinful men, be crucified, and rise on the third day.' "

8Then they remembered his words.*m* 9They returned from the tomb and reported all these things to the eleven and all the others.*n* 10The women who told the apostles

---

a *23:55* Lit. *with him*   b *24:3* Other mss. lack *of the Lord Jesus*   c *24:5* Lit. *they*   d *24:6* Other mss. lack *He is not here, but has been raised*

23:49
a Ps 38:11;
Matt 27:55;
Mark 15:40;
John 19:25

23:50
b Matt 27:57;
Mark 15:42;
John 19:38

23:51
c Mark 15:43;
Lk 2:25,38

23:53
d Matt 27:59;
Mark 15:46

23:54
e Matt 27:62

23:55
f Mark 15:47;
Lk 8:2

23:56
g Exod 20:10;
Mark 16:1

24:1
h Matt 28:1;
Mark 16:1;
Lk 23:56;
John 20:2

24:2
i Matt 28:2;
Mark 16:4

24:3
j Mark 16:5;
Lk 24:23

24:4
k John 20:12;
Acts 1:10

24:6
l Matt 16:21;
17:23; Mark 8:31;
9:31; Lk 9:22

24:8
m John 2:22

24:9
n Matt 28:8;
Mark 16:10

24:10
a Lk 8:3

about it were Mary Magdalene, Joanna, Mary the mother of James, and the others.*a* ¹¹But these words seemed to them to be nonsense, and they wouldn't believe them.*b* ¹²Peter, however, got up and ran to the tomb. He stooped down and saw only the linen cloths. Then he went home wondering about what had happened.*ac*

24:11
b Mark 16:11;
Lk 16:25

Jesus Meets Two Disciples
(Mark 16:12–13)

24:12
c John 20:3,6

¹³On the same day, two of them were going to a village called Emmaus, about seven miles*b* from Jerusalem.*d* ¹⁴They were talking with each other about all these things that had taken place. ¹⁵While they were talking and discussing, Jesus himself approached and began to walk with them,*e* ¹⁶but their eyes were prevented from recognizing him.*f*

24:13
d Mark 16:12

24:15
e Matt 18:20;
Lk 18:36

¹⁷He asked them, "What are you discussing with each other as you're walking along?" They stood still and looked gloomy. ¹⁸The one whose name was Cleopas answered him, "Are you the only visitor to Jerusalem who doesn't know what happened there these days?"*g* ¹⁹He asked them, "What things?" They answered him, "The things about Jesus of Nazareth,*c* who was a prophet, mighty in what he did and said before God and all the people,*h* ²⁰and how our high priests and leaders handed him over to be condemned to death and had him crucified.*i* ²¹But we kept hoping that he would be the one to redeem*d* Israel. What is more, this is now the third day since these things occurred.*j* ²²Even some of our women have startled us! They were at the tomb early this morning*k* ²³and didn't find his body there, so they came back and told us that they had actually seen a vision of angels who said he was alive. ²⁴Then some of those who were with us went to the tomb and found it just as the women had said, but they didn't see him."*l*

24:16
f John 20:14; 21:4

24:18
g John 19:25

24:19
h Matt 21:11;
Lk 7:16; John 3:2;
4:19; 6:14;
Acts 2:22; 7:22

24:20
i Lk 23:1;
Acts 13:27-28

24:21
j Lk 1:68; 2:38;
Acts 1:6

²⁵Then Jesus*e* said to them, "O how foolish you are and how slow of heart to believe everything the prophets said! ²⁶The Christ*f* had to suffer these things and then enter his

24:22
k Matt 28:8;
Mark 16:10;
Lk 16:9-10;
John 20:18

24:24
l Lk 24:12

---

a *24:12* Other mss. lack verse 12.   b *24:13* Lit. *sixty stadia*   c *24:19* Other mss. read *the Nazorean*   d *24:21* Or *to free*   e *24:25* Lit. *he*   f *24:26* I.e. The Messiah

glory, didn't he?"[a] 27Then, beginning with Moses and all the Prophets, he explained to them all the passages of Scripture about himself.[b]

28As they came near the village where they were going, he acted as though he were going on farther.[c] 29But they urged him strongly, "Stay with us, for it is almost evening and the day is almost gone." So he went in to stay with them.[d] 30While he was at the table with them, he took the bread, blessed it, broke it in pieces, and gave it to them.[e] 31Their eyes were opened, and they knew who he was. Then he vanished from them.

32Then they said to each other, "Our hearts kept burning within us[a] as he was talking to us on the road and explaining the Scriptures to us, didn't they?" 33That same hour they got up and went back to Jerusalem and found the eleven and their companions all together. 34They kept saying, "The Lord has really risen and has appeared to Simon!"[f] 35Then they themselves began to tell what had happened on the road and how he was recognized by them when he broke the bread in pieces.

Jesus Appears to the Disciples
(Matthew 28:16–20; Mark 16:14–18; John 20:19–23; Acts 1:6–8)

36While they were talking about this, Jesus[b] himself stood among them and said to them, "Peace be with you."[c][g] 37They were startled and terrified and thought that they were seeing a ghost.[h] 38He said to them, "Why are you frightened, and why are doubts arising in your hearts? 39Look at my hands and my feet, for it is I myself. Touch me and see, for a ghost doesn't have flesh and bones as you see that I have."[i] 40After he had said this, he showed them his hands and his feet.[d] 41While they still could not believe it for joy and were full of amazement, he said to them, "Do you have anything here to eat?"[j] 42They gave him a piece of broiled fish, 43and he took it and ate it in their presence.[k]

44Then he said to them, "These are my words that I

---

a 24:32 Other mss. lack *within us*   b 24:36 Lit. *he*   c 24:36 Other mss. lack *and said to them, "Peace be with you."*   d 24:40 Other mss. lack verse 40

24:26
a Lk 24:46;
Acts 17:3;
1Peter 1:11

24:27
b Gen 3:15; 22:18;
26:4; 49:10;
Num 21:9;
Deut 18:15;
Ps 16 title,9-10;
132:11; Isa 7:14:
9:6; 40:10-11;
50:6; Jer 23:5;
33:14-15;
Ezek 34:23;
37:25; Dan 9:24;
Mic 7:20; Mal 3:1;
4:2; Lk 24:45;
John 1:45

24:28
c Gen 32:26; 42:7;
Mark 6:48

24:29
d Gen 19:3;
Acts 16:15

24:30
e Matt 14:19

24:34
f 1Cor 15:5

24:36
g Mark 16:14;
John 20:19;
1Cor 15:5

24:37
h Mark 6:49

24:39
i John 20:20,27

24:41
j Gen 45:26;
John 21:5

24:43
k Acts 10:41

24:44
a Matt 16:21;
17:22; 20:18;
Mark 8:31;
Lk 9:22; 18:6,31
24:45
b Acts 16:14
24:46
c Ps 22:1-31;
Isa 50:6; 53:2;
Lk 24:26;
Acts 17:3
24:47
d Gen 12:3;
Ps 22:27; Isa 49:6,
22; Jer 31:34;
Dan 9:24;
Hos 2:23;
Mic 4:2; Mal 1:11;
Acts 13:38,46;
1John 2:12
24:48
e John 15:27;
Acts 1:8,22; 2:32;
24:49
f Isa 44:3;
Joel 2:28;
John 14:16,26;
15:26; 16:7;
Acts 1:4; 2:1
24:50
g Acts 1:12
24:51
h 2Kings 2:11;
Mark 16:19;
John 20:17;
Acts 1:9; Eph 4:8
24:52
i Matt 28:9,17
24:53
j Acts 2:46; 5:42

spoke to you while I was still with you—that everything written about me in the Law of Moses, the Prophets, and the Psalms had to be fulfilled."*a* 45Then he opened their minds so that they might continue to understand the Scriptures.*b* 46He said to them, "Thus it is written, that the Christ**a** was to suffer and to rise from the dead on the third day,*c* 47and that repentance and forgiveness of sins is to be proclaimed in his name to all the nations, beginning at Jerusalem.*d* 48You are witnesses of these things.*e* 49I am sending on you what my Father promised. But stay here in the city until you have been clothed with power from on high."*f*

Jesus Is Taken Up to Heaven
(Mark 16:19–20; Acts 1:9–11)

50Then he led them out as far as Bethany, lifted up his hands, and blessed them.*g* 51While he was blessing them, he parted from them and was taken up to heaven.**b***h* 52They worshiped him and**c** returned to Jerusalem with great joy.*i* 53And they were continually in the Temple blessing**d** God.**e***j*

---

a 24:46 I.e. the Messiah   **b** 24:51 Other mss. lack *and was taken up to heaven*   **c** 24:52 Other mss. lack *worshiped him and*   **d** 24:53 Other mss. read *praising*; still other mss. read *praising and blessing*   **e** 24:53 Other mss. read *God. Amen*

209

THE GOSPEL ACCORDING TO
JOHN

The Word and Creation

1 ¹In the beginning, the Word existed. The Word was with God, and the Word was God.[a] ²He existed in the beginning with God.[b] ³Through him all things were made, and apart from him nothing was made that has been made.[c] ⁴In him was life, and that life brought light to humanity.[a][d] ⁵And the light shines on in the darkness, and the darkness has never put it out.[b][e]

John's Witness to the Word

⁶There was a man sent from God, whose name was John.[f] ⁷He came as a witness to testify about the light, so that all might believe through him.[g] ⁸He was not the light, but he came[c] to testify about the light. ⁹This[d] was the true light that enlightens every person by his coming into the world.[e][h]

Responses to the Word

¹⁰He was in the world, and the world was made through him. Yet the world did not recognize him.[i] ¹¹He came to his own creation,[f] yet his own people did not receive him.[j] ¹²However, to all who received him, to those who kept believing in his name, he gave authority to become God's children,[k] ¹³who were born, not merely in a physical sense,[g] or from a fleshly impulse, or from a man's desire, but of God.[l]

The Word Becomes Human

¹⁴The Word became flesh and pitched his tent[h] among us. We gazed on his glory, the kind of glory that belongs to the Father's only Son,[i] full of grace and truth.[m] ¹⁵John told the truth about him when he cried out, "This is the person about whom I said, 'The one who comes after me ranks

---

a 1:4 Lit. *was the light of people*   b 1:5 Or *understood it*   c 1:8 The Gk. lacks *he came*   d 1:9 Lit. *He*   e 1:9 Or *every person who is coming into the world*   f 1:11 Or *possessions*   g 1:13 Lit. *not of bloods*   h 1:14 Or *lived*   i 1:14 Or *unique Son*; the Gk. lacks *Son*

1:1
a Prov 8:22-23,30; John 17:5; Phil 2:6; Col 1:17; 1John 1:1-2; 5:7; Rev 1:2; 19:13

1:2
b Gen 1:1

1:3
c Ps 33:6; John 1:10; Eph 3:9; Col 1:16; Heb 1:2; Rev 4:11

1:4
d John 5:26; 8:12; 9:5; 12:35,46; 1John 5:11

1:5
e John 3:19

1:6
f Mal 3:1; Matt 3:1; Lk 3:2; John 3:33

1:7
g Acts 19:4

1:9
h Isa 49:6; John 1:4; 1John 2:8

1:10
i John 1:3; Heb 1:2; 11:3

1:11
j Lk 19:14; Acts 3:26; 13:46

1:12
k Isa 56:5; Rom 8:15; Gal 3:26; 2Peter 1:4; 1John 3:1

1:13
l John 3:5; James 1:18; 1Peter 1:23

1:14
m Isa 40:5; Matt 1:16,20; 17:2; Lk 1:31,35; 2:7; John 2:11; 11:40; Rom 1:3; Gal 4:4; Col 1:19; 2:3,9; 1Tim 3:16; Heb 2:11,14, 16-17; 2Peter 1:17

1:15
a Matt 3:11;
Mark 1:7; Lk 3:16;
John 1:32; 3:27,
30-32; 5:33; 8:58;
Col 1:17
1:16
b John 3:34;
Eph 1:6-8;
Col 1:19; 2:9-10
1:17
c Exod 20:1;
Deut 4:44; 5:1;
33:4; John 8:32;
14:6; Rom 3:24;
5:21; 6:14
1:18
d Exod 33:20;
Deut 4:12;
Matt 11:27;
Lk 10:22;
John 3:16,18;
4:14; 6:46;
1Tim 1:17; 6:16;
1John 4:9,12,20
1:19
e John 5:33
1:20
f Lk 3:15;
John 3:28;
Acts 13:25
1:21
g Deut 18:15,18;
Mal 4:5;
Matt 17:10
1:23
h Isa 40:3;
Matt 3:3;
Mark 1:3; Lk 3:4;
John 3:28
1:26
i Mal 3:1;
Matt 3:11
1:27
j John 1:15,30;
Acts 19:4
1:28
k Jdg 7:24;
John 10:40
1:29
l Exod 12:3;
Isa 53:7,11;
John 1:36;
Acts 8:32;
1Cor 15:3;
Gal 1:4; Heb 1:3;
2:17; 9:28;
1Peter 1:19; 2:24;
3:18; 1John 2:2;
3:5; 4:10; Rev 1:5;
5:6
1:30
m John 1:15,27
1:31
n Mal 3:1;
Matt 3:6; Lk 1:17,
76-77; 3:3-4

ahead of me, because he existed before me.' "*a* ¹⁶From his fullness we have all received, one gracious gift after another.*ab* ¹⁷For the Law was given through Moses; grace and truth came through Jesus Christ.*c* ¹⁸No one has ever seen God. The only God,*b* who is close to the Father's side, has revealed him.*d*

The Testimony of John the Baptist
(Matthew 3:1–12; Mark 1:2–8; Luke 3:15–17)

¹⁹This was John's testimony when the Jews sent priests and Levites to him from Jerusalem to ask him, "Who are you?"*e* ²⁰He spoke openly and did not deny it, but confessed, "I am not the Christ."*cf* ²¹So they asked him, "Well then, are you Elijah?" He said, "I am not." "Are you the Prophet?" He answered, "No."*g* ²²Then they said to him, "Who are you? We must give an answer to those who sent us. What do you say about yourself?" ²³He said,*h*

"I am the voice of one crying out in the
wilderness,
'Make the way of the Lord straight,' "*d*

as the prophet Isaiah said.

²⁴Now they had been sent from the Pharisees. ²⁵They asked him, "Why, then, are you baptizing if you are not the Christ*c* or Elijah or the Prophet?" ²⁶John answered them, "I am baptizing with*e* water. Among you is standing a man whom you do not know,*i* ²⁷the one who is coming after me. I am not worthy to untie his sandal straps."*j* ²⁸This happened in Bethany*f* on the other side of the Jordan, where John was baptizing.*k*

²⁹The next day John*g* saw Jesus coming toward him and said, "Look, the Lamb of God who takes away the sin of the world!*l* ³⁰This is the one about whom I said, 'After me comes a man who ranks ahead of me, because he existed before me.'*m* ³¹I didn't recognize him, but I came baptizing with*e* water so that he might be revealed to Israel."*n* ³²John

---

a *1:16* Lit. *grace for grace*   **b** *1:18* Other mss. read *Son*   **c** *1:20,1:25* I.e. the Messiah   **d** *1:23* Isa 40:3   **e** *1:26,1:31* Or *in*   **f** *1:28* Other mss. read *Bethabara*   **g** *1:29* Lit. *he*

also testified, "I saw the Spirit coming down from heaven like a dove, and it remained on him."[a] [33]I didn't recognize him, but the one who sent me to baptize with[a] water told me, 'The person on whom you see the Spirit descending and remaining is the one who baptizes with[a] the Holy Spirit.'[b] [34]I have seen this and have testified that this is the Son[b] of God."

The First Disciples

[35]The next day John was again standing there with two of his disciples. [36]As he watched Jesus walk by, he said, "Look, the Lamb of God!"[c] [37]When the two disciples heard him say this, they followed Jesus. [38]But when Jesus turned around and saw them following, he said to them, "What are you looking for?" They said to him, "Rabbi" (which is translated Teacher), "where are you staying?" [39]He told them, "Come, and you will see." So they went and saw where he was staying, and they stayed with him that day. It was about four o'clock in the afternoon.[c]

[40]Andrew, Simon Peter's brother, was one of the two who heard John and followed Jesus.[d][d] [41]Andrew[e] first found his brother Simon and said to him, "We have found the Messiah" (which is translated Christ).[f] [42]He led Simon[d] to Jesus. Jesus looked at him intently and said, "You are Simon, the son of John. You will be called Cephas"[g](which is translated Peter).[h][e]

Jesus Calls Philip and Nathaniel

[43]The next day Jesus decided to go away into Galilee. He found Philip and said to him, "Follow me." [44]Now Philip was from Bethsaida, the hometown of Andrew and Peter.[f] [45]Philip found Nathaniel and told him, "We have found the man about whom Moses in the Law and the prophets wrote—Jesus, the son of Joseph, from Nazareth."[g] [46]Nathaniel said to him, "Out of Nazareth? What good can that be?" Philip told him, "Come and see!"[h]

---

a1:33 Or in   **b**1:34 Other mss. read Chosen One   **c**1:39 Lit. the tenth hour   **d**1:40,1:42 Lit. him   **e**1:41 Lit. He   **f**1:41 I.e. Anointed One   **g**1:42 Cephas means rock in Aram.   **h**1:42 Peter means rock in Gk.

212

Side references

1:32
a Matt 3:16;
Mark 1:10;
Lk 3:22; John 5:32

1:33
b Matt 3:11;
Acts 1:5; 2:4;
10:44; 19:6

1:36
c John 1:29

1:40
d Matt 4:18

1:42
e Matt 16:18

1:44
f John 12:21

1:45
g Gen 3:15; 49:10;
Deut 18:18;
Isa 4:2; 7:14; 9:6;
53:2; Mic 5:2;
Zech 6:12; 9:9;
Matt 2:23; Lk 2:4;
24:27; John 21:2

1:46
h John 7:41-42,52

1:47
a Ps 32:2;
73:1 John 8:39;
Rom 2:28-29; 9:6

47Jesus saw Nathaniel coming toward him and said about him, "Look, a true Israelite, in whom there is no falsehood!"*a* 48Nathaniel said to him, "How do you know me?" Jesus answered him, "Before Philip called you, while you were under the fig tree, I saw you." 49Nathaniel replied to him, "Rabbi, you are the Son of God! You are the King of

1:49
b Matt 14:33; 21:5;
27:11,
42 John 18:37;
19:3

Israel!"*b* 50Jesus said to him, "Do you believe because I told you that I saw you under the fig tree? You will see greater things than that." 51Then he said to him, "Truly, truly I tell all of you,*a* you will see heaven standing open and the angels of God going up and coming down to the Son of Man."*c*

1:51
c Gen 28:12;
Matt 4:11; Lk 2:9,
13; 22:43; 24:4;
Acts 1:10

Jesus Changes Water into Wine

2 1On the third day there was a wedding in Cana of Galilee. The mother of Jesus was there,*d* 2and Jesus and his disciples had also been invited to the wedding. 3When the wine ran out, Jesus' mother said to him,

2:1
d Josh 19:28

"They don't have any wine." 4Jesus said to her, "How does that concern us, woman? My hour has not yet come."*e* 5His mother told the servants, "Do whatever he tells you."

6Now standing there were six stone water jars used for

2:4
e 2Sam 16:10;
19:22 John 7:6;
19:26

the Jewish rites of purification, each one holding from twenty to thirty gallons.*f* 7Jesus told the servants,*b* "Fill the jars with water." So they filled them up to the brim. 8Then he said to them, "Now draw some out and take it to the man in charge of the banquet." So they took it.

2:6
f Mark 7:3

9When the man in charge of the banquet tasted the water that had become wine (without knowing where it had come from, though the servants who had drawn the water knew), he*c* called for the bridegroom*g* 10and said to him, "Everyone

2:9
g John 4:46

serves the best wine first, and the cheap kind when people*d* are drunk. But you have kept the best wine until now!" 11Jesus did this, the first*e* of his signs, in Cana of Galilee. He revealed his glory, and his disciples believed in him.*h*

12After this, Jesus*f* went down to Capernaum—he, his

2:11
h John 1:14

mother, his brothers, and his disciples—and they remained there for a few days.*i*

2:12
i Matt 12:46

---

a *1:51* Lit. *you* (plural)   **b** *2:7* Lit. *them*   **c** *2:9* Lit. *the man in charge of the banquet*   **d** *2:10* Lit. *they*   **e** *2:11* Or *beginning*   **f** *2:12* Lit. *he*

213

Jesus Throws Merchants and Moneychangers out of the Temple
(Matthew 21:12–13; Mark 11:15–17; Luke 19:45–46)

2:13
a Exod 12:14;
Deut 16:1,16;
John 5:1; 6:4;
11:55; 16:23

¹³The Jewish Passover was near, so Jesus went up to Jerusalem.*a* ¹⁴In the Temple he found people selling cattle, sheep, and doves, as well as moneychangers sitting at their tables.*b* ¹⁵Making a whip out of cords, he drove all of them out of the Temple, including the sheep and the cattle. He scattered the coins of the moneychangers and knocked over their tables. ¹⁶Then he told those who were selling the doves, "Take these things out of here! Stop making my Father's house a marketplace!"*c* ¹⁷His disciples remembered that it was written, "Zeal for your house will consume me."*ad*

2:14
b Matt 21:12;
Mark 11:15;
Lk 19:45

2:16
c Lk 2:49

¹⁸Then the Jews said to him, "What sign can you show us as authority for doing these things?"*e* ¹⁹Jesus answered them, "Destroy this sanctuary, and in three days I will rebuild it."*f* ²⁰The Jews said, "This Sanctuary has been under construction for forty-six years, and you're going to rebuild it in three days?" ²¹But the sanctuary he was speaking about was his own body.*g* ²²After he had been raised from the dead, his disciples remembered that he had said this. So they believed the Scripture and the statement that Jesus had made.*bh*

2:17
d Ps 69:9

2:18
e Matt 12:38;
John 6:30

2:19
f Matt 26:61;
27:40;
Mark 14:58; 15:29

Jesus Knows All People

²³While Jesus*c* was in Jerusalem for the Passover Festival, many people believed in his name because they saw the signs that he was doing. ²⁴Jesus, however, did not entrust himself to them, because he knew all people ²⁵and didn't need anyone to tell him what people were like. For he himself knew what was in every person.*di*

2:21
g 1Cor 3:16; 6:19;
2Cor 6:16;
Col 2:9; Heb 8:2

2:22
h Lk 24:8

Jesus Talks with Nicodemus

3 ¹One such person belonged to the Pharisees. His name was Nicodemus, and he was a leader of the Jews. ²He came to Jesus*e* at night and said to him, "Rabbi, we know that you have come from God as a teacher, for no one

2:25
i 1Sam 16:7;
1Chr 28:9;
Matt 9:4;
Mark 2:8;
John 6:64; 16:30;
Acts 1:24;
Rev 2:23

---

a 2:17 Ps 69:9   **b** 2:22 Lit. *spoken*   **c** 2:23 Lit. *he*   **d** 2:25 Lit. *in a person*
e 3:2 Lit. *him*

3:2
a John 7:50; 9:16, 33; 19:39; Acts 2:22; 10:38

3:3
b John 1:13; Gal 6:15; Titus 3:5; James 1:18; 1Peter 1:23; 1John 3:9

3:5
c Mark 16:16; Acts 2:38

3:8
d Eccl 11:5; 1Cor 2:11

3:9
e John 6:52,60

3:11
f Matt 11:27; John 1:18; 3:24,32; 7:16; 8:28; 12:49

3:13
g Prov 30:4; John 6:33,38,51, 62; 16:28; Acts 2:34; 1Cor 15:47; Eph 4:9-10

3:14
h Num 21:9; John 8:28; 12:32

3:15
i John 3:36; 6:47

3:16
j Rom 5:8; 1John 4:9

3:17
k Lk 9:56; John 5:45; 8:15; 12:47; 1John 4:14

can perform these signs that you are doing unless God is with him."[a]

[3]Jesus replied to him, "Truly, truly I tell you, unless a person is born from above[a] he cannot see the kingdom of God."[b]

[4]Nicodemus said to him, "How can a person be born when he is old? He can't go back into his mother's womb a second time and be born, can he?"

[5]Jesus answered, "Truly, truly I tell you, unless a person is born of water and Spirit he cannot enter the kingdom of God.[bc] [6]What is born of the flesh is flesh, and what is born of the Spirit is spirit. [7]Don't be astonished that I said to you, 'All of you[c] must be born from above.'[a] [8]The wind[d] blows where it wants to. You hear its sound, but you don't know where it comes from or where it is going. That's the way it is with everyone who is born of the Spirit."[d]

[9]Nicodemus said to him, "How can that be?"[e] [10]Jesus answered him, "You're the teacher of Israel, and you can't understand this? [11]Truly, truly I tell you, we know what we're talking about, and we testify about what we've seen. Yet you people[e] do not accept our testimony.[f] [12]If I have told you people[e] about earthly things and you do not believe, how will you believe if I tell you about heavenly things?

[13]"No one has gone up to heaven except the one who came down from heaven, the Son of Man who is in heaven.[fg] [14]Just as Moses lifted up the serpent in the wilderness, so must the Son of Man be lifted up,[h] [15]so that everyone who believes in him may have eternal life.[gi]

[16]"For this is how God loved the world: He gave his only[h] Son so that everyone who believes in him would not perish but have eternal life.[j] [17]For God sent the Son into the world, not to condemn the world, but that the world might be saved through him.[k] [18]Whoever believes in him is not

---

a 3:3,3:7 Or *again*   b 3:5 Other mss. read *of heaven*   c 3:7 Lit. *You* (plural)   d 3:8 The same Gk. word can be translated both *wind* and *spirit*.   e 3:11,3:12 Lit. *you* (plural)   f 3:13 Other mss. lack *who is in heaven*   g 3:15 The quotation possibly concludes with this verse instead of with verse 21.   h 3:16 Or *unique*

condemned, but whoever does not believe has already been condemned, because he has not believed in the name of God's only[a] Son.[a] 19And this is the basis for judgment: The light has come into the world, but people loved the darkness more than the light because their actions were evil.[b] 20For everyone who practices wickedness hates the light and does not come to the light, so that his actions may not be exposed.[bc] 21But whoever does what is true comes to the light, so that all may see[c] that his actions have been done in God."

John the Baptist Talks about Jesus

22After this, Jesus and his disciples went into the Judean countryside. He spent some time there with them and began baptizing.[d] 23John was also baptizing in Aenon, near Salim, because there was plenty of water there. People[d] kept coming and were being baptized,[e] 24since John had not yet been thrown into prison.[f]

25Then a controversy about ritual purification sprang up between John's disciples and a Jew.[e] 26They went to John and told him, "Rabbi, the man who was with you on the other side[f] of the Jordan, the one about whom you testified—look, he's baptizing, and all are going to him!"[g] 27John replied, "No one can receive anything unless it has been given to him from heaven.[h] 28You yourselves are my[g] witnesses that I said, 'I am not the Christ,[h] but I have been sent ahead of him.'[i] 29It is the bridegroom who gets the bride, yet the bridegroom's friend, who merely[i] stands by and listens for him, is overjoyed to hear the bridegroom's voice. That's why this joy of mine is now complete.[j] 30He must become more important, but I must become less important."

The One Who Comes from Above

31The one who comes from above is over everything. The one who is of the earth belongs to the earth and speaks about earthly things.[j] The one who comes from heaven is

---

a3:18 Or *unique*   b3:20 Other mss. read *exposed that they are evil*
c3:21 Lit. *so that it may be revealed*   d3:23 Lit. *They*   e3:25 Other mss.
read *the Jews*   f3:26 I.e., the east side   g3:28 Other mss. lack *my*
h3:28 I.e. the Messiah   i3:29 The Gk. lacks *merely*   j3:31 Lit. *of the earth*

3:18
a John 5:24; 6:40, 47; 20:31

3:19
b John 1:4,9-11; 8:12

3:20
c Job 24:13,17; Eph 5:13

3:22
d John 4:2

3:23
e 1Sam 9:4; Matt 3:5-6

3:24
f Matt 14:3

3:26
g John 1:7,15,27, 34

3:27
h 1Cor 4:7; Heb 5:4; James 1:17

3:28
i Mal 3:1; Mark 1:2; Lk 1:17; John 1:20,27

3:29
j Song 5:1; Matt 22:2; 2Cor 11:2; Eph 5:25,27; Rev 21:9

3:31
a Matt 28:18;
John 1:15,27;
3:13; 6:33; 8:23;
Rom 9:5;
1Cor 15:47;
Eph 1:21; Phil 2:9

3:32
b John 3:11; 8:26;
15:15

3:33
c Rom 3:4;
1John 5:10

3:34
d John 1:16; 7:16

3:35
e Matt 11:27;
28:18; Lk 10:22;
John 5:20,22;
13:3; 17:2;
Heb 2:8

3:36
f Hab 2:4;
John 1:12;
6:15-16,47;
Rom 1:17;
1John 5:10

4:1
g John 3:22,26

4:5
h Gen 33:19;
48:22 Josh 24:32

4:9
i 2Kings 17:24;
Lk 9:52-53;
Acts 10:28

4:10
j Isa 12:3;
44:3 Jer 2:13;
Zech 13:1; 14:8

over everything.[a] [32]He testifies about what he has seen and heard, yet no one accepts his testimony.[b] [33]The person who has accepted his testimony has acknowledged that God is truthful.[ac] [34]For the one whom God sent speaks the words of God, because God[b] does not give the Spirit in limited measure.[d] [35]The Father loves the Son and has put everything in his hands.[e] [36]The one who believes in the Son has eternal life, but the one who disobeys the Son will not see life. Instead, the wrath of God remains on him.[f]

Jesus Meets a Samaritan Woman

4 [1]Now when Jesus[c] realized that the Pharisees had heard that he was making and baptizing more disciples than John[g]—[2]although it was not Jesus who did the baptizing but his disciples—[3]he left Judea and went back to Galilee. [4]Now it was necessary for him to go through Samaria. [5]So he came to a town in Samaria called Sychar, near the piece of land that Jacob had given to his son Joseph.[h] [6]Jacob's Well was also there, and Jesus, tired out by the journey, sat down by the well. It was about twelve noon.[d]

[7]A Samaritan woman came to draw some water, and Jesus said to her, "Please give me a drink." [8]For his disciples had gone off into town to buy food. [9]The Samaritan woman said to him, "How can you, a Jew, ask for a drink from me, a Samaritan woman?" For Jews do not have anything to do with Samaritans.[ei] [10]Jesus answered her, "If you knew the gift of God, and who it is who is saying to you, 'Please give me a drink,' you would have been the one to ask him, and he would have given you living water."[j] [11]The woman[f] said to him, "Sir, you don't have a bucket, and the well is deep. Where are you going to get this living water? [12]You're not greater than our ancestor Jacob, who gave us the well and drank from it, along with his sons and his flocks, are you?" [13]Jesus answered her, "Everyone who drinks this water will become thirsty again. [14]But whoever drinks the water that I

---

a 3:33 Or *true*   b 3:34 Lit. *he*   c 4:1 Other mss. read *the Lord*   d 4:6 Lit. *the sixth hour*   e 4:9 Other mss. lack *For Jews do not have anything to do with Samaritans.*   f 4:11 Other mss. read *She*

will give him will never become thirsty again. The water that I will give him will become in him a well of water springing up to eternal life."[a] [15]The woman said to him, "Sir, give me this water, so that I won't get thirsty or have to keep coming here to draw water."[b]

[16]He said to her, "Go and call your husband, and come back here." [17]The woman answered him, "I don't have a husband." Jesus said to her, "You are quite right in saying, 'I don't have a husband.' [18]For you have had five husbands, and the man you have now is not your husband. What you have said is true." [19]The woman said to him, "Sir, I see that you are a prophet![c] [20]Our ancestors worshiped on this mountain. But you Jews[a] say that the place where people should worship is in Jerusalem."[d] [21]Jesus said to her, "Believe me, woman, the hour is coming when you Samaritans[a] will worship the Father neither on this mountain nor in Jerusalem.[e] [22]You don't know what you're worshiping. We know what we're worshiping, for salvation comes from the Jews.[f] [23]Yet the hour is coming, and is now here, when true worshipers will worship the Father in spirit[b] and truth. Indeed, the Father is looking for people like that to worship him.[g] [24]God is spirit,[c] and those who worship him must worship in spirit[b] and truth."[h] [25]The woman said to him, "I know that the Messiah is coming" (who is called Christ). "When he comes, he will tell us everything."[i] [26]Jesus said to her, "I am he, the one who is speaking to you."[j]

[27]At this point his disciples arrived, and they were amazed that he was talking to a woman. Yet no one said, "What do you want from her?"[d] or, "Why are you talking to her?" [28]Then the woman left her water jar and went back to town. She told the people, [29]"Come and see a man who told me everything I've ever done! Could he possibly be the Christ?"[e][k] [30]The people[f] left the town and started on their way to him.

[31]Meanwhile, the disciples were urging him, "Rabbi, have something to eat." [32]But he said to them, "I have food to eat that you know nothing about." [33]So the disciples began

---

4:14
[a]John 6:35,58; 7:38

4:15
[b]John 6:34; 17:2-3; Rom 6:23; 1John 5:20

4:19
[c]Lk 7:16; 24:19; John 6:14; 7:40

4:20
[d]Deut 12:5,11; Jdg 9:7; 1Kings 9:3; 2Chr 7:12

4:21
[e]Mal 1:11; 1Tim 2:8

4:22
[f]2Kings 17:29; Isa 2:3; Lk 24:47; Rom 9:4-5

4:23
[g]John 1:17; Phil 3:3

4:24
[h]2Cor 3:17

4:25
[i]John 4:29,39

4:26
[j]Matt 26:63-64; Mark 14:61-62; John 9:37

4:29
[k]John 4:25

---

[a]4:20,4:21 Lit. *you* (plural)   [b]4:23,4:24 Or *the Spirit*   [c]4:24 Or *Spirit*
[d]4:27 Lit. *want*   [e]4:29 I.e. the Messiah   [f]4:30 Lit. *They*

4:34
a Job 23:12;
John 6:38; 17:4;
19:30

to say to one another, "No one has brought him anything to eat, has he?" 34Jesus told them, "My food is doing the will of the one who sent me and completing his work.*a* 35You say, don't you, 'In four more months the harvest will be here?' Look, I tell you, open your eyes and observe that the fields are ready**a** for harvesting!**b** 36The one who harvests is already receiving his wages and gathering a crop for eternal life, so that the one who sows and the one who harvests may rejoice together.*c* 37For in this respect the saying is true: 'One person sows, and another person harvests.'**b** 38I have sent you to harvest what you have not labored for. Others have labored, and you have entered into their labor."

4:35
b Matt 9:37;
Lk 10:2

4:36
c Dan 12:3

39Now many of the Samaritans of that town believed in Jesus**c** because of the woman's testimony when she testified, "He told me everything I've ever done."*d* 40So when the Samaritans came to him, they asked him to stay with them, and he stayed there for two days. 41And many more believed because of his word. 42They kept telling the woman, "It is no longer because of what you said that we believe, for we have heard him ourselves, and we know that he really is the Savior of the world."*e*

4:39
d John 4:29

4:42
e John 17:8;
1 John 4:14

Jesus Heals an Official's Son

43Two days later, Jesus**d** went from that place to Galilee. 44For Jesus himself had testified that a prophet has no honor in his own country.*f* 45When he arrived in Galilee, the Galileans welcomed him because they had seen all that he had done in Jerusalem during the festival. For they, too, had gone to the festival.*g*

4:44
f Matt 13:57;
Mark 6:4; Lk 4:24

4:45
g Deut 16:16;
John 2:23; 3:2

46So he came again to Cana in Galilee, where he had turned the water into wine. Meanwhile, in Capernaum there was a government official whose son was ill.*h* 47When this man heard that Jesus had come from Judea to Galilee, he went to him and begged him to come down and heal his son, for he was about to die. 48Jesus told him, "Unless you people**e** see signs and wonders, you will never believe."*i* 49The official said to him, "Sir,**f** please come down before my

4:46
h John 2:1,11

4:48
i 1 Cor 1:22

a 4:35 Lit. *white*   **b** 4:37 Mic 6:15   **c** 4:39 Lit. *in him*   **d** 4:43 Lit. *he*
e 4:48 Lit. *you* (plural)   **f** 4:49 Or *Lord,*

little boy dies." ⁵⁰Jesus said to him, "Go home. Your son will live." The man believed what Jesus told him and started on his way.

⁵¹While he was on his way down, his servants met him and told him that his child[a] was alive. ⁵²So he asked them at what hour he had begun to recover, and they told him, "The fever left him yesterday at one o'clock in the afternoon."[b] ⁵³Then the father realized that this was the very hour when Jesus had said to him, "Your son will live." And he himself believed, along with his whole family.

⁵⁴Now this was the second sign that Jesus did after coming from Judea to Galilee.

The Healing at the Pool

5 ¹Later on, there was a[c] festival of the Jews, and Jesus went up to Jerusalem.[a] ²Near the Sheep Gate in Jerusalem is a pool called Bethesda[d] in Hebrew. It has five colonnades,[e][b] ³and under these a large number of sick people were lying—blind, lame, or paralyzed—waiting for the movement of the water.[f] ⁴For at certain times an angel of the Lord would go down into the pool and stir up the water. And the one who stepped in first after the stirring of the water was healed of whatever disease he had.[g]

⁵One particular man was there who had been ill for thirty-eight years. ⁶When Jesus saw him lying there and knew that he had already been there a long time, he said to him, "Do you want to get well?" ⁷The sick man answered him, "Sir, I don't have anyone to put me into the pool when the water is stirred up. While I'm trying to get there, someone else steps down ahead of me." ⁸Jesus said to him, "Stand up, pick up your mat, and walk!"[c] ⁹The man immediately became well, and he picked up his mat and started walking. Now that day was a Sabbath.[d]

¹⁰So the Jews said to the man who had been healed, "It is the Sabbath, and it is not lawful for you to carry your mat."[e]

---

a 4:51 Other mss. read *son*　b 4:52 Lit. *the seventh hour*　c 5:1 Other mss. read *the*　d 5:2 Other mss. read *Bethzatha*; still other mss. read *Bethsaida*　e 5:2 I.e. columns supporting the roof　f 5:3 Other mss. lack *waiting for the movement of the water*　g 5:4 Other mss. lack v. 4.

5:1
a Lev 23:2;
Deut 16:1;
John 2:13

5:2
b Neh 3:1; 12:39

5:8
c Matt 9:6;
Mark 2:11;
Lk 5:24

5:9
d John 9:14

5:10
e Exod 20:10;
Neh 13:19;
Jer 17:21;
Matt 12:2;
Mark 2:24; 3:4;
Lk 6:2; 13:14

5:14
a Matt 12:45;
John 8:11

5:17
b John 9:4; 14:10

5:18
c John 7:19; 10:30,
33; Phil 2:6

5:19
d John 5:30; 8:28;
9:4; 12:49; 14:10

5:20
e Matt 3:17;
John 3:35;
2Peter 1:17

5:21
f Lk 7:14; 8:54;
John 11:25,43

5:22
g Mal 1:11;
Matt 11:27; 28:18;
John 3:35; 17:2;
Acts 17:31;
1Peter 4:5

5:23
h 1John 2:23

5:24
i John 3:16,18;
6:40,47; 8:51;
20:31; 1John 3:14

5:25
j John 5:28;
Eph 2:1,5; 5:14;
Col 2:13

5:27
k Dan 7:13-14;
John 5:22;
Acts 10:42; 17:31

[11]But he answered them, "The man who made me well told me, 'Pick up your mat and walk.' " [12]They asked him, "Who is the man who told you, 'Pick it up and walk'?" [13]But the man who had been healed did not know who it was, for Jesus had slipped away from the crowd in that place. [14]Later on, Jesus found him in the Temple and told him, "See, you have become well. Stop sinning or something worse may happen to you."[a] [15]The man went off and told the Jews[a] that it was Jesus who had made him well. [16]So the Jews[a] began persecuting Jesus because he kept doing such things on the Sabbath. [17]But Jesus[b] answered them, "My Father has been working until now, and I, too, am working."[b] [18]So the Jews[a] were trying all the harder to kill him, because he was not only breaking the Sabbath but was also calling God his own Father, thus making himself equal to God.[c]

The Authority of the Son

[19]Jesus said to them, "Truly, truly I tell you, the Son can do nothing on his own accord, but only what he sees the Father doing. For what he does, the Son does likewise.[d] [20]For the Father loves the Son and shows him everything he is doing. And he will show him even greater works than these, so that you may be amazed.[e] [21]Just as the Father raises the dead and gives them life, so also the Son gives life to those he chooses.[f] [22]For the Father judges no one, but has given all judgment to the Son,[g] [23]so that all may honor the Son as they honor the Father. The one who does not honor the Son does not honor the Father who sent him.[h]

[24]"Truly, truly I tell you, the one who hears my word and believes in the one who sent me has eternal life and does not come under judgment, but has passed from death to life.[i] [25]Truly, truly I tell you, the hour is coming, and is now here, when the dead will hear the voice of the Son of God, and those who hear it will live.[j] [26]For just as the Father has life in himself, so also he has granted the Son to have life in himself. [27]And he has given him authority to pass judgment, because he is the Son of Man.[k] [28]Don't be amazed at this, because the hour is coming when all who are in their

a 5:15,5:16,5:18 I.e. Jewish leaders   b 5:17 Other mss. read he

graves will hear his voice ²⁹and will come out—those who have done what is good to the resurrection of life, and those who have practiced what is evil to the resurrection of condemnation.ᵃᵃ ³⁰I can do nothing on my own accord. As I hear, I judge, and my judgment is just, because I do not seek my own will but the will of the one who sent me."ᵇ

Jesus' Greater Testimony

³¹"If I testify about myself, my testimony is not true.ᶜ ³²There is another who testifies about me, and I knowᵇ that the testimony he gives about me is true.ᵈ ³³You have sent messengersᶜ to John, and he has testified to the truth.ᵉ ³⁴I myself do not accept human testimony, but I am saying these things so that you may be saved. ³⁵That man was a lamp that burns and brightly shines, and for a while you were willing to rejoice in his light.ᶠ ³⁶But I have a greater testimony than John's, for the works that the Father has given me to complete, the very works that I am doing, testify on my behalf that the Father has sent me.ᵍ ³⁷Moreover, the Father who sent me has himself testified on my behalf. You have never heard his voice or seen his appearance,ʰ ³⁸nor do you have his word abiding in you, because you do not believe in the one whom he sent. ³⁹You study the Scriptures, for you suppose that in them you have eternal life. Yet they testify about me.ⁱ ⁴⁰But you are not willing to come to me to have life.ʲ

⁴¹"I do not accept human praise.ᵏ ⁴²I know that you do not have the love of God in you. ⁴³I have come in my Father's name, and you do not accept me. Yet if another man comes in his own name, you will accept him. ⁴⁴How can you believe when you accept each other's praise and do not look for the praise that comes from the only God?ᵈˡ ⁴⁵Do not suppose that I will be the one to accuse you before the Father. Your accuser is Moses, on whom you have set your hope.ᵐ ⁴⁶For if you believed Moses, you would believe me, for it was about me that he wrote.ⁿ ⁴⁷But if you do not believe what he wrote, how will you believe my words?"

ᵃ5:29 Or *of judgment*   ᵇ5:32 Other mss. read *you know*   ᶜ5:33 The Gk. lacks *messengers*   ᵈ5:44 Other mss. read *the only One*

Cross-references (margin):

5:29
ᵃIsa 26:19;
Dan 12:2;
Matt 25:32-33,46;
1Cor 15:52;
1Thes 4:16

5:30
ᵇMatt 26:39;
John 4:34; 5:19;
6:38

5:31
ᶜJohn 8:14;
Rev 3:14

5:32
ᵈMatt 3:17; 17:5;
John 8:18;
1John 5:6-7,9

5:33
ᵉJohn 1:15,19,27,
32

5:35
ᶠMatt 13:20;
21:26; Mark 6:20;
2Peter 1:19

5:36
ᵍJohn 3:2; 10:25;
15:24; 1John 5:9

5:37
ʰDeut 4:12;
Matt 3:17; 17:5;
John 1:18; 6:27;
8:18; 1Tim 1:17;
1John 4:12

5:39
ⁱDeut 18:15,18;
Isa 8:20; 34:16;
Lk 16:29; 24:27;
John 1:45; 5:27;
Acts 17:11

5:40
ʲJohn 1:11; 3:19

5:41
ᵏJohn 5:34;
1Thes 2:6

5:44
ˡJohn 12:43;
Rom 2:29

5:45
ᵐRom 2:12

5:46
ⁿGen 3:15; 12:3;
18:18; 22:18;
49:10;
Deut 18:15,18;
John 1:45;
Acts 26:22

6:1
a Matt 14:15;
Mark 6:35;
Lk 9:10,12

Jesus Feeds More Than Five Thousand
(Matthew 14:13–21; Mark 6:30–44; Luke 9:10–17)

6 ¹After this, Jesus went away to the other side of the Sea of Galilee (or Tiberias).*a* ²A large crowd kept following him because they had seen the signs that he was performing on the sick. ³But Jesus went up on a hillside and sat down there with his disciples.

6:4
b Lev 23:5,7;
Deut 16:1;
John 2:13; 5:1

⁴Now the Passover, the festival of the Jews, was near.*b* ⁵When Jesus looked up and saw that a large crowd was coming toward him, he said to Philip, "Where can we buy bread for these people to eat?"*c* ⁶Jesus*a* said this to test him, for he himself knew what he was going to do. ⁷Philip answered him, "Two hundred denarii*b* worth of bread is not enough for each of them to get a little."*d* ⁸One of his disciples, Andrew, who was Simon Peter's brother, said to him, ⁹"There's a little boy here who has five barley loaves and two small fish. But what are they among so many people?"*e* ¹⁰Jesus said, "Have the people sit down." Now there was plenty of grass in that place. So the men sat down, numbering about five thousand. ¹¹Then Jesus took the loaves, gave thanks, and distributed them to those who were seated. He also distributed*c* the fish, as much as they wanted. ¹²When they were completely satisfied, he told his disciples, "Collect the pieces that are left over so that nothing is lost." ¹³So they collected them and filled twelve baskets with the pieces of the five barley loaves left over by those who had eaten.

6:5
c Matt 14:14;
Mark 6:35;
Lk 9:12

6:7
d Num 11:21-22

6:9
e 2Kings 4:43

¹⁴When the people saw the sign*d* that he had done, they kept saying, "Truly this is the Prophet who was to come into the world!"*f* ¹⁵Then Jesus, realizing that they were about to come and take him by force to make him king, withdrew*e* again to the hillside by himself.

6:14
f Gen 49:10;
Deut 18:15,18;
Matt 11:3;
John 1:21; 4:19,
25; 7:40

Jesus Walks on the Sea
(Matthew 14:22–27; Mark 6:45–52)

¹⁶When evening came, his disciples went down to the sea,*g* ¹⁷got into a boat, and started across the sea to

6:16
g Matt 14:23;
Mark 6:47

---

a 6:6 Lit. *He*   *b* 6:7 The denarius was the usual day's wage for a laborer. *c* 6:11 Lit. *Likewise also*   *d* 6:14 Other mss. read *signs*   *e* 6:15 Other mss. read *fled*

Capernaum. Darkness had already fallen, and Jesus had not yet come to them. ¹⁸A strong wind was blowing, and the sea was getting rough. ¹⁹They had rowed about three or four miles[a] when they saw Jesus walking on the sea and coming near the boat. They became terrified. ²⁰But he said to them, "It is I. Stop being afraid!" ²¹So they were glad to take him into the boat, and immediately the boat reached the land toward which they were going.

Jesus the Bread of Life

²²The next day, the crowd that had remained on the other side of the sea noticed that only one boat had been there, and no other, and that Jesus had not gotten into that boat with his disciples. Instead, his disciples had gone away by themselves. ²³Other small boats from Tiberias arrived near the place where they had eaten the bread after the Lord had given thanks.[b] ²⁴When the crowd saw that neither Jesus nor his disciples were there, they got into these boats and went to Capernaum to look for Jesus.

²⁵When they had found him on the other side of the sea, they asked him, "Rabbi, when did you get here?" ²⁶Jesus replied to them, "Truly, truly I tell you, you are looking for me, not because you saw signs, but because you ate the loaves and were completely satisfied. ²⁷Do not work for the food that perishes but for the food that lasts for eternal life, which the Son of Man will give you. For it is on him that God the Father has set his seal."[a] ²⁸Then they said to him, "What must we do to perform the works of God?" ²⁹Jesus answered them, "This is the work of God: to believe in the one whom he has sent."[b] ³⁰So they said to him, "What sign are you going to do so that we may see it and believe in you? What work are you performing?[c] ³¹Our ancestors ate the manna in the wilderness, just as it is written, 'He gave them bread from heaven to eat.' "[cd] ³²Jesus said to them, "Truly, truly I tell you, it was not Moses who gave you the bread from heaven, but it is my Father who gives you the true bread from heaven. ³³For the bread of God is the one

---

a 6:19 Lit. *twenty-five or thirty stadia*   b 6:23 Other mss. lack *after the Lord had given thanks*   c 6:31 Ps 78:24; Exod 16:15; Num 11:7-9

6:27
a Matt 3:17; 17:5;
Mark 1:11; 9:7;
Lk 3:22; 9:35;
John 1:33; 4:14;
5:37; 6:54; 8:18;
Acts 2:22;
2Peter 1:17

6:29
b 1John 3:23

6:30
c Matt 12:38; 16:1;
Mark 8:11;
1Cor 1:22

6:31
d Exod 16:15;
Num 11:7;
Neh 9:15;
Ps 78:24-25;
1Cor 10:3

6:34
a John 4:15

6:35
b John 4:14; 6:48,
58; 7:37

6:36
c John 6:26,64

6:37
d Matt 24:24;
John 6:45;
10:28-29;
2Tim 2:19;
1John 2:19

6:38
e Matt 26:39;
John 4:34; 5:30

6:39
f John 10:28;
17:12; 18:9

6:40
g John 3:15-16;
4:14; 6:27,47,54

6:42
h Matt 13:55;
Mark 6:3; Lk 4:22

6:44
i Song 1:4;
John 6:65

6:45
j Isa 54:13;
Jer 31:34; Mic 4:2;
John 10:37;
Heb 8:10; 10:16

6:46
k Matt 11:27;
Lk 10:22;
John 1:18; 5:37;
7:29; 8:19

6:47
l John 3:16,18,36;
6:40

6:48
m John 6:33,35

6:49
n John 6:31

6:50
o John 6:51,58

6:51
p John 3:13;
Heb 10:5,10

6:52
q John 3:9; 7:43;
9:16; 10:19

who comes down from heaven and gives life to the world."

34Then they said to him, "Sir, give us this bread all the time."a 35Jesus said to them, "I am the bread of life. The one who comes to me will never become hungry, and the one who believes in me will never become thirsty.b 36I told you that you have seen me,a yet you do not believe.c 37Everything the Father gives me will come to me, and the one who comes to me I will never turn away.d 38For I have come down from heaven, not to do my own will, but the will of the one who sent me.e 39And this is the will of the one who sent me, that I should not lose anything that he has given me, but should raise it to life on the last day.f 40For this is my Father's will, that everyone who sees the Son and believes in him should have eternal life, and I will raise him to life on the last day."g

41Then the Jewsb began grumbling about him because he said, "I am the bread that came down from heaven." 42They kept saying, "This is Jesus, the son of Joseph, isn't it, whose father and mother we know? So how can he say, 'I have come down from heaven'?"h 43Jesus answered them, "Stop grumbling among yourselves. 44No one can come to me unless the Father who sent me draws him, and I will raise him to life on the last day.i 45It is written in the Prophets, 'And all of them will be taught by God.'c Everyone who has listened to the Father and has learned anything comes to me.j 46Not that anyone has seen the Father except the one who comes from God. This one has seen the Father.k 47Truly, truly I tell you, the one who believes in med has eternal life.l 48I am the bread of life.m 49Your ancestors ate the manna in the wilderness and died.n 50This is the bread that comes down from heaven, so that a person may eat it and not die.o 51I am the living bread that came down from heaven. If anyone eats this bread, he will live forever. And the bread I will give for the life of the world is my flesh."p

52Then the Jews debated angrily with each other, saying, "How can this man give us his flesh to eat?"q 53So Jesus told them, "Truly, truly I tell you, unless you eat the flesh of the

a 6:36 Other mss. lack me   b 6:41 I.e. Jewish leaders   c 6:45 Isa 54:13
d 6:47 Other mss. lack in me

Son of Man and drink his blood, you do not have life in yourselves.*a* *54*The one who eats my flesh and drinks my blood has eternal life, and I will raise him to life on the last day.*b* *55*For my flesh is real*a* food, and my blood is real*a* drink. *56*The person who eats my flesh and drinks my blood remains in me, and I in him.*c* *57*Just as the living Father sent me and I live because of the Father, so the one who feeds on me will also live because of me. *58*This is the bread that came down from heaven, not the kind that your ancestors ate. They died, but the one who eats this bread will live forever."*d* *59*He said this while teaching in the synagogue at Capernaum.

The Words of Eternal Life

*60*When many of his disciples heard this, they said, "This is a difficult statement. Who can accept*b* it?"*e* *61*But Jesus, knowing in himself that his disciples were grumbling about this, said to them, "Does this offend you? *62*What if you saw the Son of Man going up to the place where he was before?*f* *63*It is the Spirit who gives life; the flesh is useless. The words that I have spoken to you are spirit and are life.*g* *64*But there are some among you who do not believe." For from the beginning Jesus knew those who wouldn't believe, as well as the one who would betray him.*h* *65*So he said, "That's why I told you that no one can come to me unless it be granted him by the Father."*i*

*66*As a result,*c* many of his disciples turned back and no longer associated*d* with him.*j* *67*So Jesus said to the twelve, "You don't want to leave, too, do you?" *68*Simon Peter answered him, "Lord, to whom would we go? You have the words of eternal life.*k* *69*Besides, we have believed and remain convinced that you are the Holy One of God."*el* *70*Jesus answered them, "I chose you twelve, didn't I? Yet one of you is a devil."*m* *71*Now he was speaking about Judas, the son of Simon Iscariot.*f* For this man, even though he was one of the twelve, was going to betray him.

---

a*6:55* Or *true*　**b***6:60* Lit. *listen to*　**c***6:66* Or *From this time*　**d***6:66* Lit. *walked*　**e***6:69* Other mss. read *the Christ, the Son of the living God*　**f***6:71* Other mss. read *Judas Iscariot, the son of Simon*

6:53
a Matt 26:26,28

6:54
b John 4:14; 6:27, 40,63

6:56
c 1 John 3:24; 4:15-16

6:58
d John 6:49-51

6:60
e Matt 11:6; John 6:66

6:62
f Mark 16:19; John 3:13; Acts 1:9; Eph 4:8

6:63
g 2Cor 3:6

6:64
h John 2:24-25; 6:36; 13:11

6:65
i John 6:44-45

6:66
j John 6:60

6:68
k Acts 5:20

6:69
l Matt 16:16; Mark 8:29; Lk 9:20; John 1:49; 11:27

6:70
m Lk 6:13; John 13:27

7:1
ᵃ John 5:16,18

7:2
ᵇ Lev 23:34

7:3
ᶜ Matt 12:46;
Mark 3:31;
Acts 1:14

7:5
ᵈ Mark 3:21

7:6
ᵉ John 2:4; 8:8,20,
30

7:7
ᶠ John 3:19; 15:19

7:8
ᵍ John 8:6,30

7:11
ʰ John 11:56

7:12
ⁱ Matt 21:46;
Lk 7:16;
John 6:14,40;
9:16; 10:19

7:13
ʲ John 9:22; 12:42;
19:38

7:15
ᵏ Matt 13:54;
Mark 6:2; Lk 4:22;
Acts 2:7

7:16
ˡ John 3:11; 8:28;
12:49; 14:10,24

7:17
ᵐ John 8:43

The Unbelief of Jesus' Brothers

7 ¹After this, Jesus traveled aboutᵃ in Galilee, for he didn't want to travelᵇ in Judea because the Jewsᶜ were trying to kill him.ᵃ ²Now the Jewish Festival of Tabernaclesᵈ was approaching.ᵇ ³So his brothers said to him, "You should leave this place and go to Judea, so that your disciples can see the works that you're doing.ᶜ ⁴For no one acts in secret if he wants to be known publicly. If you're going to do these things, you should reveal yourself to the world!" ⁵For not even his brothers believed in him.ᵈ ⁶Jesus told them, "My time has not yet come, but your time is always here.ᵉᵉ ⁷The world cannot hate you, but it hates me because I testify against it that its works are evil.ᶠ ⁸Go up to the festival yourselves. I am not yetᶠ going to this festival, for my time has not yet fully come."ᵍ ⁹After saying this, he remained in Galilee.

Jesus Arrives in Jerusalem

¹⁰But after his brothers had gone up to the festival, he went up himself, not openly but, as it were,ᵍ in secret. ¹¹The Jewsᶜ kept looking for him at the festival, saying, "Where is that man?"ʰ ¹²And there was a great deal of discussion about him among the crowds.ʰ Some were saying, "He is a good man," while others were saying, "No, he is deceiving the crowd!"ⁱ ¹³No one, however, would speak openly about him for fear of the Jews.ᶜʲ

Jesus Openly Declares His Authority

¹⁴Halfway through the festival, Jesus went up to the Temple and began teaching. ¹⁵The Jewsᶜ were astonished and remarked, "How can this man be so educated when he has never gone to school?"ᵏ ¹⁶Jesus replied to them, "My teaching is not mine but comes from the one who sent me.ˡ ¹⁷If anyone wants to do his will, he will know whether this teaching is from God or whether I am speaking on my own.ᵐ ¹⁸The one who speaks on his own seeks his own praise. But

---

ᵃ7:1 Lit. *walked*   ᵇ7:1 Lit. *to walk*   ᶜ7:1,7:11,7:13,7:15 I.e. Jewish leaders   ᵈ7:2 Or *Booths*   ᵉ7:6 Lit. *ready*   ᶠ7:8 Other mss. lack *yet*   ᵍ7:10 Other mss. lack *as it were*   ʰ7:12 Other mss. read *crowd*

the one who seeks the praise of him who sent him is true, and there is nothing false in him.[a] 19Moses gave you the Law, didn't he? Yet none of you is keeping the Law. Why are you trying to kill me?"[b] 20The crowd answered, "You have a demon! Who is trying to kill you?"[c] 21Jesus answered them, "I performed one work, and all of you are astonished. 22Moses gave you circumcision—not that it is from Moses, but from the Patriarchs—and so you circumcise a man on the Sabbath.[d] 23If a man receives circumcision on the Sabbath so that the Law of Moses may not be broken, are you angry with me because I made a man perfectly well on the Sabbath?[e] 24Stop judging by appearances, but judge with righteous judgment!"[f]

Is This the Christ?

25Then some of the people of Jerusalem began saying, "This is the man they are trying to kill, isn't it? 26And look, he is speaking in public, and they are not saying anything to him! Can it be that the authorities really know that this is the Christ?[a][g] 27We know where this man comes from. But when the Christ[a] comes, no one will know where he comes from."[h] 28At this point Jesus, still teaching in the Temple, shouted, "So you know me and know where I have come from? I have not come on my own accord. But the one who sent me is true, and he is the one you do not know.[i] 29I know him because I have come from him and he sent me."[j] 30Then they tried to seize him, but no one laid a hand on him because his hour had not yet come.[k] 31However, many in the crowd believed in him, saying, "When the Christ[a] comes, he won't do more signs than this man has done, will he?"[l]

Officers Are Sent to Arrest Jesus

32The Pharisees heard the crowd debating these things about him, so the high priests and the Pharisees sent officers to arrest him. 33Then Jesus said, "I will be with you only a little while longer, and then I am going back to the one who sent me.[m] 34You will look for me but will not find me.[b] And

---

a7:26,7:27,7:31 I.e. the Messiah   b7:34 Other mss. lack *me*

7:18
a John 5:41; 8:50

7:19
b Exod 24:3;
Deut 33:4;
Matt 12:14;
Mark 3:6;
John 1:17; 5:16,
18; 10:31,39;
11:53; Acts 7:38

7:20
c John 8:48,52;
10:20

7:22
d Gen 17:10;
Lev 12:3

7:23
e John 5:8-9,16

7:24
f Deut 1:16-17;
Prov 24:23;
John 8:15;
James 2:1

7:26
g John 7:48

7:27
h Matt 13:55;
Mark 6:3; Lk 4:22

7:28
i John 1:18; 5:32,
43; 8:14,26,42,55;
Rom 3:4

7:29
j Matt 11:27;
John 10:15

7:30
k Mark 11:18;
Lk 19:47; 20:19;
John 8:20,37,44;
20:19

7:31
l Matt 12:23;
John 3:2; 8:30

7:33
m John 13:33;
16:16

7:34
a Hos 5:6;
John 8:21; 13:33

7:35
b Isa 11:12;
James 1:1;
1Peter 1:1

7:37
c Lev 23:36;
Isa 55:1;
John 6:35;
Rev 22:17

7:38
d Deut 18:15;
Prov 18:4;
Isa 12:3;
44:3 John 4:14

7:39
e Isa 44:3;
Joel 2:28;
John 12:16; 16:7;
Acts 2:17,33,38

7:40
f Deut 18:15,18;
John 1:21; 6:14

7:41
g John 1:46; 4:42;
6:52,69

7:42
h 1Sam 16:1,4;
Ps 132:11;
Jer 23:5; Mic 5:2;
Matt 2:5; Lk 2:4

7:43
i John 7:12; 9:16;
10:19

7:44
j John 7:30

7:46
k Matt 7:29

7:48
l John 12:42;
Acts 6:7;
1Cor 1:20,26; 2:8

where I am, you cannot come."*a* 35Then the Jews*a* said to one another, "Where does this man intend to go so that we will not find him? Surely he's not going to the Dispersion*b* among the Greeks and teach the Greeks, is he?*b* 36What does this statement mean that he made,*c* 'You will look for me but will not find me,' and 'Where I will be, you cannot come'?"

Rivers of Living Water

37On the last and most important day of the festival, Jesus stood up and shouted, "If anyone is thirsty, let him come to me*d* and drink!*c* 38The one who believes in me, as the Scripture has said, will have rivers of living water flowing from his heart."*d* 39Now he said this about the Spirit, whom those who were believing in him were to receive. For the Spirit*e* was not yet present,*f* because Jesus had not yet been glorified.*e*

Division among the People

40When they heard these words, some in the crowd were saying, "This really is the Prophet,"*f* 41while others were saying, "This is the Christ!"*g* But some were saying, "The Christ doesn't come from Galilee, does he?*g* 42Doesn't the Scripture say that the Christ is from David's family and from Bethlehem, the village where David lived?"*h* 43So there was a division in the crowd because of him.*i* 44Some of them were wanting to seize him, but no one laid hands on him.*j*

The Unbelief of the Authorities

45Then the officers returned to the high priests and Pharisees, who said to them, "Why didn't you bring him?" 46The officers answered, "No man ever spoke like that!"*k* 47Then the Pharisees replied to them, "You haven't been deceived, too, have you? 48None of the authorities or Pharisees has believed in him, has he?*l* 49But this mob that does not know the Law—they are accursed!" 50One of their number, Nicodemus (the man who had previously gone to him), said

---

a 7:35 I.e. Jewish leaders   b 7:35 I.e. the Jewish communities outside of Israel   c 7:36 Lit. *said*   d 7:37 Other mss. lack *to me*   e 7:39 Other mss. read *Holy Spirit*   f 7:39 Other mss. read *given*   g 7:41 I.e. the Messiah

to them,[a] [51]"Surely our Law does not condemn[a] a person without first hearing from him and finding out what he is doing, does it?"[b] [52]They answered him, "You aren't from Galilee, too, are you? Search and see that no prophet comes from Galilee."[c] [53]Then each of them went to his own home.

The Woman Caught in Adultery

[1]Jesus, however, went to the Mount of Olives. [2]At daybreak he appeared again in the Temple, and all the people came to him. So he sat down and began to teach them. [3]But the scribes and the Pharisees brought a woman who had been caught in adultery.[b] After setting her before them,[c] [4]they said to him, "Teacher, this woman has been caught in the very act of adultery. [5]Now in the Law, Moses commanded us to stone such women to death. What do you say?"[d] [6]They said this to test him, so that they might have a charge against him. But Jesus bent down and began to write on the ground with his finger. [7]When they persisted in questioning him, he straightened up and said to them, "Let the person among you who is without sin be the first to throw a stone at her."[e] [8]Then he bent down again and continued writing on the ground.[d] [9]When they heard this, they went away one by one,[e] beginning with the oldest,[f] and he was left alone with the woman standing there.[c][f] [10]Then Jesus stood up and said to her, "Woman, where are your accusers?[g] Hasn't anyone condemned you?" [11]She said, "No one, sir."[h] Then Jesus said, "I don't condemn you either. Go home, and from now on do not sin any more."[i][g]

Jesus the Light of the World

[12]Later on Jesus spoke to them again, saying, "I am the light of the world. The one who follows me will never walk in darkness, but will have the light of life."[h] [13]The Pharisees said to him, "You are testifying about yourself. Your

---

a 7:51 Or *judge*　　**b** 8:3 Other mss. read *in sin*　　**c** 8:3,8:9 Lit. *in the middle*
d 8:8 Other mss read *on the ground the sins of each one of them*
e 8:9 Other mss. read *one by one, being convicted by their conscience*
f 8:9 Other mss. read *from the oldest to the youngest*　　**g** 8:10 Other mss.
read *where are they?*　　**h** 8:11 Or *Lord*　　**i** 8:11 Other mss. lack 7:53-8:11

7:50
a John 3:2

7:51
b Deut 1:17; 17:8; 19:15

7:52
c Isa 9:1-2;
Matt 4:15;
John 1:41,46

8:5
d Lev 20:10;
Deut 22:22

8:7
e Deut 17:7;
Rom 2:1

8:9
f Rom 2:22

8:11
g Lk 9:56; 12:14;
John 3:17; 5:14

8:12
h John 1:4-5,9;
3:19; 9:5;
12:35-36,46

8:13
a John 5:31

8:14
b John 7:28; 9:29

8:15
c John 3:17; 7:24;
12:47; 18:36

8:16
d John 8:29; 16:32

8:17
e Deut 17:6;
19:15; Matt 18:16;
2Cor 13:1;
Heb 10:28

8:18
f John 5:37

8:19
g John 8:55; 14:7;
16:3

8:20
h Mark 12:41;
John 7:8,30

8:21
i John 7:34; 13:24,
33

8:23
j John 3:31; 15:19;
17:16; 1John 4:5

8:24
k Mark 16:16;
John 8:21

8:26
l John 3:32; 7:28;
15:15

8:28
m John 3:11,14;
5:19,30; 12:32;
Rom 1:4

testimony is not valid."[aa] [14]Jesus answered them, "Even though I am testifying about myself, my testimony is valid[a] because I know where I have come from and where I am going. But you do not know where I come from or where I am going.[b] [15]You are judging by human standards,[b] but I am not judging anyone.[c] [16]Yet even if I should judge, my judgment would be valid,[a] for it is not I alone who judges, but I and the one who sent me.[d] [17]In your own Law it is written that the testimony of two people is valid.[ae] [18]I am testifying about myself, and the Father who sent me is testifying about me."[f] [19]Then they said to him, "Where is this Father of yours?" Jesus replied, "You do not know me or my Father. If you had known me, you would have known my Father also."[g] [20]He spoke these words in the treasury, while he was teaching in the Temple. Yet no one arrested him, because his hour had not yet come.[h]

The One from Above

[21]Later on he said to them again, "I am going away, and you will look for me but will die in your sins. You cannot come where I am going."[i] [22]So the Jews said, "He isn't going to kill himself, is he? Is that why he said,[c] 'You cannot come where I am going'?" [23]He said to them, "You are from below, I am from above. You are of this world, but I am not of this world.[j] [24]That is why I told you that you will die in your sins. For unless you believe that I am he, you will die in your sins."[k] [25]Then they said to him, "Who are you?" Jesus told them, "What have I been telling you all along?[d] [26]I have much to say about you and to condemn you for.[e] But the one who sent me is truthful,[a] and what I have heard from him I declare to the world."[l] [27]They didn't realize that he was talking to them about the Father. [28]So Jesus told them, "When you have lifted up the Son of Man, then you will know that I am he, and that I do nothing on my own authority. Instead, I speak only what the Father has taught me.[m] [29]Moreover, the one who sent me is with me. He has

---

a 8:13,8:14,8:16,8:17,8:26 Or *true*　b 8:15 Lit. *according to the flesh*　c 8:22 Lit. *Because he said*　d 8:25 Or *from the beginning*　e 8:26 Lit. *to condemn*

never left me alone because I always do what pleases him."[a]
30While he was saying these things, many believed in him.[b]

Freedom and Slavery

31So Jesus said to those Jews who had believed in him, "If you continue in my word, you are really my disciples. 32And you will know the truth, and the truth will set you free."[c] 33They replied to him, "We are Abraham's descendants and have never been slaves to anybody. So how can you say, 'You will be set free'?"[d] 34Jesus answered them, "Truly, truly I tell you that everyone who commits sin is a slave of sin.[a][e] 35The slave does not remain in the household forever, but the son does remain forever.[f] 36So if the Son sets you free, you will be free indeed!"[g]

The Real Children of Abraham

37"I know that you are Abraham's descendants. Yet you are trying to kill me because my word finds no reception among you.[h] 38I declare what I have seen in my[b] Father's presence, and you are doing what you have heard from your father."[i] 39They replied to him, "Our father is Abraham!" Jesus said to them, "If you were Abraham's children, you would be doing what Abraham did.[c][j] 40But now you are trying to kill me, a man who has told you the truth that I heard from God. Abraham would not have done that.[k] 41You are doing your father's works."[l]

They said to him, "We are not illegitimate children. We have one Father, God himself." 42Jesus told them, "If God were your Father, you would have loved me, because I came from God and am here. For I have not come on my own accord, but he sent me.[m] 43Why don't you understand my language? It's because you can't listen to my words.[n] 44You belong to your father the devil, and you want to carry out the desires of your father. He was a murderer from the beginning and has never been truthful,[d] since there is no truth in him. Whenever he tells a lie he speaks in character, for he is a liar and the father of lies.[o] 45But it is because I speak the

---

a 8:34 Other mss. lack *of sin*   b 8:38 Other mss. read *the*   c 8:39 Lit. *the works of Abraham*   d 8:44 Lit. *stood by the truth*

Cross-references (margin):

8:29 [a] John 4:34; 5:30; 6:38; 14:10-11,15

8:30 [b] John 7:31; 10:42; 11:45

8:32 [c] Rom 6:14,18,22; 8:2; James 1:25; 2:12

8:33 [d] Lev 25:42; Matt 3:9; John 8:39

8:34 [e] Rom 6:16,20; 2Peter 2:19

8:35 [f] Gal 4:30

8:36 [g] Rom 8:2; Gal 5:1

8:37 [h] John 7:19,40

8:38 [i] John 3:32; 5:19, 30; 14:10,24

8:39 [j] Matt 3:9; John 3:33; Rom 2:28; 9:7; Gal 3:7,29

8:40 [k] John 8:26,37

8:41 [l] Isa 63:16; 64:8; Mal 1:6

8:42 [m] John 5:43; 7:28-29; 16:27; 17:8,25; 1John 5:1

8:43 [n] John 7:17

8:44 [o] Matt 13:38; 1John 3:8; Jude 1:6

8:47
a John 10:26-27;
1 John 4:6

8:48
b John 7:20; 8:20,
52

8:50
c John 5:41; 7:18

8:51
d John 5:24; 11:26

8:52
e Zech 1:5;
Heb 11:13

8:54
f John 5:31,41;
16:14; 17:1;
Acts 3:13

8:55
g John 7:28-29

8:56
h Lk 10:24;
Heb 11:13

8:58
i Exod 3:14;
Isa 43:13;
John 17:5,24;
Col 1:17; Rev 1:8

8:59
j Lk 4:30;
John 10:31,39;
11:8

9:2
k John 9:34

truth that you do not believe me. ⁴⁶Can any of you prove me guilty of sin? If I am telling the truth, why don't you believe me? ⁴⁷The one who belongs to God listens to the words of God. The reason you do not listen is because you do not belong to God."ᵃ

Jesus Is Superior to Abraham

⁴⁸The Jewsᵃ replied to him, "Surely we are right in saying that you are a Samaritan and have a demon, aren't we?"ᵇ ⁴⁹Jesus answered, "I don't have a demon. On the contrary, I honor my Father, and you dishonor me. ⁵⁰I don't seek my own glory. There is one who seeks it, and he is the Judge.ᶜ ⁵¹Truly, truly I tell you, if anyone keeps my word, he will never see death at all."ᵈ ⁵²Then the Jewsᵃ said to him, "Now we really know that you have a demon. Abraham died, and so did the prophets, but you say, 'If anyone keeps my word, he will never taste death at all.'ᵉ ⁵³You aren't greater than our father Abraham, who died, are you? The prophets also died. Who are you making yourself out to be?"

⁵⁴Jesus answered, "If I were trying to glorify myself, my glory would mean nothing. It is my Father who glorifies me, of whom you say, 'He is our God.'ᶠ ⁵⁵You don't know him, but I know him. If I were to say that I don't know him, I would be a liar like you. But I do know him and keep his word.ᵍ ⁵⁶Your father Abraham rejoiced that he would see my day, and he saw it and was glad."ʰ ⁵⁷Then the Jews said to him, "You are not even fifty years old, yet you have seen Abraham?"ᵇ ⁵⁸Jesus said to them, "Truly, truly I tell you, before there was an Abraham, I am!"ⁱ ⁵⁹At this, they picked up stones to throw at him, but Jesus hid himself and went out of the Temple.ʲ

Jesus Heals a Blind Man

9 ¹As he was walking along, he saw a man who had been blind from birth. ²His disciples asked him, "Rabbi, who sinned, this man or his parents, that caused him to be born blind?"ᵏ ³Jesus answered, "Neither

---

a 8:48,8:52 I.e. Jewish leaders   b 8:57 Other mss. read *Abraham has seen you?*

this man nor his parents sinned. This happened so that[a] the works of God might be revealed in him.[a] [4]I[b] must work the works of the one who sent me[c] while it is day. Night is coming, when no one can work.[b] [5]As long as I am in the world, I am the light of the world."[c] [6]After saying this, he spit on the ground and made mud with the saliva. Then he spread the mud on the man's eyes[d] [7]and told him, "Go and wash in the pool of Siloam"(which is translated Sent One). So he went off and washed and came back seeing.[e]

[8]Then the neighbors and those who had previously seen him as a beggar said, "This is the man who used to sit and beg, isn't it?" [9]Some were saying, "It is he," while others were saying, "No, but it is someone like him." He himself kept saying, "It is I!" [10]So they said to him, "How, then, were your eyes opened?" [11]He said, "The man named Jesus made some mud, spread it on my eyes, and told me, 'Go to Siloam and wash.' So off I went and washed, and I received my sight."[f] [12]They said to him, "Where is that man?" He said, "I don't know!"

The Pharisees Investigate the Healing

[13]So they brought to the Pharisees the man who had once been blind. [14]Now it was a Sabbath day when Jesus made the mud and opened his eyes. [15]So the Pharisees also began to ask him how he had received his sight. He told them, "He put mud on my eyes, then I washed, and now I can see." [16]Some of the Pharisees began to remark, "This man is not from God because he does not keep the Sabbath." But others were saying, "How can a sinful man perform such signs?" And there was a division among them.[g] [17]So they said again to the blind man, "What do you say about him, for it was your eyes he opened?" He said, "He is a prophet."[h]

[18]The Jews[d] did not believe[e] that he had been blind and had been given sight until they summoned his parents[f] [19]and asked them, "Is this your son, the one you say was

---

a[9:3] Lit. *But so that*   b[9:4] Other mss. read *We*   c[9:4] Other mss. read *us*   d[9:18] I.e. Jewish leaders   e[9:18] Lit. *believe about him*   f[9:18] Lit. *the parents of the man who had been given sight*

9:3
a John 11:4

9:4
b John 4:34; 5:19, 36; 11:9; 12:35; 17:4

9:5
c John 1:5,9; 3:19; 8:12; 12:35,46

9:6
d Mark 7:33; 8:23

9:7
e 2Kings 5:14; Neh 3:15

9:11
f John 9:6-7

9:16
g John 3:2; 7:12, 43; 9:33; 10:19

9:17
h John 4:19; 6:14

9:22
a John 5:34; 7:13;
12:42; 16:2;
19:38; Acts 5:13

9:24
b Josh 7:19;
1Sam 6:5;
John 6:16

9:29
c John 8:14

9:30
d John 3:10

9:31
e Job 27:9;
35:12 Ps 18:41;
34:15; 66:18;
Prov 1:28; 15:29;
28:9; Isa 1:15;
Jer 11:11; 14:12;
Ezek 8:18;
Mic 3:4;
Zech 7:13

9:33
f John 9:16

9:34
g John 9:2

9:35
h Matt 14:33;
16:16; Mark 1:1;
John 10:36;
1John 5:13

9:37
i John 4:26

born blind? How does he now see?" ²⁰His parents replied, "We know that this is our son and that he was born blind. ²¹But we don't know how it is that he now sees, and we don't know who opened his eyes. Ask him. He is of age and can speak for himself." ²²His parents said this because they were afraid of the Jews.ᵃ For the Jewsᵃ had already agreed that anyone who acknowledged that Jesusᵇ was the Christᶜ would be thrown out of the synagogue.ᵃ ²³That's why his parents said, "He is of age. Ask him."

²⁴So for a second time they summoned the man who had been blind and told him, "Give glory to God! We know that this man is a sinner."ᵇ ²⁵But he responded, "I don't know whether he is a sinner or not. The one thing I do know is that I used to be blind and now I can see!" ²⁶Then they said to him, "What did he do to you? How did he open your eyes?" ²⁷He answered them, "I've already told you, but you didn't listen. Why do you want to hear it again? You don't want to become his disciples, too, do you?" ²⁸At this, they turned on him furiously and said, "You are his disciple, but we are disciples of Moses! ²⁹We know that God has spoken to Moses, but we do not know where this fellow comes from."ᶜ ³⁰The man answered them, "This is an amazing thing! You don't know where he comes from, yet he opened my eyes.ᵈ ³¹We know that God doesn't listen to sinners, but he does listen to anyone who worships him and does his will.ᵉ ³²Never since creation has it been heard that anyone opened the eyes of a man who was born blind. ³³If this man were not from God, he couldn't do anything like that."ᶠ ³⁴They said to him, "You were born entirely in sins, and you are trying to instruct us?" And they threw him out.ᵍ

Spiritual Blindness

³⁵Jesus heard that they had thrown him out. So when he found him, he said, "Do you believe in the Son of Man?"ᵈʰ ³⁶He answered, "And who is he, sir?ᵉ Tell me, so thatᶠ I may believe in him." ³⁷Jesus said to him, "You have seen him. He is the person who is talking with you."ⁱ ³⁸He said, "Lord, I

---

a 9:22 I.e. Jewish leaders   **b** 9:22 Lit. *he*   **c** 9:22 I.e. the Messiah
d 9:35 Other mss. read *Son of God*   **e** 9:36 Or *Lord*   **f** 9:36 Lit. *So that*

do believe," and worshiped him. ³⁹Then Jesus said, "I have come into this world for judgment, so that those who are blind may see, and those who see may become blind."ᵃ

⁴⁰Some of the Pharisees who were near him overheard this and said to him, "We aren't blind, too, are we?"ᵇ ⁴¹Jesus told them, "If you were blind, you would not have any sin. But now that you insist, 'We see,' your sin remains."ᶜ

The Illustration of the Sheepfold

10 ¹"Truly, truly I tell you, the person who does not enter the sheepfold through the gate, but climbs in by some other way, is a thief and a bandit. ²The one who enters through the gate is the shepherd of the sheep. ³It is to him the gatekeeper opens the gate, and it is his voice the sheep hear. He calls his own sheep by name and leads them out. ⁴When he has driven out all his own, he goes ahead of them, and the sheep follow him because they recognize his voice. ⁵They will never follow a stranger, but will run away from him because they do not recognize the voice of strangers." ⁶Jesus used this illustration with them, but they didn't understand what he was saying to them.

Jesus the Good Shepherd

⁷So again Jesus said, "Truly, truly I tell you, I am the gate for the sheep. ⁸All who came before meᵃ are thieves and bandits, but the sheep did not listen to them. ⁹I am the gate. If anyone enters through me, he will be saved. He will come in and go out and find pasture.ᵈ ¹⁰The thief comes only to steal, slaughter, and destroy. I have come that they may have life, and have it abundantly.

¹¹"I am the good shepherd. The good shepherd lays downᵇ his life for the sheep.ᵉ ¹²The hired hand, who is not the shepherd and does not own the sheep, sees the wolf coming and deserts the sheep and runs away. So the wolf snatches them and scatters them.ᶠ ¹³For he is a hired hand, and the sheep do not matter to him. ¹⁴I am the good shepherd. I know my own and my own know me,ᵍ ¹⁵just as the

---

9:39
ᵃMatt 13:13; John 3:17; 5:22, 27; 12:47

9:40
ᵇRom 2:19

9:41
ᶜJohn 15:22,24

10:9
ᵈJohn 14:6; Eph 2:18

10:11
ᵉIsa 40:11; Ezek 34:12,23; 37:24; Heb 13:20; 1Peter 2:25; 5:4

10:12
ᶠZech 11:16-17

10:14
ᵍ2Tim 2:19

ᵃ10:8 Other mss. lack *before me*   ᵇ10:11 Other mss. read *gives*

10:15
a Matt 11:27;
John 15:13

10:16
b Isa 56:8;
Ezek 37:22;
Eph 2:14;
1Peter 2:25

10:17
c Isa 53:7-8,12;
Heb 2:9

10:18
d John 2:19; 6:38;
15:10; Acts 2:24,
32

10:19
e John 7:43; 9:16

10:20
f John 7:20; 8:48,
52

10:21
g Exod 4:11;
Ps 94:9; 146:8;
John 9:6-7,32-33

10:23
h Acts 3:11; 5:12

10:25
i John 3:2; 5:36;
10:38

10:26
j John 8:47;
1John 4:6

10:27
k John 10:4,14

10:28
l John 6:37;
17:11-12; 18:9

10:29
m John 14:28;
17:2,6

10:30
n John 17:11,22

10:31
o John 8:59

Father knows me and I know the Father. And I lay down[a] my life for the sheep.[a] [16]I have other sheep that do not belong to this fold. I must lead these also, and they will listen to my voice. So there will be one flock and one shepherd.[b] [17]This is why the Father loves me, because I lay down my life in order to take it back again.[c] [18]No one is taking it from me; I lay it down of my own free will. I have the authority to lay it down, and I have the authority to take it back again. This is a command that I have received from my Father."[d]

[19]Once again there was a division among the Jews[b] because of these words.[e] [20]Many of them were saying, "He has a demon and is insane. Why bother listening to him?"[f] [21]Others were saying, "These are not the words of a man who is demon-possessed. A demon cannot open the eyes of the blind, can it?"[g]

Jesus Is Rejected by the Jews

[22]Now[c] the Festival of Hanukkah[d] took place in Jerusalem. It was winter, [23]and Jesus was walking around in the Temple inside the open porch of Solomon.[h] [24]So the Jews surrounded him and said to him, "How long are you going to keep us in suspense? If you are the Christ,[e] tell us so plainly." [25]Jesus answered them, "I have told you, but you do not believe it. The works that I do in my Father's name testify on my behalf,[i] [26]but you do not believe because you do not belong to my sheep.[f][j] [27]My sheep hear my voice. I know them, and they follow me.[k] [28]I give them eternal life, and they will never perish, and no one will snatch them out of my hand.[l] [29]What my Father has given me is greater than all else, and no one can snatch it from the Father's hand.[m] [30]I and the Father are one."[n]

[31]Again the Jews[b] picked up stones to stone him to death.[o] [32]Jesus replied to them, "I have shown you many good works from my[g] Father. For which of them are you going to stone me?" [33]The Jews answered him, "We are not

---

a 10:15 Other mss. read *give*   **b** 10:19,10:31 I.e. Jewish leaders
c 10:22 Other mss. read *Then*   **d** 10:22 Lit. *Festival of Dedication*
e 10:24 I.e. the Messiah   **f** 10:26 Other mss. read *my sheep, just as I told you*   **g** 10:32 Other mss. read *the*

going to stone you for a good work but for blasphemy, because you, a mere man, are making yourself God!"[a] 34Jesus replied to them, "Is it not written in your[a] Law, 'I said, "You are gods" '?[bb] 35If he called those to whom the word of God came 'gods' (and the Scripture cannot be set aside),[c] 36how can you say to the one whom the Father has consecrated and sent into the world, 'You are blaspheming,' because I said, 'I am the Son of God'?[d] 37If I am not doing my Father's works, do not believe me.[e] 38But if I am doing them, even though you do not believe me, believe the works, so that you may know and understand[c] that the Father is in me and I am in the Father."[f] 39Again they tried to seize him, but he slipped away out of their hands.[g]

40Then he went away again across the Jordan to the place where John had been baptizing at first, and he remained there.[h] 41Many people came to him and kept saying, "John never performed a sign, but all the things that John said about this man were true!"[i] 42And many believed in him there.[j]

The Death of Lazarus

11 1Now a certain man was ill, Lazarus from Bethany, the village of Mary and her sister Martha.[k] 2Mary was the woman who anointed the Lord with perfume and wiped his feet with her hair. Her brother Lazarus was the one who was ill.[l] 3So the sisters sent word to Jesus,[d] saying, "Lord, the one whom you love is ill." 4But when Jesus heard it, he said, "This illness is not meant to end in death. It is for God's glory, so that the Son of God may be glorified through it."[m] 5Now Jesus loved Martha and her sister and Lazarus. 6Yet, when he heard that Lazarus[e] was ill, he stayed where he was for two days.[n]

7After this he said to the disciples, "Let's go back to Judea." 8The disciples said to him, "Rabbi, the Jews were just now trying to stone you to death, and you are going back there again?"[o] 9Jesus replied, "There are twelve hours in the day, aren't there? If anyone walks during the day he does

---

a*10:34* Other mss. read *the*   b*10:34* Ps 82:6   c*10:38* Other mss. read *believe*   d*11:3* Lit. *sent to him*   e*11:6* Lit. *he*

10:33
a John 5:18

10:34
b Ps 82:6

10:35
c Rom 13:1

10:36
d Lk 1:35;
John 3:17;
5:17-18,30,36-37;
6:27; 8:42; 9:35,
37

10:37
e John 15:24

10:38
f John 5:36;
14:10-11; 17:21

10:39
g John 7:30,44;
8:59

10:40
h John 1:28

10:41
i John 3:30

10:42
j John 8:30; 11:45

11:1
k Lk 10:38-39

11:2
l Matt 26:7;
Mark 14:3;
John 12:3

11:4
m John 9:3,40

11:6
n John 10:40

11:8
o John 10:31

11:9
a John 9:4

11:10
b John 12:35

11:11
c Deut 31:16;
Dan 12:2;
Matt 9:24;
Acts 7:60;
1Cor 15:18,51

11:22
d John 9:31

11:24
e Lk 14:14;
John 5:29

11:25
f John 1:4; 3:36;
5:21; 6:35,39-40,
44; 14:6; Col 3:4;
1John 1:1-2;
5:10-11

11:27
g Matt 16:16;
John 4:42; 6:14,69

not stumble, because he sees the light of this world.*a* [10]But if anyone walks at night he stumbles, because the light is not in him."*b* [11]These were the things he said. Then after this he told them, "Our friend Lazarus has fallen asleep, but I am leaving to wake him up."*c* [12]So the disciples said to him, "Lord, if he has fallen asleep, he will get well." [13]Jesus, however, had been speaking about his death, but they thought that he was speaking about resting or sleeping. [14]Then Jesus told them plainly, "Lazarus has died. [15]For your sake I am glad that I was not there, so that you may believe. But let's go to him." [16]Then Thomas, who was called the Twin,*a* said to his fellow disciples, "Let's go, too, so that we may die with him!"

Jesus the Resurrection and the Life

[17]When Jesus arrived, he found that Lazarus*b* had already been in the tomb for four days. [18]Now Bethany was near Jerusalem, about two miles*c* away, [19]and many of the Jews had come to Martha and Mary to console them about their brother. [20]As soon as Martha heard that Jesus was coming, she went and met him, while Mary stayed at home. [21]Martha said to Jesus, "Lord, if you had been here, my brother would not have died. [22]But even now I know that whatever you ask of God, God will give it to you."*d* [23]Jesus told her, "Your brother will rise again." [24]Martha said to him, "I know that he will rise again in the resurrection on the last day."*e* [25]Jesus said to her, "I am the resurrection and the life.*d* The person who believes in me, even though he dies, will live.*f* [26]Indeed, everyone who lives and believes in me will never die. Do you believe that?" [27]She said to him, "Yes, Lord, I believe that you are the Christ,*e* the Son of God, the one who was to come into the world."*g*

[28]When she had said this, she went away and called her sister Mary and told her privately, "The Teacher is here and is calling for you!" [29]As soon as Mary*f* heard this, she got up quickly and went to him. [30]Now Jesus had not yet arrived at

---

a *11:16* Gk. *Didymus*	**b** *11:17* Lit. *he*	**c** *11:18* Lit. *fifteen stadia*
d *11:25* Other mss. lack *and the life*	**e** *11:27* I.e. the Messiah	**f** *11:29* Lit. *she*

the village but was still at the place where Martha had met him. [31]When the Jews who had been with her, consoling her in the house, saw Mary get up quickly and go out, they followed her, thinking that she had gone to the tomb to cry there.[a] [32]As soon as Mary came to where Jesus was and saw him, she fell down at his feet and said to him, "Lord, if you had been here, my brother would not have died."[b] [33]When Jesus saw her crying, and the Jews who had come with her crying, he was greatly troubled in spirit and deeply moved. [34]He said, "Where have you put him?" They said to him, "Lord, come and see." [35]Jesus burst into tears.[c] [36]So the Jews said, "See how much he loved him!" [37]But some of them said, "Surely the one who opened the eyes of the blind man could have kept this man from dying, couldn't he?"[d]

Jesus Brings Lazarus Back to Life

[38]Groaning deeply again, Jesus came to the tomb. It was a cave, and a stone was lying against it. [39]Jesus said, "Remove the stone." Martha, the dead man's sister, told him, "Lord, there must be a stench by now, because he's been dead for four days." [40]Jesus said to her, "I told you that if you believed you would see God's glory, didn't I?"[e] [41]So they removed the stone. Then Jesus looked upward and said, "Father, I thank you for hearing me. [42]I know that you always hear me, but I have said this for the sake of the crowd standing here, so that they may believe that you sent me."[f] [43]After saying this, he shouted with a loud voice, "Lazarus, come out!" [44]The dead man came out, his hands and feet tied with strips of cloth, and his face wrapped in a handkerchief. Jesus told them, "Untie him, and let him go."[g]

The Jewish Council Plans to Kill Jesus
(Matthew 26:1; Mark 14:1–2; Luke 22:1–2)

[45]Many of the Jews who had come with Mary and had observed what Jesus did believed in him.[h] [46]Some of them, however, went to the Pharisees and told them what Jesus had done. [47]So the high priests and the Pharisees assembled the Council[a] and said, "What are we going to do? This man

a 11:47 Or Sanhedrin

11:31
a John 11:19

11:32
b John 11:21

11:35
c Lk 19:41

11:37
d John 9:6

11:40
e John 11:4,23

11:42
f John 12:30

11:44
g John 20:7

11:45
h John 2:23;
10:42; 12:11,18

11:47
a Ps 2:2;
Matt 26:3;
Mark 14:1;
Lk 22:2;
John 12:19;
Acts 4:16

11:49
b Lk 3:2;
John 18:14;
Acts 4:6

11:50
c John 18:14

11:52
d Isa 49:6;
John 10:16;
Eph 2:14-17;
1 John 2:2

11:54
e 2 Chr 13:19;
John 4:1,3; 7:1

11:55
f John 2:13; 5:1;
6:4

11:56
g John 11:7

12:1
h John 11:1,43

12:2
i Matt 26:6;
Mark 14:3

12:3
j Lk 10:38-39;
John 11:2

is performing many signs.[a] [48]If we let him go on like this, everyone will believe in him, and the Romans will come and destroy both our Temple[a] and our nation." [49]But one of them, Caiaphas, who was high priest that year, told them, "You don't know anything![b] [50]You don't realize that it is better for you[b] to have one man die for the people than to have the whole nation destroyed."[c] [51]Now he did not say this on his own initiative. As high priest that year, he prophesied that Jesus would die for the nation, [52]and not only for the nation, but that he would also gather into one the children of God who were scattered abroad.[d] [53]So from that day on they resolved to put him to death.

[54]As a result, Jesus no longer walked openly among the Jews.[c] Instead, he went from there to a town called Ephraim in the region near the wilderness. There he remained with his disciples.[e]

[55]Now the Jewish Passover was approaching, and before the Passover many people from the countryside went up to Jerusalem to purify themselves.[f] [56]They kept looking for Jesus and saying to one another as they stood in the Temple, "What do you think? Surely he won't come to the festival, will he?"[g] [57]Now the high priests and the Pharisees had given orders that whoever knew where he was should tell them so that they could arrest him.

Mary Anoints Jesus
(Matthew 26:6–13; Mark 14:3–9)

12 [1]Six days before the Passover, Jesus arrived in Bethany, where Lazarus lived,[d] the man whom Jesus had raised from the dead.[h] [2]There they gave a dinner for him. Martha served, and Lazarus was one of those at the table with him.[i] [3]Mary took a pound of very expensive perfume made of pure nard and anointed Jesus' feet. She wiped his feet with her hair, and the house became filled with the fragrance of the perfume.[j] [4]But Judas Iscariot, one of his disciples, who was going to betray him, said,

---

a *11:48* Lit. *place*   **b** *11:50* Other mss. read *for us*   **c** *11:54* I.e. Jewish leaders   **d** *12:1* Lit. *was*

5"Why wasn't this perfume sold for three hundred denarii[a] and the money[b] given to the destitute?" 6He said this, not because he cared about the destitute, but because he was a thief. He was in charge of the moneybag and would steal what was put into it.[a] 7Then Jesus said, "Leave her alone, so that she might keep it for the day of my burial. 8For you will always have the destitute with you, but you will not always have me."[b]

The Plot against Lazarus

9When the large crowd of Jews realized that he was there, they came not only because of Jesus but also to see Lazarus, whom he had raised from the dead.[c] 10So the high priests planned to kill Lazarus, too,[d] 11since he was the reason why so many of the Jews were going away and believing in Jesus.[e]

The King Enters Jerusalem
(Matthew 21:1–11; Mark 11:1–11; Luke 19:28–40)

12The next day the large crowd that had come to the festival heard that Jesus was coming into Jerusalem.[f] 13So they took branches of palm trees and went out to meet him, shouting,[g]

> "Hosanna![c]
> How blessed is the one who comes
>> in the name of the Lord,[d] the King of Israel!"

14Then Jesus found a young donkey and sat on it, as it is written:[h]

> 15"Stop being afraid, daughter[e] of Zion.[i]
> Look, your king is coming,
>> sitting on a donkey's colt!"[f]

16At first his disciples didn't understand these things. However, when Jesus had been glorified, they remembered that these things had been written about him and that peo-

---

a12:5 Three hundred denarii was about a year's wages for a laborer.
b12:5 The Gk. lacks *the money*   c12:13 Hosanna is Heb. for *Please save* or *Praise*   d12:13 Ps 118:25-26   e12:15 I.e. people   f12:15 Zech 9:9

12:6
*a*John 13:29

12:8
*b*Matt 26:11;
Mark 14:7

12:9
*c*John 11:43-44

12:10
*d*Lk 16:31

12:11
*e*John 11:18,45

12:12
*f*Matt 21:8;
Mark 11:8;
Lk 19:35-36

12:13
*g*Ps 118:25-26

12:14
*h*Matt 21:7

12:15
*i*Zech 9:9

12:16
a Lk 18:34;
John 7:39; 14:26

12:18
b John 12:11

12:19
c John 11:47-48

12:20
d 1 Kings 8:41-42;
Acts 8:27; 17:4

12:21
e John 1:44

12:23
f John 13:32; 17:1

12:24
g 1 Cor 15:36

12:25
h Matt 10:39;
16:25; Mark 8:35;
Lk 9:24; 17:33

12:26
i John 14:3; 17:24;
1 Thes 4:17

12:27
j Matt 26:38-39;
Lk 12:50; 22:53;
John 13:21; 18:37

12:28
k Matt 3:17

12:30
l John 11:42

12:31
m Matt 12:29;
Lk 10:18;
John 14:30; 16:11;
Acts 26:18;
2 Cor 4:4; Eph 2:2;
6:12

12:32
n John 3:14; 8:28;
Rom 5:18;
Heb 2:9

12:33
o John 18:32

ple**ª** had done these things to him.*a* ¹⁷So the crowd that had been with him when he called Lazarus out of the tomb and raised him from the dead continued to testify to what they had seen.*b* ¹⁸This accounts for the crowd going out to meet him, for they had heard that he had performed this sign.*b* ¹⁹Then the Pharisees said to one another, "You see, there is nothing you can do. Look, the world has gone after him!"*c*

Some Greeks Ask to See Jesus

²⁰Now some Greeks were among those who had come up to worship at the festival.*d* ²¹They went to Philip (who was from Bethsaida in Galilee) and told him, "Sir, we would like to see Jesus."*e* ²²Philip went and told Andrew, and Andrew and Philip went and told Jesus. ²³Jesus said to them, "The hour has come for the Son of Man to be glorified.*f* ²⁴Truly, truly I tell you, unless a grain of wheat falls into the ground and dies, it remains alone. But if it dies, it produces a lot of grain.*g* ²⁵The one who loves his life will destroy it, and the one who hates his life in this world will preserve it for eternal life.*h* ²⁶If anyone serves me, he must follow me. And where I am, there my servant will also be. If anyone serves me, the Father will honor him."*i*

Jesus Speaks about His Death

²⁷"Now my soul is in turmoil, and what should I say— 'Father, save me from this hour'? No! It was for this very reason that I came to this hour.*j* ²⁸Father, glorify your name." Then a voice came from heaven, "I have glorified it, and I will glorify it again!"*k* ²⁹The crowd standing there heard this and said that it was thunder. Others were saying, "An angel has spoken to him." ³⁰Jesus replied, "This voice has come for your benefit, not for mine.*l* ³¹Now is the time for the judgment of this world to begin.*c* Now will the ruler of this world be thrown out.*m* ³²As for me, if I am lifted up from the earth, I will draw all people to myself."*n* ³³He said this to indicate the kind of death he was about to die.*o* ³⁴Then the crowd answered him, "We have learned**ᵈ** from

a 12:16 Lit. *they*   **b** 12:17 The Gk. lacks *to what they had seen*   **c** 12:31 Lit. *Now is the judgment of this world*   **d** 12:34 Lit. *heard*

the Law that the Christ[a] remains forever. So how can you say that the Son of Man must be lifted up? Who is this Son of Man?"[a] 35Jesus said to them, "The light is among you only for a short time. Walk while you have the light, so that the darkness may not overtake you. The person who walks in the darkness is in the darkness and does not know where he is going.[b] 36As long as you have the light, believe in the light, so that you may become children of light." After Jesus had said this, he went away and hid from them.[c]

The Unbelief of the Jews

37Although he had performed numerous signs in their presence, they did not believe in him, 38so that the word that the prophet Isaiah spoke might be fulfilled when he said:[d]

"Lord, who has believed our message,
and to whom has the arm[b] of the Lord been
revealed?"[c]

39For this reason they could not believe, for Isaiah also said,

40"He has blinded their eyes[e]
and hardened their heart,
so that they might not perceive with their eyes,
and understand with their heart and turn,
and I would heal them."[d]

41Isaiah said this when[e] he saw his glory and spoke about him.[f] 42Yet many people, even some of the authorities, believed in him, but because of the Pharisees they did not admit it for fear that they would be thrown out of the synagogue.[g] 43For they loved the praise of people more than the praise of God.[h]

Judgment by Jesus' Word

44Then Jesus said loudly, "The one who believes in me does not believe in me but in the one who sent me.[i] 45The one who sees me sees the one who sent me.[j] 46I have come into the world as light, so that everyone who believes in me

---

a 12:34 I.e. the Messiah   b 12:38 I.e. power   c 12:38 Isa 53:1
d 12:40 Isa 6:9-10   e 12:41 Other mss. read *because*

12:34
a Ps 89:36-37;
110:4; Isa 9:7;
53:8; Ezek 37:25;
Dan 2:44; 7:14,
27; Mic 4:7

12:35
b Jer 13:16;
John 1:9; 8:12;
11:10; 12:5,46;
Eph 5:8;
1 John 2:11

12:36
c Lk 16:8;
John 8:59; 11:54;
Eph 5:8;
1 Thes 5:5;
1 John 2:9-11

12:38
d Isa 53:1;
Rom 10:16

12:40
e Isa 6:9-10;
Matt 13:14

12:41
f Isa 6:1

12:42
g John 7:13; 9:22

12:43
h John 5:44

12:44
i Mark 9:37;
1 Peter 1:21

12:45
j John 14:9

12:46
a John 3:19; 8:12;
9:5,39; 12:35-36

12:47
b John 3:17; 5:45;
8:15,26

12:48
c Deut 18:19;
Mark 16:16;
Lk 10:16

12:49
d Deut 18:18;
John 8:38; 14:10

13:1
e Matt 26:2;
John 12:23; 17:1,
11

13:2
f Lk 22:3;
John 13:27

13:3
g Matt 11:27;
28:18; John 3:35;
8:42; 16:28; 17:2;
Acts 2:36;
1Cor 15:27;
Heb 2:8

13:4
h Lk 22:27;
Phil 2:7-8

13:6
i Matt 3:14

13:7
j John 13:12

13:8
k John 3:5;
1Cor 6:11;
Eph 5:26;
Titus 3:5;
Heb 10:22

13:10
l John 15:3

13:11
m John 6:64

will not remain in the darkness.*a* 47If anyone hears my words and does not keep them, I do not condemn him, for I did not come to condemn the world but to save it.*ab* 48The one who rejects me and does not receive my words has something to judge him. The word that I have spoken will judge him on the last day.*c* 49For I have not spoken on my own authority. Instead, the Father who sent me has himself given me a commandment about what to say and how to speak.*d* 50And I know that his commandment is eternal life. What I speak, therefore, I speak just as the Father has told me."

Jesus Washes the Disciples' Feet

13 1Now before the Passover Festival, Jesus realized that his hour had come to leave this world and return to the Father. Having loved his own who were in the world, he loved them to the end.*be* 2By supper time, the devil had already put it into the heart of Judas, the son of Simon Iscariot, to betray him.*f* 3Jesus, knowing that the Father had given all things into his hands, and that he had come from God and was returning to God,*g* 4got up from the table, removed his outer robe, and took a towel and fastened it around his waist.*h* 5Then he poured some water into a basin and began to wash the disciples' feet and to dry them with the towel that was tied around his waist.

6Then he came to Simon Peter, who said to him, "Lord, are you going to wash my feet?"*i* 7Jesus answered him, "You do not realize now what I am doing, but later on you will understand."*j* 8Peter said to him, "You must never wash my feet!" Jesus answered him, "Unless I wash you, you have no part with me."*k* 9Simon Peter said to him, "Lord, not just my feet, but my hands and my head as well!" 10Jesus told him, "The person who has bathed does not need to wash, except for his feet, but is entirely clean. And you men*c* are clean, though not all of you."*l* 11For he knew who was going to betray him. That's why he said, "Not all of you are clean."*m*

12When he had washed their feet and put on his outer

---

a 12:47 Lit. *save the world*   **b** 13:1 Or *loved them completely*   **c** 13:10 Lit. *you* (plural)

robe, he sat down again and said to them, "Do you realize what I have done to you? 13You call me Teacher and Lord, and you are right[a] because that is what I am.[a] 14So if I, your Lord and Teacher, have washed your feet, you must also wash one another's feet.[b] 15For I have given you an example, so that you may do as I have done to you.[c] 16Truly, truly I say to you, a servant is not greater than his master, and a messenger is not greater than the one who sent him.[d] 17If you understand these things, how blessed you are if you put them into practice![e] 18I'm not talking about all of you. I know the ones I have chosen. But the Scripture must be fulfilled: 'The one who ate bread with me[b] has lifted up his heel against[c] me.'[d][f] 19I'm telling you this now, before it happens, so that when it does happen you may believe that I am he.[g] 20Truly, truly I tell you, the one who receives whomever I send receives me, and the one who receives me receives the one who sent me."[h]

Jesus Predicts His Betrayal
(Matthew 26:20–25; Mark 14:17–21; Luke 22:21–23)

21After saying this, Jesus was deeply troubled in spirit and declared solemnly, "Truly, truly I tell you, one of you is going to betray me!"[i] 22The disciples began looking at one another, completely mystified about whom he was speaking. 23One of his disciples, the one whom Jesus kept loving, was sitting very close to him.[j] 24So Simon Peter motioned to this man to ask Jesus of whom he was speaking. 25Leaning forward on Jesus' chest, he asked him, "Lord, who is it?" 26Jesus answered, "He is the one to whom I will give this piece of bread after I have dipped it in the dish."[e]

Then he took a piece of bread, dipped it, and gave it to Judas, the son of Simon Iscariot.[f] 27After he had taken the piece of bread, Satan entered him. Then Jesus said to him, "Do quickly what you are going to do!"[k] 28Now no one at the table knew why he said this to him. 29Some thought that, since Judas had the moneybag, Jesus was telling him to buy

---

13:13
[a] Matt 23:8,10; Lk 6:46; 1Cor 8:6; 12:3; Phil 2:11

13:14
[b] Lk 22:27; Rom 12:10; Gal 6:1-2; 1Peter 5:5

13:15
[c] Matt 11:29; Phil 2:5; 1Peter 2:21; 1John 2:6

13:16
[d] Matt 10:24; Lk 6:40; John 15:20

13:17
[e] James 1:25

13:18
[f] Ps 41:9; Matt 26:23; John 13:21

13:19
[g] John 14:29; 16:4

13:20
[h] Matt 10:40; 25:40; Lk 10:16

13:21
[i] Matt 26:21; Mark 14:18; Lk 22:21; John 12:27; Acts 1:17; 1John 2:19

13:23
[j] John 19:26; 20:2; 21:7,20,24

13:27
[k] Lk 22:3; John 6:70

---

a 13:13 Lit. *you speak well*　b 13:18 Other mss. read *ate my bread*　c 13:18 I.e. has turned against　d 13:18 Ps 41:9　e 13:26 The Gk. lacks *in the dish*　f 13:26 Other mss. read *Judas Iscariot, the son of Simon*

13:29
a John 12:6

13:31
b John 12:23;
14:13; 1 Peter 4:11

13:32
c John 12:23; 17:1,
4-6

13:33
d John 7:34; 8:21

13:34
e Lev 19:18;
John 15:12,17;
Eph 5:2;
1 Thes 4:9;
James 2:8;
1 Peter 1:22;
1 John 2:7-8; 3:11,
23; 4:21

13:35
f 1 John 2:5; 4:20

13:36
g John 21:18;
2 Peter 1:14

13:37
h Matt 26:33-35;
Mark 14:29-31;
Lk 22:33-34

14:1
i John 14:27; 16:3,
22

14:2
j John 13:33,36

14:3
k John 12:26;
14:18,28; 17:24;
Acts 1:11;
1 Thes 4:17

what they needed for the festival or to give something to the destitute.*a* 30So Judas**a** took the piece of bread and immediately went outside. And it was night.

The New Commandment

31When he had gone out, Jesus said, "The Son of Man is now glorified, and God has been glorified in him.*b* 32If God has been glorified in him,**b** God will also glorify the Son of Man**c** in himself, and he will glorify him at once.*c* 33Little children, I am with you only a little longer. You will look for me, but what I told the Jews**d** I now tell you, 'Where I am going, you cannot come.'*d* 34I am giving you a new commandment to love one another. Just as I have loved you, you also should love one another.*e* 35This is how everyone will know that you are my disciples, if you have love for one another."*f*

Jesus Predicts Peter's Denial
(Matthew 26:31–34; Mark 14:27–31; Luke 22:31–34)

36Simon Peter said to him, "Lord, where are you going?" Jesus answered him, "I am going where you cannot follow me now, though you will follow later on."*g* 37Peter said to him, "Lord,**e** why can't I follow you now? I would lay down my life for you!"*h* 38Jesus answered him, "Would you lay down your life for me? Truly, truly I tell you, a rooster will certainly not crow until you have denied me three times."

Jesus the Way to the Father

14 1"Do not let your hearts be troubled. Believe**f** in God, believe also in me.*i* 2There are many rooms in my Father's house. If there were not, would I have told you that I am going away to prepare a place for you?*j* 3And if I am going away to prepare a place for you, I will come again and will welcome you into my presence, so that you may be where I am.*k* 4You know where I am going, and you know the way." 5Thomas said to him, "Lord, we don't know where you are going, so how can we know the

---

a 13:30 Lit. *he*   **b** 13:32 Other mss. lack *If God has been glorified in him*   **c** 13:32 Lit. *him*   **d** 13:33 I.e. Jewish leaders   **e** 13:37 Other mss. lack *Lord*   **f** 14:1 Or *You believe*

way?" [6]Jesus said to him, "I am the way, the truth, and the life. No one comes to the Father except through me.*a* [7]If you have known me, you will also know my Father. From now on you know him and have seen him."*b*

[8]Philip said to him, "Lord, show us the Father, and that will satisfy us." [9]Jesus said to him, "Have I been with you all this time, Philip, and you still do not know me? The person who has seen me has seen the Father. So how can you say, 'Show us the Father'?*c* [10]You believe, don't you, that I am in the Father and the Father is in me? The words that I say to you I do not speak on my own. It is the Father who dwells in me who does his works.*d* [11]Believe me, I am in the Father and the Father is in me. Otherwise, believe me[a] because of the works themselves.*e*

[12]"Truly, truly I tell you, the one who believes in me will also do the works that I am doing. He will do even greater works than these because I am going to the Father.*f* [13]I will do whatever you ask in my name, so that the Father may be glorified in the Son.*g* [14]If you ask me[a] for anything in my name, I will do it.

The Promise of the Helper

[15]"If you love me, keep[b] my commandments.*h* [16]I will ask the Father to give[c] you another Helper, to be with you always.*i* [17]He is the Spirit of truth, whom the world cannot receive, for it neither sees him nor recognizes him. But you recognize him, for he abides with you and will be in[d] you.*j* [18]I am not going to forsake you like orphans. I will come back to you.*k* [19]In a little while the world will no longer see me, but you will see me. Because I live, you will live also.*l* [20]On that day you will know that I am in my Father and that you are in me and that I am in you.*m* [21]The person who has my commandments and keeps them is the one who loves me. The one who loves me will be loved by my Father, and I, too, will love him and reveal myself to him."*n* [22]Judas (not Iscariot) said to him, "Lord, how is it that you are going to reveal yourself to us and not to the world?"*o* [23]Jesus

---

a 14:11,14:14 Other mss. lack *me*   b 14:15 Other mss. read *you will keep*
c 14:16 Lit. *and he will give*   d 14:17 Or *among*

14:6
a John 1:4,17;
8:32; 10:9; 11:25;
Heb 9:8

14:7
b John 8:19

14:9
c John 12:45;
Col 1:15; Heb 1:3

14:10
d John 5:19; 7:16;
8:28; 10:38;
12:49; 14:20;
17:21,23

14:11
e John 5:36; 10:38

14:12
f Matt 21:21;
Mark 16:17;
Lk 10:17

14:13
g Matt 7:7; 21:22;
Mark 11:24;
Lk 11:9;
John 15:7,16;
16:23-24;
James 1:5;
1John 3:22; 5:14

14:15
h John 14:21,23;
15:10,14;
1John 5:3

14:16
i John 15:26; 16:7;
Rom 8:15,26

14:17
j John 15:26;
16:13; 1Cor 2:14;
1John 2:27; 4:6

14:18
k Matt 28:20;
John 14:3,28

14:19
l John 16:16;
1Cor 15:20

14:20
m John 10:38;
14:10; 17:21,23,
26

14:21
n John 14:15,23;
1John 2:5; 5:3

14:22
o Lk 6:16

14:23
a John 14:15;
1 John 2:24;
Rev 3:20

14:24
b John 5:19,38;
7:16; 8:28; 12:49;
14:10

14:26
c Lk 24:49;
John 2:22; 12:16;
14:16; 15:26;
16:7,13;
1 John 2:20,27

14:27
d John 3:1;
Phil 4:7; Col 3:15

14:28
e John 5:18; 10:30;
14:3,12,18; 16:16;
20:17; Phil 2:6

14:29
f John 13:19; 16:4

14:30
g John 12:31;
16:11

14:31
h John 10:18;
Phil 2:8; Heb 5:8

15:2
i Matt 15:13

15:3
j John 13:10;
17:17; Eph 5:26;
1 Peter 1:22

15:4
k Col 1:23;
1 John 2:6

15:5
l Hos 14:8;
Phil 1:11; 4:13

15:6
m Matt 3:10; 7:19

answered him, "If anyone loves me, he will keep my word. Then my Father will love him, and we will go to him and make Our home within him.[a] 24The one who does not love me does not keep my words. The word that you hear is not mine, but comes from the Father who sent me.[b]

25"I have told you this while I am still with you. 26But the Helper, the Holy Spirit, whom the Father will send in my name, will teach you all things and remind you of all that I have told you.[c] 27I am leaving peace with you. I am giving you my own peace. I am not giving it to you as the world gives. So do not let your hearts be troubled, and do not let them be afraid.[d] 28You have heard me tell you, 'I am going away, but I am coming back to you.' If you loved me, you would rejoice that I am going to the Father, for the Father is greater than I am.[e] 29I have told you this now, before it happens, so that when it does happen you will believe.[f] 30I will not talk with you much longer, for the ruler of this world is coming. He has no power over me.[a][g] 31But I am doing what the Father has commanded me to let the world know that I love the Father. Get up! Let us leave this place."[h]

Jesus the True Vine

15 1"I am the true vine, and my Father is the vine-grower. 2He removes every branch in me that does not produce fruit, and he prunes[b] every branch that does produce fruit so that it might produce more fruit.[i] 3You are already clean because of the word that I have spoken to you.[j] 4Abide in me, and I will abide in you. Just as the branch cannot produce fruit by itself unless it abides in the vine, neither can you unless you abide in me.[k] 5I am the vine, you are the branches. The one who abides in me while I abide in him[c] produces much fruit, for apart from me you can do nothing.[l] 6Unless a person abides in me, he is thrown away like a branch and dries up. People gather such branches[d] and throw them into the fire, and they are burned.[m] 7If you abide in me and my words abide in you, you can ask for anything you want, and it will be

---

a 14:30 Lit. *has nothing in me*   b 15:2 Or *cleanses*   c 15:5 Lit. *and I in him*
d 15:6 Lit. *They gather them*

yours.*a* 8This is how my Father is glorified, when you produce a lot of fruit and prove to be my disciples.*b* 9Just as the Father has loved me, so I have loved you. So abide in my love. 10If you keep my commandments, you will abide in my love, just as I have kept my Father's commandments and abide in his love.*c* 11I have told you this so that my joy may be in you, and that your joy may be complete.*d*

12"This is my commandment: that you love one another as I have loved you.*e* 13No one shows**a** greater love than when he lays down his life for his friends.*f* 14You are my friends if you do what I command you.*g* 15I do not call you servants anymore, because a servant does not know what his master is doing. But I have called you friends, because I have made known to you everything that I have heard from my Father.*h* 16You have not chosen me, but I have chosen you. I have appointed you to go and produce fruit that will last,**b** so that whatever you ask the Father in my name, he will give it to you.*i* 17I am giving you these commandments so that you may love one another."*j*

The World's Hatred

18"If the world hates you, you should realize that it hated me before you.*k* 19If you belonged to the world, the world would love you as its own. But because you do not belong to the world and I have chosen you out of it,**c** the world hates you.*l* 20Remember the word that I spoke to you: 'A servant is not greater than his master.' If they persecuted me, they will also persecute you. If they kept my word, they will also keep yours.*m* 21They will do all these things to you on account of my name, because they do not know the one who sent me.*n* 22If I had not come and spoken to them, they would not have any sin. But now they have no excuse for their sin.*o* 23The person who hates me also hates my Father.*p* 24If I had not done among them the works that no one else did, they would not have any sin. But now they have seen and hated both me and my Father.*q* 25But this happened so

---

a 15:13 Lit. *has*   **b** 15:16 Lit. *produce fruit, and your fruit is to last*
c 15:19 Lit. *out of the world*

15:7
a John 14:13-14;
15:16; 16:23

15:8
b Matt 5:16;
John 8:31; 13:35;
Phil 1:11

15:10
c John 14:15,21,23

15:11
d John 16:24;
17:13; 1John 1:4

15:12
e John 13:34;
1Thes 4:9;
1Peter 4:8;
1John 3:11; 4:21

15:13
f John 10:11,15;
Rom 5:7-8;
Eph 5:2;
1John 3:16

15:14
g Matt 12:50;
John 14:15,23

15:15
h Gen 18:17;
John 17:26;
Acts 20:27

15:16
i Matt 28:19;
Mark 16:15;
John 1:7; 6:70;
13:18; 14:13;
Col 1:6;
1John 4:10,19

15:17
j John 15:12

15:18
k 1John 3:1,13

15:19
l John 17:14;
1John 4:5

15:20
m Ezek 3:7;
Matt 10:24;
Lk 6:40;
John 13:16

15:21
n Matt 10:22;
24:9; John 16:3

15:22
o John 9:41;
Rom 1:20;
James 4:17

15:23
p 1John 2:23

15:24
q John 3:2; 7:31;
9:32

15:25
a Ps 35:19; 69:4
15:26
b Lk 24:49;
John 14:17,26;
16:7,13;
Acts 2:33;
1John 5:6
15:27
c Lk 1:2; 24:48;
Acts 1:8,21-22;
2:32; 3:15; 4:20,
33; 5:32; 10:39;
13:31; 1Peter 5:1;
2Peter 1:16;
1John 1:1-2
16:1
d Matt 11:6;
24:10; 26:31
16:2
e John 9:22,34;
12:42; Acts 8:1;
9:1; 26:9-11
16:3
f John 15:21;
Rom 10:2;
1Cor 2:8;
1Tim 1:13
16:4
g Matt 9:15;
John 13:19; 14:29
16:5
h John 7:33; 13:3;
14:28; 16:10,16
16:6
i John 14:1; 16:22
16:7
j John 7:39; 14:16,
26; 15:26;
Acts 2:33; Eph 4:8
16:9
k Acts 2:22-37
16:10
l John 3:14; 5:32;
Acts 2:32
16:11
m Lk 10:18;
John 12:31;
Acts 26:18;
Eph 2:2; Col 2:15;
Heb 2:14
16:12
n Mark 4:33;
1Cor 3:2;
Heb 5:12
16:13
o John 14:17,26;
15:26; 1John 2:20,
27
16:15
p Matt 11:27;
John 3:35; 13:3;
17:10
16:16
q John 7:33; 13:3,
33; 14:19,28;
16:10

that[a] the word written in their Law might be fulfilled: 'They hated me for no reason.'[b][a]

[26]"When the Helper comes, whom I will send to you from the Father, the Spirit of Truth who comes from the Father, he will testify on my behalf.[b] [27]You will testify also, because you have been with me from the beginning."[c]

16

[1]"I have told you this to keep you from falling away.[c][d] [2]They will throw you out of the synagogues. Yes, an hour is coming when the one who kills you will think he is serving God![e] [3]They will do this because they have not known the Father or me.[f] [4]But I have told you this so that when their hour comes you may remember that I told you about them. I did not tell you this in the beginning, because I was with you."[g]

The Work of the Spirit

[5]"But now I am going to the one who sent me. Yet none of you asks me, 'Where are you going?'[h] [6]But because I have told you this, sorrow has filled your hearts.[i] [7]However, I am telling you the truth. It is for your advantage that I am going away, for if I do not go away the Helper will not come to you. But if I go, I will send him to you.[j] [8]When he comes, he will convict the world of sin, righteousness, and judgment— [9]of sin, because they do not believe in me;[k] [10]of righteousness, because I am going to the Father and you will no longer see me;[l] [11]and of judgment, because the ruler of this world has been judged.[d][m]

[12]"I still have a lot to say to you, but you cannot bear it now.[n] [13]Yet when the Spirit of Truth comes, he will guide you into all truth. For he will not speak on his own accord, but will speak whatever he hears and will declare to you the things that are to come.[o] [14]He will glorify me, for he will take what is mine and declare it to you. [15]All that the Father has is mine. That is why I said, 'He will take what is mine and declare it to you.'[p]

[16]"In a little while you will no longer see me, then in a little while you will see me again."[q] [17]At this point, some of

a 15:25 Lit. *But so that*   b 15:25 Ps 35:19; 69:4   c 16:1 Or *from stumbling*
d 16:11 Or *condemned*

his disciples said to each another, "What does he mean by telling us, 'In a little while you will no longer see me, then in a little while you will see me again,' and 'because I am going to the Father'?" 18They kept saying, "What is this 'in a little while' that he keeps talking about? We don't know what he means." 19Jesus knew that they wanted to ask him a question, so he said to them, "Are you discussing among yourselves what I meant when I said, 'In a little while you will no longer see me, then in a little while you will see me again'? 20Truly, truly I tell you, you will cry and mourn, but the world will rejoice. You will be deeply distressed, but your pain will turn into joy. 21When a woman is in labor she has pain, for her hour has come. Yet when she has given birth to her child, she doesn't remember the agony anymore because of the joy of having brought a human being into the world.*a* 22Now you are having pain. But I will see you again, and your hearts will rejoice, and no one will take your joy away from you.*b* 23On that day, you will not ask me for anything. Truly, truly I tell you, whatever you ask the Father for in my name, he will give it to you.*ac* 24So far you haven't asked for anything in my name. Keep asking and you will receive, so that your joy may be complete.*d*

25"I have said these things to you in figurative language. The hour is coming when I will no longer speak to you in figurative language, but will tell you plainly about the Father. 26On that day, you will ask in my name. I am not telling you that I will ask the Father on your behalf.*e* 27For the Father himself loves you because you have loved me and have believed that I came from God.*bf* 28I left the Father and have come into the world. Now*c* I am leaving the world and going back to the Father."*g*

29His disciples said, "Well, now you're speaking plainly and not using figurative language. 30Now we know that you know everything and do not need to have anyone ask you questions. Because of this, we believe that you have come from God."*h* 31Jesus answered them, "Do you now believe? 32Listen, the hour is coming, indeed it has already come,

---

a 16:23 Other mss. read *ask the Father for, he will give it to you in my name*
b 16:27 Other mss. read *from the Father* c 16:28 Lit. *Again*

16:21
a Isa 26:17

16:22
b Lk 24:41,52;
John 14:1,27;
16:6; 20:20;
Acts 2:46; 13:52;
1Peter 1:8

16:23
c Matt 7:7;
John 14:13; 15:16

16:24
d John 15:11

16:26
e John 16:23

16:27
f John 3:13; 14:21,
23,30; 17:8

16:28
g John 13:3

16:30
h John 16:17,27;
17:8

16:32
a Matt 26:31;
Mark 14:27;
John 8:29;
14:10-11; 20:10

16:33
b Isa 9:6;
John 14:1,27;
15:19-21;
Rom 5:1; 8:37;
Eph 2:14;
Col 1:20;
2Tim 3:12;
1John 4:4; 5:4

17:1
c John 12:23;
13:32

17:2
d Dan 7:14;
Matt 11:27; 28:18;
John 2:6,9,24;
3:35; 5:27; 6:37;
1Cor 15:25,27;
Phil 2:10; Heb 2:8

17:3
e Isa 53:11;
Jer 9:24;
John 3:34;
5:36-37; 6:29,57;
7:29; 10:36;
11:42; 1Cor 8:4;
1Thes 1:9

17:4
f John 4:34; 5:36;
9:3; 13:31; 14:13,
31; 15:10; 19:30

17:5
g John 1:1-2;
10:30; 14:9;
Phil 2:6; Col 1:15,
17; Heb 1:3,10

17:6
h Ps 22:22;
John 6:37,39;
10:29; 15:19;
17:2,9,11,26

17:8
i John 8:28; 12:49;
14:10,25; 16:27,
30

17:9
j 1John 5:19

17:10
k John 16:15

17:11
l John 1:21; 10:30;
13:1; 16:28;
1Peter 1:5;
Jude 1:1

17:12
m Ps 109:8;
John 6:39,70;
10:28; 13:18;
18:9; Acts 1:20;
Heb 2:13;
1John 2:19

when you will be scattered, each of you to his own home, and you will leave me alone. Yet I am not alone, for the Father is with me.*a* 33I have told you this so that in me you may have peace. In the world you will have trouble, but be courageous—I have overcome the world!"*b*

Jesus Prays for Himself, His Disciples, and His Future Followers

17 1After Jesus had said this, he looked up to heaven and said, "Father, the hour has come. Glorify your Son, so that the Son may glorify you.*c* 2For*a* you have given him authority over all humanity so that he might give eternal life to all those you gave him.*d* 3And this is eternal life: to know you, the only true God, and the one whom you sent—Jesus Christ.*e* 4I glorified you on earth by completing the task you gave me to do.*f* 5So now, Father, glorify me in your presence with the glory I had with you before the world existed.*g* 6I have made your name known to the men you gave me from the world. They were yours, and you gave them to me, and they have kept your word.*h* 7Now they realize that everything you gave me comes from you, 8for the words that you gave me I have given to them. They have received them and know for sure that I came from you. And they have believed that you sent me.*i* 9I am asking on their behalf. I am not asking on behalf of the world, but on behalf of those you gave me, for they are yours.*j* 10All that is mine is yours, and what is yours is mine, and I have been glorified in them.*k* 11I am no longer in the world, but they are in the world, and I am coming to you. Holy Father, protect them by your name, the name*b* that you gave me, so that they may be one, as we are one.*l* 12While I was with them, I protected them by your name that you gave me. I guarded them, and not one of them became lost except the one who was destined for*c* destruction, so that the Scripture might be fulfilled.*m*

13"And now I am coming to you, and I say these things in the world so that they may have my joy completed in themselves. 14I have given them your word, and the world

---

a 17:2 Lit. *Just as*   **b** 17:11 Lit. *the one*   **c** 17:12 Lit. *the son of*

has hated them, for they do not belong to the world, just as I do not belong to the world.*a* 15I am not asking you to take them out of the world but to protect them from the evil one.*b* 16They do not belong to the world, just as I do not belong to the world.*c* 17Sanctify them by the truth. Your word is truth.*d* 18Just as you sent me into the world, so I have sent them into the world.*e* 19It is for their sakes that I sanctify myself, so that they, too, may be sanctified by the truth.*f*

20"I ask not only on behalf of these, but also on behalf of those who will believe in me through their message, 21that they may all be one. Just as you, Father, are in me and I am in you, may they also be one*a* in us, so that the world may believe that you sent me.*g* 22I have given them the glory that you gave me, so that they may be one, just as we are one.*h* 23I am in them, and you are in me. May they be completely one, so that the world may know that you sent me and that you have loved them as you loved me.*i* 24Father, I want those you have given me to be with me where I am and to see my glory, which you gave me because you loved me before the creation of the world.*j*

25"Righteous Father, the world has never known you. Yet I have known you, and these men have known that you sent me.*k* 26I made your name known to them, and will continue to make it known, so that the love you have for me*b* may be in them and I myself may be in them."*l*

Jesus Is Betrayed and Arrested
(Matthew 26:47–56; Mark 14:43–40; Luke 22:47–53)

18 1After Jesus had said this, he went with his disciples across the Kidron valley to a place where there was a garden, which he and his disciples entered.*m* 2Now Judas, who betrayed him, also knew the place because Jesus often met there with his disciples.*n* 3So Judas took a detachment of soldiers and some officers from the high priests and the Pharisees and went there with lanterns, torches, and weapons.*o* 4Then Jesus, knowing everything that was going to happen, went forward and said to them, "Who are you looking for?" 5They answered him,

---

a17:21 Other mss. lack *one*   b17:26 Lit. *the love with which you loved me*

17:14
a John 8:16,23;
15:18-19; 17:8;
1John 3:13

17:15
b Matt 6:13;
Gal 1:4;
2Thes 3:3;
1John 5:18

17:16
c John 17:14

17:17
d 2Sam 7:28;
Ps 119:142,151;
John 8:40; 15:3;
Acts 15:9;
Eph 5:26;
1Peter 1:22

17:18
e John 20:21

17:19
f 1Cor 1:2,30;
1Thes 4:7;
Heb 10:10

17:21
g John 10:16,38;
14:11; 17:11,
22-23; Rom 12:5;
Gal 3:28

17:22
h John 14:20;
1John 1:3; 3:24

17:23
i Col 3:14

17:24
j John 4:5; 12:26;
14:3; 1Thes 4:17

17:25
k John 7:29; 8:55;
10:8,15; 15:21;
16:3,27

17:26
l John 15:9,15;
17:6

18:1
m 2Sam 15:23;
Matt 26:36;
Mark 14:32;
Lk 22:39

18:2
n Lk 21:37; 22:39

18:3
o Matt 26:47;
Mark 14:43;
Lk 22:47;
Acts 1:16

18:9
a John 17:12

18:10
b Matt 26:51;
Mark 14:47;
Lk 22:49-50

18:11
c Matt 20:22;
26:39,42

18:13
d Matt 26:57;
Lk 3:2

18:14
e John 11:50

18:15
f Matt 26:58;
Mark 14:54;
Lk 22:54

18:16
g Matt 26:69;
Mark 14:66;
Lk 22:54

"Jesus from Nazareth."[a] Jesus said to them, "I am he." Judas, the man who betrayed him, was standing with them. [6]When Jesus[b] told them, "I am he," they backed away and fell to the ground. [7]So he asked them again, "Who are you looking for?" They said, "Jesus from Nazareth."[a] [8]Jesus replied, "I told you that I am he. So if you are looking for me, let these men go." [9]This was to fulfill the word that he had spoken, "I did not lose a single one of those you gave me."[a] [10]Then Simon Peter, who had a sword, drew it and struck the high priest's servant, cutting off his right ear. The servant's name was Malchus.[b] [11]Jesus told Peter, "Put your sword back into its sheath. Shouldn't I drink the cup that the Father has given me?"[c]

Jesus before the High Priest
(Matthew 26:57–58; Mark 14:53–54; Luke 22:54)

[12]Then the soldiers, along with their commander[c] and the Jewish officers, arrested Jesus and tied him up. [13]First they brought him to Annas, for he was the father-in-law of Caiaphas, the high priest that year.[d] [14]Caiaphas was the person who had advised the Jews that it was better to have one man die for the people.[e]

Peter Denies Jesus
(Matthew 26:69–70; Mark 14:66–68; Luke 22:55–57)

[15]Simon Peter and another disciple were following Jesus. Since the other disciple was known to the high priest, he accompanied Jesus into the courtyard of the high priest.[f] [16]Peter, however, stood outside the gate. So this other disciple who was known to the high priest went out and spoke to the gatekeeper and brought Peter inside.[g] [17]The young woman at the gate said to Peter, "You aren't one of this man's disciples, too, are you?" He said, "I am not." [18]Meanwhile, the servants and officers were standing around a charcoal fire they had built and were warming themselves because it was cold. Peter was also standing with them, keeping himself warm.

---

a 18:5,18:7 Or *Jesus the Nazarene*; the Gk. *Nazoraios* may be a word play between Heb. *netser*, meaning *branch* (see Isa 11:1), and the name *Nazareth.*   b 18:6 Lit. *he*   c 18:12 Gk. *chiliarchos*

The High Priest Questions Jesus
(Matthew 26:59–66; Mark 14:55–64; Luke 22:66–71)

¹⁹Then the high priest questioned Jesus about his disciples and about his own teaching. ²⁰Jesus answered him, "I have spoken publicly to the world. I have always taught in the synagogue or in the Temple, where all Jews meet together, and I have said nothing in secret.ᵃ ²¹Why do you question me? Question those who heard what I said. These are the people who know what I said." ²²When he said this, one of the officers standing nearby slapped Jesus on the face and said, "Is that any way to answer the high priest?"ᵇ ²³Jesus answered him, "If I have said anything wrong, tell me what it was.ᵃ But if I have told the truth, why do you hit me?" ²⁴Then Annas sent him, with his hands tied, to Caiaphas the high priest.ᶜ

Peter Denies Jesus Again
(Matthew 26:71–75; Mark 14:69–72; Luke 22:58–62)

²⁵Meanwhile, Simon Peter was standing and warming himself. They said to him, "You aren't one of his disciples, too, are you?" He denied it by saying, "I am not!"ᵈ ²⁶Then one of the high priest's servants, a relative of the man whose ear Peter had cut off, said, "I saw you in the garden with him, didn't I?" ²⁷Peter again denied it, and immediately a rooster crowed.ᵉ

Pilate Questions Jesus
(Matthew 27:1–2; Mark 15:1–5; Luke 23:1–5)

²⁸Then they led Jesus from Caiaphas to the governor's headquarters.ᵇ It was early in the morning, and the Jewsᶜ did not go into the headquarters for fear that they might become unclean and be unable to eat the Passover meal.ᶠ ²⁹So Pilate came out to them and said, "What accusation are you bringing against this man?" ³⁰They answered him, "If he weren't a criminal, we wouldn't have handed him over to you." ³¹Pilate told them, "You take him and try him according to your Law." The Jews said to him, "It is not legal for us

---

ᵃ18:23 Lit. *about the wrong*   ᵇ18:28 Lit. *to the praetorium*   ᶜ18:28 Lit. *they*

18:20
ᵃMatt 26:55;
Lk 4:15;
John 7:14,26,28;
8:2

18:22
ᵇJer 20:2;
Acts 23:2

18:24
ᶜMatt 26:57

18:25
ᵈMatt 26:69,71;
Mark 14:69;
Lk 22:58

18:27
ᵉMatt 26:74;
Mark 14:72;
Lk 22:60;
John 13:38

18:28
ᶠMatt 27:2;
Mark 15:1;
Lk 23:1;
Acts 3:13; 10:28;
11:3

18:32
a Matt 20:19;
John 12:32-33

to put anyone to death." ³²This was to fulfill what Jesus had said[a] when he indicated the kind of death he was to die.[a]

³³So Pilate went back into the governor's headquarters,[b] summoned Jesus, and said to him, "Are you the king of the Jews?"[b] ³⁴Jesus replied, "Are you asking this on your own initiative, or did others tell you about me?" ³⁵Pilate replied, "I am not a Jew, am I? It is your own nation and high priests who have handed you over to me. What have you done?" ³⁶Jesus answered, "My kingdom does not belong to this world. If my kingdom belonged to this world, my servants would fight to keep me from being handed over to the Jews.[c] But for now my kingdom is not from here."[c]

³⁷Pilate said to him, "So you are a king?" Jesus answered, "You say that I am a king. I was born for this, and I came into the world for this: to testify to the truth. Everyone who belongs to the truth listens to my voice."[d] ³⁸Pilate said to him, "What is 'truth'?" After he said this, he went out to the Jews[c] again and told them, "I find no basis for a charge against him.[e] ³⁹But you have a custom that I release one person for you at Passover. Do you want me to release for you the king of the Jews?"[f] ⁴⁰At this, they shouted out again, "Not this fellow, but Barabbas!" Now Barabbas was a revolutionary.[d][g]

18:33
b Matt 27:11

18:36
c Dan 2:44; 7:14;
Lk 12:14;
John 6:15; 8:15;
1 Tim 6:13

18:37
d John 8:47;
1 John 3:19; 4:6

18:38
e Matt 27:24;
Lk 23:4;
John 19:4,6

18:39
f Matt 27:15;
Mark 15:6;
Lk 23:17

18:40
g Lk 23:19;
Acts 3:14

Jesus Is Sentenced to Death
(Matthew 27:15–31; Mark 15:6–20; Luke 23:13–25)

19 ¹Then Pilate had Jesus taken away and whipped.[h] ²The soldiers twisted some thorns into a crown, put it on his head, and threw a purple robe on him. ³They kept coming up to him and saying, "Long live the king of the Jews!" Then they began to slap him on the face. ⁴Pilate went outside again and told the Jews,[e] "Look, I am bringing him out to you to let you know that I find no basis for a charge against him."[i] ⁵Then Jesus came outside, wearing the crown of thorns and the purple robe. Pilate said to them, "Here is the man!" ⁶When the high

19:1
h Matt 20:19;
27:26;
Mark 15:15;
Lk 18:33

19:4
i John 18:6,38

---

a 18:32 Lit. *the word of Jesus that he said*   b 18:33 Lit. *into the praetorium*   c 18:36,38 I.e. Jewish leaders   d 18:40 Or *bandit*   e 19:4 Lit. *them*

priests and the officials saw him, they shouted, "Crucify him! Crucify him!" Pilate told them, "You take him and crucify him. I find no basis for a charge against him."*a* 7The Jews answered Pilate,**a** "We have a Law, and according to that Law he must die because he made himself out to be the Son of God."*b*

8When Pilate heard this, he became even more afraid. 9Returning to his headquarters,**b** he said to Jesus, "Where are you from?" But Jesus gave him no reply.*c* 10So Pilate said to him, "Aren't you going to speak to me? You realize, don't you, that I have the authority to release you and the authority to crucify you?" 11Jesus answered him, "You have no authority over me at all, except what was given to you from above. That's why the one who handed me over to you is guilty of a greater sin."*d* 12From then on, Pilate tried to release him, but the Jews kept shouting, "If you release this fellow, you're not a friend of Caesar! Anyone who claims to be a king is defying Caesar!"*e*

13When Pilate heard these words, he brought Jesus outside and sat down on the judgment seat in a place called The Pavement, which in Hebrew is called Gabbatha. 14Now it was the Preparation Day for the Passover, about twelve noon.*c* He said to the Jews, "Here is your king!"*f* 15Then they shouted, "Take him away! Take him away! Crucify him!" Pilate said to them, "Should I crucify your king?" The high priests responded, "We have no king but Caesar!"*g* 16Then Pilate**d** handed him over to be crucified, and they took Jesus away.*h*

Jesus Is Crucified
(Matthew 27:32–44; Mark 15:21–32; Luke 23:26–43)

17Carrying the cross all by himself, he went out to what is called The Place of a Skull, which in Hebrew is called Golgotha.*i* 18There they crucified him, along with two others, one on each side of him with Jesus in the middle. 19Pilate wrote an inscription and put it on the cross. It read,

---

a19:7 Lit. *him*   **b**19:9 Lit. *to the praetorium*   **c**19:14 Lit. *the sixth hour*
d19:16 Lit. *he*

19:6
a Acts 3:13

19:7
b Lev 24:16;
Matt 26:65;
John 5:18; 10:33

19:9
c Isa 53:7;
Matt 27:12,14

19:11
d Lk 22:53;
John 7:30

19:12
e Lk 23:2;
Acts 17:7

19:14
f Matt 27:62

19:15
g Gen 49:10

19:16
h Matt 27:26,31;
Mark 15:15;
Lk 23:24

19:17
i Num 15:36;
Matt 27:31,33;
Mark 15:21-22;
Lk 23:26,33;
Heb 13:12

19:19
a Matt 27:37;
Mark 15:26;
Lk 23:38

"Jesus from Nazareth,*a* the King of the Jews."*a* ²⁰Many Jews read this inscription, because the place where Jesus was crucified was near the city. It was written in Hebrew, Latin, and Greek. ²¹Then the Jewish high priests told Pilate, "Don't write, 'The King of the Jews,' but that this fellow said, 'I am the King of the Jews.' " ²²Pilate replied, "What I have written I have written."

19:23
b Matt 27:35;
Mark 15:24;
Lk 23:34

²³When the soldiers had crucified Jesus, they took his clothes and divided them into four parts, one for each soldier, and took his cloak*b* as well. The cloak was seamless, woven in one piece from the top down.*b* ²⁴So they said to each other, "Let's not tear it. Instead, let's throw dice to see who gets it." This was to fulfill the Scripture that says,*c*

19:24
c Ps 22:18

> "They divided my clothes among themselves,
> and for my clothing they threw dice."*c*

So that is what the soldiers did.

19:25
d Matt 27:55;
Mark 15:40;
Lk 23:49; 24:18

²⁵Meanwhile, standing near Jesus' cross were his mother, his mother's sister, Mary the wife of Clopas, and Mary Magdalene.*d* ²⁶When Jesus saw his mother and the disciple whom he kept loving standing there, he said to his mother, "Woman, here is your son."*e* ²⁷Then he said to the disciple, "Here is your mother." And from that hour the disciple took her into his own home.*f*

19:26
e John 2:4; 13:23;
20:2; 21:7,20,24

19:27
f John 1:11; 16:32

Jesus Dies on the Cross
(Matthew 27:45–56; Mark 15:33–41; Luke 23:44–49)

19:28
g Ps 69:21

²⁸After this, when Jesus realized that everything was now completed, he said (in order to fulfill the Scripture), "I'm thirsty."*g* ²⁹A jar of sour wine was standing there, so they put a sponge full of the wine on a branch of hyssop and held it to his mouth.*h* ³⁰After Jesus had taken the wine, he said, "It is finished." Then he bowed his head and released his spirit.*i*

19:29
h Matt 27:48

19:30
i John 17:4

a 19:19 Or *Jesus the Nazarene*; the Gk. *Nazoraios* may be a word play between Heb. *netser*, meaning *branch* (see Isa 11:1), and the name *Nazareth*.   **b** 19:23 Lit. *and his tunic*   **c** 19:24 Ps 22:18

Jesus' Side Is Pierced

19:31
a Deut 21:23;
Mark 15:42;
John 19:42

³¹Since it was the Preparation Day, the Jews did not want to leave the bodies on the crosses during the Sabbath, for that was a particularly important Sabbath. So they asked Pilate to have the men's legs broken and the bodies removed.ᵃᵃ ³²So the soldiers went and broke the legs of the first man and then of the other man who had been crucified with him. ³³But when they came to Jesus and saw that he was already dead, they did not break his legs. ³⁴Instead, one of the soldiers pierced his side with a spear, and blood and water immediately came out.ᵇ ³⁵The one who saw this has testified, and his testimony is true. He knows he is telling the truth so that you, too, may believe. ³⁶For these things happened so that the Scripture might be fulfilled: "None of his bones will be broken."ᵇᶜ ³⁷In addition, another passage of Scripture says, "They will look on the one whom they pierced."ᶜᵈ

19:34
b 1John 5:6,8

19:36
c Exod 12:46;
Num 9:12;
Ps 34:20

19:37
d Ps 22:16-17;
Zech 12:10;
Rev 1:7

Jesus Is Buried

(Matthew 27:57–61; Mark 15:42–47; Luke 23:50–56)

³⁸Later on, Joseph of Arimathea, who was a disciple of Jesus (though a secret one because he was afraid of the Jews), asked Pilate to let him remove the body of Jesus. Pilate gave him permission, and he came and removed his body.ᵉ ³⁹Nicodemus, the man who had first come to Jesus at night, also arrived, bringing a mixture of myrrh and aloes weighing about a hundred pounds.ᶠ ⁴⁰They took the body of Jesus and wrapped it in linen cloths along with spices, according to the burial custom of the Jews.ᵍ ⁴¹A garden was located in the place where he was crucified, and in that garden was a new tomb in which no one had yet been placed. ⁴²Because it was the Jewish Preparation Day, and because the tomb was nearby, they put Jesus there.ʰ

19:38
e Matt 27:57;
Mark 15:42;
Lk 23:50;
John 9:22; 12:42

19:39
f John 3:1-2; 7:50

19:40
g Acts 5:6

19:42
h Isa 53:9;
John 19:31

---

a 19:31 Lit. *to have their legs broken and removed*   b 19:36 Exod 12:46; Num 9:12; Ps 34:20   c 19:37 Zech 12:10

20:1
a Matt 28:1;
Mark 16:1;
Lk 24:1

20:2
b John 13:23;
19:26; 21:7,20,24

20:3
c Lk 24:12

20:5
d John 19:40

20:7
e John 11:44

20:9
f Ps 16:10;
Acts 2:25-31;
13:34-35

20:11
g Mark 16:5

20:14
h Matt 28:9;
Mark 16:9;
Lk 24:16,31;
John 21:4

Jesus Is Raised from the Dead
(Matthew 28:1–10; Mark 16:1–8; Luke 24:1–12)

20 ¹On the first day of the week, early in the morning and while it was still dark, Mary Magdalene went to the tomb and noticed that the stone had been removed from the tomb.*ᵃ* ²So she ran off and went to Simon Peter and the other disciple, whom Jesus kept loving. She told them, "They have taken the Lord out of the tomb, and we don't know where they have put him!"*ᵇ* ³So Peter and the other disciple set out to go to the tomb.*ᶜ* ⁴The two of them were running together, but the other disciple ran faster than Peter and came to the tomb first. ⁵Bending over to look inside, he noticed the linen cloths lying there but didn't go in.*ᵈ* ⁶At this point Simon Peter arrived, following him, and went straight into the tomb. He observed that the linen cloths were lying there, ⁷and that the handkerchief that had been on Jesus' head was not lying with the linen cloths but was rolled up in a separate place.*ᵉ* ⁸Then the other disciple, who arrived at the tomb first, went inside, looked, and believed. ⁹For they did not yet understand the Scripture that said that**ᵃ** he had to rise from the dead.*ᶠ* ¹⁰So the disciples went back to their homes.

Jesus Appears to Mary Magdalene
(Mark 16:9–11)

¹¹Meanwhile, Mary stood crying outside the tomb. As she cried, she bent over and looked into**ᵇ** the tomb.*ᵍ* ¹²She saw two angels in white clothes who were sitting down, one at the head and the other at the foot of the place where Jesus' body had been lying. ¹³They said to her, "Woman, why are you crying?" She told them, "Because they have taken away my Lord, and I don't know where they have put him." ¹⁴After she had said this, she turned around and noticed Jesus standing there, without realizing that it was Jesus.*ʰ* ¹⁵Jesus said to her, "Woman, why are you crying? Who are you looking for?" Thinking he was the gardener, she said to him, "Sir, if you have carried him away, tell me where you have put him, and I will take him away." ¹⁶Jesus

---

a 20:9 Lit. *the Scripture that*   **b** 20:11 Lit. *bent over into*

said to her, "Mary!" She turned around and said to him in Hebrew, "Rabbouni!" (which means Teacher). 17Jesus told her, "Don't hold on to me, for I have not yet ascended to the Father. But go to my brothers and tell them, 'I am ascending to my Father and your Father, to my God and your God.' "[a] 18So Mary Magdalene went and announced to the disciples, "I have seen the Lord!" She also told them what he had said to her.[b]

Jesus Appears to the Disciples
(Matthew 28:16–20; Mark 16:14–18; Luke 24:36–49)

19It was the evening of the first day of the week, and the doors of the house where the disciples had met were locked because they were afraid of the Jews.[a] Jesus came and stood among them. He said to them, "Peace be with you."[c] 20After saying this, he showed them his hands and his side, and when they saw the Lord the disciples were overjoyed.[d] 21Jesus said to them again, "Peace be with you. Just as the Father has sent me, so I am sending you."[e] 22When he had said this, he breathed on them and said to them, "Receive the Holy Spirit. 23If you forgive people's sins, they are forgiven. If you retain people's sins, they are retained."[f]

Jesus Appears to Thomas

24Thomas, one of the twelve, who was called the Twin,[b] wasn't with them when Jesus came.[g] 25So the other disciples kept telling him, "We have seen the Lord!" But he told them, "Unless I see the nail marks in his hands, put my finger into them,[c] and put my hand into his side, I will never believe!"

26A week later his disciples were again inside, and Thomas was with them. Even though the doors were shut, Jesus came and stood among them and said, "Peace be with you." 27Then he said to Thomas, "Put your finger here, and look at my hands. Take your hand, and put it into my side. Stop doubting, but believe."[h] 28Thomas answered him, saying "My Lord and my God!" 29Jesus said to him, "Is it because you have seen me that you have believed? How

---

a 20:19 I.e. Jewish leaders   b 20:24 Gk. *Didymus*   c 20:25 Lit. *into the nail marks*

20:17
a Ps 22:22;
Matt 28:10;
John 16:28;
Rom 8:29;
Eph 1:17;
Heb 2:11

20:18
b Matt 28:10;
Lk 24:10

20:19
c Mark 16:14;
Lk 24:36;
1Cor 15:5

20:20
d John 16:22

20:21
e Matt 28:18;
John 17:18-19;
2Tim 2:2; Heb 3:1

20:23
f Matt 16:19;
18:18

20:24
g John 11:16

20:27
h 1John 1:1

20:29
a 2Cor 5:7;
1Peter 1:8

blessed are those who have never seen me and yet have believed!"*a*

The Purpose of the Book

20:30
b John 21:25

[30]Jesus performed many other signs in the presence of his*a* disciples that are not recorded in this book.*b* [31]But these have been recorded so that you may believe that Jesus is the Christ,*b* the Son of God, and so that through believing you may have life in his name.*c*

Jesus Appears to Seven of His Disciples

20:31
c Lk 1:4;
John 3:15-16;
5:24; 1Peter 1:9

21 [1]Later on, Jesus revealed himself again to the disciples at the Sea of Tiberias, and he revealed himself in this way. [2]Simon Peter, Thomas (called the Twin),*c* Nathaniel from Cana in Galilee, the sons of Zebedee, and two of his other disciples were together.*d* [3]Simon Peter said to them, "I'm going fishing." They told him, "We'll go with you, too." So they went out and got into the boat but didn't catch a thing that night.

21:2
d Matt 4:21;
John 1:45

[4]Just as dawn was breaking, Jesus stood on the shore. The disciples didn't realize it was Jesus.*e* [5]Jesus said to them, " Children, you don't have any fish, do you?" They answered him, "No."*f* [6]He told them, "Throw the net on the right hand side of the boat, and you'll catch*d* some." So they threw it out and were unable to haul it in because it was so full of fish.*g*

21:4
e John 20:14

[7]That disciple whom Jesus kept loving said to Peter, "It's the Lord!" When Simon Peter heard that it was the Lord, he put back on his clothes, for he was practically naked, and jumped into the sea.*h* [8]But the other disciples came in the boat, dragging the net full of fish. They were only about a hundred yards*e* away from the shore.

21:5
f Lk 24:41

[9]When they arrived at the shore, they saw a charcoal fire with fish lying on it, and some bread. [10]Jesus told them, "Bring me some of the fish you've just caught." [11]So Simon Peter went aboard and dragged the net ashore. It was full of large fish, one hundred and fifty-three of them. And although there were so many of them, the net was not torn.

21:6
g Lk 5:4,6-7

---

a 20:30 Other mss. read *the*   b 20:31 I.e. the Messiah   c 21:2 Gk. *Didymus*   d 21:6 Lit. *find*   e 21:8 Lit. *two hundred cubits*

21:7
h John 13:23; 20:2

21:12
a Acts 10:41

12Then Jesus said to them, "Come, have breakfast." Now none of the disciples dared to ask him, "Who are you?", for they knew it was the Lord.*a* 13Jesus went and took the bread and gave it to them, and did*a* the same with the fish. 14This was now the third time that Jesus revealed himself to the disciples after he had been raised from the dead.*b*

21:14
b John 20:19,26

Jesus Speaks with Peter

15When they had finished breakfast, Jesus said to Simon Peter, "Simon, son of John, do you love me more than these?" He said to him, "Yes, Lord, you know that I love you." Jesus*b* told him, "Feed my lambs." 16Then he said to him a second time, "Simon, son of John, do you love me?" He said to him, "Yes, Lord, you know that I love you." Jesus*b* told him, "Take care of my sheep."*c* 17He said to him a third time, "Simon, son of John, do you love me?" Peter was deeply hurt that he had said to him a third time, "Do you love me?" So he said to him, "Lord, you know everything. You know that I love you!" Jesus told him, "Feed my sheep.*d*

21:16
c Acts 20:28;
Heb 13:20;
1Peter 2:25; 5:2.4

21:17
d John 2:24-25;
16:30

18"Truly, truly I tell you, when you were young, you would fasten your belt and go wherever you liked. But when you get old, you will stretch out your hands, and someone else will fasten your belt and take you where you don't want to go."*e* 19Now he said this to show by what kind of death he would glorify God. After saying this, he told him, "Keep following me."*f*

21:18
e John 13:36;
Acts 12:3-4

Jesus and the Beloved Disciple

20Peter turned around and noticed the disciple whom Jesus kept loving following them. He was the one who had put his head on Jesus' chest at the supper and had said, "Lord, who is the one who is going to betray you?"*g* 21When Peter saw him, he said, "Lord, what about him?" 22Jesus said to him, "If it is my will for him to remain until I come, how does that concern you? You must keep following me!"*h* 23So the rumor spread among the brothers*c* that this disciple wasn't going to die. Yet Jesus didn't say to him that he

21:19
f 2Peter 1:14

21:20
g John 13:23,25;
20:2

---

a *21:13* The Gk. lacks *did*   b *21:15,21:16* Lit. *He*   c *21:23* I.e. Jesus' followers

21:22
h Matt 16:27-28;
25:31; 1Cor 4:5;
11:26; Rev 2:25;
3:11; 22:7,20

21:24
a John 19:35;
3 John 1:12

wasn't going to die, but, "If it is my will for him to remain until I come, how does that concern you?"

24This is the disciple who is testifying to these things and has written them down. We know that his testimony is true.*a*

25Of course, Jesus also did many other things, and I suppose that if every one of them were written down the world couldn't contain the books that would be written.*b*

21:25
b Amos 7:10;
John 20:30

THE BOOK OF
ACTS

Introduction

1 ¹In my first book, Theophilus, I wrote about every-thing Jesus did and taught from the beginning,*a* ²up to the day when he was taken up to heaven**a** after giving orders by the Holy Spirit to the apostles he had chosen.*b* ³After he had suffered, he had shown himself alive to them by many convincing proofs, appearing to them through a period of forty days and telling them about the kingdom of God.*c*

The Promise of the Holy Spirit

⁴While he was meeting with them, he ordered them, "Do not leave Jerusalem, but wait for the Father's promise, about which you heard me speak.*d* ⁵For John baptized with**b** water, but you will be baptized with**b** the Holy Spirit not many days from now."*e*

⁶Now those who had come together began to ask him, "Lord, is this the time when you will restore the kingdom to Israel?"*f* ⁷He answered them, "It is not for you to know what times or periods the Father has set by his own authority.*g* ⁸But you will receive power when the Holy Spirit comes on you, and you will be my witnesses in Jerusalem, in all Judea and Samaria, and to the ends of the earth."*h*

Jesus Goes Up to Heaven

⁹After saying this, he was taken up while they were watching, and a cloud took him out of their sight.*i* ¹⁰While he was going and they were gazing up toward heaven, two men in white robes were standing right beside them.*j* ¹¹They asked, "Men of Galilee, why do you stand looking up toward heaven? This same Jesus, who has been taken up from you into heaven, will come back in the same way you saw him go up into heaven."*k*

---

a 1:2 *The* Gk. lacks *to heaven*   **b** 1:5 Or *in*

1:1
a Lk 1:3

1:2
b Matt 28:19;
Mark 16:15,19;
Lk 9:51;
24:51 John 20:21;
Acts 10:41-42;
24:9; 1Tim 3:16

1:3
c Mark 16:14;
Lk 24:36;
John 20:19,26;
21:1,14;
1Cor 15:5

1:4
d Lk 24:43,49;
John 14:16,26-27;
15:26; 16:7;
Acts 2:33

1:5
e Joel 3:18;
Matt 3:11;
Acts 2:4;
11:15-16; 19:4

1:6
f Isa 1:26;
Dan 7:27;
Amos 9:11;
Matt 24:3

1:7
g Matt 24:36;
Mark 13:32;
1Thes 5:1

1:8
h Lk 24:48-49;
John 15:27;
Acts 2:1,4,32;
15:22

1:9
i Lk 24:51;
John 6:62;
Acts 6:2

1:10
j Matt 28:3;
Mark 16:5;
Lk 24:4;
John 20:12;
Acts 10:3,30

1:11
k Dan 7:13;
Matt 24:30;
Mark 13:26;
Lk 21:27;
John 14:3;
Acts 2:7; 13:31;
1Thes 1:10; 4:16;
2Thes 1:10;
Rev 1:7

A New Apostle Takes the Place of Judas

1:12
a Lk 24:52

12Then they returned to Jerusalem from the Mount of Olives,ᵃ which is near Jerusalem, a Sabbath day's journey away.ᵇᵃ 13When they came into the city, they went to the upstairs room where they had been staying. They were Peter and John; James and Andrew; Philip and Thomas; Bartholomew and Matthew; James the son of Alphaeus and Simon the Zealot; and Judas the sonᶜ of James.ᵇ 14With one mind all of them kept devoting themselves to prayer, along with the women, including Mary the mother of Jesus, and his brothers.ᶜ

1:13
b Matt 10:2-4;
Lk 6:15;
Acts 9:37,39;
20:8; Jude 1:1

1:14
c Matt 13:55;
Lk 23:49,55;
24:10; Acts 2:1,46

15At that timeᵈ Peter got up among the brothers (there were about 120 people present) and said,ᵈ 16"Brothers, the Scripture had to be fulfilled, which the Holy Spirit spoke long ago through the voice of David about Judas, who was the guide to those who arrested Jesus.ᵉ 17For he was one of our number and was chosen to share in this ministry."ᶠ

1:15
d Rev 3:4

1:16
e Ps 41:9;
Lk 22:47;
John 13:18; 18:3

18Now this man bought a field with the money he got for his crime. Falling on his face, he burst open in the middle, and all his intestines gushed out.ᵍ 19This became known to all the residents of Jerusalem, so that this field is called in their language Hakeldama, that is, The Field of Blood.

20"For in the Book of Psalms it is written,ʰ

1:17
f Matt 10:4;
Lk 6:16;
Acts 2:25; 12:25;
20:24; 21:19

1:18
g Matt 26:15;
27:5,7-8;
2Peter 2:15

'Let his estate be desolate, and let no one live
        on it,'ᵉ

and

'Let someone else take over his office.'ᶠ

1:20
h Ps 69:25; 109:8

21Therefore, one of the men who have associated with us all the time the Lord Jesus came and went among us, 22beginning with the baptism of John until the day he was taken up from us, must become a witness with us to his resurrection."ⁱ

1:22
i Mark 1:1;
John 15:27;
Acts 1:9; 4:33;
15:8

23So they nominated two men—Joseph called Barsabbas, who also was called Justus, and Matthias.ʲ 24Then they

---

a 1:12 Lit. *from the mountain called Olives*   b 1:12 I.e. about a half mile away   c 1:13 Or *brother*   d 1:15 Lit. *In those days*   e 1:20 Ps 69:25   f 1:20 Ps 109:8

1:23
j Acts 15:22

prayed, "Lord, you know the hearts of all people. Show us which one of these two men you have chosen[a] 25to serve in this office of apostle,[a] from which Judas fell away to go to his own place."[b]

26So they drew lots for them, and when the lot fell on Matthias, he was added to the eleven apostles.

The Coming of the Holy Spirit

2 1When the day of Pentecost came, all of them were together in one place.[c] 2Suddenly, a sound like the roaring of a mighty windstorm came from heaven and filled the whole house where they were sitting.[d] 3They saw tongues like flames of fire that separated, and one rested on each of them. 4All of them were filled with the Holy Spirit and began to speak in other tongues as the Spirit gave them that ability.[e]

5Now devout Jews from every nation under heaven were living in Jerusalem. 6When that sound came, the crowd rushed together and was startled because each one heard the disciples[b] speaking in his own language. 7Stunned and amazed, they asked, "All of these people who are speaking are Galileans, aren't they?[f] 8So how is it that each one of us hears them speaking in his own native language?[c] 9We are Parthians, Medes, Elamites, people from Mesopotamia, Judea, Cappadocia, Pontus, Asia, 10Phrygia, Pamphylia, Egypt, the district of Libya near Cyrene, and visitors from Rome. 11We are Jews, proselytes, Cretans, and Arabs. Yet we hear them telling in our own tongues the great deeds of God!"

12All of them continued to be stunned and puzzled, and they kept asking one another, "What can this mean?" 13But others kept saying in derision, "They're full of sweet wine!"

Peter Addresses the Crowd

14Then Peter stood up with the eleven, raised his voice, and addressed them, "Men of Judea and everyone living in Jerusalem! You must understand something, so pay close

---

a 1:25 Lit. *to receive the place of this service and apostleship*   b 2:6 Lit. *them*
c 2:8 Lit. *in our language in which we were born*

Margin references:

1:24
a 1Sam 16:7;
1Chr 28:9; 29:17;
Jer 11:20; 17:10;
Acts 15:8;
Rev 2:23

1:25
b Acts 1:17

2:1
c Lev 23:15;
Deut 16:9;
Acts 1:14; 20:16

2:2
d Acts 4:31

2:4
e Mark 16:17;
Acts 1:5; 10:46;
19:6; 1Cor 12:10,
28,30; 13:1; 14:2

2:7
f Acts 1:11

2:15
a 1 Thes 5:7

2:17
b Isa 44:3;
Ezek 11:19;
36:27;
Joel 2:28-29;
Zech 12:10;
John 7:38;
Acts 10:45; 21:9

2:18
c Acts 21:4,9-10;
1 Cor 12:10,28;
14:1

2:19
d Joel 2:30-31

2:20
e Matt 24:29;
Mark 13:24;
Lk 21:25

2:21
f Rom 10:13

2:22
g John 3:2;
14:10-11;
Acts 10:38;
Heb 2:4

2:23
h Matt 26:24;
Lk 22:22; 24:44;
Acts 3:18; 4:28;
5:30

2:24
i Acts 2:32; 3:15;
4:10; 10:40;
13:30,34; 17:31;
Rom 4:24; 8:11;
1 Cor 6:14; 15:15;
2 Cor 4:14;
Gal 1:1; Eph 1:20;
Col 2:12;
1 Thes 1:10;
Heb 13:20;
1 Peter 1:21

2:25
j Ps 16:8

attention to my words. ¹⁵These men are not drunk as you suppose, for it's only nine o'clock in the morning.ᵃᵃ ¹⁶Rather, this is what was spoken through the prophet Joel:

¹⁷'In the last days, God says,ᵇ
    I will pour out my Spirit on everyone.ᵇ
Your sons and your daughters will prophesy,
    your young men will see visions,
        and your old men will dream dreams.
¹⁸In those days I will even pour out my Spiritᶜ
    on my slaves, men and women alike,
        and they will prophesy.
¹⁹I will work wonders in the sky aboveᵈ
    and signs on the earth below:
        blood, fire, and clouds of smoke.
²⁰The sun will turn to darkness,ᵉ
    and the moon to blood,
        before the coming of the great and glorious
        day of the Lord.
²¹Then whoever calls on the name of the Lordᶠ
    will be saved.'ᶜ

²²"Fellow Israelites, listen to these words! Jesus from Nazarethᵈ was a man accredited to you by God through miracles, wonders, and signs that God performed through him among you, as you yourselves know.ᵍ ²³This very man, after he was arrested according to the predetermined plan and foreknowledge of God, you crucified and killed by the hands of lawless men.ʰ ²⁴But God raised him up and destroyed the pains of death,ᵉ since it was impossible for him to be held in its power.ⁱ ²⁵For David says about him,ʲ

    'I always see the Lord in front of me,
        for he is at my right hand
            so that I cannot be shaken.
²⁶That is why my heart is glad
    and my tongue rejoices,

---

a *2:15* Lit. *the third hour of the day*   **b** *2:17* Lit. *on all flesh*
c *2:21* Joel 2:28-32   **d** *2:22* Or *Jesus the Nazarene; the Gk. Nazoraios* may be a word play between Heb. *netser,* meaning *branch* (see Isa 11:1), and the name *Nazareth.*   **e** *2:24* Other mss. read *of Hades*

> yes, even my body still rests securely in
> hope.
> 27For you will not abandon my soul to the grave[a]
> or allow your Holy One to experience decay.
> 28You have made the ways of life known to me,
> and you will fill me with gladness in your
> presence.'[b]

29"Brothers, I can tell you confidently that the patriarch David died and was buried, and that his tomb is among us to this day.[a] 30Therefore, since he was a prophet and knew that God had promised him with an oath to put one of his descendants on his throne,[b] 31he looked ahead and spoke about the resurrection of the Christ:[cc]

> 'He was not abandoned to the grave,[a]
> and his flesh did not experience decay.'[d]

32It was this very Jesus whom God raised, and of that we are all witnesses.[d] 33He has been exalted to the right hand of God, has received from the Father the promised Holy Spirit,[e] and has poured out what you are seeing and hearing.[e] 34For David did not go up to heaven, but he said,[f]

> 'The Lord said to my Lord,
> "Sit at my right hand,
> 35   until I make your enemies your footstool." '[f]

36Therefore, let the entire house of Israel understand beyond a doubt that God made this Jesus, whom you crucified, both Lord and Christ!"[gg]

37When they heard this, they were pierced to the heart. They asked Peter and the other apostles, "Brothers, what should we do?"[h] 38Peter answered them, "Repent and be baptized, every one of you, in the name of Jesus Christ since your sins are forgiven. Then you will receive the Holy Spirit as a gift.[hi] 39For this promise belongs to you and your

---

a 2:27,2:31 Gk. *Hades*, a reference to the realm of the dead   b 2:28 Ps 16:8-11   c 2:31 I.e. the Messiah   d 2:31 *Ps 16:10*   e 2:33 Or *the promise of the Holy Spirit*   f 2:35 Ps 110:1   g 2:36 I.e. Messiah   h 2:38 Or *the gift of the Holy Spirit*

2:29
a 1Kings 2:10;
Acts 13:36

2:30
b 2Sam 7:12-13;
Ps 132:11;
Lk 1:32,69;
Rom 1:3;
2Tim 2:8

2:31
c Ps 16:10;
Acts 13:35

2:32
d Acts 1:8; 2:24

2:33
e John 14:26;
15:26; 16:7,13;
Acts 1:4; 5:31;
10:45; Eph 4:8;
Phil 2:9;
Heb 10:12

2:34
f Ps 110:1;
Matt 22:44;
1Cor 15:25;
Eph 1:20;
Heb 1:13

2:36
g Acts 5:31

2:37
h Zech 12:10;
Lk 3:10; Acts 9:6;
16:30

2:38
i Lk 24:47;
Acts 3:19

2:39
a Joel 2:28;
Acts 3:25; 10:45;
11:15,18; 14:27;
15:3,8,14;
Eph 2:13,17

children, as well as to all those who are far away, whom the Lord our God may call to himself."[a]

[40]With many more words he continued to testify and to plead with them, saying, "Save yourselves from this corrupt generation!" [41]So those who welcomed his message were baptized, and that day about 3,000 persons were added to them.

2:42
b Acts 1:14; 2:46;
Rom 12:12;
Eph 6:18; Col 4:2;
Heb 10:25

Life Among the Believers

[42]They continually devoted themselves to the teaching of the apostles, to fellowship, to the breaking of bread, and to prayer.[b] [43]A sense of awe came over everyone, and many

2:43
c Mark 16:17;
Acts 4:33; 5:12

wonders and signs were being done by the apostles.[c] [44]All the believers were together, and they shared everything with one another.[a][d] [45]They made it their practice to sell their possessions and goods and to distribute the proceeds[b] to

2:44
d Acts 4:32,34

anyone who was in need.[e] [46]They had a single purpose and went to the Temple every day. They ate at each other's homes and shared their food with glad and humble hearts.[f] [47]They kept praising God and enjoying the good will of all

2:45
e Isa 58:7

the people. And every day the Lord was adding to them people who were being saved.[g]

2:46
f Lk 24:53;
Acts 1:14; 5:42;
20:7

A Crippled Man Is Healed

3 [1]Peter and John were going up to the Temple for the hour of prayer at three in the afternoon.[c][h] [2]Now a man who had been crippled from birth was being carried in. Every day people[d] would lay him at what was called the

2:47
g Lk 2:52;
Acts 4:33; 5:14;
11:24; Rom 14:18

Beautiful Gate so that he could beg from those who were going into the Temple.[i] [3]When he saw that Peter and John were about to go into the Temple, he asked them to give him something.

[4]Peter, along with John, looked him straight in the eye and said, "Look at us!" [5]So the man[e] watched them closely, expecting to get something from them. [6]However, Peter said, "I don't have any silver or gold, but I'll give you what I

3:1
h Ps 55:17;
Acts 2:46

3:2
i John 9:8;
Acts 14:8

---

a 2:44 Lit. *had all things in common*   *b* 2:45 Lit. *to distribute them*
c 3:1 Lit. *at the ninth hour*   *d* 3:2 Lit. *they*   *e* 3:5 Lit. *he*

do have. In the name of Jesus Christ from Nazareth, walk!"[aa] [7]Then Peter[b] took hold of his right hand and began to help him up. Immediately his feet and ankles became strong, [8]and he sprung to his feet, stood up, and began to walk. Then he went with them into the Temple, walking, jumping, and praising God.[b]

[9]When all the people saw him walking and praising God,[c] [10]they knew that he was the man who used to sit and beg at the Beautiful Gate of the Temple, and they were filled with wonder and amazement at what had happened to him.[d]

Peter Speaks to the Onlookers

[11]While he was holding on to Peter and John, all the people came running together to them in what was called Solomon's Colonnade. They were dumbfounded.[e] [12]When Peter saw this, he said to the people: "Fellow Israelites, why are you wondering about this, and why are you staring at us as if by our own power or godliness we made him walk? [13]The God of Abraham, the God of Isaac, and the God of Jacob—the God of our ancestors—has glorified his servant Jesus, whom you betrayed and rejected in the presence of Pilate, even though he had decided to let him go.[f] [14]You rejected the Holy and Righteous One and asked to have a murderer given to you,[g] [15]and you killed the source of life, whom God raised from the dead. We are witnesses to that.[h] [16]It is his name, that is, by the faith of[c] his name, that has healed this man whom you see and know. Yes, the faith that comes through him has given him this perfect health in the presence of all of you.[i]

[17]"And now, brothers, I know that you acted in ignorance like your leaders.[j] [18]This is how God fulfilled what he had predicted through the voice of all the prophets—that his Christ[d] would suffer.[k] [19]Therefore, repent and turn to him to have your sins blotted out,[l] [20]so that times of refreshing may come from the presence of the Lord and so that he may send you Jesus, the Christ[e] whom he appointed long ago.

---

a 3:6 Other mss. read *stand up and walk*   **b** 3:7 Lit. *he*   **c** 3:16 Or *by faith in*   **d** 3:18 I.e. Messiah   **e** 3:20 I.e. the Messiah

---

3:6 [a] Acts 4:10

3:8 [b] Isa 35:6

3:9 [c] Acts 4:16,21

3:10 [d] John 9:8

3:11 [e] John 10:23; Acts 5:12

3:13 [f] Matt 27:2,20; Mark 15:11; Lk 23:18,20-21; John 7:39; 12:16; 17:1; 18:40; 19:15; Acts 5:30; 13:28

3:14 [g] Ps 16:10; Mark 1:24; Lk 1:35; Acts 2:27; 4:27; 7:52; 22:14

3:15 [h] Acts 2:24,32

3:16 [i] Matt 9:22; Acts 4:10; 14:9

3:17 [j] Lk 23:34; John 16:3; Acts 13:27; 1Cor 2:8; 1Tim 1:13

3:18 [k] Ps 22:1-31; Isa 50:6; 53:5; Dan 9:26; Lk 24:44; Acts 26:22; 1Peter 1:10-11

3:19 [l] Acts 2:38

3:21
a Matt 17:11;
Lk 1:70; Acts 1:11

21Heaven must receive him until the time of universal restoration that God announced long ago through the voice of his holy prophets.*a* 22In fact, Moses said,*b*

'The Lord your God will raise up for you a prophet like me from among your brothers. You must listen to everything he tells you.*a* 23Any person who will not listen to that prophet will be utterly destroyed from among the people.'*b*

3:22
b Deut 18:15,
18-19; Acts 7:37

3:25
c Gen 12:3; 18:18;
22:18; 26:4;
28:14; Acts 2:39;
Rom 9:4,8; 15:8;
Gal 3:8,26

24"Indeed, all the prophets who have spoken, from Samuel and those who followed him, also predicted these days. 25You are the descendants of the prophets and the heirs of the covenant*c* that God made with your*d* ancestors when he said to Abraham, 'Through your descendant all the families of the earth will be blessed.'*ec* 26When God raised up his servant, he sent him first to you to bless you by turning every one of you from your evil ways."*d*

3:26
d Matt 1:21; 10:5;
15:24; Lk 24:47;
Acts 13:22,32-33,
46

Peter and John Are Tried before the Jewish Council

4 1While they were speaking to the people, the priests, the commander of the temple guards, and the Sadducees came to them. 2They were greatly disturbed that Peter and John*f* were teaching the people and declaring that in the case of Jesus there had been a resurrection from the dead.*e* 3So they arrested them and placed them in custody until the next day, since it was already evening. 4But many of those who heard their message believed, and the number of men grew to about 5,000.

4:2
e Matt 22:23;
Acts 23:8

4:6
f Lk 3:2;
John 11:49; 18:13

5The next day their rulers, elders, and scribes met in Jerusalem 6with Annas the high priest, Caiaphas, John,*g* Alexander, and the rest of the high priest's family.*f* 7They made them stand in front of them and began asking, "By what power or by what name did you do this?"*g*

4:7
g Exod 2:14;
Matt 21:23;
Acts 7:27

8Peter, filled with the Holy Spirit, said to them, "Rulers and elders of the people!*h* 9If we are being questioned today

4:8
h Lk 12:11-12

a 3:22 Deut 18:15-16   b 3:23 Deut 18:19; Lev 23:29   c 3:25 Lit.
descendants of the prophets and of the covenant   d 3:25 Other mss. read *our*
e 3:25 Gen 22:18; 26:4   f 4:2 Lit. *they*   g 4:6 Other mss. read *Jonathan*

for a good deed to someone who was sick or to learn how this man was healed, [10]you and all the people of Israel must understand that this man stands healthy before you because of the name of Jesus from Nazareth, whom you crucified but God raised from the dead.[a] [11]He is[b]

> 'the stone that was rejected by you builders,
> which has become the cornerstone.'[a]

[12]There is no salvation by anyone else, for there is no other name under heaven given among people by which we must be saved."[c]

[13]Now when they saw the boldness of Peter and John and found out that they were uneducated and ordinary men, they were amazed and realized that they had been with Jesus.[d] [14]And seeing the man who was healed standing with them, they could not say anything against them.[e] [15]So they ordered them to leave the Council[b] and began to discuss the matter among themselves. [16]They said, "What should we do with these men? For it's obvious to everybody living in Jerusalem that an unmistakable sign has been done by them, and we can't deny it.[f] [17]But to keep it from spreading any further among the people, let us warn them never again to speak to anyone in this name."

[18]So they called them in and ordered them not to speak or teach at all in the name of Jesus.[g] [19]But Peter and John answered them, "You must decide whether it is right in the sight of God to listen to you rather than God,[h] [20]for we cannot stop talking about what we have seen and heard."[i]

[21]So they threatened them even more and then let them go. They couldn't find any way to punish them, because all the people continued to praise God for what had happened.[j] [22]For the man on whom this sign of healing had been performed was more than forty years old.

The Believers Pray for Boldness

[23]After they were released, they went to their own people and told them everything the high priests and the elders had said.[k] [24]When they heard this, they all raised their

---

4:10
[a]Acts 2:24; 3:6,16

4:11
[b]Ps 118:22;
Isa 28:16;
Matt 21:42

4:12
[c]Matt 1:21;
Acts 10:43;
1 Tim 2:5-6

4:13
[d]Matt 11:25;
1 Cor 1:27

4:14
[e]Acts 3:11

4:16
[f]John 11:47;
Acts 3:9-10

4:18
[g]Acts 5:40

4:19
[h]Acts 5:29

4:20
[i]Acts 1:8; 2:32;
22:15; 1 John 1:1,3

4:21
[j]Matt 21:26;
Lk 20:6,19; 22:2;
Acts 3:7-8; 5:26

4:23
[k]Acts 12:12

---

a 4:11 Or capstone; Ps 118:22   b 4:15 Or Sanhedrin

4:24
a 2Kings 19:15

4:25
b Ps 2:1

4:27
c Matt 26:3;
Lk 1:35; 4:18;
22:2; 23:1,8;
John 10:36

4:28
d Acts 2:23; 3:18

4:29
e Acts 4:13,31;
9:27; 13:46; 14:3;
19:8; 26:26;
28:31; Eph 6:19

4:30
f Acts 2:43; 4:6,16,
27; 5:12

4:31
g Acts 2:2,4;
16:26,29

4:32
h Acts 2:44; 5:12;
Rom 15:5-6;
2Cor 13:11;
Phil 1:27; 2:2;
1Peter 3:8

4:33
i Acts 1:8,22; 2:47

4:34
j Acts 2:45

4:35
k Acts 2:45; 4:37;
5:2; 6:1

4:37
l Acts 4:34-35;
5:1-2

voices to God and said, "Master, you made heaven and earth, the sea, and everything in them.*a* 25You said by the Holy Spirit through the voice of our ancestor, your servant David,*b*

> 'Why do the Gentiles rage,
>   and the people devise useless plots?
> 26The kings of the earth take their stand,
>   and rulers meet together against the Lord
>   and against his Christ.'**a**

27"For in this city both Herod and Pontius Pilate actually met together with the Gentiles and the people of Israel against your holy servant Jesus, whom you anointed,*c* 28to do all that your hand and your will had predetermined to take place.*d* 29Lord, pay attention to their threats now, and allow your servants to speak your word with all boldness*e* 30as you stretch out your hand to heal and to perform signs and wonders through the name of your holy servant Jesus."*f*

31When they had prayed, the place where they were meeting was shaken, and all of them were filled with the Holy Spirit and continued to speak the word of God with boldness.*g*

The Believers Share Their Possessions

32Now the whole group of believers was one in heart and soul, and nobody called any of his possessions his own. Instead, they shared everything they owned.*h* 33With great power the apostles continued to testify to the resurrection of the Lord Jesus, and abundant grace was on them all.*i* 34For none of them needed anything, because all who had land or houses would sell them and bring the money received for the things sold*j* 35and lay it at the apostles' feet. Then it was distributed to anyone who needed it.*k*

36Now Joseph, a Levite and a native of Cyprus, who was named Barnabas by the apostles (which means "a son of encouragement"), 37sold a field that belonged to him and brought the money and laid it at the apostles' feet.*l*

---

a 4:26 I.e. Messiah; Ps 2:1-2

Ananias and Sapphira Are Punished

5 ¹But a man named Ananias, with the consent of his wife Sapphira, sold some property. ²With his wife's full knowledge he kept back some of the money for himself and brought only a part of it and laid it at the apostles' feet.ᵃ

³Peter asked, "Ananias, why has Satan filled your heart so that you should lie to the Holy Spirit and keep back some of the money you got for the land?ᵇ ⁴As long as it remained unsold, wasn't it your own? And after it was sold, wasn't the money at your disposal? So how could you have conceived such a thing in your heart? You did not lie to men but to God!" ⁵When Ananias heard these words, he fell down and died. And great fear seized everyone who heard about it.ᶜ ⁶The young men got up, wrapped him up, carried him outside, and buried him.ᵈ

⁷After an interval of about three hours, his wife came in, not knowing what had happened. ⁸So Peter asked her, "Tell me, did you sell the land for that price?" She answered, "Yes, that was the price." ⁹Then Peter said to her, "How could you have agreed together to test the Spirit of the Lord? Listen! The feet of the men who buried your husband are at the door, and they will carry you outside as well."ᵉ ¹⁰She instantly fell down at his feet and died. When the young men came in, they found her dead. So they carried her out and buried her next to her husband.ᶠ ¹¹And great fear seized the whole church and everyone else who heard about this.ᵍ

The Apostles Perform Many Miracles

¹²Now many signs and wonders were continuously being performed by the apostles among the people. And they were all together in Solomon's Colonnade.ʰ ¹³None of the other people dared to join them, although the people continued to hold them in high regard.ⁱ ¹⁴Nevertheless, still more believers, a vast number of both men and women, were being added to the Lord. ¹⁵As a result, peopleᵃ kept carrying their sick into the streets and placing them on

---

ᵃ5:15 Lit. *they*

5:2
ᵃ Acts 4:37

5:3
ᵇ Num 30:2;
Deut 23:21;
Eccl 5:4; Lk 22:3

5:5
ᶜ Acts 5:10-11

5:6
ᵈ John 19:40

5:9
ᵉ Matt 4:7;
Acts 5:3

5:10
ᶠ Acts 5:5

5:11
ᵍ Acts 2:43; 5:5;
19:17

5:12
ʰ Acts 2:43; 3:11;
4:32; 14:3; 19:11;
Rom 15:19;
2Cor 12:12;
Heb 2:4

5:13
ⁱ John 9:22; 12:42;
19:38; Acts 2:47;
4:21

5:15
a Matt 9:21; 14:36;
Acts 19:12

5:16
b Mark 16:17-18;
John 14:12

5:17
c Acts 4:1-2,6

5:18
d Lk 21:12

5:19
e Acts 12:7; 16:26

5:20
f John 6:68; 17:3;
1 John 5:11

5:21
g Acts 4:5-6

5:24
h Lk 22:4; Acts 4:1

5:26
i Matt 21:26

5:28
j Matt 23:35;
27:25; Acts 2:23,
36; 3:15; 4:18;
7:52

5:29
k Acts 4:19

stretchers and cots so that at least Peter's shadow might fall on some of them as he went by.[a] [16]Even from the towns around Jerusalem crowds continued coming in to bring their sick and those who were troubled by unclean spirits, and all of them were healed.[b]

The Apostles Are Tried before the Jewish Council

[17]Then the high priest and all those from the sect of the Sadducees who were with him were filled with jealousy. So they went[c] [18]and arrested the apostles and put them in the city jail.[d] [19]But at night the angel of the Lord opened the prison doors and led them out. He told them,[e] [20]"Go and stand in the Temple and keep on telling the people the whole message about this life."[f]

[21]After they heard this, they went into the Temple at daybreak and began to teach. The high priest and those who were with him arrived, called the Council[a] and all the elders of Israel together, and sent word[b] to the prison to have the men brought in.[g] [22]When the temple police got there, they did not find them in the prison. They came back and reported, [23]"We found the prison securely locked and the guards standing at the doors, but when we opened them, we found no one inside." [24]When the commander of the temple guards and the high priests heard these words, they were utterly at a loss as to what could have happened to them.[h]

[25]Then someone came and told them, "Look! The men you put in prison are standing in the Temple and teaching the people!" [26]So the commander of the temple guards went with his men to bring them back without force, because they were afraid of being stoned to death by the people.[i] [27]When they brought them back, they made them stand before the Council,[a] and the high priest began to question them. [28]He said, "We gave you strict orders not to teach in his name, didn't we? Yet you have filled Jerusalem with your teaching and are determined to bring this man's blood on us!"[j]

[29]But Peter and the apostles answered, "We must obey God rather than men.[k] [30]The God of our ancestors raised

---

a 5:21,5:27 Or *Sanhedrin*   b 5:21 The Gk. lacks *word*

Jesus to life after you hung him on a tree and killed him.[a] [31]God has exalted to his right hand this very man as our Leader and Savior in order to give repentance and forgiveness of sins to Israel.[b] [32]We are witnesses of these things, and so is the Holy Spirit, whom God has given to those who keep on obeying him."[c]

[33]When they heard this, they became furious and wanted to kill them.[d] [34]But a Pharisee named Gamaliel, a teacher of the Law who was respected by all the people, got up in the Council[a] and ordered the men to be taken outside for a little while.[e] [35]Then he said to them, "Fellow Israelites, consider carefully what you propose to do to these men. [36]For in days gone by Theudas appeared, claiming that he was important, and about 400 men joined him. He was killed, and all his followers were dispersed and disappeared. [37]After that man, at the time of the census, Judas the Galilean appeared and got people to follow him. He, too, died, and all his followers were scattered.

[38]"I'm telling you to keep away from these men for now. Leave them alone, because if this plan or movement is of human origin, it will fail.[f] [39]However, if it is from God, you won't be able to stop them, and you may even discover that you're fighting against God!" So they were convinced by him.[g]

[40]After calling in the apostles and beating them, they ordered them to stop speaking in the name of Jesus and let them go.[h] [41]They left the Council,[a] rejoicing to have been considered worthy to suffer dishonor for the sake of the Name.[i] [42]Every day in the Temple and from house to house they kept teaching and proclaiming that Jesus is the Christ.[b][j]

Seven Men Are Chosen to Help the Apostles

6 [1]In those days, as the number of the disciples was growing larger and larger, a complaint was made by the Hellenistic Jews against the Hebraic Jews that their widows were being neglected in the daily distribution of food.[k] [2]So the twelve called the whole group of disciples together and said, "It is not desirable for us to neglect the

---

a 5:34,5:41 Or *Sanhedrin*   b 5:42 I.e. the Messiah

Cross references

5:30 *a* Acts 3:13,15; 10:39; 13:29; 22:14; Gal 3:13; 1Peter 2:24

5:31 *b* Matt 1:21; Lk 24:47; Acts 2:33,36; 3:15,26; 13:38; Eph 1:7; Phil 2:9; Col 1:14; Heb 2:10; 12:2

5:32 *c* John 15:26-27; Acts 2:4; 10:44

5:33 *d* Acts 2:37; 7:54

5:34 *e* Acts 22:3

5:38 *f* Prov 21:30; Isa 8:10; Matt 15:13

5:39 *g* Lk 21:15; Acts 7:51; 9:5; 23:9; 1Cor 1:25

5:40 *h* Matt 10:17; 23:34; Mark 13:9; Acts 4:18

5:41 *i* Matt 5:12; Rom 5:3; 2Cor 12:10; Phil 1:29; Heb 10:34; James 1:2; 1Peter 4:13,16

5:42 *j* Acts 2:46; 4:20, 29

6:1 *k* Acts 2:41; 4:4, 35; 5:7,14; 9:29; 11:20

6:2
a Exod 18:17

6:3
b Deut 1:13;
Acts 1:21; 16:2;
1 Tim 3:7

6:4
c Acts 2:42

6:5
d Acts 8:5,26;
11:24; 21:8;
Rev 2:6,15

6:6
e Acts 1:24; 8:17;
9:17; 13:3;
1 Tim 4:14; 5:22;
2 Tim 1:6

6:7
f John 12:42;
Acts 12:24; 19:20;
Col 1:6

6:10
g Exod 4:12;
Isa 54:17;
Lk 21:15;
Acts 5:39

6:11
h 1 Kings 21:10,13;
Matt 26:59-60

6:14
i Dan 9:26;
Acts 25:8

word of God in order to wait on tables.*a* *3*Therefore, brothers, appoint seven men among you who have a good reputation, who are full of the Spirit and wisdom, and we will put them in charge of this work.*b* *4*Then we will devote ourselves to prayer and to the ministry of the word."*c*

*5*This suggestion pleased the whole group. So they chose Stephen, a man full of faith and the Holy Spirit, Philip, Prochorus, Nicanor, Timon, Parmenas, and Nicolaus, a proselyte**a** from Antioch.*d* *6*They had these men stand before the apostles, who prayed and laid their hands on them.*e*

*7*So the word of God**b** continued to spread, and the number of disciples in Jerusalem continued to grow rapidly. Even a large number of priests became obedient to the faith.*f*

Stephen Is Arrested

*8*Now Stephen, full of grace and power, was performing great wonders and signs among the people. *9*But some men who belonged to the Synagogue of the Freedmen (as it was called), as well as some Cyrenians, Alexandrians, and men from Cilicia and Asia, stood up and began to debate with Stephen. *10*But they couldn't resist the wisdom and the Spirit by which he kept speaking.*g*

*11*So they secretly got some men to say, "We have heard him speaking blasphemous words against Moses and God."*h* *12*They stirred up the people, the elders, and the scribes. Then they rushed at him, grabbed him, and brought him before the Council.**c** *13*They had false witnesses stand up and say, "This man never stops saying things against this Holy Place and against the Law. *14*For we have heard him say that this Jesus from Nazareth**d** will destroy this place and change the customs that Moses handed down to us."*i*

*15*Then all who were seated in the Council**c** glared at him and saw that his face was like the face of an angel.

---

a 6:5 I.e. a Gentile convert to Judaism   **b** 6:7 Other mss. read *of the Lord*
c 6:12,6:15 Or *Sanhedrin*   **d** 6:14 Or *Jesus the Nazarene*; the Gk. *Nazoraios* may be a word play between Heb. *netser*, meaning *branch* (see Isa 11:1), and the name *Nazareth*.

Stephen Defends Himself

7 ¹Then the high priest asked, "Is this true?" ²Stephen replied, "Listen, brothers and fathers! The glorious God appeared to our ancestor Abraham while he was in Mesopotamia before he settled in Haran.*a* ³He said to him, 'Leave your country and your relatives and go to the land I will show you.'*ab* ⁴So he left the country of the Chaldeans and settled in Haran. Then after the death of his father, God had him move to this country where you now live.*c* ⁵He gave him no property in it, not even a foot of land. Yet he promised to give it to him and his descendants after him as a permanent possession, even though he had no child.*d* ⁶This is what God promised: His descendants would be strangers in a foreign country, and its people*b* would enslave them and oppress them for 400 years.*e* ⁷'But I will punish the nation they serve,' said God, 'and afterwards they will leave and worship me in this place.'*cf* ⁸Then he gave Abraham*d* the covenant of circumcision, and he became the father of Isaac and circumcised him on the eighth day. Then Isaac became the father of Jacob, and Jacob of the twelve patriarchs.*g*

⁹"The patriarchs became jealous of Joseph and sold him as a slave*e* into Egypt. However, God was with him*h* ¹⁰and rescued him from all his troubles. He allowed him to win favor and show wisdom before Pharaoh, king of Egypt, who appointed him ruler of Egypt and of his whole household.*i*

¹¹"But a famine spread throughout Egypt and Canaan, and with it great suffering, and our ancestors couldn't find any food.*j* ¹²But when Jacob heard that there was grain in Egypt, he sent our ancestors on their first visit.*k* ¹³On their second visit Joseph made himself known to his brothers, and Joseph's family became known to Pharaoh.*l* ¹⁴Then Joseph sent word*f* and invited his father Jacob and all his relatives to come to him—seventy-five persons in all.*m* ¹⁵So Jacob went down to Egypt. Then he and our ancestors died.*n* ¹⁶They were brought back to Shechem and laid in the tomb

---

a7:3 Gen 12:1   **b**7:6 Lit. *they*   **c**7:7 Gen 15:13-14; Exod 3:12   **d**7:8 Lit. *him*   **e**7:9 The Gk. lacks *as a slave*   **f**7:14 The Gk. lacks *word*

7:2
a Acts 22:1

7:3
b Gen 12:1

7:4
c Gen 11:31; 12:4-5

7:5
d Gen 12:7; 13:15; 15:3,18; 17:8; 26:3

7:6
e Gen 15:13,16; Exod 12:40; Gal 3:17

7:7
f Exod 3:12

7:8
g Gen 17:9-11; 21:2-4; 25:26; 29:31; 30:5; 35:18,23

7:9
h Gen 37:4,11,28: 39:2,21,23; Ps 105:17

7:10
i Gen 41:37; 42:6

7:11
j Gen 41:54

7:12
k Gen 42:1

7:13
l Gen 45:4,16

7:14
m Gen 45:9,27; 46:27; Deut 10:22

7:15
n Gen 46:5; 49:33; Exod 1:6

7:16
a Gen 23:16;
35:19;
Exod 13:19;
Josh 24:32

7:17
b Gen 15:13;
Exod 1:7-9;
Ps 105:24-25;
Acts 15:6

7:19
c Exod 1:22

7:20
d Exod 2:2;
Heb 11:23

7:21
e Exod 2:3-10

7:22
f Lk 24:19

7:23
g Exod 2:11-12

7:26
h Exod 2:13

7:27
i Lk 12:14;
Acts 4:7

7:29
j Exod 2:15,22;
4:20; 18:3-4

7:30
k Exod 3:2

7:32
l Matt 22:32;
Heb 11:16

that Abraham bought for a sum of money from the sons of Hamor in Shechem.[a]

[17]"Now as the time approached for the fulfillment of the promise that God had made to Abraham, the people multiplied and grew more numerous in Egypt,[b] [18]until another king, who had not known Joseph, became ruler of Egypt.[a] [19]By shrewdly scheming against our people, he oppressed our ancestors and forced them to expose their infants so that they wouldn't live.[c]

[20]"At this time Moses was born. He was beautiful in the sight of God, and for three months he was cared for in his father's house.[d] [21]When he was placed outside, Pharaoh's daughter adopted him and brought him up as her own son.[e] [22]So Moses was educated in all the wisdom of the Egyptians and became a great man in speech and action.[f]

[23]"When he was forty years old, his heart was moved to visit his brothers, the descendants of Israel.[g] [24]Because he saw one of them being mistreated, he defended and avenged the man who was being mistreated by striking down the Egyptian. [25]He supposed that his brothers would understand that God was using him to rescue them, but they didn't understand. [26]The next day he showed himself to some of them while they were fighting and tried to reconcile them, saying, 'Men, you are brothers. Why should you harm each other?'[h] [27]But the man who was harming his neighbor pushed Moses[b] away and said, 'Who made you ruler and judge over us?[i] [28]You don't want to kill me like you killed the Egyptian yesterday, do you?'[c] [29]At this statement Moses fled and lived as a foreigner in the land of Midian. There he had two sons.[j]

[30]"When forty years had passed, an angel appeared to him in the flames of a burning bush in the desert near Mount Sinai.[k] [31]When Moses saw it, he was amazed at the sight, and when he approached to look at it, the voice of the Lord said,[d] [32]'I am the God of your ancestors—the God of Abraham, Isaac, and Jacob.'[e] Moses became terrified and didn't dare to look.[l] [33]Then the Lord said to him, 'Take your

---

a 7:18 Other mss. lack *of Egypt*   b 7:27 Lit. *him*   c 7:28 Exod 2:14
d 7:31 Lit. *came*   e 7:32 Exod 3:6

shoes off your feet, for the place where you are standing is holy ground.[a] [34]I have surely seen the oppression of my people in Egypt and have heard their groans, and I have come down to rescue them. Now come, I will send you to Egypt.'[ab]

[35]"This same Moses, whom they rejected by saying 'Who made you ruler and judge?', was the man whom God sent to be both their ruler and deliverer with the help of the angel who had appeared to him in the bush.[c] [36]It was he who led them out, performing wonders and signs in Egypt, at the Red Sea, and in the wilderness for forty years.[d] [37]It was this Moses who told the Israelites, 'God will raise up a prophet for you from among your own brothers, just as he did[b] me.'[e] [38]This is the one who was in the congregation in the wilderness with the angel who spoke to him on Mount Sinai and with our ancestors. He received living truths to give to us,[cf] [39]but our ancestors refused to obey him. Instead, they rejected him and in their hearts turned back to Egypt. [40]They said to Aaron, 'Make gods for us who will lead us. This Moses who led us out of the land of Egypt—we don't know what happened to him!'[dg] [41]In those days they even made a calf, offered a sacrifice to their idol, and delighted in the works of their hands.[h]

[42]"So God turned away from them and gave them over to worship the heavenly bodies. As it is written in the book of the Prophets:[i]

'O house of Israel,
    you didn't offer me slaughtered animals and
        sacrifices those forty years in the wilderness,
          did you?
[43]You even took along the tent of Moloch,
    the star of your god Rephan,
  and the images you made in order to worship them.
    So I will remove you beyond Babylon.'[e]

---

a 7:34 Exod 3:4-10   b 7:37 The Gk. lacks *he did*   c 7:38 Other mss. read *to you*   d 7:40 Exod 32:1, 23   e 7:43 Amos 5:25-27

7:33
a Exod 3:5;
Josh 5:15

7:34
b Exod 3:7

7:35
c Exod 14:19;
Num 20:16

7:36
d Exod 7:25;
12:41; 14:21,
27-29; 16:1,35;
33:1 Ps 105:27

7:37
e Deut 18:15,18;
Matt 15:5;
Acts 3:22

7:38
f Exod 19:3,17;
21:1; Deut 5:27,
31; 33:4; Isa 63:9;
John 1:17;
Rom 3:2;
Gal 3:19; Heb 2:2

7:40
g Exod 32:1

7:41
h Deut 9:16;
Ps 106:19

7:42
i Deut 4:19; 17:3;
2Kings 17:16;
21:3; Ps 81:12;
Jer 19:13;
Ezek 20:25,39;
Amos 5:25-26;
Rom 1:24;
2Thes 2:11

7:44
a Exod 25:40;
26:30; Heb 8:5

7:45
b Josh 3:14;
Neh 9:24; Ps 44:2;
78:55; Acts 13:19

7:46
c 1Sam 16:1;
2Sam 7:1;
1Kings 8:17;
1Chr 22:7;
Ps 89:19; 132:4-5;
Acts 13:22

7:47
d 1Kings 6:1; 8:20;
1Chr 17:12;
2Chr 3:1

7:48
e 1Kings 8:27;
2Chr 2:6; 6:18;
Acts 17:24

7:49
f Isa 66:1-2;
Matt 5:34-35;
23:22

7:51
g Exod 32:9; 33:3;
Lev 26:41;
Deut 10:16;
Isa 44:4; Jer 4:4;
6:10; 9:26;
Ezek 44:9

7:52
h 2Chr 36:16;
Matt 21:35; 23:34,
37; Acts 3:14;
1Thes 2:15

7:53
i Exod 20:1;
Gal 3:19; Heb 2:2

7:54
j Acts 5:33

7:55
k Acts 6:5

7:56
l Ezek 1:1;
Dan 7:13;
Matt 3:16;
Acts 10:11

⁴⁴"Our ancestors had the Tent of Testimony**ᵃ** in the wilderness constructed,**ᵇ** just as the one who spoke to Moses directed him to make it according to the pattern he had seen.*ᵃ* ⁴⁵Our ancestors brought it here with Joshua when they replaced the nations that God drove out before our ancestors, and it was here until the time of David.*ᵇ* ⁴⁶He found favor with God and asked to design a dwelling for the house**ᶜ** of Jacob,*ᶜ* ⁴⁷but it was Solomon who built a house for him.*ᵈ* ⁴⁸However, the Most High does not live in buildings made by human**ᵈ** hands. As the prophet says,*ᵉ*

⁴⁹"'Heaven is my throne,*ᶠ*
and the earth is my footstool.
What kind of house can you build for me," says
the Lord,
"or what place is there in which I can rest?
⁵⁰It was my hand that made all these things,
wasn't it?" '*ᵉ*

⁵¹"You stubborn people with uncircumcised hearts and ears! You are always opposing the Holy Spirit, just as your ancestors used to do.*ᵍ* ⁵²Which of the prophets did your ancestors fail to persecute? They killed those who predicted the coming of the Righteous One, and now you have become his betrayers and murderers.*ʰ* ⁵³You received the Law as ordained by angels, and yet you didn't obey it!"*ⁱ*

Stephen Is Stoned to Death

⁵⁴While they were listening to these things, they became more and more furious and began to grind their teeth at him.*ʲ* ⁵⁵But Stephen,**ᶠ** filled with the Holy Spirit, looked straight into heaven and saw the glory of God and Jesus standing at the right hand of God.*ᵏ* ⁵⁶He said, "Look! I see the heavens opened and the Son of Man standing at the right hand of God!"*ˡ*

⁵⁷But they raised a loud shout, held their ears shut, and together they all rushed at him. ⁵⁸They threw him out of the

---

a 7:44 I.e. the tent containing the Ark of the Covenant   **b** 7:44 The Gk. lacks *constructed*   **c** 7:46 Other mss. read *for the God*   **d** 7:48 The Gk. lacks *human*   **e** 7:50 Isa 66:1-2   **f** 7:55 Lit. *he*

city and began to stone him to death. Meanwhile, the witnesses laid their coats at the feet of a young man named Saul.*a* 59As they continued to stone Stephen, he kept praying, "Lord Jesus, receive my spirit!"*b* 60Then he knelt down and cried out with a loud voice, "Lord, don't hold this sin against them!" When he had said this, he died.*ac*

The Church Is Persecuted

8 1Now Saul heartily approved of putting him to death. That day a severe persecution broke out against the church in Jerusalem, and all of them, except for the apostles, were scattered throughout the countryside of Judea and Samaria.*d* 2Devout men buried Stephen as they mourned loudly for him.*e* 3But Saul kept trying to destroy the church. Going into one house after another, he kept dragging off men and women and throwing them in prison.*f*

Some Samaritans Become Believers

4Now those who were scattered went from place to place preaching the word.*g* 5Philip went down to the*b* city of Samaria and began to preach the Christ*c* to the people.*dh* 6The crowds, hearing and seeing the signs that he was doing, paid close attention to what was said by Philip. 7Unclean spirits screamed with a loud voice as they came out of the many people they had possessed, and many paralyzed and lame people were healed.*i* 8As a result, there was great rejoicing in that city.

9In that city there was a man named Simon. He was practicing magic and thrilling the people of Samaria, claiming to be a great man.*j* 10Everyone from the least to the greatest paid close attention to him, saying, "This man is the power of God, which is called great!" 11They paid careful attention to him because he had thrilled them for a long time with his magical performances. 12But when Philip proclaimed the good news of the kingdom of God and of the name of Jesus Christ, men and women believed and were

---

a7:60 Lit. *fell asleep*   **b**8:5 Other mss. read *a*   **c**8:5 I.e. the Messiah
d8:5 Lit. *to them*

7:58
a Lev 24:16;
Deut 13:9-10;
17:7;
1Kings 21:13;
Lk 4:29; Acts 8:1,
22:20; Heb 13:12

7:59
b Ps 31:5;
Lk 23:45;
Acts 9:14

7:60
c Matt 5:44;
Lk 6:28; 23:34;
Acts 9:40; 20:36;
21:5

8:1
d Acts 7:58; 11:19;
22:20

8:2
e Gen 23:2; 50:10;
2Sam 3:31

8:3
f Acts 7:58; 9:1,13,
21; 22:4;
26:10-11;
1Cor 15:9;
Gal 1:13; Phil 3:6;
1Tim 1:13

8:4
g Matt 10:23;
Acts 11:19

8:5
h Acts 6:5

8:7
i Mark 16:17

8:9
j Acts 5:36; 13:6

8:12
a Acts 1:3

baptized.*a* ¹³Even Simon believed, and after he was baptized, he became devoted to Philip. He was amazed to see the signs and great miracles that were happening.

8:15
b Acts 2:38

¹⁴Now when the apostles in Jerusalem heard that Samaria had accepted the word of God, they sent Peter and John to them. ¹⁵They went down and prayed for them to receive the Holy Spirit.*b* ¹⁶Before this he had not come on any of them. They had only been baptized in the name of the Lord Jesus.*c* ¹⁷Then they laid their hands on them, and they received the Holy Spirit.*d*

8:16
c Matt 28:19;
Acts 2:38; 10:48;
19:2,5

8:17
d Acts 6:6; 19:6;
Heb 6:2

¹⁸Now when Simon saw that the Spirit was given through the laying on of the apostles' hands, he offered them money ¹⁹and said, "Give me this power, too, so that when I lay my hands on someone, he will receive the Holy Spirit." ²⁰But Peter said to him, "May your money perish with you because you thought you could obtain God's free gift with money!*e* ²¹You have no part or share in this matter, because your heart isn't right before God. ²²So repent of this wickedness of yours, and pray to the Lord that, if possible, this thought of your heart may be forgiven you.*f* ²³For I see that you're turning into bitter poison and being chained by wickedness!"*g* ²⁴Simon answered, "Both of you pray**a** to the Lord for me that none of the things you have said will happen to me."*h*

8:20
e 2Kings 5:16;
Matt 10:8;
Acts 2:38; 10:45;
11:17

8:22
f Dan 4:27;
2Tim 2:25

²⁵After they had given their testimony and spoken the word of the Lord, they started back to Jerusalem, continuing to proclaim the good news in many Samaritan villages.

8:23
g Heb 12:15

Philip Tells an Ethiopian about Jesus

²⁶Now an angel of the Lord said to Philip, "Get up and go south by the road that leads from Jerusalem to Gaza. This is a desert road." ²⁷So he got up and went. An Ethiopian eunuch was there. He was a member of the court of Candace, queen of the Ethiopians, and was in charge of all her treasures. He had come to Jerusalem to worship*i* ²⁸and was returning home. He was seated in his chariot, reading the prophet Isaiah.

8:24
h Gen 20:7,17;
Exod 8:8;
Num 21:7;
1Kings 13:6;
Job 42:8;
James 5:16

²⁹The Spirit said to Philip, "Go to that chariot and stay

8:27
i Zeph 3:10;
John 12:20

a 8:24 Lit. *Pray* (plural)

close to it." [30]So Philip ran up to it and heard him reading
the prophet Isaiah out loud. He asked, "Do you understand
what you're reading?" [31]He replied, "How can I unless
someone guides me?" So he invited Philip to get in and sit
with him. [32]This was the passage of Scripture he was
reading:[a]

> "Like a sheep he was led away to be slaughtered,
>   and like a lamb is silent before its shearer,
>   so he does not open his mouth.
> [33]In his humiliation, justice was denied him.
>   Who can describe his generation?
>   For his life is taken away from the
>   earth."[a]

[34]The eunuch said to Philip, "I ask you, about whom is the
prophet speaking—about himself or about someone else?"
[35]Then Philip opened his mouth, and starting from this
Scripture told him the good news about Jesus.[b]

[36]As they were going along the road, they came to some
water. The eunuch said, "Look, there's some water. What
keeps me from being baptized?"[b][c] [38]So he ordered the chariot to stop, and Philip and the eunuch both went down into
the water, and Philip[c] baptized him. [39]When they came up
out of the water, the Spirit of the Lord snatched Philip away.
The eunuch went on his way rejoicing and did not see
Philip[d] again.[d] [40]But Philip found himself at Azotus. As he
was passing through the region,[e] he kept proclaiming the
good news in all the towns until he came to Caesarea.

Saul Becomes a Believer

9 [1]Now Saul, still breathing threats of murder against
the disciples of the Lord, went to the high priest[e] [2]and
asked him for letters to the synagogues in Damascus,
so that if he found any men or women belonging to the Way
he might bring them in chains to Jerusalem.

---

[a]8:33 Isa 53:7-8 (LXX)   [b]8:36 Other mss. read *from being baptized?"*
[37]*Philip said, "If you believe with all your heart, you may." He replied, "I*
believe that Jesus Christ is the Son of God."   [c]8:38 Lit. *he*   [d]8:39 Lit. *him*
[e]8:40 The Gk. lacks *the region*

Side margin notes

8:32
[a]Isa 53:7-8

8:35
[b]Lk 24:27;
Acts 18:28

8:36
[c]Matt 16:16;
28:19;
Mark 16:16;
John 6:69; 9:35,
38; 11:27;
Acts 9:20; 10:47;
1John 4:15; 5:5,13

8:39
[d]1Kings 18:12;
2Kings 2:16;
Ezek 3:12,14

9:1
[e]Acts 8:3;
Gal 1:13;
1Tim 1:13

9:3
a Acts 22:6; 26:12;
1Cor 15:8

9:4
b Matt 25:40

9:5
c Acts 5:39

9:6
d Lk 3:10;
Acts 2:37; 16:30

9:7
e Dan 10:7;
Acts 22:9; 26:13

9:10
f Acts 22:12

9:11
g Acts 21:39; 22:3

9:13
h Acts 9:1

9:14
i Acts 7:59; 9:21;
22:16; 1Cor 1:2;
2Tim 2:22

9:15
j Acts 13:2; 22:21;
25:22-23; 26:1,
17; Rom 1:1,5;
11:13;
1Cor 15:10;
Gal 1:15; 2:7-8;
Eph 3:7-8;
1Tim 2:7;
2Tim 1:11

9:16
k Acts 20:23;
21:11; 2Cor 11:23

9:17
l Acts 2:4; 4:31;
8:17; 13:52;
22:12-13

9:19
m Acts 26:20

³As he traveled along and was approaching Damascus, a light from heaven suddenly flashed around him.*ᵃ* ⁴He dropped to the ground and heard a voice saying to him, "Saul, Saul, why are you persecuting me?"*ᵇ* ⁵He asked, "Who are you, Lord?"**ᵃ** He said, "I am Jesus, whom you are persecuting.*ᶜ* ⁶But get up and go into the city, and it will be told you what you are to do."*ᵈ*

⁷Meanwhile, the men who were traveling with him were standing speechless, for they heard the voice but didn't see anyone.*ᵉ* ⁸When Saul got up off the ground, he couldn't see anything, even though his eyes were open. So they took him by the hand and led him into Damascus. ⁹For three days he couldn't see, and he didn't eat or drink anything.

¹⁰Now in Damascus there was a disciple named Ananias. The Lord said to him in a vision, "Ananias!" He answered, "Here I am, Lord."*ᶠ* ¹¹The Lord said to him, "Get up, go to the street called Straight, and in the home of Judas look for a man from Tarsus named Saul. At this very moment he is praying.*ᵍ* ¹²He has seen in a vision**ᵇ** a man named Ananias come in and lay his hands on him so he would see again." ¹³But Ananias answered, "Lord, I have heard many people tell how much evil this man has done to your saints in Jerusalem.*ʰ* ¹⁴He is here with authority from the high priests to put in chains all who call on your name."*ⁱ* ¹⁵But the Lord said to him, "Go, for he is a chosen instrument of mine to carry my name to the Gentiles and their kings and to the descendants of Israel.*ʲ* ¹⁶For I am going to show him how much he must suffer for my name's sake."*ᵏ*

Saul's Sight Is Restored

¹⁷So Ananias left and went to that house. He laid his hands on Saul**ᶜ** and said, "Brother Saul, the Lord Jesus, who appeared to you on the road as you were traveling, has sent me so that you may see again and be filled with the Holy Spirit."*ˡ* ¹⁸All at once something like scales fell from his eyes, and he could see again. He got up and was baptized, ¹⁹and after taking some food he felt strong again. For several days he stayed with the disciples in Damascus.*ᵐ* ²⁰He

---

a 9:5 Or *Sir*   **b** 9:12 Other mss. lack *in a vision*   **c** 9:17 Lit. *on him*

immediately started to proclaim Jesus in the synagogues, saying, "This is the Son of God."[a] 21All who heard him were astonished and said, "This is the man who harassed those who called on his name in Jerusalem, isn't it? Didn't he come here to bring them in chains to the high priests?"[b] 22But Saul grew more and more powerful and continued to confound the Jews who lived in Damascus by proving that this man was the Christ.[a][c]

23After several days had gone by, the Jews plotted to murder him,[d] 24but their plot became known to Saul. They were even watching the gates day and night to murder him,[e] 25but his disciples took him one night and let him down through the wall by lowering him in a basket.[f]

26When he arrived in Jerusalem, he tried to join the disciples, but they all were afraid of him because they wouldn't believe he was a disciple.[g] 27Barnabas, however, took him and presented him to the apostles, telling them how on the road he had seen the Lord, who had spoken to him, and how courageously he had spoken in the name of Jesus in Damascus.[h] 28So he went in and out among them in Jerusalem, speaking courageously in the name of the Lord.[i] 29He kept talking and arguing with the Hellenistic Jews, but they kept trying to murder him.[j] 30When the brothers found out about it, they took him down to Caesarea and sent him away to Tarsus.

31So the church throughout Judea, Galilee, and Samaria enjoyed peace. As it continued to be built up and to live in the fear of the Lord, it kept increasing in numbers through the encouragement of the Holy Spirit.[k]

Aeneas Is Healed

32Now when Peter was going around among all of the disciples,[b] he also came down to the saints living in Lydda.[l] 33There he found a man named Aeneas who was paralyzed and had been bedridden for eight years. 34Peter said to him, "Aeneas, Jesus Christ is healing you. Get up and put away your bed!" At once he got up.[m] 35All the people who lived in Lydda and Sharon saw him and turned to the Lord.[n]

---

a 9:22 I.e. the Messiah   b 9:32 Lit. *all of them*

9:20
a Acts 8:37

9:21
b Acts 8:1,3;
Gal 1:13,23

9:22
c Acts 18:28

9:23
d Acts 23:12; 25:3;
2Cor 11:26

9:24
e 2Cor 11:32

9:25
f Josh 2:15;
1Sam 19:12

9:26
g Acts 22:17;
Gal 1:17-18

9:27
h Acts 4:36; 13:2;
20:22

9:28
i Gal 1:18

9:29
j Acts 6:1; 11:20.
23; 2Cor 11:26

9:31
k Acts 8:1

9:32
l Acts 8:14

9:34
m Acts 3:6,16;
4:10

9:35
n 1Chr 5:16;
Acts 11:21

9:36
a 1 Tim 2:10;
Titus 3:8

9:37
b Acts 1:13

9:40
c Matt 9:25;
Mark 5:41-42;
John 11:43;
Acts 7:60

9:42
d John 11:45;
12:11

9:43
e Acts 10:6

10:2
f Acts 8:2;
10:12,22,35

10:3
g Acts 10:30;
11:13

10:6
h Acts 9:43; 11:14

Tabitha Is Healed

36In Joppa there was a disciple named Tabitha, which in Greek is Dorcas.*a* She was full of good works and acts of charity, which she was always doing.*a* 37At that time she got sick and died. When they had washed her, they laid her in an upstairs room.*b* 38As Lydda was near Joppa, the disciples heard that Peter was there and sent two men to him and begged him, "Come to us without delay!" 39So Peter got up and went with them. When he arrived, they took him upstairs. All the widows stood around him. They were crying and showing all the shirts and coats Dorcas made while she was still with them. 40But Peter made them all go outside. After he knelt down and prayed, he turned to the body and said, "Tabitha, get up!" She opened her eyes, and when she saw Peter, she sat up.*c* 41He gave her his hand and helped her up. Then he called the saints and widows and gave her back to them alive. 42This became known throughout Joppa, and many believed in the Lord.*d* 43Meanwhile, Peter*b* stayed in Joppa for several days with Simon, a leatherworker.*e*

Cornelius Has a Vision

10 1Now in Caesarea there was a man named Cornelius, a centurion*c* in what was known as the Italian Regiment. 2He was a devout man who feared God along with everyone in his home. He gave many gifts to the poor among the people and always prayed to God.*f*

3One day about three in the afternoon*d* he had a vision and clearly saw an angel of God coming to him and saying to him, "Cornelius!"*g* 4He stared at the angel*e* in terror and asked, "What is it, Lord?" He answered him, "Your prayers and your gifts to the poor have come up as a memorial before God. 5Send men now to Joppa and summon Simon, who is called Peter. 6He is a guest of Simon, a leatherworker, whose house is by the sea."*h*

7When the angel who had spoken to him had gone,

a 9:36 Both *Tabitha* (Aram.) and *Dorcas* (Gk.) mean *gazelle*   b 9:43 Lit. *he*   c 10:1 A Roman centurion commanded about 100 men.   d 10:3 Lit. *About the ninth hour of the day*   e 10:4 Lit. *at him*

Cornelius[a] summoned two of his household servants and a devout soldier, one of those who served him regularly. [8]He explained everything to them and sent them to Joppa.

Peter Has a Vision

[9]Around noon[b] the next day, while they were on their way and coming close to the town, Peter went up on the roof to pray.[a] [10]He became very hungry and wanted to eat. While the food[c] was being prepared, he fell into a trance [11]and saw heaven open and something like a large linen sheet coming down, being lowered by its four corners to the ground.[b] [12]In it were all kinds of four-footed animals, reptiles, and birds of the air.

[13]Then a voice told him,[d] "Get up, Peter! Kill something and eat it." [14]But Peter said, "Absolutely not, Lord, for I have never eaten anything that is common or unclean!"[c] [15]Again a voice came to him a second time, "You must stop calling unclean what God has made clean."[d] [16]This happened three times. Then the sheet[e] was quickly taken into heaven.

[17]While Peter was still at a loss to know what the vision he had seen could mean, the men sent by Cornelius asked for Simon's house and went to the gate. [18]They called out and asked if Simon who was called Peter was staying there. [19]Peter was still thinking about the vision when the Spirit said to him, "Look! Three men are looking for you.[e] [20]Get up, go downstairs, and don't hesitate to go with them, for I have sent them."[f]

[21]So Peter went to the men and said, "I'm the man you're looking for. Why are you here?" [22]The men replied, "Cornelius, a centurion and an upright and God-fearing man who is respected by the whole Jewish nation, was instructed by a holy angel to send for you to come to his home to hear what you have to say."[g]

[23]So Peter[a] invited them in, and they were his guests. The next day he got up and went with them, and some of the brothers from Joppa went along with him.[h]

---

a 10:7,10:23 Lit. *he*   b 10:9 Lit. *About the sixth hour*   c 10:10 Lit. *it*
d 10:13 Lit. *came to him*   e 10:16 Lit. *the vessel*

10:9
a Acts 11:5

10:11
b Acts 7:56;
Rev 19:11

10:14
c Lev 11:4; 20:25;
Deut 14:3,7;
Ezek 4:14

10:15
d Matt 15:11;
Acts 15:28;
Rom 14:14,17,20;
1Cor 10:25;
1Tim 4:4;
Titus 1:15

10:19
e Acts 11:12

10:20
f Acts 15:7

10:22
g Acts 10:1-2;
22:12

10:23
h Acts 10:45;
11:12

10:26
a Acts 14:14-15;
Rev 19:10; 22:9

10:28
b John 4:9; 18:28;
Acts 11:3; 15:8-9;
Gal 2:12,14;
Eph 3:6

10:30
c Matt 28:3;
Mark 16:5;
Lk 24:4; Acts 1:10

10:31
d Dan 10:12;
Acts 10:4;
Heb 6:10

10:34
e Deut 10:17;
2Chr 19:7;
Job 34:19;
Rom 2:11;
Gal 2:6; Eph 6:9;
Col 3:25;
1Peter 1:17

10:35
f Acts 15:9;
Rom 2:13,27;
3:22,29;
10:12-13;
1Cor 12:13;
Gal 3:28;
Eph 2:13,18; 3:6

10:36
g Isa 57:19;
Matt 28:18;
Rom 10:12;
1Cor 15:27;
Eph 1:20,22; 2:14,
16-17; Col 1:20;
1Peter 3:22;
Rev 17:14; 19:16

10:37
h Lk 4:14

10:38
i Lk 4:18; John 3:2;
Acts 2:22; 4:27;
Heb 1:9

Peter Speaks with Cornelius

²⁴They next day they arrived in Caesarea. Cornelius was expecting them and had called his relatives and close friends together. ²⁵When Peter was about to go in, Cornelius met him, bowed down at his feet, and began to worship him. ²⁶But Peter made him get up, saying, "Stand up! I, too, am only a man."*ᵃ*

²⁷As Peter*ᵃ* talked with him, he went in and found that many people had gathered. ²⁸He said to them, "You understand how wrong it is for a Jew to associate or visit with a Gentile. But God has shown me that I should stop calling anyone common or unclean.*ᵇ* ²⁹That is why I didn't hesitate when I was sent for. Now may I ask why you sent for me?"

³⁰Cornelius replied, "Four days ago at this very hour, three o'clock in the afternoon,*ᵇ* I was praying in my home. All at once a man in radiant clothes stood in front of me*ᶜ* ³¹and said, 'Cornelius, your prayer has been heard and your gifts to the poor have been remembered before God.*ᵈ* ³²So send messengers*ᶜ* to Joppa and summon Simon, who is called Peter, to come to you. He is a guest in the home of Simon, a leatherworker, by the sea.' ³³So I sent for you immediately, and it was good of you to come. All of us are here now in the presence of God to listen to everything the Lord has ordered you to say."

³⁴Then Peter opened his mouth and said, "Now I understand that God shows no partiality.*ᵉ* ³⁵Indeed, the person who fears him and does what is right is acceptable to him in any nation.*ᶠ* ³⁶He has sent his word to the descendants of Israel and brought them the good news of peace through Jesus Christ. This man is the Lord of everyone.*ᵍ* ³⁷You know what happened throughout Judea, beginning in Galilee after the baptism that John preached.*ʰ* ³⁸God anointed Jesus of Nazareth with the Holy Spirit and with power, and he went around doing good and healing all who were oppressed by the devil, because God was with him.*ⁱ* ³⁹We are witnesses of everything he did both in the land of the Jews and in

---

a *10:27* Lit. *he*   **b** *10:30* Lit. *the ninth hour*   **c** *10:32 The* Gk. lacks *messengers*

Jerusalem. They hung him on a tree and killed him,[a] 40but God raised him on the third day and allowed him to appear[b]—41not to all the people, but to us who were chosen by God to be witnesses and who ate and drank with him after he rose from the dead.[c] 42He also ordered us to preach to the people and to testify solemnly that this is the one ordained by God to be the judge of the living and the dead.[d] 43To him all the prophets testify that everyone who believes in him receives the forgiveness of sins through his name."[e]

The Gentiles Receive the Holy Spirit

44While Peter was still speaking these words, the Holy Spirit fell on all the people who were listening to his message.[f] 45Then the circumcised believers who had come with Peter were amazed that the gift of the Holy Spirit had been poured out on the Gentiles, too.[g] 46For they heard them speaking in tongues and praising God. Then Peter said, 47"No one can stop us from using water to baptize these people who have received the Holy Spirit in the same way that we did, can he?"[h] 48So he ordered them to be baptized in the name of Jesus Christ. Then they asked him to stay for several days.[i]

Peter Reports to the Church in Jerusalem

11 1Now the apostles and the brothers who were in Judea heard that the Gentiles had also accepted the word of God. 2But when Peter went up to Jerusalem, those who emphasized circumcision[a] disagreed with him.[j] 3They said, "You went to uncircumcised men and ate with them!"[k]

4Then Peter began to explain to them point by point what had happened. He said,[l] 5"I was in the town of Joppa praying when in a trance I saw a vision: Something like a large linen sheet was coming down from heaven, being lowered by its four corners, and it came right down to me.[m] 6When I examined it closely, I saw four-footed animals of the earth, wild animals, reptiles, and birds of the air. 7I also heard a voice telling me, 'Get up, Peter! Kill something and

---

a 11:2 Lit. those of the circumcision

10:39
a Acts 2:32; 5:30

10:40
b Acts 2:24

10:41
c Lk 24:30,43;
John 14:17,22;
21:13; Acts 13:31

10:42
d Matt 28:19-20;
John 5:22,27;
Acts 1:8; 17:31;
Rom 14:9,19;
2Cor 5:10;
2Tim 4:1;
1Peter 4:5

10:43
e Isa 53:11;
Jer 31:34;
Dan 9:24;
Mic 7:18;
Zech 13:1;
Mal 4:2;
Acts 15:9; 26:18,
22; Rom 10:11;
Gal 3:22

10:44
f Acts 4:31;
8:15-17; 11:15

10:45
g Acts 10:23;
11:18; Gal 3:14

10:47
h Acts 11:17;
15:8-9;
Rom 10:12

10:48
i Acts 2:38; 8:16;
1Cor 1:17

11:2
j Acts 10:45;
Gal 2:12

11:3
k Acts 10:28;
Gal 2:12

11:4
l Lk 1:3

11:5
m Acts 10:9

11:12
a John 16:13;
Acts 10:19,23;
15:7

11:13
b Acts 10:30

11:15
c Acts 2:4

11:16
d Isa 44:3;
Joel 2:28; 3:18;
Matt 3:11;
John 1:26,33;
Acts 1:5; 19:4

11:17
e Acts 10:47;
15:8-9

11:18
f Rom 10:12-13;
15:9,16

11:19
g Acts 8:1

11:20
h Acts 6:1; 9:29

11:21
i Lk 1:66;
Acts 2:47; 9:35

11:22
j Acts 9:27

eat it.' ⁸But I replied, 'Absolutely not, Lord, for nothing common or unclean has ever entered my mouth!' ⁹Then the voice from heaven answered a second time, 'You must stop calling common what God has made clean!' ¹⁰This happened three times. Then everything was pulled up to heaven again.

¹¹"At that very moment three men arrived at the house where we were staying. They had been sent to me from Caesarea. ¹²The Spirit told me to go with them and not to treat them differently. These six brothers went with me, too, and we went into the man's house.*a* ¹³Then he told us how he had seen the angel standing in his home and saying, 'Send messengers*a* to Joppa and summon Simon, who is called Peter.*b* ¹⁴He will speak words to you by which you and your entire home will be saved.'

¹⁵"When I began to speak, the Holy Spirit fell on them just as he had on us at the beginning.*c* ¹⁶Then I remembered the word of the Lord—how he had said, 'John baptized with*b* water, but you will be baptized with*b* the Holy Spirit.'*d* ¹⁷Now if God gave them the same gift that he gave us when we believed in the Lord Jesus Christ, who was I to try to stop God?"*e*

¹⁸When they heard this, they quieted down. Then they praised God, saying, "So God has given even the Gentiles the repentance that leads to life."*f*

The New Church in Antioch

¹⁹Now the people who were scattered by the persecution that started because of Stephen went as far as Phoenicia, Cyprus, and Antioch, speaking the word to no one except Jews.*g* ²⁰But among them were some men from Cyprus and Cyrene who came to Antioch and began talking to the Hellenistic Jews,*c* too, proclaiming the Lord Jesus.*h* ²¹The hand of the Lord was with them, and a large number of people believed and turned to the Lord.*i*

²²News of this came to the ears of the church in Jerusalem, and so they sent Barnabas all the way to Antioch.*j*

---

a *11:13* The Gk. lacks *messengers*   **b** *11:16* Or *in*   **c** *11:20* Other mss. read *to the Greeks*

23When he arrived, he rejoiced to see what the grace of God had done,[a] and with a hearty determination he continuously encouraged them all to remain faithful to the Lord.[a] 24For he was a good man, full of the Holy Spirit and faith. So a large crowd was brought to the Lord.[b]

25Then Barnabas left for Tarsus to look for Saul.[c] 26When he found him, he brought him to Antioch, and for a whole year they were guests of the church and taught a large crowd. It was in Antioch that the disciples were first called Christians.

27At that time some prophets from Jerusalem came down to Antioch.[d] 28One of them named Agabus got up and predicted by the Spirit that there would be a severe famine all over the world. This happened during the reign of Claudius.[e] 29So every one of the disciples decided, as he was able, to send a contribution to the brothers living in Judea.[f] 30They did this by sending Barnabas and Saul to the elders.[g]

An Angel Frees Peter from Prison

12 1About that time, Herod arrested some people who belonged to the church and mistreated them. 2He even had James the brother of John killed with a sword.[h] 3When he saw how this was agreeable to the Jews, he proceeded to arrest Peter, too. This happened during the Festival of Unleavened Bread.[i] 4When he arrested him, he put him in prison and turned him over to four squads of soldiers to guard him, planning to bring him out to the people after the Passover.[j] 5So Peter was being kept in prison, but earnest prayer to God for him was being offered by the church.

6That very night before Herod was going to bring him out, Peter, bound with two chains, was sleeping between two soldiers, and guards in front of the door were watching the prisoners. 7Suddenly an angel of the Lord appeared and a light shone in the cell. He tapped Peter on his side, woke him up, and said, "Get up quickly!" His chains fell from his wrists.[k] 8Then the angel said to him, "Tuck in your shirt and put on your sandals!" He did this. Then the angel[b] told him,

---

a 11:23 Lit. *to see the grace of God*   b 12:8 Lit. *he*

11:23
a Acts 13:43; 14:22

11:24
b Acts 5:14; 10:5,21

11:25
c Acts 9:30

11:27
d Acts 2:17; 13:1; 15:32; 21:9; 1Cor 12:28; Eph 4:11

11:28
e Acts 21:10

11:29
f Rom 15:26; 1Cor 16:1; 2Cor 9:1

11:30
g Acts 12:25

12:2
h Matt 4:21; 2C:23

12:3
i Exod 12:14-15; 23:15

12:4
j John 21:18

12:7
k Acts 5:19

12:9
a Ps 126:1;
Acts 10:3,17; 11:5

"Put on your coat and follow me!" [9]So he went out and began to follow him, not realizing that what was being done by the angel was real; he thought he was seeing a vision.*a* [10]They passed the first guard, then the second, and came to the iron gate that led into the city. It opened by itself for them, and they went outside and proceeded one block when the angel suddenly left him.*b*

12:10
b Acts 16:26

[11]Then Peter came to himself and said, "Now I'm sure that the Lord has sent his angel and rescued me from the hands of Herod and from everything the Jewish people were expecting!"*c*

12:11
c Job 5:19;
Ps 33:18-19; 34:7,
22; 41:2; 97:10;
Dan 3:28; 6:22;
2Cor 1:10;
Heb 1:14;
2Peter 2:9

[12]When he realized what had happened, he went to the house of Mary, the mother of John who was also called Mark, where a large number of people had gathered and were praying.*d* [13]When he knocked at the outer gate, a servant-girl named Rhoda came to answer it. [14]On recognizing Peter's voice, she was so overjoyed that she didn't open the gate but ran in and announced that Peter was standing at the gate. [15]They said to her, "You're out of your mind!" But she kept insisting that it was so. Then they said, "It's his angel."*e*

12:12
d Acts 4:23; 15:5,
37

[16]Meanwhile, Peter kept knocking and knocking. When they opened the gate, they saw him and were amazed. [17]He motioned to them with his hand to be quiet, and then he told them how the Lord had brought him out of the prison. He added, "Tell this to James and the brothers." Then he left and went somewhere else.*f*

12:15
e Gen 48:16;
Matt 18:10

[18]When morning came, there was no little commotion among the soldiers as to what had become of Peter. [19]Herod searched for him but didn't find him. So he questioned the guards and ordered them to be executed. Then he left Judea, went down to Caesarea, and stayed there for a while.

12:17
f Acts 13:16;
19:33; 21:40

The Death of Herod

[20]Now Herod had a violent quarrel with the people of Tyre and Sidon. So they came to him as a group. After they had won over Blastus, who took care of the king's bedroom, they asked for peace because their country depended on the king's country for food.*g* [21]So, on a day that was set, Herod put on his royal robes, sat down on the royal seat, and made

12:20
g 1Kings 5:9,11;
Ezek 27:17

a speech to them. 22The people kept shouting, "This is the voice of a god, not of a man!" 23Immediately the angel of the Lord struck him down because he did not give glory to God, and he was eaten by worms and died.*a* 24But the word of God continued to grow and spread.*b*

25When Barnabas and Saul had fulfilled their mission, they returned to*a* Jerusalem, bringing with them John who was also called Mark.*c*

Barnabas and Saul Travel to Cyprus

13 1Now Barnabas, Simeon called Niger, Lucius from Cyrene, Manaen who had been brought up with Herod the tetrarch, and Saul were prophets and teachers in the church at Antioch.*d* 2While they were worshiping the Lord and fasting, the Holy Spirit said, "Set Barnabas and Saul apart for me to do the work for which I called them."*e* 3Then they fasted and prayed, laid their hands on them, and let them go.*f*

4Being sent out by the Holy Spirit, they went to Seleucia and from there sailed to Cyprus.*g* 5Arriving in Salamis, they began to preach God's word in the Jewish synagogues. They also had John to help them.*h*

6They went through the whole island as far as Paphos. There they found a Jewish magician and false prophet named Bar-Jesus.*i* 7He was associated with the proconsul Sergius Paulus, who was an intelligent man. He sent for Barnabas and Saul because he wanted to hear the word of God. 8But Elymas the magician (that is the meaning of his name) continued to opposed them and tried to turn the proconsul away from the faith.*j*

9But Saul, also known as*b* Paul, filled with the Holy Spirit, looked him straight in the eye*k* 10and said, "You are full of every form of deception and trickery, you son of the devil, you enemy of all that is right! You will never stop perverting the straight ways of the Lord, will you?*l* 11The hand of the Lord is against you now, and you will be blind and not see the sun for a while!" At that moment a dark mist came over him, and he went around looking for someone to

---

a 12:25 Other mss. read *from*   **b** 13:9 Lit. *who was also*

12:23
a 1Sam 25:38;
2Sam 24:17;
Ps 115:1

12:24
b Isa 55:11;
Acts 6:7; 19:20;
Col 1:6

12:25
c Acts 13:5,13;
15:12,37

13:1
d Acts 11:22-27;
14:26; 15:35;
Rom 16:21

13:2
e Num 8:14;
Matt 9:38;
Acts 9:15; 14:26;
22:21; Rom 1:1:
10:15; Gal 1:15;
2:9; Eph 3:7-8;
1Tim 2:7;
2Tim 1:11;
Heb 5:4

13:3
f Acts 6:6

13:4
g Acts 4:36

13:5
h Acts 12:25;
13:46; 15:37

13:6
i Acts 8:9

13:8
j Exod 7:11;
2Tim 3:8

13:9
k Acts 4:8

13:10
l Matt 13:38;
John 8:44;
1John 3:8

13:11
a Exod 9:3;
1 Sam 5:6

13:13
b Acts 15:38

13:14
c Acts 16:13; 17:2;
18:4

13:15
d Lk 4:16;
Acts 4:27;
Heb 13:22

13:16
e Acts 10:35;
13:17,26,42-43

13:17
f Exod 1:1; 6:6;
13:14,16;
Deut 7:6-7;
Ps 105:23-24;
Acts 7:17

13:18
g Exod 16:35;
Num 14:33-34;
Ps 95:9-10;
Acts 7:36

13:19
h Deut 7:1;
Josh 14:1-2;
Ps 78:55

13:20
i Jdg 2:16;
1 Sam 3:1-21

13:21
j 1 Sam 8:5; 10:1

13:22
k 1 Sam 13:14;
15:23,26,28; 16:1,
13; 2 Sam 2:4; 5:3;
Ps 89:20;
Hos 13:11;
Acts 7:46

13:23
l 2 Sam 7:12;
Ps 132:11;
Isa 11:1;
Matt 1:21;
Lk 1:32,69;
Acts 2:30;
Rom 1:3; 11:26

13:24
m Matt 3:1; Lk 3:3

13:25
n Matt 3:11;
Mark 1:7; Lk 3:16;
John 1:20,27

lead him by the hand.*a* [12]When the proconsul saw what had happened, he believed, for he was astonished at the Lord's teaching.

Paul and Barnabas Go to Antioch in Pisidia

[13]Then Paul and his men set sail from Paphos and arrived in Perga in Pamphylia. But John left them and went back to Jerusalem.*b* [14]They left Perga and arrived in Antioch in Pisidia. On the Sabbath day they went into the synagogue and sat down.*c* [15]After the reading of the Law and the Prophets, the synagogue leaders asked them,*a* "Brothers, if you have any message of encouragement*b* for the people, you may speak."*d*

[16]Then Paul stood up, motioned with his hand, and said: "Men of Israel and you who fear God, listen!*e* [17]The God of this people Israel chose our ancestors and made them a great people during their stay in the land of Egypt, and with an uplifted arm he led them out of it.*f* [18]After he had put up with*c* them for forty years in the wilderness,*g* [19]he destroyed seven nations in the land of Canaan. Then he gave them their land as an inheritance*h* [20]for about 450 years. After that he gave them judges until the time of the prophet Samuel.*i*

[21]"Then they demanded a king, and for forty years God gave them Saul, the son of Kish, a man of the tribe of Benjamin.*j* [22]But he removed Saul*d* and made David their king, about whom he testified, 'I have found that David, the son of Jesse, is a man after my own heart, who will carry out all my wishes.'*e k* [23]It was from this man's descendants that God, as he promised, brought to Israel a Savior, who is Jesus.*l* [24]Before his coming, John had already preached a baptism of repentance to all the people in Israel.*m* [25]When John was finishing his work, he said, 'Who do you think I am? I am not the one. No, but he is coming after me, and I am not worthy to untie the sandals on his feet.'*n*

[26]"My brothers, descendants of Abraham's family, and those among you who fear God, it is to us*f* that the message

---

a 13:15 Lit. *sent to them*   **b** 13:15 Or *word of exhortation*   **c** 13:18 Other mss. read *nourished*   **d** 13:22 Lit. *him*   **e** 13:22 Ps 89:20; 1 Sam 13:14
f 13:26 Other mss. read *to you*

of this salvation has been sent.*[a]* [27]For the people who live in Jerusalem and their leaders, not knowing who he was, condemned him and fulfilled the words of the prophets that are read every Sabbath.*[b]* [28]Although they found no reason to sentence him to death, they asked Pilate to have him executed.*[c]* [29]When they had finished doing everything that was written about him, they took him down from the tree and placed him in a tomb.*[d]* [30]But God raised him from the dead,*[e]* [31]and for many days he appeared to those who had come with him to Jerusalem from Galilee. These are now his witnesses to the people.*[f]* [32]We are telling you the good news: What God promised our ancestors*[g]* [33]he has fulfilled for us, their descendants, by raising Jesus. As it is written in the Second Psalm, 'You are my Son. Today I have become your Father.'*[a][h]* [34]He raised him from the dead, never to experience decay. As he said, 'I will give you the holy promises made to David.'*[b][i]* [35]In another Psalm*[c]* he says, 'You will not let your Holy One experience decay.'*[d][j]* [36]For David, after he had served God's purpose in his own generation, died*[e]* and was laid to rest with his ancestors. And so he experienced decay.*[k]* [37]However, the man whom God raised did not experience decay.

[38]"So, brothers, you must understand that through him the forgiveness of sins is proclaimed to you,*[l]* [39]and that everyone who believes in him is justified and freed from everything that kept you from being justified by the Law of Moses.*[m]* [40]Se be careful that what the prophets said does not happen to you:*[n]* [41]'Look, you mockers! Be amazed and die! For I am doing a work in your days, a work that you would not believe even if someone told you!' "*[f]*

[42]As Paul and Barnabas*[g]* were leaving, the people kept urging them to tell them the same things the next Sabbath. [43]When the meeting of the synagogue broke up, many Jews and devout converts to Judaism followed Paul and Barnabas, who kept talking to them and urging them to continue in the grace of God.*[o]*

---

a13:33 Ps 2:7   **b**13:34 Isa 55:3 (LXX)   **c**13:35 The Gk. lacks *Psalm*
d13:35 Ps 16:10 (LXX)   **e**13:36 Lit. *fell asleep*   **f**13:41 Hab 1:5 (LXX)
g13:42 Lit. *As they*

13:26
a Matt 10:6;
Lk 24:47;
Acts 3:26; 13:46

13:27
b Lk 23:34; 24:20,
44; Acts 2:14-15;
3:17; 15:21;
26:22; 28:23;
1Cor 2:8

13:28
c Matt 27:22;
Mark 15:13-14;
Lk 23:21-22;
John 19:6,15;
Acts 3:13

13:29
d Matt 27:59;
Mark 15:46;
Lk 18:31; 23:53;
24:1; John 19:28,
30,36-38

13:30
e Matt 28:6;
Acts 2:24; 3:13,
15,26; 5:30

13:31
f Matt 28:16;
Acts 1:3,8,11;
2:32; 3:15; 5:32;
1Cor 15:5-7

13:32
g Gen 3:15; 12:3;
22:18; Acts 26:6;
Rom 4:13;
Gal 3:16

13:33
h Ps 2:7; Heb 1:5;
5:5

13:34
i Isa 55:3

13:35
j Ps 16:10;
Acts 2:31

13:36
k 1Kings 2:10;
Acts 2:29

13:38
l Jer 31:34;
Dan 9:24;
Lk 24:47;
1John 2:12

13:39
m Isa 53:11;
Rom 3:28; 8:3;
Heb 7:19

13:40
n Isa 29:14;
Hab 1:5

13:43
o Acts 11:23;
14:22 Titus 2:11;
Heb 12:15;
1Peter 5:12

13:45
a Acts 18:6;
1 Peter 4:4;
Jude 1:10

13:46
b Exod 32:10;
Deut 32:21;
Isa 55:5;
Matt 10:6; 21:43;
Acts 3:26; 18:6;
28:28; Rom 1:16;
10:19

13:47
c Isa 42:6; 49:6;
Lk 2:32

13:48
d Acts 2:47

13:50
e 2 Tim 3:1-17

13:51
f Matt 10:14;
Mark 6:11; Lk 9:5;
Acts 18:6

13:52
g Matt 5:12;
John 16:22;
Acts 2:46

14:3
h Mark 16:20;
Heb 2:4

14:4
i Acts 13:3

14:5
j 2 Tim 3:11

14:6
k Matt 10:23

⁴⁴The next Sabbath almost the whole town gathered to hear the word of the Lord.ᵃ ⁴⁵But when the Jews saw the crowds, they were filled with jealousy and began to object to the statements made by Paul and even to abuse him.ᵃ

⁴⁶Then Paul and Barnabas boldly declared, "We had to speak God's word to you first, but since you reject it and consider yourselves unworthy of eternal life, we are now going to turn to the Gentiles.ᵇ ⁴⁷For that is what the Lord ordered us to do: 'I have made you a light to the Gentiles to be the means of salvation to the very ends of the earth.' "ᵇᶜ

⁴⁸When the Gentiles heard this, they began rejoicing and glorifying the word of the Lord. Meanwhile, all who had been destined to eternal life believed,ᵈ ⁴⁹and the word of the Lord began to spread throughout the whole region.

⁵⁰But the Jews stirred up devout women of high social standing and the officials in the city, started a persecution against Paul and Barnabas, and drove them out of their territory.ᵉ ⁵¹So they shook the dust off their feet in protest against them and went to Iconium.ᶠ ⁵²Meanwhile, the disciples continued to be full of joy and of the Holy Spirit.ᵍ

Paul and Barnabas in Iconium

14 ¹In Iconium they went into the Jewish synagogue and spoke in such a way that a great number of both Jews and Greeks believed. ²But the Jews who refused to believe stirred up the Gentiles and poisoned their minds against the brothers. ³They stayed there a considerable time and continued to speak boldly for the Lord, who kept affirming his word of grace and granting signs and wonders to be done by them.ʰ ⁴But the people of the city were divided. Some were with the Jews, while others were with the apostles.ⁱ

⁵Now when an attempt was made by both Gentiles and Jews, along with their authorities, to mistreat and stone them,ʲ ⁶they found out about it and fled to the Lycaonian towns of Lystra and Derbe and to the surrounding territory.ᵏ ⁷There they kept telling the good news.

---

a *13:44* Other mss. read *of God* **b** *13:47* Isa 49:6

Paul and Barnabas in Lystra

8In Lystra there was a man sitting down who couldn't use his feet. He had been crippled from birth and had never walked.a 9He was listening to Paul as he spoke. Paula watched him closely, and when he saw that he had faith to be healed,b 10he said in a loud voice, "Stand up straight on your feet!" Then the manb jumped up and began to walk.c

11When the crowds saw what Paul had done, they shouted in the Lycaonian language, "The gods have become like men and have come down to us!"d 12They began to call Barnabas Zeus, and Paul Hermes, because he was the main speaker. 13The priest of the temple of Zeus, which was just outside the city, brought bulls and garlands to the gates. He and the crowds wanted to offer sacrifices.e 14But when the apostles Barnabas and Paul heard of it, they tore their clothes and rushed out into the crowd, shouting,f 15"Men, why are you doing this? We are merely human beings with natures like your own. We are telling you the good news to turn from these worthless things to the living God, who made heaven and earth, the sea, and everything in them.g 16In past generations he allowed all the nations to go their own ways,h 17yet he has not left himself without a witness by doing good, by giving you rain from heaven and fruitful seasons, and by filling you with food and joyful hearts."i 18Even by saying this it was all they could do to keep the crowds from offering sacrifices to them.

Paul and Barnabas Return to Antioch in Syria

19But some Jews came from Antioch and Iconium and won the crowds by persuasion. They stoned Paul and dragged him out of the town, thinking he was dead.j 20But the disciples formed a circle around him, and he got up and went back to town. The next day he went on with Barnabas to Derbe.

21As they were telling the good news in that city, they made many disciples. Then they went back to Lystra, Iconium, and Antioch,k 22strengthening the heartsc of the

---

a 14:9 Lit. *He*   b 14:10 Lit. *he*   c 14:22 Lit. *souls*

14:8
a Acts 3:2

14:9
b Matt 8:10; 9:28-29

14:10
c Isa 35:6

14:11
d Acts 8:10; 28:6

14:13
e Dan 2:46

14:14
f Matt 26:65

14:15
g Gen 1:1;
1Sam 12:21;
1Kings 16:13;
Ps 33:6; 146:6;
Jer 14:22;
Amos 2:4;
Acts 10:26;
1Cor 8:4;
1Thes 1:9;
James 5:17;
Rev 14:7; 19:10

14:16
h Ps 81:12;
Acts 17:30;
1Peter 4:3

14:17
i Lev 26:4;
Deut 11:14;
28:12; Job 5:10;
Ps 65:10; 68:9;
147:8; Jer 14:22;
Matt 5:45;
Acts 17:27;
Rom 1:20

14:19
j Acts 13:45;
2Cor 11:25;
2Tim 3:11

14:21
k Matt 28:19

14:22
a Matt 10:38;
16:24;
Lk 22:28-29;
Acts 11:23; 13:43;
Rom 8:17;
2Tim 2:11-12;
3:12

14:23
b Titus 1:5

14:26
c Acts 13:1,3;
15:40

14:27
d Acts 15:4,12;
21:19; 1Cor 16:9;
2Cor 2:12 Col 4:3;
Rev 3:8

15:1
e Gen 17:10;
Lev 12:3;
John 7:22;
Acts 7:5;
Gal 2:12;
5:2 Phil 3:2;
Col 2:8,11,16

15:2
f Gal 2:1

15:3
g Acts 14:27;
Rom 15:24;
1Cor 16:6,11

15:4
h Acts 14:27;
15:12; 21:19

15:5
i Acts 15:1

15:7
j Acts 10:20; 11:12

disciples and encouraging them to continue in the faith, saying, "We must endure many hardships to get into the kingdom of God."[a]

[23]They appointed elders for them in each church, and with prayer and fasting they entrusted them to the Lord in whom they had believed.[b] [24]Then they passed through Pisidia and came to Pamphylia. [25]They spoke the word[a] in Perga and went down to Attalia. [26]From there they sailed back to Antioch, where they had been commended to the grace of God for the work they had completed.[c] [27]When they arrived, they called the church together and told them everything that God had done with them and how he had opened a door of faith to the Gentiles.[d] [28]Then they spent a long time with the disciples.

Controversy about the Law

15 [1]Then some men came down from Judea and started to teach the brothers, "Unless you are circumcised according to the Law of Moses, you can't be saved."[e] [2]Paul and Barnabas had quite a dispute and argument with them. So Paul and Barnabas and some of the others were appointed to go up to Jerusalem to confer with the apostles and elders about this question.[f] [3]They were sent on their way by the church. As they were going through Phoenecia and Samaria, they told of the conversion of the Gentiles and brought great joy to all the brothers.[g]

[4]When they arrived in Jerusalem, they were welcomed by the church, the apostles, and the elders, and they reported everything that God had done through them.[h] [5]But some believers from the party of the Pharisees stood up and said, "They must be circumcised and ordered to keep the Law of Moses."[i]

[6]So the apostles and the elders met to consider this statement. [7]After a lengthy debate, Peter stood up and said to them, "Brothers, you know that in the early days God chose me to be the one among you through whom the Gentiles would hear the message of the gospel and believe.[j]

---

a 14:25 Other mss. read *the word of the Lord*; still other mss. read *the word of God*

⁸God, who knows everyone's heart, showed them he approved by giving them the Holy Spirit, just as he did to us.ᵃ ⁹He made no distinction between them and us, because he cleansed their hearts by faith.ᵇ ¹⁰So why do you test God by putting on the disciples' neck a yoke that neither our ancestors nor we could carry?ᶜ ¹¹We certainly believe that it is through the grace of the Lord Jesus Christ that we are saved, just as they are."ᵈ

¹²The whole crowd was silent as they listened to Barnabas and Paul tell about all the signs and wonders that God had done through them among the Gentiles.ᵉ ¹³After they had finished speaking, James responded by saying, "Brothers, listen to me.ᶠ ¹⁴Simeon has explained how God first showed his concern for the Gentiles by taking from among them a people for his name.ᵍ ¹⁵This agrees with the words of the prophets. As it is written,

> ¹⁶'After this, I will come backʰ
>   and set up David's fallen tent again.
>   I will restore its ruined places and set it
>   up again
> ¹⁷so that the rest of the people may search for the
>   Lord,
>   including all the Gentiles who are called by
>   my name,
>   declares the Lord.
> He is the one who has been doing these things
> ¹⁸   that have always been known.'ᵃ

¹⁹Therefore, I have decided that we should not trouble these Gentiles who are turning to God.ⁱ ²⁰Instead, we should write to them to keep away from things polluted by idols, from sexual immorality, from anything strangled,ᵇ and from blood.ʲ ²¹After all, Moses has had people to proclaim him in every city for generations, and on every Sabbath he is read aloud in the synagogues."ᵏ

---

a 15:18 Amos 9:11-12; Isa 45:21   b 15:20 Other mss. lack *from anything strangled*

15:8
ᵃ 1Chr 28:9;
Acts 1:24; 10:44

15:9
ᵇ Acts 10:15,28,
43; Rom 10:11;
1Cor 1:2;
1Peter 1:23

15:10
ᶜ Matt 23:4;
Gal 5:1

15:11
ᵈ Rom 3:24;
Eph 2:8;
Titus 2:11; 3:4-5

15:12
ᵉ Acts 14:27

15:13
ᶠ Acts 12:17

15:14
ᵍ Acts 15:7

15:16
ʰ Amos 9:11-12

15:19
ⁱ Acts 15:28;
1Thes 1:9

15:20
ʲ Gen 9:4; 35:2;
Exod 20:3,23;
Lev 3:17;
Deut 12:16,23;
Ezek 20:30;
1Cor 6:9,18; 8:1;
Gal 5:19; Eph 5:3;
Col 3:5;
1Thes 4:3;
1Peter 4:3;
Rev 2:14,20;
13:20,28

15:21
ᵏ Acts 13:15,27

The Reply of the Church

15:22
a Acts 1:23

[22]Then the apostles, the elders, and the whole church decided to choose some of their men to send with Paul and Barnabas to Antioch. These were Judas, who was called Barsabbas, and Silas, who were leaders among the brothers.[a] [23]They wrote this letter for them to deliver:[a]

15:24
b Acts 15:1;
Gal 2:4; 5:12;
Titus 1:10-11

"From[b] the apostles and the elders, your brothers, to their Gentile brothers in Antioch, Syria, and Cilicia. Greetings. [24]We have heard that some men, coming from us without instructions from us, have said things to trouble you and have unsettled your minds.[cb] [25]So we have unanimously decided to choose men and send them to you with our dear Barnabas and Paul, [26]who have risked their lives for the sake of our Lord Jesus Christ.[c] [27]We have sent Judas and Silas to tell you the same things by word of mouth. [28]For it seemed good to the Holy Spirit and to us not to place on you any burden but these essential requirements: [29]to keep away from food sacrificed to idols, from blood, from anything strangled,[d] and from sexual immorality. If you avoid these things, you will prosper. Goodbye."[d]

15:26
c Acts 13:50;
14:19;
1Cor 15:30;
2Cor 11:23,26

15:29
d Lev 17:14;
Acts 15:20; 21:25;
Rev 2:14,20

[30]So the men were sent on their way and arrived in Antioch. They gathered the congregation together and delivered the letter. [31]When the people[e] read it, they were pleased with the encouragement it brought them.[f] [32]Then Judas and Silas, who were also prophets, said much to encourage and strengthen the brothers.[e]

[33]After staying there for some time, they were sent back with a greeting[g] from the brothers to those who had sent

15:32
e Acts 14:22;
18:23

a 15:23 Lit. *They wrote through their hand*   b 15:23 The Gk. lacks *From*
c 15:24 Other mss. read *your minds, saying, 'You must be circumcised and keep the Law.'*   d 15:29 Other mss. lack *from anything strangled*
e 15:31 Lit. *they*   f 15:31 The Gk. lacks *it brought them*   g 15:33 Lit. *sent back with peace*

them.ª*a* 35Both Paul and Barnabas stayed in Antioch and taught and proclaimed the word of the Lord along with many others.*b*

Paul and Barnabas Disagree

36Some days after this, Paul said to Barnabas, "Let's go back and visit the brothers in every town where we proclaimed the word of the Lord and see how they're doing."*c* 37Barnabas persisted in wanting to take along John, who was called Mark.*d* 38Paul, however, did not think it was right to be taking along the man who had deserted them in Pamphylia and had not gone with them into the work.*e* 39The disagreement was so sharp that they parted ways. Barnabas took Mark and sailed to Cyprus, 40while Paul chose Silas and left after the brothers had commended him to the grace of the Lord.*bf* 41He went through Syria and Cilicia and strengthened the churches.*g*

Timothy Joins Paul in Lystra

16 1He also went to Derbe and Lystra. Here there was a disciple named Timothy, the son of a Jewish woman who was a believer, but his father was a Greek.*h* 2He was highly regarded by the brothers in Lystra and Iconium.*i* 3Paul wanted this man to go with him, so he took him and had him circumcised because of the Jews who lived in those places. For everyone knew that his father was a Greek.*j*

4As they went from town to town, they delivered the decisions reached by the apostles and elders in Jerusalem for them to obey.*k* 5So the churches continued to be strengthened in the faith and to increase in numbers every day.*l*

Paul Has a Vision

6Then they went through the region of Phrygia and Galatia because they had been prevented by the Holy Spirit from speaking the word in Asia. 7They went as far as Mysia

---

a*15:33* Other mss. read *sent them.* 34*But it seemed good to Silas to remain there, and Judas went back alone.*   b*15:40* Other mss. read *of God*

15:33
a 1Cor 16:11;
Heb 11:31

15:35
b Acts 13:1

15:36
c Acts 13:4,13-14,
51; 14:1,6,24-25

15:37
d Acts 12:12,25;
13:5; Col 4:10;
2Tim 4:11

15:38
e Acts 13:13

15:40
f Acts 14:26

15:41
g Acts 16:5

16:1
h Acts 14:6; 19:22;
Rom 16:21;
1Cor 4:17;
Phil 2:19;
1Thes 3:2;
1Tim 1:2;
2Tim 1:2,5

16:2
i Acts 6:3

16:3
j 1Cor 9:20;
Gal 2:3; 5:2

16:4
k Acts 15:28-29

16:5
l Acts 15:41

16:8
ᵃ2Cor 2:12;
2Tim 4:13

and tried to enter Bithynia, but the Spirit of Jesus did not let them. ⁸So they passed by Mysia and went down to Troas.ᵃ

⁹During the night Paul had a vision. A man from Macedonia was standing there and pleading with him, "Come over to Macedonia and help us!"ᵇ ¹⁰As soon as he had seen the vision, we immediately looked for a way to go to Macedonia, for we were convinced that God had called us to tell them the good news.ᶜ

16:9
ᵇActs 10:30

16:10
ᶜ2Cor 2:13

Paul and Silas in Philippi

¹¹Sailing from Troas, we went straight to Samothrace, the next day to Neapolis, ¹²and from there to Philippi, a leading city of the districtᵃ of Macedonia and a Roman colony. We were in this city for several days.ᵈ

16:12
ᵈPhil 1:1

¹³On the Sabbath day we went out of the gate and along the river, where we thought there was a place of prayer. We sat down and began talking to the women who had gathered there. ¹⁴A woman named Lydia, a dealer in purple goods from the city of Thyatira, was listening to us. She was a worshiper of God, and the Lord opened her heart to listen carefully to what was being said by Paul.ᵉ ¹⁵When she and her family were baptized, she urged us, "If you are convinced that I am a believer in the Lord, come and stay at my home." And she continued to insist that we do so.ᶠ

16:14
ᵉLk 24:45

16:15
ᶠGen 19:3;
33:11 Jdg 19:21;
Lk 24:29;
Heb 13:2

¹⁶Once, as we were going to the place of prayer, we met a slave girl who had a spirit of fortune-telling and brought her owners a great deal of money by predicting the future.ᵍ ¹⁷She would follow Paul and us and shout, "These men are servants of the Most High God and are proclaiming to youᵇ a way of salvation!" ¹⁸She kept doing this for many days until Paul became annoyed, turned to the spirit, and said, "I command you in the name of Jesus Christ to come out of her!" And it came out that very moment.ᶜʰ

16:16
ᵍ1Sam 28:7;
Acts 19:24

16:18
ʰMark 1:25,34;
16:17

¹⁹When her owners realized that their hope of making money was gone, they grabbed Paul and Silas and dragged them before the authorities in the public square.ᵈⁱ ²⁰They brought them before the magistrates and said, "These men

16:19
ⁱMatt 10:18;
Acts 19:25-26;
2Cor 6:5

a 16:12 Other mss. read *a city of the first district*   b 16:17 Other mss. read *to us*   c 16:17 Lit. *that hour*   d 16:20 Or *in the marketplace*

are stirring up a lot of trouble in our city. They are Jews[a] [21]and are advocating customs that we are not allowed to accept or practice as Romans."

[22]The crowd joined in the attack against them. Then the magistrates had them stripped of their clothes and ordered them beaten with sticks.[b] [23]After giving them a severe beating, they threw them in jail and ordered the jailer to keep them under tight security. [24]Having received these orders, he put them into the inner cell and fastened their feet in leg irons.

[25]Around midnight, Paul and Silas were praying and singing hymns to God. The other prisoners were listening to them. [26]Suddenly, there was an earthquake so violent that the foundations of the prison were shaken. All the doors immediately flew open, and everyone's chains were unfastened.[c]

[27]When the jailer woke up and saw the prison doors wide open, he drew his sword and was about to kill himself, for he thought the prisoners had escaped. [28]But Paul shouted in a loud voice, "Don't hurt yourself, for we are all here!" [29]The jailer[a] asked for torches and rushed inside. He was trembling as he knelt in front of Paul and Silas. [30]Then he took them outside and asked, "Sirs, what must I do to be saved?"[d] [31]They answered, "Believe on the Lord Jesus, and you and your family will be saved."[e] [32]Then they spoke the word of the Lord[b] to him and everyone in his home.

[33]At that hour of the night he took them and washed their wounds. Then he and his entire family were baptized immediately. [34]He brought them upstairs into his house and set food before them, and he and everyone in his house were thrilled to be believers in God.[f]

[35]When day came, the magistrates sent guards and said, "Release those men." [36]The jailer reported these words to Paul, saying, "The magistrates have sent word to release you. So come out now and go in peace." [37]But Paul told them, "They have had us beaten publicly without a trial and have thrown us into jail, even though we are Roman

---

a [16:29] Lit. *He*   b [16:32] Other mss. read *of God*

16:20
a 1Kings 18:17;
Acts 17:6

16:22
b 2Cor 6:5; 11:23,
25; 1Thes 2:2

16:26
c Acts 4:31; 5:19;
12:7,10

16:30
d Lk 3:10;
Acts 2:37; 9:6

16:31
e John 3:16,36;
6:47; 1John 5:10

16:34
f Lk 5:29; 19:6

16:37
a Acts 22:25

16:39
b Matt 8:34

16:40
c Acts 16:14

17:2
d Lk 4:16;
Acts 9:20; 13:5,
14; 14:1; 16:13;
19:8

17:3
e Lk 24:26,46;
Acts 18:28;
Gal 3:1

17:4
f Acts 15:22,27,32,
40; 28:24

17:5
g Rom 16:21

17:6
h Acts 16:20

17:7
i Lk 23:2;
John 19:12;
1 Peter 2:15

17:10
j Acts 9:14,25

citizens. Now are they going to throw us out secretly? Certainly not! Have them come and escort us out."*a*

38The guards reported these words to the magistrates, and they were afraid when they heard that they were Roman citizens. 39So they came, apologized to them, and escorted them out. Then they asked them to leave the city.*b* 40Leaving the jail, they went to Lydia's house. They saw the brothers, encouraged them, and then left.*c*

Paul and Silas in Thessalonica

17 1They traveled through Amphipolis and Apollonia and came to Thessalonica, where there was a Jewish synagogue. 2As usual, Paul went in, and on three Sabbaths he discussed with them the Scriptures.*d* 3He explained and showed them that the Christ*a* had to suffer and rise from the dead. He said, "This very Jesus whom I proclaim to you is the Christ."*ae*

4Some of them were persuaded to join Paul and Silas, especially a large crowd of devout Greeks and the wives of many prominent men.*f* 5But the Jews became jealous. They took some contemptible characters who used to hang out in the public square,*b* formed a mob, and started a riot in the city. They attacked Jason's home and searched it for Paul and Silas in order to bring them out to the people.*g* 6When they didn't find them, they dragged Jason and some other brothers before the city officials and shouted, "These fellows who have turned the world upside down have come here, too,*h* 7and Jason has welcomed them as his guests. All of them oppose the emperor's decrees by saying that there is another king—Jesus!"*i*

8The crowd and the city officials were upset when they heard this. 9But after they had gotten a bond from Jason and the others, they let them go.

Paul and Silas in Berea

10That night the brothers immediately sent Paul and Silas away to Berea. When they arrived, they went into the Jewish synagogue.*j* 11These people were more receptive

---

a 17:3 I.e. the Messiah   **b** 17:5 Or *in the marketplace*

than those in Thessalonica. They were very willing to receive the message, and every day they carefully examined the Scriptures to see if those things were so.[a] [12]Many of them believed, including a large number of prominent Greek women and men.

[13]But when the Jews in Thessalonica found out that the word of God had been proclaimed by Paul also in Berea, they went there to upset and incite the crowds. [14]The brothers immediately sent Paul away to the coast, but Silas and Timothy stayed there.[b]

Paul in Athens

[15]The men who escorted Paul took him all the way to Athens. After receiving instructions to have Silas and Timothy join him as soon as possible, they left.[c] [16]While Paul was waiting for them in Athens, his spirit was stirred to its depths to see the city full of idols.[d] [17]So he began holding discussions in the synagogue with the Jews and other worshipers, as well as every day in the public square[a] with anyone who happened to be there. [18]Some Epicurean and Stoic philosophers also debated with him. Some asked, "What is this blabbermouth trying to say?" Others said, "He seems to be preaching about foreign gods." This was because he was telling the good news about Jesus and the resurrection.

[19]Then they took him, brought him before the Areopagus,[b] and asked, "May we know what this new teaching of yours is? [20]It sounds rather strange to our ears, so we would like to know what it means." [21]Now all the Athenians and the foreigners living there used to spend their time in nothing else than repeating or listening to the latest ideas.

[22]So Paul stood up in front of the Areopagus[b] and said, "Men of Athens, I see that you are very religious in every way. [23]For as I was walking around and looking closely at the objects you worship, I even found an altar with this written on it: 'To an unknown god.' So I'm telling you about the unknown object you worship. [24]The God who made the world and everything in it is the Lord of heaven and earth.

---

a 17:17 Or *in the marketplace*   b 17:19,17:22 I.e. the city council

308

17:11
a Isa 34:16;
Lk 16:29;
John 5:39

17:14
b Matt 10:23

17:15
c Acts 18:5

17:16
d 2Peter 2:8

17:24
a Matt 11:25;
Acts 7:48; 14:15

17:25
b Gen 2:7;
Num 16:22;
Job 12:10; 27:3;
33:4; Ps 50:8;
Isa 42:5; 57:16;
Zech 12:1

17:26
c Deut 32:8

17:27
d Acts 14:17;
Rom 1:20

17:28
e Col 1:17;
Titus 1:12;
Heb 1:3

17:29
f Isa 40:18

17:30
g Lk 24:47;
Acts 14:16;
Rom 3:25;
Titus 2:11-12;
1Peter 1:14; 4:3

17:31
h Acts 2:24; 10:42;
Rom 2:16; 14:10

18:2
i Rom 16:3;
1Cor 16:19;
2Tim 4:19

18:3
j Acts 20:34;
1Cor 4:12;
1Thes 2:9;
2Thes 3:8

18:4
k Acts 17:2

He doesn't live in shrines made by human hands,*a* 25and he isn't served by hands as if he needed anything. He himself gives everyone life, breath, and everything.*b* 26From one man*a* he made every nation of humanity to live all over the earth, fixing the seasons of the year and the boundaries they live in,*c* 27so that they might look for God,*b* somehow reach for him, and find him. Of course, he is never far from any one of us.*d* 28For we live, move, and exist because of him, as some of your own poets have said: 'For we are his children, too.'*ce* 29So if we are God's children, we shouldn't think that the divine being is like gold, silver, or stone, or is an image carved by human imagination and skill.*f* 30Though God has overlooked those times of ignorance, he now commands everyone everywhere to repent,*g* 31for he has set a day when he is going to judge the world with justice*d* through a man he has appointed. He has given proof of this to everyone by raising him from the dead."*h*

32When they heard about a resurrection of the dead, some began joking about it, while others said, "We will hear you again about this." 33And so Paul left the meeting.*e* 34Some men joined him and became believers. With them were Dionysius, who was a member of the Areopagus,*f* a woman named Damaris, and some others along with them.

Paul in Corinth

18 1After this Paul*g* left Athens and went to Corinth. 2There he found a Jew named Aquila, a native of Pontus, who had recently come from Italy with his wife Priscilla because Claudius had ordered all the Jews to leave Rome. Paul*h* went to visit them,*i* 3and because they had the same trade he stayed with them. They worked together because they were tentmakers by trade.*j* 4Every Sabbath he would argue in the synagogue and try to persuade both Jews and Greeks.*k*

---

a 17:26 Other mss. read *From one blood*   **b** 17:27 Other mss. read *for the Lord*   **c** 17:28 This quotation is from the *Phainomena* (5) of Aratus, a poet of Cicilian origin (3rd century BC), though Cleanthes the Stoic (3rd century BC) used almost identical language.   **d** 17:31 Or *in righteousness*   **e** 17:33 Lit. *went out from the middle of them*   **f** 17:34 I.e. the city council   **g** 18:1 Lit. *he*   **h** 18:2 Lit. *He*

⁵But when Silas and Timothy arrived from Macedonia, Paul devoted himself entirely to the word[a] as he solemnly assured the Jews that Jesus is the Christ.[ba] ⁶But when they began to oppose him and insult him, he shook out his clothes in protest and told them, "Your blood be on your own heads! I am innocent. From now on I will go to the Gentiles."[b]

⁷Then he left that place and went to the home of a man named Titius[c] Justus, who worshiped God. His house was next door to the synagogue. ⁸Now Crispus, the leader of the synagogue, believed in the Lord, along with his whole family. Many Corinthians who heard Paul also believed and were baptized.[c]

⁹One night the Lord said to Paul in a vision, "Stop being afraid to speak out! Do not be silent![d] ¹⁰For I am with you, and no one will lay a hand on you or harm you, because I have many people in this city."[e] ¹¹So he lived there for a year and a half and continued to teach the word of God among them.

¹²While Gallio was proconsul of Achaia, the Jews united in an attack on Paul and brought him before the judge's seat. ¹³They said, "This man is persuading people to worship God in ways that are contrary to the Law." ¹⁴Paul was about to open his mouth when Gallio said to the Jews, "If there were some misdemeanor or crime involved, it would be reasonable to put up with you Jews.[f] ¹⁵But since it is a question about words, names, and your own Law, you will have to take care of that yourselves. I refuse to be a judge in these matters." ¹⁶So he drove them away from the judge's seat. ¹⁷Then all of them[d] took Sosthenes, the synagogue leader, and began beating him in front of the judge's seat. But Gallio paid no attention to any of this.[g]

Paul's Return Trip to Antioch

¹⁸After staying there for quite a while longer, Paul said goodbye to the brothers and sailed for Syria, accompanied by Priscilla and Aquila. In Cenchraea he had his hair cut,

---

a 18:5 Other mss. read *to the Spirit*   **b** 18:5 I.e. the Messiah
c 18:7 Other mss. read *Titus*   **d** 18:17 Other mss. read *all of the Greeks*

Cross references (margin):

18:5
a Job 32:18;
Acts 17:3,14-15, 28

18:6
b Lev 20:9,11-12;
2Sam 1:16;
Neh 5:13;
Ezek 3:18-19;
18:13; 33:4,9;
Matt 10:14;
Acts 13:45-46,51;
20:26; 28:28;
1Peter 4:4

18:8
c 1Cor 1:14

18:9
d Acts 23:11

18:10
e Jer 1:18-19;
Matt 28:20

18:14
f Acts 23:29;
25:11,19

18:17
g 1Cor 1:1

18:18
a Num 6:18;
Acts 21:24;
Rom 16:1

18:21
b Acts 19:21;
20:16; 1Cor 4:19;
Heb 6:3;
James 4:15

18:23
c Acts 14:22;
15:32,41; Gal 1:2;
4:14

18:24
d 1Cor 1:12; 3:5-6;
4:6; Titus 3:13

18:25
e Acts 19:3;
Rom 12:11

18:27
f 1Cor 3:6

18:28
g Acts 9:22; 17:3,5

19:1
h 1Cor 1:12; 3:5-6

19:2
i 1Sam 3:7;
Acts 8:16

19:3
j Acts 18:25

since he was under a vow.*ᵃ* ¹⁹When they arrived in Ephesus, he left them there. Then he went into the synagogue and had a discussion with the Jews. ²⁰They asked him to stay longer, but he refused. ²¹As he told them goodbye, he said, "I will come back**ᵃ** to you again if it is God's will." Then he set sail from Ephesus.*ᵇ* ²²When he arrived in Caesarea, he went up to Jerusalem,**ᵇ** greeted the church, and went back to Antioch.

²³After spending some time there, he departed and went from place to place through the region of Galatia and Phrygia, strengthening all the disciples.*ᶜ*

Apollos Preaches in Ephesus

²⁴Meanwhile, a Jew named Apollos arrived in Ephesus. He was a native of Alexandria and an eloquent man, one powerful in the Scriptures.*ᵈ* ²⁵He had been instructed in the Lord's way. With spiritual fervor he kept speaking and teaching accurately about Jesus, although he knew only about John's baptism.*ᵉ* ²⁶He began to speak boldly in the synagogue, but when Priscilla and Aquila heard him, they took him home and explained God's way to him more accurately.

²⁷When he wanted to cross over to Achaia, the brothers wrote and urged the disciples to welcome him. On his arrival he greatly helped those who through grace had believed.*ᶠ* ²⁸He successfully refuted the Jews in public and proved by the Scriptures that Jesus is the Christ.**ᶜ***ᵍ*

Paul in Ephesus

19 ¹It was while Apollos was in Corinth that Paul passed through the inland districts and came to Ephesus. He found a few disciples there*ʰ* ²and asked them, "Did you receive the Holy Spirit when you believed?" They answered him, "No, we haven't even heard that there is a Holy Spirit."*ⁱ* ³He then asked, "Then into what were you baptized?" They answered, "Into John's baptism."*ʲ*

---

a 18:21 Other mss. read *I must at all costs keep the approaching festival in Jerusalem, but I will come back.*   **b** 18:22 The Gk. lacks *to Jerusalem*
c 18:28 I.e. the Messiah

311

4Then Paul said, "John baptized with a baptism of repentance, telling the people to believe in the one who was to come after him, that is, in Jesus."*a* 5On hearing this, they were baptized in the name of the Lord Jesus.*b* 6When Paul laid his hands on them, the Holy Spirit came on them, and they began to speak in tongues and to prophecy.*c* 7There were about twelve men in all.

8He went into the synagogue and spoke there boldly for three months, holding discussions and persuading them about the kingdom of God.*d* 9But when some people became stubborn, refused to believe, and slandered the Way before the people, he left them, took his disciples away from them, and had daily discussions in the lecture hall of Tyrannus.*ae* 10This went on for two years, so that all who lived in Asia, Jews and Greeks alike, heard the word of the Lord.*f*

11God continued to do extraordinary miracles by Paul's hands.*g* 12When the handkerchiefs and aprons that had touched his skin were taken to the sick, their diseases left them, and the evil spirits went out of them.*h*

13Then some Jews who went around trying to drive out demons attempted to use the name of the Lord Jesus on those who had evil spirits, saying, "I command you by that Jesus whom Paul preaches!"*i* 14Seven sons of a Jewish high priest named Sceva were doing this. 15But the evil spirit said to them, "I know Jesus, and I know Paul, but who are you?"

16Then the man with the evil spirit jumped on them, got the better of them, and so violently overpowered all of them that they fled out of the house naked and bruised. 17When this became known to everyone living in Ephesus, Jews and Greeks alike, fear came on all of them, and the name of the Lord Jesus began to be held in high honor.*j* 18Many who became believers kept coming and confessing and telling about their practices.*k* 19Moreover, many people who had practiced magic gathered their books and burned them in front of everybody. They estimated the price of them and found they were worth 50,000 silver coins. 20In that way the word of the Lord kept spreading and triumphing.*l*

---

a *19:9* Other mss. read *of a certain Tyrannus from the fifth hour to the tenth*

19:4
a Matt 3:11;
John 1:15,27,30;
Acts 1:5; 11:16;
13:24-25

19:5
b Acts 8:16

19:6
c Acts 2:4; 6:6;
8:17; 10:46

19:8
d Acts 1:3; 17:2;
18:4; 28:23

19:9
e Acts 9:2; 22:4;
24:14,23;
2Tim 1:15;
2Peter 2:2;
Jude 1:10

19:10
f Acts 20:31

19:11
g Mark 16:20;
Acts 14:3

19:12
h 2Kings 4:29;
Acts 5:15

19:13
i Matt 12:27;
Mark 9:38;
Lk 9:49

19:17
j Lk 1:65; 7:16;
Acts 2:43; 5:5,11

19:18
k Matt 3:6

19:20
l Acts 6:7; 12:24

19:21
a Acts 18:21;
20:22; 23:11;
Rom 15:24-28;
Gal 2:1

²¹After these things had happened, Paul resolved in the Spirit to go through Macedonia and Achaia and then to go on to Jerusalem, saying, "After I have gone there, I must also see Rome."*a* ²²So he sent two of his helpers, Timothy and Erastus, to Macedonia, while he himself stayed in Asia a while longer.*b*

A Riot in Ephesus

19:22
b Acts 13:5;
Rom 16:23;
2Tim 4:20

²³Now just about that time a great commotion broke out concerning the Way.*c* ²⁴A silversmith named Demetrius provided a large income for the skilled workers by making silver shrines of Artemis.*d* ²⁵He called a meeting of these men and others who were engaged in similar trades and said, "Men, you well know that we get a good income from this business. ²⁶You also see and hear that, not only in Ephesus, but almost all over Asia, this man Paul has won over and taken away a large crowd by telling them that gods made by human*a* hands are not gods at all.*e* ²⁷There is a danger not only that our business will lose its reputation but also that the temple of the great goddess Artemis will be brought into contempt and that she will be robbed of her majesty that brought all Asia and the world to worship her."

19:23
c Acts 9:2;
2Cor 1:8

19:24
d Acts 16:16,19

19:26
e Ps 115:4;
Isa 44:10-20;
Jer 10:3

²⁸When they heard this, they became furious and began to shout, "Great is Artemis of the Ephesians!" ²⁹The city was filled with confusion, and the people*b* rushed into the theater together, dragging with them Gaius and Aristarchus, Paul's fellow travelers from Macedonia.*f* ³⁰Paul wanted to go into the crowd, but the disciples wouldn't let him. ³¹Even some officials of the province of Asia who were his friends sent him a message urging him not to risk his life in the theater.

19:29
f Acts 20:4; 27:2;
Rom 16:23;
1Cor 1:14;
Phlm 1:24;
Col 4:10

³²Meanwhile, some were shouting one thing, some another. For the assembly was confused, and most of them didn't know why they were meeting. ³³Some of the crowd concluded it was because of Alexander, since the Jews had pushed him to the front. So Alexander motioned for silence and tried to make a defense before the people.*g* ³⁴But when they found out that he was a Jew, they all started to shout in

19:33
g Acts 12:17;
1Tim 1:20;
2Tim 4:14

---

a *19:26* The Gk. lacks *human*   **b** *19:29* Lit. *they*

unison for about two hours, "Great is Artemis of the Ephesians!"

35When the city recorder had quieted the crowd, he said, "Men of Ephesus, who in the world[a] doesn't know that this city of Ephesus is the keeper of the temple of the great Artemis and of the statue that fell down from heaven?[b] 36Since these things cannot be denied, you must be quiet and not do anything reckless. 37For you have brought these men here, although they neither rob temples nor blaspheme our[c] goddess. 38So if Demetrius and his workers have a charge against anyone, the courts are open and there are proconsuls. They should accuse one another there. 39But if you want anything else, it must be settled in the regular assembly. 40For we are in danger of being charged with rioting today, and there is no good reason we can give to justify this commotion." After saying this, he dismissed the assembly.

Paul's Trip to Macedonia, Greece, and Troas

20 1When the uproar was over, Paul sent for the disciples and encouraged them. Then he said goodbye to them and left to go to Macedonia.[a] 2He went through those regions and encouraged the people[d] with many words. Then he went to Greece 3and stayed there for three months. When he was about to sail for Syria, a plot was made against him by the Jews. So he decided to go back through Macedonia.[b] 4He was accompanied by Sopater (the son of Pyrrhus) from Beroea, Aristarchus and Secundus from Thessalonica, Gaius from Derbe, Timothy, and Tychicus and Trophimus from Asia.[c] 5These men went on ahead and were waiting for us in Troas. 6After the days of Unleavened Bread, we sailed from Philippi. Five days later we joined them in Troas and stayed there for seven days.[d]

7On the first day of the week, when we had met to break bread, Paul began to address the people.[d] Since he intended to leave the next day, he went on speaking until midnight.[e] 8Now there were many lamps in the upstairs room where we were meeting.[f]

---

a 19:35 Lit. *who among people*   **b** 19:35 Or *from Zeus*   **c** 19:37 Other mss. read *your*   **d** 20:2,20:7 Lit. *them*

Margin references

20:1
a 1Cor 16:5;
1Tim 1:3

20:3
b Acts 9:23; 23:12;
25:3; 2Cor 11:26

20:4
c Acts 16:1; 19:29;
21:29; 27:2;
Eph 6:21; Col 4:7,
10; 2Tim 4:12,20;
Titus 3:12

20:6
d Exod 12:14-15;
23:15; Acts 16:8;
2Cor 2:12;
2Tim 4:13

20:7
e Acts 2:42,46;
1Cor 10:16;
11:20; 16:2;
Rev 1:10

20:8
f Acts 1:13

20:10
a 1Kings 17:21;
2Kings 4:34;
Matt 9:24

⁹A young man named Eutychus, who was sitting in a window, began to sink off into a deep sleep as Paul kept speaking longer and longer. Overcome by sleep, he fell down from the third floor and was picked up dead. ¹⁰But Paul went down, bent over*a* him, took him into his arms, and said, "Stop being alarmed, for his life is in him."*a* ¹¹Then he went back upstairs, broke the bread, and ate. He talked with them for a long time, until dawn, and then left. ¹²Then they took the boy away alive and were greatly relieved.

20:16
b Acts 2:1; 18:21;
19:21; 21:4,12;
24:17; 1Cor 16:8

Paul's Trip to Miletus

¹³We went ahead to the ship and sailed for Assos, where we were intending to pick up Paul. He had arranged it this way, since he had planned to travel there on foot. ¹⁴When he met us in Assos, we took him on board and went to Mitylene. ¹⁵We sailed from there and on the following day arrived off Chios. The next day we crossed over to Samos and stayed at Trogyllium.*b* The day after that we came to Miletus. ¹⁶Paul had decided to sail past Ephesus to avoid spending time in Asia. He was in a hurry to get to Jerusalem for the day of Pentecost, if that was possible.*b*

20:18
c Acts 18:19; 19:1,
10

Paul Meets with the Ephesian Elders

¹⁷From Miletus he sent messengers*c* to Ephesus to ask the elders of the church to meet with him. ¹⁸When they came to him, he said to them, "You know how I lived among you the entire time from the first day I set foot in Asia.*c* ¹⁹I served the Lord with all humility, with tears, and with trials that came to me through the plots of the Jews.*d* ²⁰I never shrank from telling you anything that would help you nor from teaching you publicly and from house to house.*e* ²¹I testified to both Jews and Greeks about repentance toward God and faith toward our Lord Jesus.*df*

20:19
d Acts 20:3

20:20
e Acts 20:27

20:21
f Mark 1:15;
Lk 24:47;
Acts 2:38; 18:5

a *20:10* Lit. *fell on*   b *20:15* Other mss. omit *and stayed at Trogyllium.*   c *20:17* The Gk. lacks *messengers*   d *20:21* Other mss. read *Lord Jesus Christ*

22"And now, compelled by the Spirit, I am on my way to Jerusalem, not knowing what will happen to me there,[a] 23except that in town after town the Holy Spirit assures me that imprisonment and suffering are waiting for me.[b] 24But I don't place any value on my life, if only I can finish my race and the ministry that I received from the Lord Jesus of testifying to the gospel of God's grace.[c]

25"Now I know that none of you among whom I traveled preaching the kingdom will ever see my face again.[d] 26I therefore declare to you today that I am not responsible for the blood of any of you,[e] 27for I never shrank from telling you the whole plan of God.[f] 28Pay attention to yourselves and to the entire flock in which the Holy Spirit has made you overseers to be shepherds of God's[a] church, which he acquired with his own blood.[g] 29I know that when I'm gone savage wolves will come among you and not spare the flock.[h] 30Some of your own men will come forward and distort the truth in order to lure the disciples into following them.[i] 31So be alert! Remember that for three years, night and day, I never stopped warning each of you with tears.[j]

32"I am now entrusting you to God and to the message of his grace, which is able to build you up and give you an inheritance among all who are sanctified.[k] 33I never desired anyone's silver, gold, or clothes.[l] 34You yourselves know that I worked with my own hands to support myself and those who were with me.[m] 35In every way I showed you that by working hard like this we should help the weak and remember the words that the Lord Jesus himself said, 'It is more blessed to give than to receive.' "[b][n]

36When he had said this, he knelt down and prayed with all of them.[o] 37All of them cried and cried[c] as they put their arms around Paul and kissed him with affection.[p] 38They were especially sorrowful because of what he had said—that they would never see his face again. Then they took him to the ship.[q]

---

a 20:28 Other mss. read the Lord's   b 20:35 This saying is not recorded in the Gospels.   c 20:37 Lit. Great crying came to all

20:22 a Acts 19:21
20:23 b Acts 21:4,11; 1Thes 3:3
20:24 c Acts 1:17; 21:13; Rom 8:35; 2Cor 4:1,16; Gal 1:1; 2Tim 4:7; Titus 1:3
20:25 d Acts 20:38; Rom 15:23
20:26 e Acts 18:6; 2Cor 7:2
20:27 f Lk 7:30; John 15:15; Acts 20:20; Eph 1:11
20:28 g 1Cor 12:28; Eph 1:7,14; Col 1:14; 1Tim 4:16; Heb 9:12,14; 1Peter 1:19; 5:2; Rev 5:9
20:29 h Matt 7:15; 2Peter 2:1
20:30 i 1Tim 1:20; 1John 2:19
20:31 j Acts 19:10
20:32 k Acts 9:31; 26:18; Eph 1:18; Col 1:12; 3:24; Heb 9:15; 13:9; 1Peter 1:4
20:33 l 1Sam 12:3; 1Cor 9:12; 2Cor 7:2; 11:9; 12:17
20:34 m Acts 18:3; 1Cor 4:12; 1Thes 2:9; 2Thes 3:8
20:35 n Rom 15:1; 1Cor 9:12; 2Cor 11:9,12; 12:13; Eph 4:28; 1Thes 4:11; 5:14; 2Thes 3:8
20:36 o Acts 7:60; 21:5
20:37 p Gen 45:14; 46:29
20:38 q Acts 20:25

21:4
a Acts 20:23;
21:12

21:5
b Acts 20:36

21:6
c John 1:11

21:8
d Acts 6:5; 8:26,
40; Eph 4:11;
2 Tim 4:5

21:9
e Joel 2:28;
Acts 2:17

21:10
f Acts 11:28

21:11
g Acts 20:23;
21:33

21:13
h Acts 20:24

21:14
i Matt 6:10; 26:42;
Lk 11:2; 22:42

Paul in Tyre

21 ¹When we had torn ourselves away from them, we sailed straight to Cos, and the next day to Rhodes, and from there to Patara.ᵃ ²There we found a ship going across to Phoenecia, so we went aboard and sailed away. ³We came in sight of Cyprus, and leaving it on our left we sailed on to Syria and landed at Tyre because the ship was to unload its cargo there.

⁴So we looked up the disciples and stayed there for seven days. Through the Spirit they kept telling Paul not to go to Jerusalem.ᵃ ⁵But when our days there were ended, we left and proceeded on our journey. All of them with their wives and children accompanied us out of the city. We knelt on the beach, prayed,ᵇ ⁶and said goodbye to each other. Then we went aboard the ship, and they went back home.ᶜ

Paul in Caesarea

⁷On finishing the voyage from Tyre, we arrived at Ptolemais, greeted the brothers, and stayed with them for one day. ⁸The next day we left and came to Caesarea. We went to the home of Philip the evangelist, one of the seven, and stayed with him.ᵈ ⁹He had four unmarried daughters who could prophesy.ᵉ

¹⁰After we had been there for a number of days, a prophet named Agabus arrived from Judea.ᶠ ¹¹He came to us, took Paul's belt, and tied his own feet and hands with it. Then he said, "The Holy Spirit says, 'This is how the Jews in Jerusalem will tie up the man who owns this belt. Then they will hand him over to the Gentiles.' "ᵍ ¹²When we heard this, we and the people who lived there begged him not to go up to Jerusalem. ¹³Then Paul replied, "What do you mean by crying and breaking my heart? I'm ready not only to be tied up in Jerusalem but even to die for the name of the Lord Jesus!"ʰ ¹⁴When he could not be persuaded, we remained silent except to say, "May the Lord's will be done."ⁱ

Paul in Jerusalem

¹⁵After those days, we got ready to go up to Jerusalem.

---

a 21:1 Other mss. read *Patara and Myra*

¹⁶Some of the disciples from Caesarea went with us. They took us to the home of Mnason to be his guests. He was from Cyprus and an early disciple. ¹⁷When we arrived in Jerusalem, the brothers welcomed us warmly.*ᵃ*

¹⁸The next day Paul went with us to visit James, and all the elders were present.*ᵇ* ¹⁹After greeting them, Paul*ᵃ* related one by one the things that God had done among the Gentiles through his ministry.*ᶜ* ²⁰When they heard about it, they praised God. They told him, "You see, brother, how many thousands of believers there are among the Jews, and all of them are zealous for the Law.*ᵈ* ²¹But they have been told about you—that you teach all the Jews living among the Gentiles to forsake the Law of Moses, and that you tell them not to circumcise their children or observe the customs. ²²What is to be done? They will certainly hear that you have come. ²³So do what we tell you. We have four men who are under a vow. ²⁴Take these men, go through the purification ceremony with them, and pay the expenses to shave their heads. Then everyone will know that there's nothing in what they've been told about you, but that you yourself constantly observe and guard the Law.*ᵉ* ²⁵As for the Gentiles who have become believers, we have sent a letter with our judgment that they should keep away from food that has been sacrificed to idols, from blood, from the meat of strangled animals, and from sexual immorality."*ᶠ*

²⁶Then Paul took the men and the next day purified himself with them. Then he went into the Temple to announce the time when the days of purification would be over and when the sacrifice would be offered for each of them.*ᵍ* ²⁷When the seven days were almost over, the Jews from Asia, seeing Paul*ᵇ* in the Temple, stirred up the whole crowd. They grabbed him,*ʰ* ²⁸yelling, "Men of Israel, help! This is the man who teaches everyone everywhere to turn against our people, the Law, and this place. More than that, he has even brought Greeks into the Temple and desecrated this holy place."*ⁱ* ²⁹For they had earlier seen Trophimus the Ephesian in the city with him and had supposed that Paul

---

a *21:19* Lit. *he*   **b** *21:27* Lit. *him*

21:17
a Acts 15:4

21:18
b Acts 15:13;
Gal 1:19; 2:9

21:19
c Acts 1:17; 15:4,
12; 20:24;
Rom 15:18-19

21:20
d Acts 22:3;
Rom 10:2;
Gal 1:14

21:24
e Num 6:2,13,18;
Acts 18:18

21:25
f Acts 15:20,29

21:26
g Num 6:13;
Acts 24:18

21:27
h Acts 24:18;
26:21

21:28
i Acts 24:5-6

21:29
a Acts 20:4

had taken him into the Temple.*a* ³⁰The whole city was in chaos, and the people rushed together. They grabbed Paul and dragged him out of the Temple, and at once the doors were shut.*b*

21:30
b Acts 26:21

³¹They were trying to kill him when a report reached the tribune of the cohort that all Jerusalem was in an uproar. ³²Immediately he took some soldiers and officers and ran down to them. When they saw the tribune and the soldiers, they stopped beating Paul.*c* ³³Then the tribune came up, grabbed Paul,*a* and ordered him to be tied up with two chains. He then asked who Paul*b* was and what he had done.*d* ³⁴Some of the crowd shouted this and some that. Since he couldn't learn the facts because of the confusion, he ordered him to be taken into the barracks. ³⁵When Paul*b* got to the steps, he had to be carried by the soldiers because of the violence of the mob. ³⁶The crowd of people kept following him and shouting, "Kill him!"*e*

21:32
c Acts 23:27; 24:7

21:33
d Acts 20:23;
21:11

21:36
e Lk 23:18;
John 19:15;
Acts 22:22

Paul Speaks in His Own Defense

³⁷Just as Paul was about to be taken into the barracks, he said to the tribune, "May I say something to you?" He asked, "Do you know Greek? ³⁸You're not the Egyptian who started a revolt some time ago and led four thousand assassins into the desert, are you?"*f* ³⁹Paul replied, "I am a Jew from Tarsus in Cilicia, a citizen of no insignificant city. I beg you to let me speak to the people."*g* ⁴⁰He gave him permission, and Paul, standing on the steps, motioned with his hand for the people to be silent. When everyone had quieted down, he spoke to them in the Hebrew language.*h*

21:38
f Acts 5:36

21:39
g Acts 9:11; 22:3

21:40
h Acts 12:17

22:1
i Acts 7:2

22 ¹"Brothers and fathers, listen to the defense that I am now making before you."*i* ²When they heard him speaking to them in Hebrew, they became even more quiet, and he continued, ³"I am a Jew, born in Tarsus in Cilicia but raised in this city and educated at the feet of Gamaliel in the strict ways of our ancestral Law. I am as zealous for God as all of you are today.*j* ⁴I persecuted this Way even to the death and kept tying up both men and women and putting them in prison,*k* ⁵as the high priest and

22:3
j Deut 33:3;
2Kings 4:38;
Lk 10:39;
Acts 5:34; 21:20,
39; 26:5;
Rom 10:2;
2Cor 11:22;
Gal 1:14; Phil 3:5

22:4
k Acts 8:3;
26:9-11 Phil 3:6;
1Tim 1:13

a *21:33* Lit. *him*   **b** *21:33,21:35* Lit. *he*

the whole Council of elders can testify about me. From them I also received letters to the brothers in Damascus, and I was going there to tie up those who were there and bring them back to Jerusalem to be punished.*

6"But while I was on my way and approaching Damascus about noon, a bright light from heaven suddenly flashed around me.* 7I fell to the ground and heard a voice saying to me, 'Saul! Saul! Why are you persecuting me?' 8I answered, 'Who are you, Lord?'* He said to me, 'I am Jesus from Nazareth,* whom you are persecuting.' 9The men who were with me saw the light but didn't understand the voice of the one who was speaking to me.*

10"Then I asked, 'What am I to do, Lord?' The Lord told me, 'Get up and go into Damascus, and there you will be told everything you are destined to do.' 11Since I could not see because of the brightness of the light, the men who were with me took me by the hand and led me into Damascus.

12"A certain Ananias, who was a devout man in accordance with the Law and who was highly regarded by all the Jews living there,* 13came to me. He stood beside me and said, 'Brother Saul, receive your sight!' At that moment I could see him. 14Then he said, 'The God of our ancestors has chosen you to know his will, to see the Righteous One, and to hear his own voice,*e 15because you will be his witness to all people of what you have seen and heard.* 16What are you waiting for now? Get up, be baptized, and have your sins washed away as you call on his name.'*

17"Then I returned to Jerusalem. While I was praying in the Temple, I fell into a trance* 18and saw the Lord* saying to me, 'Hurry up and get out of Jerusalem at once, because the people* won't accept your testimony about me.'* 19I said, 'Lord, they themselves know that in every synagogue I kept imprisoning and beating those who believe in you.* 20Even when the blood of your witness Stephen was being shed, I was standing there approving it and guarding the

---

a 22:8 Or *Sir*   b 22:8 Or *Jesus the Nazarene*; the Gk. *Nazoraios* may be a word play between Heb. *netser*, meaning *branch* (see Isa 11:1), and the name *Nazareth*.   c 22:14 Lit. *the voice of his mouth*   d 22:18 Lit. *him*   e 22:18 Lit. *they*

Cross-references: 22:5 a Lk 22:66; Acts 4:5; 9:2; 26:10,12 | 22:6 b Acts 9:3; 26:12-13 | 22:9 c Dan 10:7; Acts 9:7 | 22:12 d Acts 9:17; 10:22; 1 Tim 3:7 | 22:14 e Acts 3:13-14; 5:30; 7:52; 9:15; 26:16; 1 Cor 9:1; 11:23; 15:8; Gal 1:12 | 22:15 f Acts 4:20; 23:11; 26:16 | 22:16 g Acts 2:38; 9:14; Rom 10:13; Heb 10:22 | 22:17 h Acts 9:26; 2 Cor 12:2 | 22:18 i Matt 10:14; Acts 22:14 | 22:19 j Matt 10:17; Acts 8:3; 22:4

22:20
a Lk 11:48;
Acts 7:58; 8:1;
Rom 1:32

coats of those who were killing him.'*a* 21Then he said to me, 'Go, because I will send you far away to the Gentiles.' "*b*

22Up to this point they listened to him, but then they began to shout, "Away with such a fellow from the earth! He's not fit to go on living!"*c* 23While they were yelling, tossing their coats around, and throwing dirt into the air,

22:21
b Acts 9:15; 13:2,
46-47; 18:6;
26:17; Rom 1:5;
11:13; 15:16;
Gal 1:15-16;
2:7-8; Eph 3:7-8;
1 Tim 2:7;
2 Tim 1:11

24the tribune ordered Paul*a* to be taken into the barracks and told the soldiers*b* to question him with a beating in order to find out why they were yelling at him like this. 25But when they had tied him up with the straps, Paul asked the centurion*c* who was standing there, "Is it legal for you to whip a Roman citizen who hasn't been condemned?"*d*

26When the centurion heard this, he went to the tribune and said to him, "What are you doing? This man is a Roman citizen!" 27So the tribune went and asked Paul,*a* "Tell me, are you a Roman citizen?" "Yes," he said. 28Then the tribune replied, "I paid a lot of money for this citizenship of mine." Paul said, "But I was born a citizen." 29Immediately those who were about to examine him stepped back, and the tribune was afraid when he found out that Paul*d* was a Roman citizen and that he had tied him up.

22:22
c Acts 21:36;
25:24

22:25
d Acts 16:37

Paul before the Jewish Council

30The next day, since he wanted to find out exactly what Paul*d* was being accused of by the Jews, he released him and ordered the high priests and the entire Council*e* to meet. Then he brought Paul down and had him stand before them.

23:1
e Acts 24:16;
1 Cor 4:4;
2 Cor 1:12; 4:2;
2 Tim 1:3;
Heb 13:18

23 1Paul looked straight at the Council*e* and said, "Brothers, with a clear conscience I have done my duty before God up to this very day."*e* 2Then the high priest Ananias ordered the men standing near him to strike him on the mouth.*f* 3At this Paul said to him, "God will strike you, you whitewashed wall!*f* How can you sit there and judge me according to the Law and yet in violation of the Law order me to be struck?"*g* 4The men standing

23:2
f 1 Kings 22:24;
Jer 20:2;
John 18:22

23:3
g Lev 19:35;
Deut 25:1-2;
John 7:51

---

a 22:24, 22:27 Lit. *him*   *b* 22:24 Lit *them*   *c* 22:25 A Roman centurion commanded about 100 men.   *d* 22:29, 22:30 Lit. *he*   *e* 22:30, 23:1 Or *Sanhedrin*   *f* 23:3 I.e. hypocrite

near him asked, "Do you mean to insult God's high priest?" [a]
⁵Paul answered, "I didn't realize, brothers, that he is the high priest. After all, it is written, 'You must not speak evil about a ruler of your people.' "[a]

⁶When Paul saw that some of them were Sadducees and others were Pharisees, he shouted in the Council,[b] "Brothers, I am a Pharisee and a descendant[c] of Pharisees. I am on trial concerning the hope of the resurrection of the dead."[b] ⁷After he said that, an angry quarrel broke out between the Pharisees and the Sadducees, and the assembly was divided. ⁸For the Sadducees say that there is no resurrection and that there is no such thing as an angel or spirit, but the Pharisees believe in all those things.[c] ⁹There was a great deal of shouting until some of the scribes who belonged to the party of the Pharisees stood up and argued forcefully, "We find nothing wrong with this man. What if a spirit or an angel has spoken to him?"[d]

¹⁰The quarrel was becoming violent, and the tribune was afraid that they would tear Paul to pieces. So he ordered the soldiers to go down, take him away from them by force, and bring him into the barracks. ¹¹That night the Lord stood near him and said, "Have courage! For just as you have testified about me in Jerusalem, you must testify in Rome, too."[e]

Some Jews Plot to Kill Paul

¹²In the morning, the Jews formed a conspiracy and took an oath not to eat or drink anything before they had killed Paul.[f] ¹³More than forty men formed this conspiracy. ¹⁴They went to the high priests and elders and said, "We have taken a solemn oath not to taste any food before we have killed Paul. ¹⁵Now then, you and the Council[b] must notify the tribune to bring him down to you on the pretext that you want to look into his case more carefully, but before he arrives we'll be ready to kill him."

¹⁶But the son of Paul's sister heard about the ambush, so he came and got into the barracks and told Paul. ¹⁷Then Paul called one of the centurions and said, "Take this young

23:5
[a] Exod 22:28;
Eccl 10:20;
Acts 24:17;
2Peter 2:10;
Jude 1:8

23:6
[b] Acts 24:15,21;
26:5-6; 28:20;
Phil 3:5

23:8
[c] Matt 22:23;
Mark 12:18;
Lk 20:27

23:9
[d] Acts 5:39; 22:7,
17-18; 25:25;
26:31

23:11
[e] Acts 18:9;
27:23-24

23:12
[f] Acts 23:21,30;
25:3

---

a 23:5 Exod 22:28   b 23:6,23:15 Or *Sanhedrin*   c 23:6 Or *son*

23:20
a Acts 23:12

man to the tribune, because he has something to tell him." [18]So he took him, brought him to the tribune, and said, "The prisoner Paul called me and asked me to bring this young man to you. He has something to tell you." [19]The tribune took him by the hand, stepped aside to be alone with him, and asked, "What have you got to tell me?" [20]He answered, "The Jews have agreed to ask you to bring Paul down to the Council[a] tomorrow as though they were going to examine his case more carefully.[a] [21]Don't believe them, because more

23:27
b Acts 21:33; 24:7

than forty of them are planning to ambush him. They have taken an oath not to eat or drink before they have killed him. They are ready now, just waiting for your consent." [22]The tribune dismissed the young man and ordered him not to tell anyone that he had notified him.

[23]Then he summoned two of the centurions and said, "Get two hundred soldiers ready to leave for Caesarea at nine o'clock tonight,[b] along with seventy mounted soldiers and two hundred soldiers with spears. [24]Provide an animal for Paul to ride, and take him safely to Governor Felix." [25]He wrote a letter with this message:

23:28
c Acts 22:30

[26]"From[c] Claudius Lysias to Your Excellency, Governor Felix. Greetings. [27]This man had been seized by the Jews and was about to be killed by them when I went with the guard and rescued him, having learned that he was a Roman citizen.[b] [28]I wanted to know the exact charge they were making against him, so I had him brought before their Council.[a][c] [29]I found that, although he was charged with questions about their Law, there was no charge against him deserving death or imprisonment.[d] [30]Since a plot against the man has been reported to me, I am at once sending him to you and have also ordered his accusers to present their charges against him before you."[e]

23:29
d Acts 18:15;
25:19; 26:31

23:30
e Acts 23:20; 24:8;
25:6

---

a 23:20, 23:28 Or *Sanhedrin*   **b** 23:23 Lit. *from the third hour of the night*
c 23:26 The Gk. lacks *From*

[31]So the soldiers, in keeping with their orders, took Paul and brought him by night to Antipatris. [32]The next day they let the horsemen ride on with him while they returned to their barracks. [33]When these came to Caesarea, they delivered the letter to the governor and handed Paul over to him.

[34]After reading the letter, he asked which province he was from. On learning that he was from Cilicia,[a] [35]he said, "I will hear your case when your accusers arrive." Then he ordered him to be kept in custody in Herod's palace.[ab]

Paul Presents His Case to Felix

24 [1]Five days later, the high priest Ananias arrived with some elders and Tertullius, an attorney, and they presented their case against Paul before the governor.[c] [2]When Paul[b] had been summoned, Tertullius opened the prosecution by saying, "Your Excellency Felix, since we are enjoying lasting peace through you, and since reforms for this nation are being brought about through your foresight, [3]we always and everywhere acknowledge it with profound gratitude. [4]But so as not to detain you any further, I beg you to hear us briefly with your customary graciousness. [5]For we have found this man a perfect pest and an agitator among all Jews throughout the world. He is a ringleader in the sect of the Nazarenes[cd] [6]and even tried to profane the Temple, but we arrested him.[de] [8]By examining him for yourself, you will be able to find out from him everything of which we accuse him."[f] [9]The Jews supported his accusations by asserting that these things were true.

[10]When the governor motioned for Paul to speak, he replied: "Since I know that you have been a judge over this nation for many years, I am pleased to present my defense. [11]You can verify for yourself that I went up to worship in Jerusalem no more than twelve days ago.[g] [12]They never found me debating with anyone in the Temple or stirring up a crowd in the synagogues or throughout the city,[h] [13]and

23:34
[a] Acts 21:39

23:35
[b] Matt 27:27;
Acts 24:1,10;
25:16

24:1
[c] Acts 21:27; 23:2,
30,35; 25:2

24:5
[d] Lk 23:2;
Acts 6:13; 16:20;
17:6; 21:28;
1Peter 2:12,15

24:6
[e] John 18:31;
Acts 21:28

24:8
[f] Acts 21:33; 23:30

24:11
[g] Acts 21:26;
24:17

24:12
[h] Acts 25:8; 28:17

---

a 23:35 Lit. *praetorium*   b 24:2 Lit. *he*   c 24:5 The Gk. *Nazoraios* may be a word play between Heb. *netser*, meaning *branch* (see Isa 11:1), and the name *Nazareth*.   d 24:6 Other mss. read *arrested him, and we wanted to try him under our Law.* [7]But Tribune Lysias came along and took him out of our hands with much force, [8]ordering his accusers to come before you.*

24:14
a Amos 8:14;
Acts 9:2; 23:6;
26:22; 2Tim 1:3

24:15
b Dan 12:2;
John 5:28-29;
Acts 26:6-7;
28:20,23

24:16
c Acts 23:1

24:17
d Acts 11:29-30;
20:16;
Rom 15:25;
2Cor 8:4;
Gal 2:10

24:18
e Acts 21:26-27;
26:21

24:19
f Acts 23:30; 25:16

24:21
g Acts 23:6; 28:20

24:22
h Acts 24:7

24:23
i Acts 27:3; 28:16

24:26
j Exod 23:8

24:27
k Exod 23:2;
Acts 12:3; 25:9,14

they cannot prove to you the charges they are now bringing against me. [14]However, I admit to you that in accordance with the Way, which they call a heresy,[a] I worship the God of our ancestors and believe in everything written in the Law and the Prophets.[a] [15]I have the same hope in God that they themselves cherish—that there is to be a resurrection of the righteous and the wicked.[b] [16]Therefore, I always do my best to have a clear conscience in the sight of God and people.[c] [17]After many years I have come back to my people to bring gifts for the poor and to offer sacrifices.[d] [18]They found me in the Temple doing these things just as I had completed the purification ceremony. No crowd or noisy mob was present.[e] [19]But some Jews from Asia were there, and they should be here before you to accuse me if they have anything against me.[f] [20]Otherwise, these men themselves should tell what wrong they found when I stood before the Council[b]—[21]unless it is for the one thing I shouted as I stood among them: 'It is for the resurrection of the dead that I am on trial before you today.'"[g]

[22]Felix was rather well informed about the Way, and so he adjourned the trial with the comment, "When Tribune Lysias arrives, I will decide your case."[h] [23]He ordered the centurion to guard Paul[c] but to let him have some freedom and not to keep any of his friends from caring for his needs.[i]

[24]Some days later, Felix arrived with his wife Drusilla, who was Jewish. He sent for Paul and listened to him talk about faith in Christ Jesus.[d] [25]As Paul[e] talked about righteousness, self-control, and the coming judgment, Felix became afraid and said, "For the present you may go. When I get a chance, I will send for you again." [26]At the same time, he was hoping to get money from Paul, and so he would send for him frequently to talk with him.[j]

[27]After two years had passed, Felix was succeeded by Porcius Festus. Since Felix wanted to do the Jews a favor, he left Paul in prison.[k]

---

a 24:14 Or *sect*　**b** 24:20 Or *Sanhedrin*　**c** 24:23 Lit. *him*　**d** 24:24 Other mss. lack *Jesus*　**e** 24:25 Lit. *he*

Paul Appeals to the Emperor

25:2
a Acts 24:1,15

25 ¹Three days after Festus had arrived in the province, he went up from Caesarea to Jerusalem. ²The high priests and Jewish leaders informed him of their charges against Paul. They kept urging*a* ³and begging him as a favor to have Paul**a** brought to Jerusalem. They were laying an ambush to kill him on the way.*b*

25:3
b Acts 23:12,15

⁴Festus replied that Paul was being kept in custody at Caesarea and that he himself would be going there soon. ⁵"So," he said, "have your authorities come down with me and present their charges against him, if there is anything wrong with the man."*c*

25:5
c Acts 18:14,18

⁶Festus**b** stayed with them no more than eight or ten days and then went down to Caesarea. The next day he sat on the judge's seat and ordered Paul brought in. ⁷When he arrived, the Jews who had come down from Jerusalem surrounded him and began bringing a number of serious charges against him that they couldn't prove.*d* ⁸Paul said in his defense, "I have in no way sinned against the Law of the Jews or the Temple or the emperor."*e*

25:7
d Mark 15:3;
Lk 23:2,10;
Acts 24:5,13

⁹Then Festus, wanting to do the Jews a favor, asked Paul, "Are you willing to go up to Jerusalem to be tried there before me on these charges?"*f* ¹⁰But Paul said, "I am standing before the emperor's judgment seat where I ought to be tried. I haven't done anything wrong to the Jews, as you know very well. ¹¹If I am guilty and have done something that deserves death, I don't refuse to die. But if there is nothing to their charges against me, no one can hand me over to them as a favor. I appeal to the emperor!"*g* ¹²Festus talked it over with the council and then answered, "To the emperor you have appealed; to the emperor you will go!"

25:8
e Acts 6:13; 24:12;
28:17

25:9
f Acts 24:20,27

King Agrippa Meets Paul

¹³After several days had passed, King Agrippa and Bernice came to Caesarea to welcome Festus. ¹⁴Since they were staying there for several days, Festus laid Paul's case before

25:11
g Acts 18:14;
23:29; 25:25;
26:31-32; 28:19

---

a 25:3 Lit *as a favor against him to have him*   **b** 25:6 Lit. *He*

25:14
a Acts 24:27

25:15
b Acts 25:2-3

25:16
c Acts 25:4-5

25:17
d Acts 25:6

25:19
e Acts 18:15;
23:29

25:22
f Acts 9:15

25:24
g Acts 22:22;
25:2-3,7

25:25
h Acts 23:9,29;
26:11-12,31

the king. He said, "There is a man here who was left in prison by Felix.*a* **15**When I went to Jerusalem, the high priests and the Jewish elders informed me about him and asked me to condemn him.*b* **16**I answered them that it was not the Roman custom to hand over a man for punishment until the accused met his accusers face to face and had an opportunity to defend himself against the charge.*c*

17"So they came here with me, and the next day without any delay I sat down in the judge's seat and ordered the man to be brought in.*d* **18**When his accusers stood up, they didn't accuse him of any of the crimes**a** I was expecting. **19**Instead, they had several arguments with him about their own religion and about a certain Jesus who had died, but who Paul kept claiming was alive.*e* **20**I was puzzled how I should investigate such matters and asked if he would like to go to Jerusalem and be tried there in regard to these things. **21**But Paul appealed his case and asked to be held in prison until the decision of his Majesty. So I ordered him to be held in custody until I could send him to the emperor." **22**Agrippa told Festus, "I would like to hear the man." "To-morrow," he said, "you will hear him."*f*

23The next day Agrippa and Bernice arrived with much fanfare and went into the auditorium along with the tribunes and the leading men of the city. At the command of Festus, Paul was brought in. **24**Then Festus said, "King Agrippa and all you men who are present with us! You see this man about whom the whole Jewish nation petitioned me, both in Jerusalem and here, shouting that he ought not to live any longer.*g* **25**I find that he has not done anything deserving of death. But since he has appealed to his Majesty, I have decided to send him.*h* **26**I have nothing reliable to write our Sovereign about him, so I have brought him to all of you,**b** and especially to you, King Agrippa, so that I will have something to write after he is cross-examined. **27**For it seems to me absurd to send a prisoner without specifying the charges against him."

---

a *25:18* Other mss. read *of anything*   **b** *25:26* Lit. *to you* (plural)

Paul Presents His Case to Agrippa

26 ¹Then Agrippa said to Paul, "You have permission to speak for yourself." So Paul stretched out his hand and began his defense. ²"I consider myself fortunate that it is before you, King Agrippa, that I can defend myself today against all the accusations of the Jews, ³since you are especially familiar with all the Jewish customs and controversies. I beg you, therefore, to listen patiently to me. ⁴All the Jews know how I lived from the earliest days of my youth with my own people and in Jerusalem. ⁵They have known for a long time, if they would but testify to it, that I lived as a Pharisee by the standard of the strictest sect of our religion.*ᵃ*

⁶"And now it is for the hope of the promise made by God to our ancestors that I stand here on trial.*ᵇ* ⁷Our twelve tribes, worshiping day and night with intense devotion, hope to attain it. It is for this hope, O King, that I am accused by the Jews.*ᶜ* ⁸Why is it thought incredible by all of you*ᵃ* that God should raise the dead? ⁹Indeed, I myself thought it my duty to take extreme measures against the name of Jesus from Nazareth.*ᵇᵈ* ¹⁰That is what I did in Jerusalem. I received authority from the high priests and locked many of the saints in prison. And when they were put to death, I cast my vote against them.*ᵉ* ¹¹I would even punish them frequently in every synagogue and try to make them blaspheme. Raging furiously against them, I would hunt them down even to distant cities.*ᶠ*

¹²"That is how I happened to be traveling to Damascus with authority based on a commission from the high priests.*ᵍ* ¹³On the road at noon, O King, I saw from heaven a light that was brighter than the sun flash around me and those who were traveling with me. ¹⁴All of us fell to the ground, and I heard a voice asking me in the Hebrew language, 'Saul! Saul! Why are you persecuting me? It is hurting you to keep on kicking against the goads.' ¹⁵I asked, 'Who are you, Lord?'*ᶜ* The Lord answered, 'I am Jesus,

26:5 *a* Acts 22:3; 23:6; 24:15,22 Phil 3:5

26:6 *b* Gen 3:15; 22:18; 26:4; 49:10; Deut 18:15; 2Sam 7:12; Ps 132:11; Isa 4:2; 7:14; 9:6; 40:10; Jer 23:5; 33:14-16; Ezek 34:23; 37:24; Dan 9:24; Mic 7:20; Acts 13:32; 23:6; Rom 15:8; Titus 2:13

26:7 *c* Lk 2:37; Phil 3:11; 1Thes 3:10; 1Tim 5:5; James 1:1

26:9 *d* John 16:2; 1Tim 1:13

26:10 *e* Acts 8:3; 9:14, 21; 22:5; Gal 1:13

26:11 *f* Acts 22:19

26:12 *g* Acts 9:3; 22:6

---

a *26:8* Lit. *by you* (plural)   **b** *26:9* Or *Jesus the Nazarene;* the Gk. *Nazoraios* may be a word play between Heb. *netser,* meaning *branch* (see Isa 11:1), and the name *Nazareth.*   **c** *26:15* Or *Sir*

26:16
a Acts 22:15

26:17
b Acts 22:21

26:18
c Isa 35:5; 42:7;
Lk 1:77,79;
John 8:12;
Acts 20:32;
2Cor 4:4; 6:14;
Eph 1:11,18; 4:18;
5:8; Col 1:12-13;
1Thes 5:5;
1Peter 2:9,25

26:20
d Matt 3:8;
Acts 9:20,22,29;
11:26; 13:1-52;
14:1-28; 16:1-40;
17:1-34; 18:1-28;
19:1-41; 20:1-38;
21:1-40

26:21
e Acts 21:30-31

26:22
f Lk 24:27,44;
John 5:46;
Acts 24:14; 28:23;
Rom 3:21

26:23
g Lk 2:32; 24:26,
46; 1Cor 15:20;
Col 1:18; Rev 1:5

26:24
h 2Kings 9:11;
John 10:20;
1Cor 1:23;
2:13-14; 4:10

26:29
i 1Cor 7:7

whom you are persecuting. [16]But get up and stand on your feet, for I have appeared to you for the very purpose of appointing you to be a servant and witness of what you have seen and of what I will show you.[a] [17]I will continue to rescue you from your people and from the Gentiles to whom I am sending you.[b] [18]You will open their eyes and turn them from darkness to light and from Satan's control to God, so that they might receive the forgiveness of sins and a share among those who are sanctified by faith in me.'[c]

[19]"And so, King Agrippa, I was not disobedient to the heavenly vision. [20]Instead, I first told the people in Damascus and Jerusalem, then the whole countryside of Judea, and then the Gentiles to repent, turn to God, and practice works that are consistent with such repentance.[d] [21]For this reason the Jews grabbed me in the Temple and kept trying to kill me.[e] [22]I have had help from God to this day, and so I stand here to testify to high and low alike, stating only what the prophets and Moses said would happen[f]—[23]that the Christ[a] would suffer and be the first to rise from the dead and would announce light to our people and the Gentiles."[g]

[24]As he continued to make his defense, Festus shouted, "You're out of your mind, Paul! Too much education is driving you crazy!"[h] [25]But Paul said, "I'm not out of my mind, Your Excellency Festus. I'm uttering words of sober truth. [26]Indeed, the king knows about these things, and I can speak to him freely. For I am certain that none of these things has escaped his notice, since this wasn't done in a corner. [27]King Agrippa, do you believe the prophets? I know you believe them!"

[28]Agrippa said to Paul, "Can you so quickly persuade me to become a Christian?" [29]Paul replied, "Whether quickly or not, I wish to God that not only you but everyone listening to me today would become what I am—except for these chains!"[i]

[30]Then the king, the governor, Bernice, and those who were sitting with him got up. [31]As they were leaving, they

---

a *26:23* I.e. the Messiah

began to say to each other, "This man isn't doing anything to deserve death or imprisonment."*a* 32Agrippa told Festus, "This man could have been set free if he hadn't appealed to the emperor."*b*

Paul Sails for Rome

27 1When it was decided that we should sail to Italy, they transferred Paul and some other prisoners to a centurion named Julius, who belonged to the emperor's division.*c* 2Boarding a ship from Adramyttium that was about to sail to the ports on the coast of Asia, we put out to sea. Aristarchus, a Macedonian from Thessalonica, went with us.*d*

3The next day we arrived at Sidon, and Julius treated Paul kindly and allowed him to visit his friends and receive any care he needed.*e* 4After putting out from there, we sailed on the sheltered side of Cyprus because the winds were against us. 5We sailed along the sea off Cilicia and Pamphylia and reached Myra in Lycia. 6There the centurion found an Alexandrian ship bound for Italy and put us on it. 7We sailed slowly for a number of days and with difficulty arrived off Cnidus. Then, because the wind was against us, we sailed on the sheltered side of Crete off Cape Salome. 8Sailing past it with difficulty, we came to a place called Fair Havens, near the town of Lasea.

9Much time had been lost, and because navigation had become dangerous and the day of fasting had already past, Paul began to warn them*f* 10by saying, "Men, I see that in this voyage there will be hardship and a heavy loss not only of the cargo and ship but also of our lives." 11But the centurion was persuaded by the pilot and the owner of the ship and not by what Paul said. 12Since the harbor was not a good place to spend the winter, most of the men favored putting out to sea from there on the chance that somehow they could reach Phoenix and spend the winter there. It is a harbor of Crete facing southwest and northwest.

13When a gentle breeze began to blow from the south, they thought they could achieve their purpose. So they

26:31
a Acts 23:9,29;
25:25

26:32
b Acts 25:11

27:1
c Acts 25:12,25

27:2
d Acts 19:29

27:3
e Acts 24:23;
28:16

27:9
f Lev 23:27,29

27:19
a Jonah 1:5

raised the anchor and began to sail close to the shore of Crete. ¹⁴But it was not long before a violent wind (called a northeaster) swept down from the island.ᵃ ¹⁵The ship was caught so that it couldn't face the wind, and we gave up and were swept along. ¹⁶As we drifted to the sheltered side of a small island called Cauda,ᵇ we barely managed to secure the ship's lifeboat. ¹⁷They pulled it up on deck and used ropes to brace the ship. Fearing that they would hit the large sandbank near Lybia,ᶜ they lowered the sail and drifted along. ¹⁸The next day, because we were being tossed so violently by the storm, they began to throw the cargo overboard. ¹⁹On the third day they threw the ship's equipment overboard with their own hands.ᵃ ²⁰For a number of days neither the sun nor the stars were to be seen, and the storm continued to rage until at last all hope of our being saved vanished.

27:23
b Dan 6:16;
Acts 23:11;
Rom 1:9;
2Tim 1:3

²¹After they had gone a long time without food, Paul stood among them and said, "Men, you should have listened to me and not have sailed from Crete. You would have avoided this hardship and damage. ²²But now I urge you to have courage because there will be no loss of life among you but only of the ship. ²³For just last night an angel of God, to whom I belong and whom I serve, stood by meᵇ ²⁴and said, 'Stop being afraid, Paul! You must stand before the emperor. Indeed, God has given you all who are sailing with you.' ²⁵So have courage, men, for I trust God that it will turn out just as he told me.ᶜ ²⁶However, we will have to run aground on some island."ᵈ

27:25
c Lk 1:45;
Rom 4:20-21;
2Tim 1:12

The Shipwreck

²⁷It was the fourteenth night, and we were drifting through the Adriatic Sea when about midnight the sailors suspected that land was near. ²⁸On taking soundings, they found a depth of twenty fathoms. A little later they took soundings again and found it was fifteen fathoms. ²⁹Fearing

27:26
d Acts 28:1

a 27:14 Lit. *from it*   b 27:16 Other mss. read *Clauda*   c 27:17 Lit. *hit the Syrtis* that we might run aground on the rocks, they dropped four anchors from the stern and began praying for daylight to come.

30Now the sailors were trying to escape from the ship. They had lowered the lifeboat into the sea and pretended that they were going to lay out the anchors from the bow. 31Paul told the centurion and the soldiers, "Unless these men remain in the ship, you cannot be saved." 32Then the soldiers cut the ropes that held the lifeboat and set it adrift.

33Right up to daybreak Paul kept urging all of them to eat something, saying, "Today is the fourteenth day that you have been waiting and going without food, having eaten nothing. 34So I urge you to eat something, for it will help you survive, since none of you will lose a hair from his head."*a* 35After he said this, he took some bread, thanked God in front of everyone, broke it, and began to eat.*b* 36All of them were encouraged and had something to eat. 37There were 276*a* of us on the ship.*c* 38After they had eaten all they wanted, they began to lighten the ship by dumping the wheat into the sea.

39When day came, they couldn't recognize the land, but they could see a bay with a beach on which they planned if possible to run the ship ashore. 40So they cut the anchors free and left them in the sea. At the same time they untied the ropes that held the steering oars, raised the foresail to the wind, and headed for the beach. 41But they struck a sandbar and ran the ship aground. The bow stuck and couldn't be moved, while the stern was broken to pieces by the force of the waves.*d* 42The soldiers' plan was to kill the prisoners to keep them from swimming ashore and escaping. 43However, the centurion wanted to save Paul and prevented them from carrying out their plan. He ordered those who could swim to jump overboard first and get to land. 44The rest were to follow, some on planks and others on various pieces of the ship. In this way all of them got to shore safely.*e*

---

a27:37 Other mss. read 76

27:34
a 1Kings 1:52;
Matt 10:30;
Lk 12:7; 21:18

27:35
b 1Sam 9:13;
Matt 15:36;
Mark 8:6;
John 6:11;
1Tim 4:3-4

27:37
c Acts 2:41; 7:14;
Rom 13:1;
1Peter 3:20

27:41
d 2Cor 11:25

27:44
e Acts 27:22

Paul on the Island of Malta

28:1
a Acts 27:26

28 [1]When we were safely on shore, we learned that the island was called Malta.*a* [2]The people who lived there were unusually kind to us. It had started to rain and was cold, and so they made a fire and welcomed all of us around it.*b*

28:2
b Rom 1:14;
1 Cor 14:11;
Col 3:11

[3]Paul gathered a bundle of sticks and put it on the fire. A poisonous snake was forced out by the heat and attached itself to Paul's*a* hand. [4]When the people who lived there saw the snake hanging from his hand, they said to one another, "This man must be a murderer! He may have escaped from the sea, but justice won't let him live." [5]But he shook the snake into the fire and wasn't harmed.*c* [6]They were expecting him to swell up or suddenly drop dead, but after waiting a long time and seeing nothing unusual happen to him, they changed their minds and said he was a god.*d*

28:5
c Mark 16:18;
Lk 10:19

[7]The governor of the island, whose name was Publius, owned estates in that part of the island, and he welcomed us and entertained us with great hospitality for three days. [8]The father of Publius happened to be sick in bed with fever and dysentery. Paul went to him, prayed, and healed him by placing his hands on him.*e*

28:6
d Acts 14:11

[9]After that had happened, the rest of the sick people on the island went to him and were healed. [10]They honored us in many ways, and when we were going to sail, they supplied us with everything we needed.*f*

28:8
e Mark 6:5; 7:32;
16:18; Lk 4:40;
Acts 19:11-12;
1 Cor 12:9,28;
James 5:14-15

Paul Sails from Malta to Rome

[11]Three months later, we sailed on an Alexandrian ship that had spent the winter at the island. It had the Twin Brothers as its figurehead. [12]We stopped at Syracuse and stayed there for three days. [13]Then we weighed anchor and came to Rhegium. A day later a south wind began to blow, and on the second day we came to Puteoli. [14]There we found some brothers and were invited to stay with them for seven days. And so we came to Rome.

[15]The brothers there heard about us and came as far as

28:10
f Matt 15:6;
1 Tim 5:17

a 28:3 Lit. *his*

the Forum of Appius and the Three Taverns to meet us. When Paul saw them, he thanked God and felt encouraged. [16]When we came into Rome, Paul was allowed to live by himself with the soldier who was guarding him.[a]

Paul in Rome

[17]Three days later, he called the leaders of the Jews together. When they assembled, he said to them, "Brothers, although I haven't done anything against our people or the customs of our ancestors, I was arrested in Jerusalem and handed over to the Romans.[b] [18]They examined me and wanted to let me go because there was no reason for the death penalty in my case.[c] [19]But the Jews objected and forced me to appeal to the emperor, even though I have no charge to bring against my own people.[d] [20]That's why I asked to see you and speak with you, since it is for the hope of Israel that I'm wearing this chain."[e] [21]They told him, "We haven't received any letters from Judea about you, and none of the brothers coming here has reported or mentioned anything bad about you. [22]However, we would like to hear from you what you think, because everywhere people are talking against this sect."[f]

[23]So they set a day to meet with him and came in large numbers to see him where he was staying. From morning until evening he continued to explain the kingdom of God to them, trying to convince them about Jesus from the Law of Moses and the Prophets.[g] [24]Some of them were convinced by what he said, but others wouldn't believe.[h]

[25]They disagreed with one another as they were leaving, and Paul added a statement: "How well did the Holy Spirit speak to your ancestors through the prophet Isaiah! [26]He said,[i]

> 'Go to this people and say,
> "You will listen and listen
>   but never understand,
> and you will look and look
>   but never see!
> [27]For this people's heart has become dull,
>   and their ears are hard of hearing,

28:16
a Acts 24:25; 27:3

28:17
b Acts 21:33;
24:12-13; 25:8

28:18
c Acts 22:24;
24:10; 25:8; 26:31

28:19
d Acts 25:11

28:20
e Acts 26:6-7,23;
Eph 3:1; 4:1; 6:20;
2Tim 1:16; 2:9

28:22
f Lk 2:34;
Acts 24:5,14;
1Peter 2:12; 4:14

28:23
g Lk 24:27;
Acts 17:3; 19:8;
26:6,22

28:24
h Acts 14:4; 17:4;
19:9

28:26
i Isa 6:9; Jer 5:21;
Ezek 12:2;
Matt 13:14-15;
Mark 4:12;
Lk 8:10;
John 12:40;
Rom 11:8

28:28
a Matt 21:41,43;
Acts 13:46-47;
18:6; 22:21;
26:17-18;
Rom 11:11

and they have shut their eyes
> so that they may never see with their eyes,
and listen with their ears,
> and understand with their heart
and turn and let me heal them." '**a**

28You must understand that this salvation of God has been sent to the Gentiles, and they will listen."**b***a*

30For two whole years he lived in his own rented place and welcomed everyone who came to him. 31He continued to preach the kingdom of God and to teach about the Lord Jesus Christ with perfect boldness and freedom.*b*

28:31
b Acts 4:31;
Eph 6:19

---

a *28:27* Isa 6:9-10   **b** *28:28* Other mss. read *will listen. 29When he had said these words, the Jews left, arguing intensely among themselves.*

THE LETTER OF PAUL TO THE
ROMANS

Greetings from Paul

1 [1]From[a] Paul, a servant[b] of Jesus Christ,[c] called to be an apostle and set apart for the gospel of God,[a] [2]which he had already promised through his prophets in the Holy Scriptures.[b] [3]This gospel is about[d] his Son, who according to the flesh was a descendant of David,[c] [4]and according to the spirit[e] of holiness was proved to be the mighty Son of God by the resurrection from the dead—Jesus Christ our Lord.[d]

[5]Through him we have received grace and a commission as an apostle to bring about the obedience of faith among all the Gentiles for the sake of his name.[e] [6]You, too, are among those who have been called to belong to Jesus Christ. [7]To all God's loved ones in Rome,[f] who are called to be holy.[g] May grace and peace from God our Father and the Lord Jesus Christ be yours![f]

Paul's Prayer and Desire to Visit Rome

[8]First of all, I thank my God through Jesus Christ for all of you, because the news about your faith is spreading throughout the world.[g] [9]For God, whom I serve in my spirit by announcing the gospel[h] of his Son, is my witness that I never fail to mention you[h] [10]every time I pray, asking that somehow by God's will I may at last succeed in coming to you.[i] [11]For I am longing to see you in order to share with you some spiritual gift so that you may be strengthened,[j] [12]that is, that we may be mutually encouraged by each other's faith, both yours and mine.[k]

[13]I also want you to know, brothers, that I often planned to come to you, but I was prevented from doing so until now, so that I could reap a harvest among you, just as I have among the rest of the Gentiles.[l] [14]Both to Greeks and to

---

a 1:1 The Gk. lacks *From*   b 1:1 Or *slave*   c 1:1 Other mss. read *Christ Jesus*   d 1:3 Lit. *About*   e 1:4 Or *Spirit*   f 1:7 Other mss. lack *in Rome*
g 1:7 Or *saints*   h 1:9 Lit. *in the gospel*

1:1
a Acts 9:15; 13:2; 22:21; 1Cor 1:1; Gal 1:1,15; 1Tim 1:11; 2:7; 2Tim 1:11

1:2
b Acts 26:6; Rom 3:21; 16:26; Gal 3:8; Titus 1:2

1:3
c Matt 1:6,16; Lk 1:32; John 1:14; Acts 2:30; Gal 4:4; 2Tim 2:8

1:4
d Acts 13:33; Heb 9:14

1:5
e Acts 6:7; 9:15; Rom 12:3; 15:15; 16:26; 1Cor 15:10; Gal 1:15; 2:9; Eph 3:8

1:7
f Rom 9:24; 1Cor 1:2-3; 2Cor 1:2; Gal 1:3; 1Thes 4:7

1:8
g Rom 16:19; 1Cor 1:4; Phil 1:3; Col 1:3-4; 1Thes 1:2,8

1:9
h Acts 27:23; Rom 9:1; 2Cor 1:23; Phil 1:8; 1Thes 2:5; 3:10; 2Tim 1:3

1:10
i Rom 15:23,32; 1Thes 3:10; James 4:15

1:11
j Rom 15:29

1:12
k Titus 1:4; 2Peter 1:1

1:13
l Acts 16:7; Rom 15:23; Phil 4:17; 1Thes 2:18

1:14
a 1Cor 9:16

1:16
b Ps 40:9-10;
Mark 8:38;
Lk 2:30-32; 24:47;
Acts 3:26; 13:26,
46; Rom 2:9;
1Cor 1:18; 15:2;
2Tim 1:8

1:17
c Hab 2:4;
John 3:36;
Rom 3:21;
Gal 3:11; Phil 3:9;
Heb 10:38

1:18
d Acts 17:30;
Eph 5:6; Col 3:6

1:19
e John 1:9;
Acts 14:17

1:20
f Ps 19:1;
Acts 14:17; 17:27

1:21
g 2Kings 17:15;
Jer 2:5;
Eph 4:17-18

1:22
h Jer 10:14

1:23
i Deut 4:16;
Ps 106:20;
Isa 40:18,26;
Jer 2:11;
Ezek 8:10;
Acts 17:29

1:24
j Lev 18:22;
Ps 81:12;
Acts 7:42;
1Cor 6:18;
Eph 4:18-19;
1Thes 4:4;
2Thes 2:11-12;
1Peter 4:3

1:25
k Isa 44:20;
Jer 10:14; 13:25;
Amos 2:4;
1Thes 1:9;
1John 5:20

1:26
l Lev 18:22-23;
Eph 5:12;
Jude 1:10

barbarians,[a] both to wise and to foolish people, I am a debtor.[a] 15That's why I'm so eager to proclaim the gospel to you who live in Rome,[b] too.

16For I am not ashamed of the gospel, for it is God's power for the salvation of everyone who believes, of the Jew first and of the Greek as well.[b] 17For in it God's righteousness is being revealed from faith to faith, as it is written, "The just will live by faith."[c]c

God's Wrath against Sinful Humanity

18For God's wrath is being revealed from heaven against all the ungodliness and wickedness of those who in their wickedness suppress the truth.[d] 19For what can be known about God is clear to them, because God himself has made it clear to them.[e] 20Indeed, ever since the creation of the world, his invisible attributes—his eternal power and divine nature—have been understood and observed by what he made, so that people[d] are without excuse.[f]

21Although they knew God, they didn't honor him as God or give him thanks. Instead, their thoughts turned to worthless things,[e] and their ignorant hearts were darkened.[g] 22Though claiming to be wise, they became fools[h] 23and substituted the glory of the immortal God for images that looked like mortal human beings, birds, four-footed animals, and reptiles.[i]

24For this reason, God has given them over to impurity to follow the lusts[f] of their hearts and to dishonor their bodies with one another.[j] 25They have exchanged God's truth for a lie and have worshiped and served the creation rather than the Creator, who is blessed forever. Amen![k]

26For this reason, God has given them over to degrading passions. For their females have exchanged their natural sexual function for one that is unnatural,[l] 27and their males, too, have given up the natural sexual function of females and burned with lust for one another. Males commit indecent acts with males, and so they receive among themselves

---

a 1:14 I.e. uncultured people   b 1:15 Other mss. lack *who live in Rome*
c 1:17 Hab 2:4   d 1:20 Lit. *they*   e 1:21 Lit. *they became worthless in their thoughts*   f 1:24 Lit. *to impurity in the lusts*

the punishment they deserve for deviating from what is normal.[a]

28And so, because they did not think it worthwhile to retain the full knowledge of God, God has given them over to degraded minds to perform acts that should not be done.[a] 29They are filled with every kind of wickedness, evil, greed, and hatred. They are full of envy, murder, quarreling, deceit, and viciousness. They are gossips, 30slanderers, God-haters, haughty, arrogant, boastful, inventors of evil, disobedient to their parents, 31foolish, faithless, heartless, ruthless. 32Although they know God's just requirement—that those who practice such things deserve to die—they not only do these things but even applaud others who practice them.[b]

God Will Judge Everyone

2 1Therefore, you have no excuse—every one of you who judges. For when you pass judgment on another person, you condemn yourself, since you, the judge, practice the very same things.[c] 2Now we know that God's judgment justly falls[b] on those who practice such things. 3When you judge those who practice these things but then do them yourself, do you think you will escape God's judgment? 4Do you think so little of the riches of his kindness, forbearance, and patience, not realizing that it is God's kindness that is leading you to repentance?[d]

5But because of your stubborn and unrepentant heart you are storing up wrath for yourself on the day of wrath, when God's righteous judgment will be revealed.[e] 6For he will repay everyone according to what that person has done:[f] 7eternal life to those who strive for glory, honor, and immortality by patiently doing good; 8but wrath and fury for those who in their selfish pride refuse to believe the truth and practice wickedness instead.[g] 9There will be suffering and anguish for every person who practices doing evil, for Jews first and for Greeks as well.[h] 10But there will be glory, honor, and peace for every person who practices doing

---

a 1:27 Lit. *for their deviation*   b 2:2 Lit. *is according to the truth*

1:28
a Eph 5:4

1:32
b Ps 50:18;
Hos 7:3; Rom 2:2;
6:21

2:1
c 2Sam 12:5-7;
Matt 7:1-2;
John 8:9;
Rom 1:20

2:4
d Exod 34:6;
Isa 30:18;
Rom 3:25; 9:23;
Eph 1:7; 2:4,7;
2Peter 3:9,15

2:5
e Deut 32:34;
James 5:3

2:6
f Job 34:11;
Ps 62:12;
Prov 24:12;
Jer 17:10; 32:19;
Matt 16:27;
Rom 14:12;
1Cor 3:8;
2Cor 5:10;
Rev 2:23; 20:12;
22:12

2:8
g Job 24:13;
Rom 1:18;
2Thes 1:8

2:9
h Amos 3:2;
Lk 12:47-48;
1Peter 4:17

2:10
a 1Peter 1:7

2:11
b Deut 10:17;
2Chr 19:7;
Job 34:19;
Acts 10:34;
Gal 2:6; Eph 6:9;
Col 3:25;
1Peter 1:17

2:13
c Matt 7:21;
James 1:22-23,25;
1John 3:7

2:16
d Eccl 12:14;
Matt 25:31;
John 5:22; 12:48;
Acts 10:42; 17:31;
Rom 3:6; 16:25;
1Cor 4:5;
1Tim 1:11;
2Tim 2:8; 4:1,8;
1Peter 4:5;
Rev 20:12

2:17
e Isa 45:25; 48:2;
Mic 3:11;
Matt 3:9;
John 8:33,41;
Rom 9:4,6-7;
2Cor 11:22

2:18
f Deut 4:8;
Ps 147:19-20;
Phil 1:10

2:19
g Matt 15:14;
23:16-17,19,24;
John 9:34,40-41

2:20
h Rom 6:17;
2Tim 1:13; 3:5

2:21
i Ps 50:16;
Matt 23:3

2:22
j Mal 3:8

2:23
k Rom 2:17

2:24
l 2Sam 12:14;
Isa 52:5;
Ezek 36:20,23

2:25
m Gal 5:3

2:26
n Acts 10:34-35

2:27
o Matt 12:41-42

good, for Jews first and for Greeks as well.[a] [11]For God does not show partiality.[b]

[12]For all who have sinned apart from the Law will also perish apart from the Law, and all who have sinned under the Law will be judged by the Law. [13]Those who merely[a] hear the Law are not righteous in God's sight; those who do the Law will be justified.[c] [14]For whenever Gentiles, who do not possess the Law, do instinctively what the Law requires, they are a law to themselves, even though they do not have the Law. [15]They show that what the Law requires is written in their hearts, a fact to which their own consciences testify. And so their thoughts will either accuse or excuse them [16]on that day when God, through Jesus Christ, will judge people's secrets according to my gospel.[d]

Who Is a Jew?

[17]Now if you call yourself a Jew, and rely on the Law, and boast about God,[e] [18]and know his will, and determine what is best because you have been instructed in the Law;[f] [19]and if you are sure that you are a guide for the blind, a light to those in darkness,[g] [20]an instructor of ignorant people, and a teacher of the young because you have the full content of knowledge and truth in the Law[h]—[21]as you teach others, do you fail to teach yourself? As you preach against stealing, do you steal?[i] [22]As you forbid adultery, do you commit adultery? As you treat idols with disgust, do you rob temples?[j] [23]As you boast about the Law, do you dishonor God by breaking the Law?[k] [24]As it is written, "God's name is being blasphemed among the Gentiles because of you."[b][l]

[25]For circumcision is valuable only if you obey the Law. But if you break the Law, your circumcision has become uncircumcision.[m] [26]So if a man who is uncircumcised keeps the requirements of the Law, his uncircumcision will be regarded as circumcision, won't it?[n] [27]The man who is uncircumcised physically but who keeps the Law will condemn you who break the Law, even though you have the written Law[c] and circumcision.[o]

---

a 2:13 The Gk. lacks *merely*   **b** 2:24 Isa 52:5   **c** 2:27 Lit. *what is written*

28For a person is not a Jew because of his appearance, nor is circumcision something external and physical.*a* 29Rather, a person is a Jew inwardly, and circumcision is a matter of the heart—it is spiritual, not a written Law.**a** That person's praise will come from God, not from people.*b*

Everyone Is a Sinner

3 1What advantage, then, does the Jew have? Or what is the value of circumcision? 2There are all kinds of advantages. First of all, the Jews**b** were entrusted with the utterances of God.*c* 3What if some of them were unfaithful? Their unfaithfulness cannot cancel God's faithfulness, can it?*d* 4Of course not! God is true, even if everyone else is a liar. As it is written,*e*

"You are right when you speak,**c**
and win your case when you go into court."**d**

5But if our wrongdoing serves to confirm God's righteousness, what can we say? God is not unrighteous when he vents his wrath on us, is he? (I'm talking in human terms.)*f* 6Of course not! Otherwise, how could God judge the world?*g* 7For**e** if through my falsehood God's truthfulness increases to his glory, why am I still being condemned as a sinner? 8Or can we say—as some people slander us by claiming that we say—"Let us do evil so that good will come from it"? Their condemnation is deserved!*h*

9What, then, does this mean?**f** Are we Jews**g** any better off? Not at all! For we have already accused everyone, both Jews and Greeks, of being under the power of sin.**hi** 10As it is written,*j*

"Not even one person is righteous.
11   No one understands.
No one searches for God.
12   All have turned away.
Together they have become worthless.

---

a 2:29 Lit. *what is written*   **b** 3:2 Lit. *they*   **c** 3:4 Lit. *are justified in your words*   **d** 3:4 Ps 51:4   **e** 3:7 Other mss. read *But*   **f** 3:9 Lit. *What then?*   **g** 3:9 The Gk. lacks *Jews*   **h** 3:9 Lit. *under sin*

Marginal cross-references:

2:28
a Matt 3:9;
John 8:39;
Rom 9:6-7;
Gal 6:15; Rev 2:9

2:29
b Rom 7:6;
1Cor 4:5;
2Cor 3:6; 10:18;
Phil 3:3; Col 2:11;
1Thes 2:4;
1Peter 3:4

3:2
c Deut 4:7-8;
Ps 147:19-20;
Rom 2:18; 9:4

3:3
d Num 23:19;
Rom 9:6; 10:16;
11:29; 2Tim 2:13;
Heb 4:2

3:4
e Job 40:8;
Ps 51:4; 62:9;
116:11; John 3:33

3:5
f Rom 6:19;
Gal 3:15

3:6
g Gen 18:25;
Job 8:3; 34:17

3:8
h Rom 5:20; 6:1,
15

3:9
i Rom 3:23;
Gal 3:22

3:10
j Ps 14:1-3; 53:1

3:13
a Ps 5:9;
140:3 Jer 5:16

3:14
b Ps 10:7

3:15
c Prov 1:16;
Isa 59:7-8

3:18
d Ps 36:1

3:19
e Job 5:16;
Ps 107:42;
Ezek 16:63;
John 10:34; 15:25;
Rom 1:20; 2:1-2,
9,23

3:20
f Ps 143:2;
Acts 13:39;
Rom 7:7;
Gal 2:16; 3:11;
Eph 2:8-9;
Titus 3:5

3:21
g John 5:46;
Acts 15:11; 26:22;
Rom 1:2,17;
Phil 3:9;
Heb 11:4;
1 Peter 1:10

3:22
h Rom 10:12;
Gal 3:28; Col 3:11

3:23
i Rom 3:9; 11:32;
Gal 3:22

3:24
j Matt 20:28;
Rom 4:16;
Eph 1:7; 2:8;
Col 1:14;
1 Tim 2:6;
Titus 3:5,7;
Heb 9:12;
1 Peter 1:18-19

3:25
k Lev 16:15;
Acts 13:38-39;
17:30; Col 1:20;
1 Tim 1:15;
Heb 9:15;
1 John 2:2; 4:10

No one shows kindness, not even one
person!ᵃ

¹³Their throats are open graves. *a*

With their tongues they practice deception.ᵇ

The venom of poisonous snakes is under their lips.ᶜ

14   Their mouths are full of cursing and
bitterness.ᵈᵇ

¹⁵Their feet are swift to shed blood. *c*

16   There is ruin and misery wherever they go.ᵉ

¹⁷They have not learned the path to peace.ᶠ

18   There is no reverence for God before their eyes."ᵍᵈ

¹⁹Now we know that whatever the Law says applies to those who are under the Law, so that every mouth may be silenced and the whole world may be held accountable to God. *e* ²⁰For no human being can be justified in God'sʰ sight by means of the works prescribed by the Law. For through the Law comes the full knowledge of sin. *f*

God Gives Us Righteousness through Faith

²¹But now, apart from the Law, God's righteousness is revealed and is attested by the Law and the Prophetsᵍ— ²²God's righteousness through the faith of Jesus Christⁱ for all who believe. For there is no distinction,ʰ ²³since all have sinned and continue to fall short of God's glory.ⁱ ²⁴By his grace they are justified freely through the redemption that is in Christ Jesus,ʲ ²⁵whom God offered as a place where atonement by Christ'sʰ blood could occur through faith. He did this to demonstrateʲ his righteousness, because he had waited patiently to deal with sins committed in the past.ᵏ ²⁶He wanted to demonstrateʲ at the present time that he himself is righteous and that he justifies the person who has the faith of Jesus.ᵏ

²⁷What, then, is there to boast about? That has been

---

a *3:12* Ps 14:1-3; 53:1-3; Eccl 7:20   b *3:13* Ps 5:9   c *3:13* Ps 140:3
d *3:14* Ps 10:7   e *3:16* Lit. *in their paths*   f *3:17* Isa 59:7-8; Prov 1:16
g *3:18* Ps 36:1   h *3:20,3:25* Lit. *his*   i *3:22* Or *through faith in Jesus Christ*
j *3:25,3:26* Lit. *To demonstrate*   k *3:26* Or *faith in Jesus*

eliminated. On what principle? On that of works? No, but on the principle of faith.*a* 28For*a* we hold that a person is justified by faith apart from the works prescribed by the Law.*b* 29Is God the God of the Jews only? Isn't he also the God of the Gentiles? Yes, of the Gentiles also, 30since there is only one God. And it is he who will justify the circumcised on the basis of faith and the uncircumcised by the same faith.*c* 31Do we, then, abolish the Law by this faith? Of course not! Instead, we uphold the Law.

The Example of Abraham

4 1What, then, are we to say about Abraham, our ancestor according to the flesh?*d* 2For if Abraham was justified by works, he would have had something to boast about—though not before God.*e* 3For what does the Scripture say? "Abraham believed God, and it was credited to him as righteousness."*bf*

4Now to someone who works, wages are not considered a gift but an obligation.*g* 5But to someone who doesn't work, but simply believes in the one who justifies the ungodly, his faith is credited as righteousness.*h* 6Likewise, David also speaks of the blessedness of the person whom God regards as righteous apart from works:

> 7"How blessed are those whose iniquities are
>   forgiven*i*
> and whose sins are covered!
> 8How blessed is the person whose sins
>   the Lord will never charge against him!"*c*

9Now does this blessedness come to the circumcised alone, or also to the uncircumcised? For we say, "Abraham's faith was credited to him as righteousness."*b* 10Under what circumstances was his faith credited as righteousness?*d* Was he circumcised or uncircumcised? He had not been circumcised, but was uncircumcised. 11Afterward he received the mark of circumcision as a seal of the righteousness that he had by faith while he was still uncircumcised. Therefore, he

---

a*3:28* Other mss. read *Therefore*   **b***4:3,4:9* Gen 15:6   **c***4:8* Ps 32:1-2
d*4:10* Lit. *How was it credited?*

Marginal cross-references:

3:27
a Rom 2:17,23;
4:2; 1Cor 1:29,31;
Eph 2:9

3:28
b Acts 13:38-39;
Rom 3:20-22;
8:3;
Gal 2:16

3:30
c Rom 10:12-13;
Gal 3:8,20,28

4:1
d Isa 51:2;
Matt 3:9;
John 8:33,39;
2Cor 11:22

4:2
e Rom 3:20,27-28

4:3
f Gen 15:6;
Gal 3:6;
James 2:23

4:4
g Rom 11:6

4:5
h Josh 24:2

4:7
i Ps 32:1-2

4:11
a Gen 17:10;
Lk 19:9;
Rom 4:12,16;
Gal 3:7

is the ancestor of all who believe while uncircumcised and yet are regarded as righteous.*a* [12]He is also the ancestor of the circumcised—those who are not only circumcised but are also following the example of the faith that our father Abraham had before he was circumcised.

4:13
b Gen 17:4;
Gal 3:29

The Promise Comes through Faith

4:14
c Gal 3:18

[13]For the promise that he would inherit the world did not come to Abraham or to his descendants through the Law, but through the righteousness produced by faith.*b* [14]For if those who were given the Law*a* are the heirs, then faith is useless and the promise is worthless.*c* [15]For the Law brings about wrath. But where there is no Law, neither can there be any violation of it.*d*

4:15
d Rom 3:20; 5:13,
20; 7:8,10-11;
1Cor 15:56;
2Cor 3:7,9;
Gal 3:10,19;
1John 3:4

[16]Therefore, the promise is based*b* on faith so that it may be a matter of grace and may be guaranteed for all his descendants—not only for those who were given the Law,*a* but also for those who share Abraham's faith did, who is the father of us all.*e* [17]As it is written, "I have made you the father of many nations."*c* Abraham*d* acted in faith when he stood in God's presence, who gives life to the dead and calls into existence things that don't even exist.*f* [18]Hoping in spite of hopeless circumstances, he believed that he would become "the father of many nations,"*c* as he had been told:*e* "This is how many descendants you will have."*fg* [19]He didn't weaken in faith when he thought about his own body (which was already*g* as good as dead now that he was about a hundred years old) or about Sarah's inability to have children,*h* [20]nor did he doubt God's promise out of a lack of faith. Instead, he became strong in faith, gave glory to God, [21]and was absolutely convinced that God would do what he had promised.*i* [22]That's why his faith*h* "was credited to him as righteousness."*i*

4:16
e Isa 51:2;
Rom 3:24; 9:8;
Gal 3:22

4:17
f Gen 17:5;
Rom 8:11; 9:26;
1Cor 1:28;
Eph 2:1,5;
1Peter 2:10

4:18
g Gen 15:5

4:19
h Gen 17:17;
18:11;
Heb 11:11-12

4:21
i Ps 115:3;
Lk 1:37,45;
Heb 11:19

[23]Now the words "was credited to him" were written not only for him*j* [24]but also for us. Our faith will be regarded in

---

a *4:14,4:16* Lit. *those of the Law*   b *4:16* Lit. *it is based*   c *4:17,4:18* Gen 17:5   d *4:17* Lit. *He*   e *4:18* Lit. *according to what was said*   f *4:18* Gen 15:5   g *4:19* Other mss. lack *already*   h *4:22* Lit. *it*   i *4:22* Gen 15:6

4:23
j Rom 15:4;
1Cor 10:6,11

the same way,[a] if we believe in the one who raised from the dead Jesus our Lord,[a] 25who was handed over to death for our sins and was raised to life for our justification.[b]

We Enjoy Peace with God through Jesus

5 1Therefore, since we have been justified by faith, we have[b] peace with God through our Lord Jesus Christ.[c] 2Through him we have also obtained[c] access by faith[d] to this grace in which we stand, and we boast[e] in our hope of sharing God's glory.[d]

3Not only that, we also boast[f] in our sufferings, knowing that suffering produces endurance,[e] 4endurance produces character, and character produces hope.[f] 5This hope does not disappoint us,[g] because God's love has been poured into our hearts by the Holy Spirit, who has been given to us.[g]

6For while we were still helpless,[h] Christ died for ungodly people at just the right time.[h] 7It is rare for anyone to die for a righteous person, though somebody might be brave enough to die for a good person. 8But God proves his love for us by the fact that Christ died for us while we were still sinners.[i]

9Now that we have been justified by his blood, how much more will we be saved from wrath through him![j] 10For if we were reconciled to God through the death of his Son while we were enemies, how much more will we be saved by his life because we have been reconciled![k] 11Not only that, we continue to boast in God through our Lord Jesus Christ, through whom we have now received our reconciliation.[l]

Death in Adam, Life in Christ

12Therefore, just as sin came into the world through one man, and death came through sin, so death spread to everyone, because all have sinned.[m] 13Certainly sin was in the world before the Law was given,[i] but no record of sin is kept when there is no Law.[n] 14Still, death ruled from the

---

a 4:24 Lit. *It will be regarded*   **b** 5:1 Other mss. read *let us have*   **c** 5:2 Or *let us also obtain*   **d** 5:2 Other mss. lack *by faith*   **e** 5:2 Or *let us boast*
f 5:3 Or *let us also boast*   **g** 5:5 Or *does not put us to shame*   **h** 5:6 Or *weak*
i 5:13 The Gk. lacks *was given*

Cross-references (margin):

4:24
a Acts 2:24; 13:30

4:25
b Isa 53:5-6;
Rom 3:25; 5:6;
8:32; 1Cor 15:17;
2Cor 5:21;
Gal 1:4;
Heb 9:28;
1Peter 1:21; 2:24;
3:18

5:1
c Isa 32:17;
John 16:33;
Rom 3:28,30;
Eph 2:14;
Col 1:20

5:2
d John 10:9; 14:6;
1Cor 15:1;
Eph 2:18; 3:12;
Heb 3:6; 10:19

5:3
e Matt 5:11-12;
Acts 5:41;
2Cor 12:10;
Phil 2:17;
James 1:2-3,12;
1Peter 3:14

5:4
f James 1:12

5:5
g 2Cor 1:22;
Gal 4:6;
Eph 1:13-14;
Phil 1:20

5:6
h Rom 4:25; 5:8

5:8
i John 15:13;
1Peter 3:18;
1John 3:16;
4:9-10

5:9
j Rom 1:18; 3:25;
Eph 2:13;
1Thes 1:10;
Heb 9:14;
1John 1:7

5:10
k John 5:26; 14:19;
Rom 8:32;
2Cor 4:10-11;
5:18-19; Eph 2:16;
Col 1:20-21

5:11
l Rom 2:17;
3:29-30; Gal 4:9

5:12
m Gen 2:17; 3:6;
Rom 6:23;
1Cor 15:21

5:13
n Rom 4:15;
1John 3:4

5:14
a 1Cor 15:21-22,
45

time of Adam[a] to Moses, even over those who had not sinned in the same way Adam had when he disobeyed.[b] He is a type of the one who would come.[a]

[15]But God's free gift[c] is not like Adam's offense.[d] For if many people died as the result of one man's offense, how much more have God's grace and the free gift given through the kindness of one man, Jesus Christ, been showered on

5:15
b Isa 53:11;
Matt 20:28; 26:28

many people![b] [16]Nor can the free gift be compared to what came through the man who sinned.[e] For the sentence that followed one man's offense brought condemnation, but the free gift brought justification, even after many offenses. [17]For if, through one man, death ruled because of that man's

5:18
c John 12:32;
Heb 2:9

offense, how much more will those who receive such overflowing grace and the gift of righteousness rule in life because of one man, Jesus Christ!

[18]Therefore, just as one offense resulted in condemnation for everyone, so one act of righteousness results in justification and life for everyone.[c] [19]For just as through one

5:20
d Lk 7:47;
John 15:22;
Rom 3:20; 4:15;
7:8; Gal 3:19,23;
1 Tim 1:14

man's disobedience many people were made sinners, so through one man's obedience many people will be made righteous. [20]Then Law crept in so that the offense would increase. But where sin increased, grace increased even more.[d] [21]Just as sin ruled by bringing death,[f] so grace rules by bringing justification[g] that results in eternal life through Jesus Christ our Lord.

No Longer Sin's Slaves, but God's Slaves

6:1
e Rom 3:8,15

6 [1]What should we say then? Should we go on sinning so that grace may increase?[e] [2]Of course not! How can we who died as far as sin is concerned go on living in it?[f]

6:2
f Rom 6:11; 7:4;
Gal 2:19; 6:14

[3]Or don't you know that all of us who were baptized into union with Christ Jesus were baptized into his death?[g] [4]Therefore, through baptism we were buried with him into his death so that, just as Christ was raised from the dead by

6:3
g 1Cor 15:29;
Col 3:3;
1 Peter 2:24

---

a 5:14 Lit. *from Adam*   b 5:14 Lit. *in the likeness of Adam's disobedience*   c 5:15 Lit. *the free gift*   d 5:15 Lit. *the offense*   e 5:16 Lit. *nor is the gift like the man who sinned*   f 5:21 Lit. *ruled in death*   g 5:21 Lit. *through justification*

the Father's glory, we, too, should live an entirely new life.[a] [5]For if we have become united with him in a death like his, certainly we will also be united with him in a resurrection like his.[b] [6]We know that our old selves were crucified with him so that our sinful bodies might be rendered powerless and we might no longer be slaves to sin.[c] [7]For the person who has died has been freed from sin.[d]

[8]Now if we have died with Christ, we believe that we will also live with him,[e] [9]for we know that Christ, who was raised from the dead, will never die again; death no longer has power over him.[f] [10]For when he died, he died once and for all as far as sin is concerned. But now he is alive, and he lives for God.[g] [11]So you, too, must continually consider yourselves dead as far as sin is concerned, but alive to God in Christ Jesus.[a][h]

[12]Therefore, don't let sin rule your physical bodies so that you obey their desires.[i] [13]Stop offering[b] the parts of your body[c] to sin as instruments of unrighteousness. Instead, offer yourselves to God as people who have been brought from death to life and the parts of your body[c] as instruments of righteousness to God.[j] [14]For sin will not have power over you, because you are not under Law but under grace.[k]

[15]What, then, does this mean?[d] Should we go on sinning because we are not under Law but under grace? Of course not![l] [16]Don't you know that if you offer yourselves to someone as obedient slaves, you are slaves of the one whom you obey—either of sin, which leads to death, or of obedience, which leads to righteousness?[m] [17]But thank God that, though you were once slaves of sin, you became obedient from your hearts to that form of teaching with which you have been entrusted![n] [18]And since you have been freed from sin, you have become slaves of righteousness.[o]

[19]I'm speaking in human terms because of the frailty of your flesh. Just as you once offered the parts of your body[c] as slaves to impurity and to greater and greater disobedience, so now, in the same way, you must offer the parts of

---

[a]6:11 Other mss. read *Christ Jesus our Lord*   [b]6:13 Or *Don't offer*
[c]6:13,6:19 Lit. *your members*   [d]6:15 Lit. *What then?*

6:4
[a]John 2:11; 11:40;
Rom 8:11;
1Cor 6:14;
2Cor 13:4;
Gal 6:15;
Eph 4:22-24;
Col 2:12; 3:10

6:5
[b]Phil 3:10-11

6:6
[c]Gal 2:20; 5:24;
6:14; Eph 4:22;
Col 2:11; 3:5,9

6:7
[d]1Peter 4:1

6:8
[e]2Tim 2:11

6:9
[f]Rev 1:18

6:10
[g]Lk 20:38;
Heb 9:27-28

6:11
[h]Rom 6:2;
Gal 2:19

6:12
[i]Ps 19:13;
119:133

6:13
[j]Rom 7:5;
12:1 Col 3:5;
James 4:1;
1Peter 2:24; 4:2

6:14
[k]Rom 7:4,6; 8:2;
Gal 5:18

6:15
[l]1Cor 9:21

6:16
[m]Matt 6:24;
John 8:34;
2Peter 2:19

6:17
[n]2Tim 1:13

6:18
[o]John 8:32;
1Cor 7:22;
Gal 5:1;
1Peter 2:16

6:20
a John 8:34

6:21
b Rom 1:32; 7:5

6:22
c John 8:32

6:23
d Gen 2:17;
Rom 2:7; 5:12,17,
21; James 1:15;
1 Peter 1:4

7:2
e 1 Cor 7:39

7:3
f Matt 5:32

7:4
g Rom 8:2;
Gal 2:19; 5:18,22;
Eph 2:15;
Col 2:14

7:5
h Rom 6:13,21;
Gal 5:19;
James 1:15

7:6
i Rom 2:29;
2 Cor 3:6

7:7
j Exod 20:17;
Deut 5:21;
Acts 20:33;
Rom 3:20; 13:9

7:8
k Rom 4:15; 5:20;
1 Cor 15:56

your body[a] as slaves to righteousness that leads to sanctification. 20For when you were slaves of sin, you were free as far as righteousness was concerned.[a] 21What advantage did you get from doing those things you're now ashamed of? For those things ended in death.[b] 22But now that you have been freed from sin and have become God's slaves, the advantage you have is sanctification and, in the end, eternal life.[c] 23For the wages of sin is death, but the free gift of God is eternal life in union with Christ Jesus our Lord.[d]

Now We Are Released from the Law

7 1Don't you realize, brothers—for I am speaking to people who know the Law—that the Law can press its claims over a person only as long as he is alive? 2For a married woman is bound by the Law to her husband while he is living, but if her husband dies, she is released from the Law concerning her husband.[e] 3So while her husband is living, she will be called an adulterer if she lives with another man. But if her husband dies, she is free from this Law, so that she is not an adulterer if she marries another man.[f]

4In the same way, brothers, through Christ's body you have died as far as the Law is concerned, so that you may belong to another person, the one who was raised from the dead, and may bear fruit for God.[g] 5For while we were living in the flesh, sinful passions stirred up by the Law were at work in our bodies[b] to bear fruit for death.[h] 6But now we are released from the Law and are dead to what enslaved us so that we may serve in the new life of the Spirit, not under the old written code.[i]

The Law Shows Us What Sin Is

7What should we say, then? Is the Law sinful? Of course not! In fact, I wouldn't have known sin if it had not been for the Law. For I wouldn't have known what it means to covet if the Law hadn't said, "You must not covet."[c][j] 8But sin took the opportunity provided by this commandment and produced in me all kinds of sinful desires. Clearly, without the Law sin is dead.[k]

---

a *6:19* Lit. *your members*   **b** *7:5* Lit. *members*   **c** *7:7* Exod 20:17

⁹At one time I was alive without any connection to the Law.ᵃ But when this commandment came, sin became alive, ¹⁰and I died. I found that the commandment that was intended to bring life actually brought me death.ᵃ ¹¹For sin, taking the opportunity provided by the commandment, deceived me and used it to kill me. ¹²So the Law itself is holy, and the commandment is holy, just, and good.ᵇ

The Problem of the Sin That Lives in Us

¹³Now, did something good bring me death? Of course not! Rather, sin used something good to cause my death, so that sin would be recognized as sin. Through the commandment, sin became more sinful than ever. ¹⁴For we know that the Law is spiritual, but I am mere flesh, sold into slavery to sin.ᵇᶜ ¹⁵I don't understand what I'm doing. For I don't do what I want to do, but instead do what I hate.ᵈ ¹⁶Now if I do what I don't want to do, I agree that the Law is good. ¹⁷So I am no longer the one who is doing it, but the sin that lives in me is doing it.ᶜ

¹⁸For I know that nothing good lives in me, that is, in my flesh. Although I desire to do what is right, I can't do it.ᵉ ¹⁹For I don't do the good I want to do, but instead do the evil that I don't want to do. ²⁰But if I do what I don't want to do, I am no longer the one who is doing it, but the sin that lives in me is doing it.ᶜ

²¹So I find this to be a law: even when I want to do what is good, evil is present with me. ²²For I delight in the Law of God in my inner being,ᶠ ²³but I see in my bodyᵈ a different law waging war with the law in my mind and making me a prisoner of the law of sin that exists in my body.ᵉᵍ ²⁴What a miserable person I am! Who will rescue me from this body of death? ²⁵Thank God through Jesus Christ our Lord! So with my mind I serve the Law of God, but with my flesh I serve the law of sin.ʰ

ᵃ7:9 Lit. *without the Law*   ᵇ7:14 Lit. *sold under sin*   ᶜ7:17,7:20 The Gk. lacks *is doing it*   ᵈ7:23 Lit. *in my members*   ᵉ7:23 Lit. *the sin that lives in me*

7:10
ᵃLev 18:5;
Ezek 20:11,13,21;
2Cor 3:7

7:12
ᵇPs 19:8; 119:38,
137; 1Tim 1:8

7:14
ᶜ1Kings 21:20,25;
2Kings 17:17

7:15
ᵈGal 5:17

7:18
ᵉGen 6:5; 8:21

7:22
ᶠPs 1:2;
2Cor 4:16;
Eph 3:16;
Col 3:9-10

7:23
ᵍRom 6:13,19;
Gal 5:17

7:25
ʰ1Cor 15:57

God's Spirit Makes Us His Children

8 [1]So now there is no condemnation for those who are in union with Christ Jesus.[a][a] [2]For the law of the Spirit of life in Christ Jesus has set me[b] free from the law of sin and death.[b] [3]For God has done what the Law, weakened by the flesh, could not do: He sent his own Son in the likeness of sinful flesh to deal with sin. He condemned sin in the flesh[c] [4]so that the righteous requirement of the Law might be fulfilled in us, who do not live by our flesh but by the Spirit.[d]

[5]For those who live by their flesh set their minds on the things of the flesh. But those who live by the Spirit set their minds on the things of the Spirit.[e] [6]To set our minds on the flesh leads to death, but to set our minds on the Spirit leads to life and peace.[f] [7]That's why the mind that is set on the flesh is hostile toward God. It refuses to submit to the authority of God's Law because it is powerless to do so.[g] [8]Those who are under the control of the flesh can't please God.

[9]However, you are not under the control of the flesh but under the control of the Spirit, since God's Spirit lives in you. Whoever doesn't have the Spirit of Christ doesn't belong to him.[h] [10]If Christ is in you, your bodies are dead because of sin, but the Spirit is life because of righteousness. [11]And if the Spirit of the one who raised Jesus from the dead lives in you, then the one who raised Christ from the dead will also make your mortal bodies alive by his Spirit who lives in you.[i]

[12]So then, brothers, we don't owe it to the flesh to live the way the flesh wants us to live.[j] [13]If you live by the flesh, you are going to die, but if by the Spirit you continually put to death the activities of the body, you will live.[k] [14]For all who are led by God's Spirit are God's children.[l] [15]For you have not received a spirit of slavery that leads you into fear again. Instead, you have received a spirit of adoption by which we call out, "Abba![c] Father!"[m] [16]The Spirit himself

---

8:1
[a] Rom 8:4;
Gal 5:16,25

8:2
[b] John 8:36;
Rom 6:18,22;
7:24-25;
1Cor 15:45;
2Cor 3:6;
Gal 2:19; 5:1

8:3
[c] Acts 13:39;
Rom 3:20;
2Cor 5:21;
Gal 3:13;
Heb 7:18-19;
10:1-2,10,14

8:4
[d] Rom 8:1

8:5
[e] John 3:6;
1Cor 2:14;
Gal 5:22,25

8:6
[f] Rom 6:13,21;
Gal 6:8

8:7
[g] 1Cor 2:14;
James 4:4

8:9
[h] John 3:34;
1Cor 3:16; 6:19;
Gal 4:6; Phil 1:19;
1Peter 1:11

8:11
[i] Acts 2:24;
Rom 6:4-5;
1Cor 6:14;
2Cor 4:14;
Eph 2:5

8:12
[j] Rom 6:7,14

8:13
[k] Rom 8:6;
Gal 6:8; Eph 4:22;
Col 3:5

8:14
[l] Gal 5:18

8:15
[m] Isa 56:5;
Mark 14:36;
1Cor 2:12;
Gal 4:5-6;
2Tim 1:7;
Heb 2:15;
1John 4:18

---

a *8:1* Other mss. read *Christ Jesus, who do not live by their flesh but by the Spirit*   **b** *8:2* Other mss. read *you*   **c** *8:15* Abba is Aram. for *Father.*

testifies with our spirit that we are God's children.[a]
[17]Now if we are his children, we are also his heirs. We are
God's heirs and heirs together with Christ—if, in fact, we
share in his sufferings in order to share his glory.[b]

God's Spirit Helps Us

[18]For I consider that the sufferings of this present time
are not worth comparing to the glory that will soon be revealed to us.[c] [19]For the creation is eagerly waiting for God to
reveal his children,[d] [20]because the creation was subjected to
frustration, though not by its own choice. The one who subjected it did so in the hope[e] [21]that the creation itself would
also be set free from slavery to decay in order to share the
glorious freedom of God's children. [22]For we know that all
creation has been groaning with the pains of childbirth up to
the present time.[f]

[23]However, not only creation groans.[a] We, who have the
first fruits of the Spirit, also groan inwardly as we eagerly
wait for our adoption, the redemption of our bodies.[g] [24]For
we were saved with this hope in mind.[b] Now hope that is
seen is not really hope, for who hopes for what can be seen?[h]
[25]But if we hope for what we don't see, we eagerly wait for
it with patience.

[26]In the same way, the Spirit also helps us in our weakness, for we don't know how to pray as we should. But the
Spirit himself intercedes[c] with groans too deep for words,[i]
[27]and the one who searches our hearts knows the mind of
the Spirit, for the Spirit[d] intercedes for the saints according
to God's will.[e][j] [28]And we know that he works all things
together[f] for the good of those who love God—those who
are called according to his purpose.[k] [29]For those whom he
knew beforehand are the ones he had appointed to be conformed to the image of his Son, in order that he might be
the firstborn among many brothers.[l] [30]He also called those
whom he had appointed beforehand, and justified those

8:16
[a]2Cor 1:22; 5:5;
Eph 1:13; 4:30

8:17
[b]Acts 14:22;
26:18; Gal 4:7;
Phil 1:29;
2Tim 2:11-12

8:18
[c]2Cor 4:17;
1Peter 1:6-7; 4:13

8:19
[d]2Peter 3:13;
1John 3:2

8:20
[e]Gen 3:19;
Rom 8:22

8:22
[f]Jer 12:11

8:23
[g]Lk 20:36; 21:28;
2Cor 5:2,4-5;
Eph 1:14; 4:30

8:24
[h]2Cor 5:7;
Heb 11:1

8:26
[i]Zech 12:10;
Matt 20:22;
Eph 6:18;
James 4:3

8:27
[j]1Chr 28:9;
Ps 7:9; Prov 17:3;
Jer 11:20; 17:10;
20:12; Acts 1:24;
1Thes 2:4;
1John 5:14;
Rev 2:23

8:28
[k]Rom 9:11,23-24;
2Tim 1:9

8:29
[l]Exod 33:12,17;
Ps 1:6; Jer 1:5;
Matt 7:23;
John 17:22;
Rom 11:2;
2Cor 3:18;
Eph 1:5,11;
Phil 3:21;
Col 1:15,18;
2Tim 2:19;
Heb 1:6;
1Peter 1:2;
1John 3:2; Rev 1:5

---

[a]8:23 The Gk. lacks *groans*   [b]8:24 The Gk. lacks *in mind*   [c]8:26 Other
mss. read *intercedes for us*   [d]8:27 Lit. *he*   [e]8:27 Lit. *according to God*
[f]8:28 Or *that all things work together*; other mss. read *that God works all
things together*

8:30
a John 17:22;
Rom 1:6; 9:24;
1Cor 6:11;
Eph 2:6; 4:4;
Heb 9:15;
1Peter 2:9

8:31
b Num 14:9;
Ps 118:6

8:32
c Rom 4:25; 5:6,10

8:33
d Isa 50:8-9;
Rev 12:10-11

8:34
e Job 34:29;
Mark 16:19;
Col 3:1; Heb 1:3;
7:25; 8:1; 9:24;
12:1; 1Peter 3:22;
1John 2:1

8:36
f Ps 44:22;
1Cor 15:30-31;
2Cor 4:11

8:37
g 1Cor 15:57;
2Cor 2:14;
1John 4:4; 5:4-5;
Rev 12:11

8:38
h Eph 1:21;
6:12 Col 1:16;
2:15; 1Peter 3:22

9:1
i Rom 1:9;
2Cor 1:23; 11:31;
12:19; Gal 1:20;
Phil 1:8; 1Tim 2:7

9:2
j Rom 10:1

9:3
k Exod 32:32

9:4
l Exod 4:22;
Deut 7:6; 14:1;
1Sam 4:21;
1Kings 8:11;
Ps 63:2;
78:61; 147:19;
Jer 31:9;
Acts 3:25; 13:32;
Rom 3:2;
Eph 2:12;
Heb 8:8-10; 9:1

whom he had called, and glorified those whom he had justified.[a]

Nothing Can Separate Us from God's Love

[31] What can we say about all of this? If God is for us, who can be against us?[b] [32] God[a] didn't spare his own Son but gave him up for all of us. Surely he will give us everything else along with him, won't he?[c]

[33] Who can bring an accusation against God's chosen people? God has justified them![d] [34] Who can condemn them? Christ Jesus has died, and more importantly, he has been raised and is seated at the right hand of God. He is the one who intercedes for us![e]

[35] Who can separate us from Christ's love? Can trouble, distress, persecution, hunger, nakedness, danger, or a sword?[b] [36] As it is written,[f]

> "We are being killed all day long because of you.
> We are thought of as sheep to be
> slaughtered."[c]

[37] No, in all these things we are more than conquerors through the one who loved us.[g] [38] For I am convinced that neither death, nor life, nor angels, nor rulers, nor things present, nor things to come, nor powers,[h] [39] nor anything above, nor anything below, nor anything else can separate us from the love of God in Christ Jesus our Lord.

Paul's Concern for the Jewish People

9 [1] I'm telling the truth as one who is in union with Christ. I'm not lying, for my conscience, enlightened by the Spirit, supports me in this.[i] [2] I have deep sorrow and endless heartache,[j] [3] for I wish I could be condemned[d] and cut off from Christ for the sake of my own brothers, my relatives according to the flesh.[k]

[4] They are Israelites. To them belong the adoption, the glory, the covenants,[e] the giving of the Law, the worship, and the promises.[l] [5] To them belong the patriarchs, and from

---

a 8:32 Lit. *He*   b 8:35 I.e. a violent death   c 8:36 Ps 44:22   d 9:3 Or *accursed*   e 9:4 Other mss. read *the covenant*

them, according to the flesh, Christ[a] descended, who is God over all, blessed forever! Amen.[a]

[6]But it is not as though the word of God has failed. For not all Israelites truly belong to Israel,[b] [7]and not all of Abraham's descendants are his true descendants. Instead, "It is through Isaac that descendants will be named for you."[bc] [8]That is, it is not the children of natural descent who are God's children. Instead, the children of the promise are regarded as descendants.[d]

[9]For this is the language of promise: "At this time I will return, and Sarah will have a son."[ce] [10]Not only that, but Rebecca became pregnant by our ancestor Isaac.[f] [11]Before their children[d] had been born or had done anything good or bad (so that God's plan of election might continue to operate[g] [12]according to his calling and not by works), Rebecca[e] was told, "The older child will serve the younger one."[fh] [13]As it is written, "Jacob I loved, but Esau I hated."[gi]

[14]What can we say? God isn't unrighteous, is he? Of course not![j] [15]For he says to Moses, "I will be merciful to the person I want to be merciful to, and I will be kind to the person I want to be kind to."[hk] [16]Therefore, God's choice[i] doesn't depend on a person's will or effort, but on God himself, who shows mercy. [17]For the Scripture says to Pharaoh,[l]

"I have raised you up for this reason:
  to demonstrate my power through you,
so that my name may be proclaimed
    throughout the earth."[j]

[18]Therefore, God[k] has mercy on whomever he chooses, and he hardens the heart of whomever he chooses.

God Chose People Who Are Not Jewish

[19]You may ask me, "Why does God still find fault with anybody?[l] For who can resist his will?"[m] [20]On the contrary,

---

a[9:5] I.e. the Messiah   b[9:7] Gen 21:12   c[9:9] Gen 18:10, 14   d[9:11] Lit. *they*   e[9:12] Lit. *she*   f[9:12] Gen 25:23   g[9:13] Mal 1:2-3   h[9:15] Exod 33:19   i[9:16] Lit. *it*   j[9:17] Exod 9:16   k[9:18] Lit. *he*   l[9:19] Lit. *Why does he still find fault?*

9:5
a Deut 10:15;
Jer 23:6; Lk 3:23;
John 1:1;
Acts 20:28;
Rom 1:3; 11:28;
Heb 1:8;
1 John 5:20

9:6
b Num 23:19;
John 8:39;
Rom 2:28-29; 3:8;
4:12,16; Gal 6:16

9:7
c Gen 21:12;
Gal 4:23;
Heb 11:18

9:8
d Gal 4:28

9:9
e Gen 18:10,14

9:10
f Gen 25:21

9:11
g Rom 4:17; 8:28

9:12
h Gen 25:23

9:13
i Deut 21:15;
Prov 13:24;
Mal 1:2-3;
Matt 10:37;
Lk 14:26;
John 12:25

9:14
j Deut 32:4;
2 Chr 19:7;
Job 8:3; 34:10;
Ps 92:15

9:15
k Exod 33:19

9:17
l Exod 9:16;
Gal 3:8,22

9:19
m 2 Chr 20:6;
Job 9:12; 23:13;
Dan 4:35

9:20
a Isa 29:16; 45:9;
64:8

9:21
b Prov 16:4;
Jer 18:6;
2Tim 2:20

9:22
c 1Thes 5:9;
1Peter 2:8;
Jude 1:4

9:23
d Rom 2:4;
8:28-30; Eph 1:7;
Col 1:27

9:24
e Rom 3:29

9:25
f Hos 2:23;
1Peter 2:10

9:26
g Hos 1:10

9:27
h Isa 10:22-23;
Rom 11:5

9:28
i Isa 28:22

9:29
j Isa 1:9; 13:19;
Jer 50:40;
Lam 3:22

who you are—mere man that you are—to talk back to God? Can an object that was molded say to the one who molded it, "Why did you make me like this?"*a* 21A potter has the right to do what he wants to with his clay, doesn't he? He can make something for a special occasion or something for ordinary use from the same lump.*b*

22If God wants to demonstrate his wrath and reveal his power, can't he be extremely patient with the objects of his wrath that are made for destruction?*c* 23Can't he also reveal his glorious riches to the objects of his mercy that he has prepared ahead of time for glory?*d* 24This includes us whom he has called, not only Jews but Gentiles as well.*e* 25As he says in Hosea,*f*

> "Those who are not my people
>   I will call my people,
> and the one who was not loved
>   I will call my loved one.**a**
>   26In the very place where it was said to them,*g*
>   'You are not my people,'
>   they will be called children of the
>   living God."**b**

27Isaiah also calls out concerning Israel,*h*

> "Although the descendants of Israel
>   are as numerous as the grains of sand on the
>   seashore,
>   only a few will be saved.
>   28For the Lord will carry out his plan*i*
>   and shorten it in righteousness,**c**
> because he will carry out his plan on the earth
>   decisively."**d**

29And as Isaiah predicted,*j*

> "If the Lord of the Heavenly Armies
>   had not left us some descendants,
> we would have become like Sodom

---

a 9:25 Hos 2:23   **b** 9:26 Hos 1:10   **c** 9:28 Other mss. lack *in righteousness*
d 9:28 Isa 10:22-23

and would have been compared to
Gomorrah."[a]

9:30
[a] Rom 1:17; 4:11;
10:20

[30]So what can we say? Gentiles, who were not seeking righteousness, have attained righteousness, the righteousness that comes through faith.[a] [31]But Israel, who did seek the righteousness that is based on the Law, did not arrive at that Law.[b] [32]Why not? Because they didn't seek it on the basis of faith, but as if it were based on works. They stumbled over the stone that causes people to stumble.[c] [33]As it is written,[d]

9:31
[b] Rom 10:2; 11:7;
Gal 5:4

9:32
[c] Lk 2:34;
1Cor 1:23

"Look! I am placing a stone in Zion
that people will stumble over,
a large rock that will make them fall.
Whoever believes in him will not be
ashamed."[b]

9:33
[d] Ps 118:22;
Isa 8:14; 28:16;
Matt 21:42;
Rom 10:11;
1Peter 2:6-8

The Person Who Believes Will Be Saved

10 [1]Brothers, my heart's desire and prayer to God on behalf of the Jews[c] is that they would be saved. [2]I can testify on their behalf that they have a zeal for God, but it is not in keeping with full knowledge.[e] [3]For they are ignorant of the righteousness that comes from God while they try to establish their own, and they have not submitted to God's righteousness.[f] [4]For Christ is the culmination[d] of the Law as far as righteousness is concerned for everyone who believes.[g]

[5]For Moses writes about the righteousness that comes from the Law as follows: "The person who obeys these things will find life in them."[e][h] [6]But the righteousness that comes from faith says, "Don't say in your heart, 'Who will go up to heaven?' (that is, to bring Christ down),[i] [7]or 'Who will go down into the depths?' (that is, to bring Christ back from the dead)." [8]But what does it say? "The message is near you. It's in your mouth and in your heart."[f] This is the message of faith that we proclaim.[j]

[9]So if you declare with your mouth that Jesus is Lord,

10:2
[e] Acts 21:20; 22:3;
Rom 9:31;
Gal 1:14; 4:17

10:3
[f] Rom 1:17; 9:30;
Phil 3:9

10:4
[g] Matt 5:17;
Gal 3:24

10:5
[h] Lev 18:5;
Neh 9:29;
Ezek 20:11,13,21;
Gal 3:12

10:6
[i] Deut 30:12-13

10:8
[j] Deut 30:14

---

a 9:29 Isa 1:9   b 9:33 Isa 28:16   c 10:1 Lit. *on behalf of them*   d 10:4 Or *end*   e 10:5 Lev 18:5   f 10:8 Deut 9:4; 30:12-14

and believe in your heart that God raised him from the dead, you will be saved.[a] [10]For a person believes with his heart and is justified, and a person declares with his mouth and is saved. [11]For the Scripture says, "Whoever believes in him will not be ashamed."[ab] [12]For there is no difference between Jews and Greeks, because they all have the same Lord, who gives richly to all who call on him.[c] [13]So then, "Everyone who calls on the name of the Lord will be saved."[bd]

[14]But how can people[c] call on someone they have not believed? And how can they believe in someone they have not heard about? And how can they hear without someone proclaiming him?[e] [15]And how can they proclaim him without being sent? As it is written,[f]

> "How beautiful are the feet of those
> who bring the good news!"[d]

[16]But not everyone has obeyed the gospel. For Isaiah asks, "Lord, who has believed our message?"[eg] [17]So faith comes from listening, and listening comes through the word of Christ.[f]

[18]But I ask, "Didn't they hear?" Certainly they did! In fact,[h]

> "Their voice has gone out into the whole world,
> and their words to the ends of the earth."[g]

[19]Again I ask, "Didn't Israel understand?" Moses was the first to say,[i]

> "I will make you jealous
> of those who are not a nation.
> I will make you angry
> about a nation that doesn't understand."[h]

[20]Isaiah said very boldly,[j]

10:9
[a] Matt 10:32; Lk 12:8; Acts 8:37

10:11
[b] Isa 28:16; 49:23 Jer 17:7; Rom 9:33

10:12
[c] Acts 10:36; 15:9; Rom 3:22,29; Gal 3:28; Eph 1:7; 2:4,7; 1 Tim 2:5

10:13
[d] Joel 2:32; Acts 2:21; 9:14

10:14
[e] Titus 1:3

10:15
[f] Isa 52:7; Nah 1:15

10:16
[g] Isa 53:1; John 12:38; Rom 3:3; Heb 4:2

10:18
[h] 1 Kings 18:10; Ps 19:4; Matt 4:8; 24:14; 28:19; Mark 16:15; Col 1:6,23

10:19
[i] Deut 32:21; Rom 11:11; Titus 3:3

10:20
[j] Isa 65:1; Rom 9:30

---

a 10:11 Isa 28:16 b 10:13 Joel 2:32 c 10:14 Lit. they d 10:15 Isa 52:7 e 10:16 Isa 53:1 f 10:17 Other mss. read of God g 10:18 Ps 19:4 h 10:19 Deut 32:21

"I was found by those who weren't looking
　　　　for me.
I was revealed to those who weren't asking
　　　　for me."^a

10:21
a Isa 65:2

²¹Then he said about Israel,^a

"All day long I have stretched out my hands
to a disobedient and rebellious people."^b

God's Love for the Jews

11:1
b 1Sam 12:22;
Jer 31:37;
2Cor 11:22;
Phil 3:5

11 ¹So I ask, "God hasn't rejected his people, has he?" Of course not! I'm an Israelite myself, a descendant of Abraham from the tribe of Benjamin.^b ²God hasn't rejected his people whom he chose^c long ago. Don't you know what the Scripture says in the story about Elijah,^d when he pleads with God against Israel?^c ³"Lord, they've killed your prophets and demolished your altars. I'm the only one left, and they're trying to take my life."^{ed} ⁴But what was the divine reply to him? "I've kept 7,000 people for myself who have not knelt to worship Baal."^{fe} ⁵So it is at the present time: there is a remnant, chosen by grace.^f ⁶But if this was by grace, then it wasn't on the basis of works. Otherwise, grace would no longer be grace.^g

11:2
c Rom 8:29

11:3
d 1Kings 19:10,14

11:4
e 1Kings 19:18

11:5
f Rom 9:27

⁷What does this mean?^g It means that Israel failed to obtain what it was striving for, but those who were chosen obtained it. However, the rest were hardened.^h ⁸As it is written,ⁱ

11:6
g Deut 9:4-5;
Rom 4:4-5;
Gal 5:4

11:7
h Rom 9:31; 10:3

"To this day God has given them a spirit of deep
　　　　sleep.^h
Their eyes don't see, and their ears don't
　　　　hear."ⁱ

⁹And David says,^j

"Let their table become a snare and a trap,

11:8
i Deut 29:4;
Isa 6:9; 29:10;
Jer 5:21;
Ezek 12:2;
Matt 13:14;
John 12:40;
Acts 28:26-27

---

a *10:20* Isa 65:1　　**b** *10:21* Isa 65:2 (LXX)　　**c** *10:2* Lit. *knew*　　**d** *10:2* Lit. *says in Elijah*　　**e** *11:3* 1 Kings 19:10, 14　　**f** *11:4* 1 Kings 19:18　　**g** *11:7* Lit. *What then?*　　**h** *11:8* I.e. an attitude of unresponsiveness　　**i** *11:8* Deut 29:4; Isa 29:10

11:9
j Ps 69:22

a stumbling block and a punishment for them.
¹⁰Let their eyes be darkened so that they
                cannot see,ᵃ
        and keep their backs forever bent."ᵃ

¹¹So I ask, "They haven't stumbled so as to fall, have they?" Of course not! On the contrary, because of their stumbling salvation has come to the Gentiles to make the Jewsᵇ jealous.ᵇ ¹²Now if their stumbling means riches for the world, and if their fall means riches for the Gentiles, how much more will their full inclusion mean!

¹³I am now speaking to you Gentiles. Because I am an apostle to the Gentiles, I am glorifying my ministryᶜ ¹⁴so that I can make my peopleᶜ jealous and save some of them.ᵈ ¹⁵For if their rejection means the reconciliation of the world, what will their acceptance mean but life from the dead? ¹⁶If the first part of the dough is holy, the whole batch is, too. If the root is holy, the branches are, too.ᵉ

¹⁷Now if some of the branches have been broken off, and you, a wild olive branch, have been grafted in their place to share the rich root of the olive tree,ᶠ ¹⁸don't boast about being better than the other branches.ᵈ If you boast, remember that you don't support the root, but the root supports you.ᵍ ¹⁹You say, "Branches were cut off so that I could be grafted in." ²⁰That's right! They were broken off because of their unbelief, but you remain only because of faith. So don't be arrogant, but be afraid!ᵉʰ ²¹If God didn't spare the natural branches, he certainly won't spare you either.

²²Note, then, the kindness and severity of God: his severity toward those who fell, but God's kindness toward you—if you continue in his kindness. Otherwise, you, too, will be cut off.ⁱ ²³If the Jewsᶠ do not continue in their unbelief, they will be grafted in again, because God is able to graft them in.ʲ ²⁴For if you have been cut off from what is

---

a *11:10* Ps 69:22-23; 35:8   **b** *11:11* Lit. *them*   **c** *11:14* Lit. *flesh*
d *11:18* Lit. *don't brag about the branches*   **e** *11:20* Or *be reverent*
f *11:23* Lit. *they*

naturally a wild olive tree and, contrary to nature, have
been grafted into a cultivated olive tree, how much easier it
will be for these natural branches to be grafted back into
their own olive tree!

25For I want you to understand this secret, brothers, so
that you won't claim to be wiser than you are. A partial
hardening has come on Israel until the full number of the
Gentiles is included.ᵃ 26In this way, all Israel will be saved.
As it is written,ᵇ

> "The Deliverer will come from Zion.
>   He will remove ungodliness from Jacob.
> 27This is my covenant with themᶜ
>   when I take away their sins."ᵃ

28As regards the gospel, they are enemies for your sake.
But as regards election, they are loved because of their an-
cestors.ᵈ 29For God's gifts and calling never change.ᵉ 30For
just as you disobeyed God in the past but now have received his mercy because of their disobedience,ᶠ 31so they,
too, have disobeyed in the present so that they mayᵇ receive
mercy because of the mercy shown to you. 32For God has
locked all people in the prison of their own disobedience in
order to have mercy on them all.ᵍ

33O how deep are God's riches, wisdom, and knowledge! How impossible to explain his judgments or to understand his ways!ʰ

> 34"Who has known the mind of the Lord?ⁱ
>   Who has become his adviser?ᶜ
> 35Who has given him somethingʲ
>   only to have him pay it back?"ᵈ

36For everything is from him, by him, and for him. Glory
belongs to him forever! Amen.ᵏ

ᵃ11:27 Isa 59:20-21   ᵇ11:31 Other mss. read *may now*   ᶜ11:34 Isa
40:13 (LXX)   ᵈ11:35 Job 41:3

11:25
ᵃLk 21:24;
Rom 12:7,16;
2Cor 3:14;
Rev 7:9

11:26
ᵇPs 14:7;
Isa 59:20

11:27
ᶜIsa 27:9;
Jer 31:31;
Heb 8:8; 10:16

11:28
ᵈDeut 7:8; 9:5;
10:15

11:29
ᵉNum 23:19

11:30
ᶠEph 2:2; Col 3:7

11:32
ᵍRom 3:9;
Gal 3:22

11:33
ʰJob 11:7;
Ps 36:6; 92:5

11:34
ⁱJob 15:8; 36:22;
Isa 40:13;
Jer 23:18;
1Cor 2:16

11:35
ʲJob 35:7; 41:11

11:36
ᵏ1Cor 8:6;
Gal 1:5; Col 1:16;
1Tim 1:17;
2Tim 4:18;
Heb 13:21;
1Peter 5:11;
2Peter 3:18;
Jude 1:25; Rev 1:6

12:1
a Ps 50:13-14;
Rom 6:13,16,19;
1Cor 6:13,20;
2Cor 10:1;
Heb 10:20;
1Peter 2:5
12:2
b Eph 1:18; 4:23;
5:10,17;
Col 1:21-22; 3:10;
1Thes 4:3;
1Peter 1:14;
1John 2:15
12:3
c Prov 25:27;
Eccl 7:16;
Rom 1:5; 11:20;
15:15; 1Cor 3:10;
12:7,11; 15:10;
Gal 2:9; Eph 3:2,
7-8; 4:7
12:4
d 1Cor 12:12;
Eph 4:16
12:5
e 1Cor 10:17;
12:20,27;
Eph 1:23; 4:25
12:6
f Acts 11:27;
Rom 4:3;
1Cor 12:4,10,28;
13:2; 14:1,6,29,
31; 1Peter 4:10-11
12:7
g Acts 13:1;
Gal 6:6; Eph 4:11;
1Tim 5:17
12:8
h Matt 6:1-3;
Acts 15:32; 20:28;
1Cor 14:3;
2Cor 9:7;
1Tim 5:17;
Heb 13:7,24;
1Peter 5:2
12:9
i Ps 34:14; 36:4;
97:10; Amos 5:15;
1Tim 1:5;
1Peter 1:22
12:10
j Phil 2:3;
Heb 13:1;
1Peter 1:22; 2:17;
3:8; 5:5;
2Peter 1:7
12:12
k Lk 10:20; 18:1;
21:19; Acts 2:42;
12:5; Rom 5:2;
15:13; Eph 6:18;
Phil 3:1; 4:4;
Col 4:2;
1Thes 2:17; 5:16;
1Tim 6:11;
Heb 3:6; 10:36;
12:1 James 1:4;
5:7;

Dedicate Your Lives to God

12 [1]Therefore, brothers, because of God's mercies, I urge you to offer your bodies as living sacrifices that are holy and pleasing to God, for this is a reasonable way for you to worship.[aa] [2]Stop being[b] conformed to this world, but continue to be transformed by the renewing of your minds so that you may be able to determine what is God's will—what is proper,[c] pleasing, and perfect.[b]

[3]Because of the grace given to me, I ask every one of you not to think of yourself more highly than you should think, but to have a sober view of yourself, based on the measure of faith that God has assigned each of you.[c] [4]We have many parts in one body, but these parts don't all have the same function.[d] [5]In the same way, even though we are many people, we are one body in Christ and individual parts connected to each other.[e] [6]We have different gifts based on the grace that was given to us. So if your gift is prophecy, use your gift[d] in proportion to your faith.[f] [7]If your gift is serving, devote yourself to serving others.[e] If it is teaching, devote yourself to teaching others.[fg] [8]If it is encouraging, devote yourself to encouraging others.[g] If it is sharing, share generously.[h] If it is leading, lead enthusiastically.[i] If it is helping, help cheerfully.[jh]

[9]Your love must be without hypocrisy. Hate what is evil. Hold on to what is good.[i] [10]Be devoted to each other with mutual affection. Excel in showing respect for each other.[j] [11]Don't be lazy in showing such devotion. Be on fire with the Spirit. Serve the Lord.[k] [12]Be joyful in hope. Be patient in trouble. Be persistent in prayer.[k] [13]Supply the needs of the saints. Extend hospitality to strangers.[l]

[14]Bless those who persecute you. Keep on blessing them,

1Peter 2:19-20; 4:13 **12:13** *l* 1Cor 16:1; 2Cor 9:1,12; 1Tim 3:2; Titus 1:8; Heb 6:10; 13:2,16; 1Peter 4:9; 1John 3:17

---

a 12:1 Lit. *to God, your reasonable worship*   **b** 12:2 Or *Don't be*   **c** 12:2 Or *good*   **d** 12:6 Lit. *If prophecy*   **e** 12:7 Lit. *If serving, in serving*   **f** 12:7 Lit. *If teaching, in teaching*   **g** 12:8 Lit. *If encouraging, in encouragement*   **h** 12:8 Lit. *The one who shares, with generosity*   **i** 12:8 Lit. *The one who leads, with enthusiasm*   **j** 12:8 Lit. *The one who helps, with cheerfulness*   **k** 12:11 Other mss. read *the time*

and never curse them.[a] [15]Rejoice with those who are rejoicing. Cry with those who are crying.[b] [16]Live in harmony with each other. Don't be arrogant, but associate with humble people. Don't think that you are wiser than you really are.[c]

[17]Don't pay anyone back with evil for the evil he does to you.[a] Instead, focus your thoughts on what is right in the sight of all people.[d] [18]If possible, so far as it depends on you, live in peace with all people.[e] [19]Don't take revenge, dear friends. Instead, leave room for God's[b] wrath. For it is written, "Vengeance belongs to me. I will pay them back, says the Lord."[c][f] [20]But "if your enemy is hungry, feed him. If he is thirsty, give him a drink. If you do this, you will pile burning coals on his head."[d][g] [21]Don't be conquered by evil, but conquer evil with good.

Obey Your Government

13 [1]Every person must be subject to the governing authorities, for no authority exists except by God's permission.[e] The existing authorities have been established by God,[h] [2]so that whoever resists the authorities opposes what God has established, and those who resist will bring judgment on themselves.[i]

[3]For the authorities are not a terror to good conduct, but to bad. Would you like to live without being afraid of the authorities? Then do what is right, and you will receive their approval.[j] [4]For they are God's servants working for your good. But if you do what is wrong, you should be afraid, for they have the right to bear the sword.[f] Indeed, they are God's servants to execute wrath on anyone who does wrong. [5]Therefore, it is necessary for you to be subject, not only because of God's[b] wrath but also because of your own conscience.[k]

[6]That is also why you pay taxes. For rulers[g] are God's servants faithfully devoting themselves to their work.[h] [7]Pay everyone whatever you owe them—taxes to whom taxes are

---

12:14
[a]Matt 5:44;
Lk 6:28; 23:34;
Acts 7:60;
1Cor 4:12;
1Peter 2:23; 3:9

12:15
[b]1Cor 12:26

12:16
[c]Ps 131:1-2;
Prov 3:7; 26:12;
Isa 5:21; Jer 45:5;
Rom 11:25; 15:5;
1Cor 1:10;
Phil 2:2; 3:16;
1Peter 3:8

12:17
[d]Prov 20:22;
Matt 5:39;
Rom 14:16;
2Cor 8:21;
1Thes 5:15;
1Peter 3:9

12:18
[e]Mark 9:50;
Rom 14:19;
Heb 12:14

12:19
[f]Lev 19:18;
Deut 32:35;
Prov 24:29;
Rom 12:17;
Heb 10:30

12:20
[g]Exod 23:4-5;
Prov 25:21-22;
Matt 5:44

13:1
[h]Prov 8:15-16;
Dan 2:21; 4:32;
John 19:11;
Titus 3:1;
1Peter 2:13

13:2
[i]Titus 3:1

13:3
[j]1Peter 2:14; 3:13

13:5
[k]Eccl 8:2;
1Peter 2:19

13:7
a Matt 22:21;
Mark 12:17;
Lk 20:35

13:8
b Rom 13:10;
Gal 5:14;
Col 3:14;
1 Tim 1:5;
James 2:8

13:9
c Exod 20:13;
Lev 19:18;
Deut 5:17;
Matt 19:18; 22:39;
Mark 12:31;
Gal 5:14;
James 2:8

13:10
d Matt 22:40;
Rom 13:8

13:11
e 1 Cor 15:34;
Eph 5:14;
1 Thes 5:5-6

13:12
f Eph 5:11; 6:13;
Col 3:8; 1 Thes 5:8

13:13
g Prov 23:20;
Lk 21:34;
1 Cor 6:9; Eph 5:5;
Phil 4:8;
1 Thes 4:12;
James 3:14;
1 Peter 2:12; 4:3

13:14
h Gal 3:27; 5:16;
Eph 4:24;
Col 3:10;
1 Peter 2:11

14:1
i Rom 15:1,7;
1 Cor 8:9,11; 9:22

14:2
j Rom 14:14;
1 Cor 10:25;
1 Tim 4:4;
Titus 1:15

14:3
k Col 2:16

14:4
l James 4:12

due, tolls to whom tolls are due, respect to whom respect is due, honor to whom honor is due. [a]

Love One Another

[8] Stop owing[a] anyone anything—except to love one another. For the one who loves another has fulfilled the Law. [b] [9] For the commandments, "You must not commit adultery; you must not murder; you must not steal; you must not covet," [b] and every other commandment are summed up in this statement: "Love your neighbor as yourself." [cc] [10] Love never does anything that is harmful to a neighbor. Therefore, love fulfills the Law. [d]

Live in the Light of Christ's Return

[11] This is necessary because you know the times—that it's time for you to wake up from sleep. For our salvation is nearer now than when we became believers. [e] [12] The night is almost over, and the day is near. So we should put away the works of darkness and put on the armor of light. [f] [13] We should live honorably, as people who live in the light of day. [d] No wild parties, drunkenness, sexual immorality, promiscuity, rivalry, or jealousy! [g] [14] Instead, put on the Lord Jesus Christ, and stop obeying[e] your flesh and its desires. [h]

How to Treat Believers Who Are Weak in Faith

14 [1] Welcome the person who is weak in faith, but not for the purpose of arguing over differences of opinion. [i] [2] One person believes that he can eat anything, while the weak person eats only vegetables. [j] [3] The person who eats should not despise the person who does not eat, and the person who does not eat should not criticize the person who eats, because God has accepted him. [k] [4] Who are you to criticize someone else's servant? His own Lord will determine whether[f] he stands or falls. And stand he will, because God[g] is able to make him stand. [l]

[5] One person decides that one day is better than another, while another person decides that all days are the same.

---

a *13:8* Or *Don't owe*   b *13:9* Exod 20:13-15, 17; Deut 5:17-19, 21
c *13:9* Lev 19:18   d *13:13* Lit. *as in the day*   e *13:14* Or *don't obey*
f *14:4* Lit. *To his own Lord*   g *14:4* Other mss. read *the Lord*

Every person must be convinced in his own mind.*a* 6The person who observes a special day,ᵃ observes it to honor the Lord. The person who eats, eats to honor the Lord, since he gives thanks to God. And the person who does not eat, refrains from eating to honor the Lord; yet he, too, gives thanks to God.*b* 7For no one lives to himself, and no one dies to himself.*c* 8If we live, we live to honor the Lord, and if we die, we die to honor the Lord. So whether we live or die, we belong to the Lord. 9For this reason Christ died and came back to life, so that he would become the Lord of both the dead and the living.*d*

10So why do you criticize your brother? Or why do you despise your brother? All of us will stand before the judgment seat of God.**b**e 11For it is written,*f*

"As certainly as I live, says the Lord,
　　every knee will bow to me,
　　　　and every tongue will praise God."ᶜ

12Therefore, each of us will have to give an account to God.*g*

13So let us stop criticizing**d** each other. Instead, decide never to put a stumbling block or hindrance in the way of a brother.*h* 14I know and am persuaded in the Lord Jesus that nothing is unclean in and of itself. But it is unclean to a person who thinks it's unclean.*i* 15For if your brother is being hurt by what you eat, you are no longer living by love. Don't destroy the person for whom Christ died by what you eat!*j* 16So stop allowing**e** your good to be spoken of as evil.*k* 17For God's kingdom doesn't consist of food and drink, but of righteousness, peace, and joy produced by the Holy Spirit.*l* 18The person who serves Christ in this way is pleasing to God and respected by people.*m*

19So let us keep on pursuing those things that bring peace and that lead to building one another up.*n* 20Stop destroying**f** God's work because of food. Everything is clean, but it's wrong to make another person fall because of what you eat.*o* 21The right thing to do is to avoid eating meat,

---

a*14:6* Lit. *the day*　b*14:10* Other mss. read *of Christ*　c*14:11* Isa 49:18; 45:23　d*14:13* Or *let us not criticize*　e*14:16* Or *don't allow*　f*14:20* Or *Don't destroy*

14:5
ᵃGal 4:10;
Col 2:16

14:6
ᵇ1Cor 10:31;
Gal 4:10;
1Tim 4:3

14:7
ᶜ1Cor 6:19-20;
Gal 2:20;
1Thes 5:10;
1Peter 4:2

14:9
ᵈActs 10:36;
2Cor 5:15

14:10
ᵉMatt 25:31-32;
Acts 10:42; 17:31;
2Cor 5:10;
Jude 1:14-15

14:11
ᶠIsa 45:23;
Phil 2:10

14:12
ᵍMatt 12:36;
Gal 6:5;
1Peter 4:5

14:13
ʰ1Cor 8:9,13;
10:32

14:14
ⁱActs 10:15;
Rom 10:2,20;
1Cor 8:7,10;
10:25; 1Tim 4:4;
Titus 1:15

14:15
ʲ1Cor 8:11

14:16
ᵏRom 12:17

14:17
ˡ1Cor 8:8

14:18
ᵐ2Cor 8:21

14:19
ⁿPs 34:14;
Rom 12:18; 15:2;
1Cor 14:12;
1Thes 5:11

14:20
ᵒMatt 15:11;
Acts 10:15;
Rom 10:14;
14:15;
1Cor 8:9-12;
Titus 1:15

14:21
a 1Cor 8:13

14:22
b 1John 3:21

14:23
c Titus 1:15

15:1
d Rom 14:1;
Gal 6:1

15:2
e Rom 14:19;
1Cor 9:19,22;
10:24,33; 13:5;
Phil 2:4-5

15:3
f Ps 69:9;
Matt 26:39;
John 5:30; 6:38

15:4
g Rom 4:23-24;
1Cor 9:9-10;
10:11;
2Tim 3:16-17

15:5
h Rom 12:16;
1Cor 1:10;
Phil 3:16

15:6
i Acts 4:24,32

15:7
j Rom 5:2; 14:1,3

15:8
k Matt 15:24;
John 1:11;
Acts 3:25-26;
13:46; Rom 3:3;
2Cor 1:20

15:9
l Ps 18:49;
John 10:16;
Rom 9:23

15:10
m Deut 32:43

drinking wine, or doing anything else that makes your brother stumble or become upset or weak.ª*a* ²²As for the faith you do have, have it as your own conviction before God. How blessed is the person who has no reason to condemn himself because of what he approves!*b* ²³But the person who has doubts is condemned if he eats, because he doesn't act in faith. And anything that is not done in faith is sin.*c*

Please Others, Not Yourselves

15 ¹So those of us who are strong must be patient with the weaknesses of those who aren't strong and must stop pleasing ourselves.*d* ²Each of us must please our neighbor for the good purpose of building him up.*e* ³For not even Christ pleased himself. Instead, as it is written, "The insults of those who insult you have fallen on me."ᵇ*f* ⁴For everything written long ago was written for our instruction, so that we would have hope through the endurance and encouragement that the Scriptures give us.ᶜ*g*

⁵May God, the source of endurance and encouragement, allow you to live in harmony with each other as you follow Christ Jesus.ᵈ*h* ⁶Then, with one mind and one voice, you will glorify the God and Father of our Lord Jesus Christ.*i*

⁷Therefore, accept one another just as Christ accepted you,ᵉ for the glory of God.*j* ⁸I tell you that Christ became a servant of the circumcised to revealᶠ God's truth. As a result, he fulfilledᵍ the promises given to our forefathers.*k* ⁹Moreover, the Gentiles glorify God for his mercy as well. As it is written,*l*

> "That is why I will confess you among the
> Gentiles
> and I will sing praises to your name."ʰ

¹⁰Scriptureⁱ says again,*m*

> "Rejoice, you Gentiles, with his people!"ʲ

---

a 14:21 Other mss. lack *or become upset or weak*   **b** 15:3 Ps 69:9
c 15:4 Lit. *of the Scriptures*   **d** 15:5 Lit. *according to Christ Jesus*
e 15:7 Other mss. read *us*   **f** 15:8 Lit. *on behalf of*   **g** 15:8 Or *confirmed*
h 15:9 Ps 18:49   **i** 15:10 Lit. *It*   **j** 15:10 Deut 32:43

[11]And again,[a]

"Praise the Lord, all you Gentiles!
Let all the nations[a] praise him."[b]

[12]Again, Isaiah says,[b]

"There will be a Root[c] from Jesse.
He will rise to rule the Gentiles,
and the Gentiles will hope in him."[d]

[13]Now may God, the source of hope, fill you with all joy and peace as you believe, so that you may overflow with hope by the power of the Holy Spirit.[c]

Paul's Desire to Take the Gospel to the Whole World

[14]I am convinced,[e] my brothers, that you, too, are filled with goodness and full of all the knowledge you need to be able to instruct each other.[d] [15]However, on some points I have written to you rather boldly, both as a reminder to you and because of the grace given me by God[e] [16]to be a minister of Christ Jesus to the Gentiles in the priestly service of the gospel of God. As a result, the offering of the Gentiles will be acceptable because it has been sanctified by the Holy Spirit.[f]

[17]Therefore, in Christ Jesus I have the right to boast about my work for God.[g] [18]For I am bold enough to tell you only about what Christ has accomplished through me: the bringing of Gentiles to obedience. By my words and actions,[h] [19]by the power of signs and wonders, and by the power of God's Spirit,[f] I have fully proclaimed the gospel of Christ from Jerusalem as far as Illyricum.[i] [20]My one ambition is to proclaim the gospel where the name of Christ is not known, so that I don't build on someone else's foundation.[j] [21]As it is written,[k]

"Those who were never told about him will see,
and those who never heard will
understand."[g]

---

a[15:11] Lit. *all peoples*   b[15:11] Ps 117:1   c[15:12] I.e. Descendant
d[15:12] Isa 11:10   e[15:14] Lit. *convinced about you*   f[15:19] Other mss.
read *of the Holy Spirit*   g[15:21] Isa 52:15

15:11
a Ps 117:1

15:12
b Isa 11:1,10;
Rev 5:5; 22:16

15:13
c Rom 12:12;
14:17

15:14
d 1Cor 8:1,7,10;
2Peter 1:12;
1John 2:21

15:15
e Rom 1:5; 12:3;
Gal 1:15;
Eph 3:7-8

15:16
f Isa 66:20;
Rom 11:13;
Gal 2:7-9;
Phil 2:17;
1Tim 2:7;
2Tim 1:11

15:17
g Heb 5:1

15:18
h Acts 21:19;
Rom 1:5; 16:26;
Gal 2:8

15:19
i Acts 19:11;
2Cor 12:12

15:20
j 2Cor 10:13,
15-16

15:21
k Isa 52:15

15:22
a Rom 1:13;
1Thes 2:17-18

15:23
b Acts 19:21;
Rom 1:11; 15:32

15:24
c Acts 15:3

15:25
d Acts 19:21;
20:22; 24:17

15:26
e 1Cor 16:1-2;
2Cor 8:1; 9:2,12

15:27
f Rom 11:17;
1Cor 9:11;
Gal 6:6

15:28
g Phil 4:17

15:29
h Rom 1:11

15:30
i 2Cor 1:11;
Phil 2:1; Col 4:12

15:31
j 2Cor 8:4;
2Thes 3:2

15:32
k Acts 18:21;
Rom 1:10;
1Cor 4:19; 16:18;
2Cor 7:13;
2Tim 1:16;
James 4:15

15:33
l Rom 16:20;
1Cor 14:33;
2Cor 13:11;
Phil 4:9;
1Thes 5:23;
2Thes 3:16;
Heb 13:20

16:1
m Acts 18:18

16:2
n Phil 2:29;
3John 1:5-6

16:3
o Acts 18:2,18,26;
2Tim 4:19

Paul's Plan to Visit Rome

22That's why I have so often been kept from coming to you.*a* 23But now, having no further opportunities in these regions, I have the desire to come to you, as I have had for many years.*b* 24Now that I am on my way to Spain, I hope to see you when I come your way and, after I have enjoyed your company for a while, to be sent on by you.*c*

25Right now, however, I'm going to Jerusalem to minister to the saints.*d* 26For the believers in*a* Macedonia and Achaia have been eager to share their resources with the poor among the saints in Jerusalem.*e* 27Yes, they were eager to do this, and in fact are obligated to help them, for if the Gentiles have shared in their spiritual blessings, they are obligated to be of service to them in material things.*f*

28So when I have completed this and have put my seal on this contribution of theirs,*b* I will visit you on my way to Spain.*g* 29I know that when I come to you I will come with the full blessing of Christ.*c**h*

30Now I encourage you, brothers, through our Lord Jesus Christ and by the love that the Spirit produces, to join me in my struggle, earnestly praying to God for me*i* 31that I will be rescued from the unbelievers in Judea, that my ministry to Jerusalem will be acceptable to the saints,*j* 32and that by the will of God I may come to you with joy and be refreshed when I am with you.*k*

Doxology

33May the God of peace be with all of you! Amen.*l*

Personal Greetings

16 1Now I commend to you our sister Phoebe, a deaconess in the church at Cenchreae.*m* 2Welcome her in the Lord as is appropriate for saints, and provide her with anything she may need from you, for she has assisted many people, including me.*n*

3Greet Prisca*d* and Aquila, my co-workers in Christ Jesus.*o* 4They risked their necks for my life. I'm thankful to

---

a 15:26 The Gk. lacks *the believers in*   **b** 15:28 Lit. *have sealed to them this fruit*   **c** 15:29 Other mss. read *of the gospel of Christ*   **d** 16:3 I.e. Priscilla

them, and so are all the churches among the Gentiles. [5]Also greet the church in their house. Greet my dear friend Epaenetus, who was the first person to become a believer[a] in Christ in Asia.[a] [6]Greet Mary, who has worked very hard for you. [7]Greet Andronicus and Junias,[b] my fellow Jews who are in prison with me and are prominent among the apostles. They also were united with Christ before I was.[b] [8]Greet Ampliatus, my dear friend in the Lord. [9]Greet Urbanus, our co-worker in Christ, and my dear friend Stachys. [10]Greet Apelles, who has been approved by Christ. Greet those who belong to the family of Aristobulus. [11]Greet Herodion, my fellow Jew. Greet those who are united with the Lord who belong to the family of Narcissus. [12]Greet Tryphaena and Tryphosa, who have worked hard for the Lord. Greet dear Persis, who has worked very hard for the Lord. [13]Greet Rufus, the one chosen by the Lord, and his mother, who has been a mother to me, too.[c] [14]Greet Asyncritus, Phlegon, Hermes, Patrobas, Hermas, and the brothers who are with them. [15]Greet Philologus and Julia, Nereus and his sister, Olympas, and all the saints who are with them. [16]Greet each other with a holy kiss. All the churches of Christ greet you.[d]

Final Warning

[17]Now I urge you, brothers, to watch out for those who create divisions and sinful enticements in opposition to the teaching you have learned. Stay away from them![e] [18]For such people are not serving Christ our Lord but their own desires. By their smooth talk and flattering words they deceive the hearts of the unsuspecting.[f] [19]For your obedience has become known to everyone, and I am happy for you. But I want you to be wise about what is good and innocent about what is evil.[g] [20]The God of peace will soon crush Satan under your feet. May the grace of our Lord Jesus Christ be with you![c][h]

Final Greeting

[21]Timothy, my co-worker, greets you, as do Lucius,

---

a *16:5* Lit. *who was the first fruits*   **b** *16:7* Or *Junia*   **c** *16:20* Other mss. lack *May the grace of our Lord Jesus Christ be with you!*

16:5
a 1Cor 16:15,19; Col 4:15

16:7
b Gal 1:22

16:13
c 2John 1:1

16:16
d 1Cor 16:20; 2Cor 13:12; 1Thes 5:26; 1Peter 5:14

16:17
e Acts 15:1,5,24; 1Cor 5:9,11; 2Thes 3:6,14; 1Tim 6:3; 2Tim 3:5; Titus 3:10; 2John 1:10

16:18
f Phil 3:19; Col 2:4; 1Tim 6:5; 2Tim 3:6; Titus 1:10; 2Peter 2:3

16:19
g Matt 10:16; Rom 1:8; 1Cor 14:20

16:20
h Gen 3:15; Rom 3:24; 15:33; 1Cor 16:23; 2Cor 13:14; Phil 4:23; 1Thes 5:28; 2Thes 3:1-18; Rev 22:21

16:21
a Acts 13:1; 16:1;
17:5; 20:4;
Phil 2:19; Col 1:1;
1Thes 3:2;
1Tim 1:2;
Heb 13:23
16:23
b Acts 19:22;
1Cor 1:14;
2Cor 4:20
16:25
c Rom 2:16;
1Cor 2:7; Eph 1:9;
3:3-5,9,20;
Col 1:26-27;
1Thes 3:13;
2Thes 2:17;
3:3 Jude 1:24
16:26
d Acts 6:7;
Rom 1:5; 15:18;
Eph 1:9;
2Tim 1:10;
Titus 1:2-3;
1Peter 1:20
16:27
e 1Tim 1:17; 6:16;
Jude 1:25

Jason, and Sosipater, my fellow Jews.*a* 22I, Tertius, who wrote this letter, greet you in the Lord. 23Gaius, who is host to me and the whole church, greets you. Erastus, the city treasurer, and our brother Quartus, greet you.*ab*

Final Doxology

25Now to the one who is able to strengthen you by my gospel and the message that I preach about Jesus Christ, by revealing the secret that was kept in silence for a very long time*c* 26but now has been made known through the prophets to all the Gentiles, in keeping with the decree of the eternal God to bring them to the obedience of faith*d*—27to the only wise God, through Jesus Christ, be the glory forever! Amen.*e*

------

a *16:23* Other mss. read *greet you.* 24*May the grace of our Lord Jesus Christ be with all of you!*

THE LETTER OF PAUL CALLED
FIRST CORINTHIANS

Paul Greets the Church in Corinth

1 ¹From[a] Paul, called to be an apostle of Christ Jesus[b] by the will of God, and from our brother Sosthenes,[a] ²to the church of God in Corinth, to those who have been sanctified in Christ Jesus and called to be holy,[c] together with all those everywhere who continually call on the name of our Lord Jesus Christ—their Lord[d] and ours.[b] ³May grace and peace from God our Father and the Lord Jesus Christ be yours![c]

You Are Rich

⁴I always thank my[e] God for you because of the grace of God given you in Christ Jesus.[d] ⁵For in him you have become rich in every way—in speech and knowledge of every kind.[e] ⁶In this way, our testimony about Christ has been confirmed among you.[f] ⁷Therefore, you don't lack any spiritual gift as you eagerly wait for our Lord Jesus Christ to be revealed.[g] ⁸He will keep you strong until the end, so that you will be blameless on the day of our Lord Jesus Christ.[h] ⁹Faithful is the God by whom you were called into fellowship with his Son Jesus Christ our Lord.[i]

Divisions in the Church

¹⁰Brothers, I urge all of you in the name of our Lord Jesus Christ to be in agreement[f] and not to have divisions among you, so that you may be perfectly united in your understanding and opinions.[j] ¹¹My brothers, some members of Chloe's family have made it clear to me that there are quarrels among you. ¹²This is what I mean: Each of you is saying, "I belong to Paul," or "I belong to Apollos," or "I belong to Cephas,"[g] or "I belong to Christ."[k]

¹³Has Christ been divided? Paul wasn't crucified for

---

a 1:1 The Gk. lacks *From*   b 1:1 Other mss. read *Jesus Christ*   c 1:2 Or *to be saints*   d 1:2 Lit. *theirs*   e 1:4 Other mss. lack *my*   f 1:10 Lit. *to say the same thing*   g 1:12 I.e. Peter

1:1
a Acts 18:17;
Rom 1:1;
2Cor 1:1; Eph 1:1;
Col 1:1

1:2
b John 17:19;
Acts 9:14,21;
15:9; 22:16;
Rom 1:7; 3:22;
10:12; 1Cor 8:6;
2Tim 1:9;
2:22 Jude 1:1

1:3
c Rom 1:7;
2Cor 1:2; Eph 1:2;
1Peter 1:2

1:4
d Rom 1:8

1:5
e 1Cor 12:8;
2Cor 8:7

1:6
f 1Cor 2:1;
2Tim 1:8; Rev 1:2

1:7
g Phil 3:20;
Titus 2:13;
2Peter 3:12

1:8
h Col 1:22;
1Thes 3:13; 5:23

1:9
i Isa 49:7;
John 15:4; 17:21;
1Cor 10:13;
1Thes 5:24;
2Thes 3:3;
Heb 10:23;
1John 1:3; 4:13

1:10
j Rom 12:16; 15:5;
2Cor 13:11;
Phil 2:2; 3:16;
1Peter 3:8

1:12
k John 1:42;
Acts 18:24; 19:1;
1Cor 3:4; 16:12

1:13
a 2Cor 11:4;
Eph 4:5

1:14
b Acts 18:8;
Rom 16:23

1:16
c 1Cor 16:15,17

1:17
d 1Cor 2:1,4,13;
2Peter 1:16

1:18
e Acts 17:18;
Rom 1:16;
1Cor 1:24; 2:14;
15:2; 2Cor 2:15

1:19
f Job 5:12-13;
Isa 29:14; Jer 8:9

1:20
g Job 12:17,20,24;
Isa 33:18; 44:25;
Rom 1:22

1:21
h Matt 11:25;
Lk 10:21;
Rom 1:20-21,28

1:22
i Matt 12:38; 16:1;
Mark 8:11;
Lk 11:16;
John 4:48

1:23
j Isa 8:14;
Matt 11:6; 13:57;
Lk 2:34;
John 6:60,66;
Rom 9:32;
1Cor 15:14,18;
Gal 5:11;
1Peter 2:8

1:24
k Rom 1:4,16;
1Cor 1:18; Col 2:3

1:26
l John 7:48

1:27
m Ps 8:2;
Matt 11:25;
James 2:5

you, was he? You weren't baptized in Paul's name, were you?[a] [14]I thank God[a] that I didn't baptize any of you except Chrispus and Gaius,[b] [15]so no one can say that you were baptized in my name. [16](Yes, I also baptized the family of Stephanus. Beyond that, I'm not sure whether I baptized anyone else.)[c] [17]For Christ didn't send me to baptize but to preach the gospel, not with eloquent wisdom, for in that case the cross of Christ would be emptied of its power.[d]

Christ Is God's Power and Wisdom

[18]For the message about the cross is nonsense to those who are being destroyed, but it is God's power to us who are being saved.[e] [19]For it is written,[f]

> "I will destroy the wisdom of the wise,
> and the intelligence of the intelligent I will
> reject."[b]

[20]Where is the wise person? Where is the scholar? Where is the philosopher of this age? God has turned the wisdom of the world into nonsense, hasn't he?[g] [21]For since in the wisdom of God the world through its wisdom did not know God, God decided through the nonsense of our preaching to save those who believe.[h] [22]Jews ask for signs, and Greeks look for wisdom,[i] [23]but we preach Christ crucified. He is a stumbling block to Jews and nonsense to Gentiles,[j] [24]but to those who are called, both Jews and Greeks, Christ is God's power and God's wisdom.[k] [25]For God's nonsense is wiser than human wisdom,[c] and God's weakness is stronger than human strength.[c]

[26]Brothers, think about your own calling. Not many of you were wise by human standards,[d] not many were powerful, not many were of noble birth.[l] [27]But God chose what is nonsense in the world to make the wise feel ashamed. God chose what is weak in the world to make the strong feel ashamed.[m] [28]And God chose what is insignificant in the world, what is despised, what is nothing, in order to destroy

---

a *1:14* Other mss. read *I thank my God*; still other mss. read *I am thankful* **b** *1:19* Isa 29:14   **c** *1:25* Lit. *than men*   **d** *1:26* Lit. *according to the flesh*

what is something,[a] 29so that no human being[a] may boast in God's presence.[b] 30It is because of him that you are in union with Christ Jesus, who for us has become wisdom from God, as well as our righteousness, sanctification, and redemption.[c] 31Therefore, as it is written, "The person who boasts must boast in the Lord."[bd]

Preaching in the Power of God

2 1When I came to you, brothers, I didn't come and tell you about God's secret[c] with rhetorical language or wisdom.[e] 2For while I was with you I resolved to know nothing except Jesus Christ and him crucified.[f] 3It was in weakness, fear, and great trembling that I came to you.[g] 4My message and my preaching were not accompanied by clever words of wisdom, but by a display of the Spirit's power,[h] 5so that your faith would not be based on human wisdom but on God's power.[i]

God's Spirit Reveals Everything

6However, when we are among mature people, we do speak a message of wisdom,[d] but not the wisdom of this world or of the rulers of this world, who are passing off the scene.[j] 7Instead, we speak about God's secret wisdom that has been hidden, which God destined for our glory before the world began.[ek] 8None of the rulers of this world understood it, for if they had, they would not have crucified the Lord of Glory.[l] 9But as it is written,[m]

> "No eye has seen, no ear has heard,
>   and no mind has imagined
> the things that God has prepared
>   for those who love him."[f]

10But[g] God has revealed those things to us by his Spirit. For the Spirit searches everything, even the deep things of God.[n] 11Is there anyone who can understand his own thoughts except by his own inner spirit? In the same way,

---

a1:29 Lit. *no flesh*   b1:31 Jer 9:24   c2:1 Other mss. read *testimony*
d2:6 Lit. *speak wisdom*   e2:7 Lit. *before the ages*   f2:9 Isa 64:4
g2:10 Other mss. read *For*

1:28
a Rom 4:17;
1Cor 2:6

1:29
b Rom 3:27;
Eph 2:9

1:30
c Jer 23:5-6;
John 17:19;
Rom 4:25;
1Cor 1:24;
2Cor 5:21;
Eph 1:7; Phil 3:9

1:31
d Jer 9:23-24;
2Cor 10:17

2:1
e 1Cor 1:4,6,13,
17; 2Cor 10:10;
11:6

2:2
f Gal 6:14; Phil 3:8

2:3
g Acts 18:1,6,12;
2Cor 4:7; 10:1,10;
11:30; 12:5,9;
Gal 4:13

2:4
h Rom 15:19;
1Cor 1:17; 2:1;
1Thes 1:5;
2Peter 1:16

2:5
i 2Cor 4:7; 6:7

2:6
j 1Cor 1:20,28;
3:1,13,19; 14:20;
2Cor 1:12;
Eph 4:13;
Phil 3:15;
Heb 5:14;
James 3:15

2:7
k Rom 16:25-26;
Eph 3:5,9;
Col 1:26;
2Tim 1:9

2:8
l Matt 11:25;
Lk 23:34;
John 7:48; 16:3;
Acts 3:17; 13:27;
2Cor 3:14

2:9
m Isa 64:4

2:10
n Matt 13:11;
16:17; John 14:26;
16:13; 1John 2:27

2:11
a Prov 20:27;
27:19; Jer 17:9;
Rom 11:33-34

2:12
b Rom 8:15

2:13
c 1Cor 1:4,17;
2Peter 1:16

2:14
d Matt 16:23;
Rom 8:5-7;
1Cor 1:18,
23 Jude 1:19

2:15
e Prov 28:5;
1Thes 5:21;
1John 4:1

2:16
f Job 15:8;
Isa 40:13;
Jer 23:18;
John 15:15;
Rom 11:34

3:1
g 1Cor 2:14-15;
Heb 5:13

3:2
h John 16:12;
Heb 5:12-13;
1Peter 2:2

3:3
i 1Cor 1:11; 11:18;
Gal 5:20-21;
James 3:16

3:4
j 1Cor 1:12

3:5
k Rom 12:3,6;
1Cor 4:1;
2Cor 3:3;
1Peter 4:11

3:6
l Acts 18:4,8,11,
24,27; 19:1;
1Cor 1:30; 4:15;
9:1; 15:1,10;
2Cor 3:5;
10:14-15

3:7
m 2Cor 12:11;
Gal 6:3

3:8
n Ps 62:12;
Rom 2:6;
1Cor 4:5;
Gal 6:4-5;
Rev 2:23; 22:12

3:9
o Acts 15:4;
2Cor 6:1;
Eph 2:20; Col 2:7;
Heb 3:3-4;
1Peter 2:5

no one can know the thoughts of God except God's Spirit.*a* [12]Now, we have not received the spirit of the world but the Spirit who comes from God, so that we can understand the things that were freely given to us by God.*b* [13]We don't speak about these things in words taught us by human wisdom, but in words*a* taught by the Spirit, as we explain spiritual things to spiritual people.*bc* [14]A person who isn't spiritual doesn't accept the things of God's Spirit, for they are nonsense to him. He can't understand them because they are spiritually evaluated.*d* [15]The spiritual person evaluates everything but is subject to no one else's evaluation.*e* [16]For*f*

> "Who has known the mind of the Lord
>   so that he can advise him?"*c*

However, we have the mind of Christ.

Spiritual Immaturity

3 [1]Brothers, I couldn't talk to you as spiritual people but as worldly people, as mere infants in Christ.*g* [2]I gave you milk to drink, not solid food, because you weren't ready for it. Why, you're still not ready for it!*h* [3]That's because you are still worldly. As long as there is jealousy and quarreling among you, you are worldly and living by human standards, aren't you?*i* [4]For when one says, "I belong to Paul," and another, "I belong to Apollos," you are merely human, aren't you?*j*

[5]What is Apollos anyhow? Or what is Paul? Mere servants through whom you came to believe, as the Lord gave to each of us his task.*k* [6]I did the planting, Apollos did the watering, but God kept everything growing.*l* [7]So neither the one who plants nor the one who waters is significant, but God, who keeps everything growing, is the one who matters.*m* [8]The one who plants and the one who waters have the same goal, and each will receive a reward for his own work.*n* [9]For we are God's co-workers. You are God's farmland and God's building.*o*

---

a 2:13 Lit. *in things*   **b** 2:13 Or *in spiritual words*   **c** 2:16 Isa 40:13

Christ Is Our Foundation

[10]As an expert builder using the grace that God gave me, I laid the foundation, and someone else is building on it. But each person must be careful how he builds on it.[a] [11]After all, no one can lay any other foundation than the one that is already laid, and that is Jesus Christ.[b] [12]Whether a person builds on this foundation with gold, silver, expensive stones, wood, hay, or straw, [13]the workmanship of each person will become evident, for the day[a] will show what it is, because it will be revealed with fire, and the fire will test the quality of each person's work.[c] [14]If what a person has built on the foundation survives, he will receive a reward.[b][d] [15]If his work is burned up, he will suffer loss. However, he himself will be saved, but it will be like going through fire.[e]

[16]You know that you are God's sanctuary and that God's Spirit lives in you, don't you?[f] [17]If anyone destroys God's sanctuary, God will destroy him, for God's sanctuary is holy. And you are that sanctuary!

True Wisdom

[18]Let no one deceive himself. If any of you thinks he is wise in the ways of this world,[c] he must become a fool to become really wise.[g] [19]For the wisdom of this world is nonsense in God's sight. For it is written,[h]

> "He catches the wise with their own trickery,"[d]

[20]and again,[i]

> "The Lord knows that the thoughts of the wise
> are worthless."[e]

[21]So let no one boast about men. For everything belongs to you,[j] [22]whether Paul, Apollos, Cephas, the world, life, death, the present, or the future—everything belongs to you, [23]but you belong to Christ, and Christ belongs to God.[k]

---

a 3:13 I.e. the day of judgment　b 3:14 Or *receive wages*　c 3:18 Lit. *wise in this world*　d 3:19 Job 5:13　e 3:20 Ps 94:11

3:10
a Rom 1:5; 12:3; 15:20; 1Cor 4:15; 15:6; 1Peter 4:11; Rev 21:14

3:11
b Isa 28:16; Matt 16:18; 2Cor 11:4; Gal 1:7; Eph 2:20

3:13
c Lk 2:35; 1Cor 4:5; 1Peter 1:7; 4:12

3:14
d 1Cor 4:5

3:15
e Jude 1:23

3:16
f 1Cor 6:19; 2Cor 6:16; Eph 2:21-22; Heb 3:6; 1Peter 2:5

3:18
g Prov 5:7; Isa 5:21

3:19
h Job 5:13; 1Cor 1:20; 2:6

3:20
i Ps 94:11

3:21
j 1Cor 1:12; 4:4-6; 2Cor 4:5,15

3:23
k Rom 14:8; 1Cor 11:3; 2Cor 10:7; Gal 3:29

4:1
a Matt 24:45;
Lk 12:42;
1Cor 3:5; 9:17;
2Cor 6:4;
Col 1:25;
Titus 1:7;
1Peter 4:10

4:4
b Job 9:2;
Ps 130:3; 143:2;
Prov 21:2;
Rom 3:20; 4:2

4:5
c Matt 7:1;
Rom 2:1,16,29;
14:4,10,13;
1Cor 3:13;
2Cor 5:10;
Rev 20:12

4:6
d Rom 12:3;
1Cor 1:12; 3:4,21;
5:2,6

4:7
e John 3:27;
James 1:17;
1Peter 4:10

4:8
f Rev 3:17

4:9
g Ps 44:22;
Rom 8:36;
1Cor 15:30-31;
2Cor 4:11; 6:9;
Heb 10:33

4:10
h 2Kings 9:11;
Acts 17:18; 26:24;
1Cor 1:18; 2:3,14;
3:18; 2Cor 13:9

4:11
i Job 22:6;
Acts 23:2;
Rom 8:35;
2Cor 4:8;
11:23-27;
Phil 4:12

4:12
j Matt 5:44;
Lk 6:28; 23:34;
Acts 7:60; 18:3;
20:34;
Rom 12:14,20;
1Thes 2:9;
2Thes 3:8;
1Tim 4:10;
1Peter 2:23; 3:9

4:13
k Lam 3:45

Faithful Servants of Christ

4 [1]A person should think of us as servants of Christ and managers entrusted with God's secrets.*a* [2]Now it is required of managers that each one should prove to be trustworthy.*a* [3]It is a very small thing to me that I should be examined by you or by any human court. In fact, I don't even examine myself. [4]For my conscience is clear,**b** but that does not vindicate me. It is the Lord who examines me.*b* [5]Therefore, you must stop judging before the proper time, before the Lord comes, for he will bring to light what is hidden in darkness and reveal the motives of our hearts. Then each person will receive his praise from God.*c*

Fools for Christ's Sake

[6]Brothers, I have applied all this to Apollos and myself for your benefit, so that you may learn from us not to go beyond what is written. Then you will stop boasting about one person at the expense of another.*d*

[7]For who makes you superior? What do you have that you didn't receive? And if you did receive it, why do you boast as though you didn't receive it?*e* [8]You already have all you want! You've already become rich! You've become kings without us! I wish you really were kings so that we could be kings with you!*f*

[9]For it seems to me that God has put us apostles on display at the end of the procession, like men condemned to death. We have become a spectacle for the world, for angels, and for people to stare at.*g* [10]We are fools for Christ's sake, but you are wise in Christ. We are weak, but you are strong. You are honored, but we are dishonored.*h* [11]To this very hour we are hungry, thirsty, dressed in rags, brutally treated, and homeless.*i* [12]We wear ourselves out from working with our own hands. When insulted, we bless. When persecuted, we endure.*j* [13]When slandered, we answer with kind words. Up to this moment we have become the filth of the world, the scum of the universe!*k*

---

a 4:2 Or *should be found faithful*   **b** 4:4 Lit. *I don't know of anything against me*

Fatherly Advice

[14]I'm not writing this to make you feel ashamed, but to warn you as my dear children.[a] [15]You may have ten thousand guardians in Christ, but not many fathers. For in Christ Jesus I became your father through the gospel.[b] [16]So I urge you to become imitators of me.[c] [17]That's why I sent Timothy to you. He is my dear and dependable child in the Lord and will help you remember my way of life in Christ Jesus as I teach it everywhere in every church.[d]

[18]Some of you have become arrogant, as though I were not coming to you.[e] [19]But I will come to you soon if it's the Lord's will. Then I'll discover, not only what these arrogant people are saying, but also what power they have,[f] [20]for the kingdom of God isn't just talk but power.[g] [21]Which do you prefer? Should I come to you with a stick, or in love and with a gentle spirit?[h]

Disciplining for Sexual Immorality

5 [1]It is actually reported that sexual immorality exists among you, and of a kind that isn't found even among the Gentiles. A man is actually living with his father's wife![i] [2]And you are being arrogant instead of being filled with grief and seeing to it that the man who did this is removed from among you.[j] [3]Even though I am away from you physically, I am with you in spirit. I have already passed judgment on the man who did this, as though I were present with you.[k] [4]When you are gathered together in the name of our Lord Jesus and my spirit and the power of our Lord Jesus are present,[l] [5]hand this man over to Satan for the destruction of his flesh,[a] so that his spirit may be saved on the day of the Lord.[b][m]

[6]Your boasting is not good. You know that a little yeast leavens the whole batch of dough, don't you?[n] [7]Get rid of the old yeast so that you may be a new batch of dough, since you are to be free from yeast. For Christ, our Passover lamb, has been sacrificed.[o] [8]So let us keep celebrating the festival, not with the old yeast or with the yeast of vice and

---

a5:5 Or *sinful nature*　　**b**5:5 Other mss. read *Lord Jesus*; still other mss. read *our Lord Jesus Christ*

4:14
a 1Thes 2:11
4:15
b Acts 18:11;
Rom 15:20;
1Cor 3:6;
Gal 4:19;
James 1:18
4:16
c 1Cor 11:1;
Phil 3:17;
1Thes 1:6;
2Thes 3:9
4:17
d Acts 19:22;
1Cor 7:17; 11:2;
14:33; 16:10;
Phil 2:19;
1Thes 3:2;
1Tim 1:2;
2Tim 1:2
4:18
e 1Cor 5:2
4:19
f Acts 18:21;
19:21;
Rom 15:32;
1Cor 16:5;
2Cor 1:15,23;
Heb 6:3;
James 4:15
4:20
g 1Cor 2:4;
1Thes 1:5
4:21
h 2Cor 10:2; 13:10
5:1
i Lev 18:8;
Deut 22:30;
27:20; 2Cor 7:12;
Eph 5:3
5:2
j 1Cor 4:18;
2Cor 7:7,10
5:3
k Col 2:5
5:4
l Matt 16:19;
18:18; John 20:23;
2Cor 2:10; 13:3,
10
5:5
m Job 2:6;
Ps 109:6;
Acts 26:18;
1Tim 1:20
5:6
n 1Cor 3:21; 4:19;
5:2; 15:33;
Gal 5:9;
2Tim 2:17;
James 4:16
5:7
o Isa 53:7;
John 1:29; 19:14;
1Cor 15:3;
1Peter 1:19;
Rev 5:6,12

5:8
a Exod 12:15;
13:6; Deut 16:3;
Matt 16:6,12;
Mark 8:15;
Lk 12:1

5:9
b 1Cor 5:2,7;
2Cor 6:14;
Eph 5:11;
2Thes 3:14

5:10
c John 17:15;
1Cor 1:20; 10:27;
1John 5:19

5:11
d Matt 18:17;
Rom 16:17;
Gal 2:12;
2Thes 3:6,14;
2John 1:10

5:12
e Mark 4:11;
1Cor 6:1-4;
Col 4:5;
1Thes 4:12;
1Tim 3:7

5:13
f Deut 13:5; 17:7;
21:21; 22:21-22,
24

6:2
g Ps 49:14;
Dan 7:22;
Matt 19:28;
Lk 22:30;
Rev 2:26; 3:21;
20:4

6:3
h 2Peter 2:4;
Jude 1:6

6:4
i 1Cor 5:12

6:7
j Prov 20:22;
Matt 5:39-40;
Lk 6:29;
Rom 12:17,19;
1Thes 5:15

6:8
k 1Thes 4:6

6:9
l 1Cor 15:50;
Gal 5:21; Eph 5:5;
1Tim 1:9;
Heb 12:14; 13:4;
Rev 22:15

wickedness, but with the bread of purity and truth that has no yeast.[a]

9I wrote to you in my letter to stop associating with people who are sexually immoral[b]—10not at all meaning the people of this world who are immoral, or greedy people, robbers, or idolaters. In that case you would have to leave this world.[c] 11But now I am writing to you to stop associating with any so-called brother if he is sexually immoral, greedy, an idolater, a slanderer, a drunk, or a robber. You must even stop eating with such a person.[d] 12After all, is it my business to judge outsiders? You are to judge those who are inside, aren't you?[e] 13God will judge outsiders. "Put that wicked man away from you."[a][f]

Morality in Legal Matters

6 1When one of you has a complaint against another, does he dare to take it before the unrighteous and not before the saints? 2You know that the saints will rule the world, don't you? And if the world is going to be ruled by you, can't you handle insignificant cases?[g] 3You know that we will rule angels, not to mention things in this life, don't you?[h] 4So if you have cases dealing with this life, why do you appoint as judges people who have no standing in the church?[i] 5I say this to make you feel ashamed. Has it come to this, that there isn't one person among you who is wise enough to settle disagreements between brothers?[b] 6Instead, one brother goes to court against another brother, and before unbelievers at that! 7The very fact that you have lawsuits among yourselves is already a defeat for you. Why not rather be wronged? Why not rather be cheated?[j] 8Instead, you yourselves practice doing wrong and cheating others, and brothers at that![k]

9You know that wicked people won't inherit the kingdom of God, don't you? Stop deceiving yourselves! Sexually immoral people, idolaters, adulterers, male prostitutes, homosexuals,[l] 10thieves, greedy people, drunks, slanderers, and robbers won't inherit the kingdom of God. 11That's what some of you were! But you were washed, you were

---

a *5:13* Deut 17:7 (LXX)   **b** *6:5* Lit. *between his brother*

sanctified, you were justified in the name of our Lord Jesus Christ and in*a* the Spirit of our God.*a*

Morality in Sexual Matters

[12]Everything is permissible for me, but not everything is helpful. Everything is permissible for me, but I won't allow anything to control me.*b* [13]Food is for the stomach, and the stomach is for food, but God will put an end to both of them. The body is not meant for sexual immorality but for the Lord, and the Lord for the body.*c* [14]God raised the Lord, and by his power he will also raise us.*d*

[15]You know that your bodies are parts of Christ, don't you? Should I take the parts of Christ and make them parts of a prostitute? Certainly not!*e* [16]You know that the person who unites himself with a prostitute becomes one body with her, don't you? For it is said, "The two will become one flesh."*bf* [17]But the person who unites himself with the Lord becomes one spirit with him.*g*

[18]Keep on running away from sexual immorality. Any other sin that a person commits is outside his body, but the person who sins sexually sins against his own body.*h* [19]You know that your body is a sanctuary of the Holy Spirit who is in you, whom you have received from God, don't you? You do not belong to yourselves,*i* [20]because you were bought for a price. Therefore glorify God with your bodies.*j*

Concerning Marriage

7 [1]Now concerning the things you wrote about: It's good for a man not to touch a woman.*ck* [2]But because sexual immorality is so rampant,*d* every man should have his own wife, and every woman should have her own husband.

[3]A husband should fulfill his obligation to his wife, and a wife should do the same for her husband.*l* [4]A wife doesn't have authority over her own body, but her husband does. In the same way, a husband doesn't have authority over his own body, but his wife does. [5]Don't withhold yourselves

---

a 6:11 Or *by*   b 6:16 Gen 2:24   c 7:1 I.e. not to get married   d 7:2 Lit. *because of instances of sexual immorality*

6:11
a 1Cor 1:30; 12:2;
Eph 2:2; 4:22; 5:8;
Col 3:7; Titus 3:3;
Heb 10:22

6:12
b 1Cor 10:23

6:13
c Matt 15:17;
Rom 14:17;
1Cor 6:15,19-20;
Eph 5:23;
Col 2:22-23;
1Thes 4:3,7

6:14
d Rom 6:5,8; 8:11;
2Cor 4:14;
Eph 1:19-20

6:15
e Rom 12:5;
1Cor 12:27;
Eph 4:12,15-16;
5:30

6:16
f Gen 2:24;
Matt 19:5;
Eph 5:31

6:17
g John 17:21-23;
Eph 4:4; 5:30

6:18
h Rom 1:24;
6:12-13;
1Thes 4:4;
Heb 13:4

6:19
i Rom 14:7-8;
1Cor 3:16;
2Cor 6:16

6:20
j Acts 20:28;
1Cor 7:23;
Gal 3:13;
Heb 9:12;
1Peter 1:18-19;
2Peter 2:1;
Rev 5:9

7:1
k 1Cor 7:8,26

7:3
l Exod 21:10;
1Peter 3:7

7:5
a Exod 19:15;
1Sam 21:4-5;
Joel 2:16;
Zech 7:3;
1Thes 3:5

7:6
b 1Cor 7:12,25;
2Cor 8:8; 11:17

7:7
c Matt 19:12;
Acts 26:29;
1Cor 9:5; 12:11

7:8
d 1Cor 7:1,26

7:9
e 1Tim 5:14

7:10
f Mal 2:14,16;
Matt 5:32; 19:6,9;
Mark 10:11-12;
Lk 16:18;
1Cor 7:12,25,40

7:12
g 1Cor 7:6

7:14
h Mal 2:15

7:15
i Rom 12:18;
14:19;
1Cor 14:33;
Heb 12:14

7:16
j 1Peter 3:1

7:17
k 1Cor 4:17;
2Cor 11:28

7:18
l Acts 15:1,5,19,
24,28; Gal 5:2

from each other unless you agree to do so for a set time in order to devote yourselves to prayer.a Then you should come together again so that Satan doesn't tempt you through your lack of self-control.a 6But I say this as a concession, not as a command.b 7I would like everyone to be like me. However, each person has a special gift from God, one this and another that.c

8I say to those who are unmarried, especially to widows: It's good for them to remain like me.d 9However, if they can't control themselves, they should get married, for it is better to marry than to burn with passion.be 10To married people I give this command (not really I, but the Lord): A wife must not leave her husband.f 11But if she does leave him, she must remain unmarried or else be reconciled to her husband. Likewise, a husband must not abandonc his wife.

12I (not the Lord) say to the rest of you: If a brother has a wife who is an unbeliever and she is willing to live with him, he must not abandonc her.g 13And if a woman has a husband who is an unbeliever and he is willing to live with her, she must not abandonc him. 14For the unbelieving husband has been sanctified because of his wife, and the unbelieving wife has been sanctified because of her husband.d Otherwise, your children would be unclean, but now they are holy.h 15But if the unbelieving partnere leaves, let him go. In such cases the brother or sister is not bound; God has called youf to live in peace.i 16Wife, how do you know whether you will save your husband? Husband, how do you know whether you will save your wife?j

Live according to God's Call

17Nevertheless, everyone should live the life that the Lord gave him and to which God called him. This is my rule in all the churches.k 18Was anyone circumcised when he was called? He shouldn't try to change that. Was anyone uncircumcised when he was called? He shouldn't get circumcised.l 19Circumcision is nothing, and uncircumcision is

a 7:5 Other mss. read *to fasting and prayer*   b 7:9 The Gk. lacks *with passion*   c 7:11,7:12,7:13 Or *divorce*   d 7:14 Other mss. read *brother*   e 7:15 Lit. *the unbeliever*   f 7:15 Other mss. read *us*

nothing, but obeying God's commandments is everything.ª ᵃ ²⁰Everyone should stay in the calling in which he was called. ²¹Were you a slave when you were called? Don't let that bother you. Of course, if you have a chance to become free, take advantage of the opportunity. ²²For the slave who has been called in the Lord is the Lord's free person. In the same way, the free person who has been called is Christ's slave.ᵇ ²³You were bought for a price. Stop becoming slaves of people.ᶜ ²⁴Brothers, everyone should stay in the calling he was in when called by God.ᵈ

Concerning Unmarried Women

²⁵Now concerning unmarried women:ᵇ Although I don't have any command from the Lord, I will give you my opinion as one who by the Lord's mercy is trustworthy.ᵉ ²⁶In view of the present crisis, I think it is prudent for a man to stay as he is.ᶠ ²⁷Have you been bound to a wife? Stop trying to get free. Have you been freed from a wife? Stop looking for a wife. ²⁸But if you do get married, you have not sinned. And if a virgin gets married, she has not sinned. However, these people will experience distress,ᶜ and I want to spare you that.

²⁹This is what I mean, brothers: The time has been shortened. From now on, those who have wives should live as though they had none,ᵍ ³⁰and those who mourn as though they did not mourn, and those who rejoice as though they were not rejoicing, and those who buy as though they didn't own a thing, ³¹and those who use the things in the world as though they were not dependent on them. For the world in its present form is passing away.ʰ

³²I want you to be free from concerns. An unmarried man is concerned about the affairs of the Lord, that is, about how he can please the Lord.ⁱ ³³But a married man is concerned about the affairs of this world, that is, about how he can please his wife, ³⁴and so his attention is divided. An unmarried woman or virgin is concerned about the affairs of the Lord, so that she may be holy in body and spirit. But a

---

ª 7:19 The Gk. lacks *is everything*   ᵇ 7:25 Lit. *virgins*   ᶜ 7:28 Lit. *distress in the flesh*

Cross references

7:19
ª John 15:14;
Gal 5:6; 6:15;
1 John 2:3; 3:24

7:22
ᵇ John 8:36;
Rom 6:18,22;
1 Cor 9:21;
Gal 5:13; Eph 6:6;
1 Peter 2:16

7:23
ᶜ Lev 25:42;
1 Cor 6:20;
1 Peter 1:18-19

7:24
ᵈ 1 Cor 7:20

7:25
ᵉ 1 Cor 4:2; 7:6,10,
40; 2 Cor 8:8,10;
1 Tim 1:12,16

7:26
ᶠ 1 Cor 7:1,8

7:29
ᵍ Rom 13:11;
1 Peter 4:7;
2 Peter 3:8-9

7:31
ʰ Ps 39:6;
1 Cor 9:18;
James 1:10; 4:14;
1 Peter 1:24; 4:7;
1 John 2:17

7:32
ⁱ 1 Tim 5:5

7:34
a Lk 10:40

7:38
b Heb 13:4

7:39
c Rom 7:2;
2Cor 6:14

7:40
d 1Cor 7:25;
1Thes 4:8

8:1
e Acts 15:20,29;
Rom 14:3,10,14,
22; 1Cor 10:19

8:2
f 1Cor 13:8-9,12;
Gal 6:3; 1Tim 6:4

8:3
g Exod 33:12,17;
Nah 1:7;
Matt 7:23;
Gal 4:9;
2Tim 2:19

8:4
h Deut 4:39; 6:4;
Isa 41:24; 44:8;
Mark 12:29;
1Cor 10:19; 12:6;
Eph 4:6; 1Tim 2:5

8:5
i John 10:34

8:6
j Mal 2:10;
John 1:3; 13:13;
Acts 2:36; 17:28;
Rom 11:36;
1Cor 12:3;
Eph 4:5-6;
Phil 2:11; Col 1:6;
Heb 1:2

8:7
k Rom 14:14,23;
1Cor 10:28-29

married woman is concerned about the affairs of this world, that is, about how she can please her husband.[a] 35I'm saying this for your benefit, not to put a noose around your necks, but to promote good order and unhindered devotion to the Lord.

36If a man thinks he is not behaving properly toward his virgin,[a] and if his passion is too strong and he feels he ought to, let him do what he wants; he isn't sinning. Let them get married. 37However, if a man stands firm in his resolve and feels no necessity but has made up his mind to keep her a virgin, he will be acting appropriately. 38So then the man who marries the virgin acts appropriately, but the man who refrains from marriage does even better.[b]

39A wife is bound to her husband as long as he lives. But if her husband dies, she is free to marry anyone she wishes, only in the Lord.[c] 40However, in my opinion she will be happier[b] if she stays as she is. And I think that I, too, have God's Spirit.[d]

Concerning Food Offered to Idols

8 1Now concerning food offered to idols: We know that we all possess knowledge. Knowledge puffs up, but love builds up.[e] 2If anyone thinks he knows something, he has not yet learned it as he ought to know it.[f] 3But if anyone loves God, he is known by him.[c][g]

4Now concerning eating food offered to idols: We know that no idol is real in the world and that there is only one God.[h] 5For even if there are "gods" in heaven and on earth (as indeed there are many so-called "gods" and "lords"),[i] 6yet for us there is only one God, the Father, from whom everything came into being and for whom we live. And there is only one Lord, Jesus Christ, through whom everything came into being and through whom we live.[j]

7But not everyone has this knowledge. Some people are so accustomed to idols that they still think they are eating food offered to an idol, and since their conscience is weak, it becomes contaminated.[k] 8However, food will not bring us

---

a 7:36 I.e., virgin fiancée, but possibly virgin daughter.   b 7:40 Or *more blessed*   c 8:3 I.e. Other mss. omit *by him*

closer to God. We are no worse off if we do not eat, and no better off if we do.[a]

[9] But you must see to it that this right of yours does not become a stumbling block to the weak.[b] [10] For if anyone with a weak conscience sees you who have this knowledge eating in an idol's temple, he will be encouraged to eat what has been offered to idols, won't he?[c] [11] In that case, the weak brother for whom Christ died is destroyed by your knowledge.[d] [12] When you sin against your brothers in this way and wound their weak consciences, you are sinning against Christ.[e] [13] Therefore, if food causes my brother to fall, I will never eat meat again, in order to keep my brother from falling.[f]

The Rights of an Apostle

9 [1] I am free, am I not? I am an apostle, am I not? I have seen Jesus our Lord, have I not? You are my work in the Lord, aren't you?[g] [2] If I am not an apostle to other people, surely I am one to you, for you are the seal of my apostleship in the Lord![h]

[3] This is my defense to those who would examine me: [4] We have the right to eat and drink, don't we?[i] [5] We have the right to take a believing wife with us like the other apostles, the Lord's brothers, and Cephas,[a] don't we?[j] [6] Or is it only Barnabas and I who have no right to refrain from working for a living?[k]

[7] Who would ever go to war at his own expense? Who plants a vineyard and does not eat any of its grapes? Or who takes care of a flock and does not drink any of its milk?[l] [8] I am not saying this on human authority, am I? The Law says the same thing, doesn't it? [9] For in the Law of Moses it is written, "You must not muzzle an ox while it is treading out the grain."[b] God isn't only concerned about oxen, is he?[m] [10] Isn't he really speaking on our behalf? Yes, this was written on our behalf, because the one who plows should plow in hope, and the one who threshes should thresh in hope of sharing in the crop.[n] [11] If we have sown spiritual seed among you, is it too much if we reap material benefits from you?[o]

---

a 9:5 I.e. Peter   b 9:9 Deut 25:4

8:8
a Rom 14:17

8:9
b Rom 14:13,20;
Gal 5:13

8:10
c 1Cor 10:28,32

8:11
d Rom 14:15,20

8:12
e Matt 25:40,45

8:13
f Rom 14:21;
2Cor 11:29

9:1
g Acts 9:3,15,17;
13:2; 18:9; 22:14,
18; 23:11; 26:17;
1Cor 3:6; 4:15;
15:8; 2Cor 12:12;
Gal 2:7-8;
1Tim 2:7;
2Tim 1:11

9:2
h 2Cor 3:2; 12:12

9:4
i 1Cor 9:14;
1Thes 2:6;
2Thes 3:9

9:5
j Matt 8:14; 13:55;
Mark 6:3; Lk 6:15;
Gal 1:19

9:6
k 2Thes 3:8-9

9:7
l Deut 20:6;
Prov 27:13;
John 21:15;
1Cor 3:6-8;
2Cor 10:4;
1Tim 1:18; 6:12;
2Tim 2:3; 4:7;
1Peter 5:2

9:9
m Deut 25:4;
1Tim 5:18

9:10
n 2Tim 2:6

9:11
o Rom 15:27;
Gal 6:6

9:12
a Acts 20:33;
1Cor 9:15,18;
2Cor 11:7,9,12;
12:13; 1Thes 2:6

9:13
b Lev 6:16,26; 7:6;
Num 5:9-10;
18:8-20;
Deut 10:9; 18:1

9:14
c Matt 10:10;
Lk 10:7; Gal 6:6;
1Tim 5:17

9:15
d Acts 18:3; 20:34;
1Cor 4:12; 9:12;
2Cor 11:10;
1Thes 2:9;
2Thes 3:8

9:16
e Rom 1:14

9:17
f 1Cor 3:8,14; 4:1;
Gal 2:7; Phil 1:17;
Col 1:25

9:18
g 1Cor 7:31;
10:33; 2Cor 4:5;
11:7

9:19
h Matt 18:15;
1Cor 9:1;
Gal 5:13;
1Peter 3:1

9:20
i Acts 16:3; 18:18;
21:23

9:21
j Rom 2:12,14;
1Cor 7:22;
Gal 3:2

9:22
k Rom 11:14;
15:1; 1Cor 7:16;
10:33; 2Cor 11:29

9:24
l Gal 2:2; 5:7;
Phil 2:16; 3:14;
2Tim 4:7;
Heb 12:1

¹²If others enjoy this right over you, don't we have a stronger claim? But we didn't use this right. On the contrary, we put up with everything in order not to put an obstacle in the way of the gospel of Christ.ᵃ

¹³You know that those who work in the Temple get their food from the Temple and that those who serve at the altar get their share of its offerings, don't you?ᵇ ¹⁴In the same way, the Lord has ordered that those who proclaim the gospel should make their living from the gospel.ᶜ

¹⁵But I haven't used any of these rights, and I'm not writing this so that they may be applied in my case. I would rather die than let anyone deprive me of my reason forᵃ boasting.ᵈ ¹⁶For if I preach the gospel, I have nothing to boast about, for this obligation has been laid on me. How terrible it would be for me if I didn't preach the gospel!ᵉ ¹⁷For if I do this voluntarily, I get a reward. But if I am unwilling to do it, I am still entrusted with an obligation.ᶠ ¹⁸What, then, is my reward? To be able to preach the gospel free of charge, and so never resort to using my rights in the gospel.ᵍ

¹⁹Although I am free from all people, I made myself a slave to all of them to win more of them.ʰ ²⁰To the Jews I became like a Jew to win Jews. To those under the Law I became like a man under the Law, in order to win those under the Law (although I myself am not under the Law).ⁱ ²¹To those who don't have the Law, I became like a man who doesn't have the Law, in order to win those who don't have the Law (although I am not free from God's Law, but am under the law of Christ).ʲ ²²To the weak I became weak to win the weak. I have become all things to all people so that by all possible means I might save some of them.ᵏ ²³I do all this for the sake of the gospel in order to have a share in its blessings.

²⁴You know that in a race all the runners run but only one wins the prize, don't you? You must run in such a way that you may be victorious.ˡ ²⁵Everyone who enters an athletic contest practices self-control in everything. They do it

a 9:15 The Gk. lacks *reason for*

to win a wreath that dies, but we to win one that never dies.*a* ²⁶That is the way I run, with a clear goal in mind. That is the way I box, not like someone punching the air.*b* ²⁷No, I keep on beating my body and making it my slave so that, after I have preached to others, I myself will not somehow be disqualified.*c*

Warnings About Idolatry

10 ¹For I don't want you to be ignorant, brothers, of the fact that all of our ancestors were under the cloud, and they all went through the sea,*d* ²and they all were baptized into Moses in the cloud and in the sea, ³and they all ate the same spiritual food,*e* ⁴and they all drank the same spiritual drink, for they continually drank from the spiritual Rock that went with them, and that Rock was Christ.*f* ⁵But God wasn't pleased with most of them, and so they were struck down in the wilderness.*g*

⁶Now these things became examples for us so that we won't set our hearts on evil as they did.*h* ⁷Let us stop being idolaters, as some of them were. As it is written, "The people sat down to eat and drink and got up to play."*a i* ⁸Let us stop sinning sexually, as some of them were doing, and on a single day 23,000 fell dead.*j* ⁹Let us stop putting the Lord*b* to the test, as some of them were doing, and were destroyed by snakes.*k* ¹⁰You must stop complaining, as some of them were doing, and were destroyed by the destroying angel.*l* ¹¹These things happened to them to serve as an example, and they were written down as a warning for us in whom the climax of the ages has been realized.*m*

¹²Therefore, the person who thinks he is standing securely should watch out that he doesn't fall.*n* ¹³No temptation has overtaken you that is unusual for human beings. But God is faithful, and he will not allow you to be tempted beyond your strength. Instead, along with the temptation he will also provide a way out, so that you may be able to endure it.*o*

Jer 29:11; 1Cor 1:9; 2Peter 2:9

---

a *10:7* Exod 32:6   **b** *10:9* Other mss. read *Christ*

9:25
a Eph 6:12;
1Tim 6:12;
2Tim 2:5; 4:7-8;
James 1:12;
1Peter 1:4; 5:4;
Rev 2:10; 3:11
9:26
b 2Tim 2:5
9:27
c Jer 6:30;
Rom 6:18-19;
8:13; 2Cor 13:5-6;
Col 3:5
10:1
d Exod 13:21;
14:22; 40:34;
Num 9:18; 14:14;
33:8; Deut 1:33;
Josh 4:23;
Neh 9:12,19;
Ps 78:13-14;
105:39
10:3
e Exod 16:15,35;
Neh 9:15,20;
Ps 78:24
10:4
f Exod 17:6;
Num 20:11;
Ps 78:15
10:5
g Num 14:29,32,
35; 26:64-65;
Ps 106:26;
Heb 3:17;
Jude 1:5
10:6
h Num 11:4,
33-34; Ps 106:14
10:7
i Exod 32:6;
1Cor 10:14
10:8
j Num 25:1,9;
Ps 106:29;
1Cor 6:18;
Rev 2:14
10:9
k Exod 17:2,7;
Num 21:5-6;
Deut 6:16;
Ps 78:18,56; 95:9;
106:14
10:10
l Exod 12:23; 16:2;
17:2; Num 14:2,
29,37; 16:41,49;
2Sam 24:16;
1Chr 21:15
10:11
m Rom 15:4;
1Cor 7:29; 9:10;
Phil 4:5;
Heb 10:25,37;
1John 2:18
10:12
n Rom 11:20
10:13
o Ps 125:3;

10:14
a 1Cor 10:7;
2Cor 6:17;
1John 5:21

10:15
b 1Cor 8:1

10:16
c Matt 26:26-28;
Acts 2:42,46;
1Cor 11:23-24

10:17
d Rom 12:5;
1Cor 12:27

10:18
e Lev 3:3; 7:15;
Rom 4:1,12; 9:3,
5; 2Cor 11:18;
Gal 6:16

10:19
f 1Cor 8:4

10:20
g Lev 17:7;
Deut 32:17;
Ps 106:37;
Rev 9:20

10:21
h Deut 32:38;
2Cor 6:15-16

10:22
i Deut 32:21;
Ezek 22:14

10:23
j 1Cor 6:12

10:24
k Rom 15:1-2;
1Cor 13:5; 15:33;
Phil 2:4,21

10:25
l 1Tim 4:4

10:26
m Exod 19:5;
Deut 10:14;
Ps 24:1; 50:12;
1Cor 10:28

10:27
n Lk 10:7

10:28
o Deut 10:14;
Ps 24:1;
1Cor 8:10,12;
10:26

10:29
p Rom 14:16

10:30
q Rom 14:6;
1Tim 4:3-4

[14]And so, my dear friends, keep on running away from idolatry.[a] [15]I'm talking to sensible people. Decide for yourselves what I'm saying.[b] [16]The cup of blessing that we bless is a sign of our sharing in the blood of Christ, isn't it? The bread that we break is a sign of our sharing in the body of Christ, isn't it?[c] [17]Because there is one loaf, we who are many are one body, because all of us partake of the one loaf.[d]

[18]Look at the Israelites from a human point of view.[a] Those who eat the sacrifices share in what is on the altar, don't they?[e] [19]Am I suggesting that an offering made to idols means anything, or that an idol itself means anything?[f] [20]Hardly! What they offer they offer to demons and not to God, and I don't want you to become partners with demons.[g] [21]You can't drink the cup of the Lord and the cup of demons. You can't eat at the table of the Lord and at the table of demons.[h] [22]Are we trying to provoke the Lord to jealousy? We're not stronger than he is, are we?[i]

All to the Glory of God

[23]Everything is permissible, but not everything is helpful. Everything is permissible, but not everything builds others[b] up.[j] [24]No one should seek his own welfare, but rather his neighbor's.[k]

[25]Eat anything that is sold in the meat market without raising any question about it on the ground of conscience,[l] [26]for, "The earth and everything in it belong to the Lord."[c][m] [27]If an unbeliever invites you to his house and you wish to go, eat whatever is set before you, raising no question on the ground of conscience.[n] [28]However, if someone says to you, "This was offered in sacrifice," don't eat it, both out of consideration for the one who told you and because of conscience.[o] [29]I mean, of course, his conscience, not yours. For why should my freedom be judged by someone else's conscience?[p] [30]If I eat with thankfulness, why should I be denounced because of what I am thankful for?[q]

[31]Therefore, whether you eat or drink, or whatever you

---

a *10:18* Lit. *Israel according to the flesh*   **b** *10:23* The Gk. lacks *others*
c *10:26* Ps 24:1

do, do everything to the glory of God.[a] 32Stop being[a] stumbling blocks to Jews or Greeks or to the church of God,[b] 33just as I myself try to please everybody in every way, not looking for my own advantage but for that of many people, so that they might be saved.[c]

Be Imitators of Me

11 1Be imitators of me, as I am of Christ.[d] 2I praise you for remembering me in everything and for carefully following the traditions, just as I passed them on to you.[e]

Advice about Uncovering the Head in Worship

3Now I want you to realize that Christ is the head of every man, and man is the head of the woman, and God is the head of Christ.[f] 4Every man who prays or prophesies with something on his head dishonors his head,[g] 5and every woman who prays or prophesies with her head uncovered dishonors her head, which is the same as having her head shaved.[h] 6So if a woman doesn't cover her head, she should cut off her hair. If it's a disgrace for a woman to cut off her hair or shave her head, let her cover her own head.[i]

7A man shouldn't cover his own head, because he exists as God's image and glory. But the woman is man's glory,[j] 8for man didn't come from woman, but woman from man;[k] 9and man wasn't created for woman, but woman for man.[l] 10This is why a woman should have authority over her own head: because of the angels.[m]

11In the Lord, however, woman is not independent of man, nor is man of woman.[n] 12For as woman came from man, so man comes through woman. But everything comes from God.[o] 13Decide for yourselves: Is it proper for a woman to pray to God with her head uncovered?[b] 14Nature itself teaches you neither that it is disgraceful for a man to have long hair[c] 15nor that hair is a woman's glory, for hair is given as a substitute for coverings. 16But if anyone wants to

---

a 10:32 Or *Don't be*   b 10:13 Or *It is proper . . . uncovered, isn't it?*
c 10:14 The Gk. lacks *long*

10:31
a Col 3:17;
1 Peter 4:11

10:32
b Acts 20:28;
Rom 14:13;
1 Cor 8:13; 11:22;
2 Cor 6:3;
1 Tim 3:5

10:33
c Rom 15:2;
1 Cor 9:19,22,24

11:1
d 1 Cor 4:16;
Eph 5:1; Phil 3:17;
1 Thes 1:6;
2 Thes 3:9

11:2
e 1 Cor 4:17; 7:17

11:3
f Gen 3:16;
John 14:28;
1 Cor 3:23;
15:27-28;
Eph 5:23;
Phil 2:7-9;
1 Tim 2:11-12;
1 Peter 3:1,5-6

11:4
g 1 Cor 12:10,28;
14:1

11:5
h Deut 21:12;
Acts 21:9

11:6
i Num 5:18;
Deut 22:5

11:7
j Gen 1:26-27;
5:1; 9:6

11:8
k Gen 2:21-22

11:9
l Gen 2:18,21,23

11:10
m Gen 24:65;
Eccl 5:6

11:11
n Gal 3:28

11:12
o Rom 11:36

11:16
a 1Cor 7:17;
14:33; 1Tim 6:4

argue about this, we don't have any custom like this, nor do any of God's churches.*a*

Concerning the Lord's Supper
(Matthew 26:26–29; Mark 14:22–25; Luke 22:14–20)

11:18
b 1Cor 1:10-12;
3:3

[17]I'm not praising you in giving you the following instructions: When you gather, it is not for the better but for the worse. [18]In the first place, I hear that when you gather as a church there are divisions among you, and I partly believe it.*b* [19]Of course, there must be factions among you to show which of you are genuine!*c*

11:19
c Deut 13:3;
Matt 18:7;
Lk 2:35; 17:1;
Acts 20:30;
1Tim 4:1;
2Peter 2:1-2;
1John 2:19

[20]When you gather in the same place, it is not to eat the Lord's Supper. [21]For as you eat, each of you rushes to eat his own supper, and one person goes hungry while another gets drunk.*d* [22]You have homes in which to eat and drink, don't you? Or do you despise God's church and humiliate those who have nothing? What should I say to you? Should I praise you? I won't praise you for this!*e*

11:21
d 2Peter 2:13;
Jude 1:12

11:22
e 1Cor 10:32;
James 2:6

[23]For I received from the Lord what I also passed on to you: The Lord Jesus, on the night he was betrayed, took a loaf of bread,*f* [24]gave thanks for it, and broke it in pieces, saying, "This is my body that is[a] for you. Keep doing this in memory of me." [25]He did the same with the cup after the supper, saying, "This cup is the new covenant in my blood. As often as you drink from it, keep doing this in memory of me." [26]For as often as you eat this bread and drink from this cup, you proclaim the Lord's death until he comes.*g*

11:23
f Matt 26:26;
Mark 14:22;
Lk 22:19;
1Cor 15:3;
Gal 1:1,11-12

11:26
g John 14:3;
21:22; Acts 1:11;
1Cor 4:5; 15:23;
1Thes 4:16;
2Thes 1:10;
Jude 1:14; Rev 1:7

[27]Therefore, whoever eats the bread or drinks from the cup in an unworthy manner will be held responsible for the Lord's body and blood.*h* [28]A person must examine himself and then eat the bread and drink from the cup.*i* [29]For the one who eats and drinks[b] without recognizing the body[c] eats and drinks judgment on himself. [30]That's why so many of you are weak and sick and a considerable number are dying.*d* [31]But if we judged ourselves correctly, we would not be judged.*j* [32]Now, while we are being judged by the Lord,

11:27
h Num 9:10,13;
John 6:51,63-64;
13:27; 1Cor 10:21

11:28
i 2Cor 13:5;
Gal 6:4

11:31
j Ps 32:5;
1John 1:9

---

a 11:24 Other mss. read *that is broken;* still other mss. read *that is given*
b 11:29 Other mss. read *drinks in an unworthy manner*   **c** 11:29 Other mss. read *the Lord's body*   **d** 11:30 Lit. *are falling asleep*

we are being disciplined so that we won't be condemned along with the world.*a*

33Therefore, my brothers, when you gather to eat, wait for each other. 34If anyone is hungry, he should eat at home, so that when you gather it will not bring judgment on you. And when I come I will give instructions concerning the other matters.*b*

Concerning Spiritual Gifts

12 1Now concerning spiritual gifts, brothers, I don't want you to be ignorant.*c* 2You know that when you were Gentiles, you were enticed and led away to idols that couldn't even speak.*d* 3So I want you to know that no one who is speaking by God's Spirit can say, "Jesus is cursed," and no one can say, "Jesus is Lord," except by the Holy Spirit.*e*

4Now gifts vary, but the Spirit is the same;*f* 5and ministries vary, but the Lord is the same;*g* 6and results vary, but God is the same, and it is he who produces all the results in everyone.*h*

7To each person has been given the ability to display the Spirit for the common good.*i* 8To one has been given a message of wisdom by the Spirit; to another the ability to speak with knowledge according to the same Spirit;*j* 9to another faith by the same Spirit; to another gifts of healing by that one Spirit;*k* 10to another miraculous results; to another prophecy; to another the ability to distinguish between spirits; to another various kinds of tongues; and to another the interpretation of tongues.*l* 11One and the same Spirit produces all these results and gives what he wants to each person.*m*

The Unity and Diversity of Spiritual Gifts

12For just as the body is one and yet has many parts, and all the parts of the body, though many, form one body, so it is with Christ.*n* 13For by*a* one Spirit all of us—Jews and

---

a 12:13 Or *in*

11:32
a Ps 94:12-13;
Heb 12:5-11

11:34
b 1Cor 4:19; 7:17;
11:21-22 Titus 1:5

12:1
c 1Cor 14:1,37

12:2
d Ps 115:5;
1Cor 6:11;
Eph 2:11-12;
1Thes 1:9;
Titus 3:3;
1Peter 4:3

12:3
e Matt 16:17;
Mark 9:39;
John 15:26;
2Cor 3:5;
1John 4:2-3

12:4
f Rom 12:4;
Eph 4:4; Heb 2:4;
1Peter 4:10

12:5
g Rom 12:6-8;
Eph 4:11

12:6
h Eph 1:23

12:7
i Rom 12:6-8;
1Cor 14:26;
Eph 4:7;
1Peter 4:10-11

12:8
j 1Cor 1:5; 2:6-7;
13:2; 2Cor 8:7

12:9
k Matt 17:19-20;
Mark 16:18;
1Cor 13:2;
2Cor 4:13 James
5:14

12:10
l Mark 16:17;
Acts 2:4; 10:46;
Rom 12:6;
1Cor 12:28-29;
13:1-2; 14:1,29;
Gal 3:5; 1John 4:1

12:11
m John 3:8;
Rom 12:6;
1Cor 7:7;
2Cor 10:13;
Eph 4:7; Heb 2:4

12:12
n Rom 12:4-5;
1Cor 12:27;
Gal 3:16;
Eph 4:4,16

12:13
a John 6:63;
7:37-39; Rom 6:5;
Gal 3:28;
Eph 2:13-14,16;
Col 3:11

Greeks, slaves and free—were baptized into one body and were all privileged to drink from one Spirit.*a*

¹⁴For the body doesn't consist of only one part, but of many. ¹⁵If the foot says, "Since I'm not a hand, I'm not part of the body," that doesn't make it any less a part of the body, does it? ¹⁶And if the ear says, "Since I'm not an eye, I'm not part of the body," that doesn't make it any less a part of the body, does it? ¹⁷If the whole body were an eye, where would the sense of hearing be? If the whole body[a] were an ear, where would the sense of smell be? ¹⁸At this very time God has arranged the parts, every one of them, in the body just as he wanted to.*b* ¹⁹If they were all one part, where would the body be? ²⁰So there are many parts, but one body.

12:18
b Rom 12:3;
1 Cor 3:5,11;
12:28

²¹The eye can't say to the hand, "I don't need you," or the head to the feet, "I don't need you." ²²On the contrary, those parts of the body that seem to be weaker are in fact indispensable, ²³and the parts of the body that we think are less honorable are treated with special honor, and we make our less attractive parts more attractive. ²⁴However, our attractive parts don't need this. But God has put the body together and has given special honor to the parts that lack it, ²⁵so that there should be no disharmony in the body, but that its parts should have the same concern for each other. ²⁶If one part suffers, every part suffers with it. If one part is praised, every part rejoices with it.

12:27
c Rom 12:5;
Eph 1:23; 4:12;
5:23,30; Col 1:24

²⁷Now, you are Christ's body and individual parts of it.*c* ²⁸God has appointed in the church first of all apostles, second prophets, third teachers, then those who perform miracles, those who have gifts of healing, those who help others, administrators, and various kinds of tongues.*d* ²⁹Not all are apostles, are they? Not all are prophets, are they? Not all are teachers, are they? Not all perform miracles, do they? ³⁰Not all have the gift of healing, do they? Not all speak in tongues, do they? Not all interpret, do they? ³¹So keep on desiring[b] the better gifts. And now I will show you the best way of all.*e*

12:28
d Num 11:17;
Acts 13:1;
Rom 12:6,8;
1 Cor 12:9-10;
Eph 2:20; 3:5;
4:11; 1 Tim 5:17;
Heb 13:17,24

12:31
e 1 Cor 14:1,39

a 12:17 The Gk. lacks *body*   **b** 12:31 Or *You are desiring*

The Supremacy of Love

13 ¹If I speak in the tongues of humans and angels but don't have love, I have become a reverberating gong or a clashing cymbal. ²If I have the gift of prophecy and can understand all secrets and every form of knowledge, and if I have absolute faith so as to move mountains but don't have love, I am nothing.*ᵃ* ³Even if I give away all that I have and surrender my body so that I may boast**ᵃ** but don't have love, I get nothing out of it.*ᵇ*

4   *Love is always**ᵇ** patient,ᶜ*
     *Love is always**ᵇ** kind,*
     Love is never envious
     Or vaunted up with pride.

     Nor is she conceited,
5   *And never is she rude,ᵈ*
     Never does she think of self
     Or ever get annoyed.

     She never is resentful,
6   *Is never glad with sin,ᵉ*
     But always glad to side with truth,
     *Whene'er the truth should win.***ᶜ**

7   *She bears up under everything,ᶠ*
     Believes the best in all,
     There is no limit to her hope,
     And never will she fall.

⁸Love never breaks down. If there are prophecies, they will be done away with. If there are tongues, they will cease. If there is knowledge, it will be done away with. ⁹For what we know is incomplete and what we prophesy is incomplete.ᵍ ¹⁰But when what is complete**ᵈ** comes, then what is incomplete will be done away with.

¹¹When I was a child, I spoke like a child, thought like a child, and reasoned like a child. When I became a man, I gave up my childish ways. ¹²Now we see only a blurred

---

a 13:3 Other mss. read *my body to be burned*   **b** 13:4 The Gk. lacks *always*
c 13:6 Lit. *but rejoices in the truth*   **d** 13:10 Or *when that which is perfect*

Side references:

13:2
ᵃ Matt 7:22; 17:20;
Mark 11:23;
Lk 17:6;
1 Cor 12:8-10,28;
14:1

13:3
ᵇ Matt 6:1-2

13:4
ᶜ Prov 10:12;
1 Peter 4:8

13:5
ᵈ 1 Cor 10:24;
Phil 2:4

13:6
ᵉ Ps 10:3;
Rom 1:32;
2 John 1:4

13:7
ᶠ Rom 15:1;
Gal 6:2;
2 Tim 2:24

13:9
ᵍ 1 Cor 8:2

13:12
a Matt 18:10;
2Cor 3:18; 5:7;
Phil 3:12;
1John 3:2

reflection in a mirror, but then we will see face to face. Now what I know is incomplete, but then I will know fully, even as I have been fully known.*a*

¹³Right now three things remain: faith, hope, and love. But the greatest of these is love.

Prophecy and Tongues

14 ¹Keep on pursuing love, and keep on desiring spiritual gifts, especially the ability to prophesy.*b* ²For the person who speaks in a tongue doesn't speak to people but to God. Indeed, no one understands him, because he is speaking secrets in the Spirit.*ac* ³But the person who prophesies speaks to people for their upbuilding, encouragement, and comfort. ⁴The person who speaks in a tongue builds himself up, but the person who prophesies builds the church up. ⁵I wish that all of you could speak in tongues, but especially that you could prophesy. The person who prophesies is more important than the person who speaks in a tongue, unless he interprets it so that the church may be built up.

⁶Now, brothers, if I come to you speaking in tongues, what good will I be to you unless I speak to you in some revelation, knowledge, prophecy, or teaching?*d* ⁷In the same way, lifeless instruments like the flute or harp produce sounds. But if there's no difference in the notes, how can a person tell what tune is being played? ⁸For example, if a bugle doesn't sound a clear call, who will get ready for battle? ⁹In the same way, unless you speak an intelligible message with your tongue, how will anyone know what is being said? You'll be talking into the air!

¹⁰There are, I suppose, many different languages*b* in the world, yet none of them is without meaning. ¹¹If I don't know the meaning of the language,*c* I will be a foreigner to the speaker and the speaker will be a foreigner to me. ¹²In the same way, since you're so desirous of spiritual gifts, you must keep on desiring them for the upbuilding of the church.

¹³Therefore, the person who speaks in a tongue should

14:1
b Num 11:25,29;
1Cor 12:31

14:2
c Acts 2:4; 10:46

14:6
d 1Cor 14:26

a 14:2 Or *with his spirit*   b 14:10 Or *sounds*   c 14:11 Or *sound*

pray for the ability to interpret it. [14]For if I pray in a tongue, my spirit prays, but my mind is not productive. [15]What does this mean? I will pray with my spirit, but I will also pray with my mind. I will sing psalms with my spirit, but I will also sing psalms with my mind.[a] [16]Otherwise, if you say a blessing with your spirit, how can an otherwise uneducated person[a] say "Amen" to your thanksgiving, since he doesn't know what you're saying?[b] [17]It's good for you to give thanks, but it doesn't build up the other person. [18]I thank God that I speak in tongues more than all of you. [19]But in church I would rather speak five words with my mind to instruct others than 10,000 words in a tongue.

[20]Brothers, stop being[b] children in your thinking. In evil be infants, but in thinking be adults.[c] [21]In the Law it is written,[d]

> "Through people of strange tongues
>   and through the mouths of foreigners
> I will speak to this people,
>   but even then they will not listen to me,"[c]

says the Lord.
[22]Tongues, then, are meant to be a sign, not for believers, but for unbelievers, while prophecy is meant, not for unbelievers, but for believers. [23]Now if the whole church gathers in the same place and everyone is speaking in tongues, when uneducated people or unbelievers come in, they'll say that you're out of your mind, won't they?[e] [24]But if everyone is prophesying, when an unbeliever or an uneducated person comes in, he will be convicted by all and examined by all. [25]The secrets in his heart will become known, and so he will bow down to the ground and worship God, declaring, "God is truly among you!"[f]

Maintain Order in the Church

[26]So what does this mean, brothers? When you gather, everyone has a psalm, teaching, revelation, tongue, or interpretation. Everything must be done for upbuilding.[g] [27]If

14:15 [a]Ps 47:7; Eph 5:19; Col 3:16

14:16 [b]1Cor 11:24

14:20 [c]Ps 131:2; Matt 11:25; 18:3; 19:14; Rom 16:19; 1Cor 3:1; Eph 4:14; Heb 5:12-13; 1Peter 2:2

14:21 [d]Isa 28:11-12; John 10:34

14:23 [e]Acts 2:13

14:25 [f]Isa 45:14; Zech 8:23

14:26 [g]1Cor 12:7-10; 14:6; 2Cor 12:19; Eph 4:12

---

a 14:16 Lit. *the person who occupies the place of the uneducated*　　b 14:20 Or *don't be*　　c 14:21 Isa 28:11-12

14:29
a 1Cor 12:10

14:30
b 1Thes 5:19-20

14:32
c 1John 4:1

14:33
d 1Cor 11:16

14:34
e Gen 3:16;
1Cor 11:3;
Eph 5:22;
Col 3:18;
1Tim 2:11-12;
Titus 2:5;
1Peter 3:1

14:37
f 2Cor 10:7;
1John 4:6

14:39
g 1Cor 12:31;
1Thes 5:20

14:40
h 1Cor 14:33

15:1
i Rom 5:2;
Gal 1:11

15:2
j Rom 1:16;
1Cor 1:21;
Gal 3:4

15:3
k Ps 22:15;
Isa 53:5-6;
Dan 9:26;
Zech 13:7;
Lk 24:26,46;
Acts 3:18; 26:23;
1Cor 11:2,23;
Gal 1:12;
1Peter 1:11; 2:24

anyone speaks in a tongue, only two or three at the most should do so, one at a time, and somebody must interpret. [28]If an interpreter isn't present, he should remain silent in the church and speak to himself and God.

[29]Two or three prophets should speak, and the others should weigh carefully what is said.[a] [30]If a revelation is made to another person who is seated, the first person should be silent.[b] [31]For everyone can prophesy in turn, so that everyone can be instructed and everyone can be encouraged. [32]The spirits of prophets are subject to the prophets.[c] [33]For God[a] is not a God of disorder but of peace. As in all the churches of the saints,[d] [34]the women must keep silent in the churches. They are not allowed to speak out, but must place themselves in submission, as the Law also says.[e] [35]If they want to learn anything, they should ask their own husbands at home, for it is inappropriate for a woman to speak out in church.[b]

[36]Did God's word originate with you? Are you the only people it has reached? [37]If anyone thinks he is a prophet or a spiritual person, he must acknowledge that what I am writing to you is the Lord's command.[f] [38]But if anyone ignores this, he should be ignored.[c]

[39]Therefore, my brothers, desire the ability to prophesy, and don't prevent others from speaking in tongues.[g] [40]But everything must be done in a proper and orderly way.[h]

The Resurrection of Christ

15 [1]Now I'm making known to you, brothers, the gospel that I proclaimed to you, which you accepted, on which you have taken your stand,[i] [2]and by which you are also being saved if you hold firmly to the message I proclaimed to you—unless, of course, your faith was worthless.[j]

[3]For I passed on to you the most important points of[d] what I received: Christ died for our sins in keeping with the Scriptures,[k] [4]he was buried, he was raised on the third day

---

a 14:33 Lit. *he*   b 14:35 Other mss. place vss. 34 and 35 after vs. 40.
c 14:38 Other mss. read *If he is ignorant of this, he should remain ignorant*
d 15:3 Or *to you as matters of great importance*

in keeping with the Scriptures—and is still alive!*ᵃ*—⁵and he was seen by Cephas,**ᵃ** and then by the twelve.*ᵇ* ⁶After that, he was seen by more than 500 brothers at one time, most of whom are still alive, though some have died.**ᵇ** ⁷Next he was seen by James, then by all the apostles,*ᶜ* ⁸and finally he was seen by me, as though I were born abnormally late.*ᵈ*

⁹For I am the least of the apostles and not even fit to be called an apostle because I persecuted God's church.*ᵉ* ¹⁰But by God's grace I am what I am, and his grace shown to me wasn't wasted. Instead, I worked harder than all the others—not I, of course, but God's grace that was with me.*ᶠ* ¹¹So, whether it was I or they, this is what we preach, and this is what you believed.

The Resurrection of the Dead

¹²Now if we preach that Christ has been raised from the dead, how can some of you keep claiming there is no resurrection of the dead? ¹³If there is no resurrection of the dead, then Christ hasn't been raised,*ᵍ* ¹⁴and if Christ hasn't been raised, then our message means nothing and your**ᶜ** faith means nothing. ¹⁵In addition, we are found to be false witnesses about God because we testified on God's behalf that he raised Christ—whom he didn't raise if in fact it's true that the dead aren't raised.*ʰ* ¹⁶For if the dead aren't raised, then Christ hasn't been raised, ¹⁷and if Christ hasn't been raised, your faith is worthless and you're still in your sins.*ⁱ* ¹⁸Yes, even those who have died**ᵇ** in Christ are lost. ¹⁹If we have set our hopes on Christ in this life only, we deserve more pity than any other people.*ʲ*

²⁰But at this moment Christ stands risen from the dead, the first one offered in the harvest of those who have died.**ᵇ**ᵏ ²¹For since death came through a man, the resurrection of the dead also came through a man.*ˡ* ²²For as in Adam all die, so also in Christ will all be made alive. ²³However, this will happen to each person in the proper order: first Christ,**ᵈ** then those who belong to Christ when he comes.*ᵐ* ²⁴Then the end will come, when he hands over the kingdom to God the

---

a15:5 I.e. Peter   **b**15:6,15:18,15:20 Lit. *have fallen asleep*   **c**15:14 Other mss. read *our*   **d**15:23 Lit. *Christ the first fruits*

15:4 ᵃPs 2:7; 16:10; Isa 53:10; Hos 6:2; Lk 24:26, 46; Acts 2:25-31; 13:33-35; 26:22-23; 1Peter 1:11

15:5 ᵇMatt 28:17; Mark 16:14; Lk 24:34,36; John 20:19,26; Acts 10:41

15:7 ᶜLk 24:50; Acts 1:3-4

15:8 ᵈActs 9:4,17; 22:14,18; 1Cor 9:1

15:9 ᵉActs 8:3; 9:1; Gal 1:13; Eph 3:8; Phil 3:6; 1Tim 1:13

15:10 ᶠMatt 10:20; Rom 15:18-19; 2Cor 3:5; 11:23; 12:11; Gal 2:8; Eph 2:7-8; 3:7; Phil 2:13

15:13 ᵍ1Thes 4:14

15:15 ʰActs 2:24,32; 4:10,33; 13:30

15:17 ⁱRom 4:25

15:19 ʲ2Tim 3:12

15:20 ᵏActs 26:23; 1Cor 15:23; Col 1:18; 1Peter 1:3; Rev 1:5

15:21 ˡJohn 11:25; Rom 5:12,17; 6:23

15:23 ᵐ1Cor 15:20; 1Thes 4:15-17

15:24
a Dan 7:14,27

15:25
b Ps 110:1;
Acts 2:34-35;
Eph 1:22;
Heb 1:13; 10:13

15:26
c 2Tim 1:10;
Rev 20:14

15:27
d Ps 8:6;
Matt 28:18;
Heb 2:8;
1Peter 3:22

15:28
e 1Cor 3:23; 11:3;
Phil 3:21

15:30
f 2Cor 11:26;
Gal 5:11

15:31
g Rom 8:36;
1Cor 4:9;
2Cor 4:10-11;
11:23; 1Thes 2:19

15:32
h Eccl 2:24;
Isa 22:13; 56:12;
Lk 12:19;
2Cor 1:8

15:33
i 1Cor 5:6

15:34
j Rom 13:11;
1Cor 6:5;
Eph 5:14;
1Thes 4:5

15:35
k Ezek 37:3

15:36
l John 12:24

Father after he has done away with every ruler and every authority and power.[a] 25For he must rule until God[a] puts all his enemies under his feet.[b] 26The last enemy to be done away with is death,[c] 27for "God[a] has put everything under his feet."[b] When he says, "Everything has been put under him," this clearly excludes the one who put everything under him.[d] 28But when everything has been put under him, then the Son himself will also become subject to the one who put everything under him, so that God may be all in all.[e]

29Otherwise, what will those people do who are being baptized for the dead? If the dead aren't raised at all, why are they being baptized for them? 30And why in fact are we being endangered every hour?[f] 31I face death every day! That is as certain, brothers,[c] as it is that I'm proud of you in Christ Jesus our Lord.[g] 32If I have fought with wild animals in Ephesus from merely human motives, what do I get out of it? If the dead aren't raised,[h]

"Let's eat and drink, for tomorrow we die."[d]

33Stop being deceived:[i]

"Wicked friends lead to evil ends."[e]

34Come back to your senses as you should, and stop sinning! For some of you—I say this to your shame—are without a true knowledge of God.[j]

The Resurrection Body

35But someone will ask, "How are the dead raised? What kind of body will they have when they come back?"[k] 36You fool! The seed you plant doesn't come to life unless it dies,[l] 37and what you plant isn't the form that it will be, but a bare kernel, whether it's wheat or something else. 38But God gives the plant[f] the form he wants it to have, and to each kind of seed its own form. 39Not all flesh is the same.[g] Humans have one kind of flesh,[h] animals in general have

---

a 15:25,15:27 Lit. *he*   b 15:27 Ps 8:6   c 15:31 Other mss. lack *brothers*
d 15:32 Isa 22:13   e 15:33 Menander, *Thais* (218)   f 15:38 The Gk. lacks *the plant*   g 15:39 Lit. *the same flesh*   h 15:39 The Gk. lacks *of flesh*

another,[a] birds have another,[a] and fish have still another. [40]There are heavenly bodies and earthly bodies, but the splendor of those in heaven is of one kind, and that of those on earth is of another. [41]One kind of splendor belongs to the sun, another[b] to the moon, and still another[b] to the stars. In fact, one star differs from another star in splendor.

[42]This is how it will be at the resurrection of the dead. What is planted is decaying, what is raised can't decay.[a] [43]The body[c] is planted in dishonor but raised in splendor. It is planted in weakness but raised in power.[b] [44]It is planted a physical body but raised a spiritual body. If there is a physical body, there is also a spiritual body.[d]

[45]This, indeed, is what is written: "The first man, Adam, became a living being."[e] The last Adam became a life-giving spirit.[c] [46]The spiritual doesn't come first, but the physical and then the spiritual. [47]The first man came from the dust of the earth; the second man came from heaven.[d] [48]Those who are made of the dust are like the man from the dust. Those who are heavenly are like the man who is from heaven.[e] [49]Just as we have borne the likeness of the man who was made from dust, we will[f] also bear the likeness of the man from heaven.[f]

[50]Brothers, this is what I mean: Flesh and blood can't inherit the kingdom of God, and what decays can't inherit what doesn't decay.[g] [51]Let me tell you a secret. Not all of us will die, but all of us will be changed[h]—[52]in a moment, in the blinking of an eye, at the sound of the last trumpet. Indeed, that trumpet[g] will sound, and then the dead will be raised never to decay, and we will be changed.[i] [53]For what is decaying must put on what can't decay, and what is dying must put on what can't die.[j] [54]Now, when what is decaying puts on what can't decay, and what is dying puts on what can't die, then the saying that is written will be fulfilled: "Death has been swallowed up in victory!"[h][k]

---

a*15:39* Lit. *another kind of flesh*   b*15:41* Lit. *another kind of splendor*
c*15:43* Lit. *It*   d*15:44* The Gk. lacks *body*   e*15:45* Gen 2:7
f*15:49* Other mss. read *we should*   g*15:52* Lit. *it*   h*15:54* Isa 25:8

15:42
a Dan 12:3;
Matt 13:43

15:43
b Phil 3:21

15:45
c Gen 2:7;
John 5:21; 6:33
39-40,54,57;
Rom 5:14;
Phil 3:21; Col 3:4

15:47
d Gen 2:7; 3:19:
John 3:13,31

15:48
e Phil 3:20-21

15:49
f Gen 5:3;
Rom 8:29;
2Cor 3:18; 4:1˜;
Phil 3:21;
1John 3:2

15:50
g Matt 16:17;
John 3:3,5

15:51
h Phil 3:21;
1Thes 4:15-17

15:52
i Zech 9:14;
Matt 24:31;
John 5:25;
1Thes 4:16

15:53
j 2Cor 5:4

15:54
k Isa 25:8;
Heb 2:14-15;
Rev 20:14

15:55
a Hos 13:14

15:56
b Rom 4:15; 5:13;
7:5,13

15:57
c Rom 7:25;
1John 5:4-5

15:58
d 1Cor 3:8;
2Peter 3:14

16:1
e Acts 11:29;
24:17;
Rom 15:26;
2Cor 8:4; 9:1,12;
Gal 2:10

16:2
f Acts 20:7;
Rev 1:10

16:3
g 2Cor 8:19

16:4
h 2Cor 8:4,19

16:5
i Acts 19:21;
2Cor 1:16

16:6
j Acts 15:3; 17:15;
21:5; Rom 15:24;
2Cor 1:16

16:7
k Acts 18:21;
1Cor 4:19;
James 4:15

16:9
l Acts 14:27; 19:9;
2Cor 2:12;
Col 4:3; Rev 3:8

16:10
m Acts 19:22;
Rom 16:21;
1Cor 4:17;
Phil 2:20,22;
1Thes 3:2

16:11
n Acts 15:33;
1Tim 4:12

55"Where, O death, is your victory?[a]
Where, O death, is your sting?"[a]

56Now the sting of death is sin, and the power of sin is the Law.[b] 57But thanks be to God, who gives us the victory through our Lord Jesus Christ![c]

58Therefore, my dear brothers, be steadfast, unmovable, always excelling in the work of the Lord, because you know that your work isn't wasted in the Lord.[d]

Concerning the Collection for the Saints

16 1Now concerning the collection for the saints, you should follow the directions I gave to the churches of Galatia.[e] 2On the first day of the week, each of you should set aside and save some of your money in proportion to what you have, so that no collections will have to be made when I come.[f] 3When I arrive, I will send with letters the men you approve to take your gift to Jerusalem.[g] 4If it's worthwhile for me to go, too, they can go with me.[h]

Plans for Travel

5I will visit you when I go through Macedonia—for I intend to go through Macedonia[i]—6and will probably stay with you or even spend the winter. Then you can send me on my way, wherever I decide to go.[j] 7I don't want to see you now just in passing, because I hope to spend some time with you if the Lord permits.[k] 8However, I will be staying on in Ephesus until Pentecost, 9because a door has opened wide for me to do effective work, although many people are opposing me.[l]

10If Timothy comes, see to it that he doesn't have anything to be afraid of while he is with you. He's doing the Lord's work as I am,[m] 11and so no one should treat him with contempt. Send him on his way in peace so that he may come to me, because I'm expecting him along with the brothers.[n]

12Now concerning our brother Apollos, I strongly urged

---

a 15:55 Hos 13:14

him to visit you with the other[a] brothers, but he wasn't inclined to go just now. However, he will come when the time is right.[a]

Final Instructions

[13]Remain alert. Keep standing firm in your faith. Keep on being courageous and strong.[b] [14]Everything you do should be done in love.[c]

[15]Now I urge you, brothers—for you know that the members of the family of Stephanas were the first converts in Achaia, and that they have devoted themselves to serving the saints[d]—[16]to submit yourselves to people like these and to anyone else who shares their labor and hard work.[e] [17]I'm glad that Stephanas, Fortunatus, and Achaicus came here, because they have supplied what was lacking from you.[f] [18]They refreshed my spirit—and yours, too. So you are to appreciate men like that.[g]

Final Greetings

[19]The churches in Asia greet you. Aquila and Prisca[b] and the church in their house greet you warmly in the Lord.[h] [20]All the brothers greet you. Greet one another with a holy kiss.[i] [21]I, Paul, am writing this greeting with my own hand.[j]

[22]If anyone doesn't love the Lord, let him be cursed! May our Lord come![c][k] [23]May the grace of the Lord Jesus be with you![l] [24]My love is with all of you in Christ Jesus.[d]

---

a[16:12] *The* Gk. lacks *other*　b[16:19] I.e. Priscilla　c[16:22] Lit. *Marana tha*
d[16:24] Other mss. read *Jesus. Amen*

16:12
a 1Cor 1:12; 3:5

16:13
b Matt 24:42;
25:13; 1Cor 15:1;
Eph 6:10;
Phil 1:27;
4:1 Col 1:11;
1Thes 3:8; 5:6;
2Thes 2:15;
1Peter 5:8

16:14
c 1Cor 14:1;
1Peter 4:8

16:15
d Rom 16:5;
1Cor 1:16;
2Cor 8:4; 9:1;
Heb 6:10

16:16
e Heb 6:10; 13:17

16:17
f 2Cor 11:9;
Phil 2:30

16:18
g Phil 2:29;
Col 4:8;
1Thes 5:12

16:19
h Rom 16:5,15

16:20
i Rom 16:16

16:21
j Col 4:18;
2Thes 3:17

16:22
k Gal 1:8-9;
Eph 6:24;
Jude 1:14-15

16:23
l Rom 16:20

THE LETTER OF PAUL CALLED
SECOND CORINTHIANS

1:1
a 1Cor 1:1;
Eph 1:1; Phil 1:1;
Col 1:1-2;
1Tim 1:1

Paul Greets the Church in Corinth

1 ¹From*ᵃ* Paul, an apostle of Christ Jesus by the will of God, and Timothy our brother, to the church of God that is in Corinth, with all the holy people*ᵇ* throughout Achaia.*ᵃ* ²May grace and peace from God our Father and the Lord Jesus Christ be yours!*ᵇ*

1:2
b Rom 1:7;
1Cor 1:3; Gal 1:3;
Phil 1:2; Col 1:2;
1Thes 1:1;
2Thes 1:2

The God of All Comfort

³Blessed be the God and Father of our Lord Jesus Christ! He is the Father of mercies and the God of all comfort,*ᶜ* ⁴who comforts us in all our suffering, so that we may be able to comfort others in all their suffering, since we ourselves are being comforted by God. ⁵For just as Christ's sufferings overflow to us, so our comfort overflows through Christ.*ᵈ* ⁶If we suffer, it is for your comfort and salvation. If we are comforted, it is for your comfort when you patiently endure the same sufferings that we are suffering.*ᵉ* ⁷Our hope for you is unshaken, because we know that as you share our sufferings, you also share our comfort.*ᶠ*

1:3
c Eph 1:3;
1Peter 1:3

1:5
d Acts 9:4;
2Cor 4:10;
Col 1:24

1:6
e 2Cor 4:15

How God Rescued Paul

⁸Brothers, we don't want you to be ignorant about the suffering we experienced in Asia. We were so crushed beyond our ability to endure that we even despaired of living.*ᵍ* ⁹In fact, we felt within ourselves that we had received the sentence of death, so that we would not rely on ourselves but on the God who raises the dead.*ʰ* ¹⁰He has rescued us from a terrible death, and he will continue to rescue us. Yes, the one on whom we have set our hope will rescue us again,*ⁱ* ¹¹as you also help us by your prayers on our behalf. Then prayers of thanksgiving will be uttered by many people on our behalf because of the favor shown us through the prayers of many.*ʲ*

1:7
f Rom 8:17;
2Tim 2:12

1:8
g Acts 19:23;
1Cor 15:32; 16:9

1:9
h Jer 17:5,7

1:10
i 2Peter 2:9

1:11
j Rom 15:30;
2Cor 4:15;
Phil 1:19

---

a *1:1 The* Gk. lacks *From*   **b** *1:1* Or *the saints*

397

Paul's Reason for Boasting

[12]For this is what we boast about: Our conscience testifies that we have conducted ourselves in the world with pure motives and godly sincerity, without earthly wisdom but with God's grace—and especially towards you.[a] [13]For what we are writing you is nothing more than what you can read and also understand. I hope you will understand completely, [14]just as you have already understood us partially, so that on the day of our[a] Lord Jesus we can be your reason to boast, even as you are ours.[b]

Why Paul's Visit Was Postponed

[15]It was because of this confidence that I planned to come to you first, so that you might receive a double blessing.[c] [16]I planned to leave you in order to go[b] to Macedonia, and then come back to you from Macedonia, and let you send me on to Judea.[d]

[17]When I planned this, I didn't do it lightly, did I? Are my plans so fickle[c] that I can say "Yes" and "No"[d] at the same time?[e] [18]As certainly as God is faithful, our word to you isn't "Yes" and "No." [19]For God's Son, Jesus Christ, who was preached among you by us—by me, Silvanus, and Timothy—was not "Yes" and "No." But with him it is always "Yes."[f] [20]For all God's promises are "Yes" in him. And so through him we can say "Amen,"[e] to the glory of God.[g] [21]Now the one who makes us—and you as well—secure in union with Christ and has anointed us is God.[h] [22]He has put his seal on us and has given us the Spirit in our hearts as a down payment.[i]

[23]I call upon God as a witness on my behalf that it was in order to spare you that I didn't return to Corinth.[j] [24]It's not that we're trying to lord it over your faith. On the contrary, we are workers with you to promote your joy, because you have been standing firm in the faith.[k]

---

a[1:14] Other mss. read *the*   b[1:16] Lit. *To go through you*   c[1:17] Lit. *according to the flesh*   d[1:17] Lit. *"Yes, yes" and "No, no"*   e[1:20] Lit. *through him is the "Amen"*

1:12
a 1Cor 2:4,13; 2Cor 2:17; 4:2

1:14
b 2Cor 5:12; Phil 2:16; 4:1; 1Thes 2:19-20

1:15
c Rom 1:11; 1Cor 4:19

1:16
d 1Cor 16:5-6

1:17
e 2Cor 10:2

1:19
f Mark 1:1; Lk 1:35; Acts 9:20; Heb 13:8

1:20
g Rom 15:8-9

1:21
h 1John 2:20,27

1:22
i 2Cor 5:5; Eph 1:13-14; 4:30; 2Tim 2:19; Rev 2:17

1:23
j Rom 1:9; 1Cor 4:21; 2Cor 2:3; 11:31; 12:20; 13:2,10; Gal 1:20; Phil 1:8

1:24
k Rom 11:20; 1Cor 3:5; 15:1; 1Peter 5:3

2:1
a 2Cor 1:23;
12:20-21; 13:10

Paul's Painful Visit

2 [1]Now[a] I decided not to pay you another painful visit.[a] [2]After all, if I were to grieve you, who should make me happy but the person I'm making sad? [3]This is the very reason I wrote you, so that when I did come I might not be made sad by those who should have made me happy. For I had confidence in all of you that my gladness would be for all of you.[b] [4]For I wrote to you out of great sorrow and anguish of heart—along with many tears—not to make you sad but to let you know how much love I have for you.[c]

2:3
b 2Cor 7:16; 8:22;
12:21; Gal 5:10

2:4
c 2Cor 7:8-9,12

Forgive the Person Who Sinned

[5]But if anyone has caused grief, he didn't cause me any grief. To some extent—I don't want to emphasize this too much[b]—it has affected[c] all of you.[d] [6]This punishment by the majority is severe enough for such a man.[e] [7]So forgive and comfort him, or else he'll drown in his excessive grief.[f] [8]That's why I'm urging you to assure him of your love. [9]I had also written to you to see if you would stand the test and be obedient in every way.[g] [10]When you forgive someone, I do, too. Indeed, what I have forgiven—if there was anything to forgive—I did[d] in the presence of Christ for your benefit, [11]so that we may not be outsmarted by Satan. After all, we are not unaware of his intentions.

2:5
d 1Cor 5:1;
Gal 4:12

2:6
e 1Cor 5:4-5;
1Tim 5:20

2:7
f Gal 6:1

2:9
g 2Cor 7:15; 10:6

Paul's Anxiety and Relief

[12]When I went to Troas on behalf of the gospel of Christ, a door, in fact, stood wide open for me in the Lord.[h] [13]But my spirit couldn't find any relief, because I couldn't find Titus, my brother. So I said goodbye to them and went on to Macedonia.[i]

[14]But thanks be to God! He always leads us triumphantly in Christ and through us spreads everywhere the fragrance of knowing him.[j] [15]To God we are the aroma of Christ among those who are being saved and among those who are being lost.[k] [16]To some people we are a deadly

2:12
h Acts 16:8; 20:6;
1Cor 16:9

2:13
i 2Cor 7:5-6

2:14
j Song 1:3

2:15
k 1Cor 1:18;
2Cor 4:3

---

a 2:1 Other mss. read *For*   **b** 2:5 The Gk. lacks *too much*   **c** 2:5 The Gk. lacks *it has affected*   **d** 2:10 The Gk. lacks *I did*

fragrance,[a] while to others we are a living fragrance.[b] Who is qualified for this?[a] [17]At least we aren't commercializing God's word like so many others. Instead, in Christ we speak with sincerity, like people who are sent from God and are accountable to God.[cb]

Ministers of the New Covenant

3 [1]Are we beginning to recommend ourselves again? Unlike some people, we don't need letters of recommendation to you or from you, do we?[c] [2]You are our letter, written in our hearts and known and read by everyone.[d] [3]You are demonstrating that you are Christ's letter, produced by our service, written not with ink but with the Spirit of the living God, not on tablets of stone but on tablets of human hearts.[e]

[4]Such is the confidence that we have in God through Christ. [5]By ourselves we are not qualified to claim that anything comes from us. Rather, our credentials come from God,[f] [6]who has also qualified us to be ministers of a new covenant, which is not written but spiritual, because the written text[d] brings death, but the Spirit gives life.[g]

[7]Now if the ministry of death that was inscribed in letters of stone came with such glory that the people of Israel could not gaze on Moses' face (because the glory was fading away from it),[h] [8]won't the Spirit's ministry have even more glory?[i] [9]For if the ministry of condemnation has glory, then the ministry of justification has an overwhelming glory.[j] [10]In fact, that which once had glory lost its glory, because the other glory surpassed it. [11]For if that which fades away came[e] through glory, how much more does that which is permanent have glory?

[12]Since we have such a hope, we speak with great boldness,[k] [13]not like Moses, who kept covering his face with a veil to keep the people of Israel from gazing at the end of what was fading away.[l] [14]However, their minds were

---

a 2:16 Lit. *a fragrance of death to death*   b 2:16 Lit. *a fragrance of life to life*
c 2:17 Lit. *as from God and before God*   d 3:6 Lit. *what is written*
e 3:11 The Gk. lacks *came*

2:16
a Lk 2:34;
John 9:39;
1Cor 15:10;
2Cor 3:5-6;
1Peter 2:7-8

2:17
b 2Cor 1:12; 4:2;
11:13; 2Peter 2:3

3:1
c Acts 18:27;
2Cor 5:12; 10:8,
12; 12:11

3:2
d 1Cor 9:2

3:3
e Exod 24:12;
34:1 Ps 40:8;
Jer 31:33;
Ezek 11:19;
36:26; 1Cor 3:5;
Heb 8:10

3:5
f John 15:5;
1Cor 15:10;
2Cor 2:16;
Phil 2:13

3:6
g Jer 31:31;
Matt 26:28;
John 6:63;
Rom 2:27,29;
3:20; 4:15; 7:6.
9-11; 8:2;
1Cor 3:5; 15:10;
2Cor 5:18;
Gal 3:10; Eph 3:7;
Col 1:25,29;
1Tim 1:11-12;
2Tim 1:11;
Heb 8:6,8

3:7
h Exod 34:1,28-30,
35; Deut 10:1;
Rom 7:10

3:8
i Gal 3:5

3:9
j Rom 1:17; 3:21

3:12
k 2Cor 7:4;
Eph 6:19

3:13
l Exod 34:33,35;
Rom 10:4;
Gal 3:23

3:14
a Isa 6:10;
Matt 13:11,14;
John 12:40;
Acts 28:26;
Rom 11:7-8,25;
2Cor 4:4

3:16
b Exod 34:34;
Isa 25:7;
Rom 11:23,26

3:17
c 1Cor 15:45;
2Cor 3:6

3:18
d Rom 8:29;
1Cor 13:12;
15:49; 2Cor 4:4,6;
Col 3:10;
1Tim 1:11

4:1
e 1Cor 7:25;
2Cor 3:6;
1Tim 1:13

4:2
f 2Cor 2:17; 5:11;
6:4,7; 7:14;
1Thes 2:3,5

4:3
g 1Cor 1:18;
2Cor 2:15;
2Thes 2:10

4:4
h Isa 6:10;
John 1:18; 12:31,
40,45; 14:9,30;
16:11; 2Cor 3:6,
8-9,11,14,18;
Eph 6:12; Phil 2:6;
Col 1:15; Heb 1:3

4:5
i 1Cor 1:13,23;
9:19; 10:33;
2Cor 1:24

4:6
j Gen 1:3;
2Cor 1:4;
1Peter 2:9;
2Peter 1:19

4:7
k 1Cor 2:5;
2Cor 5:1; 12:9

4:8
l 2Cor 7:5

4:9
m Ps 37:24

4:10
n Rom 8:17;
1Cor 15:31;
2Cor 1:5,9;
Gal 6:17;
Phil 3:10;
2Tim 2:11-12;
1Peter 4:13

hardened, for to this day the same veil is still there when they read the old covenant. Only in union with Christ is that veil removed.*aa* [15]Yet even to this day, when Moses is read, a veil covers their hearts. [16]But whenever a person turns to the Lord, the veil is removed.*b*

[17]Now the Lord is the Spirit, and where the Lord's Spirit is, there is freedom.*c* [18]As all of us reflect the glory of the Lord with unveiled faces, we are being transformed into the same image with ever-increasing glory. This comes from the Lord, who is the Spirit.*bd*

Treasure in Clay Jars

4 [1]Therefore, since we have this ministry through the mercy shown to us, we don't get discouraged.*e* [2]Instead, we have renounced secret and shameful ways. We don't use trickery or pervert God's word. By clear statements of the truth we commend ourselves to everyone's conscience before God.*f*

[3]So if our gospel is veiled, it is veiled to those who are dying.*cg* [4]In their case, the god of this world has blinded the minds of those who don't believe to keep them from seeing the light of the glorious gospel of Christ, who is the image of God.*h*

[5]For we don't preach ourselves but Jesus Christ as Lord, and ourselves as merely your servants for Jesus' sake.*i* [6]For God, who said, "Let light shine out of darkness,"*d* has shone in our hearts to give us the light of the knowledge of God's glory in the face of Jesus Christ.*ej*

[7]But we have this treasure in clay jars to show that its extraordinary power comes from God and not from us.*k* [8]In every way we're troubled but not crushed, frustrated but not in despair,*l* [9]persecuted but not abandoned, struck down but not destroyed.*m* [10]We are always carrying around the death of Jesus in our bodies, so that the life of Jesus may be clearly shown in our bodies.*n* [11]While we are alive, we are

---

a 3:14 Lit. *is it removed*   **b** 3:18 Lit. *from glory to glory, just as by the Lord's Spirit*   **c** 4:3 Or *being destroyed*   **d** 4:6 Gen 1:3   **e** 4:6 Other mss. lack *Jesus*; still other mss. read *Christ Jesus*

constantly being handed over to death for Jesus' sake, so that the life of Jesus may be clearly shown in our dying bodies.*ᵃ* ¹²And so death is at work in us, but life is at work**ᵃ** in you.*ᵇ*

¹³Now since we have the same spirit of faith in keeping with what is written—"I believed, and so I spoke"**ᵇ**—we also believe, and so we speak.*ᶜ* ¹⁴We know that the one who raised the Lord Jesus will also raise us with Jesus and present us to God**ᶜ** together with you.*ᵈ* ¹⁵All this is for your sake so that, as his grace spreads, it will increase the thanksgiving of more and more people to the glory of God.*ᵉ*

¹⁶That's why we're not discouraged. No, even if our outer man is wearing out, our inner man is being renewed day by day.*ᶠ* ¹⁷This light, temporary nature of our suffering is producing for us an eternal weight of glory, far beyond any comparison,*ᵍ* ¹⁸because we don't look for things that can be seen but for things that can't be seen. For things that can be seen are temporary, but things that can't be seen are eternal.*ʰ*

Life in an Earthly Tent

5 ¹We know that if the earthly tent we live in is torn down, we have a building in heaven that comes from God, an eternal house not built by human**ᵈ** hands.*ⁱ* ²For in this one we sigh, since we long to put on our heavenly dwelling.*ʲ* ³Of course, if we do put it on, we will not be found without a body.*ᵉᵏ* ⁴So while we are still in this tent, we sigh under our burdens, because we don't want to put it off but to put it on, so that our dying bodies may be swallowed up by life.*ˡ* ⁵God has prepared us for this and has given us his Spirit as a guarantee.*ᵐ*

⁶So we are always confident, and we know that as long as we are at home in this body we are away from the Lord. ⁷For we live by faith, not by sight.*ⁿ* ⁸We are confident, then, and would prefer to be away from this body and to live with the Lord.*ᵒ* ⁹So whether we are at home or away from home,

---

a *4:12 The* Gk. lacks *is at work*　　**b** *4:13* Ps 116:10　　**c** *4:14* The Gk. lacks *to God*　　**d** *5:1 The* Gk. lacks *human*　　**e** *5:3* Lit. *found naked*

402

Side references:

4:11
a Ps 44:22;
Rom 8:36;
1Cor 15:31,49

4:12
b 2Cor 13:9

4:13
c Ps 116:10;
Rom 1:12;
2Peter 1:1

4:14
d Rom 8:11;
1Cor 6:14

4:15
e 1Cor 3:21;
2Cor 1:6,11; 8:19;
9:11-12 Col 1:24;
2Tim 2:10

4:16
f Rom 7:22;
Eph 3:16;
Col 3:10;
1Peter 3:4

4:17
g Matt 5:12;
Rom 8:18;
1Peter 1:6; 5:10

4:18
h Rom 8:24;
2Cor 5:7;
Heb 11:1

5:1
i Job 4:19;
2Cor 4:7;
2Peter 1:13-14

5:2
j Rom 8:23

5:3
k Rev 3:18; 16:15

5:4
l 1Cor 15:53-54

5:5
m Isa 29:23;
Rom 8:23;
2Cor 1:22;
Eph 1:14; 2:10;
4:30

5:7
n Rom 8:24-25;
1Cor 13:12;
2Cor 4:18;
Heb 11:1

5:8
o Phil 1:23

5:10
a Matt 25:31-32;
Rom 2:6; 14:10;
Gal 6:7; Eph 6:8;
Col 3:24-25;
Rev 22:12

5:11
b Job 31:23;
2Cor 4:2;
Heb 10:31;
Jude 1:23

5:12
c 2Cor 1:14; 3:1

5:13
d 2Cor 11:1,16-17;
12:6,11

5:14
e Rom 5:15

5:15
f Rom 6:11-12;
14:7-8; 1Cor 6:19;
Gal 2:20;
1Thes 5:10;
1Peter 4:2

5:16
g Matt 12:50;
John 6:63; 15:14;
Gal 5:6;
Phil 3:7-8;
Col 3:11

5:17
h Isa 43:18-19;
65:17; Rom 8:9;
16:7; Gal 5:6;
6:15; Eph 2:15;
Rev 21:5

5:18
i Rom 5:10;
Eph 2:16;
Col 1:20;
1John 2:2; 4:10

5:19
j Rom 3:24-25

5:20
k Job 33:23;
Mal 2:7; 2Cor 3:6;
6:1; Eph 6:20

5:21
l Isa 53:6,9,12;
Rom 1:17; 5:19;
10:3; Gal 3:13;
1Peter 2:22,24;
1John 3:5

our goal is to be pleasing to him. ¹⁰For all of us must appear before the judgment seat of Christ, so that each of us may receive what he deserves for what he has done in his body, whether good or worthless.ᵃᵃ

Christ's Love Controls Us

¹¹Therefore, since we know the fear of the Lord, we try to persuade people. We ourselves are perfectly known to God. I hope we are also really known to your consciences.ᵇ ¹²We are not recommending ourselves to you again but are giving you a reason to be proud of us, so that you can answer those who are proud of outward things rather than inward character.ᵇᶜ ¹³So if we were crazy, it was for God; if we are sane, it is for you.ᵈ ¹⁴The love of Christ controls us, for we are convinced of this: that one person died for all people; therefore, all people have died.ᵉ ¹⁵He died for all people, so that those who live should no longer live for themselves but for the one who died and rose for them.ᶠ

¹⁶So then, from now on we don't think of anyone from a human point of view.ᶜ Even if we did think of Christ from a human point of view,ᶜ we don't think of him that way any more.ᵍ ¹⁷If anyone is in Christ, he is a new creation. What was old has disappeared, and now everything has become new!ʰ

¹⁸All of this comes from God, who has reconciled us to himself through Christ and has given us the ministry of reconciliation.ⁱ ¹⁹For in Christ God was reconciling the world to himself by not counting their sins against them, and he has committed to us the message of reconciliation.ʲ

²⁰Therefore, we are Christ's representatives, since God is pleading through us. We plead on Christ's behalf: "Be reconciled to God!"ᵏ ²¹Godᵈ made the one who did not know sin to be sin for us, so that we might become God's righteousness in him.ˡ

---

a 5:10 Or *bad* **b** 5:12 Lit. *rather than the heart* **c** 5:16 Lit. *according to the flesh* **d** 5:21 Lit. *He*

Workers with God

6 [1]Since we are working with God,[a] we plead with you not to accept God's grace in vain.[a] [2]For he says,[b]

> "At the right time I heard you,
> and on a day of salvation I helped you."[b]

Listen, now is really the "right time"! Now is the "day of salvation"!

We Are God's Servants

[3]We don't put an obstacle in anyone's way. Otherwise, fault may be found with our ministry.[c] [4]Instead, in every way we demonstrate that we are God's servants by tremendous endurance in the midst of difficulties, hardships, and calamities;[d] [5]in beatings, imprisonments, and riots; in hard work, sleepless nights, and hunger;[e] [6]with purity, knowledge, patience, and kindness; with the Holy Spirit, genuine love, [7]truthful speech, and divine power; through the weapons of righteousness in the right and left hands;[f] [8]through honor and dishonor; through ill repute and good repute; perceived[c] as deceivers and yet true, [9]as unknown and yet well-known, as dying and yet—as you see—very much alive, as punished and yet not killed,[g] [10]as sorrowful and yet always rejoicing, as poor and yet enriching many, as having nothing and yet possessing everything.

[11]We have spoken frankly[d] to you, Corinthians. Our hearts are wide open.[h] [12]We haven't cut you off, but you have cut off your own feelings toward us.[i] [13]Do us a favor—I ask you as my children—and open wide your hearts.[j]

Relating with Unbelievers

[14]Stop becoming[e] unevenly yoked with unbelievers. What partnership can righteousness have with lawlessness? What fellowship can light have with darkness?[k] [15]What harmony exists between Christ and Beliar,[f] or what do a believer and an unbeliever have in common? [16]What

---

a 6:1 Lit. *working together*　**b** 6:2 Isa 49:8　**c** 6:8 The Gk. lacks *perceived*
d 6:11 Lit. *Our mouth is open*　**e** 6:14 Or *Don't become*　**f** 6:15 I.e. the devil

Cross-references:
6:1 [a] 1Cor 3:9; 2Cor 5:20; Heb 12:15
6:2 [b] Isa 49:8
6:3 [c] Rom 14:13; 1Cor 9:12; 10:32
6:4 [d] 1Cor 4:1
6:5 [e] 2Cor 11:23
6:7 [f] 1Cor 2:4; 2Cor 4:2; 7:14; 10:4; Eph 6:11,13; 2Tim 4:7
6:9 [g] Ps 118:18; 1Cor 4:9; 2Cor 1:9; 4:2, 10-11; 5:11; 11:6
6:11 [h] 2Cor 7:3
6:12 [i] 2Cor 12:15
6:13 [j] 1Cor 4:14
6:14 [k] Deut 7:2-3; 1Sam 5:2-3; 1Kings 18:21; 1Cor 5:9; 7:39; 10:21; Eph 5:7,11

6:16
a Exod 29:45;
Lev 26:12;
Jer 31:33; 32:38;
Ezek 11:20;
36:28; 37:26;
Zech 8:8; 13:9;
1 Cor 3:16; 6:19;
Eph 2:21-22;
Heb 3:6

agreement can a temple of God make with idols? For we[a] are the temple of the living God, just as God said:[a]

> "I will live and walk among them.
> I will be their God,
> and they will be my people."[b]

[17]Therefore,[b]

6:17
b Isa 52:11;
2 Cor 7:1;
Rev 18:4

> "Get away from them
> and separate yourselves from them," says the Lord,
> "and don't touch anything unclean.
> Then I will welcome you.
> [18]I will be your Father,[c]
> and you will be my sons and daughters,"
> says the Lord Almighty.[c]

6:18
c Jer 31:1,9;
Rev 21:7

Cleanse Yourselves in Holiness

7:1
d 2 Cor 6:17-18;
1 John 3:3

7 [1]Since we have these promises, dear friends, we should cleanse ourselves from everything that contaminates body and spirit by perfecting holiness in the fear of God.[d]

Encouraged by the Corinthians

7:2
e Acts 20:33;
2 Cor 12:17

[2]Make room for us in your hearts![d] We haven't treated anyone unjustly, harmed anyone, or cheated anyone.[e] [3]I'm not saying this to condemn you. I told you before that you are in our hearts to die together and to live together.[f] [4]I have great confidence in you. I'm very proud of you. I'm very much encouraged. I'm overjoyed in all our troubles.[g]

7:3
f 2 Cor 6:11-12

7:4
g 1 Cor 1:4;
2 Cor 1:4,14;
3:12 Phil 2:17;
Col 1:24

[5]For even when we came to Macedonia, our bodies had no rest. We suffered in a number of ways. Outwardly there were conflicts, inwardly there were fears.[h] [6]Yet God, who comforts those who feel miserable, comforted us by the arrival of Titus,[i] [7]and not only by his arrival but also by the comfort he had received from you. He told us about your

7:5
h Deut 32:25;
2 Cor 2:13; 4:8

7:6
i 2 Cor 1:4; 2:13

---

a *6:16* Other mss. read *you* (plural)   **b** *6:16* Lev 26:12; Ezek 37:27
c *6:18* Isa 52:11; Ezek 20:34, 41; 2 Sam 7:8, 14   **d** *7:2 The* Gk. lacks *in your hearts*

longing for me, your sorrow, and your eagerness to take my side, and this made me even happier.

8If I made you sad with my letter, I don't regret it, although I did regret it then. I see that the letter caused you sorrow, though only for a while.*a* 9Now I'm happy, not because you had such sorrow, but because your sorrow led you to repentance. For you were sorry in a godly way, and so you were not hurt by us in any way. 10For having sorrow in a godly way results in repentance that leads to salvation and leaves no regrets. But the sorrow of the world produces death.*b*

11See what great earnestness godly sorrow has produced in you! How ready you are to clear yourselves, how indignant, how alarmed, how full of longing and enthusiasm, how eager to seek justice! In every way you have demonstrated that you are innocent in this matter. 12So, even though I wrote to you, it wasn't because of the man who did the wrong or because of the man who was hurt. But I wrote to you so that*a* your devotion to us might be made perfectly clear to you before God.*c*

13This is what comforted us. In addition to our own comfort, we were even more delighted at the joy of Titus, because his spirit had been set at rest by all of you.*d* 14If I have been doing some boasting about you to him, I have never been ashamed of it. Since everything we told you was true, our boasting to Titus has also proved to be true. 15His heart goes out to you even more as he remembers how obedient all of you were and how you welcomed him with fear and trembling.*e* 16I'm glad that I can have complete confidence in you.*f*

The Collection for the Christians in Jerusalem

8 1We want you to know, brothers, about God's grace that was given to the churches of Macedonia. 2In spite of a terrible ordeal of suffering, their abundant joy, along with their deep poverty, has resulted in the abundance of their generosity.*g* 3I can testify that by their own free will they have given to the utmost of their ability, yes,

---

a 7:12 Lit. *But so that*

7:8
a 2Cor 2:4

7:10
b 2Sam 12:13;
Prov 17:22;
Matt 26:75

7:12
c 2Cor 2:4

7:13
d Rom 15:32

7:15
e 2Cor 2:9;
Phil 2:12

7:16
f 2Thes 3:4

8:2
g Mark 12:44

8:4
a Acts 11:29;
24:17;
Rom 15:25-26;
1Cor 16:1,3-4;
2Cor 9:1

8:6
b 2Cor 8:17; 12:18

8:7
c 1Cor 1:5; 12:8;
2Cor 9:8

8:8
d 1Cor 7:6

8:9
e Matt 8:20;
Lk 9:58; Phil 2:6-7

8:10
f Prov 19:17;
Matt 10:42;
1Cor 7:25;
2Cor 9:2;
1Tim 6:18-19;
Heb 13:16

8:12
g Mark 12:43-44;
Lk 21:3

8:15
h Exod 16:18

8:17
i 2Cor 8:6

8:18
j 2Cor 12:18

even beyond their ability. [4]They begged us earnestly for the privilege[a] of participating in this ministry to the saints.[a] [5]We didn't expect that! They gave themselves to the Lord first and then to us, since this was God's will. [6]So we urged Titus to finish this work of kindness[b] among you in the same way that he had started it.[b] [7]Indeed, the more your faith, speech, knowledge, enthusiasm, and love for us increase, the more we want you to be rich in this work of kindness.[cc]

[8]I'm not commanding you but testing the genuineness of your love by the enthusiasm of others.[d] [9]For you know the grace of our Lord Jesus Christ. He was rich, yet for your sakes he became poor, in order to make you rich through his poverty.[e]

[10]I'm giving you my opinion on this matter because it will be helpful to you. Last year you were not only willing to do something but had already started to do it.[f] [11]Now finish doing it, so that your eagerness to undertake it may be matched by its completion, in keeping with what you have. [12]For if the eagerness is there, the gift[d] is acceptable according to what you have, not according to what you don't have.[g]

[13]Not that others should have relief while you have hardship. Rather, it's a question of fairness. [14]At the present time, your surplus fills their need, so that their surplus may fill your need. In this way things are fair. [15]As it is written,[h]

> "The person who had much didn't have too
> much,
> and the person who had little didn't have
> too little."[e]

Titus and His Companions

[16]But thanks be to God! He placed in the heart of Titus the same dedication to you that I have. [17]He welcomed my request and eagerly went to visit you by his own free will.[i] [18]With him we have sent the brother who is praised in all the churches for spreading the gospel.[fj] [19]More than that, he

---

a *8:4* Or *for the grace*   b *8:6* Or *this grace*   c *8:7* Or *in this grace*
d *8:12* Lit. *it*   e *8:15* Exod 16:18   f *8:18* Lit. *in the gospel*

has also been selected by the churches to travel with us while we are administering this work of kindness[a] for the glory of the Lord and as evidence of our eagerness to help.[b][a] [20]We're trying to avoid any criticism of the way we are administering this great undertaking. [21]We intend to do what's right, not only in the sight of the Lord, but also in the sight of people.[b]

[22]We have also sent with them our brother whom we have often tested in many ways and found to be dedicated. Now he is more dedicated than ever because he has so much confidence in you.

[23]As for Titus, he is my partner and fellow worker on your behalf. Our brothers, emissaries[c] from the churches, are the glory of Christ.[c] [24]Therefore, give to the churches a demonstration of your love and a reason for why we boast about you.[d]

Why Giving Is Important

9 [1]I don't need to write to you any further about the ministry to the saints.[e] [2]I know how willing you are, and I boast about you to the people of Macedonia, saying[d] that Achaia has been ready since last year, and your enthusiasm has stimulated most of them.[f] [3]I've sent the brothers so that our boasting about you in this matter may not prove to be an idle boast, and so that you may stand ready, just as I said.[g] [4]Otherwise, if any Macedonians come with me and find out that you aren't ready, we would be humiliated—to say nothing of you—in this undertaking. [5]So I thought it necessary to urge these brothers to visit you ahead of me, to make arrangements in advance for this gift you promised, and to have it ready as something given generously and not forced.

[6]Remember[e] this: The person who sows sparingly will also reap sparingly, and the person who sows generously will also reap generously.[h] [7]Each of you must give what you have decided in your heart, not with regret or under compulsion, since God loves a cheerful giver.[i] [8]Besides, God is

---

a 8:19 Or *this grace*　b 8:19 The Gk. lacks *to help*　c 8:23 Or *apostles*
d 9:2 The Gk. lacks *saying*　e 9:6 Lit. *Now*

Cross-references

8:19
[a] 1Cor 16:3-4;
2Cor 4:15

8:21
[b] Rom 12:17;
Phil 4:8;
1Peter 2:12

8:23
[c] Phil 2:25

8:24
[d] 2Cor 7:14; 9:2

9:1
[e] Acts 11:29;
Rom 15:26;
1Cor 16:1;
2Cor 8:4;
Gal 2:10

9:2
[f] 2Cor 8:10,19,24

9:3
[g] 2Cor 8:6,17-18,22

9:6
[h] Prov 11:24;
19:17; 22:9;
Gal 6:7,9

9:7
[i] Exod 25:2; 35:5;
Deut 15:7;
Prov 11:25;
Rom 12:8;
2Cor 8:12

9:8
a Prov 11:24-25;
28:27; Phil 4:19

9:9
b Ps 112:9

9:10
c Isa 55:10;
Hos 10:12;
Matt 6:1

9:11
d 2Cor 1:11; 4:15

9:12
e 2Cor 8:14

9:13
f Matt 5:16;
Heb 13:16

9:14
g 2Cor 8:1

9:15
h James 1:17

10:1
i Rom 12:1;
2Cor 12:5,7,9-10

10:2
j 1Cor 4:21;
2Cor 13:2,10

10:4
k Jer 1:10;
Acts 7:22;
1Cor 2:5;
2Cor 6:7; 13:3-4;
Eph 6:13;
1Thes 5:8;
1Tim 1:18;
2Tim 2:3

10:5
l 1Cor 1:19; 3:19

10:6
m 2Cor 2:9; 7:15;
13:2,10

able to make every blessing of yours overflow for you, so that in every situation you will always have all you need for any good work.*a* *9*As it is written,*b*

> "He scatters everywhere and gives to the poor;
> his righteousness lasts forever."**a**

*10*Now he who supplies seed to the sower and bread to eat will also supply you with seed and multiply it and enlarge the harvest of your righteousness.*c* *11*In every way you will grow richer and become even more generous, and this will produce thanksgiving to God because of us.*d* *12*This ministry you render is not only fully supplying the needs of the saints, but it is also overflowing with more and more prayers of thanksgiving to God.*e* *13*Because of the proof that this service of yours brings, you will glorify God because of your obedience to your confession of the gospel of Christ and because of your generosity in sharing with them and everyone else.*f* *14*And so in their prayers for you they will long for you because of God's exceptional grace that was shown to you.*g* *15*Thanks be to God for his indescribable gift!*h*

Paul's Authority to Speak Forcefully

10 *1*Now I myself, Paul, plead with you with the gentleness and kindness of Christ—I who am humble when I'm face to face with you but forceful toward you when I'm away!*i* *2*I beg you that when I come I won't need to be courageous by daring to oppose some people who think that we are living according to the flesh.*j* *3*Of course, we are living in the flesh, but we don't fight in a fleshly way. *4*For the weapons of our warfare are not those of the flesh. Instead, they have the power of God to demolish fortresses. We tear down arguments*k* *5*and every proud obstacle that is raised against the knowledge of God. We take every thought captive in order to obey Christ.*l* *6*We're ready to punish every act of disobedience when your obedience is complete.*m*

*7*Look at the plain facts! If anyone is confident that he

---

a *9:9* Ps 112:9

belongs to Christ, he should remind himself of this: Just as he belongs to Christ, so do we.[a] [8]So if I boast a little too much about our authority, which the Lord gave us to build you up and not to tear you down, I will not be ashamed of it.[b]

[9]I don't want you to think that I'm trying to frighten you with my letters. [10]For someone is saying,[a] "His letters are impressive and forceful, but his bodily presence is weak and his speech contemptible."[c] [11]Someone like this should take note of the following: What we say by letter when we are absent is what we will do when present!

Paul's Reason for Boasting

[12]We wouldn't dare put ourselves in the same class with or compare ourselves to those who recommend themselves. When they measure themselves by themselves and compare themselves to themselves, they show how foolish they are.[d] [13]We won't boast about what can't be evaluated. Instead, we will stay within the field that God assigned us, so as to reach even you.[e] [14]It's not as though we were overstepping our limits when we came to you. We were the first to reach you with the gospel of Christ.[f] [15]We aren't boasting about the work done by others that can't be evaluated. On the contrary, we cherish the hope that your faith may continue to grow and enlarge our sphere of action among you until it overflows.[g] [16]Then we can preach the gospel in the regions far beyond you without boasting about things already accomplished by someone else.

[17]"The person who boasts must boast in the Lord."[b][h] [18]It isn't the person who commends himself who is approved, but the person whom the Lord commends.[i]

Paul Contrasts Himself with False Apostles

11 [1]I wish you would put up with a little foolishness of mine. Yes, do put up with me![j] [2]I am jealous of you with God's own jealousy, because I promised you in marriage to one husband, to present you as a pure virgin to Christ.[k] [3]However, I'm afraid that just as the

---

a 10:10 The Gk. lacks *For someone is saying*　　b 10:17 Jer 9:24

10:7
a John 7:24;
1Cor 3:23; 9:1;
14:37; 2Cor 5:12;
11:18,23;
1John 4:6

10:8
b 2Cor 7:14; 12:6;
13:10

10:10
c 1Cor 1:17; 2:1,
3-4; 2Cor 2:1;
11:6; 12:5,7,9;
Gal 4:13

10:12
d 2Cor 3:1; 5:12

10:13
e 2Cor 10:15

10:14
f 1Cor 3:5,10;
4:15; 9:1

10:15
g Rom 15:20

10:17
h Isa 65:16;
Jer 9:24;
1Cor 1:31

10:18
i Prov 27:2;
Rom 2:29;
1Cor 4:5

11:1
j 2Cor 5:13; 11:16

11:2
k Lev 21:13;
Hos 2:19-20;
1Cor 4:15;
Gal 4:17-18;
Col 1:28

11:3
a Gen 3:4;
John 8:44;
Eph 6:24; Col 2:4,
8,18; 1Tim 1:3;
4:1; Heb 13:9;
2Peter 3:17

11:4
b Gal 1:7-8

11:5
c 1Cor 15:10;
2Cor 12:11;
Gal 2:6

11:6
d 1Cor 1:17; 2:1,
13; 2Cor 4:2;
5:11; 10:10;
12:12; Eph 3:4

11:7
e Acts 18:3;
1Cor 9:6,12;
2Cor 10:1

11:9
f Acts 20:33;
2Cor 12:13-14,16;
Phil 4:10,15-16;
1Thes 2:9;
2Thes 3:8-9

11:10
g Rom 9:1;
1Cor 9:15

11:11
h 2Cor 6:11; 7:3;
12:15

11:12
i 1Cor 9:12

11:13
j Acts 15:24;
Rom 16:18;
2Cor 2:17;
Gal 1:7;
6:12 Phil 1:15;
3:2; Titus 1:10-11;
2Peter 2:1;
1John 4:1; Rev 2:2

11:14
k Gal 1:8

11:15
l 2Cor 3:9;
Phil 3:19

11:16
m 2Cor 11:1; 12:6,
11

11:17
n 1Cor 7:6,12;
2Cor 6:4

11:18
o Phil 3:3-4

11:19
p 1Cor 4:10

serpent deceived Eve by its tricks, so your minds may somehow be lured away from sincere and pure[a] devotion to Christ.[a] [4]For if someone comes along and preaches another Jesus than the one we preached, or should you receive a different spirit from the one you received or a different gospel from the one you accepted, you're all too willing to listen.[b] [5]I don't think I'm inferior in any way to those "super-apostles."[c] [6]Even though I may be untrained as an orator, I am not so in the field of knowledge. We have made this clear to all of you in every possible way.[d]

[7]Did I commit a sin when I humbled myself by proclaiming to you the gospel of God free of charge, so that you could be exalted?[e] [8]I robbed other churches by accepting support from them in order to serve you. [9]When I was with you and needed something, I didn't bother any of you, because our brothers who came from Macedonia supplied everything I needed. I kept myself from being a burden to you in any way, and I will continue to do so.[f]

[10]As surely as the truth of Christ is in me, my boasting will not be silenced in the regions of Achaia.[g] [11]Why? Because I don't love you? God knows that I do![h]

[12]But I'll go on doing what I'm doing in order to deny an opportunity to those people who want an opportunity to be recognized as our equals in the work they're boasting about.[i] [13]Such people are false apostles, dishonest workers who are masquerading as apostles of Christ.[j] [14]And no wonder, since Satan himself masquerades as an angel of light.[k] [15]So it's not surprising if his servants also masquerade as servants of righteousness. Their doom[b] will match their deeds![l]

Paul's Sufferings as an Apostle

[16]I'll say it again: No one should think that I'm a fool. But if you do, then treat me like a fool so that I can also boast a little.[m] [17]When I talk as a confident boaster, I'm not talking with the Lord's authority but like a fool.[n] [18]Since many people boast in a fleshly way, I'll do it, too.[o] [19]You're wise, so you'll gladly put up with fools.[p] [20]You put up with

---

a 11:3 Other mss. lack *and pure*   **b** 11:15 Lit. *end*

anyone who makes you his slaves, devours what you have, takes what is yours, orders you around, or slaps your face!*a*

²¹I'm ashamed to admit it, but we have been too weak for that. Whatever anyone else dares to claim—I'm talking like a fool—I can claim it, too.*b* ²²Are they Hebrews? So am I. Are they Israelites? So am I. Are they Abraham's descendants? So am I.*c* ²³Are they Christ's servants? I'm insane to talk like this, but I'm a far better one! I've been involved in far greater efforts, far more imprisonments, countless beatings, and have faced death more than once.*d* ²⁴Five times I received from the Jews forty lashes minus one.*e* ²⁵Three times I was beaten with a stick, once I was pelted with stones, three times I was shipwrecked, and I drifted on the sea for a day and a night.*f* ²⁶I've been involved in frequent journeys, in dangers from rivers, dangers from robbers, dangers from my own people, dangers from the Gentiles, dangers in the city, dangers in the open country, dangers at sea, dangers from false brothers,*g* ²⁷in toil and hardship, through many a sleepless night, through hunger and thirst, through many periods of fasting, through coldness and nakedness.*h* ²⁸Besides everything else, I have a daily burden because of my anxiety about all the churches.*i* ²⁹Who is weak without me being weak, too? Who is caused to stumble without me becoming indignant?*j*

³⁰If I must boast, I will boast about the things that show how weak I am.*k* ³¹The God and Father of the Lord Jesus, who is blessed forever, knows that I'm not lying.*l* ³²In Damascus, the governor under King Aretas put guards around the city of Damascus to catch me,*m* ³³but I was let down in a basket through an opening in the wall and escaped from his hands.

Paul's Thorn

12 ¹I must boast, although it doesn't do any good. I'll go on to visions and revelations from the Lord. ²I know a man in Christ. Fourteen years ago—whether in his body or outside of his body, I don't know, but God knows—that man was snatched away to the third heaven.*n* ³I know that this man—whether in his body or outside of his body, I don't know, but God knows—⁴was

11:20
a Gal 2:4; 4:9

11:21
b 2Cor 10:10;
Phil 3:4

11:22
c Acts 22:3;
Rom 11:1;
Phil 3:5

11:23
d Acts 9:16; 20:23;
21:11;
1Cor 15:10,30-32;
2Cor 1:9-10; 4:1ˉ;
6:4-5,9

11:24
e Deut 25:3

11:25
f Acts 14:19;
16:22; 27:41

11:26
g Acts 9:23; 13:50;
14:5; 17:5; 19:23;
20:3; 21:31;
23:10-11; 25:3

11:27
h Acts 20:31;
1Cor 4:11;
2Cor 6:5

11:28
i Acts 20:18;
Rom 1:14

11:29
j 1Cor 8:13; 9:22

11:30
k 2Cor 12:5,9-10

11:31
l Rom 1:9; 9:1,5;
2Cor 1:23;
Gal 1:2; 1Thes 2:5

11:32
m Acts 9:24-25

12:2
n Acts 14:6; 22:17;
Rom 16:7;
2Cor 5:17;
Gal 1:22

12:4
a Lk 23:43

12:5
b 2Cor 11:30

12:6
c 2Cor 10:8; 11:16

12:7
d Job 2:7;
Ezek 28:24;
Lk 13:16;
Gal 4:13-14

12:8
e Deut 3:23-27;
Matt 26:44

12:9
f 2Cor 11:30;
1Peter 4:14

12:10
g Rom 5:3;
2Cor 7:4; 13:4

12:11
h 1Cor 3:7; 15:8-9;
2Cor 11:1,5,
16-17; Gal 2:6-8;
Eph 3:8

12:12
i Rom 15:18-19;
1Cor 9:2;
2Cor 4:2; 6:4;
11:6

12:13
j 1Cor 1:7; 9:12;
2Cor 11:7,9

12:14
k Acts 20:33;
1Cor 4:14-15;
10:33; 2Cor 13:1

12:15
l John 10:11;
2Cor 1:6; 6:12-13;
Phil 2:17;
Col 1:24;
1Thes 2:8;
2Tim 2:10

12:16
m 2Cor 11:9

12:17
n 2Cor 7:2

snatched away to Paradise and heard things that can't be expressed in words, things that no human being has a right even to mention.[a] [5]I'll boast about this man, but as for myself I will boast only about my weaknesses.[b] [6]However, if I did want to boast, I wouldn't be a fool, because I'd be telling the truth. But I'm not going to do it in order to keep anyone from thinking more of me than what he sees and hears about me.[c]

[7]To keep me from becoming conceited because of the exceptional nature of these revelations, a thorn was given to me and placed in my body.[a] It was Satan's messenger to torment me so that I wouldn't become conceited.[d] [8]I begged the Lord three times to take it away from me,[e] [9]but he told me, "My grace is all you need, for my power is perfected in weakness." So I'll most happily boast about my weaknesses, so that Christ's power may rest on me.[f] [10]That's why I take such pleasure in weaknesses, insults, hardships, persecutions, and difficulties for Christ's sake, for when I'm weak, then I'm strong.[g]

Concern for the Corinthians

[11]I have become a fool. You forced me to be one. Really, I should have been commended by you, for I am not in any way inferior to your "super-apostles," even if I am nothing.[h] [12]The signs of an apostle were performed among you with utmost patience—signs, wonders, and works of power.[i] [13]How were you treated worse than the other churches, except that I didn't bother you for help? Forgive me for this wrong![j] [14]Here I'm ready to visit you for a third time, and I won't bother you for help. I don't want your things but you. Children shouldn't have to support[b] their parents, but parents their children.[k] [15]I'll be very glad to spend my money and myself for you. Do you love me less because I love you so much?[l]

[16]Granting that I haven't been a burden to you, was I a clever schemer who trapped you by some trick?[m] [17]I didn't take advantage of you through any of the men I sent you, did I?[n] [18]I encouraged Titus to visit you, and I sent along

a 12:7 Lit. *was given to me in the flesh*　b 12:14 Lit. *to save up for*

with him the brother you know so well. Titus didn't take advantage of you, did he? We conducted ourselves with the same spirit, didn't we? We took the very same steps, didn't we?[a]

19Have you been thinking all along that we're trying to defend ourselves before you? We are speaking before God in Christ, and everything, dear friends, is meant to build you up.[b] 20I'm afraid that I may come and somehow find you not as I want to find you, and that you may find me not as you want to find me. Perhaps there will be quarreling, jealousy, angry feelings, selfishness, slander, gossip, arrogance, and disorderly conduct.[c] 21I'm afraid that when I come my God may again humble me before you. I may have to grieve over many who formerly lived in sin and haven't repented of their impurity, sexual immorality, and promiscuity that they once practiced.[d]

Final Warnings

13 1This will be the third time I'm coming to you. "Every accusation must be verified by two or three witnesses."[a][e] 2I've already warned those who sinned previously and all the rest. Although I'm absent now, I'm warning them as I did on my second visit: If I come back, I won't spare you,[f] 3since you want proof that Christ is speaking through me. He is not weak in dealing with you but is making his power felt among you.[g] 4Though he was crucified in weakness, he lives by God's power. We are weak with him, but by God's power we will live for you.[h]

5Keep examining yourselves to see whether you are continuing in the faith. Test yourselves! You know, don't you, that Jesus Christ lives in you? Could it be that you're failing the test?[i] 6I hope you will realize that we haven't failed our test. 7We pray to God that you won't do anything wrong—not to show that we haven't failed the test, but so that you may do what is right, even if we seem to have failed.[j] 8For we can't do anything against the truth, but only

---

a13:1 Deut 19:15

Cross-references (margin)

12:18
a 2Cor 8:6,16,18, 22

12:19
b Rom 9:1; 1Cor 10:33; 2Cor 5:12; 11:31

12:20
c 1Cor 4:21; 2Cor 10:2; 13:2, 10

12:21
d 1Cor 5:1; 2Cor 2:1,4; 13:2

13:1
e Num 35:30; Deut 17:6; 19:15; Matt 18:16; John 8:17; 2Cor 12:14; Heb 10:28

13:2
f 2Cor 1:23; 10:2; 12:21

13:3
g Matt 10:20; 1Cor 5:4; 9:2; 2Cor 2:10

13:4
h Rom 6:4; 2Cor 10:3-4; Phil 2:7-8; 1Peter 3:18

13:5
i Rom 8:10; 1Cor 9:27; 11:28; Gal 4:19

13:7
j 2Cor 6:9

13:9
a 1Cor 4:10;
2Cor 11:30; 12:5,
9-10; 1Thes 3:10

13:10
b 1Cor 4:21;
2Cor 2:3; 10:2,8;
12:20-21 Titus
1:13

13:11
c Rom 12:16,18;
15:5,33;
1Cor 1:10;
Phil 2:2; 3:16;
1Peter 3:8

13:12
d Rom 16:16;
1Cor 16:20;
1Thes 5:26;
1Peter 5:14

13:13
e Rom 16:24;
Phil 2:1

for the truth. ⁹We're glad when we are weak and you are strong. That's what we're praying for—your maturity.*a*

¹⁰Here's why I'm writing this while I'm away from you: When I come I don't want to be severe in using the authority the Lord gave me to build you up and not to tear you down.*b*

Final Greetings and Benediction

¹¹Finally, brothers, goodbye. Keep on growing to maturity. Keep listening to my appeals. Continue agreeing with each other and living in peace. Then the God of love and peace will be with you.*c* ¹²Greet one another with a holy kiss. All the saints greet you.*d*

¹³May the grace of the Lord Jesus Christ, the love of God, and the fellowship of the Holy Spirit be with all of you!*e*

THE LETTER OF PAUL TO THE
GALATIANS

Greetings from Paul

1 ¹From[a] Paul—an apostle not sent from men or by a man, but by Jesus Christ and God the Father who raised him from the dead[a]—²and all the brothers who are with me, to the churches in Galatia.[b] ³May grace and peace from God our Father and the Lord Jesus Christ be yours![c] ⁴He gave himself for our sins in order to rescue us from this present evil age according to the will of our God and Father.[d] ⁵To him be the glory forever and ever! Amen.

There Is No Other Gospel

⁶I am astonished that you are so quickly deserting the one who called you by the grace of Christ to follow[b] a different gospel,[e] ⁷which is not really another one. To be sure, there are certain people who are troubling you and want to distort the gospel about Christ.[f] ⁸But even if we or an angel from heaven should proclaim to you[c] a gospel contrary to what we proclaimed to you, let that person be condemned![g] ⁹What we have told you in the past I am now telling you again: If anyone proclaims to you a gospel contrary to what you received, let that person be condemned![h] ¹⁰Am I now trying to win the approval of people or of God? Or am I trying to please people? If I were still trying to please people, I would not be Christ's servant.[d][i]

Jesus Himself Gave Paul His Message

¹¹For[e] I want you to know, brothers, that the gospel that was proclaimed by me is not of human origin.[j] ¹²For I did not receive it from a man, nor was I taught it, but I received it[f] through a revelation of Jesus Christ.[k] ¹³For you have heard about my earlier life in Judaism—how I kept violently persecuting God's church and was trying to destroy it.[l] ¹⁴I

---

a1:1 The Gk. lacks *From*   **b**1:6 Lit. *for*   **c**1:8 Other mss. lack *to you*
d1:10 Or *slave*   **e**1:11 Other mss. read *Now*   **f**1:12 The Gk. lacks *I received it*

1:1
*a*Acts 2:24; 9:6;
22:10,15,21;
26:16;
Gal 1:11-12;
Titus 1:3

1:2
*b*1Cor 16:1;
Phil 2:22; 4:21

1:3
*c*Rom 1:7;
1Cor 1:3;
2Cor 1:2; Eph 1:2;
Phil 1:2; Col 1:2;
1Thes 1:1;
2Thes 1:2;
2John 1:3

1:4
*d*Isa 65:17;
Matt 20:28;
John 15:19; 17:14;
Rom 4:25;
Gal 2:20;
Titus 2:14;
Heb 2:5; 6:5;
1John 5:19

1:6
*e*Gal 5:8

1:7
*f*Acts 15:1,24;
2Cor 2:17; 11:4,
13; Gal 5:10,12

1:8
*g*1Cor 16:22

1:9
*h*Deut 4:2;
12:32 Prov 30:6;
Rev 22:18

1:10
*i*1Sam 24:7;
Matt 28:14;
1Thes 2:4;
James 4:4;
1John 3:9

1:11
*j*1Cor 15:1

1:12
*k*1Cor 15:1,3;
Gal 1:1; Eph 3:3

1:13
*l*Acts 8:3; 9:1;
22:4; 26:11;
1Tim 1:13

1:14
a Jer 9:14;
Matt 15:2;
Mark 7:5;
Acts 22:3; 26:9;
Phil 3:6

1:15
b Isa 49:1,5;
Jer 1:5; Acts 9:15;
13:2; 22:14-15;
Rom 1:1

1:16
c Matt 16:17;
Acts 9:15; 22:21;
26:17-18;
Rom 11:13;
1Cor 15:50;
2Cor 4:6; Eph 3:8;
6:12

1:18
d Acts 9:26

1:19
e Matt 13:55;
Mark 6:3;
1Cor 9:5

1:20
f Rom 9:1

1:21
g Acts 9:30

1:22
h Rom 16:7;
1Thes 2:14

2:1
i Acts 15:2

2:2
j Acts 15:12;
Phil 2:16;
1Thes 3:5

2:4
k Acts 15:1,24;
2Cor 11:20,26;
Gal 3:25; 4:3,9;
5:1,13

2:5
l Gal 2:14; 3:1;
4:16

advanced in Judaism beyond many of my contemporaries, because I was far more zealous for the traditions of my ancestors.[a]

15But when God, who set me apart before I was born and who called me by his grace, was pleased[b] 16to reveal to me his Son so that I would proclaim him among the Gentiles, I did not confer with another human being[a] at any time,[c] 17nor did I go up to Jerusalem to see[b] those who were apostles before me. Instead, I went away to Arabia and then came back to Damascus.

18Then three years later I went up to Jerusalem to get acquainted with Cephas, and I stayed with him for fifteen days.[d] 19But I didn't see any other apostle except James, the Lord's brother.[e] 20(I declare before God that[c] what I am writing to you is not a lie.)[f] 21Then I went to the regions of Syria and Cilicia.[g] 22But I was unknown by sight to the churches of Christ in Judea.[h] 23The only thing they kept hearing was this: "The man who used to persecute us is now proclaiming the faith he once tried to destroy!" 24So they kept glorifying God for what had happened to me.[d]

How Paul Was Accepted by the Apostles in Jerusalem

2 1Then fourteen years later I again went up to Jerusalem with Barnabas, taking Titus with me.[i] 2I went in response to a revelation, and in a private meeting with the reputed leaders I set before them the gospel I proclaim among the Gentiles. I did this because I was afraid that[e] I was running or had run for nothing.[j] 3But not even Titus, who was with me, was forced to be circumcised, even though he was a Greek. 4However, false brothers were secretly brought in; they slipped in to spy on the freedom we have in Christ Jesus so that they might enslave us.[k] 5But we did not give in to them for a moment, so that the truth of the gospel might always remain with you.[l]

6Now those who were reputed to be important added nothing to my message.[f] (What sort of people they were

---

a 1:16 Lit. *with flesh and blood*   **b** 1:17 The Gk. lacks *see*   **c** 1:20 Lit. *Before God*   **d** 1:24 Lit. *glorifying God for me*   **e** 2:2 Lit. *Lest somehow*   **f** 2:6 Lit. *to me*

makes no difference to me, since God pays no attention to outward appearances.)*a* *7*In fact, they saw that I had been entrusted with the gospel for the uncircumcised, just as Peter had been entrusted with the gospel for the circumcised.*b* *8*For the one who worked through Peter by making him an apostle to the circumcised also worked through me by sending me to the Gentiles.*c* *9*So when James, Cephas,*a* and John (who were reputed to be leaders)*b* recognized the grace that had been given me, they gave Barnabas and me the right hand of fellowship, agreeing that we should go to the Gentiles and they to the circumcised.*d* *10*The only thing they asked us to do was to remember the poor, the very thing I was eager to do.*e*

Paul Confronts Cephas in Antioch

*11*But when Cephas came to Antioch, I opposed him to his face, because he was clearly wrong.*cf* *12*For until some men came from James, he was in the habit of eating with the Gentiles, but after they came, he drew back and would not associate himself with them, because he was afraid of the circumcision party.*g* *13*The other Jews also joined him in this hypocrisy, to the extent that even Barnabas was caught up in their hypocrisy. *14*But when I saw that they were not acting consistently with the truth of the gospel, I told Cephas in front of everyone, "Though you're a Jew, you live like a Gentile and not like a Jew. So how can you insist that the Gentiles must live like Jews?"*h*

*15*We ourselves are Jews by birth, and not Gentile sinners.*i* *16*Yet we know that a person is not justified by the works of the Law, but by the faith of Jesus Christ.*d* We, too, have believed in Christ Jesus so that we might be justified by the faith of Christ*e* and not by the works of the Law, for no human being*f* will be justified by the works of the Law.*j*

*17*Now if we, while trying to be justified in Christ, have been found to be sinners, does that mean that Christ is a minister of sin? Of course not!*k* *18*For if I rebuild something

---

a*2:9* I.e. Peter   b*2:9* Lit. *pillars*   c*2:11* Or *was self-condemned*   d*2:16* Or *by faith in Jesus Christ*   e*2:16* Or *by faith in Christ*   f*2:16* Lit. *no flesh*

2:6
a Acts 10:34;
Rom 2:11;
2Cor 12:11;
Gal 6:3

2:7
b Acts 13:46;
Rom 1:5; 11:13;
1Thes 2:4;
1Tim 2:7;
2Tim 1:11

2:8
c Acts 9:15; 13:2;
22:21; 26:17-18;
1Cor 15:10;
Gal 1:16; 3:5;
Col 1:29

2:9
d Matt 16:18;
Rom 1:5; 12:3,6;
15:15;
1Cor 15:10;
Eph 2:20; 3:8;
Rev 21:14

2:10
e Acts 11:30;
24:17;
Rom 15:25;
1Cor 9:1-27;
16:1;
2Cor 8:1-13

2:11
f Acts 15:35

2:12
g Acts 10:28; 11:3

2:14
h Acts 10:28; 11:3;
Gal 2:5;
1Tim 5:20

2:15
i Matt 9:11;
Acts 15:10-11;
Eph 2:3,12

2:16
j Ps 143:2;
Acts 13:38-39;
Rom 1:17; 3:20,
22,28; 8:3;
Gal 3:11,24;
Heb 7:18-19

2:17
k 1John 3:8-9

2:19
a Rom 6:11,14;
7:4,6; 8:2;
2Cor 5:15;
1Thes 5:10;
Heb 9:14;
1Peter 4:2

2:20
b Rom 6:6;
2Cor 5:15;
Gal 3:21; 5:24;
6:14; Eph 5:2;
1Thes 5:10;
Titus 2:14;
1Peter 4:2

2:21
c Rom 11:6;
Gal 3:21; 5:4;
Heb 7:11

3:1
d Gal 2:14; 5:7

3:2
e Acts 2:38; 8:15;
10:47; 15:8;
Rom 10:16-17;
Gal 3:14;
Eph 1:13; Heb 6:4

3:3
f Gal 4:9;
Heb 7:16; 9:10

3:4
g Heb 10:35-36;
2John 1:8

3:5
h 2Cor 3:8

3:6
i Gen 15:6;
Rom 4:3,9,21-22;
James 2:23

3:7
j John 8:39;
Rom 4:11-12,16

3:8
k Gen 12:3; 18:18;
22:18; Acts 3:25;
Rom 9:17;
Gal 3:22

3:10
l Deut 27:26;
Jer 11:3

3:11
m Hab 2:4;
Rom 1:17;
Gal 2:16;
Heb 10:38

that I tore down, I demonstrate that I am a wrongdoer. [19]For through the Law I died to the Law so that I might live for God. I have been crucified with Christ.[a] [20]I no longer live, but Christ lives in me, and the life that I now live in the flesh I live by the faith of the Son of God,[a] who loved me and gave himself for me.[b] [21]I do not set aside the grace of God. For if righteousness comes through the Law, then Christ died for nothing.[c]

Believers Are Approved by God

3 [1]You foolish Galatians! Who put you under a spell? Wasn't Jesus Christ clearly portrayed as crucified before your very eyes?[d] [2]I want to learn only one thing from you: Did you receive the Spirit by doing the works[b] of the Law or by believing what you heard?[c][e] [3]Are you so foolish? Having started out with the Spirit, are you now ending up with the flesh?[f] [4]Did you suffer so much for nothing? (If it really was for nothing!)[g] [5]Does God[d] supply you with the Spirit and work miracles among you because you do the works[b] of the Law or because you believe what you heard?[c][h] [6]In the same way, Abraham "believed God, and it was credited to him as righteousness."[e][i]

[7]You see, then, that those who have faith are Abraham's real descendants.[j] [8]Because the Scripture saw ahead of time that God would justify the Gentiles by faith, it announced the gospel to Abraham beforehand when it said, "Through you all nations[f] will be blessed."[g][k] [9]Therefore, those who believe are blessed together with Abraham, the one who believed.

[10]Certainly all who depend on the works of the Law are under a curse. For it is written, "A curse on everyone who doesn't obey everything that is written in the book of the Law!"[h][l] [11]Now it's obvious that no one is justified in the sight of God by the Law, because "The just will live by faith."[i][m] [12]But the Law has nothing to do with faith. Instead,

---

a *2:20* Or *by faith in the Son of God*   **b** *3:2,3:5* Lit. *through the works*
c *3:2,3:5* Lit. *through the hearing of faith*   **d** *3:5* Lit. *he*   **e** *3:6* Gen 15:6
f *3:8* Or *all the Gentiles*   **g** *3:8* Gen 12:3   **h** *3:10* Deut 27:26   **i** *3:11* Hab 2:4

"The person who keeps the commandments[a] will have life in them."[b][a] [13]Christ redeemed us from the curse of the Law by becoming a curse for us. For it is written, "A curse on everyone who is hung on a tree!"[c][b] [14]This happened in order that[d] the blessing promised to Abraham[e] would come to the Gentiles through Christ Jesus, so that we might receive the promised Spirit[f] through faith.[c]

[15]Brothers, let me use an example from everyday life.[g] Once a person's will has been ratified, no one can cancel it or add conditions to it.[d] [16]Now the promises were spoken to Abraham and to his descendant. It doesn't say "descendants," referring to many, but "your descendant,"[h] referring to one person, who is Christ.[e] [17]This is what I mean: The Law that came 430 years later did not cancel the covenant previously ratified by God so as to nullify the promise.[f] [18]For if the inheritance comes by the Law, it no longer comes by the promise. But it was by a promise that God so graciously gave it to Abraham.[g]

[19]Why, then, was the Law given?[i] It was added because of transgressions until the descendant to whom the promise was given came. It was put into effect through angels by means of an intermediary.[h] [20]Now an intermediary involves more than one party, but God has acted on his own.[j][i] [21]So is the Law in conflict with the promises of God? Of course not! For if a law had been given that could give us life, then certainly righteousness would come through the Law.[j] [22]But the Scripture has put everything under the power of sin, so that what was promised by the faith of Christ[k] might be given to those who believe.[k]

[23]Now before this faith came, we were held in custody and carefully guarded under the Law in preparation for the faith that was to be revealed. [24]So the Law was our guardian until Christ came, so that we might be justified by faith.[l]

---

a 3:12 Lit. *who does them*   b 3:12 Lev 18:5   c 3:13 Deut 21:23   d 3:14 Lit. *In order that*   e 3:14 Lit. *the blessing of Abraham*   f 3:14 Or *the promise of the Spirit*   g 3:15 Lit. *I'm speaking according to man*   h 3:16 Gen 12:7   i 3:19 Lit. *Why then the Law?*   j 3:20 Lit. *God is one*   k 3:22 Or *by faith in Christ*

3:12
a Lev 18:5;
Neh 9:29;
Ezek 20:11;
Rom 4:4-5;
10:5-6; 11:6

3:13
b Deut 21:23;
Rom 8:3;
2Cor 5:21;
Gal 4:5

3:14
c Isa 32:15;
44:3 Jer 31:33;
32:40;
Ezek 11:19;
36:27;
Joel 2:28-29;
Zech 12:10;
John 7:39;
Acts 2:33;
Rom 4:9,16

3:15
d Heb 9:17

3:16
e Gen 12:3,7;
17:7; 1Cor 12:12;
Gal 3:8

3:17
f Exod 12:40-41;
Rom 4:13,15;
Gal 4:21

3:18
g Rom 4:14; 8:17

3:19
h Exod 20:19,
21-22; Deut 5:5,
22-23,27,31;
John 1:17; 15:22;
Acts 7:38,53;
Rom 4:15; 5:20;
7:8,13; Gal 1:16;
1Tim 1:9; 2:5;
Heb 2:2

3:20
i Rom 3:29-30

3:21
j Gal 2:21

3:22
k Rom 3:9,19,23;
4:11-12,16;
11:32; Gal 3:8

3:24
l Matt 5:17;
Acts 13:39;
Rom 10:4;
Gal 2:16;
Col 2:17;
Heb 9:9-10

3:26
a John 1:12;
Rom 8:14-16;
Gal 4:5;
1John 3:1-2
3:27
b Rom 6:3; 13:14
3:28
c John 10:16;
17:20-21;
Rom 10:12;
1Cor 12:13;
Gal 5:6;
Eph 2:14-16; 4:4,
15; Col 3:11
3:29
d Gen 21:10,12;
Rom 8:17; 9:7;
Gal 4:7,28;
Eph 3:6;
Heb 11:18
4:3
e Gal 2:4; 4:9;
5:1 Col 2:8,20;
Heb 9:10
4:4
f Gen 3:15; 49:10;
Isa 7:14;
Dan 9:24;
Mic 5:3;
Matt 1:23; 5:17;
Mark 1:15;
Lk 1:31; 2:7,27;
John 1:14;
Rom 1:3;
Eph 1:10; Phil 2:7;
Heb 2:14
4:5
g Matt 20:28;
John 1:12;
Gal 3:13,26;
Eph 1:5,7;
Titus 2:14;
Heb 9:12;
1Peter 1:18-19
4:6
h Rom 5:5; 8:15
4:7
i Rom 8:16-17;
Gal 3:29
4:8
j Rom 1:25;
1Cor 12:2;
Eph 2:11-12;
1Thes 1:9; 4:5
4:9
k Rom 8:3;
1Cor 8:3; 13:12;
Gal 3:3; Col 2:20;
2Tim 2:19;
Heb 7:18
4:10
l Rom 14:5;
Col 2:16
4:11
m Gal 2:2; 5:2,4;
1Thes 3:5
4:12
n 2Cor 2:5

[25]But now that this faith has come, we are no longer under the control of a guardian.

You Are God's Children

[26]For all of you are God's children through faith in Christ Jesus.*a* [27]Indeed, all of you who were baptized into Christ have clothed yourselves with Christ.*b* [28]A person is no longer a Jew or a Greek, a slave or a free person, a male or a female. For all of you are one in Christ Jesus.*c* [29]And if you belong to Christ, then you are Abraham's descendants and heirs according to the promise.*d*

4 [1]What I'm saying is this: As long as an heir is a child, he is no better off than a slave, even though he owns everything. [2]But he is placed under the control of guardians and trustees until the time set by the father. [3]It was the same way with us. While we were children, we were slaves to the basic principles of the world.*ae* [4]But when the fullness of time had come, God sent his Son, born of a woman, born under the Law,*f* [5]in order to redeem those who were under the Law, so that we might receive adoption as his children.*g* [6]Because you are his children, God has sent the Spirit of his Son into our*b* hearts to cry out, "Abba!*c* Father!"*h* [7]So you are no longer a slave but a child, and if you are a child, then you are also an heir through God.*i*

[8]But in the past, when you didn't know God, you were slaves to things that are not really gods at all.*dj* [9]But now that you know God, or rather have been known by God, how can you turn back again to those powerless and bankrupt basic principles?*e* Why do you want to become their slaves all over again?*k* [10]You are observing days, months, seasons, and years.*l* [11]I'm afraid for you. Maybe my work for you has been wasted!*m*

Paul's Concern for the Galatians

[12]I beg you, brothers, to become like me, since I became like you. You didn't do anything wrong to me.*n* [13]You know

---

a 4:3 Or *the elemental spirits of the universe*   **b** 4:6 Other mss. read *your*   **c** 4:6 Abba is Aram. for *Father.*   **d** 4:8 Lit. *gods by nature*   **e** 4:9 Or *elemental spirits*

that it was because I was ill[a] that I brought you the gospel the first time.[a] 14Even though my condition put you to the test, you didn't despise or reject me. On the contrary, you welcomed me as if I were an angel of God, as Christ Jesus himself.[b] 15What happened to your positive attitude?[b] For I testify that if it had been possible, you would have torn out your eyes and given them to me. 16So have I now become your enemy for telling you the truth?[c]

17These people[c] are devoted to you, but not in a good way. They want you to avoid me so that you will be devoted to them.[d] 18(Now it's always good to be devoted to a good cause, even when I'm not with you.) 19My children, I am suffering birth pains for you again until Christ is formed in you.[e] 20I wish I were with you right now so that I could change the tone of my voice, because I'm completely baffled by you.

You Are Children of a Free Woman

21Tell me, those of you who want to live under the Law: Are you really listening to what the Law says? 22For it is written that Abraham had two sons, one by a slave woman and the other by a free woman.[f] 23Now the son of the slave woman was conceived according to the flesh, but the son of the free woman was conceived through a promise.[g] 24This is being said as an allegory, for these women represent two covenants. The one woman, Hagar, is from Mount Sinai, and her children are born into slavery.[h] 25Now Hagar is Mount Sinai in Arabia and corresponds to present-day Jerusalem, because she is in slavery along with her children. 26But the heavenly Jerusalem is the free woman, and she is our mother.[d][i] 27For it is written,[j]

> "Rejoice, you childless woman,
>   who cannot give birth to any children!
> Break into song and shout,
>   you who feel no pains of childbirth!
> For the children of the deserted woman

---

a 4:13 Lit. *because of a weakness of the flesh*   b 4:15 Lit. *your blessedness*
c 4:17 Lit. *They*   d 4:26 Other mss. read *the mother of us all*

4:13
a 1Cor 2:3;
2Cor 11:30; 12:7,
9; Gal 1:6

4:14
b 2Sam 19:27;
Zech 12:8;
Mal 2:7;
Matt 10:40;
Lk 10:16;
John 13:20;
1Thes 2:13

4:16
c Gal 2:5,14

4:17
d Rom 10:2;
1Cor 11:2

4:19
e 1Cor 4:15;
James 1:18

4:22
f Gen 16:15; 21:2

4:23
g Gen 18:10,14;
21:1-2;
Rom 9:7-8;
Heb 11:11

4:24
h Deut 33:2

4:26
i Isa 2:2;
Heb 12:22;
Rev 3:12; 21:2,10

4:27
j Isa 54:1

422

4:28
a Acts 3:25;
Rom 9:8; Gal 3:29

4:29
b Gen 21:9;
Gal 5:11; 6:12

4:30
c Gen 21:10,12;
John 8:35;
Gal 3:8,22

4:31
d John 8:36;
Gal 5:1,13

5:1
e John 8:32;
Acts 15:10;
Rom 6:18;
Gal 2:4; 4:9;
1Peter 2:16

5:2
f Acts 15:1; 16:3

5:3
g Gal 3:10

5:4
h Rom 9:31-32;
Gal 2:21;
Heb 12:15

5:5
i Rom 8:24-25;
2Tim 4:8

5:6
j 1Cor 7:19;
Gal 3:28; 6:15;
Col 3:11;
1Thes 1:3;
James 2:18,20,22

5:7
k 1Cor 9:24;
Gal 3:1

5:8
l Gal 1:6

5:9
m 1Cor 5:6; 15:33

5:10
n 2Cor 2:3; 8:22;
10:6; Gal 1:7

5:11
o 1Cor 1:23;
15:30; Gal 4:29;
6:12,17

are more numerous than the children
of the woman who has a husband."[a]

[28]So you,[b] brothers, are children of the promise, like Isaac.[a] [29]But just as then the son who was conceived according to the flesh persecuted the son who was conceived according to the Spirit, so it is now.[b] [30]But what does the Scripture say? "Drive out the slave woman and her son, for the son of the slave woman must never share the inheritance with the son of the free woman."[cc] [31]So then, brothers, we are not children of the slave woman but of the free woman.[d]

Live in the Freedom That Christ Provides

5 [1]Christ has set us free so that we may enjoy the benefits of freedom.[d] So keep on standing firm in it, and stop attaching yourselves to the yoke of slavery again.[e] [2]Listen! I, Paul, am telling you that if you allow yourselves to be circumcised, Christ will be of no benefit to you.[f] [3]Again, I insist[e] that everyone who allows himself to be circumcised is obligated to obey the entire Law.[g] [4]Those of you who are trying to be justified by the Law have been cut off from Christ. You have fallen away from grace.[h] [5]For through the Spirit, by faith, we eagerly wait for the hope of righteousness.[i] [6]For in Christ Jesus neither circumcision nor uncircumcision matters. What matters is faith[f] that is active through love.[j]

[7]You were running beautifully! Who stopped you from obeying the truth?[k] [8]Such influence does not come from the one who calls you.[l] [9]A little yeast spreads through the whole batch of dough.[m] [10]I am confident[g] in the Lord that you will take no other view of the matter. However, the one who is troubling you will suffer God's judgment,[h] whoever he is.[n] [11]As for me, brothers, if I am still preaching the necessity of circumcision,[i] why am I still being persecuted? In that case the offense of the cross has been removed.[o] [12]I wish

---

a 4:27 Isa 54:1   b 4:28 Other mss. read *we*   c 4:30 Gen 21:10   d 5:1 Lit. *has set us free for freedom*   e 5:3 Lit. *testify*   f 5:6 Lit. *But faith*   g 5:10 Lit. *confident about you*   h 5:10 Lit. *suffer judgment*   i 5:11 Lit. *preaching circumcision*

that those who are unsettling you would castrate themselves!*a*

13For you, brothers, were called to freedom. Only don't turn your freedom into an opportunity to gratify your flesh, but through love serve one another.*b* 14For the whole Law is summarized in a single statement: "You must love your neighbor as yourself."*ac* 15But if you bite and devour one another, be careful that you aren't destroyed by each other. 16So I say, live by the Spirit, and you will never fulfill the desires of the flesh.*d* 17For what the flesh wants is opposed to the Spirit, and what the Spirit wants is opposed to the flesh. They are opposed to each other, and so you don't do what you want to do.*e* 18But if you are being led by the Spirit, you are not under the Law.*f*

19Now the works of the flesh are obvious: sexual immorality, impurity, promiscuity,*g* 20idolatry, witchcraft,**b** hatred, rivalry, jealously, outbursts of anger, quarrels, conflicts, factions, 21envy, murder,**c** drunkenness, wild partying, and things like that. I'm telling you now, as I've told you in the past, that people who practice such things will not inherit the kingdom of God.*h* 22But the fruit of the Spirit is love, joy, peace, patience, kindness, goodness, faithfulness,**d***i* 23gentleness, and self-control. There is no law against such things.*j* 24Now those who belong to Christ Jesus have crucified their flesh with its passions and desires.*k* 25If we live by the Spirit, let us also be guided by the Spirit.*l* 26Let us stop being arrogant, provoking one another, and envying one another.*m*

Help Each Other

1Brothers, if a person is caught doing something wrong, those of you who are spiritual should restore that person in a spirit of gentleness. Watch out for yourself so that you are not tempted as well.*n* 2Practice carrying each other's burdens. In this way you will fulfill the law of Christ.*o* 3For if anyone thinks he's something when

---

a5:14 Lev 19:18   **b**5:20 Or *sorcery*   **c**5:21 Other mss. lack *murder*
d5:22 Or *faith*

5:12
a Josh 7:25;
Acts 15:1-2,24;
1Cor 5:13;
Gal 1:8-9
5:13
b 1Cor 8:9; 9:19;
Gal 6:2;
1Peter 2:16;
2Peter 2:19;
Jude 1:4
5:14
c Lev 19:18;
Matt 7:12;
22:39-40;
Rom 13:8-9;
James 2:8
5:16
d Rom 6:12; 8:1,4,
12; 13:14;
Gal 5:25;
1Peter 2:11
5:17
e Rom 7:15,19,23;
8:6-7
5:18
f Rom 6:14; 8:2
5:19
g 1Cor 3:3;
Eph 5:3; Col 3:5;
James 3:14-15
5:21
h 1Cor 6:9;
Eph 5:5; Col 3:6;
Rev 22:15
5:22
i John 15:2;
Rom 15:14;
1Cor 13:7;
Eph 5:9; Col 3:12;
James 3:17
5:23
j 1Tim 1:9
5:24
k Rom 6:6; 13:14;
Gal 2:20;
1Peter 2:11
5:25
l Rom 8:4-5;
Gal 5:16
5:26
m Phil 2:3
6:1
n Rom 14:1; 15:1;
1Cor 2:15; 3:1;
4:21; 7:5; 10:12;
2Thes 3:15;
2Tim 2:25;
Heb 12:13;
James 5:19
6:2
o John 13:14-15,
34; 15:12;
Rom 15:1;
Gal 5:13;
1Thes 5:14;
James 2:8;
1John 4:21

6:3
a Rom 12:3;
1Cor 8:2;
2Cor 3:5; 12:11;
Gal 2:6

6:4
b Lk 18:11;
1Cor 11:28;
2Cor 13:5

6:5
c Rom 2:6;
1Cor 3:8

6:6
d Rom 15:27;
1Cor 9:11,14

6:7
e Job 13:9;
Lk 16:25;
Rom 2:6;
1Cor 6:9; 15:33;
2Cor 9:6

6:8
f Job 4:8;
Prov 11:18; 22:8;
Hos 8:7; 10:12;
Rom 8:13;
James 3:18

6:9
g Matt 24:13;
1Cor 15:58;
2Thes 3:13;
Heb 3:6,14;
10:36; 12:3,5;
Rev 2:10

6:10
h John 9:4; 12:35;
Eph 2:19;
1Thes 5:15;
1Tim 6:18;
Titus 3:8; Heb 3:6

6:12
i Gal 2:3,14; 5:11;
Phil 3:18

6:14
j Rom 6:6;
Gal 2:20; Phil 3:3,
7-8

6:15
k 1Cor 7:19;
2Cor 5:17;
Gal 5:6; Col 3:11

6:16
l Ps 125:5;
Rom 2:29; 4:12;
9:6-8; Gal 3:7,9,
29; Phil 3:3,16

6:17
m 2Cor 1:5; 4:10;
11:23; Gal 5:11;
Col 1:24

6:18
n 2Tim 4:22

he's really nothing, he's only fooling himself.*a* *4*Each person must approve his own actions. Then he can be proud of his own accomplishments and not those of his neighbor.*b* *5*For everyone must carry his own load.*c*

*6*The person who is taught the word should share all his goods with his teacher.*d* *7*Stop being*a* deceived; God is not to be ridiculed. A person harvests whatever he plants.*e* *8*The person who plants in his flesh will harvest decay from the flesh, but the person who plants in the Spirit will harvest eternal life from the Spirit.*f* *9*Let us not get tired of doing what is good, for at the right time we will reap a harvest—if we don't give up.*g* *10*So then, whenever we have the opportunity, let us practice doing good to everyone, especially to the family of faith.*h*

A Final Warning Against Circumcision

*11*Look at how large these letters are because I'm writing with my own hand! *12*These people who want to impress others by their flesh are trying to force you to be circumcised, simply to avoid being persecuted for the cross of Christ.*i* *13*Why, not even those who are circumcised obey the Law! They simply want you to be circumcised so that they can boast about your flesh. *14*But may I never boast about anything except the cross of our Lord Jesus Christ, by which the world has been crucified to me, and I to the world!*j* *15*For neither circumcision nor uncircumcision matters. Rather, what matters is being a new creation.*bk* *16*Now may peace be on all those who live by this principle, and may mercy be on the Israel of God.*l* *17*From now on, let no one make trouble for me, for I carry the scars of Jesus on my own body.*m*

Final Greeting

*18*May the grace of our Lord Jesus Christ be with your spirit, brothers! Amen.*n*

---

a *6:7* Or *Don't be*   **b** *6:15* Lit. *Rather a new creation*

THE LETTER OF PAUL TO THE
EPHESIANS

Greetings from Paul

1 ¹From[a] Paul, an apostle of Christ Jesus by God's will, to his holy and faithful people[b] in Ephesus[c] who are in union with Christ Jesus.[a] ²May grace and peace from God our Father and the Lord Jesus Christ be yours![b]

The Many Blessings of Salvation

³Blessed be the God and Father of our Lord Jesus Christ! He has blessed us in Christ with every spiritual blessing in the heavenly realm,[c] ⁴just as he chose us in him before the foundation of the world to be holy and blameless in his presence. In love[d] ⁵he predestined us for adoption to himself through Jesus Christ, according to the pleasure of his will,[e] ⁶so that we would praise[d] his glorious grace that he gave us in the Beloved One.[f] ⁷In him we have redemption through his blood, the forgiveness of our offenses, according to the riches of God's[e] grace[g] ⁸that he lavished on us, along with all wisdom and understanding, ⁹when he made known to us the secret of his will. This was according to his plan that he set forth in Christ[fh] ¹⁰to usher in[g] the fullness of the times and to gather up all things in Christ, both things in heaven and things on earth.[i]

¹¹In Christ[f] we were also chosen when we were set apart beforehand[h] according to the purpose of the one who does everything according to the intention of his will.[j] ¹²He did this so that we[i] who had already fixed our hope on Christ might live for his praise and glory.[k] ¹³You, too, have heard the word of truth, the gospel of your salvation, and have believed in him. You were sealed in him with the promised Holy Spirit,[l] ¹⁴who is the guarantee of our inheritance until

1:12 [k]Eph 1:6,14; 2Thes 2:13 James 1:18 1:13 [l]John 1:17; 2Cor 1:22; 6:7; Eph 4:30

a 1:1 The Gk. lacks *From*   b 1:1 Or *to the saints and faithful*   c 1:1 Other mss. lack *in Ephesus*   d 1:6 Lit. *to the praise of*   e 1:7 Lit. *his*   f 1:9,1:11 Lit. *him*   g 1:10 Or *administer*   h 1:11 Or *predestined*   i 1:12 Lit. *So that we*

1:1
[a] Rom 1:7;
1Cor 4:17;
2Cor 1:1;
Eph 6:21; Col 1:2
1:2
[b] Gal 1:3; Titus 1:4
1:3
[c] 2Cor 1:3;
1Peter 1:3
1:4
[d] Lk 1:75;
Rom 8:28;
Eph 2:10; 5:27;
Col 1:22;
1Thes 4:7;
2Thes 2:13;
2Tim 1:9;
Titus 2:12;
James 2:5;
1Peter 1:2,20; 2:9
1:5
[e] Matt 1:24;
Lk 12:32;
John 1:12;
Rom 8:15,29-30;
1Cor 1:21;
2Cor 6:18;
Gal 4:5; Eph 1:9;
8:11; 1John 3:1
1:6
[f] Matt 3:17; 17:5;
John 3:35; 10:17;
Rom 3:24; 5:15
1:7
[g] Acts 20:28;
Rom 2:4; 3:24;
9:23; Eph 2:7; 3:8,
16; Phil 4:19;
Col 1:14;
Heb 9:12;
1Peter 1:18-19;
Rev 5:9
1:9
[h] Rom 16:25;
Eph 3:4,9,11;
Col 1:26;
2Tim 1:9
1:10
[i] 1Cor 3:22-23;
11:3; Gal 4:4;
Eph 2:15; 3:15;
Phil 2:9-10;
Col 1:20; Heb 1:2;
9:10; 1Peter 1:20
1:11
[j] Isa 46:10-11;
Acts 20:32; 26:18;
Rom 8:17;
Eph 1:5; Col 1:12;
3:24; Titus 3:7;
James 2:5;
1Peter 1:4

1:14
a Lk 21:28;
Acts 20:28;
Rom 8:23;
2Cor 1:22; 5:5;
Eph 1:6,12; 4:30
1Peter 2:9

1:15
b Col 1:4

1:16
c Rom 1:9;
Phil 1:3-4;
Col 1:3;
1Thes 1:2;
2Thes 1:3

1:17
d John 20:17;
Col 1:9

1:18
e Acts 26:18;
Eph 2:12; 4:4,11

1:19
f Eph 3:7;
Col 1:29; 2:12

1:20
g Ps 110:1;
Acts 2:24,33;
7:55-56; Col 3:1;
Heb 1:3; 10:12

1:21
h Rom 8:38;
Phil 2:9-10;
Col 1:16; 2:10,15;
Heb 1:4

1:22
i Ps 8:6;
Matt 28:18;
1Cor 15:27;
Eph 4:15-16;
Col 1:18;
Heb 2:7-8

1:23
j Rom 12:5;
1Cor 12:6,12,27;
Eph 4:10,12; 5:23,
30; Col 1:18,24;
2:10; 3:11

2:1
k John 5:24;
Eph 2:5; 4:18;
Col 2:13

2:2
l 1Cor 6:11;
Eph 4:22; 5:6;
6:12; Col 1:21;
3:6-7; 1John 5:19

2:3
m Ps 51:5;
Rom 5:12,14;
Gal 5:16;
Titus 3:3;
1Peter 4:3

2:4
n Rom 10:12;
Eph 1:7

the redemption of God's own possession,[a] to his praise and glory.[a]

Paul's Prayer for the Ephesians

[15]Therefore, because I have heard about your faith in the Lord Jesus and your love[b] for all the saints,[b] [16]I never stop giving thanks for you as I mention you in my prayers.[c] [17]I pray that[c] the God of our Lord Jesus Christ, the Father most glorious,[d] would give you a spirit of wisdom and revelation through knowing Christ[e] fully.[d] [18]Then, with the eyes of your hearts enlightened, you will know the hope of his calling, the riches of his glorious inheritance among the saints,[e] [19]and the unlimited greatness of his power for us who believe, according to the working of his mighty strength.[f] [20]He put this power to work[f] in Christ when he raised him from the dead and seated him at his right hand in the heavenly realm.[g] [21]He is far above every ruler, authority, power, dominion, and every name that can be named, not only in the present age but also in the one to come.[h] [22]God[g] has put everything under his feet and has made him the head of everything for the good of the church,[h][i] [23]which is his body, the fullness of the one who fills everything in every way.[i][j]

God Has Brought Us from Death to Life

2 [1]You used to be dead because of your offenses and sins,[k] [2]in which you once lived according to the ways of this present world and according to the ruler of the power of the air, the spirit that is now active in those who are disobedient.[j][l] [3]All of us once behaved like[k] them in the lusts of our flesh, fulfilling the desires of our flesh and senses. By nature we deserved wrath,[l] just like everyone else.[m] [4]But God, who is rich in mercy, because of his great love for us[m][n] [5]even when we were dead because of our offenses, made us alive together with[n] Christ (by grace you

---

a 1:14 Lit. *of the possession*   **b** 1:15 Other mss. lack *your love*   **c** 1:17 Lit. *That*   **d** 1:17 Lit. *the Father of glory*   **e** 1:17 Lit. *knowing him*   **f** 1:19 Lit. *Which he put to work*   **g** 1:22 Lit. *He*   **h** 1:22 Lit. *for the church*   **i** 1:23 Or *who fills all in all*   **j** 2:2 Lit. *the sons of disobedience*   **k** 2:3 Or *lived among*   **l** 2:3 Lit. *were children of wrath*   **m** 2:4 Lit. *love with which he loved us*   **n** 2:5 Other mss. read *in*

have been saved),[a] [6]raised us up with him, and seated us with him in the heavenly realm in Christ Jesus.[b] [7]He did this so that[a] in the coming ages he might display the limitless riches of his grace in kindness toward us in Christ Jesus.[c] [8]By that grace you have been saved through faith. This does not come from you. It is the gift of God[d] [9]and not the result of works, so that no one can boast.[e] [10]For we are his masterpiece,[b] created in Christ Jesus for good works that God prepared long ago to be our way of life.[cf]

All Believers Are One in Christ

[11]So then, remember that at one time you were Gentiles by birth[d] and were called "the uncircumcision" by what is called "the circumcision" made in the flesh by hands.[g] [12]At that time you were without Christ, excluded from citizenship in Israel,[e] and strangers to the covenants of promise. You had no hope and were in the world without God.[h] [13]But now, in Christ Jesus, you who once were far away have been brought near by the blood of Christ.[i]

[14]For it is he who is our peace. In his flesh he made both groups one by tearing down the wall of hostility that divided them.[fj] [15]He did away with the Law with its commandments and regulations so that he could create in himself one new humanity from the two, thus making peace,[k] [16]and could reconcile both groups to God in one body through the cross, on which he killed the hostility.[l] [17]He came and proclaimed peace for you who were far away and for you who were near.[m] [18]Through him, both of us[g] have access to the Father in one Spirit.[n]

[19]That is why you are no longer strangers and foreigners but fellow citizens with the saints and members of God's household.[o] [20]You have been built on the foundation of the

Rom 5:2; 1Cor 12:13; Eph 3:12; 4:4; Heb 4:16; 10:19-20; 1Peter 3:18 **2:19** *o* Gal 6:10; Eph 3:15; Phil 3:20; Heb 12:22-23

a 2:7 Lit. *So that*   **b** 2:10 Or *workmanship*   **c** 2:10 Lit. *so that we might walk in them*   **d** 2:11 Lit. *in the flesh*   **e** 2:12 Or *the commonwealth of Israel*   **f** 2:14 Lit. *the dividing wall, the hostility*   **g** 2:18 I.e. both Jews and Gentiles

2:5
a Rom 5:6,8,10; 6:4-5; Eph 5:1; Col 2:12-13; 3:1,3
2:6
b Eph 1:20
2:7
c Titus 3:4
2:8
d Matt 16:17; John 6:44,65; Rom 3:24; 4:16; 10:14-15,17; Eph 1:19; 2:5; Phil 1:29; 2Tim 1:9
2:9
e Rom 3:20,27-28; 4:2; 9:11; 11:6; 1Cor 1:29-31; 2Tim 1:9; Titus 3:5
2:10
f Deut 32:6; Ps 100:3; Isa 19:25; 29:23; 44:21 John 3:3,5; 1Cor 3:9; 2Cor 5:5,17; Eph 1:4; 4:24; Titus 2:14
2:11
g Rom 2:28-29; 1Cor 12:2; Eph 5:8; Col 1:21; 2:11,13
2:12
h Ezek 13:9; John 10:16; Rom 9:4,8; Gal 4:8; Eph 4:18; Col 1:21; 1Thes 4:5,13
2:13
i Acts 2:39; Gal 3:28; Eph 2:17
2:14
j Mic 5:5; John 10:16; 16:33; Acts 10:36; Rom 5:1; Gal 3:28; Col 1:20
2:15
k 2Cor 5:17; Gal 6:15; Eph 4:24; Col 1:22; 2:14,20
2:16
l Rom 6:6; 8:3; Col 1:20-22; 2:14
2:17
m Ps 148:14; Isa 57:19; Zech 9:10; Acts 2:39; 10:36; Rom 5:1; Eph 5:13-14
2:18
n John 10:9; 14:6;

2:20
a Ps 118:22;
Isa 28:16;
Matt 16:18; 21:42;
1Cor 3:9-10;
12:28; Gal 2:9;
Eph 4:11-12;
1Peter 2:4-5;
Rev 21:14
2:21
b 1Cor 3:17; 6:19;
2Cor 6:16;
Eph 4:15-16
2:22
c 1Peter 2:5
3:1
d Acts 21:33;
28:17,20;
Gal 5:11; Eph 4:1;
6:20; Phil 1:7,
13-14,16;
Col 1:24; 4:3,18;
2Tim 1:8; 2:9-10
3:2
e Acts 9:15; 13:2;
Rom 1:5; 11:13;
12:3; 1Cor 4:1;
Gal 1:16; Eph 1:8;
4:7; Col 1:25
3:3
f Acts 22:17,21;
26:17-18;
Rom 16:25;
Gal 1:12;
Eph 1:9-10;
Col 1:26-27
3:4
g 1Cor 4:1;
Eph 6:19
3:5
h Acts 10:28;
Rom 16:25;
Eph 2:20; 3:9
3:6
i Gal 3:14,28-29;
Eph 2:14-16
3:7
j Rom 1:5; 15:16,
18; Eph 1:19;
Col 1:20,23,25
3:8
k 1Cor 15:9;
Gal 1:16; 2:8;
Eph 1:7; Col 1:27;
1Tim 1:13,15; 2:7;
2Tim 1:11
3:9
l Ps 33:6; John 1:3;
Rom 16:25;
1Cor 2:7; Eph 1:9;
3:3,5;
Col 1:16,26;
Heb 1:2
3:10
m Rom 8:38;
1Cor 2:7;
Eph 1:21;
Col 1:16;
1Tim 3:16;
1Peter 1:12; 3:22

apostles and prophets, Christ Jesus himself being the cornerstone.[aa] [21]In him the whole building is joined together and rises into a holy sanctuary in the Lord.[b] [22]You, too, are being built in him along with the others into a dwelling place of God in the Spirit.[c]

Paul's Ministry to the Gentiles

3 [1]For this reason I, Paul, am the prisoner of Christ Jesus for the sake of you Gentiles.[d] [2]Surely you have heard about the responsibility of administering God's grace that was given to me on your behalf,[e] [3]and how this secret was made known to me through a revelation, just as I wrote about briefly in the past.[f] [4]By reading this, you will be able to grasp my understanding of the secret about Christ.[g] [5]In previous generations, this secret was not[b] made known to people[c] as it has now been revealed by the Spirit to God's[d] holy apostles and prophets:[h] [6]the Gentiles are fellow heirs, fellow members of the body, and fellow sharers of what was promised[e] in Christ Jesus through the gospel.[i]

[7]I have become a servant of this gospel[f] according to the gift of God's grace that was given me by the working of his power.[j] [8]To me, the very least of all the saints, this grace was given so that I might proclaim to the Gentiles the immeasurable wealth of Christ[k] [9]and help everyone see how this secret, which was hidden for ages in God who created all things, has been at work.[l] [10]He did this so that[g] now, through the church, the wisdom of God in all its variety might be made known to the rulers and authorities in the heavenly realm.[m] [11]This was in keeping with the eternal purpose that God[h] carried out through Christ Jesus our Lord,[n] [12]in whom we have boldness and confident access through his faithfulness.[i][o] [13]So then, I ask you not to become discouraged because of my troubles on your behalf. They are your glory![p]

3:11 *n* Eph 1:9 **3:12** *o* Eph 2:18; Heb 4:16 **3:13** *p* Acts 14:22; 2Cor 1:6; Eph 3:1; Phil 1:14; 1Thes 3:3

---

a *2:20* Or *capstone*   **b** *3:5* Lit. *it was not*   **c** *3:5* Lit. *the sons of men*
d *3:5* Lit. *his*   **e** *3:6* Lit. *of the promise*   **f** *3:7* The Gk. lacks *of this gospel*
g *3:10* Lit. *So that*   **h** *3:11* Lit. *he*   **i** *3:12* Or *through faith in him*

To Know Christ's Love

[14]This is the reason I bow my knees before the Father of our Lord Jesus Christ,[a] [15]from whom every family[b] in heaven and on earth receives its name.[a] [16]I pray that God would give you,[c] according to his glorious riches, strength in your inner being and power through his Spirit.[b] [17]Then Christ will make his home in your hearts through faith, and you will be rooted and grounded in love.[c] [18]This way you will be able to understand, along with all the saints, what is wide, long, high, and deep[d]—[19]that is, you will know the love of Christ, which goes far beyond knowledge, and will be filled with all the fullness of God.[e]

[20]Now to the one who can do infinitely more than all we can ask or imagine according to the power that is working among[d] us[f]—[21]to him be glory in the church and in Christ Jesus to all generations, forever and ever! Amen.[g]

Christ's Gifts to the Church

4 [1]I, therefore, a prisoner in the Lord, encourage you to live in a way that is worthy of the calling to which you have been called.[h] [2]With all humility and gentleness, along with patience, accept one another in love.[i] [3]Do your best to maintain the unity of the Spirit by means of the bond of peace.[j] [4]There is one body and one Spirit. In the same way, you were called to the one hope of your calling.[k] [5]There is one Lord, one faith, one baptism,[l] [6]one God and Father of all, who is above everything, through everything, and in everything.[m]

[7]Now to each one of us grace has been given according to the measure of Christ's gift.[n] [8]That's why the Scripture says,[e][o]

> "When he went up to the highest place
> he led captives into captivity
> and gave gifts to people."[f]

[9]Now what does this "he went up" mean except that he also

---

a 3:14 Other mss. lack *of our Lord Jesus Christ*   **b** 3:15 Or *all fatherhood*
c 3:16 Lit. *That he would give you*   **d** 3:20 Or *in*   **e** 4:8 Lit. *it says*
f 4:8 Ps 68:18

3:15
[a] Eph 1:10;
Phil 2:9-11

3:16
[b] Rom 7:22; 9:23;
2Cor 4:16;
Eph 1:7; 6:10;
Phil 4:19;
Col 1:11,27

3:17
[c] John 14:23;
Eph 2:22;
Col 1:23; 2:7

3:18
[d] Rom 10:3,11-12;
Eph 1:18

3:19
[e] John 1:16;
Eph 1:23;
Col 2:9-10

3:20
[f] Rom 16:25;
1Cor 2:9; Eph 2:7;
Col 1:29;
Jude 1:24

3:21
[g] Rom 11:36;
16:27; Heb 13:21

4:1
[h] Eph 3:1;
Phil 1:27;
Col 1:10;
1Thes 2:12

4:2
[i] Acts 20:19;
Gal 5:22-23;
Col 3:12-13

4:3
[j] Col 3:14

4:4
[k] Rom 12:5;
1Cor 12:4,11-13;
Eph 1:18; 2:16

4:5
[l] 1Cor 1:13; 8:6;
12:5; 2Cor 11:4;
Gal 3:27-28;
Eph 1:13;
Heb 6:6; Jude 1:3

4:6
[m] Mal 2:10;
Rom 11:36;
1Cor 8:6; 12:6

4:7
[n] Rom 12:3,6;
1Cor 12:11

4:8
[o] Jdg 5:12;
Ps 68:18; Col 2:15

4:9
a John 3:13; 6:33, 62

4:10
b Acts 1:9,11; 2:33; 1Tim 3:16; Heb 4:14; 7:26; 8:1; 9:24

4:11
c Acts 20:28; 21:8; Rom 12:7; 1Cor 12:28; Eph 2:20; 2Tim 4:5

4:12
d 1Cor 12:7; 14:26; Eph 1:23; Col 1:24

4:13
e 1Cor 14:20; Col 1:28; 2:2

4:14
f Isa 28:9; Matt 11:7; Rom 16:18; 1Cor 14:20; 2Cor 2:17; Heb 13:9

4:15
g Zech 8:16; 2Cor 4:2; Eph 1:22; 2:21; 4:25; Col 1:18; 1John 3:18

4:16
h Col 2:19

4:17
i Rom 1:21; Eph 2:1-3,22; Col 3:7; 1Peter 4:3

4:18
j Acts 26:18; Rom 1:21; Gal 4:8; Eph 2:12; 1Thes 4:5

4:19
k Rom 1:24,26; 1Tim 4:2; 1Peter 4:3

4:21
l Eph 1:13

4:22
m Rom 6:6; Eph 2:2-3,17; Col 2:11; 3:7-9; Heb 12:1; 1Peter 2:1; 4:3

4:23
n Rom 12:2; Col 3:10

4:24
o Rom 6:4; 2Cor 5:17; Gal 6:15; Eph 2:10; 6:11 Col 3:10

had gone down[a] into the lower parts of the earth?[b][a] [10]The one who went down is the same one who went up above all the heavens so that he might fill everything.[b] [11]It is he who gifted some to be apostles, others to be prophets, others to be evangelists, and still others to be pastors and teachers.[c] [12]Their purpose is to perfect the saints, to do the work of ministry, and to build up the body of Christ[d] [13]until all of us are united in the faith and in the full knowledge of God's Son, and until we attain mature adulthood and the full standard of development in Christ.[e] [14]Then we will no longer be little children, tossed like waves and blown about by every wind of doctrine, by people's trickery, or by clever strategies that would lead us astray.[f] [15]Instead, by speaking the truth in love, we will grow up completely into the one who is the head, that is, into Christ.[g] [16]In him the whole body is united and held together by every ligament with which it is supplied. As each individual part does its job, the body's growth is promoted so that it builds itself up in love.[h]

The Old Life and the New

[17]So I tell you and insist on[c] in the Lord not to live any longer like the Gentiles live, thinking worthless thoughts.[d][i] [18]They are darkened in their understanding and separated from the life of God because of their ignorance and hardness of heart.[j] [19]Since they have lost all sense of shame, they have abandoned themselves to sensuality and practice every kind of sexual perversion without restraint.[k] [20]That is not the way you came to know Christ! [21]Surely you have listened to him and have been taught by him, since truth is in Jesus.[l] [22]Regarding your former way of life, you were taught to strip off[e] your old man, which is being ruined by its deceptive desires,[m] [23]to be renewed in the spirit of your minds,[n] [24]and to clothe yourselves with the new man, which was created according to the likeness of God[f] in righteousness and true holiness.[o]

---

a 4:9 Other mss. read *had first gone down* **b** 4:9 Or *to the lower parts, that is, the earth* **c** 4:17 Or *testify* **d** 4:17 Lit. *in the worthlessness of their mind* **e** 4:22 The Gk. lacks *you were taught* **f** 4:24 Lit. *according to God*

Living As God's People

[25]Therefore, stripping off falsehood, "let each of us speak the truth to his neighbor,"[a] for we are members of one another.[a] [26]"Be angry, yet do not sin."[b] Don't let the sun go down on your wrath,[b] [27]and don't give the devil any opportunity to work.[cc] [28]The thief must no longer steal. Instead, he must work hard and do what is good with his own hands so that he will have something to give to the needy.[d]

[29]Let no filthy talk come out of your mouths, but only what is good for building up as the need may be. This way you will give grace to those who hear you.[e] [30]Don't cause God's Holy Spirit to be sad.[d] You were marked with a seal by him for the day of redemption.[f] [31]Let all bitterness, wrath, anger, quarreling, and slander be put away from you, along with all hatred.[g] [32]Be kind to one another, compassionate, forgiving one another just as God has forgiven you[e] in Christ.[h]

5 [1]So be imitators of God, as his dear children.[i] [2]Live in love as Christ also loved us[f] and gave himself for us as an offering and sacrifice, a fragrant aroma to God.[j] [3]Don't let sexual sin, impurity of any kind, or greed even be mentioned among you, as is proper for saints.[k] [4]Obscene, flippant, or vulgar talk is totally inappropriate. Instead, let there be thanksgiving.[l] [5]For you know very well that no immoral or impure person, or anyone who is greedy (that is, an idolater), has an inheritance in the kingdom of Christ and of God.[m]

Living in the Light

[6]Don't let anyone deceive you with meaningless words. It is because of these things that God's wrath comes on those who are disobedient.[g][n] [7]So don't be partners with them. [8]Once you were darkness, but now you are light in the Lord. Live as children of light.[o] [9]The fruit of the light[h] consists in

Rom 1:18; Eph 2:2; Col 2:4,8,18; 2Thes 2:3 **5:8** o Isa 9:2; Matt 4:16; Lk 16:8; John 8:12; 12:36,46; Acts 26:18; Rom 1:21; 2Cor 3:18; 4:6; Eph 2:11-12; 4:18; 1Thes 5:5; Titus 3:3; 1Peter 2:9; 1John 2:9

a 4:25 Zech 8:16   b 4:26 Ps 4:4   c 4:27 Lit. *an opportunity*   d 4:30 Or *grieved*   e 4:32 Other mss. read *us*   f 5:2 Other mss. read *you*   g 5:6 Lit. *the sons of disobedience*   h 5:9 Other mss. read *Spirit*

4:25
a Zech 8:16;
Rom 12:5;
Eph 4:15; Col 3:9
4:26
b Ps 4:4; 37:8
4:27
c 2Cor 2:10-11;
James 4:7;
1Peter 5:9
4:28
d Lk 3:11;
Acts 20:35;
1Thes 4:11;
2Thes 3:8,11-12
4:29
e Matt 12:36;
Eph 5:4; Col 3:8,
16; 4:6;
1Thes 5:11
4:30
f Isa 7:13; 63:10;
Ezek 16:43;
Lk 21:28;
Rom 8:23;
Eph 1:13-14;
1Thes 5:19
4:31
g Col 3:8,19;
Titus 3:2-3;
James 4:11;
1Peter 2:1
4:32
h Matt 6:14;
Mark 11:25;
2Cor 2:10;
Col 3:12-13
5:1
i Matt 5:45,48;
Lk 6:36; Eph 4:32
5:2
j Gen 8:21;
Lev 1:9;
John 13:34; 15:12;
2Cor 2:15;
Gal 1:4; 2:20;
1Thes 4:9;
Heb 7:27; 9:14.
26; 10:10,12;
1John 3:11,16,23;
4:21
5:3
k Rom 6:13;
1Cor 5:1; 6:18;
2Cor 12:21;
Eph 4:19-20;
Col 3:5; 1Thes 4:3
5:4
l Matt 12:35;
Rom 1:28;
Eph 4:29
5:5
m 1Cor 6:9;
Gal 5:19,21;
Col 3:5;
1Tim 6:17;
Rev 22:15
5:6
n Jer 29:8;
Matt 24:4;

5:9
a Gal 5:22
5:10
b Rom 12:2;
Phil 1:10;
1Thes 5:21;
1Tim 2:3
5:11
c Lev 19:17;
Rom 6:21; 13:12;
1Cor 5:9,11;
10:20; 2Cor 6:14;
Gal 6:8;
2Thes 3:6,14;
1Tim 5:20
5:12
d Rom 1:24,26;
Eph 1:3
5:13
e John 3:20-21;
Heb 4:13
5:14
f Isa 60:1;
John 5:25;
Rom 6:4-5;
13:11-12;
1Cor 15:34;
Eph 2:5; Col 3:1;
1Thes 5:6
5:15
g Col 4:5
5:16
h Eccl 11:2;
12:1 John 12:35;
Gal 6:10;
Eph 6:15; Col 4:5
5:17
i Rom 12:2;
Col 4:5;
1Thes 4:3; 5:18
5:18
j Prov 20:1;
23:29-30;
Isa 5:11,22;
Lk 21:34
5:19
k Acts 16:25;
1Cor 14:26;
Col 3:16;
James 5:13
5:20
l Ps 34:1; Isa 63:7;
Col 3:17;
1Thes 5:18;
2Thes 1:3;
Heb 13:15;
1Peter 2:5; 4:11
5:21
m Phil 2:3;
1Peter 5:5
5:22
n Gen 3:16;
1Cor 14:34;
Eph 6:5; Col 3:18;
Titus 2:5;
1Peter 3:1
5:23
o 1Cor 11:3;
Eph 1:22-23; 4:15;
Col 1:18

every form of goodness, righteousness, and truth.*a* [10]Determine what pleases the Lord,*b* [11]and have nothing to do with the unfruitful works of darkness. Instead, expose them for what they are.*c* [12]For it is shameful even to mention what is done by people*a* in secret.*d* [13]But everything that is exposed to the light becomes visible,*e* [14]for everything that is visible is light. That's why it says,*f*

> "Wake up, O sleeper!
>   Arise from the dead,
>   And Christ will shine on you."**b**

Wise Behavior

[15]So be careful how you live. Don't be unwise but wise,*g* [16]making the best use of time*c* because the days are evil.*h* [17]Don't be foolish, but understand what the Lord's will is.*i* [18]Stop getting*d* drunk with wine, which leads to wild living. Instead, keep on being filled with the Spirit.*j* [19]Then you will recite to one another psalms, hymns, and spiritual songs. You will sing and make music to the Lord with your hearts.*k* [20]You will always give thanks to God the Father for everything in the name of our Lord Jesus Christ.*l* [21]And you will submit yourselves to one another out of reverence for*e* Christ.*m*

[22]Wives, submit yourselves*f* to your husbands as to the Lord.*n* [23]For the husband is the head of his wife as Christ is the head of the church. It is he who is the Savior of the body.*o* [24]As the church is submissive to Christ, so wives must be submissive*g* to their husbands in everything.*p*

[25]Husbands, love your wives as Christ loved the church and gave himself for it.*q* [26]He did this to make*h* it holy by cleansing it, washing it with water and the word.*r* [27]Then he could present the church to himself in all its glory, without a spot or wrinkle or anything of the kind, but holy and

5:24 *p* Col 3:20,22; Titus 2:9 **5:25** *q* Acts 20:28; Gal 1:4; 2:20; Eph 2:2; Col 3:19; 1Peter 3:7 **5:26** *r* John 3:5; 15:3;
17:17; Titus 3:5; Heb 10:22; 1John 5:6

---

a 5:12 Lit. *them*   **b** 5:14 The source of this quote is unknown.   **c** 5:16 Or
buying up the time   **d** 5:18 Or *Don't get*   **e** 5:21 Or *in the fear of*
f 5:22 Other mss. lack *submit yourselves*   **g** 5:24 Lit. *so wives*   **h** 5:26 Lit.
To make

without fault.*a* ²⁸In the same way, husbands must love their wives as they love their own bodies.**a** A man who loves his wife loves himself. ²⁹For no one has ever hated his own body. Instead, he feeds and takes care of it, as Christ takes care of**b** the church.

³⁰For we are parts of his body—of his flesh and of his bones.**c***b* ³¹"That's why a man will leave his father and mother and be united with his wife, and the two will become one flesh."**d***c* ³²This is a great secret, but I am talking about Christ and the church. ³³But each individual man among you must love his wife as he loves**e** himself, and a wife must respect her husband.*d*

Advice for Children and Parents

6 ¹Children, obey your parents in the Lord,**f** for this is the right thing to do.*e* ²"Honor your father and mother." This is a very important commandment with a promise:*f* ³"so that it may go well for you, and you may have a long life on the earth."**g**

⁴Fathers, don't make your children angry. Instead, bring them up in the training**h** and instruction of the Lord.*g*

Advice for Slaves and Masters

⁵Slaves, obey your earthly masters with fear and trembling. Do this with sincerity,**i** as when you obey Christ.**j***h* ⁶Don't do this only while being watched in order to please them. Obey like**k** slaves of Christ who do God's will from the heart.*i* ⁷Serve willingly, as if you were serving the Lord and not merely people.**l** ⁸You know that everyone will receive a reward from the Lord for whatever good he has done, whether he is a slave or free.*j*

⁹Masters, treat your slaves**m** the same way. Don't threaten them, for you know that both of you have the same Master in heaven. There is no favoritism with him.*k*

---

a5:28 Lit. *as their own bodies*   **b**5:29 The Gk. lacks *takes care of*
c5:30 Other mss. lack *of his flesh and of his bones*   **d**5:31 Gen 2:24
e5:33 The Gk. lacks *he loves*   **f**6:1 Other mss. lack *in the Lord*
g6:3 Exod 20:12; Deut 5:16   **h**6:4 Or *discipline*   **i**6:5 Lit. *With sincerity*
j6:5 Lit. *as to Christ*   **k**6:6 Lit. *But like*   **l**6:7 Lit. *as to the Lord and not people*   **m**6:9 Lit. *them*

5:27
a Song 4:7;
2Cor 11:2;
Eph 1:4; Col 1:22

5:30
b Gen 2:23;
Rom 12:5;
1Cor 6:15; 12:27

5:31
c Gen 2:24;
Matt 19:5;
Mark 10:7-8;
1Cor 6:16

5:33
d Eph 5:25;
Col 3:19;
1Peter 3:6

6:1
e Prov 23:22;
Col 3:20

6:2
f Exod 20:12;
Deut 5:16; 27:16;
Jer 35:18;
Ezek 22:7;
Mal 1:6;
Matt 15:4;
Mark 7:10

6:4
g Gen 18:19;
Deut 4:9; 6:7,20;
11:19; Ps 78:4;
Prov 19:18; 22:6;
29:17; Col 3:21

6:5
h 1Chr 29:17;
2Cor 7:15;
Phil 2:12;
Col 3:22;
1Tim 6:1;
Titus 2:9;
1Peter 2:18

6:6
i Col 3:22-23

6:8
j Rom 2:6;
2Cor 5:10;
Gal 3:28;
Col 3:11,24

6:9
k Lev 25:43;
John 13:13;
Rom 2:11;
1Cor 7:22;
Col 3:25; 4:1

6:10
a Eph 1:19; 3:16;
Col 1:11

6:11
b Rom 13:12;
2Cor 6:7;
Eph 6:13;
1Thes 5:8

6:12
c Matt 16:17;
Lk 22:53;
John 12:31; 14:30;
Rom 8:38;
1Cor 15:50;
Eph 1:21;
2:2 Col 1:13; 2:15

6:13
d 2Cor 10:4;
Eph 5:16; 6:11

6:14
e Isa 11:5; 59:17;
Lk 12:35;
2Cor 6:7;
1Thes 5:8;
1Peter 1:13

6:15
f Isa 52:7;
Rom 10:15

6:16
g 1John 5:4

6:17
h Isa 59:17;
1Thes 5:8;
Heb 4:12;
Rev 1:16; 2:16;
19:15

6:18
i Matt 26:41;
Mark 13:33;
Lk 18:1;
Rom 12:12;
Eph 1:16; Phil 1:4;
Col 4:2;
1Thes 5:17;
1Tim 2:1

6:19
j Acts 4:29;
2Cor 3:12;
Col 4:3; 2Thes 3:1

6:20
k Acts 26:29;
28:20,31;
2Cor 5:20;
Eph 3:1; Phil 1:7,
13-14,20;
1Thes 2:2;
2Tim 1:16; 2:9

6:21
l Acts 20:4;
Col 4:7;
2Tim 4:12;
Titus 3:12

6:22
m Col 4:8

Putting on the Whole Armor of God

¹⁰Finally, be strong in the Lord and in his mighty strength.*a* ¹¹Put on the whole armor of God so that you may be able to stand against the devil's strategies.*ab* ¹²For our*b* struggle is not against a human opponent,*c* but against rulers, against authorities, against cosmic powers in the darkness around us,*d* against evil spiritual forces in the heavenly realm.*c* ¹³For this reason, take up the whole armor of God so that you may be able to take a stand in that evil day. When you have done everything you could, you will be able to stand firm.*d*

¹⁴Take a stand, then! Fasten the belt of truth around your waist. Put on the breastplate of righteousness.*e* ¹⁵Put shoes on your feet so that you are ready to proclaim the gospel of peace.*ef* ¹⁶In addition to all of these, pick up the shield of faith. With it you will be able to put out all the flaming arrows of the evil one.*g* ¹⁷Also take the helmet of salvation and the sword of the Spirit, which is the word of God.*h*

¹⁸Pray in the Spirit at all times with every kind of prayer and request there is. For the same reason be alert with every kind of effort and request for all the saints.*i* ¹⁹Pray also for me,*f* so that, when I open my mouth, the right words will be given to me. Then I will boldly make known the secret of the gospel,*j* ²⁰for whose sake I am an ambassador in chains. I desire to declare it as boldly as I should!*gk*

Final Greeting

²¹So that you may know what has happened to me and how I am doing, Tychicus, our dear brother and a faithful minister in the Lord, will tell you everything.*l* ²²I'm sending him to you for this very reason, so that you may know how we're doing and that he may encourage your hearts.*m* ²³May the brothers have peace and love, with faith, from God the

---

a *6:11* Or *schemes*   **b** *6:12* Other mss. read *your*   **c** *6:12* Lit. *flesh and blood*   **d** *6:12* Lit. *this darkness*   **e** *6:15* Lit. *in readiness for the gospel of peace*   **f** *6:19* Lit. *And for me*   **g** *6:20* Lit. *as I should speak*

Father and the Lord Jesus Christ!*a* 24May all who love the Lord Jesus Christ with sincerity have his grace!*ab*

---

a6:24 Other mss. read *his grace. Amen*

6:23
a 1 Peter 5:14

6:24
b Titus 2:7

THE LETTER OF PAUL TO THE
PHILIPPIANS

1:1
a 1Cor 1:2

1:2
b Rom 1:7;
2Cor 1:2;
1Peter 1:2

1:3
c Rom 1:8-9;
1Cor 1:4;
Eph 1:15-16;
Col 1:3;
1Thes 1:2;
2Thes 1:3

1:5
d Rom 12:13;
15:26; 2Cor 8:1;
Phil 4:14-15

1:6
e John 6:29;
Phil 1:10;
1Thes 1:3

1:7
f 2Cor 3:2; 7:3;
Eph 3:1; 6:20;
Phil 1:17; 4:14;
Col 4:3,18;
2Tim 1:8

1:8
g Rom 1:9; 9:1;
Gal 1:20;
Phil 2:26; 4:1;
1Thes 2:5

1:9
h 1Thes 3:12

1:10
i Acts 24:16;
Rom 2:18; 12:2;
1Cor 1:8;
Eph 5:10;
1Thes 3:13; 5:23

1:11
j John 15:4-5,8;
Eph 1:12,14; 2:10;
Col 1:6

1:13
k Phil 4:22

Greetings from Paul and Timothy

1 ¹From[a] Paul and Timothy, servants[b] of Christ Jesus, to all the holy ones[c] in Philippi who are united with Christ Jesus, with their overseers[d] and deacons.[e][a] ²May grace and peace from God our Father and the Lord Jesus Christ be yours![b]

Paul's Prayer for the Philippians

³I thank my God every time I remember you,[f][c] ⁴always praying with joy in every one of my prayers for all of you ⁵because of your partnership in the gospel from the first day until now.[d] ⁶I am convinced of this, that the one who began a good work among[g] you will bring it to completion by the day of Christ Jesus.[e] ⁷For it's only right for me to think this way about all of you, because I have you in my heart.[h] Both in my imprisonment and in the defense and confirmation of the gospel, all of you are partners with me in grace.[f] ⁸For God is my witness how much I long for all of you with the compassion of Christ Jesus.[g]

⁹And this is my prayer, that your love will keep on growing more and more in full knowledge and perfect insight,[h] ¹⁰so that you may be able to determine what is best and may be pure and blameless until the day of Christ,[i] ¹¹having been filled with the fruit of righteousness that comes through Jesus Christ to the glory and praise of God.[j]

The Priority of the Gospel in Everything

¹²Now I want you to know, brothers, that what has happened to me has actually turned out for the progress of the gospel. ¹³As a result, it has become clear to the whole imperial guard and to everyone else that I am in prison because of Christ.[k] ¹⁴Moreover, because of my imprisonment most of

---

a *1:1 The* Gk. lacks *From*   **b** *1:1* Or *slaves*   **c** *1:1* Or *saints*   **d** *1:1* Or *bishops*   **e** *1:1* Or *ministers*   **f** *1:3* Or *every time you remember me*   **g** *1:6* Or *in*   **h** *1:7* Or *you have me in your heart*

the brothers have been made confident in the Lord to speak God's word more boldly and courageously than ever before.

[15]Some are preaching Christ because of their envy and rivalry, while others do so[a] because of their good will.[a] [16]The latter are motivated by love,[b] because they know that I have been appointed for the defense of the gospel. [17]The former proclaim Christ out of selfish ambition and without sincerity, thinking that they will stir up trouble for me during my imprisonment.[b]

[18]But what does it matter?[c] Just this, that in every way, whether in pretense or in truth, Christ is being proclaimed, and because of this I am joyful. Yes, I will continue to be joyful, [19]because I know that this will result in my deliverance through your prayers and the help that comes from the Spirit of Jesus Christ.[c] [20]This is according to my eager expectation and hope that I will have nothing to be ashamed of. Instead, because of my[d] boldness Christ will be exalted in my body, now as always, whether I live or die.[e][d]

[21]For to me, to continue to live is Christ, and to die is gain. [22]If I continue to live in this body, that will produce more results.[f] Yet I don't know which I would prefer. [23]I can't decide between the two. I have the desire to leave this life and be with Christ, for that is far better.[e] [24]But for your sake it's better that I remain in this body.

[25]Since I'm convinced of this, I know that I will continue to live and be with all of you for the sake of your progress and joy in the faith.[f] [26]Then your boasting in Christ Jesus will increase along with mine[g] through my coming again to you.[g]

Standing Firm in One Spirit

[27]The only thing that matters is that you live as good citizens in a manner that is worthy of the gospel of Christ. Then, whether I come to see you or whether I stay away, I may hear all about you—that you are standing firm in one spirit, struggling with one mind for the faith of the gospel,[h]

---

a1:15 The Gk. lacks *do so*　**b**1:16 Lit. *The latter out of love*　**c**1:18 Lit. *What then?*　**d**1:20 Lit. *with all*　**e**1:20 Lit. *by life or by death*　**f**1:22 Lit. *that to me is fruitful labor*　**g**1:26 Lit. *in me*

1:15
a Phil 2:3

1:17
b Phil 1:7

1:19
c Rom 8:9;
2Cor 1:11

1:20
d Rom 5:5; 8:19;
Eph 6:19-20

1:23
e 2Cor 5:8;
2Tim 4:6

1:25
f Phil 2:24

1:26
g 2Cor 1:14; 5:12

1:27
h 1Cor 1:10;
Eph 4:1; Phil 4:1;
Col 1:10;
1Thes 2:12; 4:1;
Jude 1:3

1:28
a Rom 8:17;
2Thes 1:5;
2Tim 2:11
1:29
b Acts 5:41;
Rom 5:3; Eph 2:8
1:30
c Acts 16:19;
Col 2:1; 1Thes 2:2
2:1
d 2Cor 13:14;
Col 3:12
2:2
e John 3:29;
Rom 12:16; 15:5;
1Cor 1:10;
2Cor 13:11;
Phil 1:27;
3:16; 4:2;
1Peter 3:8
2:3
f Rom 12:10;
Gal 5:26;
Eph 5:21;
Phil 1:15-16;
James 3:14;
1Peter 5:5
2:4
g 1Cor 10:24,33;
13:5
2:5
h Matt 11:29;
John 13:15;
1Peter 2:21;
1John 2:6
2:6
i John 1:1-2; 5:18;
10:33; 17:5;
2Cor 4:4;
Col 1:15; Heb 1:3
2:7
j Ps 22:6; Isa 42:1;
49:3,6; 52:13;
53:3,11;
Ezek 34:23-24;
Dan 9:26;
Zech 3:8;
Matt 20:28;
Mark 9:12;
Lk 22:27;
John 1:14;
Rom 1:3; 8:3;
15:3; Gal 4:4;
Heb 2:14,17
2:8
k Matt 26:39,42;
John 10:18;
Heb 5:8; 12:2
2:9
l John 17:1-2,5;
Acts 2:33;
Eph 1:20-21;
Heb 1:4; 2:9
2:10
m Isa 45:23;
Matt 28:18;
Rom 14:11;
Rev 5:13

²⁸and that you are not intimidated by your opponents in any way. This is evidence that they will be destroyed and that you will be saved, and that from God.*ᵃ* ²⁹For you have been given the privilege*ᵃ* for Christ's sake not only to believe in him but also to suffer for him.*ᵇ* ³⁰You have the same struggle that you saw in me and now hear that I'm still having.*ᵇᶜ*

Unity through Humility

2 ¹So if there is any encouragement in Christ, if there is any comfort of love, if there is any fellowship in the Spirit, if there is any compassion and sympathy,*ᵈ* ²then fill me with joy by having the same attitude, sharing the same love, being united in spirit, keeping one purpose in mind.*ᵉ* ³Don't act out of selfish ambition or conceit. Instead, with humility think of others as being better than yourselves.*ᶠ* ⁴Don't be concerned about your own interests, but also be concerned about*ᶜ* the interests of others.*ᵍ* ⁵Have the same attitude among yourselves that was also in Christ Jesus:*ᵈʰ*

> ⁶*In God's own form existed he,*ⁱ
>   *And shared with God equality,*
>   *Deemed nothing needed grasping.*
> ⁷*Instead, poured out in emptiness,*ʲ
>   *A servant's form did he possess,*
>   *A mortal man becoming.*
> *In human form he chose to be,*
> 8   *And lived in all humility,*ᵏ
>   *Death on a cross obeying.*
> ⁹*Now lifted up by God to heaven,*ˡ
>   *A name above all others given,*
>   *This matchless name possessing.*
> ¹⁰*And so, when Jesus' name is called,*ᵐ
>   *The knees of everyone will fall,*ᵉ
>   *Where'er they are residing.*ᶠ

---

a 1:29 Lit. *it has been given you*   **b** 1:30 Lit. *hear in me*   **c** 2:4 The Gk. lacks *be concerned about*   **d** 2:5 Verses 6-11 probably represent an early Christian hymn.   **e** 2:10 Or *every knee should bend*   **f** 2:10 Lit. *in heaven, on earth, and under the earth*

> 11*Then every tongue in one accord,*[a]
> *Will say that Jesus Christ is Lord,*
> *While God the Father praising.*

Blameless Living

12And so, my dear friends, just as you have always obeyed, not only when I was with you but even more now that I'm absent, continue to work out your salvation with fear and trembling.[b] 13For it is God who is producing in you both the desire and the ability to do what pleases him.[c] 14Do everything without complaining or arguing.[d] 15Then you will be blameless and innocent, God's children without any faults among a crooked and perverse generation. You will shine like stars among them in the world[e] 16as you hold out[a] the word of life. Then I can boast in the day of Christ that I didn't run in vain or work hard in vain.[f]

17Even if I'm being poured out like an offering as part of the sacrifice and service I offer[b] for your faith, I am joyful, and I share my joy with all of you.[g] 18In the same way, you also should be joyful and share your joy with me.

News about Paul's Companions

19Now I hope in the Lord Jesus to send Timothy to you soon so that I can be encouraged when I learn of your condition.[h] 20I don't have anyone else like him who takes a genuine interest in your welfare.[i] 21All the others look after their own interests, not after those of Jesus Christ.[j] 22But you know his proven worth. Like a son with his father, he has worked hard[c] with me in the gospel.[k] 23I hope to send him as soon as I see how things are going to turn out for me. 24I am also confident in the Lord that I will come to visit you soon.[d][l]

25Meanwhile, I thought it best to send Epaphroditus—my brother, fellow worker, and fellow soldier, but your messenger and minister to my need—back to you.[m] 26For he has been longing for[e] all of you and is troubled because you heard that he was sick.[n] 27Indeed he was sick, to the point of

---

a *2:16* Or *hold firmly to* **b** *2:17* The Gk. lacks *I offer* **c** *2:22* Or *has served*
d *2:24* Lit. *will come soon* **e** *2:26* Other mss. read *longing to see*

2:11 [a] John 13:13; Acts 2:36; Rom 14:9; 1Cor 8:6; 12:3

2:12 [b] Eph 6:5; Phil 1:5

2:13 [c] 2Cor 3:5; Heb 13:21

2:14 [d] Rom 14:1; 1Cor 10:10; 1Peter 4:9

2:15 [e] Deut 32:5; Matt 5:14,16,45; Eph 5:1,8; 1Peter 2:12

2:16 [f] 2Cor 1:14; Gal 2:2; 1Thes 2:19; 3:5

2:17 [g] Rom 15:16; 2Cor 7:4; Col 1:24; 2Tim 4:6

2:19 [h] Rom 16:21; 1Thes 3:2

2:20 [i] Ps 55:13

2:21 [j] 1Cor 10:24,33; 13:5; 2Tim 4:10, 16

2:22 [k] 1Cor 4:17; 1Tim 1:2; 2Tim 1:2

2:24 [l] Phil 1:25

2:25 [m] 2Cor 8:23; 11:9; Phil 4:18

2:26 [n] Phil 1:3

2:29
a 1Cor 16:18;
1Thes 5:12;
1Tim 5:17

2:30
b 1Cor 16:17;
Phil 4:10

3:1
c 2Cor 13:11;
Phil 4:4;
1Thes 5:16

3:2
d Isa 56:10;
Rom 2:28;
2Cor 11:13;
Gal 5:2,15

3:3
e Deut 10:16;
30:6; Jer 4:4;
John 4:23-24;
Rom 2:29;
4:11-12; 7:6;
Gal 6:14; Col 2:11

3:4
f 2Cor 11:18,21

3:5
g Gen 17:12;
Acts 23:6; 26:4-5;
Rom 11:1;
2Cor 11:22

3:6
h Lk 1:6; Acts 8:3;
9:1; 22:3;
Rom 10:5;
Gal 1:13-14

3:7
i Matt 13:44

3:8
j Isa 53:11;
Jer 9:23-24;
John 17:3;
1Cor 2:2; Col 2:2

3:9
k Rom 1:17;
3:21-22; 9:30;
10:3,5-6; Gal 2:16

death. But God had mercy on him, and not only on him but also on me, so that I would not have one sorrow on top of another.*a* [28]I'm especially eager to send him so that you will have the joy of seeing him again, and I will feel relieved. [29]So welcome him in the Lord with all joy, and make sure you honor such people highly.*a* [30]For he came close to death for the work of Christ,*b* risking his life to complete what was lacking in your service to me.*b*

Warning against Pride

3 [1]So then,*c* my brothers, be joyful in the Lord. It's no trouble for me to write the same things to you, and it's for your safety.*c*

[2]Beware of the dogs! Beware of the evil workers! Beware of the mutilators!*d**d* [3]For it is we who are the circumcision*e*— we who worship in the Spirit of God*f* and take pride in Christ Jesus. We have not placed any confidence in the flesh,*e* [4]although I could have confidence in the flesh. If anyone thinks he can place confidence in the flesh, I have more reason to think so.*g**f* [5]Having been circumcised on the eighth day, I am of the nation of Israel, from the tribe of Benjamin, a Hebrew of Hebrews. As far as the Law is concerned, I was a Pharisee.*g* [6]As far as zeal is concerned, I was a persecutor of the church. As far as the righteousness that is in the Law is concerned, I was perfect.*h*

[7]But whatever things were assets to me, these I now consider a loss for the sake of Christ.*i* [8]What is more, I continue to consider all these things as a loss for the sake of the surpassing value of knowing Christ Jesus my Lord. It's because of him that I have experienced the loss of all those things. I consider them rubbish*h* in order to gain Christ*j* [9]and be found in him, not having a righteousness of my own that comes from the Law, but one that comes through the faith of Christ.*i* This is the righteousness that comes from God and is by faith.*k* [10]I want to know Christ*j*—that is, what

---

a 2:27 Lit. *sorrow on sorrow*   *b* 2:30 Other mss. read *of the Lord*   *c* 3:1 Or *Furthermore*   *d* 3:2 Lit. *the mutilation*; Gk. *katatome* (a cutting off) *e* 3:3 Gk. *peritome* (a cutting around)   *f* 3:3 Other mss. read *worship God in the Spirit*   *g* 3:4 Lit. *I more*   *h* 3:8 Or *dung*   *i* 3:9 Or *through faith in Christ*   *j* 3:10 Lit. *To know him*

his resurrection power is like and what it means to share in his sufferings by becoming like him in his death,[a] [11]though I hope to experience the resurrection from the dead.[b]

Pursuing the Goal

[12]It's not that I've already reached this goal or have already become perfect. But I keep pursuing it, hoping somehow to embrace it just as I have been embraced by Christ Jesus.[c] [13]Brothers, I don't consider myself to have embraced it.[a] But this one thing I do: forgetting what lies behind and straining forward to what lies ahead,[d] [14]I keep pursuing the goal to win the prize[b] of God's heavenly call in Christ Jesus.[e]

[15]Therefore, those of us who are mature[c] should think this way. And if you think differently about anything, God will show you how to think.[d][f] [16]However, we should live up to what we have achieved so far.[g]

True and False Teachers

[17]Join together in imitating me, brothers, and pay close attention to those who live by the example we have given you.[e][h] [18]I have often told you, and now tell you even with tears, that many live as enemies of the cross of Christ.[i] [19]Their destiny is destruction, their god is their belly, and their glory is in their shame. Their minds are set on worldly things.[j]

[20]Our citizenship, however, is in heaven, and it is from there that we eagerly wait for a Savior, the Lord Jesus Christ.[k] [21]He will change our humble bodies and make them like his glorious body through the power that enables him to bring everything under his authority.[l]

Closing Exhortations

4 [1]Therefore, my dear brothers whom I long for, my joy and my crown, stand firm in the Lord in this way, dear friends.[m]

[2]I encourage Euodia and I encourage Syntyche to have the same attitude in the Lord.[n] [3]Yes, I also ask you, my true

---

a3:13 Other mss. read *embraced it yet*   **b**3:14 Lit. *the goal for the prize*
c3:15 Or *perfect*   **d**3:15 Lit. *show you this*   **e**3:17 Lit. *the example you have in us*

3:10
[a]Rom 6:3-5; 8:17;
2Cor 4:10-11;
2Tim 2:11-12;
1Peter 4:13

3:11
[b]Acts 26:7

3:12
[c]1Tim 6:12;
Heb 12:23

3:13
[d]Ps 45:10;
Lk 9:62;
1Cor 9:24,26;
2Cor 5:16;
Heb 6:1

3:14
[e]2Tim 4:7-8;
Heb 3:1; 12:1

3:15
[f]1Cor 2:6; 14:20;
Gal 5:10

3:16
[g]Rom 12:16;
15:5; Gal 6:16;
Phil 2:2

3:17
[h]1Cor 4:16;
11:1 Phil 4:9;
1Thes 1:6;
1Peter 5:3

3:18
[i]Gal 1:7; 2:21;
6:12 Phil 1:15-16

3:19
[j]Hos 4:7;
Rom 8:5; 16:18;
2Cor 11:12,15;
Gal 6:13;
1Tim 6:5;
Titus 1:11;
2Peter 2:1

3:20
[k]Acts 1:11;
1Cor 1:7; Eph 2:6,
19; Col 3:1,3;
1Thes 1:10;
Titus 2:13

3:21
[l]1Cor 15:26-27,
43,48-49;
Eph 1:19; Col 3:4;
1John 3:2

4:1
[m]2Cor 1:14;
Phil 1:8,27; 2:16;
1Thes 2:19-20

4:2
[n]Phil 2:2; 3:16

4:3
a Exod 32:32;
Ps 69:28;
Dan 12:1;
Lk 10:20;
Rom 16:3;
Phil 1:27; Rev 3:5;
13:8; 20:12; 21:27

4:4
b Rom 12:12;
Phil 3:1;
1Thes 5:16;
1Peter 4:13

4:5
c 2Thes 2:2;
Heb 10:25;
James 5:8-9;
1Peter 4:7;
2Peter 3:8-9

4:6
d Ps 55:22;
Prov 16:3;
Matt 6:25;
Lk 12:22;
1Peter 5:7

4:7
e John 14:27;
Rom 5:1; Col 3:15

4:8
f 1Thes 5:22

4:9
g Rom 15:33;
16:20;
1Cor 14:33;
2Cor 13:11;
Phil 3:17;
1Thes 5:23;
Heb 13:20

4:10
h 2Cor 11:9

4:11
i 1Tim 6:6,8

4:12
j 1Cor 4:11;
2Cor 6:10; 11:27

4:13
k John 15:5;
2Cor 12:9

4:14
l Phil 1:7

4:15
m 2Cor 11:8-9

4:17
n Rom 15:28;
Titus 3:14

partner,[a] to help these women. They have struggled with me in the gospel along with Clement and the rest of my fellow workers, whose names are in the Book of Life.[a]

[4] Always be joyful in the Lord. I'll say it again: Be joyful![b] [5] Let your gentleness be known to all people. The Lord is near.[c] [6] Never worry about anything, but in every situation let your needs be made known to God in prayers and requests, with thanksgiving.[d] [7] Then God's peace, which goes beyond anything we can imagine, will guard your hearts and minds in Christ Jesus.[e]

[8] Finally, brothers, whatever is true, whatever is honorable, whatever is fair, whatever is pure, whatever is acceptable, whatever is commendable, if there is anything of excellence and if there is anything praiseworthy—keep your thoughts on these things.[f] [9] Likewise, what you've learned and received and heard and seen in me—keep practicing these things. Then the God of peace will be with you.[g]

The Philippians' Gifts

[10] Now I am very joyful in the Lord, because once again you have shown your concern for me. Of course, you were concerned for me but didn't have an opportunity to show it.[b][h] [11] I'm not saying this because I'm in any need. For I've learned to be content in whatever situation I'm in.[i] [12] I know how to be humble, and I know how to prosper. In each and every situation I've learned the secret of being full and of going hungry, of having too much and of having too little.[j] [13] I can do all things through him[c] who strengthens me.[k] [14] Nevertheless, it was kind of you to share my troubles.[l]

[15] You Philippians also know that in the early days[d] of the gospel, when I left Macedonia, no church participated with me in the matter of giving and receiving except for you.[m] [16] Even while I was in Thessalonica, you provided for my needs twice. [17] It's not that I'm looking for a gift. I'm looking for your resources to increase.[e][n] [18] I have been paid in full and have more than enough. I am fully supplied, now

---

a 4:3 Or *loyal Syzygus* **b** 4:10 The Gk. lacks *to show it* **c** 4:13 Other mss. read *Christ* **d** 4:15 Lit. *in the beginning* **e** 4:17 Lit. *for the profit that accumulates to your account*

that I have received from Epaphroditus what you sent—a
fragrant aroma, a sacrifice acceptable and pleasing to God.*
¹⁹My God will fully supply your every need according to his
glorious riches in Christ Jesus.*ᵇ ²⁰Glory belongs to our God
and Father forever and ever! Amen.*ᶜ

Final Greeting

²¹Greet every saint in Christ Jesus. The brothers who are
with me send their greetings to you.*ᵈ ²²All the saints, especially those of the emperor'sᵃ household, greet you.*ᵉ

²³May the grace of the Lord Jesus Christ be with your
spirit! Amen.ᵇᶠ

---

a 4:22 Or *Caesar's*   **b** 4:23 Other mss. lack *Amen*

4:18
*ᵃ*2Cor 9:12;
Phil 2:25;
Heb 13:16

4:19
*ᵇ*Ps 23:1;
2Cor 9:8; Eph 1:7;
3:16

4:20
*ᶜ*Rom 16:27;
Gal 1:5

4:21
*ᵈ*Gal 1:2

4:22
*ᵉ*Phil 1:13

4:23
*ᶠ*Rom 16:24

THE LETTER OF PAUL TO THE
COLOSSIANS

1:1
a Eph 1:1

Greetings from Paul

1 [1]From[a] Paul, an apostle of Christ Jesus by the will of God, and Timothy our brother,[a] [2]to the holy[b] and faithful brothers in Colossae who are in union with Christ.[b]

May grace and peace from God our Father[c] be yours!

1:2
b 1Cor 4:17;
Gal 1:3; Eph 6:21

Paul's Prayer for the Colossians

[3]We give thanks to God, the Father of our Lord Jesus Christ, praying always for you.[c] [4]For we have heard about your faith in Christ Jesus and the love that you have for all the saints, [5]based on the hope laid up for you in heaven. Some time ago you heard about this hope[d] in the word of truth, the gospel [6]that has come to you. Just as it is bearing fruit and spreading all over the world, so it has been doing among[e] you from the day you heard it and came to know the grace of God in truth. [7]You learned about this gospel[f] from Epaphras, our dear fellow servant, who is a faithful minister of Christ on your[g] behalf. [8]He has told us about your love in the Spirit.[d]

1:3
c 1Cor 1:4;
Eph 1:16

1:8
d Rom 15:30

1:9
e Rom 12:2;
1Cor 1:5; Eph 1:8,
15-16; 5:10,17;
Col 1:3-4

Christ Is Above All

[9]For this reason, since the day we heard about this, we haven't stopped praying for you and asking that you may be filled with the full knowledge of God's[h] will in all spiritual wisdom and understanding.[e] [10]Then you will live in a manner worthy of the Lord and be fully pleasing to him[i] as you bear fruit in every good work and grow in the full knowledge of God.[f] [11]You are being strengthened with all power according to his glorious might, so that you might patiently endure everything with joy[g] [12]and might thank the

1:10
f John 15:16;
2Cor 9:8; Eph 4:1;
Phil 1:11,27;
1Thes 2:12;
4:1 Titus 3:1;
Heb 13:21

1:11
g Acts 5:41;
Rom 5:3;
Eph 3:16; 4:2;
6:10

---

a *1:1 The Gk. lacks From*   **b** *1:2 Or to the saints*   **c** *1:2 Other mss. read from God our Father and the Lord Jesus Christ*   **d** *1:5 Lit. about it*   **e** *1:6 The Gk. lacks it has been doing*   **f** *1:7 Lit. Just as you learned*   **g** *1:7 Other mss. read our*   **h** *1:9 Lit. his*   **i** *1:10 Lit. to all pleasing*

Father, who has enabled us[a] to share in the saints' inheritance in the light.[a] 13He has rescued us from the power of darkness and has brought us into the kingdom of the Son whom he loves.[b] 14In him we have redemption, the forgiveness of sins.[c]

15He is the image of the invisible God, the firstborn of[b] all creation.[d] 16For in[c] him all things in heaven and on earth were created, things visible and invisible, whether they are kings,[d] lords, rulers, or powers. All things have been created through him and for him.[e] 17He himself existed before all things, and in[c] him all things hold together.[f] 18He is also the head of the body, which is the church. He is the beginning, the firstborn from the dead, so that he himself might have first place in everything.[g] 19For God[e] was pleased to have all of his fullness live in him.[h] 20Through him he also reconciled all things to himself, whether things on earth or things in heaven. He did this by making peace through the blood of his cross.[i]

21You who were once alienated and hostile in mind, doing evil deeds,[f][j] 22he has now reconciled by the death of his physical body so that he might present you holy, blameless, and without fault before him.[k] 23However, you must remain firmly established and steadfast in the faith, without being moved from the hope of the gospel that you heard, which has been proclaimed to every creature under heaven and of which I, Paul, have become a servant.[g][l]

Paul's Service in the Church

24Now I am rejoicing in my sufferings for you and completing in my flesh whatever remains of Christ's sufferings on behalf of his body, which is the church.[m] 25I became its servant[g] according to God's commission that was given to me for you, so that I might fulfill the ministry of the word of God.[h][n] 26This secret was hidden throughout the ages and generations but has now been revealed to his saints.[o] 27God

1:26 o Matt 13:11; Rom 16:25; 1Cor 2:7; Eph 3:9; 2Tim 1:10

a 1:12 Other mss. read *you*   b 1:15 Or *over*   c 1:16,1:17 Or *by*
d 1:16 Lit. *thrones*   e 1:19 Lit. *he*   f 1:21 Lit. *in evil deeds*   g 1:23,1:25 Or
minister   h 1:25 Lit. *to fulfill the word of God*

1:12
a Acts 26:18;
Eph 1:11; 5:20;
Col 3:15

1:13
b Eph 6:12;
1Thes 2:12;
Heb 2:14;
1Peter 2:9;
2Peter 1:11

1:14
c Eph 1:7

1:15
d 2Cor 4:4;
Heb 1:3; Rev 3:14

1:16
e John 1:3;
Rom 8:38; 11:36;
1Cor 8:6;
Eph 1:21; 3:9;
Col 2:10,15;
Heb 1:2; 2:10;
1Peter 3:22

1:17
f John 1:1,3; 17:5;
1Cor 8:6

1:18
g Acts 26:23;
1Cor 11:3; 15:20,
23; Eph 1:10,22;
4:15; 5:23;
Rev 1:5

1:19
h John 1:16; 3:34;
Col 2:9; 3:11

1:20
i 2Cor 5:18;
Eph 1:10; 2:14-15

1:21
j Eph 2:1-2,12,19;
4:18;
Titus 1:15-16

1:22
k Lk 1:75; Eph 1:4;
2:15-16; 5:27;
1Thes 4:7;
Titus 2:14;
Jude 1:24

1:23
l John 15:6;
Acts 1:17;
Rom 10:18;
2Cor 3:6; 4:1;
5:18; Eph 3:7,17;
Col 1:6; 2:7; 3:25;
1Tim 2:7

1:24
m Rom 5:3;
2Cor 1:5-6; 7:4;
Eph 1:23; 3:1,13;
Phil 3:10;
2Tim 1:8; 2:10

1:25
n 1Cor 9:17;
Gal 2:7; Eph 3:2;
Col 3:23

1:27
a Rom 9:23;
2Cor 2:14;
Eph 1:7; 3:8;
1Tim 1:1

1:28
b Acts 20:20,27,
31; 2Cor 11:2;
Eph 5:27;
Col 1:22

1:29
c 1Cor 15:10;
Eph 1:19; 3:7,20;
Col 2:1

2:1
d Phil 1:30;
Col 1:29;
1Thes 2:2

2:2
e 2Cor 1:6;
Phil 3:8; Col 1:9;
3:14

2:3
f 1Cor 1:24; 2:6-7;
Eph 1:8; Col 1:9

2:4
g Rom 16:18;
2Cor 11:13;
Eph 4:14; 5:6;
Col 2:8,18

2:5
h 1Cor 5:3; 14:40;
1Thes 2:17;
1Peter 5:9

2:6
i 1Thes 4:1;
Jude 1:3

2:7
j Eph 2:21-22;
3:17; Col 1:23

2:8
k Jer 29:8;
Matt 15:2;
Rom 16:17;
Gal 1:14; 4:3,9;
Eph 5:6; Col 1:22;
2:18,20;
Heb 13:9

2:9
l John 1:14;
Col 1:19

2:10
m John 1:16;
Eph 1:20-21;
Col 1:16;
1Peter 3:22

2:11
n Deut 10:16;
30:6; Jer 4:4;
Rom 2:29; 6:6;
Eph 4:22; Phil 3:3;
Col 3:8-9

2:12
o Acts 2:24;
Rom 6:4;
Eph 1:19; 3:7;
Col 3:1

wanted to make known to them the glorious riches of this secret among the Gentiles—which is Christ in you, the hope of glory.[a] 28It is he whom we proclaim as we admonish everyone and teach everyone with all wisdom, so that we may present everyone mature[a] in Christ.[b] 29I work hard and struggle to do this according to his energy that powerfully works in me.[c]

2 1For I want you to know how much I struggle for you, for those in Laodicea, and for all who have never seen me face to face.[b][d] 2Because they are united in love, I pray that their hearts may be encouraged by all the riches that come from a complete understanding of the full knowledge of Christ, who is the secret of God.[e] 3In him are hidden all the treasures of wisdom and knowledge.[f] 4I say this so that no one will mislead you with nice-sounding rhetoric.[g] 5Although I am absent in body, I am with you in spirit, rejoicing to see how stable you are and how firm your faith in Christ is.[h]

Fullness of Life

6So then, just as you received Christ Jesus the Lord, continue to live in him.[i] 7For you have been rooted in him, and now[c] you are being built up and strengthened in the faith, just as you were taught, while you overflow with thanksgiving.[j]

8See to it that no one enslaves you through philosophy and empty deceit according to human tradition, according to the basic principles of the world,[d] and not according to Christ.[k] 9For in him the whole fullness of God lives in bodily form.[l] 10You have been brought to fullness in him, who is the head of every ruler and authority.[m] 11In him you were circumcised with a circumcision performed without human hands by stripping off the corrupt nature in the circumcision performed by Christ.[n] 12When you were buried with him in baptism, you were also raised with him through faith in the power of God, who raised him from the dead.[o] 13Even when

---

a 1:28 Or *complete*   **b** 2:1 Lit. *my face in the flesh*   **c** 2:7 The Gk. lacks *now*
d 2:8 Or *the elemental spirits of the universe*

you were dead because of your offenses and the uncircumcision of your flesh, God[a] made you alive with him when he forgave us all of our offenses.[a] [14]He has erased the charges that were brought against us with their decrees that were hostile to us. He took those charges away when he nailed them to the cross.[b] [15]He disarmed the rulers and the authorities and made a public spectacle of them, triumphing over them in the cross.[bc]

[16]Therefore, let no one judge you in matters of food and drink or with respect to a festival, a new moon, or a Sabbath day.[d] [17]These are a shadow of the things to come, but the reality[c] belongs to Christ.[e] [18]Let no one who delights in humility and the worship of angels cheat you out of the prize by boasting about what he has seen.[d] Such a person is puffed up without cause by his carnal mind.[f] [19]He doesn't hold on to the head, from whom the whole body, which is nourished and held together by its joints and ligaments, grows with a growth that comes from God.[g]

The New Life in Christ

[20]If you have died with Christ to the basic principles of the world,[e] why are you submitting to its decrees as though you still lived in the world?[h] [21]"Don't handle this! Don't taste or touch that!"[i] [22]All of these things will be destroyed through use because they are based on human commands and teachings.[j] [23]These things have the appearance of wisdom in promoting self-made religion, humility, and harsh treatment of the body, but they have no value against self-indulgence.[k]

Keep Focusing on Christ

3 [1]Therefore, if you have been raised with Christ, keep focusing on the things that are above, where Christ is seated at the right hand of God.[l] [2]Keep your minds on things that are above, not on things that are on the earth. [3]For you have died, and your life is hidden with Christ in

---

a 2:13 Lit. he　b 2:15 Lit. in it　c 2:17 Or substance　d 2:18 Other mss. read what he has not seen　e 2:20 Or the elemental spirits of the universe

2:13
a Eph 2:1,5-6,11

2:14
b Eph 2:15-16

2:15
c Gen 3:15;
Ps 68:18;
Isa 53:12;
Matt 12:29;
Lk 10:18;
11:22 John 12:31;
16:11; Eph 4:8;
6:12; Heb 2:14

2:16
d Rom 14:2-3,5,
10,13,17;
1 Cor 8:8;
Gal 4:10

2:17
e Heb 8:5; 9:9;
10:1

2:18
f Ezek 13:3;
Col 2:4; 1 Tim 1:7

2:19
g Eph 4:15-16

2:20
h Rom 6:3,5; 7:4,
6; Gal 2:19; 4:3,9;
Eph 2:15; Col 2:3

2:21
i 1 Tim 4:3

2:22
j Isa 29:13;
Matt 15:9;
Titus 1:14

2:23
k Col 4:8;
1 Tim 4:8

3:1
l Rom 6:5; 8:34;
Eph 1:20; 2:6;
Col 2:12

3:3
a Rom 6:2;
2Cor 5:7;
Gal 2:20; Col 1:5;
2:20
3:4
b John 11:25; 14:6;
1Cor 15:43;
Phil 3:21;
1John 3:2
3:5
c Rom 6:13; 8:13;
Gal 5:24; Eph 5:3,
5; 1Thes 4:5
3:6
d Rom 1:18;
Eph 2:2; 5:6;
Rev 22:15
3:7
e Rom 6:19-20;
7:5; 1Cor 6:11;
Eph 2:2; Titus 3:3
3:8
f Eph 4:22,29; 5:4;
Heb 12:1;
James 1:21;
1Peter 2:1
3:9
g Lev 19:11;
Eph 4:22,24-25
3:10
h Rom 12:2;
Eph 2:10; 4:23-24
3:11
i Rom 10:12;
1Cor 12:13;
Gal 3:28; 5:6;
Eph 1:23; 6:8
3:12
j Gal 5:22;
Eph 4:2,24,32;
Phil 2:1;
1Thes 1:4;
1Peter 1:2;
2Peter 1:10
3:13
k Mark 11:25;
Eph 4:2,32
3:14
l John 13:34;
Rom 13:8;
1Cor 13:1-13;
Eph 4:3;
5:2 Col 2:2;
1Thes 4:9;
1Tim 1:5;
1Peter 4:8;
1John 3:23; 4:21
3:15
m Rom 14:17;
1Cor 7:15;
Eph 2:16-17; 4:4;
Phil 4:7; Col 2:7,
17
3:16
n 1Cor 14:26;
Eph 5:19; Col 4:6
3:17
o Rom 1:8;
1Cor 10:31;

God.[a] [4]When Christ your[a] life is revealed, then you, too, will be revealed with him in glory.[b]

[5]So put to death your worldly impulses:[b] sexual sin, impurity, passion, evil desire, and greed (which is idolatry).[c] [6]It is because of these things that the wrath of God is coming on those who are disobedient.[c][d] [7]You used to behave like this when you were living among them.[e] [8]But now you must also get rid of anger, wrath, malice, slander, obscene language from your mouth, and all such sins.[f] [9]Stop lying to one another, for you have stripped off the old man with its practices[g] [10]and have clothed yourselves with the new man, which is being renewed into full knowledge according to the image of the one who created it.[h] [11]Where this happens, there is no Greek or Jew, circumcised or uncircumcised, barbarian, Scythian,[d] slave, or free person. Instead, Christ is all and in all.[i]

[12]Therefore, as God's chosen ones, holy and loved, clothe yourselves with compassion, kindness, humility, meekness,[e] and patience.[j] [13]Put up with one another and forgive each other if anyone has a complaint against another. Just as the Lord[f] has forgiven you, you also should forgive.[g][k] [14]Above all, clothe yourselves with[h] love, which ties everything together in unity.[l] [15]Also, let the peace of Christ rule in your hearts, to which you were called in one body. And be thankful![m] [16]Let the word of Christ[i] live in you with all richness and wisdom, teaching and admonishing one another with psalms, hymns, and spiritual songs. Sing to God with thankfulness in your hearts.[n] [17]Whatever you do, in word or deed, do everything in the name of the Lord Jesus, giving thanks to God the Father through him.[o]

Family Duties

[18]Wives, submit yourselves to your husbands, as is

Eph 5:20; Col 1:12; 2:7; 1Thes 5:18; Heb 13:15

a 3:4 Other mss. read *our*   b 3:5 Lit. *the parts that are on the earth*
c 3:6 Lit. *on the sons of disobedience*   d 3:11 I.e. uncivilized person
e 3:12 Or *gentleness*   f 3:13 Other mss. read *Christ*   g 3:13 Lit. *so you also*
h 3:14 The Gk. lacks *clothe yourselves with*   i 3:16 Other mss. read *of God*;
still other mss. read *of the Lord*

fitting in the Lord.*a* 19Husbands, love your wives, and don't be harsh with**a** them.*b*

20Children, obey your parents in everything, for this is pleasing to the Lord.*c* 21Fathers, don't make your children resentful, or they'll become discouraged.*d*

22Slaves, obey your earthly masters in everything, not only while being watched in order to please them, but with a sincere heart, fearing the Lord.*e* 23Whatever you do, work at it wholeheartedly as though you were doing it for the Lord**b** and not merely for people.*f* 24You know that it is from the Lord that you will receive the inheritance as a reward. It is the Lord Christ whom you are serving!*g* 25For the person who does what is wrong will be paid back for what he has done. There is no favoritism.*h*

4 1Masters, treat your slaves with justice and fairness, for you know that you also have a master in heaven.*i*

Closing Exhortations

2Devote yourselves to prayer. Be alert when you pray**c** with thanksgiving.*j* 3At the same time also pray for us—that God would open before us a door for the word so that we may tell the secret about Christ, for which I have been imprisoned.*k* 4May I reveal it as clearly as I should!**d**

5Behave wisely toward unbelievers,**e** making the best use of your time.*l* 6Let your speech always be gracious, seasoned with salt, so that you may know how you ought to answer everyone.*m*

Greetings from Paul and His Fellow Workers

7Tychicus will tell you everything that has happened to me. He is a dear brother, a faithful minister, and a fellow servant in the Lord.*n* 8I am sending him to you for this very reason, so that you may know how we are doing and that he may encourage your hearts.*o* 9He is coming with Onesimus, that faithful and dear brother, who is one of you. They will tell you everything that is happening here.

---

a3:19 Or *bitter toward*　　**b**3:23 Lit. *wholeheartedly as for the Lord*
c4:2 Lit. *Be alert in it*　　**d**4:4 Lit. *as I should speak*　　**e**4:5 Lit. *outsiders*

3:18
*a*Eph 5:3,22;
Titus 2:5;
1Peter 3:1

3:19
*b*Eph 4:31; 5:25,
28,33; 1Peter 3:7

3:20
*c*Eph 5:24;
6:1 Titus 2:9

3:21
*d*Eph 6:4

3:22
*e*Eph 6:5;
Col 2:20;
1Tim 6:1 Titus 2:9;
1Peter 2:18

3:23
*f*Eph 6:6-7

3:24
*g*1Cor 7:22;
Eph 6:8

3:25
*h*Deut 10:17;
Rom 2:11;
Eph 6:9;
1Peter 1:17

4:1
*i*Eph 6:9

4:2
*j*Lk 18:1;
Rom 12:12;
Eph 6:18; Col 2:7;
3:15;
1Thes 5:17-18

4:3
*k*Matt 13:11;
1Cor 4:1; 16:9;
2Cor 2:12;
Eph 6:19-20;
Phil 1:7; Col 1:26;
2:2; 2Thes 3:1

4:5
*l*Eph 5:15-16;
1Thes 4:12

4:6
*m*Eccl 10:12;
Mark 9:50;
Col 3:16;
1Peter 3:15

4:7
*n*Eph 6:21

4:8
*o*Eph 6:22

4:10
a Acts 15:37;
19:29; 20:4; 27:2;
2Tim 4:11

4:12
b Matt 5:48;
Rom 15:30;
1Cor 2:6; 14:20;
Phil 3:15; Col 1:7;
Heb 5:14

4:14
c 2Tim 4:10-11

4:15
d Rom 16:5;
1Cor 16:19

4:16
e 1Thes 5:27

4:17
f 1Tim 4:6

4:18
g 1Cor 16:21;
2Thes 3:17;
Heb 13:3,25

[10]Aristarchus, my fellow prisoner, sends his greetings, as does Mark, the cousin of Barnabas. You have received instructions about him. If he comes to you, welcome him.[a] [11]Jesus, who is called Justus, also greets you. These are the only ones of the circumcision who are fellow workers for the kingdom of God. They have been an encouragement to me. [12]Epaphras, who is one of you, a servant[a] of Christ Jesus, sends you his greetings. He is always wrestling in his prayers for you, so that you may stand mature[b] and completely convinced of the entire will of God.[b] [13]For I can testify on his behalf that he has a deep concern for you and for those in Laodicea and in Hieropolis. [14]Luke, the beloved physician, and Demas greet you.[c] [15]Give my greetings to the brothers in Laodicea, especially to Nympha and the church that is in her house.[d] [16]When this letter has been read among you, have it read also in the church of the Laodiceans. And make sure that you read the one from Laodicea.[e] [17]Tell Archippus, "See that you complete the ministry you've received in the Lord."[f]

Final Greeting

[18]This greeting is by my own hand—"Paul." Remember my imprisonment. May grace be yours! Amen.[c][g]

---

a *4:12* Or *slave*   **b** *4:12* Or *complete*   **c** *4:18* Other mss. lack *Amen*

451

THE LETTER OF PAUL CALLED
FIRST THESSALONIANS

Greetings from Paul, Silvanus, and Timothy

1 [1]From[a] Paul, Silvanus,[b] and Timothy, to the church of the Thessalonians in union with God the Father and the Lord Jesus Christ. May grace and peace from God our Father and the Lord Jesus Christ be yours![ca]

Paul's Prayer for the Thessalonians

[2]We always thank God for all of you when we mention you in our prayers.[b] [3]In the presence of our God and Father, we constantly remember how your faith is active, your love is hard at work, and your hope in our Lord Jesus Christ is enduring.[c] [4]Brothers whom God loves, we know that he has chosen you.[d] [5]For the gospel we brought[d] didn't come to you in words only, but also with power, with the Holy Spirit, and with deep conviction. Indeed,[e] you know what kind of people we proved to be while we were with you, acting on your behalf.[e]

[6]You became imitators of us and of the Lord. In spite of a great deal of suffering, you welcomed the word with the joy that the Holy Spirit produces.[ff] [7]As a result, you became a model for all the believers in Macedonia and Achaia. [8]From you the word of the Lord has spread out not only in Macedonia and Achaia, but also in every place where your faith in God has become known. As a result, we don't need to say anything.[g]

[9]People[g] keep telling us what kind of welcome you gave us. They also report how[h] you turned away from idols to serve a living and true God[h] [10]and to wait for his Son whom he raised from the dead to come back[i] from heaven. This Jesus is the one who rescues us from the coming wrath.[i]

---

a 1:1 The Gk. lacks *From*   b 1:1 I.e. Silas   c 1:1 Other mss. lack *from God our Father and the Lord Jesus Christ*   d 1:5 Lit. *our gospel*   e 1:5 Lit. *Just as*   f 1:6 Or *the joy of the Holy Spirit*   g 1:9 Lit. *They*   h 1:9 Lit. *And how*   i 1:10 The Gk. lacks *to come back*

1:1
a 2Cor 1:19;
Eph 1:2;
2Thes 1:1;
1Peter 5:12

1:2
b Rom 1:8;
Eph 1:16

1:3
c John 6:29;
Rom 16:6;
Gal 5:6;
1Thes 2:13; 3:6;
2Thes 1:3,11;
Heb 6:10;
James 2:17

1:4
d Col 3:12;
2Thes 2:13

1:5
e Mark 16:20;
1Cor 2:4; 4:20;
2Cor 6:6; Col 2:2;
1Thes 2:1,5,
10-11; 2Thes 3:7;
Heb 2:3

1:6
f Acts 5:41;
1Cor 4:16;
11:1 Phil 3:17;
1Thes 2:14;
2Thes 3:9;
Heb 10:34

1:8
g Rom 1:8; 10:18;
2Thes 1:4

1:9
h 1Cor 12:2;
Gal 4:8; 1Thes 2:1

1:10
i Matt 3:7;
Acts 1:11; 2:24;
Rom 2:7; 5:9;
Phil 3:20;
1Thes 4:16; 5:9;
2Thes 1:7;
Titus 2:13;
2Peter 3:12;
Rev 1:7

2:1
a 1Thes 1:5,9

2:2
b Acts 16:22;
17:2 Phil 1:30;
Col 2:1; 1Thes 1:5

2:3
c 2Cor 7:2;
1Thes 2:5;
2Peter 1:16

2:4
d Prov 17:3;
Rom 8:27;
1Cor 7:25; 9:17;
Gal 1:10; 2:7;
1Tim 1:11-12;
Titus 1:3

2:5
e Acts 20:33;
Rom 1:9;
2Cor 2:17; 4:2;
7:2; 12:17

2:6
f John 5:41,44;
12:43; 1Cor 9:1-2,
4-6,12,18;
2Cor 10:1-2,
10-11; 11:9;
12:13-14; 13:10;
2Thes 3:8-9;
1Tim 5:17

2:7
g 1Cor 2:3; 9:22;
2Cor 13:4;
2Tim 2:24

2:8
h Rom 1:11;
15:29; 2Cor 12:15

2:9
i Acts 20:34;
1Cor 4:12;
2Cor 11:9;
12:13-14;
2Thes 3:8

2:10
j 2Cor 7:2;
1Thes 1:5;
2Thes 3:7

2:12
k 1Cor 1:9;
Eph 4:1; Phil 1:27;
Col 1:10;
1Thes 4:1; 5:24;
2Thes 2:14;
2Tim 1:9

2:13
l Matt 10:40;
Gal 4:14;
1Thes 1:3;
2Peter 3:2

Paul Recalls His Visit to the Thessalonians

2 ¹You yourselves know, brothers, that our visit to you was not a waste of time.*a* ²As you know, we suffered persecution and were mistreated in Philippi. Yet we were encouraged by our God to tell you his**a** gospel in spite of strong opposition.*b* ³For our appeal does not spring from deceit, impure motives, or trickery.*c* ⁴Rather, because we have been approved by God to be entrusted with the gospel, we speak as we do, not trying to please people but God, who tests our motives.*d*

⁵As you know, we didn't come with words of flattery or with a scheme to make money. God is our witness!*e* ⁶We didn't seek praise from people—from you or from anyone else*f*—⁷even though as apostles of Christ we might have made such demands. Instead, we were gentle**b** among you, like a nursing mother tenderly caring for her own children.*g* ⁸We cared so deeply for you that we were determined to share with you not only the gospel of God but our very lives. That's how dear you were to us.*h* ⁹You remember, brothers, our labor and toil. We worked night and day so that we would not become a burden to any of you while we proclaimed the gospel of God to you.*i* ¹⁰You and God are witnesses of how pure, honest, and blameless our conduct was among you who believe.*j* ¹¹You know very well that we treated each of you the way a father treats**c** his children. ¹²We comforted and encouraged you, urging you to live in a manner worthy of the God who calls**d** you into his kingdom and glory.*k*

Paul Remembers How the Thessalonians Welcomed the Gospel

¹³Here is another reason why we constantly give thanks to God: When you received God's word, which you heard from us, you didn't accept it as the word of humans but for what it really is—the word of God, which is at work in you who believe.*l* ¹⁴For you, brothers, became imitators of the churches of God in Judea that are united with Christ Jesus.

---

a 2:2 Lit. *God's*   **b** 2:7 Other mss. read *infants*   **c** 2:11 *The* Gk. lacks *treats*   **d** 2:12 Other mss. read *called*

You suffered the same persecutions from the people of your own country as they did from those Jews*[a]* [15]who killed the Lord Jesus and the*[a]* prophets and have persecuted us. They are displeasing to God and are the enemies of all people,*[b]* [16]because they try to keep us from telling the Gentiles how they can be saved. The result is that they are always adding to the measure of their sins. However, wrath has come on them at last!*[c]*

[17]Brothers, although we have been separated from you for a little while—in person but not in heart—we desire with great eagerness to see you again face to face.*[d]* [18]That's why we wanted to come to you. Certainly I, Paul, time and again wanted to come,*[b]* but Satan blocked our way.*[e]* [19]After all, who is our hope, joy, or reason for*[c]* boasting in the presence of our Lord Jesus at his coming? It's you, isn't it?*[f]* [20]Yes, you are our glory and joy!

Timothy's Report to Paul

3 [1]Therefore, when we could stand it no longer, we decided to remain alone in Athens*[g]* [2]and send Timothy, our brother and co-worker for God in the gospel of Christ,*[d]* to strengthen and encourage you in your faith,*[h]* [3]so that no one would be shaken by these persecutions. Indeed, you yourselves know that we were destined for this.*[i]* [4]In fact, when we were with you, we told you ahead of time that we were going to suffer persecution. And as you know, that's what happened.*[j]* [5]But when I could stand it no longer, I sent Timothy*[e]* to find out about your faith. I was afraid that the tempter had tempted you in some way, and that our work had been a waste of time.*[k]*

[6]But Timothy has just now come back to us from you and has told us the good news about your faith and love. He also told us that you always have fond memories of us and want to see us, just as we want to see you.*[l]* [7]That's why, brothers, in all our distress and persecution we have been encouraged about you by your faith.*[m]* [8]For now we can go on living, as long as you continue to stand firm in the Lord.*[n]*

---

a 2:15 Other mss. read *their own*   **b** 2:18 Lit. *time and again*   **c** 2:19 Lit. *crown of*   **d** 3:2 Other mss. lack *of Christ*   **e** 3:5 Lit. *I sent*

2:14
a Acts 17:5,13;
Gal 1:22;
Heb 10:33-34

2:15
b Esth 3:8;
Matt 5:12; 23:34,
37; Lk 13:33-34;
Acts 2:23; 3:15;
5:30; 7:52

2:16
c Gen 15:16;
Matt 23:32; 24:6,
14; Lk 11:52;
Acts 13:50; 14:5,
19; 17:5,13;
18:12; 19:9;
22:21-22

2:17
d 1Cor 5:3;
Col 2:5;
1Thes 3:10

2:18
e Rom 1:13; 15:22

2:19
f Prov 16:31;
1Cor 15:23;
2Cor 1:14;
Phil 2:16; 4:1;
1Thes 3:13;
Rev 1:7; 22:12

3:1
g Acts 17:15;
1Thes 3:5

3:2
h Rom 16:21;
1Cor 16:10;
2Cor 1:19

3:3
i Acts 9:16; 14:22;
20:23; 21:11;
1Cor 4:9;
Eph 3:13;
2Tim 3:12;
1Peter 2:21

3:4
j Acts 20:24

3:5
k 1Cor 7:5;
2Cor 11:3;
Gal 2:2; 4:11;
Phil 2:16;
1Thes 3:1

3:6
l Acts 18:1,5;
Phil 1:8

3:7
m 2Cor 1:4; 7:6-7,
13

3:8
n Phil 4:1

3:9
a 1Thes 1:2
3:10
b Acts 26:7;
Rom 1:10-11;
15:32; 2Cor 13:9,
11 Col 4:12;
1Thes 2:17;
2Tim 1:3
3:11
c Mark 1:3
3:12
d 1Thes 4:9-10;
5:15; 2Peter 1:7
3:13
e Zech 14:5;
1Cor 1:8;
Phil 1:10;
1Thes 5:23;
2Thes 2:17;
1John 3:20-21
Jude 1:14
4:1
f Phil 1:27;
Col 1:10; 2:6;
1Thes 2:12
4:3
g Rom 12:2;
1Cor 6:15,18;
Eph 3,17,27;
Col 3:5
4:4
h Rom 6:19;
1Cor 6:15,18
4:5
i Rom 1:24,26;
1Cor 15:34;
Gal 4:8; Eph 2:12;
4:17-18; Col 3:5;
2Thes 1:8
4:6
j Lev 19:11,13;
1Cor 6:8;
2Thes 1:8
4:7
k Lev 11:44; 19:2;
1Cor 1:2;
Heb 12:14;
1Peter 1:14-15
4:8
l Lk 10:16;
1Cor 2:10; 7:40;
1John 3:24
4:9
m Jer 31:34;
Matt 22:39;
John 6:45; 13:34;
14:26; 15:12;
Eph 5:2;
1Thes 5:1;
Heb 8:11;
1Peter 4:8;
1John 2:20,27;
3:11,23; 4:21
4:10
n 1Thes 1:7; 3:12
4:11
o Acts 20:35;
Eph 4:28;
2Thes 3:7-8,
11-12; 1Peter 4:15

[9]How can we thank God enough for you in return for all the joy that we have in God's presence because of you?[a] [10]We pray very hard night and day that we may see you again face to face, so that we can supply whatever is lacking in your faith.[b]

[11]Now may our God and Father and our Lord Jesus guide us to you.[c] [12]May the Lord greatly increase your love[a] for each other and for all people, just as we love you.[bd] [13]Then you[c] will be strong in holiness and blameless in the presence of our God and Father when our Lord Jesus comes with all his saints.[de]

Instructions on the Way Christians Should Live

4 [1]Now then, brothers, you learned from us how you ought to live and to please God, as in fact you are doing. We ask and encourage you in the Lord to do so even more.[f] [2]You know what instructions we gave you through the Lord Jesus. [3]For it is God's will that you be sanctified: You must abstain from sexual immorality;[g] [4]each of you must know how to control his own body[e] in holiness and honor,[h] [5]not with passion and lust like the Gentiles who don't know God;[i] [6]and you must never take advantage of or exploit a brother in this regard. For the Lord is an avenger in all these things, just as we already told you and warned you.[j] [7]For God did not call us to impurity but to holiness.[k] [8]Therefore, whoever rejects this instruction[f] is not rejecting human authority but God, who gives you his Holy Spirit.[l]

[9]Now you don't need anyone to write to you about brotherly love, since you have been taught by God to love each other.[m] [10]In fact, you are showing love to all the brothers throughout Macedonia. But we encourage you, brothers, to do this even more.[n] [11]Also, make it your goal to live quietly, to mind your own business, and to work with your own hands, as we instructed you.[o] [12]Then you will win the

---

a 3:12 Lit. *cause you to increase and abound in love*   b 3:12 Lit. *as we for you*
c 3:13 Lit. *your hearts*   d 3:13 Or *holy ones*; other mss. read *saints. Amen*
e 4:4 Lit. *vessel*   f 4:8 Lit. *this*

respect of outsiders, and you won't be dependent on anyone.[a]

Comfort about Christians Who Have Died

13But we don't want you to be ignorant, brothers, about those who have died, so that you may not grieve like other people who have no hope.[b] 14Since we believe that Jesus died and rose again, even so it is through Jesus that God will bring back with him those who have died.[c] 15For this we declare to you by the word of the Lord, that we who are alive and who remain until the coming of the Lord will by no means precede those who have died.[d] 16With a shout of command, with the archangel's call, and with the sound of God's trumpet, the Lord himself will come down from heaven, and the dead in Christ will rise first.[e] 17Then we who are alive and who remain will be caught up in the clouds together with them to meet the Lord in the air. Thus we will be with the Lord forever.[f] 18So then, encourage one another with these words.[g]

Be Ready for the Day of the Lord

5 1Now you don't need to have anything written to you about times and dates, brothers.[h] 2You yourselves know very well that the Day of the Lord will come like a thief in the night.[i] 3When people[a] say, "There is peace and security," destruction will strike them as suddenly as labor pains come to[b] a pregnant woman. They won't be able to escape.[j]

4But, brothers, you are not in the darkness, so that day won't surprise you like a thief.[k] 5For all of you are children of light and children of day. We do not belong to the night or to darkness.[l] 6Therefore, we must not fall asleep like others do, but we must stay awake and be sober.[m] 7People who go to sleep, go to sleep at night; people who get drunk, get drunk at night.[n] 8But since we belong to the day, we must be sober. We must put on the breastplate of faith and love, and the hope of salvation as a helmet.[o] 9For God has not destined us for wrath but for obtaining salvation through our

---

a 5:3 Lit. *they*　　b 5:3 Lit. *as labor pains to*

4:12
[a] Rom 13:13;
2Cor 8:21;
Col 4:5;
1Peter 2:12

4:13
[b] Lev 19:28;
Deut 14:2;
2Sam 12:20;
Eph 2:12

4:14
[c] 1Cor 15:13,18,
23; 1Thes 3:13

4:15
[d] 1Kings 13:17-18;
20:35; 1Cor 15:51

4:16
[e] Matt 24:30-31;
Acts 1:11;
1Cor 15:23,52;
2Thes 1:7

4:17
[f] John 12:26; 14:3;
17:24; Acts 1:9;
1Cor 15:51;
Rev 11:12

4:18
[g] 1Thes 5:11

5:1
[h] Matt 24:3,36;
Acts 1:7;
1Thes 4:9

5:2
[i] Matt 24:43-44;
25:13;
Lk 12:39-40;
2Peter 3:10;
Rev 3:3; 16:15

5:3
[j] Isa 13:6-9;
Jer 13:21;
Hos 13:13;
Lk 17:27-29;
21:34-35;
2Thes 1:9

5:4
[k] Rom 13:12-13;
1John 2:8

5:5
[l] Eph 5:8

5:6
[m] Matt 24:42;
25:5,13;
Rom 13:11-13;
1Peter 5:8

5:7
[n] Lk 21:34,36;
Acts 2:15;
Rom 13:13;
1Cor 15:34;
Eph 5:14

5:8
[o] Isa 59:17;
Eph 6:14,16-17

Lord Jesus Christ.[a] 10He died for us so that, whether we are
awake or asleep, we will live together with him.[b] 11So then,
encourage one another and build each other up, as you are
doing.[c]

Paul Gives Final Instructions to the Church

12Brothers, we ask you to show your appreciation for
those who work among you, set an example for you in the
Lord, and instruct[a] you.[d] 13Hold them in the highest regard
in love because of their work. Live in peace with each other.[e]
14We urge you, brothers, to instruct[a] those who are disorderly,[b] cheer up those who are discouraged, and help those
who are weak. Be patient with everyone.[f] 15Make sure that
no one pays back evil for evil. Instead, always pursue what
is good for each other and for everyone else.[g] 16Always be
joyful.[h] 17Continually be prayerful.[i] 18In everything be
thankful, because this is God's will in Christ Jesus for you.[j]
19Don't put out the Spirit's fire.[c][k] 20Don't despise prophecies.[l] 21Instead, test everything. Hold on to what is good,[m]
22but keep away from every kind of evil.[n]

Final Greeting

23May the God of peace himself make you holy in every
way. And may your whole being—spirit, soul, and body—be
kept blameless at the coming of our Lord Jesus Christ.[o]
24The one who calls you is faithful, and he will do this.[p]
25Brothers, pray[d] for us.[q] 26Greet all the brothers with a holy
kiss.[r] 27I order you by the Lord to have this letter read to all
the brothers.[s] 28May the grace of our Lord Jesus Christ be
with you! Amen.[e][t]

5:9 [a] Rom 9:22; 1Thes 1:10; 2Thes 2:13-14; 1Peter 2:8; Jude 1:4
5:10 [b] Rom 14:8-9; 2Cor 5:15
5:11 [c] 1Thes 4:18
5:12 [d] 1Cor 16:18; Phil 2:29; 1Tim 5:17; Heb 13:7,17
5:13 [e] Mark 9:50
5:14 [f] Rom 14:1; 15:1; Gal 5:22; 6:1-2; Eph 4:2; Col 3:12; 2Thes 3:11-12; 2Tim 4:2; Heb 12:12
5:15 [g] Lev 19:18; Prov 20:22; 24:29; Matt 5:39,44; Rom 12:17; 1Cor 6:7; Gal 6:10; 1Thes 3:12; 1Peter 3:9
5:16 [h] 2Cor 6:10; Phil 4:4
5:17 [i] Lk 18:1; 21:36; Rom 12:12; Eph 6:18; Col 4:2; 1Peter 4:7
5:18 [j] Eph 5:20; Col 3:17
5:19 [k] 1Cor 14:30; Eph 4:30; 1Tim 4:14; 2Tim 1:6
5:20 [l] 1Cor 14:1,39
5:21 [m] 1Cor 2:11,15; Phil 4:8; 1John 4:1
5:22 [n] 1Thes 4:12
5:23 [o] 1Cor 1:8; Phil 4:9; 1Thes 3:13

5:24 [p] 1Cor 1:9; 10:13; 2Thes 3:3 **5:25** [q] Col 4:3; 2Thes 3:1 **5:26** [r] Rom 16:16 **5:27** [s] Col 4:16; 2Thes 3:14
5:28 [t] Rom 16:20,24; 2Thes 3:18

a *5:12,5:14* Or *admonish* **b** *5:14* Or *idle* **c** *5:19* I.e. stifle the Spirit's work **d** *4:25* Other mss. read *also pray* **e** *4:28* Other mss. lack *Amen*

THE LETTER OF PAUL CALLED
SECOND THESSALONIANS

Greetings from Paul, Silvanus, and Timothy

1 ¹From[a] Paul, Silvanus,[b] and Timothy, to the church of the Thessalonians in union with God our Father and the Lord Jesus Christ.[a] ²May grace and peace from God our Father and the Lord Jesus Christ be yours![b]

³At all times we are obligated to thank God for you, brothers. It's right to do this[c] because your faith is growing all the time and the love of every one of you for each other is increasing.[c] ⁴As a result, we speak proudly about you among God's churches—about your endurance and faith through all the persecutions and afflictions you are experiencing.[d]

⁵This is evidence of God's righteous judgment and is intended to make you worthy of God's kingdom, for which you are suffering.[e] ⁶Certainly it is right for God to pay back those who afflict you with affliction[f] ⁷and to give us who are afflicted relief when the Lord Jesus is revealed from heaven with his mighty angels[g] ⁸in a blazing fire. He will take revenge on those who refuse to acknowledge[d] God and on those who refuse to obey the gospel of our Lord Jesus.[h] ⁹Such people will suffer the punishment of eternal destruction by being separated from the Lord's presence and from his glorious power[i] ¹⁰when he comes to be glorified by his saints and to be regarded with wonder on that day by all who have believed—including you, because you believed our testimony.[j]

¹¹With this in mind, we always pray for you, asking that[e] our God will make you worthy of his calling and that through his power he will help you accomplish every good desire and faithful work.[k] ¹²That way the name of our Lord Jesus will be glorified by you, and you by him, according to the grace of our God and Lord, Jesus Christ.[l]

---

a *1:1 The* Gk. lacks *From*   **b** *1:1 I.e. Silas*   **c** *1:3 Lit. As is right*   **d** *1:8 Or who do not know*   **e** *1:11 Lit. for you, that*

1:1
a 2Cor 1:19;
1Thes 1:1

1:2
b 1Cor 1:3

1:3
c 1Thes 1:2-3; 3:6,
9; 2Thes 2:13

1:4
d 2Cor 7:14; 9:2;
1Thes 1:3; 2:14,
19-20

1:5
e Phil 1:28;
1Thes 2:14

1:6
f Rev 6:10

1:7
g 1Thes 4:16;
Jude 1:14;
Rev 14:13

1:8
h Ps 79:6;
Rom 2:8;
1Thes 4:5;
Heb 10:27; 12:29;
2Peter 3:7;
Rev 21:8

1:9
i Deut 33:2;
Isa 2:19;
Phil 3:19;
2Thes 2:8;
2Peter 3:7

1:10
j Ps 68:35; 89:7

1:11
k 1Thes 1:3;
2Thes 1:5

1:12
l 1Peter 1:7; 4:14

The Lawless One

2:1
a Matt 24:31;
Mark 13:27;
1 Thes 4:16-17

2 ¹Brothers, about the coming of our Lord Jesus Christ and our gathering to meet him,ᵃ we ask youᵃ ²not to be so quickly upsetᵇ or alarmed when someone claims that we saidᶜ either by some spirit, conversation, or letter that the Day of the Lord has already come.ᵇ ³Don't let anyone deceive you in any way. That day cannot come unlessᵈ the rebellionᵉ takes place first and the man of sin,ᶠ who is destined for destruction,ᵍ is revealed.ᶜ ⁴He opposes and exalts himself above every so-called god and object of worship. As a result, he seats himself in the Sanctuary of God and declares himself to be God.ᵈ

2:2
b Matt 24:4;
Eph 5:6; 1 John 4:1

2:3
c Dan 7:25;
Matt 24:4;
John 17:12;
Eph 5:6; 1 Tim 4:1;
1 John 2:18;
Rev 13:11

2:4
d Isa 14:13;
Ezek 28:2,6,9;
Dan 7:25; 11:36;
1 Cor 8:5;
Rev 13:6

⁵Don't you remember that I repeatedly told you about these things when I was still with you? ⁶You know what it is that is now holding him back, so that he will be revealed when his time comes. ⁷For the secret of this lawlessness is already at work, but only until the person now holding it back gets out of the way.ᵉ ⁸Then the Lawless One will be revealed, whom the Lord will destroy with the breath of his mouth, rendering him powerless by the manifestation of his coming.ᶠ ⁹The coming of the lawless oneʰ will be accompanied by the power of Satan. He will use every kindⁱ of power, including miraculous signs, lying wonders,ᵍ ¹⁰and every type of evil to deceiveʲ those who are dying, those who refused to love the truth that would save them.ᵏʰ ¹¹For this reason, God will send them a powerful delusion so that they will believe the lie.ⁱ ¹²Then all who have not believed the truth but have taken pleasure in unrighteousness will be condemned.ʲ

2:7
e 1 John 2:18; 4:3

2:8
f Job 4:9; Isa 11:4;
Dan 7:10-11;
Hos 6:5;
2 Thes 1:8-9;
Heb 10:27;
Rev 2:16; 19:15,
20-21

2:9
g Deut 13:1;
Matt 24:24;
John 8:41;
Eph 2:2;
Rev 13:13; 18:23;
19:21

2:10
h 2 Cor 2:15; 4:3

¹³At all times we are obligated to thank God for you, brothers who are loved by the Lord, because God chose you to be the first fruitsˡ for salvation through sanctification by the Spirit and through faith in the truth.ᵏ ¹⁴With this purpose in mind, he called you through our proclamation of the

2:11
i 1 Kings 22:22;
Ezek 14:9;
Matt 24:5,11;
Rom 1:24;
1 Tim 4:1

2:12
j Rom 1:32

2:13
k Lk 1:75; Eph 1:4;
1 Thes 1:4;
2 Thes 1:3;
1 Peter 1:2

---

a 2:1 Lit. *to him*   b 2:2 Lit. *shaken in mind*   c 2:2 Lit. *as though by us*
d 2:3 Lit. *For unless*   e 2:3 Or *apostasy*   f 2:3 Other mss. read *man of lawlessness*   g 2:3 Lit. *the son of destruction*   h 2:9 Lit. *his coming*
i 2:9 Lit. *In every kind*   j 2:10 Lit. *every evil deception*   k 2:10 Lit. *so that they might be saved*   l 2:13 Other mss. read *from the beginning*

gospel[a] so that you would obtain the glory of our Lord Jesus Christ.[a] [15]So then, brothers, stand firm, and cling to the traditions that you were taught by us, either by word of mouth[b] or by our letter.[b]

[16]May our Lord Jesus Christ himself and God our Father, who loved us and by his grace gave us eternal comfort[c] and good hope,[c] [17]encourage your hearts and strengthen you in every good work and word.[d]

An Example to Follow

3 [1]Finally, brothers, pray for us—that the word of the Lord may spread rapidly, and that it may be honored the way it is among you.[e] [2]Also pray that[d] we may be rescued from worthless and evil people, since not everyone holds to the faith.[ef] [3]But the Lord is faithful and will strengthen you and protect you from the evil one.[g] [4]We have confidence in the Lord[f] that you are doing and will continue to do what we command.[h] [5]May the Lord direct your hearts to the love of God and to the endurance of Christ.[i]

[6]In the name of our Lord Jesus Christ we command you, brothers, to keep away from every brother who is leading a disorderly life[g] and not living according to[h] the tradition that they received[i] from us.[j] [7]For you yourselves know what you must do to imitate us. We didn't lead a disorderly life[j] among you.[k] [8]We didn't eat anyone's food without paying for it. Instead, with toil and labor we worked night and day in order not to be a burden to any of you.[l] [9]It's not as though we didn't have that right. Rather, we wanted to give[k] you an example to follow.[m] [10]While we were with you, we gave this order: "If anyone doesn't want to work he shouldn't eat."[n]

[11]We hear that some of you are leading disorderly lives.[l] You're not busy working[m]—you're busy interfering[n] in other

2:14
[a] John 17:22;
1 Thes 2:12;
1 Peter 5:10

2:15
[b] 1 Cor 11:2;
16:13; Phil 4:1;
2 Thes 3:6

2:16
[c] 2 Thes 1:1-2;
1 Peter 1:3;
1 John 4:10;
Rev 1:5

2:17
[d] 1 Cor 1:8;
1 Thes 3:13;
1 Peter 5:10

3:1
[e] Eph 6:19;
Col 4:3;
1 Thes 5:25

3:2
[f] Acts 28:24;
Rom 10:16; 15:31

3:3
[g] John 17:15;
1 Cor 1:9;
1 Thes 5:24;
2 Peter 2:9

3:4
[h] 2 Cor 7:16;
Gal 5:10

3:5
[i] 1 Chr 29:18

3:6
[j] Rom 16:17;
1 Cor 5:11,13;
1 Thes 4:11; 5:14;
2 Thes 2:15;
3:11-12,14;
1 Tim 6:5;
2 John 1:10

3:7
[k] 1 Cor 4:16; 11:1;
1 Thes 1:6-7; 2:10

3:8
[l] Acts 18:3; 20:34;
2 Cor 11:9;
1 Thes 2:9

3:9
[m] 1 Cor 9:6;
1 Thes 2:6;
2 Thes 2:7

3:10
[n] Gen 3:19;
1 Thes 4:11

---

a 2:14 Lit. *through our gospel*   b 2:15 Lit. *by word*   c 2:16 Or *encouragement*   d 3:2 Lit. *Also that*   e 3:2 Or *has faith*   f 3:4 Lit. *in the Lord concerning you*   g 3:6 Or *is living in idleness*   h 3:6 Lit. *not according to*   i 3:6 Other mss. read *you received*   j 3:7 Or *We were not idle*   k 3:9 Lit. *Rather to give*   l 3:11 Or *are living in idleness*   m 3:11 Gk. *ergazomenous* (working)   n 3:11 Gk. *periergazomenous* (uselessly working)

3:11
a 1 Thes 4:11;
2 Thes 3:6;
1 Tim 5:13;
1 Peter 4:15

3:12
b Eph 4:28;
1 Thes 4:11

3:13
c Gal 6:9

3:14
d Matt 18:17;
1 Cor 5:9,11;
2 Thes 3:6

3:15
e Lev 19:17;
1 Thes 5:14;
Titus 3:10

3:16
f Rom 15:33;
16:20;
1 Cor 14:33;
2 Cor 13:11;
1 Thes 5:23

3:17
g 1 Cor 16:21;
Col 4:18

3:18
h Rom 16:24

people's lives!*a* [12]We order and encourage such people by the Lord Jesus Christ to do their work quietly and to earn their own living.*b* [13]Brothers, do not get tired of doing what is right.*c*

[14]If anyone does not obey what we say*a* in this letter, take note of him. Have nothing to do with him so that he will feel ashamed.*d* [15]Yet, don't treat him like an enemy, but warn*b* him like a brother.*e* [16]May the Lord of peace give you his peace at all times and in every way. May the Lord be with all of you.*f*

Final Greeting

[17]I, Paul, am writing this greeting with my own hand. This is the mark in every letter of mine. It's the way I write.*g* [18]May the grace of our Lord Jesus Christ be with all of you. Amen.*ch*

---

a *3:14* Lit. *our word*   **b** *3:15* Or *instruct*   **c** *3:18* Other mss. lack *Amen*

THE LETTER OF PAUL CALLED
FIRST TIMOTHY

Greetings from Paul

1 [1]From[a] Paul, an apostle of Christ Jesus by the command of God our Savior and Christ Jesus our hope,[a] [2]to Timothy, my genuine child in the faith. May grace, mercy, and peace from God the Father and Christ Jesus our Lord be yours![b]

A Warning Against False Teachers

[3]When I was on my way to Macedonia, I urged you to stay in Ephesus so that you could instruct certain people to stop teaching false doctrine[c] [4]and occupying themselves with myths and endless genealogies. These things promote controversies rather than God's ongoing purpose, which involves faith.[d] [5]The goal of this instruction is love that flows from a pure heart, from a clear conscience, and from a sincere faith.[e] [6]Some people have left these qualities behind and have turned to fruitless discussion.[f] [7]They want to be teachers of the Law, yet they don't understand either what they're talking about or the things about which they speak so confidently.[g]

[8]Of course, we know that the Law is good if a person uses it legitimately,[h] [9]that is, if he understands that the Law is not intended for righteous[b] people but for lawbreakers and rebels, for ungodly people and sinners, for those who are unholy and irreverent, for those who kill their fathers, their mothers, or other people,[i] [10]for those involved in sexual immorality, for homosexuals, for kidnappers,[c] for liars, for false witnesses, and for whatever else goes against the healthy teaching[j] [11]that agrees with the glorious gospel of the blessed God, which he entrusted to me.[k]

[12]I thank Christ Jesus our Lord, who gives me strength, that he has considered me faithful and has appointed me to his service.[l] [13]In the past I was a blasphemer, a persecutor,

---

a 1:1 *The* Gk. lacks *From*   b 1:9 Or *innocent*   c 1:10 Or *slave traders*

1:1
a Acts 9:15;
Gal 1:1,11;
Col 1:27;
1 Tim 2:3; 4:10;
Titus 1:3; 2:10;
3:4; Jude 1:25

1:2
b Acts 16:1;
1 Cor 4:17;
Gal 1:3; Phil 2:19;
1 Thes 3:2;
2 Tim 1:2;
Titus 1:4;
1 Peter 1:2

1:3
c Acts 20:1,3;
Gal 1:6-7;
Phil 2:24;
1 Tim 6:3,10

1:4
d 1 Tim 4:7; 6:4,
20; 2 Tim 2:14,16,
23; Titus 1:14; 3:9

1:5
e Rom 13:8,10;
Gal 5:14;
2 Tim 2:22

1:6
f 1 Tim 6:4,20

1:7
g 1 Tim 6:4

1:8
h Rom 7:12

1:9
i Gal 3:19; 5:23

1:10
j 1 Tim 6:3;
2 Tim 4:3;
Titus 1:9; 2:1

1:11
k 1 Cor 9:17;
Gal 2:7; Col 1:25;
1 Thes 2:4;
1 Tim 2:7; 6:15;
2 Tim 1:11;
Titus 1:3

1:12
l 1 Cor 7:25;
2 Cor 3:5-6; 4:1;
12:9; Col 1:25

1:13
a Lk 23:34;
John 9:39,41;
Acts 3:17; 8:3;
9:1; 26:9;
1Cor 15:9;
Phil 3:6
1:14
b Lk 7:47;
Rom 5:20;
1Cor 15:10;
2Tim 1:13
1:15
c Matt 9:13;
Mark 2:17;
Lk 5:32; 19:10;
Rom 5:8;
1Tim 3:1; 4:9;
2Tim 2:11;
1John 3:5
1:16
d Acts 13:39;
2Cor 4:1
1:17
e 1Chr 29:11;
Ps 10:16; 145:13;
Dan 7:14;
John 1:18;
Rom 1:23; 16:27;
1Tim 6:15-16;
Heb 11:27;
1John 4:12
1:18
f 1Tim 4:14;
6:12-14,20;
2Tim 2:2-3; 4:7
1:19
g 1Tim 3:9; 6:9
1:20
h Acts 13:45;
1Cor 5:5;
2Tim 2:14,17
2:2
i Ezra 6:10;
Jer 29:7;
Rom 13:1
2:3
j Rom 12:2;
1Tim 1:1; 5:4;
2Tim 1:9
2:4
k Ezek 18:23;
John 3:16-17;
17:3; 2Tim 2:25;
Titus 2:11;
2Peter 3:9
2:5
l Rom 3:29-30;
10:12; Gal 3:20;
Heb 8:6; 9:15
2:6
m Matt 20:28;
Mark 10:45;
Rom 5:6;
1Cor 1:6; Gal 4:4;
Eph 1:7,9; 3:5;
2Thes 1:10;
2Tim 1:8;
Titus 1:3; 2:14

and a violent*a* man. But I received mercy because I acted ignorantly in my unbelief,*a* [14]and the grace of our Lord overflowed toward me,*b* along with the faith and love that are in Christ Jesus.*b* [15]This saying is trustworthy and deserves complete acceptance:*cc*

> To this world Christ Jesus came,
> Sinful people to reclaim.*d*

I am the worst*e* of them. [16]However, for that very reason I received mercy, so that in me, as the worst*e* sinner,*f* Christ Jesus might demonstrate all of his patience as an example for those who would believe in him for eternal life.*d* [17]Now to the King Eternal—the immortal, invisible, and only God—be honor and glory forever and ever! Amen.*e*

Guidelines for Behavior in the Church

[18]Timothy, my child, I'm giving you this instruction in keeping with the prophecies made earlier about you, so that by following them you may continue to fight the good fight*f* [19]with faith and a good conscience. By ignoring their consciences,*g* some people have destroyed their faith like a wrecked ship.*g* [20]These include Hymenaeus and Alexander, whom I handed over to Satan so that they may learn not to blaspheme.*h*

Prayer and Submission to Authority

2 [1]First of all, then, I urge you to offer petitions, prayers, intercessions, and expressions of thanks for all people, [2]for kings, and for everyone who has authority, so that we can lead a quiet and peaceful life with all godliness and dignity.*hi* [3]This is good and acceptable in the sight of God our Savior,*j* [4]who wants all people to be saved and to come to a full knowledge of the truth.*k* [5]There is one God. There is also one mediator between God and humans—a human, Christ Jesus.*l* [6]He gave himself as a ransom for all people, a fact that was acknowledged at the right time.*m* [7]For this

---

a *1:13* Or *an arrogant*   **b** *1:14* The Gk. lacks *toward me*   **c** *1:15* This formula accompanied early Christian sayings on which full reliance could be placed.   **d** *1:15* Or *save*   **e** *1:15,1:16* Or *foremost*   **f** *1:16* The Gk. lacks *sinner*   **g** *1:19* Lit. *By ignoring it*   **h** *2:2* Or *seriousness*

reason I was appointed to be a preacher, an apostle, and a teacher of the Gentiles in faith and truth. (I'm telling you the truth.[a] I'm not lying.)[a]

⁸So I want the men to offer prayers in every place, lifting up holy hands without being angry or argumentative.[b] ⁹Women, for their part, should display their beauty by dressing modestly and decently in appropriate clothes, not by braiding their hair or by wearing gold, pearls, or expensive clothes.[c] ¹⁰Their beauty should be displayed through good works.[b] This is proper for women who claim to have reverence for God.[d]

¹¹A woman must learn quietly with full submission. ¹²Moreover, I don't allow a woman to teach or to have authority over a man. Instead, she is to be quiet.[e] ¹³For Adam was formed first, then Eve.[f] ¹⁴And it wasn't Adam who was deceived. It was the woman who was deceived and became a lawbreaker.[g] ¹⁵However, she (and all women)[c] will be saved by having children,[d] if they continue to have faith, love, and holiness, along with good judgment.[e]

Qualifications for Leaders in the Church

3 ¹This saying is trustworthy:[fh]

The one who would an elder be,
A noble task desires he.

²Therefore, an elder must be blameless. He must be the husband of one wife,[g] stable, sensible, respectable, a lover of strangers, and teachable.[hi] ³He must not drink excessively or be a violent person, but he must be gentle. He must not be argumentative or a lover of money.[j] ⁴He must manage his own family well and have children who are submissive

---

a 2:7 Other mss. read *the truth in Christ*   b 2:10 Lit. *But through good works*   c 2:15 The Gk. lacks *(and all women)*   d 2:15 Or *will be kept safe when having children;* or *will be saved through the birth of the Child*   e 2:15 Or *modesty*   f 3:1 This formula accompanied early Christian sayings on which full reliance could be placed.   g 3:2 Or *devoted to his wife;* lit. *a man of one woman*   h 3:2 Or *able to teach*

Cross-references (margin)

2:7
a Rom 9:1; 11:13; 15:16; Gal 1:16; Eph 3:7-8; 2 Tim 1:11

2:8
b Ps 134:2; Isa 1:15; Mal 1:11; John 4:21

2:9
c 1 Peter 3:3

2:10
d 1 Peter 3:4

2:12
e 1 Cor 14:34; Eph 5:24

2:13
f Gen 1:27; 2:18, 22; 1 Cor 11:8-9

2:14
g Gen 3:6; 2 Cor 11:3

3:1
h Acts 20:28; Eph 4:12; Phil 1:1; 1 Tim 1:15

3:2
i 1 Tim 5:9; 2 Tim 2:24; Titus 1:6

3:3
j 1 Tim 3:8; 2 Tim 2:24; Titus 1:7; 1 Peter 5:2

3:4
a Titus 1:6

3:6
b Isa 14:12

3:7
c Acts 22:12;
1Cor 5:12;
1Thes 4:12;
1Tim 6:9;
2Tim 2:26

3:8
d Lev 10:9;
Ezek 44:21;
Acts 6:3; 1Tim 6:3

3:9
e 1Tim 1:19

3:11
f Titus 2:3

3:13
g Matt 25:21

3:15
h Eph 2:21-22;
2Tim 2:20

3:16
i Matt 3:16; 28:2;
Mark 16:5;
Lk 2:13; 24:4,
51 John 1:14,
32-33; 15:26;
16:8-9; 20:12;
Acts 1:19; 10:34;
13:46,48;
Rom 1:4; 10:18;
Gal 2:8;
Eph 3:5-6,8,10;
Col 1:6,23,27-28;
1Tim 2:7;
1Peter 1:12; 3:18,
22; 1John 1:2; 5:6

and respectful in every way.[a] [5]For if a man doesn't know how to manage his own family, how can he take care of God's church? [6]He must not be a recent convert, or he might become arrogant and fall into the condemnation of the devil.[b] [7]He must be well thought of by non-Christians,[a] or he might fall into disgrace and the trap set for him by[b] the devil.[c]

[8]Deacons, too, must be serious. They must not be two-faced,[c] addicted to wine, or greedy for money.[d] [9]They must hold firmly to the secret of the faith with clear consciences.[e] [10]But they must first be tested. Then, if they prove to be blameless, they may become deacons. [11]Their wives[d] must also be serious. They must not be gossips, but they must be stable and trustworthy in everything.[f] [12]Deacons must be husbands of one wife[e] and must manage their children and their families well. [13]Those deacons who serve well gain an excellent reputation for themselves and will have great assurance in their faith in Christ Jesus.[g]

[14]I hope to come to you soon. However, I'm writing this to you [15]in case I'm delayed so that you may know how a person is to behave in God's household, which is the church of the living God, the pillar and foundation of the truth.[h] [16]By common confession, the secret of our godly worship is great:[f][i]

> In flesh was he[g] revealed to sight,
> Kept righteous by the Spirit's might,
> Adored by angels singing.[h]
> To nations was he manifest,
> Believing souls found peace and rest,[i]
> Our Lord in heaven reigning![j]

---

a 3:7 Lit. *outsiders*   **b** 3:7 Lit. *the trap of*   **c** 3:8 Lit. *double-worded*   **d** 3:11 Or *Deaconesses*   **e** 3:2 Or *devoted to their wives;* lit. *men of one woman*   **f** 3:16 What follows probably represents an early Christian hymn or creed.   **g** 3:16 Other mss. read *God*   **h** 3:16 Lit. *he was seen by angels*   **i** 3:16 Lit. *he was believed in the world*   **j** 3:16 Lit. *he was taken up in glory*

A Prophecy About the Future

4 [1]Now the Spirit says clearly that in the last times some people will abandon the faith by following deceitful spirits, the teachings of demons,[a] [2]and the hypocrisy of liars, whose consciences have been burned by a hot iron.[b] [3]They will try to stop people from marrying and from eating certain foods, which God created to be received with thanksgiving by those who believe and know the truth.[c] [4]For everything God created is good, and nothing should be rejected if it is received with thanksgiving,[d] [5]because it is sanctified by the word of God and prayer.

How to Be a Good Servant of Christ Jesus

[6]If you continue to point these things out to the brothers, you will be a good servant of Christ Jesus, nourished by the words of the faith and the healthy teaching that you have followed closely.[e] [7]Don't have anything to do with godless myths and fables of old women. Rather, train yourself in godliness.[f] [8]Physical exercise is of limited value, but[g]

> *Godliness is very dear,*
> *A pledge of life, both now and e'er.*

[9]This saying is trustworthy and deserves complete acceptance.[a][h] [10]To this end we work hard and struggle,[b] because we have set our hope on the living God, who is the Savior of all people, especially of those who believe.[i]

[11]These are the things you must insist on and teach.[j] [12]Don't let anyone look down on you because you are young. Instead, be an example for other believers in your speech, behavior, love, faith, and purity.[k] [13]Until I arrive, concentrate on the public reading of Scripture,[c] on exhorting, and on teaching. [14]Don't neglect[d] the gift that is in you. It was given to you through prophecy, accompanied by the laying on of the elders' hands.[l] [15]Think on these things. Devote your life to them so that everyone can see your progress. [16]Pay close attention to your life and your

---

a 4:9 This formula accompanied early Christian sayings on which full reliance could be placed.   b 4:10 Other mss. read *suffer abuse*
c 4:13 Lit. *on the reading*   d 4:14 Or *Stop neglecting*

4:1
a Dan 11:35, 37-38;
John 16:13;
2 Thes 2:3;
2 Tim 3:1,13;
1 Peter 1:20;
2 Peter 2:1; 3:3;
1 John 2:18;
Jude 1:4,18;
Rev 9:20; 16:14

4:2
b Matt 7:15;
Rom 16:18;
Eph 4:19;
2 Peter 2:3

4:3
c Gen 1:29; 9:3;
Rom 14:3,6,17;
1 Cor 7:28,36,38;
8:8; 10:30;
Col 2:20-21;
Heb 13:4

4:4
d Rom 14:14,20;
1 Cor 10:25;
Titus 1:15

4:6
e 2 Tim 3:14-15

4:7
f 1 Tim 1:4; 6:20;
2 Tim 2:16,23; 4:4;
Titus 1:14;
Heb 5:14

4:8
g Ps 37:4; 84:11;
112:2-3; 145:19;
Matt 6:33; 19:29;
Mark 10:30;
Rom 8:28;
1 Cor 8:8;
Col 2:23;
1 Tim 6:6

4:9
h 1 Tim 1:15

4:10
i Ps 36:6; 107:2,6;
1 Cor 4:11-12;
1 Tim 6:17

4:11
j 1 Tim 6:2

4:12
k 1 Cor 16:11;
Titus 2:7,15;
1 Peter 5:3

4:14
l Acts 6:6; 8:17;
13:3; 19:6;
1 Tim 1:18; 5:22;
2 Tim 1:6

4:16
a Ezek 33:9;
Acts 20:28;
Rom 11:14;
1 Cor 9:22;
James 5:20

5:1
b Lev 19:32

5:3
c 1 Tim 5:5,16

5:4
d Gen 45:10-11;
Matt 15:4;
Eph 6:1-2;
1 Tim 2:3

5:5
e Lk 2:37; 18:1;
Acts 26:7;
1 Cor 7:32

5:6
f James 5:5

5:7
g 1 Tim 1:3; 4:11;
6:17

5:8
h Isa 58:7;
Matt 18:17;
Gal 6:10;
2 Tim 3:5;
Titus 1:16

5:9
i Lk 2:36; 1 Tim 3:2

5:10
j Gen 18:4; 19:2;
Lk 7:38,44;
John 13:5,14;
Acts 16:15;
Heb 13:2;
1 Peter 4:9

5:13
k 2 Thes 3:11

teaching. Persevere in these things. For if you do this, you will save both yourself and those who listen to you.*a*

How to Treat Other Believers

5 ¹Never speak harshly to an older man, but appeal to him as if he were your father. Treat younger men*a* like brothers,*b* ²older women like mothers, and younger women like sisters, with absolutely purity.

³Honor widows who are really widows.*bc* ⁴But if a widow has children or grandchildren, they must first learn to respect their own family by repaying their parents. This is pleasing in God's sight.*d* ⁵A woman who is really a widow and is left all alone has placed her hope in God and devotes herself to petitions and prayers night and day.*e* ⁶But the widow*c* who lives for pleasure is dead while she lives.*f*

⁷Continue to give these instructions so that the people*d* may be blameless.*g* ⁸If anyone doesn't take care of his own relatives, especially his immediate family, he has denied the faith and is worse than an unbeliever.*h* ⁹A widow may be put on the widows' list*e* if she is at least sixty years old and has been the wife of one husband.*fi* ¹⁰She must be well known for her good works as a woman who has raised children, welcomed strangers, washed the saints' feet, helped the suffering, and devoted herself to doing good in every way.*j*

¹¹But don't include younger widows on your list.*g* For whenever their natural desires cause them to lose their devotion to Christ, they want to remarry. ¹²They receive condemnation for having rejected the faith they first accepted.*h* ¹³At the same time, they also learn how to be lazy while going from house to house. Not only this, but they even become gossips and are busy interfering in other people's lives, saying things they shouldn't say.*k*

¹⁴So I want younger widows to remarry, have children,

---

a 5:1 Lit. *Younger men*   *b 5:3* I.e. who have no families   *c 5:6* Lit. *the one*   *d 5:7* Lit. *they*   *e 5:9* Lit. *the list*   *f 5:9* Or *devoted to her husband;* lit. *a woman of one man*   *g 5:11* The Gk. lacks *on your list*   *h 5:12* Lit. *their first faith*

manage their homes, and not give the enemy any chance to ridicule them.[a] [15]For some widows[a] have already turned away to follow Satan. [16]If any woman[b] is a believer and has relatives who are widows, she should help them. The church should not be burdened so that it can help those who really are widows.[b]

[17]Elders who handle their duties[c] well should be considered worthy of double honor,[d] especially those who work hard at preaching and teaching.[c] [18]For the Scripture says, "You must not muzzle an ox while it is treading out grain,"[e] and "A worker deserves his pay."[f][d] [19]Don't accept an accusation against an elder unless it is supported by two or three witnesses.[e] [20]As for those who keep on sinning, reprimand them in front of everyone so that the others will also be afraid.[f] [21]In the sight of God, Christ Jesus, and the chosen angels, I solemnly call on you to carry out these instructions without prejudice, doing nothing on the basis of partiality.[g] [22]Don't ordain[g] anyone hastily. Don't participate in the sins of others. Keep yourself pure.[h] [23]Stop drinking only water, but use a little wine for your stomach because of your frequent illnesses.[i]

[24]The sins of some people are obvious, going ahead of them to judgment. The sins of[h] others follow them there.[j] [25]In the same way, good works are obvious, and those that aren't can't remain hidden.

6 [1]All who are under the yoke of slavery should regard their own masters to be deserving of the highest respect,[i] so that the name of God and our teaching may not be discredited.[j][k] [2]Moreover, those who have believing masters should not be disrespectful to them because they are fellow believers.[k] Rather, they must serve them even better, because those who benefit from their service are believers and dear to them. These are the things you must teach and exhort.[l]

---

a 5:15 Lit. *some*   b 5:16 Other mss. read *man or woman*   c 5:17 Or *who rule*   d 5:17 Or *double compensation*   e 5:18 Deut 25:4   f 5:18 Matt 10:10   g 5:22 Lit. *lay hands on*   h 5:24 Lit. *Those of*   i 6:1 Or *of full honor*   j 6:1 Or *slandered*   k 6:2 Lit. *brothers*

5:14
a 1 Cor 7:9;
1 Tim 6:1;
Titus 2:8

5:16
b 1 Tim 5:3,5

5:17
c Acts 28:10;
Rom 12:8;
1 Cor 9:10,14;
Gal 6:6; Phil 2:29;
1 Thes 5:12-13;
Heb 13:7,17

5:18
d Lev 19:13;
Deut 24:14-15;
25:4; Matt 10:10;
Lk 10:7; 1 Cor 9:9

5:19
e Deut 19:15

5:20
f Deut 13:11;
Gal 2:11,14;
Titus 1:13

5:21
g 1 Tim 6:13;
2 Tim 2:14; 4:1

5:22
h Acts 6:6; 13:3;
1 Tim 4:14;
2 Tim 1:6;
2 John 1:11

5:23
i Ps 104:15

5:24
j Gal 5:19

6:1
k Isa 52:5;
Rom 2:24;
Eph 6:5; Col 3:22;
Titus 2:5,8-9;
1 Peter 2:18

6:2
l Col 4:1;
1 Tim 4:11

6:3
a 1 Tim 1:3,10;
2 Tim 1:13; 4:3;
Titus 1:1,9

6:4
b 1 Cor 8:2;
1 Tim 1:4,7;
2 Tim 2:23;
Titus 3:9

6:5
c Rom 16:17;
1 Cor 11:16;
1 Tim 1:6;
2 Tim 3:5,8;
Titus 1:11;
2 Peter 2:3

6:6
d Ps 37:16;
Prov 15:16; 16:8;
Heb 13:5

6:7
e Job 1:21;
Ps 49:17;
Prov 27:24;
Eccl 5:15

6:8
f Gen 28:20;
Heb 13:5

6:9
g Prov 15:27;
20:21; 28:20;
Matt 13:22;
1 Tim 1:19; 3:7;
James 5:1

6:10
h Exod 23:8;
Deut 16:19

6:11
i Deut 33:1;
2 Tim 2:22; 3:17

6:12
j 1 Cor 9:25-26;
Phil 3:12,14;
1 Tim 1:18; 6:19;
2 Tim 4:7;
Heb 13:23

6:13
k Deut 32:39;
1 Sam 2:6;
Matt 27:11;
John 5:21; 18:37;
1 Tim 5:21;
Rev 1:5; 3:14

6:14
l Phil 1:6,10;
1 Thes 3:13; 5:23

6:15
m 1 Tim 1:11,17;
Rev 17:14; 19:16

6:16
n Exod 33:20;
John 6:46;
Eph 3:21;
Phil 4:20;
1 Tim 1:17;
Jude 1:25;
Rev 1:6; 4:11;
7:12

Rules for Godly Living

³If anyone teaches false doctrine and refuses to agree with the healthy words of our Lord Jesus Christ and godly teaching,*a* ⁴he is a conceited person and doesn't understand anything. He has an unhealthy craving for arguments and debates. This produces jealousy, rivalry, slander, evil suspicions,*b* ⁵and incessant conflict between people who are depraved in mind and deprived of truth. They think that godliness is a way to make a profit.*ac* ⁶Of course, godliness with contentment does bring a great profit.*d* ⁷For we didn't bring anything into the world, and surely*b* we can't take anything out of it.*e* ⁸So as long as we have food and clothes, we'll be satisfied with these.*f* ⁹But people who want to get rich keep toppling into temptation and are trapped by many stupid and harmful desires that plunge them into destruction and ruin.*g* ¹⁰For the love of money is a root of all kinds of evil. Some people, in their eagerness to get rich, have wandered away from the faith and pierced themselves with much pain.*h*

¹¹But you, man of God, must flee from all these things. Instead, you must pursue righteousness, godliness, faithfulness,*c* love, endurance, and gentleness.*i* ¹²Fight the good fight for the faith. Keep your hold on eternal life, to which you were called and about which you gave a good testimony in front of many witnesses.*j* ¹³In the sight of God, who gives life to everything, and in the sight of Christ Jesus, who gave a good testimony before Pontius Pilate, I solemnly charge you*k* ¹⁴to keep this command stainless and blameless until the appearance of our Lord Jesus Christ.*l* ¹⁵At the right time God*d* will make him known. He is the blessed and only Ruler, the King of kings and Lord of lords.*m* ¹⁶He alone has endless life and lives in inaccessible light. No one has ever seen him, nor can anyone see him. Honor and eternal power belong to him! Amen.*n*

¹⁷Tell those who are rich in the present world not to be arrogant and not to place their confidence in anything as

---

a 6:5 Other mss. read *make a profit. Stay away from such people.*
b 6:7 Other mss. lack *surely*   **c** 6:11 Or *faith*   **d** 6:15 Lit. *he*

uncertain as riches. Instead, they are to place their confidence in God,[a] who lavishly provides us with everything for our enjoyment.[a] [18]They are to do good, to be rich in good works, to be generous, and to share.[b] [19]By doing this they store up a treasure for themselves that is a good foundation for the future, so that they can take hold of the life that is real.[c]

Final Greeting

[20]Timothy, guard what has been entrusted to you. Avoid the pointless discussions and contradictions of what is falsely called knowledge.[d] [21]Although some claim to have it, they have abandoned the faith. May grace be with all of you![b][e]

---

a6:17 Lit. *Instead in God*   **b**6:21 Lit. *with you* (plural). Other mss. read *you! Amen*

6:17
[a]Job 31:24;
Ps 52:7; 62:10;
Prov 23:5;
Mark 10:24;
Lk 12:21;
Acts 14:17; 17:25;
1Thes 1:9;
1Tim 3:15; 4:10
6:18
[b]Lk 12:21;
Rom 12:13;
Gal 6:6;
1Tim 5:10;
Titus 3:8;
Heb 13:16;
James 2:5
6:19
[c]Matt 6:20; 19:21;
Lk 12:33; 16:9;
1Tim 6:12
6:20
[d]1Tim 1:4,6; 4:7;
2Tim 1:14; 2:14,
16,23; Titus 1:9,
14; 3:9; Rev 3:3
6:21
[e]1Tim 1:6,19;
2Tim 2:18

THE LETTER OF PAUL CALLED
SECOND TIMOTHY

1:1
a 2Cor 1:1;
Eph 3:6; Titus 1:2;
Heb 9:15

1:2
b 1Tim 1:2

1:3
c Acts 22:3; 23:1;
24:14; 27:23;
Rom 1:8-9;
Gal 1:14;
Eph 1:16;
1Thes 1:2; 3:10

1:4
d 2Tim 4:9,21

1:5
e Acts 16:1;
1Tim 1:5; 4:6

1:6
f 1Thes 5:19;
1Tim 4:14

1:7
g Lk 24:49;
Acts 1:8;
Rom 8:15

1:8
h Rom 1:16;
Eph 3:1; Phil 1:7;
Col 1:24;
1Tim 2:6;
2Tim 4:5; Rev 1:2

1:9
i Rom 3:20; 8:28;
9:11; 16:25;
Eph 1:4; 3:11;
1Thes 4:7;
1Tim 1:1 Titus 1:2;
3:4-5; Heb 3:1;
1Peter 1:20

1:10
j Rom 16:26;
1Cor 15:54-55;
Eph 1:9; Col 1:26;
Titus 1:3;
Heb 2:14;
1Peter 1:20

1:11
k Acts 9:15;
Eph 3:7-8;
1Tim 2:7;
2Tim 4:17

Greetings from Paul

1 [1]From[a] Paul, an apostle of Christ Jesus by God's will in keeping with the promise of life that is in Christ Jesus,[a] [2]to Timothy, my dear child. May grace, mercy, and peace from God the Father and Christ Jesus our Lord be yours![b]

Paul's Advice for Timothy

[3]I constantly thank my God—whom I serve[b] with a clear conscience, as my ancestors did—when I remember you in my prayers night and day.[c] [4]I remember your tears and long to see you so that I can be filled with joy.[d] [5]I'm reminded of your sincere faith, which lived first in your grandmother Lois and your mother Eunice. I'm convinced that this faith[c] also lives in you.[e] [6]For this reason, I'm reminding you to fan into flames the gift of God that is within you through the laying on of my hands.[f] [7]For God didn't give us a spirit of timidity but one of power, love, and self-discipline.[d][g]

[8]Therefore, never be ashamed of the testimony about our Lord or of me, his prisoner. Instead, by God's power, join me in suffering for the sake of the gospel.[h] [9]He saved us and called us with a holy calling, not according to our own works but according to his own purpose and grace, which was given to us in Christ Jesus before the world began.[e][i] [10]Now, however, it has been revealed through the coming of our Savior Christ Jesus, who has destroyed death and through the gospel has brought life and release from death into full view.[j] [11]For the sake of this gospel[f] I was appointed to be a preacher, an apostle, and a teacher of the Gentiles.[g][k] [12]That's why I suffer as I do. However, I'm not ashamed, for I know the one in whom I have put my trust, and I'm

---

a *1:1 The* Gk. lacks *From*   **b** *1:3* Or *worship*   **c** *1:5* Lit. *it*   **d** *1:7* Or *good judgment*   **e** *1:9* Or *before time began;* Lit. *before eternal ages*   **f** *1:11* Lit. *For which*   **g** *1:11* Other mss. lack *of the Gentiles*

convinced that he is able to protect what he has entrusted to me[a] until that day.[a] 13Hold on to the pattern of healthy teachings that you have heard from me, along with the faith and love that are in Christ Jesus.[b] 14With the help of the Holy Spirit who lives in us, protect the good treasure that has been entrusted to you.[c]

News About Paul's Helpers

15You know that everyone in Asia has abandoned me, including Phygelus and Hermogenes.[d] 16May the Lord grant mercy to the family of Onesiphorus, for he often took care of[b] me and wasn't ashamed that I was a prisoner.[e] 17Instead, when he arrived in Rome he searched diligently for me and found me. 18May the Lord grant that he finds mercy from the Lord on that day. You know very well how much he assisted me in Ephesus.[f]

Remain Committed to Christ Jesus

2 1As for you, my child, be strong in the grace that is in Christ Jesus.[g] 2What you've heard from me through many witnesses entrust to faithful people who will be able to teach others as well.[h] 3Join me in suffering like a good soldier of Christ Jesus.[i] 4No one serving in the military gets mixed up in civilian matters. His aim is to please his commanding officer.[j] 5Moreover, no one who is an athlete wins a prize unless he competes according to the rules.[k] 6Furthermore, it is the hard working farmer who should have the first share of the crops.[l] 7Think about what I'm saying. The Lord will help you to understand all these things.

8Meditate on[c] Jesus Christ, who was raised from the dead and is a descendant of David. This is the gospel I tell others.[d][m] 9Because of it I'm experiencing trouble, even to the point of being chained like a criminal. However, God's word is not chained.[n] 10For that reason, I endure everything for the sake of those who have been chosen so that they, too,

---

a 1:12 Or *what I have entrusted to him*   b 1:16 Or *refreshed*   c 2:8 Or *Remember*   d 2:8 Lit. *of David, according to my gospel*

1:12
a Eph 3:1;
1Tim 6:20;
2Tim 1:18; 2:9;
4:8; 1Peter 4:19

1:13
b Rom 2:20; 6:17;
1Tim 1:10,14; 6:3;
2Tim 2:2; 3:14;
Titus 1:9;
Heb 10:23;
Rev 2:25

1:14
c Rom 8:11;
1Tim 6:20

1:15
d Acts 19:10;
2Tim 4:10,16

1:16
e Matt 5:7;
Acts 28:20;
Eph 6:20;
2Tim 1:8; 4:19

1:18
f Matt 25:34-40;
2Thes 1:10;
2Tim 1:12;
Heb 6:10

2:1
g Eph 6:10;
1Tim 1:2;
2Tim 1:2

2:2
h 1Tim 1:18; 3:2;
2Tim 1:13; 3:10,
14; Titus 1:9

2:3
i 1Tim 1:18;
2Tim 1:8; 4:5

2:4
j 1Cor 9:25

2:5
k 1Cor 9:25-26

2:6
l 1Cor 9:10

2:8
m Acts 2:30;
13:23; Rom 1:3-4;
2:16; 1Cor 15:1,4,
20

2:9
n Acts 9:16; 28:31;
Eph 3:1; 6:19-20;
Phil 1:7,13-14:
Col 4:3,18;
2Tim 1:12

2:10
a 2Cor 1:6;
Eph 3:13;
Col 1:24

2:11
b Rom 6:5,8;
2Cor 4:10;
1Tim 1:15

2:12
c Matt 10:33;
Mark 8:38;
Lk 12:9;
Rom 8:17;
1Peter 4:13

2:13
d Num 23:19;
Rom 3:3; 9:6

2:14
e 1Tim 1:4; 5:21;
6:4,13; 2Tim 4:1;
Titus 3:9,11

2:16
f 1Tim 4:7; 6:20;
Titus 1:14

2:17
g 1Tim 1:20

2:18
h 1Cor 15:12;
1Tim 6:21

2:19
i Num 16:5;
Nah 1:7;
Matt 24:24;
John 10:14,27;
Rom 8:35;
1John 2:19

2:20
j Rom 9:21;
1Tim 3:15

2:21
k Isa 52:11;
2Tim 3:17;
Titus 3:1

2:22
l Acts 9:14;
1Cor 1:2;
1Tim 1:5; 4:12;
6:11

2:23
m 1Tim 1:4; 4:7;
6:4; 2Tim 2:16;
Titus 3:9

may receive the salvation that is in Christ Jesus along with eternal glory.[a] [11]This saying is trustworthy:[a][b]

> *In dying with Christ,*[b] *true life we gain.*[c]
> [12] *Enduring, we with him shall reign.*[c]
> *Who him denies, he will disclaim.*
> [13] *Our faith may fail, his never wanes*[d]—
> *For thus he is, he cannot change!*[d]

[14]Remind others about these things, and warn them in the sight of God[e] not to argue over words. Arguing[f] doesn't do any good but only destroys those who are listening.[e] [15]Do your best to present yourself to God as an approved worker who has nothing to be ashamed of as he teaches the word of truth correctly. [16]However, avoid pointless discussions. For people will become more and more ungodly,[f] [17]and what they say will spread everywhere like gangrene. Hymenaeus and Philetus are like that.[g] [18]They have abandoned the truth by claiming that the resurrection has already taken place, and so they destroy the faith of others.[h]

[19]However, God's solid foundation still stands. It has this inscription on it: "The Lord knows those who belong to him,"[g] and "Everyone who calls on the name of the Lord must turn away from evil."[h][i] [20]In a large house there are not only utensils made of gold and silver, but also those made of wood and clay. Some are for special use, while others are for ordinary use.[j] [21]Therefore, if anyone stops associating with[i] these people, he will become a special utensil, set apart for the owner's use, prepared for every good work.[k]

[22]Flee from youthful passions. Instead, pursue righteousness, faithfulness,[j] love, and peace together with those who call on the Lord with a pure heart.[l] [23]Don't have anything to do with foolish and stupid discussions, because you know they breed arguments.[m] [24]A servant[k] of the Lord must not argue. Instead, he must be kind to everyone, teachable,[l]

---

a *2:11 This* formula accompanied early Christian sayings on which full reliance could be placed. **b** *2:11* Lit. *with him* **c** *2:11* Lit. *we will live with him* **d** *2:13* Lit. *he cannot deny himself* **e** *2:14* Other mss. read *of the Lord* **f** *2:14* Lit. *It* **g** *2:19* Num 16:5 **h** *2:19* Num 16:26 **i** *2:21* Lit. *cleanses himself from* **j** *2:22* Or *faith* **k** *2:24* Or *slave* **l** *2:24* Or *able to teach*

willing to suffer wrong,[a] 25and gentle in refuting his opponents. After all, maybe God will allow them to repent and to come to a full knowledge of the truth.[b] 26Then they might escape from the devil's snare, even though they've been held captive by him to do his will.[c]

What People Will Be Like in the Last Days

3 1You must realize, however, that in the last days difficult times will come.[d] 2People will be lovers of themselves, lovers of money, boastful, arrogant, abusive, disobedient to their parents, ungrateful, unholy,[e] 3unfeeling, uncooperative, slanderous, degenerate, brutal, hateful of what is good,[f] 4traitors, reckless, conceited, and lovers of pleasure rather than lovers of God.[g] 5They will hold to an outward form of godliness but deny its power. Stay away from such people.[h] 6For some of these men go into homes and deceive foolish women who are burdened with sins and swayed by all kinds of desires.[i] 7These women are always studying but are never able to arrive at a full knowledge of the truth.[j] 8Just as Jannes and Jambres opposed Moses, so these men oppose the truth. They are depraved in mind and their faith is a counterfeit.[k] 9But they won't get very far because, as in the case of those two men,[a] their stupidity will be plain to everyone.[l]

Continue to Teach the Truth

10But you have observed my teaching, my way of life, my purpose, my faith, my patience, my love, my endurance,[m] 11and my persecutions and sufferings that happened to me in Antioch, Iconium, and Lystra. What persecutions I endured! Yet the Lord rescued me from all of them.[n] 12Indeed, all who want to live a godly life in union with Christ Jesus will be persecuted.[o] 13But evil people and impostors will go from bad to worse as they deceive others and are themselves deceived.[p]

14But as for you, continue in what you have learned and found to be true, because you know from whom you learned it.[q] 15From infancy you have known the Holy

---

a 3:9 The Gk. lacks two men

2:24
a 1 Tim 3:2-3;
Titus 1:9; 3:2
2:25
b Acts 8:22;
Gal 6:1; 1 Tim 2:4;
6:11; 2 Tim 3:7;
Titus 1:1;
1 Peter 3:15
2:26
c 1 Tim 3:7
3:1
d 1 Tim 4:1;
2 Tim 4:3;
2 Peter 3:3;
1 John 2:18;
Jude 1:18
3:2
e Rom 1:30;
Phil 2:21;
1 Tim 1:20; 6:4;
2 Peter 2:3,
12 Jude 1:10,16
3:3
f Rom 1:31;
2 Peter 3:3
3:4
g Phil 3:19;
2 Peter 2:10,13;
Jude 1:4,19
3:5
h 2 Thes 3:6;
1 Tim 5:8; 6:5;
Titus 1:16
3:6
i Matt 23:14;
Titus 1:11
3:7
j 1 Tim 2:4
3:8
k Exod 7:11;
Rom 1:28;
2 Cor 13:5;
1 Tim 6:5;
Titus 1:16
3:9
l Exod 7:12; 8:18;
9:11
3:10
m Phil 2:22;
1 Tim 4:6
3:11
n Ps 34:19;
Acts 13:45,50;
14:2,5,19;
2 Cor 1:10;
2 Tim 4:7
3:12
o Josh 17:14;
Ps 34:19;
Matt 16:24;
Acts 14:22;
1 Cor 15:19;
1 Thes 3:3
3:13
p 2 Thes 2:11;
1 Tim 4:1;
2 Tim 2:16
3:14
q 2 Tim 1:13; 2:2

3:15
a John 5:39

3:16
b Rom 15:4;
2Peter 1:20-21

3:17
c 1Tim 6:11;
2Tim 2:21

4:1
d Acts 10:42;
1Tim 5:21; 6:13;
2Tim 2:14

4:2
e 1Tim 4:13; 5:20;
Titus 1:13; 2:15

4:3
f 1Tim 1:10;
2Tim 3:1,6

4:4
g 1Tim 1:4; 4:7;
Titus 1:14

4:5
h Acts 21:8;
Eph 4:11;
2Tim 1:8; 2:3

4:6
i Phil 1:23; 2:17;
2Peter 1:14

4:7
j 1Cor 9:24-25;
Phil 3:14;
1Tim 6:12;
Heb 12:1

4:8
k 1Cor 9:25;
2Tim 1:12;
James 1:12;
1Peter 5:4;
Rev 2:10

4:10
l Col 4:15;
1John 2:15

4:11
m Acts 12:25;
15:37; Col 4:10,
14; 2Tim 1:15

4:12
n Acts 20:4;
Eph 6:12; Col 4:7;
Titus 3:12

Scriptures that are able to give you the wisdom you need for salvation through faith in Christ Jesus.*a* [16]All Scripture is inspired by God and is useful for teaching, for reproof, for correction, and for training in righteousness,*b* [17]so that the man of God may be complete and thoroughly equipped for every good work.*c*

Complete the Task Entrusted to You

4 [1]In the presence of God and Christ Jesus, who is going to judge those who are living and those who are dead, and in view of his appearing and his kingdom, I solemnly appeal to you*d* [2]to proclaim the message. Be ready to do this*a* whether or not the time is convenient. Refute, warn, and encourage with the utmost patience when you teach.*e* [3]For the time will come when people will not put up with healthy doctrine but with itching ears will surround themselves with teachers who cater to their own needs.*f* [4]They will refuse to listen to the truth and will turn to myths.*g* [5]But you must be clear-headed about everything. Endure suffering. Do the work of an evangelist. Devote yourself completely to your ministry.*h*

[6]For I'm already being poured out as an offering, and the time for my departure has come.*i* [7]I have fought the good fight. I have completed the race. I have kept the faith.*j* [8]The crown of righteousness is now waiting for me. The Lord, the righteous Judge, will give it to me on that day, and not only to me but also to all who eagerly wait for his appearing.*k*

Final Instructions to Timothy

[9]Do your best to come to me soon. [10]For Demas, having fallen in love with this present world, has abandoned me and has gone to Thessalonica. Crescens has gone to Galatia, and Titus to Dalmatia.*l* [11]Only Luke is with me. Get Mark and bring him with you, for he is useful in my ministry.*m* [12]I have sent Tychicus to Ephesus.*n*

[13]When you come, bring the coat I left with Carpus in

---

a *4:2 The* Gk. lacks *to do this*

Troas, as well as the scrolls and especially the parchments.[a] [14]Alexander the metalworker did me a great deal of harm. The Lord will pay him back for what he did.[a] [15]You, too, must watch out for him, for he violently opposed our message.

[16]At my first trial no one came to my defense. Everyone abandoned me. May it not be held against them![b] [17]However, the Lord stood by me and gave me strength so that through me the message could be fully proclaimed and all the Gentiles could hear it. I was rescued out of a lion's mouth.[c] [18]The Lord will rescue me from every evil attack[b] and will take me safely to[c] his heavenly kingdom. Glory belongs to him forever and ever! Amen.[d]

Final Greeting

[19]Greet Prisca[d] and Aquila and the family of Onesiphorus.[e] [20]Erastus stayed in Corinth, and I left Trophimus in Miletus because he was sick.[f] [21]Do your best to come to me before winter. Eubulus sends you greetings, as do Pudens, Linus, Claudia, and all the brothers.[g]

[22]May the Lord be with your spirit. Grace be with all of you![e] Amen.[fh]

---

a 4:13 Parchments were writing materials made from animal skins.
b 4:18 Lit. *evil work*   c 4:18 Or *will preserve me for*   d 4:19 I.e. Priscilla
e 4:22 Lit. *with you* (plural)   f 4:22 Other mss. lack *Amen*

4:14
a 2Sam 3:39;
Ps 28:4;
Acts 19:33;
1 Tim 1:20;
Rev 18:6

4:16
b Acts 7:60;
2Tim 1:15

4:17
c Ps 22:21;
Matt 10:19;
Acts 9:15; 23:11;
26:17-18; 27:23;
Eph 3:8;
2Peter 2:9

4:18
d Ps 121:7;
Rom 11:36;
Gal 1:5;
Heb 13:21

4:19
e Acts 18:2;
Rom 16:3;
2Tim 1:16

4:20
f Acts 19:22; 20:4;
21:29; Rom 16:23

4:21
g 2Tim 4:9

4:22
h Gal 6:18

THE LETTER OF PAUL TO
TITUS

1:1
a 1 Tim 3:16; 6:3;
2 Tim 2:25

Greetings from Paul

1 ¹From*a* Paul, a servant*b* of God, and yet an apostle of Jesus Christ for the faith of God's elect and the full knowledge of the truth that leads to*c* godliness,*a* ²which is based on the hope of eternal life that God, who cannot lie, promised before the world*d* began.*b* ³At the right time he revealed his message through the proclamation that I was entrusted with by the command of God our Savior.*c* ⁴To Titus, a genuine child in the faith we share. May grace and peace*e* from God the Father and Christ Jesus our Savior be yours!*d*

1:2
b Num 23:19;
Rom 16:25;
1 Tim 2:13;
2 Tim 1:1,9;
Titus 3:7;
1 Peter 1:20

1:3
c 1 Thes 2:4;
1 Tim 1:1,11; 2:3;
4:10; 2 Tim 1:10

1:4
d Rom 1:12;
2 Cor 2:13; 4:13;
7:13; 8:6,16,23;
12:18; Gal 2:3;
Eph 1:2; Col 1:2;
1 Tim 1:2;
2 Tim 1:2;
2 Peter 1:1

1:5
e Acts 14:23;
1 Cor 11:34;
2 Tim 2:2

1:6
f 1 Tim 3:2,4,12

1:7
g Lev 10:9;
Matt 24:45;
1 Cor 4:1-2;
Eph 5:18;
1 Tim 3:3,8;
1 Peter 5:2

1:8
h 1 Tim 3:2

1:9
i 2 Thes 2:15;
1 Tim 1:10,15; 4:9;
6:3; 2 Tim 1:13;
2:2; 4:3; Titus 2:1

Qualifications for Leaders in the Church

⁵The reason I left you in Crete was to complete what still needed to be done and to appoint elders in every city as I myself commanded you.*e* ⁶An elder must be*f* blameless. He must be the husband of one wife*g* and have children who are believers and who are not accused of having wild lifestyles or of being rebellious.*f* ⁷Because an overseer is God's administrator, he must be blameless. He must not be arrogant or irritable. He must not drink too much, be a violent person, or use shameful ways to make money.*g* ⁸Instead, he must be a lover of strangers, a lover of goodness, sensible, honest, moral, and self-controlled.*h* ⁹He must be devoted to the trustworthy message that is in agreement with our teaching. Then he will be able to encourage others with healthy doctrine and refute those who oppose it.*i*

Guard What Is True

¹⁰For there are many people who are rebellious, especially those who are converts from Judaism.*h* They speak

---

a *1:1* The Gk. lacks *From*   **b** *1:1* Or *slave*   **c** *1:1* Lit. *that is according to*
d *1:2* Or *the ages*   **e** *1:4* Other mss. read *grace, mercy, and peace*   **f** *1:6* Lit.
If anyone is   **g** *1:6* Or *devoted to his wife*; lit. *a man of one woman*
h *1:10* Lit. *those of the circumcision*

utter nonsense and deceive people.[a] ¹¹They must be silenced, because they are the kind of people who ruin whole families by teaching what they shouldn't teach in order to make money in a shameful way.[b] ¹²One of their very own prophets said,[c]

> "Liars ever, men of Crete,
>   Savage brutes that live to eat."[a]

¹³That testimony is true. For this reason, refute them sharply so that they may become healthy in the faith[d] ¹⁴and not pay attention to Jewish myths or commands given by people who reject the truth.[e] ¹⁵Everything is clean to those who are clean. But nothing is clean to those who are corrupt and unbelieving. Indeed, their very way of thinking and their consciences have been corrupted.[f] ¹⁶They claim to know God, but they deny him by their actions. They are detestable, disobedient, and disqualified to do anything good.[g]

Guidelines for Christian Living

2 ¹But as for you, teach what is consistent with healthy doctrine.[h] ²Older men are to be sober, serious, sensible, and sound in faithfulness,[b] love, and endurance.[i]
³Likewise, older women are to show their reverence for God by their behavior. They are not to be gossips or addicted to alcohol, but to be examples[c] of goodness.[j] ⁴They should encourage the younger women to be lovers of their husbands, lovers of their children,[k] ⁵sensible, pure, managers of their households, and kind, and to submit themselves to their husbands. Then the word of God will not be discredited.[d][l]
⁶Likewise, encourage the younger men to be sensible. ⁷Always set an example of good works. When you teach, show[e] integrity and dignity.[m] ⁸Use wholesome speech that cannot be condemned. Then any opponent will be ashamed because he cannot say anything bad about us.[n]
⁹Slaves are to submit themselves to their masters in everything, aiming to please them and not argue with them[o]

---

a1:12 Epimenides (6th to 5th century BC)   **b**2:2 Or *faith*   **c**2:3 Or *teachers*   **d**2:5 Or *blasphemed*   **e**2:7 Lit. *In teaching*

1:10 *a*Acts 15:1; Rom 16:18; 1Tim 1:6

1:11 *b*Matt 23:14; 1Tim 6:5; 2Tim 3:6

1:12 *c*Acts 17:28

1:13 *d*2Cor 13:10; 2Tim 4:2; Titus 2:2

1:14 *e*Isa 29:13; Matt 15:9; Col 2:22; 1Tim 1:4; 4:7; 2Tim 4:4

1:15 *f*Lk 11:39-41; Rom 14:14,20,23; 1Cor 6:12; 10:23, 25; 1Tim 4:3-4

1:16 *g*Rom 1:28; 2Tim 3:5,8; Jude 1:4

2:1 *h*1Tim 1:10; 6:3; 2Tim 1:13; Titus 1:9

2:2 *i*Titus 1:13

2:3 *j*1Tim 2:9-10; 3:11; 1Peter 3:3-4

2:4 *k*1Tim 5:14

2:5 *l*Rom 2:24; 1Cor 14:34; Eph 5:22; Col 3:18; 1Tim 2:11; 6:1; 1Peter 3:1,5

2:7 *m*Eph 6:24; 1Tim 4:12; 1Peter 5:3

2:8 *n*Neh 5:9; 2Thes 3:14; 1Tim 5:14; 6:3; 1Peter 2:12,15; 3:16

2:9 *o*Eph 5:24; 6:5; Col 3:22; 1Tim 6:1-2; 1Peter 2:18

2:10
a Matt 5:16;
Phil 2:15
2:11
b Lk 3:6; John 1:9;
Rom 5:15;
1Tim 2:4;
Titus 3:4-5;
1Peter 5:12
2:12
c Lk 1:75;
Rom 6:19;
Eph 1:4; Col 1:22;
1Thes 4:7;
1Peter 4:2;
1John 2:16
2:13
d Acts 24:15;
1Cor 1:7;
Phil 3:20; Col 1:5,
23; 3:4; 2Tim 4:1,
8; Titus 1:2; 3:7;
Heb 9:28;
1Peter 1:7;
2Peter 3:12;
1John 3:2
2:14
e Exod 15:16;
19:5; Deut 7:6;
14:2; 26:18;
Gal 1:4; 2:20;
Eph 2:10; 5:2;
1Tim 2:6;
Titus 3:8;
Heb 9:14;
1Peter 2:9
2:15
f 1Tim 4:12;
2Tim 4:2
3:1
g Rom 13:1;
Col 1:10;
2Tim 2:21;
Heb 13:21;
1Peter 2:13
3:2
h Eph 4:2,31;
Phil 4:5; Col 3:12;
2Tim 2:24-25
3:3
i 1Cor 6:11;
Eph 2:1; Col 1:21;
3:7; 1Peter 4:3
3:4
j 1Tim 2:3;
Titus 2:11
3:5
k John 3:3,5;
Rom 3:20; 9:11;
11:6; Gal 2:16;
Eph 2:4,8-9; 5:26;
2Tim 1:9;
1Peter 3:21
3:6
l Ezek 36:25;
Joel 2:28;
John 1:16;
Acts 2:33; 10:45;
Rom 5:5

[10]or steal from them. Instead, they are to show complete and perfect loyalty so that in every way they will make the teaching about God our Savior more attractive.[a]

[11]For the grace of God has appeared, bringing salvation to all people.[b] [12]It trains us to renounce ungodly living and worldly passions so that we can live sensible, honest, and godly lives in the present world[c] [13]as we wait for the blessed hope and the glorious appearance of our great God and Savior, Jesus Christ.[d] [14]He gave himself for us to set us free from every wrong and to cleanse us so that we could be his special people who are enthusiastic about good works.[e]

[15]These are the things you should say. Encourage and refute with full authority. Don't let anyone look down on you.[f]

Concentrate on Doing What Is Good

3 [1]Remind believers[a] to submit themselves to rulers and authorities, to be obedient, and to be ready to do any honorable kind of work.[g] [2]They shouldn't insult[b] anyone or be argumentative. Instead, they should be gentle and show perfect courtesy to everyone.[h] [3]After all, we ourselves were once foolish, disobedient, and misled. We were slaves to many kinds of lusts and pleasures, spending our days in malice and jealousy. We were despised, and we hated one another.[i] [4]However,[j]

> *In grace our Savior God appeared,*
> *His love for mankind to make clear.*
> [5]*'Twas not for deeds that we had done,[k]*
> *But by his steadfast love[c] alone,*
> *He saved us through a second birth,*
> *Renewed us by the Spirit's[d] work,*
> [6]*And poured him out upon us, too,[l]*
> *Through Jesus Christ our Savior true.*
> [7]*And so, made right by his own grace,[m]*
> *Eternal life we now embrace.[e]*

3:7 m Rom 3:24; 8:23-24; Gal 2:16; Titus 1:2; 2:11

---

a 3:1 Lit. *them*   **b** 3:2 Or *slander*   **c** 3:5 Or *his mercy*   **d** 3:5 Lit. *the Holy Spirit's*   **e** 3:7 Lit. *we have become heirs according to the hope of eternal life*

[8]This saying is trustworthy.[a] I want you to insist on these things so that those who have put their faith in God will devote themselves to good works. These things are good and helpful to other people.[a]

[9]But avoid foolish controversies, arguments about gene-alogies, quarrels, and fights about the Law. These things are useless and worthless.[b] [10]Have nothing to do with a person who causes divisions after you have warned him once or twice.[c] [11]You know that a person like this is corrupt and keeps on sinning, and so he brings on his own condemnation.[d]

Final Instructions to Titus

[12]As soon as I send Artemas to you, or perhaps Tychi-cus, do your best to come to me at Nicopolis. For I have decided to spend the winter there.[e] [13]Do all you can to send Zenas the expert in the Law and Apollos on their way, and see that they have everything they need.[f]

[14]Our own people should also learn to devote them-selves to good works when urgent needs arise so that they can live productive lives.[g]

Final Greeting

[15]All who are with me send you greetings. Greet those who love us in the faith. May grace be with all of you! Amen.[b]

---

[a]3:8 This formula accompanied early Christian sayings on which full reliance could be placed.   [b]3:15 Other mss. lack *Amen*

3:8
[a] 1 Tim 1:15;
Titus 1:9,14; 2:14

3:9
[b] 1 Tim 1:4;
2 Tim 2:14,23;
Titus 1:14

3:10
[c] Matt 18:17;
Rom 16:17;
2 Cor 13:2;
2 Thes 3:6,14;
2 Tim 3:5;
2 John 1:10

3:11
[d] Acts 13:46

3:12
[e] Acts 20:4;
2 Tim 4:12

3:13
[f] Acts 18:24

3:14
[g] Rom 15:28;
Phil 1:11; 4:17;
Col 1:10;
Titus 3:8;
2 Peter 1:8

THE LETTER OF PAUL TO
PHILEMON

1:1
a Eph 3:1;
4:1 Phil 2:25;
2 Tim 1:8

1:2
b Rom 16:5;
1 Cor 16:19;
Phil 2:25;
Col 4:17

1:3
c Eph 1:2

1:4
d Eph 1:16;
1 Thes 1:2;
2 Thes 1:3

1:5
e Eph 1:15; Col 1:4

1:6
f Phil 1:9,11

1:7
g 2 Cor 7:13;
2 Tim 1:16

1:8
h 1 Thes 2:6

1:9
i Phlm 1:1

1:10
j 1 Cor 4:15;
Gal 4:19; Col 4:9

1:13
k 1 Cor 16:17;
Phil 2:30

1:14
l 2 Cor 9:7

Greetings from Paul

¹From**ᵃ** Paul, a prisoner of Christ Jesus, and Timothy our brother, to Philemon our dear friend**ᵇ** and fellow worker,*ᵃ* ²to Apphia our sister, to Archippus our fellow soldier, and to the church in your house.*ᵇ* ³May grace and peace from God our Father and the Lord Jesus Christ be yours!**ᶜ***ᶜ*

Paul's Prayer for Philemon

⁴I always thank my God when I mention you**ᵈ** in my prayers.*ᵈ* ⁵For I hear about your love and the faith that you have toward the Lord Jesus and for all the saints.*ᵉ* ⁶I pray that**ᵉ** the sharing of your faith may become effective as you fully acknowledge every blessing that is ours**ᶠ** in Christ.*ᶠ* ⁷For I have gotten a lot of joy and encouragement from your love, because the hearts of the saints have been refreshed, brother, through you.*ᵍ*

Paul's Plea for Onesimus

⁸For this reason, although in Christ I have complete freedom to order you to do what is proper,*ʰ* ⁹I prefer to make my appeal on the basis of love. I, Paul, as an old man and now a prisoner of Christ Jesus,*ⁱ* ¹⁰appeal to you for my child Onesimus, whose father I have become during my imprisonment.*ʲ* ¹¹Once he was useless to you, but now he is very useful**ᵍ** both to you and to me. ¹²I am sending him, that is, my own heart, back to you. ¹³I wanted to keep him with me so that he could serve me in your place during my imprisonment for the gospel.*ᵏ* ¹⁴Yet I didn't want to do anything without your consent, so that your good deed might not be something forced, but voluntary.*ˡ* ¹⁵Perhaps this is why he was separated from you for a while, so that you

---

a *1:1 The* Gk. lacks *From*   **b** *1:1 Or* our beloved Philemon   **c** *1:3 Here* yours *is plural in the* Gk.   **d** *1:4 From verse 4 through verse 21,* you *and* your *are singular.*   **e** *1:6 Lit. That*   **f** *1:6 Other mss. read* yours *(plural)*   **g** *1:11 The* name Onesimus *means* useful.

could have him back forever,[a] [16]no longer as a slave but better than a slave—as a dear brother, especially to me, but even more so to you, both in the flesh[a] and in the Lord.[b][b]

[17]So if you consider me a partner, welcome him as you would welcome[c] me.[c] [18]If he has wronged you in any way or owes you anything, charge it to my account. [19]I, Paul, am writing this with my own hand: I will repay it. (I won't mention to you that you owe me your very life.) [20]Yes, brother, I desire this favor from you in the Lord. Refresh my heart in Christ![d] [21]Confident of your obedience, I am writing to you because I know that you will do even more than I ask.[e] [22]Meanwhile, prepare a guest room for me, too, for I am hoping through your prayers to be returned to you.[f]

Greetings from Paul's Fellow Workers

[23]Epaphras, my fellow prisoner in Christ Jesus, sends greetings to you,[d][g] [24]and so do Mark, Aristarchus, Demas, and Luke, my fellow workers.[h] [25]May the grace of our[e] Lord Jesus Christ be with your spirit! Amen.[f][i]

---

a*1:16* I.e. as a person   b*1:16* I.e. as a Christian   c*1:17* The Gk. lacks *you would welcome*   d*1:23* Here *you* is singular in the Gk.   e*1:25* Other mss. read *the*   f*1:25* Other mss. lack *Amen*.

1:15
a Gen 45:5,8

1:16
b Matt 23:8;
Col 3:22;
1 Tim 6:2

1:17
c 2 Cor 8:23

1:20
d Phlm 1:7

1:21
e 2 Cor 7:16

1:22
f 2 Cor 1:11;
Phil 1:25; 2:24

1:23
g Col 1:7; 4:12

1:24
h Acts 12:12,25;
19:29; 27:2;
Col 4:10,14;
2 Tim 4:11

1:25
i 2 Tim 4:22

THE LETTER TO THE
HEBREWS

1:1
a Num 12:6,8

God Has Spoken to Us

1 ¹God, having spoken in former times in fragmentary fashion to our forefathers by the prophets,*a* ²has in these last days spoken to us by a Son whom he appointed to be the heir of everything and through whom he made the universe.*b* ³He is the reflection*a* of God's glory and the exact likeness of his being. He holds everything together by his powerful word. After he had provided a cleansing from sins, he sat down at the right hand of the Highest Majesty*c* ⁴and became as much superior to the angels as the name he has inherited is better than theirs.*d*

1:2
b Deut 4:30;
Ps 2:8;
Matt 21:38; 28:18;
John 1:3,17; 3:35;
15:15; Rom 8:17;
1Cor 8:6; Gal 4:4;
Eph 1:10;
Col 1:16; Heb 2:3

1:3
c Ps 110:1;
John 1:4,14; 14:9;
2Cor 4:4;
Eph 1:20;
Col 1:15,17;
Heb 7:27; 8:1;
9:12,14,16; 10:12;
12:2; 1Peter 3:22;
Rev 4:11

God's Son Is Superior to the Angels

⁵For to which of the angels did God**b** ever say, "You are my Son. Today I have become your Father"?**c** Or again, "I will be his Father, and he will be my Son"?**d**e ⁶And again, when he brings**e** his firstborn into the world, he says, "Let all God's angels worship him."**f**f ⁷Now about the angels he says, "He makes his angels winds and his servants flames of fire."**g**g ⁸But about the Son he says,*h*

1:4
d Eph 1:21;
Phil 2:9-10

1:5
e 2Sam 7:14;
1Chr 22:10; 28:6;
Ps 2:7; 89:26-27;
Acts 13:33;
Heb 5:5

"Your throne, O God,
 is forever and ever,
 and the scepter of your kingdom
is a righteous scepter.
 ⁹You have loved righteousness*i*
 and hated wickedness.
That is why God, your God,
 anointed you rather than your companions
 with the oil of gladness."**h**

1:6
f Deut 32:43;
Ps 97:7;
Rom 8:29;
Col 1:18;
1Peter 3:22;
Rev 1:5

1:7
g Ps 104:4

1:8
h Ps 45:6-7

1:9
i Isa 61:1;
Acts 4:27; 10:38

---

a 1:3 Or *radiance*   **b** 1:5 Lit. *he*   **c** 1:5 Ps 2:7   **d** 1:5 2 Sam 7:14   **e** 1:6 Or *And when he again brings*   **f** 1:6 Deut 32:43 (LXX); Ps 97:7   **g** 1:7 Ps 104:4   **h** 1:9 Ps 45:6-7

[10]And,[a]

"In the beginning, Lord,
 you laid the foundation of the earth,
  and the heavens are the work of your
   hands.
[11]They will come to an end,[b]
 but you will remain forever.
  They will all wear out like clothes.
[12]You will roll them up like a robe,
 and they will be changed like clothes.
But you remain the same,
 and your years will never end."[a]

[13]But to which of the angels did he ever say,[c]

"Sit at my right hand
 until I make your enemies a footstool for
  your feet"?[b]

[14]All of them are spirits on a divine mission, sent to serve those who are about to inherit salvation, aren't they?[d]

We Must Not Neglect Our Salvation

2 [1]For this reason we must pay closer attention to what we have heard, or we may drift away. [2]For if the message spoken by angels was reliable, and every violation and act of disobedience received its just punishment,[e] [3]how will we escape if we neglect a salvation as great as this? It was first proclaimed by the Lord himself, and then it was confirmed to us by those who heard him,[f] [4]while God added his testimony through signs, wonders, various miracles, and gifts of the Holy Spirit distributed according to his will.[g]

Jesus Is the Source of Our Salvation

[5]For he didn't put the coming world we are talking about under the control of angels.[h] [6]Instead, someone has declared somewhere,[i]

---

a *1:12 Ps* 102:25-27 **b** *1:13 Ps* 110:1

1:10
a Ps 102:25

1:11
b Isa 34:4; 51:6;
Matt 24:35;
2Peter 3:7,10;
Rev 21:1

1:13
c Ps 110:1;
Matt 22:44;
Mark 12:36;
Lk 20:42;
Heb 10:3,12

1:14
d Gen 19:16;
32:1-2,24;
Ps 34:7; 91:11;
103:20-21;
Dan 3:28; 7:10;
10:11; Matt 18:10;
Lk 1:19; 2:9,13;
Acts 12:7; 27:23;
Rom 8:17;
Titus 3:7;
James 2:5;
1Peter 3:7

2:2
e Num 15:30-31;
Deut 4:3; 17:2,5,
12; 27:26; 33:2;
Ps 68:17;
Acts 7:53;
Gal 3:19

2:3
f Matt 4:17;
Mark 1:14; Lk 1:2;
Heb 1:2;
10:28-29; 12:25

2:4
g Mark 16:20;
Acts 2:22,43;
14:3; 19:11;
Rom 15:18-19;
1Cor 2:4; 12:4,7,
11; Eph 1:5,9

2:5
h Heb 6:5;
2Peter 3:13

2:6
i Job 7:17; Ps 8:4;
144:3

2:8
a Matt 28:18;
1Cor 15:25,27;
Eph 1:22;
Heb 1:13

2:9
b John 3:16; 12:32;
Acts 2:33;
Rom 5:18; 8:32;
2Cor 5:15;
Phil 2:7-9;
1Tim 2:6;
1John 2:2; Rev 5:9

2:10
c Lk 13:32; 24:46;
Acts 3:15; 5:31;
Rom 11:36;
Heb 5:9; 12:2

2:11
d Matt 28:10;
John 20:17;
Acts 17:26;
Rom 8:29;
Heb 10:10,14

2:12
e Ps 22:22,25

2:13
f Ps 18:2; Isa 8:18;
12:2; John 17:6,9,
11-12; 20:29

2:14
g John 1:14;
Rom 8:3;
1Cor 15:54-55;
Phil 2:7; Col 2:15;
2Tim 1:10

2:15
h Lk 1:74;
Rom 8:15;
2Tim 1:7

2:17
i Phil 2:7;
Heb 4:15; 5:1-2

2:18
j Heb 4:15-16;
5:2; 7:25

"What is man that you should remember him,
  or the son of man that you should care for him?
⁷You made him a little lower than the angels,
  yet you crowned him with glory and honor
8   and put everything under his feet."ᵃᵃ

Now when God*b* put everything under him, he left nothing outside his control. However, at the present time we do not see everything put under him. ⁹But we do see someone who was made a little lower than the angels. He is Jesus, who is now crowned with glory and honor because he suffered death, so that by the grace of*c* God he might experience*d* death for everyone.*b*

¹⁰In bringing many children to glory, it was fitting that God, for whom and through whom everything exists, should make the source of their salvation perfect through suffering.*c* ¹¹For both the one who sanctifies and those who are being sanctified all have the same Father.*e* That is why Jesus*b* is not ashamed to call them brothers*d* ¹²when he says, "I will announce your name to my brothers. I will praise you within the congregation."*fe* ¹³And again, "I will trust him."*g* And again, "I am here with the children God has given me."*hf*

¹⁴Since the children have flesh and blood, he also shared the same things, so that by his death he might destroy the one who has the power of death (that is, the devil)*g* ¹⁵and might free those who were slaves all their lives because they were terrified by death.*h* ¹⁶For it is clear that he did not come to help angels. No, he came to help Abraham's descendants. ¹⁷Thus he had to become like his brothers in every way, so that he could be a merciful and faithful high priest in service to God and could atone for the people's sins.*i* ¹⁸Because he himself suffered when he was tempted, he is able to help those who are being tempted.*j*

---

a 2:8 Ps 8:5-7 (LXX)   **b** 2:8,2:11 Lit. *he*   **c** 2:9 Other mss. read *so that apart from*   **d** 2:9 Lit. *taste*   **e** 2:11 Lit. *are all of one*   **f** 2:12 Ps 22:22   **g** 2:13 Isa 8:17 (LXX)   **h** 2:13 Isa 8:18

Christic Is Superior to Moses

3 [1]Therefore, holy brothers, partners in a heavenly calling, keep your focus on Jesus, the apostle and high priest of our confession.[a] [2]He was faithful to the one who appointed him, just as Moses was in all God's[a] household.[b] [3]For he is worthy of greater glory than Moses in the same way that the builder of a house has greater honor than the house itself.[c] [4]After all, every house is built by someone, but God is the builder of everything.[d] [5]Moses was faithful in all God's[a] household as a servant who was to testify to what would be said later.[e] [6]But Christ is faithful[b] as the Son in charge of God's[a] household. We are his household, if we hold on to our courage and the hope we are proud of.[c][f]

A Rest for the People of God

[7]Therefore, as the Holy Spirit says,[g]

"Today, if you hear his voice, [8]do not harden
    your hearts
  as they did when they provoked me during
    the time of testing in the wilderness.
[9]There your ancestors tested me,
  even though they had seen my works
10   for forty years.
That is why I was indignant with that
  generation and said,
  'They are always going astray in their hearts,
  and they have not known my ways.'
[11]So in my anger I swore a solemn oath
  that they would never enter my rest."[d]

[12]See to it, my brothers, that no evil, unbelieving heart is found in any of you, as shown by your turning away from the living God. [13]Instead, continue to encourage one another every day, as long as it is called "Today," so that none of you may be hardened by the deceitfulness of sin. [14]For we are Christ's partners only if we hold on to our original confidence to the end.[e][h] [15]As it is said,[i]

---

a 3:2,3:5,3:6 Lit. *his* **b** 3:6 The Gk. lacks *is faithful* **c** 3:6 Lit. *the pride of our hope* **d** 3:11 Ps 95:7-11 **e** 3:14 Other mss. lack *to the end*

3:1
a Rom 1:7; 15:8;
1Cor 1:2; Eph 4:1;
Phil 3:14;
2Thes 1:11;
2Tim 1:9;
Heb 2:17; 4:14;
5:5; 6:20; 8:1;
9:11; 10:21;
2Peter 1:10

3:2
b Num 12:7;
Heb 12:5

3:3
c Zech 6:12;
Matt 16:18

3:4
d Eph 2:10; 3:9;
Heb 1:2

3:5
e Exod 14:31;
Num 12:7;
Deut 3:24; 18:15,
18-19; Josh 1:2;
8:31; Heb 3:2

3:6
f Matt 10:22;
24:13; Rom 5:2;
1Cor 3:16; 6:19;
2Cor 6:16;
Eph 2:21-22;
Col 1:23;
1Tim 3:15;
Heb 1:2; 2:14;
6:11; 10:35;
1Peter 2:5

3:7
g 2Sam 23:2;
Ps 95:7; Acts 1:16;
Heb 3:15

3:14
h Heb 3:6

3:15
i Heb 3:7

3:16
a Num 14:2,4,11,
24,30; Deut 1:34,
36,38

"Today, if you hear his voice,
>   you must not harden your hearts as they did
>   when they provoked me."a

3:17
b Num 14:22,29;
26:65; Ps 106:26;
1Cor 10:5;
Jude 1:5

16Who heard him and provoked him? Was it not all those who came out of Egypt led by Moses?ba 17And with whom was he angry for forty years? Was it not with those who sinned and whose bodies fell in the wilderness?b 18And to whom did he swear that they would never enter his rest, if not to those who disobeyed him?c 19So we see that they couldn't enter because of their unbelief.d

3:18
c Num 14:30;
Deut 1:34-35

We Must Enter the Rest

4 1Therefore, as long as the promise of entering his rest remains valid, let us be afraid lest someone among you fails to reach it.e 2For we have had the good news told to us as well as to them, but the message they heard didn't help them, because they were not united by faith with those who listened to it. 3For we who have believed are entering that rest, just as he has said,f

3:19
d Heb 4:6

4:1
e Heb 12:15

"In my anger I swore a solemn oath
>   that they should never enter my rest,"c

even though his works had been finished since the foundation of the world. 4For somewhere he has spoken about the seventh day as follows: "On the seventh day God rested from all his works,"dg 5and again in this place, "They will never enter my rest."c

4:3
f Ps 95:11;
Heb 3:11,14

6Therefore, since it is still true that some will enter it, and since those who once heard the good news failed to enter it because of their disobedience,h 7he again fixes a definite day—"Today"—saying long afterward through David, as already quoted,i

4:4
g Gen 2:2;
Exod 20:11; 31:17

"Today, if you hear his voice,
>   do not harden your hearts."a

8For if Joshuae had given them rest, he would not have

4:6
h Heb 3:19

---

a 3:15,4:7 Ps 95:7-8   b 3:16 Lit. out of Egypt by Moses   c 4:3,4:5 Ps 95:11
d 4:4 Gen 2:2   e 4:8 The Gk. (Jesus) appears to be a word play on the
name Joshua.

4:7
i Ps 95:7; Heb 3:7

spoken later about another day. ⁹There remains, therefore, a Sabbath rest for the people of God. ¹⁰For the one who enters God's^a rest has himself rested from his own works, just as God did from his.^b ¹¹Let us, therefore, make every effort to enter that rest, so that no one may fail by following their example of disobedience.^a

¹²For the word of God is living and active. It is sharper than any double-edged sword, piercing until it divides soul and spirit, joints and marrow, as it judges the thoughts and purposes of the heart.^b ¹³No creature can hide from him. Everything is naked and helpless before the eyes of the one to whom we must give an account.^c

Our Compassionate High Priest

¹⁴Therefore, since we have a great high priest who has gone through the heavens, Jesus the Son of God, let us continue to hold on to our confession.^d ¹⁵For we do not have a high priest who is incapable of sympathizing with our weaknesses, but one who was tempted in every respect as we are, yet without sin.^e ¹⁶So let us keep on coming with boldness to the throne of grace, so that we may obtain mercy and find grace to help us in our time of need.^f

Qualifications for the Priesthood

5 ¹For every high priest selected from among men is appointed to officiate on their behalf^c in matters relating to God, that is, to offer gifts and sacrifices for sins.^g ²He can deal gently with people who are ignorant and easily deceived, because he himself is subject to weakness.^h ³For that reason he has to offer sacrifices for his own sins, as well as for those of the people.ⁱ ⁴No one takes this honor upon himself. Instead, he is called to it by God, just as Aaron was.^j

Christ's Qualifications as High Priest

⁵In the same way, Christ did not take upon himself the glory of being a high priest. It was God who said^d to him,^k

---

a4:10 Lit. *his*   b4:10 Lit. *just as God from his*   c5:1 Lit. *on behalf of men*
d5:5 Lit. *He said*

488

4:11
^aHeb 3:12,18-19

4:12
^bProv 5:4;
Isa 49:2;
Jer 23:29;
1Cor 14:24-25;
2Cor 10:4-5;
Eph 6:17;
1Peter 1:23;
Rev 1:16; 2:16

4:13
^cJob 26:6;
34:21 Ps 33:13-14;
90:8; 139:11-12;
Prov 15:11

4:14
^dHeb 3:1; 7:26;
9:12,24; 10:23

4:15
^eIsa 53:3;
Lk 22:28;
2Cor 5:21;
Heb 2:18; 7:26;
1Peter 2:22;
1John 3:5

4:16
^fEph 2:18; 3:12;
Heb 10:19,21-22

5:1
^gHeb 2:17; 8:3-4;
9:9; 10:11; 11:4

5:2
^hHeb 2:18; 4:15;
7:28

5:3
ⁱLev 4:3; 9:7;
16:6,15-17;
Heb 7:27; 9:7

5:4
^jExod 28:1;
Num 16:5,40;
1Chr 23:13;
2Chr 26:18;
John 3:27

5:5
^kPs 2:7;
John 8:54;
Heb 1:5

5:6
a Ps 110:4;
Heb 7:17,21

5:7
b Ps 22:1;
Matt 26:37,39,42,
44,53; 27:46,50;
Mark 14:33,36,39;
15:34,37;
Lk 22:43;
John 12:27; 17:1

5:8
c Phil 2:8; Heb 3:6

5:9
d Heb 2:10; 11:40

5:10
e Heb 5:6; 6:20

5:11
f Matt 13:15;
John 16:12;
2Peter 3:16

5:12
g 1Cor 3:1-3;
Heb 6:1

5:13
h 1Cor 13:11;
14:20; Eph 4:14;
1Peter 2:2

5:14
i Isa 7:15;
1Cor 2:14-15

6:1
j Phil 3:12-14;
Heb 5:12; 9:14

6:2
k Acts 8:14-17;
17:31-32; 19:4-6;
24:25; Rom 2:16

6:3
l Acts 18:21;
1Cor 4:19

> "You are my Son.
> Today I have become your Father."**a**

⁶He also says in another place,*a*

> "You are a priest forever
> according to the order of Melchizedek."**b**

⁷During his life on earth,**c** he offered up prayers and appeals with loud cries and tears to the one who could save him from death, and he was heard because of his devotion to God.*b* ⁸Although he was a Son, he learned obedience through his sufferings*c* ⁹and, once made perfect, he became the source of eternal salvation for all who obey him,*d* ¹⁰having been designated by God to be a high priest according to the order of Melchizedek.*e*

You Still Need Someone to Teach You

¹¹We have much to say about this,**d** but it is difficult to explain because you have become too lazy to understand.*f* ¹²In fact, though by now you should be teachers, you still need someone to teach you the basic truths of God's word.**e** You have become people who need milk instead of solid food.*g* ¹³For everyone who lives on milk is still a baby and is inexperienced in the message of righteousness.*h* ¹⁴But solid food is for mature people, whose minds are trained by practice to distinguish between good and evil.*i*

The Peril of Immaturity

6 ¹Therefore, leaving behind the elementary teachings about Christ, let us continue to be carried along to maturity, not laying again a foundation of repentance from dead works, faith toward God,*j* ²instruction about baptisms, the laying on of hands, the resurrection of the dead, and eternal judgment.*k* ³We will do this,**f** if God lets us.*l*

⁴For it is impossible to keep on restoring to repentance time and again people who have once been enlightened,

---

a 5:5 Ps 2:7   **b** 5:6 Ps 110:4   **c** 5:7 Lit. *During the days of his flesh*
d 5:11 Or *about him*   **e** 5:12 Or *oracles*   **f** 6:3 Other mss. read *Let us do this*

who have tasted the heavenly gift, who have become sharers of the Holy Spirit,[a] [5]who have tasted the goodness of God's word and the powers of the coming age,[b] [6]and who have fallen away, as long as they continue to crucify to themselves the Son of God and to expose him to public ridicule.[c]

[7]For when the ground soaks up rain that often falls on it and continues producing vegetation useful to those for whom it is cultivated, it receives a blessing from God.[d] [8]However, if it continues to produce thorns and thistles, it is worthless and in danger of being cursed, and in the end it will be burned.[e]

Be Diligent

[9]Even though we speak like this, dear friends, we are convinced of better things in your case, things that point to salvation. [10]For God is not so unjust as to forget your work and the love you have shown him[a] as you have ministered to the saints and continue to minister to them.[f] [11]But we want each of you to continue to show this same diligence to the very end, in order to give full assurance to your hope.[g] [12]Then, instead of being lazy, you will become imitators of those who are inheriting the promises through faith and patience.[h]

God's Promise Is Reliable

[13]For when God made his promise to Abraham, he swore an oath by himself, since he had no one greater to swear by.[i] [14]He said, "I will certainly bless you and give you many descendants."[b] [15]And so he obtained the promise, because he patiently waited for it.

[16]For people swear by someone greater than themselves, and an oath given as confirmation puts an end to all argument.[j] [17]In the same way, when God wanted to make the unchangeable character of his purpose perfectly clear to the heirs of his promise, he guaranteed it with an oath[k] [18]so that by these two unchangeable things, in which it is impossible for God to prove false, we who have taken refuge in him

---

a *6:10* Lit. *shown for his name*　　**b** *6:14* Gen 22:17

Cross references

6:4
[a] Matt 12:31-32;
John 4:10; 6:32;
Gal 3:2,5;
Eph 2:8; Heb 2:4;
10:26,32;
2Peter 2:20-21;
1John 5:16

6:5
[b] Heb 2:5

6:6
[c] Heb 10:29

6:7
[d] Ps 65:10

6:8
[e] Isa 5:6

6:10
[f] Prov 14:31;
Matt 10:42; 25:40;
John 13:20;
Rom 3:4; 15:25;
2Cor 8:4; 9:1,12;
1Thes 1:3;
2Thes 1:6-7;
2Tim 1:18

6:11
[g] Col 2:2;
Heb 3:6,14

6:12
[h] Heb 6:36

6:13
[i] Gen 22:16-17;
Ps 105:9; Lk 1:73

6:16
[j] Exod 22:11

6:17
[k] Rom 11:29;
Heb 11:9

6:18
a Heb 12:1

6:19
b Lev 16:15;
Heb 9:7

6:20
c Heb 3:1,5-6,10;
4:14; 7:17; 8:1;
9:24

7:1
d Gen 14:18

7:4
e Gen 14:20

7:5
f Num 18:21,26

7:6
g Gen 14:19;
Rom 4:13;
Gal 3:16

7:8
h Heb 5:6; 6:20

7:11
i Gal 2:21;
Heb 7:18-19; 8:7

might have a strong encouragement to take hold of the hope set before us.*a* [19]We have this hope[a] as an anchor for our souls, firm and secure, which reaches behind the curtain,*b* [20]where Jesus, our forerunner, went on our behalf, having become a high priest forever according to the order of Melchizedek.*c*

Christ Is Superior to Melchizedek

7 [1]Now this man Melchizedek, king of Salem and priest of the Most High God, met Abraham and blessed him when he was returning from defeating the kings.*d* [2]Abraham gave him a tenth of everything.[b] In the first place, his name means "king of righteousness." He is also king of Salem, that is, "king of peace." [3]He has no father, mother, or ancestors. He has neither beginning of days nor end of life. Like the Son of God, he continues to be a priest forever.

[4]Just look at how great this man was: Even Abraham—the patriarch himself—gave him a tenth of what he had captured![e] [5]The descendants of Levi who accept the priesthood have a commandment in the Law to collect a tenth from the people, that is, from their own brothers, even though they are also descendants of Abraham.*f* [6]But this man, whose descent is not traced from them, collected a tenth from Abraham and blessed the man who had received the promises.*g* [7]It is beyond dispute that the less important person is blessed by the more important person. [8]The men who collect the tenth die, but we are told that[c] he keeps on living.*h* [9]One might even say that Levi, who collects the tenth, paid the tenth through Abraham, [10]because he was still in the body of his ancestor when Melchizedek met him.

[11]Now if perfection could have been attained through the Levitical priesthood—for on this basis the people received the Law—what further need would there be to speak of appointing another kind of priest according to the order of Melchizedek, not one according to the order of Aaron?*i* [12]For when a change in the priesthood takes place, there must also be a change in the Law. [13]The person we are talking about belonged to a different tribe, and no one from

---

a *6:19* Lit. *We have this*   **b** *7:2* Gen 14:18-20   **c** *7:8* Or *it is declared that*

that tribe has ever served[a] at the altar. [14]For it is obvious that our Lord was a descendant of Judah, and Moses said nothing about priests coming from that tribe.[a]

[15]This point is even more obvious in that another priest who is like Melchizedek has appeared. [16]He was appointed to be a priest,[b] not on the basis of a regulation concerning his ancestry, but rather on the basis of the power of an indestructible life. [17]For it is declared about him,[b]

> "You are a priest forever
>   according to the order of Melchizedek."[c]

[18]Indeed, the cancellation of the former regulation has occurred because it was weak and ineffective[c] [19](for the Law made nothing perfect), and a better hope is introduced, by which we approach God.[d]

[20]Now, none of this happened without an oath. Others became priests without any oath, [21]but Jesus[d] became a priest with an oath when God said[e] to him,[e]

> "The Lord has taken an oath
>   and will not change his mind.
> You are a priest forever."[f]

[22]In this way, Jesus has become the guarantor of a better covenant.[f]

[23]There have been many priests, since they have been prevented by death from continuing in office. [24]But because Jesus[d] lives forever, he has a permanent priesthood. [25]Therefore, because he always lives to intercede for them, he is able to save completely[g] those who come to God through him.[g]

[26]We need such a high priest—one who is holy, innocent, pure, set apart from sinners, exalted above the heavens.[h] [27]He doesn't need to offer sacrifices every day like those high priests, first for his own sins, and then for those of the people. He did this once for all when he sacrificed himself.[i] [28]For the Law appoints as high priests men who are weak.

---

a 7:13 Lit. *from which no one has served*　b 7:16 Lit. *He was appointed*
c 7:17 Ps 110:4　d 7:21,7:24 Lit. *he*　e 7:21 Lit. *but he with an oath when he said*　f 7:21 Ps 110:4　g 7:25 Or *he is always able to save*

7:14
a Isa 11:1;
Matt 1:3; Lk 3:33;
Rom 1:3; Rev 5:5

7:17
b Ps 110:4;
Heb 5:6,10; 6:20

7:18
c Rom 8:3; Gal 4:9

7:19
d Acts 13:39;
Rom 3:20-21,28;
5:2; 8:3; Gal 2:16;
Eph 2:18; 3:12;
Heb 4:16; 6:18;
8:6; 9:9; 10:19

7:21
e Ps 110:4

7:22
f Heb 8:6; 9:15;
12:24

7:25
g Rom 8:34;
1 Tim 2:5;
Heb 9:24;
1 John 2:1

7:26
h Eph 1:20; 4:10;
Heb 4:15; 8:1

7:27
i Lev 9:7; 16:6,11,
15; Rom 6:10;
Heb 5:3; 9:7,12,
28; 10:12

7:28
a Heb 2:10; 5:1-2, 9

But God's oath,[a] which came after the Law, appoints one who is a Son, who has been made perfect forever.[a]

Christand Has a Better Ministry

8:1
b Eph 1:20;
Col 3:1; Heb 1:3;
10:12; 12:2

8 ¹Now the main point in what we are saying is this: We do have this kind of high priest, who sat down at the right hand of the throne of the Majesty in heaven[b] ²and who serves in the sanctuary, the true tabernacle set up by the Lord and not by any human.[c]

8:2
c Heb 9:8,11-12, 24

³For every high priest is appointed to offer both gifts and sacrifices. Therefore, this high priest[b] had to offer something, too.[d] ⁴Now if he were on earth, he would not even be a priest, because other men offer the gifts prescribed by the Law. ⁵They serve in a sanctuary that is a copy and shadow of the heavenly one. This is why Moses was warned when he was about to build the tabernacle: "See to it that you make everything according to the pattern shown you on the mountain."[ce] ⁶However, Jesus[d] has now entered into a ministry that is as superior to theirs as the covenant he mediates is founded on better promises.[f]

8:3
d Eph 5:2;
Heb 5:1; 9:14

8:5
e Exod 25:40;
26:30; 27:8;
Num 8:4;
Acts 7:44;
Col 2:17;
Heb 9:23; 10:1

The New Covenant Is Better Than the Old

⁷For if the first covenant had been faultless, there would have been no need to look for a second one.[g] ⁸But God[d] found something wrong with his people[e] when he said,[h]

8:6
f 2Cor 3:6,8-9;
Heb 7:22

"Look! The days are coming, says the Lord,
when I will establish a new covenant with the
house of Israel and with the house of Judah.
⁹It will not be like the covenant that I made
with their ancestors at the time when I took
them by the hand and brought them out of
the land of Egypt. Because they did not remain loyal to my covenant, I ignored them,
says the Lord. ¹⁰For this is the covenant that I
will make with the house of Israel after those
days, says the Lord:[i]

8:7
g Heb 7:11,18

8:8
h Jer 31:31-34

8:10
i Zech 8:8;
Heb 10:16

a 7:28 Lit. *But the word of the oath*   b 8:3 Lit. *this one*   c 8:5 Exod 25:40
d 8:6,8:8 Lit. *he*   e 8:8 Lit. *with them*

I will put my laws in their minds
  and write them on their hearts.
I will be their God,
  and they will be my people.
[11]Never again will everyone teach his neighbor[a]
  or his brother by saying, 'Know the Lord,'
because all of them will know me,
  from the least important to the most
    important.
[12]For I will be merciful regarding their wrong deeds,[b]
  and I will never again remember their sins."[a]

[13]In speaking of a "new" covenant, he has made the first one obsolete. And what is obsolete and aging will soon disappear.[c]

The Earthly Sanctuary and Its Ritual

9 [1]The first covenant[b] had regulations for worship and an earthly sanctuary.[d] [2]For a tabernacle was set up, and in the first part were the lampstand, the table, and the bread of the Presence.[c] This was called the Holy Place.[e] [3]Behind the second curtain was the part of the tabernacle called the Holy of Holies,[f] [4]which had the gold altar for incense and the ark of the covenant completely covered with gold. In it were the gold jar holding the manna, Aaron's staff that had budded, and the tablets of the covenant.[g] [5]Above it were the cherubim of glory overshadowing the place of atonement. (We cannot discuss these things in detail now.)[h]

[6]When everything had been arranged like this, the priests always went into the first part of the tabernacle to perform their duties.[i] [7]But only the high priest went[d] into the second part, and he only once a year, and never without blood, which he offered for himself and for the sins committed by the people in ignorance.[j] [8]The Holy Spirit was indicating by this that the way into the Holy of Holies had not yet been disclosed as long as the first part of the

---

8:11
[a]Isa 54:13;
John 6:45;
1John 2:27

8:12
[b]Rom 11:27;
Heb 10:17

8:13
[c]2Cor 5:17

9:1
[d]Exod 25:8

9:2
[e]Exod 25:23,31;
26:1,35; 40:4;
Lev 24:5

9:3
[f]Exod 26:31,33;
40:3,21; Heb 6:19

9:4
[g]Exod 16:33-34;
25:10,16,21;
26:33; 34:29;
40:3,20-21;
Num 17:10;
Deut 10:2,5;
1Kings 8:9,21;
2Chr 5:10

9:5
[h]Exod 25:18,22;
Lev 16:2;
1Kings 8:6-7

9:6
[i]Num 28:3;
Dan 8:11

9:7
[j]Exod 30:10;
Lev 16:2,11-12,
15,34; Heb 5:3;
7:27; 9:25

---

a 8:12 Jer 31:31-34   b 9:1 Lit. the first   c 9:2 Lit. the presentation of the bread   d 9:7 The Gk. lacks went

494

9:8
a John 14:6;
Heb 10:19-20

9:9
b Gal 3:21;
Heb 7:18-19;
10:1,11

9:10
c Lev 11:2;
Num 19:7;
Eph 2:15;
Col 2:16,20;
Heb 7:16

9:11
d Heb 3:1; 8:2;
10:1

9:12
e Dan 9:24;
Zech 3:9;
Acts 20:28;
Eph 1:7; Col 1:14;
Heb 9:26,28;
10:4,10;
1Peter 1:19;
Rev 1:5; 5:9

9:13
f Lev 16:14,16;
Num 19:2,17

9:14
g Lk 1:74;
Rom 1:4; 6:13,22;
Eph 2:5;
Titus 2:14;
Heb 1:3; 6:1;
7:27; 10:22;
1Peter 1:19; 3:18;
4:2; 1John 1:7;
Rev 1:5

9:15
h Rom 3:25; 5:6;
1Tim 2:5;
Heb 3:1; 7:22;
8:6; 12:24;
1Peter 3:18

9:17
i Gal 3:15

9:18
j Exod 24:6

9:19
k Exod 24:5-6,8;
Lev 14:4,6-7,49,
51-52; 16:14-15,
18

9:20
l Exod 24:8;
Matt 26:28

tabernacle was still standing.*a* [9]This is an illustration of the present time, indicating that the gifts and sacrifices being offered could not make the conscience of the worshiper perfect,*b* [10]since they deal only with food, drink, and various washings, which are required for the body until the time when things would be set right.*c*

Christ Has Offered a Superior Sacrifice

[11]But when Christ came as a high priest of the good things that have come,*a* he went*b* through the greater and more perfect tabernacle that was not made by human*c* hands and that is not a part of this creation.*d* [12]Not with the blood of goats and calves, but with his own blood he went into the Holy of Holies once for all and secured our eternal redemption.*e* [13]For if the blood of goats and bulls and the ashes of a heifer sprinkled on those who are unclean purifies them with physical cleansing,*f* [14]how much more will the blood of Christ, who through the eternal Spirit*d* offered himself unblemished to God, cleanse our*e* consciences from dead works so that we may serve the living God!*g*

Christ Is the Mediator of a New Covenant

[15]This is why he is the mediator of a new covenant, so that those who are called may receive the eternal inheritance promised them, because a death has occurred that redeems them from the offenses committed under the first covenant.*h* [16]For where there is a will, the death of the one who made it must be established, [17]because a will is in force only when somebody has died. It never takes effect as long as the one who made it is alive.*i* [18]This is why even the first covenant was not put into effect without blood.*j* [19]For after every commandment in the Law had been spoken to all the people by Moses, he took the blood of calves and goats,*f* together with some water, scarlet wool, and branches of hyssop, and sprinkled the scroll and all the people,*k* [20]saying, "This is the blood of the covenant that God ordained for you."*g l* [21]In the

---

a 9:11 Other mss. read *that are to come*   **b** 9:11 The Gk. lacks *went*
c 9:11 The Gk. lacks *human*   **d** 9:14 Other mss. read *through the Holy Spirit*   **e** 9:14 Other mss. read *your*   **f** 9:19 Other mss. lack *and goats*
g 9:20 Exod 24:8

same way, he sprinkled with the blood both the tabernacle and everything used in worship.[a] 22In fact, under the Law almost everything is cleansed with blood, and without the shedding of the blood there is no forgiveness.[b]

Christ's Perfect Sacrifice

23And so it was necessary for the copies of the things in heaven to be cleansed by these sacrifices,[a] but the heavenly things themselves with better sacrifices than these.[c] 24For Christ did not go into a sanctuary made by human[b] hands and just a copy of the true one, but into heaven itself, now to appear in God's presence on our behalf.[d] 25Nor did he go into heaven to sacrifice[c] himself again and again, the way the high priest goes into the Holy Place every year with blood that is not his own.[e] 26Then he would have had to suffer many times since the foundation of the world. But now, at the end of the ages, he has appeared once for all to remove sin by his sacrifice.[f] 27Indeed, just as people are appointed to die once and after that to be judged,[d][g] 28so Christ was sacrificed once to take away the sins of many people. And he will appear a second time, not to deal with sin,[e] but to bring salvation to those who eagerly wait for him.[h]

The Law Is a Reflection

10 1For the Law, being only a reflection[f] of the blessings to come and not their substance, can never, by the same sacrifices repeatedly offered year after year, make those who come near perfect.[i] 2Otherwise, wouldn't they have stopped offering them, because the worshipers, cleansed once for all, would no longer be aware of any sins? 3Instead, through those sacrifices there is a reminder of sins year after year,[j] 4for it is impossible for the blood of bulls and goats to take away sins.[k]

---

a9:23 Lit. *by these things*   b9:24 The Gk. lacks *human*   c9:25 Lit. *Nor to sacrifice*   d9:27 Lit. *after that the judgment*   e9:28 Lit. *a second time without sin*   f10:1 Or *shadow*

9:21
aExod 29:12,36;
Lev 8:15,19; 16:1,
15-16,18-19

9:22
bLev 17:11

9:23
cHeb 8:5

9:24
dRom 8:34;
Heb 6:20; 7:25;
8:2; 1John 2:1

9:25
eHeb 9:7

9:26
f1Cor 10:11;
Gal 4:4; Eph 1:10;
Heb 7:27; 9:12;
10:10; 1Peter 3:18

9:27
gGen 3:19;
Eccl 3:20;
2Cor 5:10;
Rev 20:12-13

9:28
hMatt 26:28;
Rom 5:15; 6:10;
Titus 2:13;
1Peter 2:24; 3:18;
2Peter 3:12;
1John 3:5

10:1
iCol 2:17;
Heb 8:5; 9:9,11,
14,23

10:3
jLev 16:21;
Heb 9:7

10:4
kMic 6:6-7;
Heb 9:11,13

10:5
a Ps 40:6; 50:8;
Isa 1:11; Jer 6:20;
Amos 5:21-22

Christ Offered One Sacrifice

⁵For this reason, when Christ[a] came into the world, he said,[a]

> "You did not want sacrifices and offerings,
>> but you prepared a body for me.
>> ⁶In burnt offerings and sin offerings
>> you never took delight.
> ⁷Then I said, 'See, I have come to do your will,
>> O God'
> (in the scroll of the Book[b] this is written
>> about me)."[c]

10:10
b John 17:19;
Heb 9:12; 13:12

10:11
c Num 28:3;
Heb 7:4,27

⁸In this passage he says, "You never wanted or took delight in sacrifices, offerings, burnt offerings, and sin offerings,"[d] which are offered according to the Law. ⁹Then he says, "See, I have come to do your will."[e] He takes away the first to establish the second. ¹⁰By his will we have been sanctified through the sacrifice of the body of Jesus Christ once for all.[b]

¹¹Day after day every priest stands and offers again and again the same sacrifices that can never take away sins.[c] ¹²But when this priest[f] had offered for all time one sacrifice for sins, "he sat down at the right hand of God."[g][d] ¹³Since that time, he has been waiting for his enemies to be made a footstool for his feet.[e] ¹⁴For by a single offering he has perfected for all time those who are being sanctified.[f]

10:12
d Col 3:1; Heb 1:3

10:13
e Ps 110:1;
Acts 2:35;
1Cor 15:25;
Heb 1:13

¹⁵The Holy Spirit also assures us of this. For he said,

> ¹⁶"This is the covenant that I will make with them[g]
>> after those days, says the Lord:
> I will put my laws in their hearts
>> and will write them on their minds,"[h]

10:14
f Heb 10:1

¹⁷and,

> "I will never again remember their sins
>> and their lawless deeds."[i]

10:16
g Jer 31:33-34;
Heb 8:10,12

a *10:5* Lit. *he*   b *10:7* I.e. the Book of Psalms   c *10:7* Ps 40:6-8
d *10:8* Ps 40:6   e *10:9* Ps 40:7   f *10:12* Lit. *this one*   g *10:12* Ps 110:1
h *10:16* Jer 31:33   i *10:17* Jer 31:34

[18]Now where there is forgiveness of these sins,[a] there is no longer any offering for sin.

How We Should Live

[19]Therefore, my brothers, since we have confidence to enter the sanctuary by the blood of Jesus,[a] [20]the new and living way that he opened for us through the curtain (that is, through his flesh),[b] [21]and since we have a great high priest over the household of God,[c] [22]let us continue to come near with sincere hearts in full assurance of faith, because our hearts have been sprinkled clean from an evil conscience and our bodies have been washed with pure water.[d] [23]Let us continue to hold firmly to the hope that we confess without wavering, for the one who made the promise is faithful.[e] [24]And let us also make it our habit to consider how to stimulate[b] one another to love and good deeds. [25]We must not continue to neglect meeting together, as is the habit of some. Instead, we must continue to encourage one another even more as you see the day coming nearer.[f]

[26]For if we choose to go on sinning after we have received the full knowledge of the truth, there is no more sacrifice for our sins.[g] [27]All that remains is a[c] terrifying prospect of judgment and a raging fire that will consume God's[d] enemies.[h] [28]Anyone who violates the Law of Moses dies without mercy "on the testimony of two or three witnesses."[e][i] [29]How much more severe a punishment do you think that person deserves who tramples on God's Son, treats as common the blood of the covenant by which it[f] was sanctified, and insults the Spirit of grace?[j] [30]For we know the one who said, "Vengeance belongs to me; I will pay them back,"[g] and again, "The Lord will judge his people."[h][k] [31]It is a terrifying thing to fall into the hands of the living God![l]

[32]But you must continue to remember those earlier days, how after you were enlightened you endured a hard and painful struggle.[m] [33]At times you were made a public spectacle through insults and persecutions, while at other times

---

a[10:18] Lit. *of these things*   b[10:24] Or *provoke*   c[10:27] Lit. *But a*
d[10:27] Lit. *the*   e[10:28] Deut 17:6   f[10:29] Or *he*   g[10:30] Deut 32:35
h[10:30] Deut 32:36; Ps 135:14

10:19
a Rom 5:2;
Eph 2:18; 3:12;
Heb 9:8,12

10:20
b John 10:9; 14:6;
Heb 9:3,8

10:21
c 1Tim 3:15;
Heb 4:14

10:22
d Ezek 36:25;
2Cor 7:1;
Eph 3:12;
Heb 4:16; 9:14;
James 1:6;
1John 3:21

10:23
e 1Cor 1:9; 10:13;
1Thes 5:24;
2Thes 3:3;
Heb 4:14; 11:11

10:25
f Acts 2:42;
Rom 13:11;
Phil 4:5;
2Peter 3:9,11,14;
Jude 1:19

10:26
g Num 15:30;
Heb 6:4;
2Peter 2:20-21

10:27
h Ezek 36:5;
Zeph 1:18; 3:8;
2Thes 1:8;
Heb 12:29

10:28
i Deut 17:2,6;
19:15; Matt 18:16;
John 8:17;
2Cor 13:1;
Heb 2:2

10:29
j Matt 12:31-32;
1Cor 11:29;
Eph 4:30;
Heb 2:3; 12:25;
13:20

10:30
k Deut 32:35-36;
Ps 50:4; 135:14;
Rom 12:19

10:31
l Lk 12:5

10:32
m Gal 3:4;
Phil 1:29-30;
Col 2:1; Heb 6:4;
2John 1:8

10:33
a 1Cor 4:9;
Phil 1:7; 4:14;
1Thes 2:14

10:34
b Matt 5:12; 6:20;
19:21; Lk 12:33;
Acts 5:41;
Phil 1:7;
1Tim 6:19;
2Tim 1:16;
James 1:2

10:35
c Matt 5:12; 10:32

10:36
d Lk 21:19;
Gal 6:9; Col 3:24;
Heb 9:15; 12:1;
1Peter 1:9

10:37
e Hab 2:3-4;
Lk 18:8;
2Peter 3:9

10:38
f Rom 1:17;
Gal 3:11

10:39
g Acts 16:30-31;
1Thes 5:9;
2Thes 2:14;
2Peter 2:20-21

11:1
h Rom 8:24-25;
2Cor 4:18; 5:7

11:2
i Heb 11:39

11:3
j Gen 1:1; Ps 33:6;
John 1:3; Heb 1:2;
2Peter 3:5

11:4
k Gen 4:4,10;
Matt 23:35;
Heb 12:24;
1John 3:12

11:5
l Gen 5:22,24

you associated with people who were treated this way.*a* [34]You suffered with prisoners and cheerfully submitted to the violent seizure of your property, because you know that you have a better and more permanent possession.*b*

[35]So don't ever lose your confidence, since it holds a great reward for you.*c* [36]You need endurance so that after you have done God's will you can receive what he has promised.*d* [37]For*e*

> "in a very little while
>> the one who is coming will return
>> and not delay,
> [38]and my righteous one will live by faith.*f*
> But if he turns back,
>> my soul will take no pleasure in him."*a*

[39]Now, we don't belong to those who turn back and are destroyed, but to those who have faith and are saved.*g*

The Meaning of Faith

11 [1]Now faith is the assurance of things we hope for, the certainty of things we cannot see.*h* [2]By it our ancestors won approval.*i* [3]By faith we understand that the universe was prepared by the word of God, so that what is seen was not made from things that are visible.*j*

[4]By faith Abel brought to God a better sacrifice than Cain did.*b* By faith*c* he was declared to be righteous, since God himself approved his offerings. And by faith*d* he continues to speak, even though he is dead.*k*

[5]By faith Enoch was taken away without experiencing death. He couldn't be found, because God had taken him away. For before he was taken, he won approval as one who pleased God.*l* [6]Now without faith it is impossible to please God, because anyone who comes to him must believe that he exists and that he rewards those who diligently search for him.

[7]By faith Noah, when warned about things not yet seen,

---

a *10:38* Isa 26:20 (LXX); Hab 2:3-4 (LXX)   **b** *11:4* The Gk. lacks *did*
c *11:4* Lit. *By it*   **d** *11:4* Lit. *by it*

reverently prepared an ark to save his family. By faith*a* he condemned the world and became heir to the righteousness that comes by faith.*a*

8By faith Abraham, when called to go to a place he would later receive as his inheritance, obeyed and went, even though he didn't know where he was going.*b* 9By faith he made his home in the promised land like a stranger, living in tents with Isaac and Jacob, who were heirs with him of the same promise.*c* 10For he was waiting for the city with permanent foundations, whose architect and builder is God.*d*

11By faith Sarah, even though she was old and barren, received the strength to conceive, because she was convinced that the one who had made the promise was faithful.*e* 12Abraham*b* was as good as dead, yet from this one man came descendants as numerous as the stars in the sky and as countless as the sand on the seashore.*f*

13All these people died having faith. They didn't receive the things that were promised, yet they saw them in the distant future and welcomed them, acknowledging that they were strangers and foreigners on earth.*g* 14People who say such things make it clear that they are looking for a country of their own.*h* 15If they had been thinking about what they had left behind, they would have had an opportunity to go back. 16Instead, they were longing for a better country, that is, a heavenly one. That is why God is not ashamed to be called their God, because he has prepared a city for them.*i*

17By faith Abraham, when he was tested, offered Isaac. The man who had received the promises was about to offer his only son,*cj* 18about whom it had been said, "It is through Isaac that descendants will be named for you."*dk* 19He was certain that God could raise people from the dead, and figuratively speaking he did get him back in this way.*l*

20By faith Isaac blessed Jacob and Esau in regard to their future.*m* 21By faith Jacob, when he was dying, blessed each of Joseph's sons "and worshiped while leaning on*e* the top of

---

a 11:7 Lit. *By it*   b 11:12 Lit. *He*   c 11:17 Lit. *unique one*; the Gk. lacks *son*   d 11:18 Gen 21:12   e 11:21 Lit. *worshiped on*

11:7
a Gen 6:13,22;
Rom 3:22; 4:13;
Phil 3:9;
1 Peter 3:20

11:8
b Gen 12:1,4;
Acts 7:2-4

11:9
c Gen 12:8; 13:3,
18; 18:1,9;
Heb 6:17

11:10
d Heb 3:4; 12:22;
13:14; Rev 21:2,
10

11:11
e Gen 17:19;
18:11,14; 21:2;
Lk 1:36;
Rom 4:21;
Heb 10:23

11:12
f Gen 22:17;
Rom 4:18-19

11:13
g Gen 23:4; 47:9;
1 Chr 29:15;
Ps 39:12; 119:19;
John 8:56;
Heb 11:27,39;
1 Peter 1:17; 2:11

11:14
h Heb 13:14

11:16
i Exod 3:6,15;
Matt 22:32;
Acts 7:32;
Phil 3:20;
Heb 13:14

11:17
j Gen 22:1,9;
James 2:21

11:18
k Gen 21:12;
Rom 9:7

11:19
l Rom 4:17,19,21

11:20
m Gen 27:27,39

11:21
a Gen 47:31; 48:5, 16,20

11:22
b Gen 50:24-25; Exod 18:19

11:23
c Exod 1:16,22; 2:2; Acts 7:20

11:24
d Exod 2:10-11

11:25
e Ps 84:10

11:26
f Heb 10:35; 13:13

11:27
g Exod 10:28-29; 12:37; 13:17-18; Heb 13:13

11:28
h Exod 12:21

11:29
i Exod 14:22,29

11:30
j Josh 6:20

11:31
k Josh 1:1; 6:23 James 2:25

11:32
l Jdg 4:6; 6:11; 11:1; 12:7; 13:24; 1Sam 1:20; 12:20; 16:1,13; 17:45

11:33
m Jdg 14:5-6; 1Sam 17:34-35; 2Sam 7:11; Dan 6:22

11:34
n Jdg 15:8,15; 1Sam 14:13; 17:51-52; 20:1; 2Sam 8:1; 1Kings 19:3; 2Kings 6:16; 20:7; Job 42:10; Ps 6:8; Dan 3:25

11:35
o 1Kings 17:22; 2Kings 4:35; Acts 22:25

11:36
p Gen 39:20; Jer 20:2; 37:15

11:37
q 1Kings 21:13; 2Kings 1:8; 2Chr 24:21; Zech 13:4; Matt 3:4; Acts 7:58; 14:19

his staff."[a] 22By faith Joseph, when his end was near, spoke about the exodus of the Israelites and gave them instructions about burying[a] his bones.[b]

23By faith Moses was hidden by his parents for three months after he was born, because they saw that he was a beautiful child and were not afraid of the king's order.[c] 24By faith Moses, when he had grown up, refused to be called a son of Pharaoh's daughter,[d] 25because he preferred being mistreated with God's people to enjoying the pleasures of sin for a short time.[e] 26He thought that being insulted for the sake of Christ[b] was of greater value than the treasures of Egypt, because he was looking ahead to his reward.[f]

27By faith he left Egypt, without being afraid of the king's anger, and he persevered because he saw the one who is invisible.[g] 28By faith he established the Passover and the sprinkling of blood to keep the destroyer of the firstborn from touching the people.[c][h] 29By faith they went through the Red Sea as if it were dry land. When the Egyptians tried to do this, they were drowned.[i]

30By faith the walls of Jericho fell down, after they had been encircled for seven days.[j] 31By faith Rahab the prostitute did not die with those who were disobedient, because she had welcomed the spies with a greeting of peace.[d][k]

32What more should I say? I don't have enough time to tell you about Gideon, Barak, Samson, Jephthah, David, Samuel, and the prophets.[l] 33Through faith they conquered kingdoms, administered justice, received promises, shut the mouths of lions,[m] 34put out raging fires, escaped death by[e] the sword, found strength in weakness, became powerful in battle, and routed foreign armies.[n] 35Women received back their dead through a resurrection. Others were brutally tortured but refused to accept release, so that they might gain a better resurrection.[o] 36Still others endured taunts and floggings, and even chains and imprisonment.[p] 37They were stoned to death, sawed in half, and killed with swords. They went around in sheepskins and goatskins. They were needy, oppressed, and mistreated.[q] 38The world wasn't worthy of

---

a 11:22 The Gk. lacks *burying*   **b** 11:26 I.e. the Messiah   **c** 11:28 Lit. *them*
d 11:31 Lit. *with peace*   **e** 11:34 Lit. *by the edge of*

them. They wandered in deserts, mountains, caves, and holes in the ground.*

39All these people won approval for their faith but didn't receive what was promised,*b* 40because God had planned something better for us so that they would not become perfect without us.*c*

We Must Look Off to Jesus

12 1Therefore, having so vast a cloud of witnesses surrounding us, and throwing off everything that hinders us and especially the sin that so easily entangles**a** us, let us keep running with endurance the race set before us,*d* 2looking off to Jesus, the Founder and Finisher of the faith, who endured the cross, disregarding its shame, for the joy now set before him, and has sat down at the right hand of the throne of God.*e*

The Father Disciplines Us

3Think about the one who endured such hostility from sinners, so that you don't become tired and give up.*f* 4In your struggle against sin, you haven't yet resisted to the point of shedding your blood.**b***g* 5You have forgotten the encouragement that is addressed to you as sons:*h*

> "My son, don't think lightly of the Lord's
> discipline
> or give up when you are corrected by him.
> 6For the Lord disciplines the one he loves,*i*
> and he punishes**c** every son he accepts."**d**

7What you endure is for the sake of discipline. God is treating you as sons. Is there a son whom his father doesn't discipline?*j* 8Now if you are without any discipline, in which all sons share, then you are illegitimate and not his sons.*k* 9Furthermore, we had earthly fathers who used to discipline us, and we respected them for it. We should even more submit to the Father of our spirits and live, shouldn't we?*l* 10For a short time they disciplined us as they thought

---

a *12:1* Other mss. read *distracts*   **b** *12:4* Lit. *resisted to blood*   **c** *12:6* Or *whips*   **d** *12:6* Prov 3:11-12

Side references:

11:38
a 1Kings 18:4; 19:9

11:39
b Heb 11:2,13

11:40
c Heb 5:9; 7:22; 8:6; 12:23; Rev 6:11

12:1
d Rom 12:12; 1Cor 9:24; Phil 3:13-14; Col 3:8; Heb 10:36; 1Peter 2:1

12:2
e Ps 110:1; Lk 24:26; Phil 2:8; Heb 1:3,13; 8:1; 1Peter 1:11; 3:22

12:3
f Matt 10:24-25; John 15:20; Gal 6:9

12:4
g 1Cor 10:13; Heb 10:32-34

12:5
h Job 5:17; Prov 3:11

12:6
i Ps 94:12; 119:75; Prov 3:12; James 1:12; Rev 3:19

12:7
j Deut 8:5; 2Sam 7:14; Prov 13:24; 19:18; 23:13

12:8
k Ps 73:1; 1Peter 5:9

12:9
l Num 16:22; 27:16; Job 12:10; Eccl 12:7; Isa 42:5; 57:16; Zech 12:1

12:10
a Lev 11:44; 19:2;
1 Peter 1:15-16

12:11
b James 3:18

12:12
c Job 4:3-4;
Isa 35:3

12:13
d Prov 4:26-27;
Gal 6:1

12:14
e Ps 34:14;
Matt 5:8;
Rom 12:18; 14:9;
2Cor 7:1; Eph 5:5;
2Tim 2:22

12:15
f Deut 29:18;
2Cor 6:1; Gal 5:4;
Heb 3:12

12:16
g Gen 25:33;
Eph 5:3; Col 3:5;
1Thes 4:3

12:17
h Gen 27:34,36,
38; Heb 6:6

12:18
i Exod 19:12,
18-19; 20:18;
Deut 4:11; 5:22;
Rom 6:14; 8:15;
2Tim 1:7

12:19
j Exod 20:19;
Deut 5:5,25;
18:16

12:20
k Exod 19:13

12:21
l Exod 19:16

12:22
m Deut 33:2;
Ps 68:17;
Gal 4:26;
Phil 3:20;
Jude 1:14;
Rev 3:12; 21:2,10

12:23
n Gen 18:25;
Exod 4:22;
Ps 94:2; Lk 10:20;
Phil 3:12; 4:3;
Heb 11:40;
James 1:18;
Rev 13:8; 14:4

12:24
o Gen 4:10;
Exod 24:8;
Heb 8:6; 9:15;
10:22; 11:4;
1Peter 1:2

12:25
p Heb 2:2-3; 3:17;
10:28-29

best. But he does it for our good, so that we may share in his holiness.*a* [11]No discipline seems pleasant at the time, but painful. Later on, however, for those who have been trained by it, it produces a harvest of righteousness and peace.*b*

Live As God's People

[12]Therefore, strengthen your tired arms and your weak knees,*c* [13]and make straight paths for your feet, so that what is lame won't become worse, but rather be healed.*d*

[14]Pursue peace with everyone, as well as holiness, without which no one will see the Lord.*e* [15]Make sure that no one fails to obtain the grace of God and that no bitter root grows up and causes you trouble, or many of you will become defiled.*f* [16]No one should be immoral or godless like Esau, who sold his birthright for a single meal.*g* [17]You know that afterwards, when he wanted to inherit the blessing, he was rejected because he couldn't find any opportunity to repent, even though he begged for it with tears.*h*

[18]You have not come to something*a* that can be touched, to a blazing fire, to darkness, to gloom,*i* [19]to a trumpet's blast, or to a voice that made the hearers beg that not another word be spoken to them.*j* [20]For they couldn't endure the command that was given: "If even an animal touches the mountain, it must be stoned to death."*bk* [21]Indeed, the sight was so terrifying that Moses said, "I am trembling with fear."*cl* [22]Instead, you have come to Mount Zion, to the city of the living God, to the heavenly Jerusalem, to tens of thousands of angels joyfully gathered together,*m* [23]to the assembly*d* of the firstborn who are enrolled in heaven, to a judge who is the God of all, to the spirits of righteous people who have been made perfect,*n* [24]to Jesus, the mediator of a new covenant, and to the sprinkled blood that speaks a better message than Abel's.*o* [25]See to it that you don't ignore the one who is speaking. For if they didn't escaped when they ignored the one who warned them on earth, how much less will we escape*e* if we turn away from the one who is from heaven!*p* [26]At that time his voice shook the earth, but

---

a 12:18 Other mss. read *to a mountain*   **b** 12:20 Exod 19:12-13
c 12:21 Deut 9:19   **d** 12:23 Or *church*   **e** 12:25 The Gk. lacks *escape*

now he has promised, "Once more I will shake not only the earth but also heaven."ᵃᵃ ²⁷The expression "once more" signifies the removal of what can be shaken, that is, what he has made, so that what can't be shaken may remain.ᵇ ²⁸Therefore, since we are receiving a kingdom that can't be shaken, we must be thankful and worship God in reverence and fear in a way that pleases him. ²⁹For our God is an all-consuming fire.ᵇᶜ

Concluding Words

13 ¹Let brotherly love continue.ᵈ ²Stop neglecting to show hospitality to strangers, for by showing hospitalityᶜ some have had angels as their guests without being aware of it.ᵉ ³Continue to remember those in prison as if you were in prison with them, as well as those who are mistreated, because you also are liable to physical punishment.ᵈᶠ

⁴Let marriage be kept honorable in every way, and the marriage bed undefiled. For God will judge those who commit sexual sins, especially those who commit adultery.ᵍ

⁵Keep your lives free from the love of money, and be content with what you have, for Godᵉ has said, "I will never leave you or abandon you."ᶠʰ ⁶And so we can confidently say, "The Lord is my helper. I will not be afraid. What can anyone do to me?"ᵍⁱ

⁷Remember your leaders who have spoken God's word to you. Think about the impact of their lives, and imitate their faith.ʲ ⁸Jesus Christ is the same yesterday and today—and forever!ᵏ

⁹Stop being carried away by all kinds of unusual teachings. It's good for the heart to be strengthened by grace, not by food lawsʰ that have never helped those who follow them.ˡ ¹⁰We have an altar, and those who serve in the tabernacle have no right to eat at it.ᵐ

¹¹For the bodies of animals, whose blood is taken into the Sanctuary by the high priest as an offering for sin, are

---

a12:26 Exod 19:18   b12:29 Deut 4:24   c13:2 Lit. *by this*   d13:3 Lit. *are in the body*   e13:5 Lit. *he*   f13:5 Deut 31:6   g13:6 Ps 118:6   h13:9 Lit. *by foods*

12:26
ᵃExod 19:18;
Hag 2:6
12:27
ᵇPs 102:26;
Matt 24:35;
2Peter 3:10;
Rev 21:1
12:29
ᶜExod 24:17;
Deut 4:24; 9:3;
Ps 50:3; 97:3;
Isa 66:15;
2Thes 1:8;
Heb 10:27
13:1
ᵈRom 12:10;
1Thes 4:9;
1Peter 1:22; 2:17;
3:8; 4:8;
2Peter 1:7;
1John 3:11; 4:7,
20,21
13:2
ᵉGen 18:3; 19:2;
Matt 25:35;
Rom 12:13;
1Tim 3:2;
1Peter 4:9
13:3
ᶠMatt 25:36;
Rom 12:15;
1Cor 12:26;
Col 4:18;
1Peter 3:8
13:4
ᵍ1Cor 6:9;
Gal 5:19,21;
Eph 5:5;
Col 3:5-6;
Rev 22:15
13:5
ʰGen 28:15;
Deut 31:6,8;
Josh 1:5;
1Chr 28:20;
Ps 37:25;
Matt 6:25,34;
Phil 4:11-12;
1Tim 6:6,8
13:6
ⁱPs 27:1; 56:4,
11-12; 118:6
13:7
ʲHeb 6:12; 13:17
13:8
ᵏJohn 8:58;
Heb 1:12; Rev 1:4
13:9
ˡRom 14:17;
Eph 4:14; 5:6;
Col 2:4,8,16;
1Tim 4:3;
1John 4:1
13:10
ᵐ1Cor 9:13;
10:18

13:11
a Exod 29:14;
Lev 4:11,21-22;
6:30; 9:11; 16:27;
Num 19:3
13:12
b John 19:17-18;
Acts 7:58
13:13
c Heb 11:26;
1 Peter 4:14
13:14
d Mic 2:10;
Phil 3:20;
Heb 11:10,16;
12:22
13:15
e Lev 7:12;
Ps 50:14,23;
69:30-31; 107:22;
116:17; Hos 14:2;
Eph 5:20;
1 Peter 2:5
13:16
f Rom 12:13;
2 Cor 9:12;
Phil 4:18;
Heb 6:10
13:17
g Ezek 3:17; 33:2,
7; Acts 20:26,28;
Phil 2:29;
1 Thes 5:12;
1 Tim 5:17;
Heb 5:7
13:18
h Acts 23:1; 24:16;
Rom 15:30;
2 Cor 1:12;
Eph 6:19; Col 4:3;
1 Thes 5:25;
2 Thes 3:1
13:20
i Isa 40:11;
Ezek 34:23;
37:24; Zech 9:11;
John 10:11,14;
Acts 2:24,32;
Rom 4:24; 8:11;
15:33; 1 Cor 6:14;
15:15; 2 Cor 4:14;
Gal 1:1; Col 2:12;
1 Thes 1:10; 5:23;
Heb 10:22;
1 Peter 1:21; 2:25;
5:4
13:21
j Gal 1:5;
Phil 2:13;
2 Thes 2:17;
2 Tim 4:18;
1 Peter 5:10;
Rev 1:6
13:22
k 1 Peter 5:12

burned outside the camp.[a] [12]That is why Jesus, in order to sanctify the people by his own blood, also suffered outside the city gate.[b] [13]So we must go to him outside the camp and endure the insults he endured.[c] [14]For we don't have a permanent city here but are looking for the one that's coming.[d] [15]Therefore, through him we should always bring God a sacrifice of praise, that is, the fruit of lips that confess his name.[e] [16]We should stop neglecting to do good and to be generous, for God is pleased with such sacrifices as these.[f]

[17]Continue to obey your leaders and to be submissive to them. They watch over your souls because they will have to give an account. Let them do this with joy and not with grief, for that would be harmful to you.[g]

[18]Pray for us, for we are sure that we have a clear conscience and desire to live honorably in every way.[h] [19]I especially ask you to do this so that I may be brought back to you sooner.

[20]Now may the God of peace, who by the blood of the eternal covenant brought back from the dead our Lord Jesus, the Great Shepherd of the sheep,[i] [21]equip you for everything good[a] to do his will, accomplishing in us[b] through Jesus Christ what pleases him. To him be glory forever and ever![c] Amen.[j]

Final Greeting

[22]I urge you, brothers, to listen patiently to my encouraging message,[d] because I have written you a short letter.[e][k] [23]You should know that our brother Timothy has been set free. If he comes soon, he will be with me when I see you.[l]

[24]Greet all your leaders and all the saints. Those who are from Italy greet you.[m]

[25]May grace be with all of you![f][n]

13:23 *l* 1 Thes 3:2; 1 Tim 6:12 **13:24** *m* Heb 13:7,17 **13:25** *n* Titus 3:15

a 13:21 Other mss. read *for every good work*   b 13:21 Other mss. read *you*
c 13:21 Other mss. lack *and ever*   d 13:22 Or *word of exhortation*
e 13:22 Lit. *written you briefly*   f 13:25 Other mss. read *with all of you! Amen*

THE LETTER OF
JAMES

Greetings from James

1 [1]From[a] James, a servant[b] of God and of the Lord Jesus Christ, to the twelve tribes in the Dispersion. Greetings.[a]

Turn to God when Tested

[2]Consider it pure joy, my brothers, when you are involved in various trials,[b] [3]because you know that the testing of your faith produces endurance.[c] [4]But you must let endurance have its full effect, so that you may be mature and complete, lacking nothing.

[5]Now if any of you lacks wisdom, he should ask God, who gives to everyone generously without a rebuke, and it will be given to him.[d] [6]But he must ask in faith, without any doubts, for the one who has doubts is like a wave of the sea that is driven and tossed by the wind.[e] [7]Such a person should not expect to receive anything from the Lord. [8]He is a double-minded person, unstable in all he undertakes.[cf]

[9]A brother of low status should boast in his exalted status, [10]and a rich person in his lowliness, because he will fade away like a flower in the grass.[g] [11]For the sun comes up with its scorching heat and dries up the grass. The flower in it drops off, and its beauty is gone. That is how the rich person will fade away in his pursuits.

Our Desires Tempt Us

[12]How blessed is the person who endures temptation! When he has passed the test, he will receive the crown of life that God[d] has promised those who keep on loving him.[h] [13]When someone is tempted, he should not say, "I am being tempted by God," because God cannot be tempted by evil,

1:1
a Deut 32:26;
John 7:35;
Acts 2:5; 8:1;
12:17; 15:13;
26:7; Gal 1:19;
2:9; Titus 1:1;
1 Peter 1:1;
Jude 1:1

1:2
b Matt 5:12;
Acts 5:41;
Heb 10:34;
1 Peter 1:6; 4:13,
16

1:3
c Rom 5:3

1:5
d 1 Kings 3:9,
11-12; Prov 2:3;
Jer 29:12;
Matt 7:7; 21:22;
Mark 11:24;
Lk 11:9;
John 14:13; 15:7;
16:23;
1 John 5:14-15

1:6
e Mark 11:24;
1 Tim 2:8

1:8
f James 4:8

1:10
g Job 14:2;
Ps 37:2; 90:5-6;
102:11; 103:15;
Isa 40:6;
1 Cor 7:31;
James 4:14;
1 Peter 1:24;
1 John 2:17

1:12
h Job 5:17;
Prov 3:11-12;
Matt 10:22;
19:28-29;
1 Cor 9:25;
2 Tim 4:8;
Heb 12:5;
James 2:5;
1 Peter 5:4;
Rev 2:10; 3:19

a 1:1 The Gk. lacks From b 1:1 Or slave c 1:8 Lit. in all his ways
d 1:12 Lit. he; other mss. read God; still other mss. read the Lord

506

1:15
a Job 15:35;
Ps 7:14;
Rom 6:21,23

1:17
b Num 23:19;
1Sam 15:29;
Mal 3:6;
John 3:27;
Rom 11:29;
1Cor 4:7

1:18
c Jer 2:3;
John 1:13; 3:3;
1Cor 4:15;
Eph 1:12;
1Peter 1:23;
Rev 14:4

1:19
d Prov 10:19;
14:17; 16:32;
17:27; Eccl 5:1-2;
7:9

1:21
e Acts 13:26;
Rom 1:16;
1Cor 15:2;
Eph 1:13; Col 3:8;
Titus 2:11;
Heb 2:3;
1Peter 1:9; 2:1

1:22
f Matt 7:21;
Lk 6:46; 11:28;
Rom 2:13;
1John 3:7

1:23
g Lk 6:47;
James 2:14

1:25
h John 13:17;
2Cor 3:18;
James 2:12

1:26
i Ps 34:13; 39:1;
1Peter 3:10

1:27
j Isa 1:16-17;
58:6-7;
Matt 25:36;
Rom 12:2;
James 4:4;
1John 5:18

and he doesn't tempt anyone. [14]Instead, each person is tempted by his own desire, being lured and trapped by it. [15]When that desire becomes pregnant, it gives birth to sin, and when that sin grows up, it gives birth to death.[a]

Live As God's Children

[16]Stop being[a] deceived, my dear brothers! [17]Every generous act of giving and every perfect gift is from above and comes down from the Father who made the heavenly lights,[b] in whom there is no inconsistency or shifting shadow.[b] [18]In accordance with his will he made us his children by the word of truth, so that we might become the most important of his creatures.[cc]

[19]You must understand this, my dear brothers. Everyone should be quick to listen, slow to speak, and slow to get angry.[d] [20]For human anger does not produce God's righteousness. [21]So rid yourselves of everything impure and every expression of wickedness, and with a gentle spirit welcome the word planted in you that can save your souls.[e]

[22]Keep on being doers of the word, and not merely hearers who deceive themselves.[f] [23]For if anyone is a hearer of the word and not a doer, he is like a man who looks at himself in a mirror.[g] [24]For he studies himself carefully and then goes off and immediately forgets what he looks like. [25]But the one who looks at the perfect law of freedom and remains committed to it, thus proving that he is not a forgetful hearer but a doer of what it requires, will be blessed in what he does.[h]

[26]If anyone thinks that he is religious and does not bridle his tongue, but instead deceives himself,[d] his religion is worthless.[i] [27]A religion that is pure and stainless in the sight of God the Father is this: to take care of orphans and widows in their suffering, and to keep oneself unstained by the world.[j]

---

a *1:16* Or *Don't be*   **b** *1:17* Lit. *the Father of lights*   **c** *1:18* Lit. *a kind of first fruits among his creatures*   **d** *1:26* Lit. *his heart*

Stop Showing Partiality

2 ¹My brothers, stop practicing[a] your faith in our glorious Lord Jesus Christ by showing partiality.[a] ²Suppose a man wearing gold rings and fine clothes comes into your assembly,[b] and a poor man in dirty clothes also comes in. ³If you give special attention to the man wearing fine clothes and say, "Please take this seat," but you say to the poor man, "Stand over there" or "Sit on the floor at my feet,"[c] ⁴you have made false distinctions among yourselves and have become critics with evil motives, haven't you?

⁵Listen, my dear brothers! God has chosen the poor in the world to become rich in faith and to be heirs of the kingdom that he promised to those who love him, hasn't he?[b] ⁶But you have humiliated the man who is poor. Aren't rich people the ones who oppress you and drag you into court?[c] ⁷Aren't they the ones who blaspheme the excellent name by which you have been called? ⁸Nevertheless, you are doing the right thing if you obey the royal law in keeping with the Scripture, "Love your neighbor as yourself."[d] ⁹But if you show partiality, you are committing sin and will be convicted by the Law as violators.[e] ¹⁰For whoever keeps the whole Law but fails in one point is guilty of breaking all of it.[f] ¹¹For the one who said, "Never commit adultery,"[e] also said, "Never murder."[f] If you do not commit adultery but you murder, you become a violator of the Law.[g] ¹²You must make it your habit to speak and act like people who are going to be judged by the law of liberty.[h] ¹³For merciless judgment will come to the one who has shown no mercy. Yet, mercy triumphs over judgment.[i]

Faith Is Shown by Works

¹⁴What good does it do, my brothers, if someone claims to have faith but doesn't have any works? This kind of faith can't save him, can it?[j] ¹⁵Suppose a brother or sister doesn't have any clothes or daily food[k] ¹⁶and one of you tells them, "Blessings on you![g] Stay warm and eat heartily." If you don't

---

a2:1 Or *don't practice*   **b**2:2 Or *synagogue*   **c**2:3 Lit. *Sit at my footstool*   **d**2:8 Lev 19:18   **e**2:11 Exod 20:14; Deut 5:18   **f**2:11 Exod 20:13; Deut 5:17   **g**2:16 Lit. *Go in peace*

2:1
a Lev 19:15; Deut 1:17; 16:19; Prov 24:23; 28:21; Matt 22:16; 1Cor 2:8; James 2:9; Jude 1:16

2:5
b Exod 20:6; 1Sam 2:30; Prov 8:17; Matt 5:3; Lk 6:20; 12:21,32; John 7:48; 1Cor 1:26,28; 2:9; 1Tim 6:18; 2Tim 4:8; James 1:12; Rev 2:9

2:6
c Acts 13:50; 17:6; 18:12; 1Cor 11:22; James 5:6

2:8
d Lev 19:18; Matt 22:39; Rom 13:8-9; Gal 5:14; 6:2

2:9
e James 2:1

2:10
f Deut 27:26; Matt 5:19; Gal 3:10

2:11
g Exod 20:13-14

2:12
h James 1:25

2:13
i Job 22:6; Prov 21:13; Matt 6:15; 18:35; 25:41-42; 1John 4:17-18

2:14
j Matt 7:26; James 1:23

2:15
k Job 31:19-20; Lk 3:11

2:16
a 1John 3:18

2:18
b James 3:13

2:19
c Matt 8:29;
Mark 1:24; 5:7;
Lk 4:34;
Acts 16:17; 19:15

2:21
d Gen 22:9,12

2:22
e Heb 11:17

2:23
f Gen 15:6;
2Chr 20:7;
Isa 41:8; Rom 4:3;
Gal 3:6

2:25
g Josh 2:1;
Heb 11:31

3:1
h Matt 23:8,14;
Lk 6:37;
Rom 2:20-21;
1Peter 5:3

3:2
i 1Kings 8:46;
2Chr 6:36;
Ps 34:13;
Prov 20:9;
Eccl 7:20;
Matt 12:37;
James 1:26;
1Peter 3:10;
1John 1:8

3:3
j Ps 32:9

3:5
k Ps 12:3; 73:8-9;
Prov 12:18; 15:2

provide for their bodily needs, what good does it do?[a] [17]In the same way, faith by itself, if it doesn't have any works, is dead.

[18]But someone may say, "You have faith, and I have works." Show me your faith without any works, and I will show you my faith by my works.[b] [19]You believe that there is one God. That's fine! Even the demons believe that and tremble with fear.[c]

[20]Do you want proof, you foolish person, that faith without works is worthless? [21]Our ancestor Abraham was justified by works when he offered his son Isaac on the altar, wasn't he?[d] [22]You see that his faith was active with his works, and by his works faith was made complete.[e] [23]And so the Scripture was fulfilled that says, "Abraham believed God, and it was credited to him as righteousness."[a] So he was called God's friend.[f] [24]You see that a person is justified by works and not by faith alone.

[25]Likewise, Rahab the prostitute was justified by works when she welcomed the messengers[b] and sent them away on a different road, wasn't she?[g] [26]For just as the body without the spirit[c] is dead, so faith without works is also dead.

Speak Wisely

3 [1]Not many of you should become teachers, my brothers, because you know that we who teach[d] will be judged more severely.[h] [2]For all of us make many mistakes. If someone doesn't make any mistakes when he speaks, he is perfect and able to control his whole body.[i] [3]If we put bits into horses' mouths to make them obey us, we can guide their whole bodies as well.[j] [4]And look at ships! They are so big that it takes strong winds to drive them, yet they are steered wherever the pilot pleases by a tiny rudder.

[5]In the same way, the tongue is a small part of the body, yet it can boast of great achievements. A huge forest can be set on fire by a little flame.[k] [6]The tongue is a fire, a world of evil. Placed among the parts of our bodies, the tongue contaminates the whole body and sets on fire the course of life,

---

a 2:23 Gen 15:6   b 2:25 Other mss. read *spies*   c 2:26 Or *without breath*
d 3:1 The Gk. lacks *who teach*

and is itself set on fire by hell.[a][a] [7]For all kinds of animals, birds, reptiles, and sea creatures can be or have been tamed by the human species, [8]but no one can tame the tongue. It is an uncontrollable evil filled with deadly poison.[b] [9]With it we bless the Lord and Father, and with it we curse those who are made in God's likeness.[c] [10]From the same mouth come blessing and cursing. It shouldn't be like this, my brothers! [11]A spring cannot pour both fresh and brackish water from the same opening, can it? [12]My brothers, a fig tree cannot produce olives, nor a grapevine figs, can it? Neither can a salt spring produce fresh water.

Live Wisely

[13]Who among you is wise and understanding? Let him show by his good life that his works are done in humility born of wisdom.[d] [14]But if you have bitter jealousy and rivalry in your hearts, stop boasting and lying against the truth.[e] [15]That kind of wisdom doesn't come from above. No, it is worldly, self-centered, and demonic.[f] [16]For wherever jealousy and rivalry exist, there is disorder and every kind of evil.[g]

[17]However, the wisdom that comes from above is first of all pure, then peace-loving, gentle, willing to yield, full of compassion and good fruits, and without a trace of partiality or hypocrisy.[h] [18]A harvest of righteousness is grown from the seed of peace[b] planted by peacemakers.[i]

Stop Fighting with Each Other

4 [1]Where do those fights and quarrels among you come from? They come from your selfish desires that are at war in your bodies, don't they?[j] [2]You want something but don't get it, so you commit murder. You covet something but can't obtain it, so you quarrel and fight. You don't get things because you don't ask for them! [3]You ask for something but don't get it because you ask for it for the wrong reason—for your own pleasure.[k]

[4]You adulterers! Don't you know that friendship with

---

a 3:6 Gk. *Gehenna*, a reference to the realm of the dead   b 3:18 Lit. *is grown in peace*

3:6
a Prov 16:27;
Matt 15:11,18-20;
Mark 7:15,20,23

3:8
b Ps 140:3

3:9
c Gen 1:26; 5:1;
9:6

3:13
d Gal 6:4;
James 1:21; 2:18

3:14
e Rom 2:17,23;
13:13

3:15
f Phil 3:19;
James 1:17

3:16
g 1 Cor 3:3;
Gal 5:20

3:17
h Rom 12:9;
1 Cor 2:6-7;
1 Peter 1:22; 2:1;
1 John 3:18

3:18
i Prov 11:18;
Hos 10:12;
Matt 5:9;
Phil 1:11;
Heb 12:11

4:1
j Rom 7:23;
Gal 5:17;
1 Peter 2:11

4:3
k Job 27:9;
35:12 Ps 18:41;
66:18; Prov 1:28;
Isa 1:15;
Jer 11:11; Mic 3:4;
Zech 7:13;
1 John 3:22; 5:14

4:4
a Ps 73:27;
John 15:19; 17:14;
Gal 1:10;
1John 2:15

4:5
b Gen 6:5; 8:21;
Num 11:29;
Prov 21:10

4:6
c Job 22:29;
Ps 138:6;
Prov 3:34; 29:23;
Matt 23:12;
Lk 1:52; 14:11;
18:14; 1Peter 5:5

4:7
d Eph 4:27; 6:11;
1Peter 5:9

4:8
e 2Chr 15:2;
Isa 1:16;
James 1:8;
1Peter 1:22;
1John 3:3

4:9
f Matt 5:4

4:10
g Job 22:29;
Matt 23:12;
Lk 14:11; 18:14;
1Peter 5:6

4:11
h Matt 7:1;
Lk 6:37; Rom 2:1;
1Cor 4:5;
Eph 4:31;
1Peter 2:1

4:12
i Matt 10:28;
Rom 14:4,13

4:13
j Prov 27:1;
Lk 12:18

4:14
k Job 7:7;
Ps 102:3;
James 1:10;
1Peter 1:24;
1John 2:17

4:15
l Acts 18:21;
1Cor 4:19; 16:7;
Heb 6:3

4:16
m 1Cor 5:6

4:17
n Lk 12:47;
John 9:41; 15:22;
Rom 1:20-21,32;
2:17-18,23

the world means hostility with God? So whoever wants to be a friend of this world is an enemy of God.*a* [5]Or do you think the Scripture means nothing when it says that the Spirit that God*a* caused to live in us jealously yearns for us?**b***b* [6]But he gives all the more grace. And so it says,*c*

> "God opposes the arrogant
>   but gives grace to the humble."**c**

[7]So submit yourselves to God. Resist the devil, and he will run away from you.*d* [8]Come close to God, and he will come close to you. Cleanse your hands, you sinners, and purify your hearts, you double-minded.*e* [9]Be miserable, mourn, and cry. Let your laughter be turned into mourning, and your joy into gloom.*f* [10]Humble yourselves before the Lord, and he will exalt you.*g*

Stop Criticizing Each Other

[11]Stop criticizing*d* each other, brothers. Whoever makes it his habit to criticize his brother or to judge his brother is judging the Law and condemning the Law. But if you condemn the Law, you are not a doer of the Law but its judge.*h* [12]There is only one Lawgiver and Judge—the one who can save and destroy. So who are you to judge your neighbor?*i*

Don't Boast about Future Plans

[13]Now listen, you who say, "Today or tomorrow we will go to such and such a town, stay there a year, conduct business, and make money."*j* [14]You don't know what tomorrow will bring. What is your life? You are a mist that appears for a little while and then vanishes.*k* [15]Instead you should say, "If the Lord wants us to, we will live and do this or that."*l* [16]But you boast about your proud intentions. All such boasting is evil.*m*

[17]So anyone who knows what is right but fails to do it is guilty of sin.*n*

---

a4:5 Lit. *he*   **b**4:5 Exod 20:5; Num 11:29   **c**4:6 Prov 3:34 (LXX)
d4:11 Or *Don't criticize*

Advice for Rich People

5 ¹Now listen, you rich people! Cry and moan over the miseries that are overtaking you.*a* ²Your riches are rotten, your clothes have been eaten by moths,*b* ³your gold and silver are corroded, and their corrosion will be used as evidence against you and will eat your flesh like fire. You have stored up treasures in these last days.*c* ⁴Look! The wages that you kept back from the workers who harvested your fields are shouting out against you, and the cries of the reapers have reached the ears of the Lord of the Heavenly Armies.*d* ⁵You have lived in luxury and pleasure on earth. You have fattened your hearts for the day of slaughter.*e* ⁶You have condemned and murdered the one who is righteous, even though he didn't resist you.*f*

Be Patient

⁷So be patient, brothers, until the coming of the Lord. See how the farmer waits for the precious crop from his land, being patient with it until it receives the fall and the spring rains.*g* ⁸You, too, must be patient. Strengthen your hearts, because the coming of the Lord is near.*h* ⁹Stop complaining**a** about each other, brothers, or you will be condemned. Look! The Judge is standing at the door.*i*

¹⁰As an example of suffering and patience, brothers, take the prophets, who spoke in the name of the Lord.*j* ¹¹We consider those who endured to be blessed. You have heard about Job's endurance and have seen the purpose of the Lord—that the Lord is compassionate and merciful.*k*

Stop Swearing Oaths

¹²Above all, brothers, stop swearing**b** oaths by heaven or by earth or by any other object.**c** Instead, let your "Yes" mean yes and your "No" mean no, or you may fall under condemnation.*l*

The Power of Prayer

¹³Is anyone of you suffering? He should keep on praying. Is anyone cheerful? He should keep on singing psalms.*m*

---

a5:9 Or *don't complain*   **b**5:12 Or *don't swear*   **c**5:12 Lit. *oath*

5:1
a Prov 11:28;
Lk 6:24; 1 Tim 6:9

5:2
b Job 13:28;
Matt 6:20;
James 2:2

5:3
c Rom 2:5

5:4
d Lev 19:13;
Deut 24:15;
Job 24:10-11;
Jer 22:13; Mal 3:5

5:5
e Job 21:13;
Amos 6:1,4;
Lk 16:19,25;
1 Tim 5:6

5:6
f James 2:6

5:7
g Deut 11:14;
Jer 5:24; Hos 6:3;
Joel 2:23;
Zech 10:1

5:8
h Phil 4:5;
Heb 10:25,37;
1 Peter 4:7

5:9
i Matt 24:33;
1 Cor 4:5;
James 4:11

5:10
j Matt 5:12;
Heb 11:35

5:11
k Num 14:18;
Job 1:21-22; 2:10;
42:10; Ps 94:12;
103:8;
Matt 5:10-11;
10:22

5:12
l Matt 5:34

5:13
m Eph 5:19;
Col 3:16

5:14
a Mark 6:13; 16:18
5:15
b Isa 33:24;
Matt 9:2
5:16
c Gen 20:17;
Num 11:2;
Deut 9:18-20;
Josh 10:12;
1Sam 12:18;
1Kings 13:6;
2Kings 4:33; 9:5,
20; 20:2,4;
Ps 10:17; 34:15;
145:18;
Prov 15:29; 28:9;
John 9:31;
1John 3:22
5:17
d 1Kings 17:1;
Lk 4:25;
Acts 14:15
5:18
e 1Kings 18:42,45
5:19
f Matt 18:15
5:20
g Prov 10:12;
Rom 11:14;
1Cor 9:22;
1Tim 4:16;
1Peter 4:8

¹⁴Is anyone of you sick? He should call for the elders of the church, and they should pray for him and anoint him with oil in the name of the Lord.*a* ¹⁵And the prayer offered in faith**a** will save the person who is sick. The Lord will restore him to health,**b** and if he has committed any sins, he will be forgiven.*b*

¹⁶So keep on confessing your sins to one another and praying for one another, so that you may be healed. The prayer of a righteous person is powerful and effective.*c* ¹⁷Elijah was a man just like us, and he prayed earnestly for it not to rain, and it did not rain on the ground for three years and six months.*d* ¹⁸Then he prayed again, and heaven sent rain, and the ground produced its crops.*e*

¹⁹My brothers, if one of you wanders away from the truth and somebody brings him back,*f* ²⁰you may be sure that whoever brings a sinner back from his wrong path will save his soul from death and cover a multitude of sins.*g*

---

a *5:15* Lit. *the prayer of faith*   **b** *5:15* Lit. *will raise him up*

THE LETTER OF
FIRST PETER

Greetings from Peter

1 ¹From[a] Peter, an apostle of Jesus Christ, to the exiles of the Dispersion in Pontus, Galatia, Cappadocia, Asia, and Bithynia,[a] ²the people chosen according to the foreknowledge of God the Father through the sanctifying work of the Spirit to be obedient to Jesus Christ and to be sprinkled with his blood. May grace and peace be yours in abundance![b]

Our Hope and Joy Are in Christ

³Blessed be the God and Father of our Lord Jesus Christ! Because of his great mercy he has given us a new birth to an ever-living hope through the resurrection of Jesus Christ from the dead[c] ⁴and to an inheritance kept in heaven for you that can't be destroyed, corrupted, or changed.[d] ⁵Through faith you are being protected by God's power for a salvation that is ready to be revealed at the end of time.[e]

⁶In this you greatly rejoice, though now for a little while you have to suffer various kinds of trials,[f] ⁷so that the genuineness of your faith, which is more valuable than gold that perishes when it is tested by fire, may result in praise, glory, and honor when Jesus Christ is revealed.[g]

⁸Though you have not seen[b] him, you love him. And even though you don't see him now, you believe in him and rejoice with an indescribable and glorious joy,[h] ⁹because you are receiving the goal of your faith, the salvation of your souls.[i]

¹⁰Even the prophets, who prophesied about the grace that was to be yours, carefully researched and investigated this salvation.[j] ¹¹They tried to find out what era or specific time the Spirit of Christ in them kept referring to when he predicted the sufferings of Christ and the glories that would

---

a 1:1 The Gk. lacks From   b 1:8 Other mss. read known

1:1
a John 7:35;
Acts 2:5,9-10;
James 1:1

1:2
b Rom 1:7; 8:29;
11:2; Eph 1:4;
2Thes 2:13;
Heb 10:22; 12:24;
1Peter 2:9;
2Peter 1:2;
Jude 1:2

1:3
c John 3:3,5;
1Cor 15:20;
2Cor 1:3; Eph 1:3;
1Thes 4:14;
Titus 3:5;
James 1:18;
1Peter 3:21

1:4
d Col 1:5;
2Tim 4:8;
1Peter 5:4

1:5
e John 10:28-29;
17:11-12,15;
Jude 1:1

1:6
f Matt 5:12;
Rom 12:12;
2Cor 4:17; 6:10;
James 1:2;
1Peter 4:13; 5:10

1:7
g Job 23:10;
Ps 66:10;
Prov 17:3;
Isa 48:10;
Zech 13:9;
Rom 2:7,10;
1Cor 3:13; 4:5;
2Thes 1:7-12
James 1:3,
12; 1Peter 4:12

1:8
h John 20:29;
2Cor 5:7;
Heb 11:1,27;
1John 4:20

1:9
i Rom 6:22

1:10
j Gen 49:10;
Dan 2:44;
Hag 2:7;
Zech 6:12;
Matt 13:17;
Lk 10:24;
2Peter 1:19-21

1:11
a Ps 22:6; Isa 53:3;
Dan 9:26;
Lk 24:25-26,44,
46; John 12:41;
Acts 26:22-23;
1Peter 3:19;
2Peter 1:21
1:12
b Exod 25:20;
Dan 8:13; 9:24;
12:5-6,9,13;
Acts 2:4;
Eph 3:10;
Heb 11:13,39,40
1:13
c Lk 12:35; 17:30;
21:34;
Rom 13:13;
1Cor 1:7;
Eph 6:14;
1Thes 5:6,8;
2Thes 1:7;
1Peter 4:7; 5:8
1:14
d Acts 17:30;
Rom 12:2;
1Thes 4:5;
1Peter 4:2
1:15
e Lk 1:74-75;
2Cor 7:1;
1Thes 4:3-4,7;
Heb 12:14;
2Peter 3:11
1:16
f Lev 11:44; 19:2;
20:7
1:17
g Deut 10:17;
Acts 10:34;
Rom 2:11;
2Cor 5:6;
7:1 Phil 2:12;
Heb 11:13; 12:28;
1Peter 2:11
1:18
h Ezek 20:18;
1Cor 6:20; 7:23;
1Peter 4:3
1:19
i Exod 12:5;
Isa 53:7;
John 1:29,36;
Acts 20:28;
1Cor 5:7; Eph 1:7;
Heb 9:12,14;
Rev 5:9
1:20
j Rom 3:25;
16:25-26; Gal 4:4;
Eph 1:10; 3:9,
11 Col 1:26;
2Tim 1:9-10;
Titus 1:2-3;
Heb 1:2; 9:26;
Rev 13:8
1:21
k Matt 28:18;
Acts 2:24,33;

follow.*a* [12]It was revealed to them that they were not serving themselves but you in regard to the things that have now been announced to you by those who brought you the good news through the Holy Spirit sent from heaven. These are things that even the angels want to look into.*b*

Be Holy

[13]Therefore, prepare your minds for action, keep a clear head, and set your hope completely on the grace to be given you when Jesus Christ is revealed.*c* [14]As obedient children, stop being**a** shaped by the desires that you once had in your ignorance.*d* [15]Instead, just as the one who called you is holy, be holy in every aspect of your life.*e* [16]For it is written, "You must be holy, because I am holy."**b***f*

[17]If you call "Father" the one who judges everyone impartially according to what he has done, you must live reverently as long as you are strangers here.*g* [18]For you know that it was not with perishable things like silver or gold that you have been ransomed from the worthless way of life handed down to you by your ancestors,*h* [19]but with the precious blood of Christ, like that of a lamb without blemish or defect.*i* [20]He was known long ago before the foundation of the world, but for your good he became publicly known at the end of time.*j* [21]Through him you believe in God, who raised him from the dead and gave him glory. As a result, your faith and hope are in God.*k*

Love One Another

[22]Now that you have obeyed the truth**c** and have purified your souls to love your brothers sincerely, you must love one another intensely and with a pure heart.*l* [23]For you have been born again, not by a seed that perishes but by one that can't perish—by the living and everlasting word of God.**d***m* [24]For**n**

3:13; Eph 1:20; Phil 2:9; Heb 2:9; 1Peter 3:22 **1:22** *l* Acts 15:9; Rom 12:9-10; 1Thes 4:9; 1Tim 1:5; Heb 13:1; 1Peter 2:17; 3:8; 4:8; 2Peter 1:7; 1John 3:18; 4:7,21 **1:23** *m* John 1:13; 3:5; James 1:18; 1John 3:9 **1:24** *n* Ps 103:15; Isa 40:6; 51:12; James 1:10

---

a *1:14* Or *don't be*   **b** *1:16* Lev 11:44-45; Lev 19:2   **c** *1:22* Other mss. read *the truth through the Spirit*   **d** *1:23* Or *by the word of the living and everlasting God*

"all human life[a] is like grass,
    and all its glory is like a flower in the grass.
The grass dries up and the flower drops off,
25   but the word of the Lord lasts forever."[b][a]

This word is the good news that was announced to you.

Live as God's Chosen People

2 ¹Therefore, rid yourselves of every kind of evil and deception, hypocrisy, jealousy, and every kind of slander.[b] ²Like newborn babies, thirst for the pure milk of the word so that by it you may grow in your salvation.[c] ³Surely you have tasted that the Lord is good![d]

⁴As you come to him, the living stone who was rejected by people but was chosen and precious in God's sight,[e] ⁵you, too, as living stones, are building yourselves up into a spiritual house and a holy priesthood, so that you may offer spiritual sacrifices that are acceptable to God through Jesus Christ.[f] ⁶This is why it says in Scripture:[g]

"See, I am laying a chosen
    and precious cornerstone[c] in Zion.
The person who believes in him will never be
    ashamed."[d]

⁷So he is precious to you who believe, but to those who do not believe,[h]

"The stone that the builders rejected
    has become the cornerstone,[c]
⁸a stone they stumble over and a rock they
    trip on."[e][i]

They keep on stumbling because they disobey the word, as they were destined to do. ⁹But you are a chosen people, a royal priesthood, a holy nation, a people to be his very own and to proclaim the wonderful deeds of the one who called you out of darkness into his marvelous light.[j]

---

a 1:24 Lit. *all flesh*   b 1:25 Isa 40:6-8   c 2:6,2:7 Or *capstone*   d 2:6 Isa 28:16   e 2:8 Ps 118:22; Isa 8:14

1:25
a Ps 102:12,26;
Isa 40:8; Lk 16:17;
John 1:1,14;
1 John 1:1,3

2:1
b Eph 4:22,25,31;
Col 3:8; Heb 12:1;
James 1:21; 5:9;
1 Peter 4:2

2:2
c Matt 18:3;
Mark 10:15;
Rom 6:4;
1 Cor 3:2; 14:20;
Heb 5:12-13;
1 Peter 1:23

2:3
d Ps 34:8; Heb 6:5

2:4
e Ps 118:22;
Matt 21:42;
Acts 4:11

2:5
f Isa 61:6; 66:21;
Hos 14:2;
Mal 1:11;
Rom 12:1;
Eph 2:21-22;
Phil 4:18;
Heb 3:6;
13:15-16;
1 Peter 2:9; 4:11

2:6
g Isa 28:16;
Rom 9:33

2:7
h Ps 118:22;
Matt 21:42;
Acts 4:11

2:8
i Exod 9:16;
Isa 8:14; Lk 2:34;
Rom 9:22,33;
1 Cor 1:23;
1 Thes 5:9;
Jude 1:4

2:9
j Exod 19:5-6;
Deut 4:20; 7:6;
10:15; 14:2;
26:18-19;
John 17:19;
Acts 20:28; 26:18;
1 Cor 3:17;
Eph 1:14; 5:8;
Col 1:13;
1 Thes 5:4-5;
2 Tim 1:9;
Titus 2:14;
1 Peter 1:2;
Rev 1:6; 5:10

2:10
a Hos 1:9-10;
2:23; Rom 9:25
2:11
b 1Chr 29:15;
Ps 39:12; 119:19;
Rom 13:14;
Gal 5:16;
Heb 11:13;
James 4:1;
1Peter 1:17
2:12
c Matt 5:16;
Lk 19:44;
Rom 12:17;
2Cor 8:21;
Phil 2:15;
Titus 2:8;
1Peter 3:16
2:13
d Matt 22:21;
Rom 13:1;
Titus 3:1
2:14
e Rom 13:3-4
2:15
f Titus 2:8;
1Peter 2:12
2:16
g 1Cor 7:22;
Gal 5:1,13
2:17
h Prov 24:21;
Matt 22:21;
Rom 12:10; 13:7;
Phil 2:3;
Heb 13:1;
1Peter 1:22
2:18
i Eph 6:5;
Col 3:22;
1Tim 6:1 Titus 2:9
2:19
j Matt 5:10;
Rom 13:5;
1Peter 3:14
2:20
k 1Peter 3:14;
4:14-15
2:21
l Matt 16:24;
John 13:15;
Acts 14:22;
Phil 2:5;
1Thes 3:3;
2Tim 3:12;
1Peter 3:18;
1John 2:6
2:22
m Isa 53:9;
Lk 23:41;
John 8:46;
2Cor 5:21;
Heb 4:15
2:23
n Isa 53:7;
Matt 27:31;
Lk 23:46;
John 8:48-49;
Heb 12:3

[10]Once you were not a people,[a]
> but now you are the people of God.
Once you had not received mercy,
> but now you have received mercy.

Live as God's Servants

[11]Dear friends, I urge you as aliens and exiles to keep on abstaining from the desires of the flesh that wage war against the soul.[b] [12]Continue to live such upright lives among the Gentiles that, when they slander you as evildoers, they may see your good works and glorify God when he visits them in judgment.[ac]

[13]For the Lord's sake submit yourselves to every human authority: whether to the king as supreme,[d] [14]or to governors who are sent by him to punish those who do wrong and to praise those who do right.[e] [15]For it is God's will that by doing right you should silence the ignorant talk[b] of foolish people.[f] [16]Live like free people, and stop using[c] your freedom as an excuse for doing evil. Instead, be God's servants.[g] [17]Show honor to everyone. Keep on loving the brothers, fearing God, and honoring the king.[h]

Suffer Patiently

[18]You household servants must submit yourselves to your masters with all respect, not only to those who are kind and fair, but also to those who are unjust.[i] [19]For it is a fine thing if, when moved by your conscience to please God, you suffer patiently when wronged.[j] [20]What credit is it if you sin and patiently receive a beating for it? But if you suffer for doing good and take it patiently, you have God's approval.[k]

[21]This is, in fact, what you were called to do, because Christ also suffered for you and left an example for you to follow in his steps.[l] [22]"He never committed a sin, and no deceit was found in his mouth."[dm] [23]When he was insulted, he did not retaliate. When he suffered, he did not threaten but made it his habit to commit the matter to the one who judges fairly.[n] [24]He himself bore our sins in his body on the

---

a 2:12 Lit. *on the day of visitation*   **b** 2:15 Lit. *the ignorance*   **c** 2:16 Or *don't use*   **d** 2:22 Isa 53:9

tree, so that we might die to those sins and live for righteousness. By his wounds you have been healed.[a] 25For you were like sheep that kept going astray, but now you have returned to the Shepherd and Overseer of your souls.[b]

Wives and Husbands

3 1In a similar way, you wives must submit yourselves to your husbands so that, even if some of them refuse to obey the word, they may be won over without a word through your conduct as wives[c] 2when they see your pure and reverent lives.[d]

3Your beauty should not be an external one, consisting of braided hair or the wearing of gold ornaments and dresses.[e] 4Instead, it should be the inner disposition of the heart, consisting in the imperishable quality of a gentle and quiet spirit, which is of great value in the sight of God.[f] 5After all, this is how holy women who set their hope on God used to make themselves beautiful in the past. They submitted themselves to their husbands, 6just as Sarah obeyed Abraham and called him lord. You have become her daughters by doing good and by not letting anything terrify you.[g]

7In a similar way, you husbands must live with your wives with understanding, because they are the weaker sex.[a] Honor them as heirs with you of the gracious gift of life, so that nothing may interfere with your prayers.[h]

When You Are Wronged

8Finally, all of you must live in harmony, be sympathetic, love as brothers, and be compassionate and humble.[i] 9Don't pay others back evil for evil or insult for insult. Instead, bless them, because you were called to inherit a blessing.[j] 10For[k]

> "the person who wants to love life
>   and see good days

---

a 3:7 Lit. *the weaker vessel*

Cross references

2:24
[a] Isa 53:4-6,11; Matt 8:17; Rom 6:2,11; 7:6; Heb 9:28

2:25
[b] Isa 53:6; Ezek 34:6,23; 37:24; John 10:11,14,16; Heb 13:20; 1 Peter 5:4

3:1
[c] Matt 18:15; 1Cor 7:16; 9:19-22; 14:34; Eph 5:22; Col 3:18; Titus 2:5

3:2
[d] 1 Peter 2:12

3:3
[e] 1 Tim 2:9; Titus 2:3

3:4
[f] Ps 45:13; Rom 2:29; 7:22; 2Cor 4:16

3:6
[g] Gen 18:12

3:7
[h] Job 42:8; Matt 5:23-24; 18:19; 1Cor 7:3; 12:23; Eph 5:25; Col 3:19; 1Thes 4:4

3:8
[i] Rom 12:10,16; 15:5; Eph 4:32; Phil 3:16; Col 3:12; Heb 13:1; 1Peter 2:17

3:9
[j] Prov 17:13; 20:22; Matt 5:39; 25:34; Rom 12:14,17; 1Cor 4:12; 1Thes 5:15

3:10
[k] Ps 34:12; James 1:26; 1Peter 2:1,22; Rev 14:5

3:11
a Ps 37:27;
Isa 1:16-17;
Rom 12:18;
14:19; Heb 12:14;
3 John 1:11

3:12
b John 9:31;
James 5:16

3:13
c Prov 16:7;
Rom 8:28

3:14
d Isa 8:12-13;
Jer 1:8;
Matt 5:10-12;
John 14:1,27;
James 1:12;
1 Peter 2:19; 4:14

3:15
e Ps 119:46;
Acts 4:8; Col 4:6;
2 Tim 2:25

3:16
f Titus 2:8;
Heb 13:18;
1 Peter 2:12

3:18
g Rom 1:4; 5:6;
8:11; 2 Cor 13:4;
Col 1:21-22;
Heb 9:26,28;
1 Peter 2:21; 4:1

3:19
h Isa 42:7; 49:9;
61:1; 1 Peter 1:12;
4:6

3:20
i Gen 6:3,5,13;
7:7; 8:18;
Heb 11:7;
2 Peter 2:5

3:21
j Rom 10:10;
Eph 5:26;
Titus 3:5;
1 Peter 1:3

3:22
k Ps 110:1;
Rom 8:34,38;
1 Cor 15:24;
Eph 1:20-21;
Col 3:1; Heb 1:3

> must keep his tongue from evil
> and his lips from speaking deceit.
> [11]He must turn away from evil and do good.*a*
> He must seek peace and pursue it.
> [12]For the eyes of the Lord are on the righteous,*b*
> and his ears are attentive to their prayer.
> But the face of the Lord is against those who do
> wrong."*a*

[13]Who will harm you if you are devoted to doing what is good?*c* [14]But even if you should suffer for doing what is right, you are blessed. Never be afraid of their threats, and never get upset.*d* [15]Instead, exalt[b] Christ as Lord in your hearts. Always be prepared to give a defense to everyone who asks you to explain the hope you have.*e* [16]But do this with[c] gentleness and respect, keeping a clear conscience, so that those who speak evil of your good conduct in Christ will be ashamed of slandering you.*f* [17]After all, if it is the will of God, it is better to suffer for doing right than for doing wrong.

[18]For Christ also suffered[d] for sins once for all, an innocent person for the guilty, so that he could bring you[e] to God. He was put to death in the sphere of the flesh but was made alive in the sphere of the spirit,[fg] [19]in which state of existence[g] he went and made a proclamation to the spirits in prison[h] [20]who disobeyed long ago in the days of Noah, when God waited patiently while the ark was being built. In it a few, that is, eight persons, were saved by water.*i* [21]Baptism, which is symbolized by that water, now saves you also, not by removing dirt from the body, but by asking God for a clear conscience based on the resurrection of Jesus Christ,*j* [22]who has gone to heaven and is at the right hand of God, where angels, authorities, and powers have been made subject to him.*k*

---

a *3:12 Ps* 34:12-16   **b** *3:15* Or *set apart*   **c** *3:16* Lit. *But with*
d *3:18* Other mss. read *died*   **e** *3:18* Other mss. read *us*   **f** *3:18* Or *Spirit*
g *3:19* The Gk. lacks *state of existence*

Good Managers of God's Grace

4 [1]Therefore, since Christ suffered in the sphere of the flesh,[a] you, too, must arm yourselves with the same determination. For the person who has suffered in the sphere of the flesh has stopped sinning,[a] [2]so that he can live the rest of his time in the flesh guided, not by human desires, but by the will of God.[b] [3]For you spent enough time in the past doing what the Gentiles like to do, living in sensuality, sinful desires, drunkenness, wild celebrations, drinking parties, and detestable idolatry.[c] [4]They insult you now because they are surprised that you are no longer joining them in the same excesses of wild living.[d] [5]They will give an account to the one who is ready to judge the living and the dead.[e] [6]Indeed, this is why the gospel was proclaimed even to those who have died, so that they could be judged in the realm of the flesh like all humans and live in the realm of the spirit[b] like God.[f]

[7]The end of everything is near. So be sensible and clearheaded for the sake of your prayers.[g] [8]Above all, continue to love each other deeply, because love covers a multitude of sins.[h] [9]Show hospitality to one another without complaining.[i] [10]As good managers of God's grace in its various forms, serve one another with the gift each of you has received.[j] [11]Whoever speaks must speak God's words.[c] Whoever serves must serve with the strength[d] that God supplies, so that in every way God may be glorified through Jesus Christ. Glory and power belong to him forever and ever! Amen.[k]

Suffering as a Christian

[12]Dear friends, stop being[e] surprised by the fiery ordeal that is taking place among you to test you, as though something strange were happening to you.[l] [13]Instead, because you are participating in the sufferings of Christ, keep on rejoicing, so that you may be glad and shout for joy when

---

a4:1 Other mss. read *suffered for us*; still other mss. read *suffered for you*
b4:6 Or *Spirit*   **c**4:11 Lit. *If anyone speaks as the words of God*   **d**4:11 Lit. *Whoever serves as with the strength*   **e**4:12 Or *don't be*

4:1
a Rom 6:2,7; Gal 5:24; Col 3:3, 5; 1Peter 3:18
4:2
b John 1:13; Rom 6:11; 14:7; 2Cor 5:15; Gal 2:20; James 1:18; 1Peter 1:14; 2:1
4:3
c Ezek 44:6; 45:9; Acts 17:30; Eph 2:2; 4:17; 1Thes 4:5; Titus 3:3; 1Peter 1:14
4:4
d Acts 13:45; 18:6; 1Peter 3:16
4:5
e Acts 10:42; 17:31; Rom 14:10,12; 1Cor 15:51-52; 2Tim 4:1 James 5:9
4:6
f 1Peter 3:19
4:7
g Matt 24:13-14; 26:41; Lk 21:34; Rom 13:12; Phil 4:5; Col 4:2; Heb 10:25; James 5:8; 1Peter 1:13; 5:8; 2Peter 3:9,11; 1John 2:18
4:8
h Prov 10:12; 1Cor 13:7; Col 3:14; Heb 13:1; James 5:20
4:9
i Rom 12:13; 2Cor 9:7; Phil 2:14; Heb 13:2
4:10
j Matt 24:45; 25:14,21; Lk 12:42; Rom 12:6; 1Cor 4:1-2,7; 12:4; Eph 4:11; Titus 1:7
4:11
k Jer 23:22; Rom 12:6-8; 1Cor 3:10; Eph 5:20; 1Tim 6:16; 1Peter 2:5; 5:11; Rev 1:6
4:12
l 1Cor 3:13; 1Peter 1:7

4:13
a Acts 5:41;
Rom 8:17;
2Cor 1:7; 4:10;
Phil 3:10;
Col 1:24;
2Tim 2:12;
James 1:1-13;
1Peter 1:5-6; 5:1,
10; Rev 1:9
4:14
b Matt 5:11;
2Cor 12:10;
James 1:12;
1Peter 2:12,19-20;
3:14,16
4:15
c 1Thes 4:11;
1Tim 5:13;
1Peter 2:20
4:16
d Acts 5:41
4:17
e Isa 10:12;
Jer 25:29; 49:12;
Ezek 9:6; Mal 3:5;
Lk 10:12,14;
23:31
4:18
f Prov 11:31;
Lk 23:31
4:19
g Ps 31:5;
Lk 23:46;
2Tim 1:12
5:1
h Lk 24:48;
Acts 1:8,22; 5:32;
10:39;
Rom 8:17-18;
Rev 1:9
5:2
i John 21:15-17;
Acts 20:28;
1Cor 9:17;
1Tim 3:3,8;
Titus 1:7
5:3
j Ps 33:12; 74:2;
Ezek 34:4;
Matt 20:25-26;
1Cor 3:9;
2Cor 1:24;
Phil 3:17;
2Thes 3:9;
1Tim 4:12 Titus
2:7
5:4
k 1Cor 9:25;
2Tim 4:8;
Heb 13:20;
James 1:12;
1Peter 1:4
5:5
l Isa 57:15; 66:2;
Rom 12:10;
Eph 5:21; Phil 2:3;
James 4:6

his glory is revealed.[a] [14]If you are insulted because of the name of Christ, you are blessed, for the glorious Spirit of God is resting on you.[a][b]

[15]Of course, none of you should suffer for being a murderer, thief, criminal, or troublemaker.[c] [16]But if you suffer for being a Christian, don't feel ashamed, but glorify God with that name.[d] [17]For the time has come for judgment to begin with the household of God. And if it begins with us, what will be the outcome for those who refuse to obey the gospel of God?[e]

> [18]"If it is hard for the righteous person to be saved,[f]
> what will happen to the ungodly and sinful
> person?"[b]

[19]So then, those who suffer according to God's will should entrust their souls to a faithful Creator and continue to do what is good.[g]

Be Shepherds of God's Flock

5 [1]Therefore, as a fellow elder, a witness of Christ's sufferings, and one who shares in the glory to be revealed, I appeal to the elders among you:[h] [2]Be shepherds of God's flock that is among you, watching over it, not because you must but because you want to, and not greedily but eagerly, as God desires.[i] [3]Don't lord it over the people entrusted to you, but be examples to the flock.[j] [4]Then, when the Chief Shepherd appears, you will receive the crown of glory that will never fade away.[k]

Be Humble and Alert

[5]In a similar way, you young people must be submissive to the elders.[c] All of you must put on the apron of humility before one another, because[l]

> "God opposes the proud,
> but gives grace to the humble."[d]

---

a 4:14 Other mss. read *on you. For their sake he is being blasphemed, but for your sake he is being glorified.*   b 4:18 Prov 11:31 (LXX)   c 5:5 Or *to those who are older*   d 5:5 Prov 3:34 (LXX)

⁶Therefore, humble yourselves under the mighty hand of God, so that at the proper time he may exalt you.ᵃ ⁷Throw all your worry on him, because he cares for you.ᵇ ⁸Be clearminded and alert. Your opponent the devil is prowling around like a roaring lion, looking for someone to devour.ᶜ ⁹Resist him and be firm in the faith, because you know that your brothers throughout the world are undergoing the same kinds of suffering.ᵈ ¹⁰After you have suffered for a little while, the God of all grace, who called you in Christ Jesusᵃ to his eternal glory, will restore you, establish you, strengthen you, and support you.ᵉ ¹¹Power belongsᵇ to him forever and ever! Amen.ᶠ

Final Greeting

¹²Through Silvanus, whom I regard as a faithful brother, I have written this short letter to encourage you and to testify that this is the true grace of God. Stand firm in it!ᵍ

¹³Your sister churchᶜ in Babylon,ᵈ chosen along with you, sends you greetings, as does my son Mark.ʰ ¹⁴Greet one another with a kiss of love. Peace be to all of you who are in Christ!ᵉⁱ

---

a*5:10* Other mss. lack *Jesus*   b*5:11* Other mss. read *Glory and power belong*   c*5:13* Lit. *She who is*   d*5:13* I.e. Rome   e*5:14* Other mss. read *Christ Jesus! Amen*

5:6
ᵃJames 4:10
5:7
ᵇPs 37:5; 55:22;
Matt 6:25;
Lk 12:11,22;
Phil 4:6; Heb 13:5
5:8
ᶜJob 1:7; 2:2;
Lk 21:34,36;
22:31;
1Thes 5:6;
1Peter 4:7;
Rev 12:12
5:9
ᵈActs 14:22;
Eph 6:11,13;
1Thes 3:3;
1Peter 2:21
5:10
ᵉ1Cor 1:9;
2Cor 4:17;
2Thes 2:17; 3:3;
1Tim 6:12;
Heb 13:21;
Jude 1:24
5:11
ᶠ1Peter 4:11;
Rev 1:6
5:12
ᵍActs 20:24;
1Cor 15:1;
2Cor 1:19;
Heb 13:22;
2Peter 1:12
5:13
ʰActs 12:12,25
5:14
ⁱRom 16:16;
1Cor 16:20;
2Cor 13:12;
Eph 6:23;
1Thes 5:26

THE LETTER OF
SECOND PETER

1:1
a Rom 1:12;
2Cor 4:13;
Eph 4:5; Titus 1:4

Greetings from Peter

1 ¹From[a] Simeon[b] Peter, a servant[c] and apostle of Jesus Christ, to those who have obtained a faith that is as valuable as ours through the righteousness of our God and Savior, Jesus Christ.[a] ²May grace and peace be yours in abundance through the full knowledge of God and of Jesus our Lord![b]

1:2
b Dan 4:1; 6:25;
1Peter 1:2;
Jude 1:2

We Are Called to Holy Living

1:3
c John 17:3;
1Thes 2:12; 4:7;
2Thes 2:14;
2Tim 1:9;
1Peter 2:9; 3:9

³His divine power has given us everything we need for life and godliness through the full knowledge of the one who called us by his own glory and excellence.[c] ⁴Through these he has given us his precious and wonderful promises, so that through them you may participate in the divine nature, seeing that you have escaped the corruption that is in the world caused by evil desires.[d] ⁵For this very reason, you must make every effort to supplement your faith with moral character, your moral character with knowledge,[e] ⁶your knowledge with self-control, your self-control with endurance, your endurance with godliness, ⁷your godliness with brotherly kindness, and your brotherly kindness with love.[f] ⁸For if you possess these qualities and they continue to increase among you, they will keep you from being ineffective and unproductive in attaining a full knowledge of our Lord Jesus Christ.[g] ⁹For the person who lacks these qualities is blind and shortsighted and has forgotten the cleansing that he has received from his past sins.[h]

1:4
d 2Cor 3:18; 7:1;
Eph 4:24;
Heb 12:10;
2Peter 2:18,20;
1John 3:2

1:5
e 1Peter 3:7;
2Peter 3:18

1:7
f Gal 6:10;
1Thes 3:12; 5:15;
1John 4:21

1:8
g John 15:2;
Titus 3:14

1:9
h Eph 5:26;
Heb 9:14;
1John 1:7; 2:9,11

¹⁰So then, my brothers, be all the more eager to make your calling and election certain, for if you keep on doing this you will never fail.[i] ¹¹In this way you will be generously granted entry into the eternal kingdom of our Lord and Savior Jesus Christ.

¹²Therefore, I intend to keep on reminding you about

1:10
i 2Peter 3:17;
1John 3:19

---

a *1:1 The* Gk. lacks *From*   b *1:1* Other mss. read *Simon*   c *1:1* Or *slave* these things, even though you already know them and are firmly established in the truth that you now have.[a] [13]Yet I think it is right to refresh your memory as long as I am living in this bodily tent,[b] [14]because I know that the removal of my bodily tent will come soon, as indeed our Lord Jesus Christ has shown me.[c] [15]And I will make every effort to see that you will always remember these things after I am gone.

Pay Attention to God's Word

[16]When we told you about the power and coming of our Lord Jesus Christ, we didn't follow any clever myths. Rather, we were eyewitnesses of his majesty.[d] [17]For he received honor and glory from God the Father when the voice of the Majestic Glory was conveyed to him as follows: "This is my Son, whom I love. I am pleased with him."[e] [18]We ourselves heard this voice that came from heaven when we were with him on the holy mountain.[f] [19]Thus we regard the message of the prophets as confirmed beyond doubt, and you will do well to pay attention to it, as to a lamp that is shining in a gloomy place, until the day dawns and the morning star rises in your hearts.[g] [20]First of all, you must understand this: No prophecy in Scripture is a matter of one's own interpretation,[h] [21]because no prophecy ever originated through a human decision. Instead, men spoke from God as they were carried along by the Holy Spirit.[i]

Warning against False Teachers

2 [1]Now there were false prophets among the people, just as there also will be false teachers among you, who will secretly introduce destructive heresies and even deny the Master who bought them, bringing swift destruction on themselves.[j] [2]Many people will follow their immoral ways, and because of them the way of truth will be maligned.[a] [3]In their greed they will exploit you with deceptive words. The ancient verdict against them is still in force, and their destruction is not asleep.[k]

[4]For if God didn't spare angels when they sinned, but threw them into hell and committed them to chains[b] of

a 2:2 Or *blasphemed*   b 2:4 Other mss. read *pits*

Cross references

1:12
[a] Rom 15:14-15;
Phil 3:1;
1 Peter 5:12;
2 Peter 3:1,17;
1 John 2:21;
Jude 1:5

1:13
[b] 2 Cor 5:1,4;
2 Peter 3:1

1:14
[c] Deut 4:21-22;
31:14;
John 21:18-19;
2 Tim 4:6

1:16
[d] Matt 17:1-2;
Mark 9:2;
John 1:14;
1 Cor 1:17; 2:1,4;
2 Cor 2:17; 4:2;
1 John 1:1; 4:14

1:17
[e] Matt 3:17; 17:5;
Mark 1:11; 9:7;
Lk 3:22; 9:35

1:18
[f] Exod 3:5;
Josh 5:15;
Matt 17:6

1:19
[g] Ps 119:105;
John 5:35;
2 Cor 4:4,6;
Rev 2:28; 22:16

1:20
[h] Rom 12:6

1:21
[i] 2 Sam 23:2;
Lk 1:70;
Acts 1:16; 3:18;
2 Tim 3:16;
1 Peter 1:11

2:1
[j] Deut 13:1;
Matt 24:11;
Acts 20:30;
1 Cor 6:20; 11:19;
Gal 3:13; Eph 1:7;
Phil 3:19;
1 Tim 4:1;
2 Tim 3:1,5;
Heb 10:29;
1 Peter 1:18;
1 John 4:1;
Jude 1:4,18;
Rev 5:9

2:3
[k] Deut 32:35;
Rom 16:18;
2 Cor 2:17;
12:17-18;
1 Tim 6:5;
Titus 1:11;
2 Peter 1:16;
Jude 1:4,15

2:4
a Job 4:18;
Lk 8:31;
John 8:44;
1John 3:8;
Jude 1:6;
Rev 20:2-3

2:5
b Gen 7:1,7,23;
Heb 11:7;
1Peter 3:19-20;
2Peter 3:6

2:6
c Gen 19:24;
Num 26:10;
Deut 29:23;
Jude 1:7

2:7
d Gen 19:16

2:8
e Ps 119:139,158;
Ezek 9:4

2:9
f Ps 34:17,19;
1Cor 10:13

2:10
g Jude 1:4,7-8,10,
16

2:11
h Jude 1:9

2:12
i Jer 12:3;
Jude 1:10

2:13
j Rom 13:13;
1Cor 11:20-21;
Phil 3:19;
Jude 1:12

2:14
k Jude 1:11

2:15
l Num 22:5,7,21,
23,28; Jude 1:11

2:17
m Jude 1:12-13

deepest darkness to be kept for judgment;*a* ⁵and if he didn't spare the ancient world but protected Noah, a preacher of righteousness, and seven others when he brought the flood on the world of ungodly people;*b* ⁶and if he condemned the cities of Sodom and Gomorrah and destroyed them by burning them to ashes, making them an example to ungodly people of what is going to happen to them;*c* ⁷and if he rescued Lot, a righteous man who was greatly distressed by the immoral conduct of lawless people*d*—⁸for as long as that righteous man lived among them, day after day he was being tortured in his righteous soul by what he saw and heard in their lawless actions*e*—⁹then the Lord knows how to rescue godly people from their trials and to hold unrighteous people for punishment on the day of judgment,*f* ¹⁰especially those who satisfy their flesh by indulging in its passions and despise authority. Being bold and arrogant, they aren't afraid to slander glorious beings.*g* ¹¹Yet even angels, although they are greater in strength and power, do not bring a slanderous accusation against them from the Lord.*h*

¹²These people, like irrational animals, are mere creatures of instinct that are born to be caught and killed. They insult what they don't understand, and like animals they, too, will be destroyed,*i* ¹³suffering wrong as punishment for their wrongdoing. They take pleasure in wild parties in broad daylight. They are stains and blemishes, reveling in their deceitful pleasures*a* while they eat with you.*j* ¹⁴With eyes full of adultery, they can't get enough of sin. They seduce unsteady souls and have had their hearts expertly trained in greed. They are doomed to a curse.*bk*

¹⁵They have left the straight path and wandered off to follow the path of Balaam, the son of Bosor,*c* who loved the reward he got for doing wrong.*l* ¹⁶But he was rebuked for his offense. A donkey that normally can't talk spoke with a human voice and restrained the prophet's insanity. ¹⁷These men are dried-up springs, mere clouds driven by a storm. Gloomy darkness is reserved for them.*m* ¹⁸By talking high-sounding nonsense and using sinful cravings of the flesh

---

a 2:13 Other mss. read *in their love feasts*   **b** 2:14 Lit. *children of a curse*
c 2:15 Other mss. read *Beor*

they entice people who have just escaped from those who live in error.[a] [19]Promising them freedom, they themselves are slaves to depravity. For a person is a slave to whatever conquers him.[b]

[20]For if, after they have escaped the world's corruptions through a full knowledge of our Lord and Savior Jesus Christ and are again entangled and conquered by them, then their last condition is worse than their former one.[c] [21]It would have been better for them not to have known the way of righteousness than to know it and turn their backs on the holy commandment that was committed to them.[d] [22]The proverb is true that describes what has happened to them: "A dog returns to its vomit,"[a] and "A pig that is washed goes back to wallow in the mud."[e]

Be Ready for the Day of the Lord

3 [1]Dear friends, this is now the second letter I'm writing to you. In them I have been trying to stimulate your pure minds by reminding you[f] [2]to recall the words spoken in the past by the holy prophets and the commandment of our Lord and Savior spoken[b] through your apostles.[g]

[3]First of all you must understand this: In the last days mockers will come and, indulging in their own lusts, will ridicule us[h] [4]by saying, "What happened to his promise to return? Ever since our ancestors died,[c] everything continues as it did from the beginning of creation."[i] [5]But they deliberately ignore the fact that long ago the heavens existed and the earth was formed by God's word out of water and with water,[j] [6]by which the world at that time was deluged with water and destroyed.[k] [7]By the same word the present heavens and earth have been reserved for fire and are being kept for the day when ungodly people will be judged and destroyed.[l]

[8]Don't forget this fact, dear friends: With the Lord a single day is like a thousand years, and a thousand years are like a single day.[m] [9]The Lord is not slow about his promise, as some people understand slowness, but is being patient

---

a 2:22 *Prov* 26:11   b 3:2 *The* Gk. lacks *spoken*   c 3:4 Lit. *fell asleep*

2:18
a Acts 2:40;
2Peter 1:4,20;
Jude 1:16

2:19
b John 8:34;
Rom 6:16;
Gal 5:13;
1Peter 2:16

2:20
c Matt 12:45;
Lk 11:26;
Heb 6:4;
10:26-27;
2Peter 1:2,4,18

2:21
d Lk 12:47-48;
John 9:41; 15:22

2:22
e Prov 26:11

3:1
f 2Peter 1:13

3:2
g Jude 1:17

3:3
h 1Tim 4:1;
2Tim 3:1;
2Peter 2:10;
Jude 1:18

3:4
i Isa 5:19;
Jer 17:15;
Ezek 12:22,27;
Matt 24:48;
Lk 12:45

3:5
j Gen 1:6,9;
Ps 24:2; 33:6;
136:6; Col 1:17;
Heb 11:3

3:6
k Gen 7:11,21-23;
2Peter 2:5

3:7
l Matt 25:41;
2Thes 1:8;
2Peter 3:10

3:8
m Ps 90:4

3:9
a Isa 30:18;
Ezek 18:23,32;
33:11; Hab 2:3;
Rom 2:4;
1Tim 2:4;
Heb 10:37;
1Peter 3:20;
2Peter 3:15
3:10
b Ps 102:26;
Isa 51:6;
Matt 24:35,43;
Mark 13:31;
Lk 12:39;
Rom 8:20;
1Thes 5:2;
Heb 1:11;
Rev 3:3; 16:15;
20:11; 21:1
3:11
c 1Peter 1:15
3:12
d Ps 50:3; Isa 34:4;
Mic 1:4; 1Cor 1:7;
Titus 2:13;
2Peter 1:10
3:13
e Isa 65:17; 66:22;
Rev 21:1,27
3:14
f 1Cor 1:8; 15:58;
Phil 1:10;
1Thes 3:13; 5:23
3:15
g Rom 2:4;
1Peter 3:20;
2Peter 3:9
3:16
h Rom 8:19;
1Cor 15:24;
1Thes 4:15
3:17
i Mark 13:23;
Eph 4:14;
2Peter 1:10-12;
2:18
3:18
j Eph 4:15;
2Tim 4:18;
1Peter 2:2;
Rev 1:6

with you. He doesn't want anyone to perish, but everyone to come to repentance.*a* ¹⁰But the day of the Lord will come like a thief. On that day*a* the heavens will disappear with a roaring sound, the elements will be destroyed by fire, and the earth and everything done on it will be exposed.*b*

¹¹Since everything will be destroyed in this way, think of the kind of holy and godly people you ought to be*c* ¹²as you look forward to and hasten the coming of the day of God, by which the heavens will be set ablaze and dissolved and the elements will melt with fire.*d* ¹³But in keeping with his promise, we are looking forward to new heavens and a new earth, where righteousness is at home.*e*

¹⁴So then, dear friends, since you are looking forward to this, make every effort to have him find you without spot or fault and at peace.*f* ¹⁵Think of our Lord's patience as salvation, just as our dear brother Paul also wrote to you according to the wisdom given him.*g* ¹⁶He speaks about this subject in all his letters. Some things in them are hard to understand, which ignorant and unstable people distort to their own destruction, as they do the rest of the Scriptures.*h*

¹⁷And so, dear friends, since you already know these things, continually be on your guard not to be carried away by the deception of lawless people. Then you won't fall from your secure position.*i* ¹⁸Instead, continue to grow in the grace and knowledge of our Lord and Savior Jesus Christ. Glory belongs to him both now and for that eternal day! Amen.*bj*

---

a *3:10* Lit. *On it*   **b** *3:18* Other mss. lack *Amen*

THE LETTER OF
FIRST JOHN

Jesus, the Word of Life

1 ¹What existed from the beginning, what we have heard, what we have seen with our eyes, what we observed and touched with our own hands—this is the[a] Word of life![a] ²This life was revealed to us, and we have seen it and testify about it. We declare to you this eternal life that was with the Father and was revealed to us.[b] ³What we have seen and heard we declare to you so that you, too, can have fellowship with us. Now this fellowship of ours is with the Father and with his Son, Jesus Christ.[c] ⁴We are writing these things[b] so that our[c] joy may be full.[d]

Through Jesus We Have Fellowship with God

⁵This is the message that we have heard from him and declare to you: God is light, and in him there is no darkness—none at all![e] ⁶If we say that we have fellowship with him but keep living in the darkness, we are lying and the truth is not in us.[f] ⁷But if we keep living in the light as he himself is in the light, we have fellowship with one another, and the blood of Jesus his Son cleanses us from all sin.[g] ⁸If we say that we don't have any sin, we are deceiving ourselves and the truth is not in us.[h] ⁹If we confess our sins, he is faithful and righteous to forgive us those sins and cleanse us from all unrighteousness.[i] ¹⁰If we say that we have never sinned, we make him a liar and his word is not in us.

Christ Is Our Advocate

2 ¹My little children, I'm writing these things to you so that you won't sin. Yet if anyone does sin, we have an advocate with the Father—Jesus Christ, one who is righteous.[j] ²It is he who is the atoning sacrifice for our sins, and not for ours only, but also for the whole world's.[k]

³This is how we can be sure that we have come to know

---

a1:1 Lit. *about the*   b1:4 Other mss. read *these things to you*   c1:4 Other mss. read *your*

1:1
a Lk 24:39;
John 1:1,14;
20:27;
2Peter 1:16;
1John 2:13; 4:14

1:2
b John 1:1-2,4;
11:25; 14:6;
21:24; Acts 2:32;
Rom 16:26;
1Tim 3:16;
1John 3:5; 5:20

1:3
c John 17:21;
Acts 4:20;
1Cor 1:9;
1John 2:24

1:4
d John 15:11;
16:24; 2John 1:12

1:5
e John 1:9; 8:12;
9:5; 12:35-36;
1John 3:11

1:6
f 2Cor 6:14;
1John 2:4

1:7
g 1Cor 6:11;
Eph 1:7;
Heb 9:14;
1Peter 1:19;
1John 2:2; Rev 1:5

1:8
h 1Kings 8:46;
2Chr 6:36;
Job 9:2; 15:14;
25:4; Prov 20:9;
Eccl 7:20;
James 3:2;
1John 2:4

1:9
i Ps 32:5;
51:2 Prov 28:13;
1John 1:7

2:1
j Rom 8:34;
1Tim 2:5;
Heb 7:25; 9:24

2:2
k John 1:29; 4 42;
11:51-52;
Rom 3:25;
2Cor 5:18;
1John 1:7; 4:10,14

2:4
a 1John 1:6,8; 4:20

2:5
b John 14:21,23;
1John 4:12-13

2:6
c Matt 11:29;
John 13:15;
15:4-5;
1Peter 2:21

2:7
d 1John 3:11;
2John 1:5

2:8
e John 1:9; 8:12;
12:35; 13:34;
15:12;
Rom 13:12;
Eph 5:8;
1Thes 5:5,8

2:9
f 1Cor 13:2;
2Peter 1:9;
1John 3:14-15

2:10
g 2Peter 1:10;
1John 3:14

2:11
h John 12:35

2:12
i Lk 24:47;
Acts 4:12; 10:43;
13:38; 1John 1:7

2:13
j 1John 1:1

2:14
k Eph 6:10

him: if we continually keep his commandments. ⁴The person who says, "I have come to know him," but doesn't continually keep his commandments is a liar. The truth is not in that person.*ᵃ* ⁵But whoever continually keeps his word is the kind of person in whom God's love has truly been perfected. This is how we can be sure that we are in union with him:*ᵇ* ⁶The one who says that he remains in him must live the same way he himself lived.*ᶜ*

We Must Obey God's Commandments

⁷Dear friends, I am not writing to you a new commandment, but an old commandment that you have had from the beginning. This old commandment is the word you have heard.*ᵈ* ⁸On the other hand, I am writing to you a new commandment that is true in him and in you. For the darkness is fading away, and the true light is already shining.*ᵉ*

⁹The person who says that he is in the light but hates his brother is still in the darkness.*ᶠ* ¹⁰The person who loves his brother remains in the light, and there is no reason for him to stumble.*ᵍ* ¹¹But the person who hates his brother is in the darkness and lives in the darkness. He doesn't know where he is going, because the darkness has blinded his eyes.*ʰ*

¹²I am writing to you, little children,*ⁱ*
    because your sins have been forgiven
        on account of his name.
¹³I am writing to you, fathers,*ʲ*
    because you have known the one who
        has existed from the beginning.
I am writing to you, young people,
    because you have overcome the evil one.
¹⁴I have written to you, little children,*ᵏ*
    because you have known the Father.
I have written to you, fathers,
    because you have known the one who
        has existed from the beginning.
I have written to you, young people,
    because you are strong
    and because God's word remains in you
        and you have overcome the evil one.

¹⁵Stop loving**ᵃ** the world and the things that are in the world. If anyone persists in loving the world, the Father's love is not in him.ᵃ ¹⁶For everything that is in the world—the desire for fleshly gratification,**ᵇ** the desire for possessions,**ᶜ** and worldly arrogance—is not from the Father but is from the world.ᵇ ¹⁷And the world and its desires are fading away, but the person who does God's will remains forever.ᶜ

Live in Christ

¹⁸Little children, it is the last hour. Just as you heard that an antichrist is coming, so now many antichrists have appeared. This is how we know it is the last hour.ᵈ ¹⁹They left us, but they weren't part of us. For if they had been part of us, they would have stayed with us. They simply made it clear that none of them was really part of us.ᵉ

²⁰You have an anointing from the Holy One and know all things.ᵈᶠ ²¹I haven't written to you because you don't know the truth, but because you do know it and because no lie comes from the truth. ²²Who is a liar but the person who denies that Jesus is the Christ?**ᵉ** The person who denies the Father and the Son is the antichrist.ᵍ ²³No one who denies the Son has the Father. The person who acknowledges the Son also has the Father.ʰ

²⁴What you have heard from the beginning must remain in you. If what you've heard from the beginning remains in you, you will also remain in the Son and in the Father.ⁱ ²⁵The message that he himself declared to us is eternal life.ʲ ²⁶I've written**ᶠ** to you about those who are trying to deceive you.ᵏ ²⁷The anointing you received from him remains in you, and you don't need anyone to teach you. Instead, because his anointing teaches you about everything and is true and not a lie, remain in union with him as he taught you to do.ᵍˡ

We Are God's Children

²⁸Even now, little children, remain in union with him.

---

a 2:15 Or *Don't love*　　**b** 2:16 Lit. *for the flesh*　　**c** 2:16 Lit. *of the eyes*
d 2:20 Other mss. read *and all of you know*　　**e** 2:22 I.e. the Messiah
f 2:26 Lit. *written these things*　　**g** 2:27 The Gk. lacks *to do*

2:15
a Matt 6:24;
Rom 12:2;
Gal 1:10;
James 4:4

2:16
b Eccl 5:11

2:17
c 1Cor 7:31;
James 1:10; 4:14;
1Peter 1:24

2:18
d Matt 24:5,24;
John 21:5;
2Thes 2:3;
1Tim 4:1;
2Tim 3:1;
Heb 1:2;
2Peter 2:1;
1John 4:3;
2John 1:7

2:19
e Deut 13:13;
Ps 41:9;
Matt 24:24;
John 6:37;
10:28-29;
Acts 20:30;
1Cor 11:19;
2Tim 2:19

2:20
f Mark 1:24;
John 10:4-5;
14:26; 16:13;
Acts 3:14;
2Cor 1:21;
Heb 1:9;
1John 2:27

2:22
g 1John 4:3;
2John 1:7

2:23
h John 14:7,9-10;
15:23; 1John 4 15;
2John 1:9

2:24
i John 14:23;
1John 1:3;
2John 1:6

2:25
j John 17:3;
1John 1:2; 5:11

2:26
k 1John 3:7;
2John 1:7

2:27
l Jer 31:33-34;
John 14:26; 16 13;
Heb 8:10-11;
1John 2:20

2:28
a 1John 3:2; 4:17

2:29
b Acts 22:14;
1John 3:7,10

3:1
c John 1:12;
15:18-19; 16:3;
17:25

3:2
d Job 19:26;
Ps 16:11; Isa 56:5;
Matt 5:8;
Rom 8:15,18,29;
1Cor 13:12;
15:49; 2Cor 4:17;
5:7; Gal 3:26; 4:6;
Phil 3:21; Col 3:4;
2Peter 1:4;
1John 5:1

3:3
e 1John 4:17

3:4
f Rom 4:15;
1John 5:17

3:5
g Isa 53:5-6,11;
2Cor 5:21;
1Tim 1:15;
Heb 1:3; 4:15;
9:26;28;
1Peter 2:22,24;
1John 1:2

3:6
h 1John 2:4; 4:8;
3John 1:11

3:7
i Ezek 18:5-9;
Rom 2:13;
1John 2:26,29

3:8
j Gen 3:15;
Matt 13:38;
Lk 10:18;
John 8:44; 16:11;
Heb 2:14

3:9
k 1Peter 1:23;
1John 5:18

3:10
l 1John 2:29; 4:8

3:11
m John 13:34;
15:12; 1John 1:5;
2:7,23; 4:7,21;
2John 1:5

Then, when he appears, we will have confidence and will not turn away from him in shame at his coming.*a* [29]If you know that he is righteous, you also know that everyone who practices righteousness has been born from God.*ab*

3 [1]See what kind of love the Father has given us in letting us be called God's children! Yet that is what we are.*b* For this reason the world doesn't recognize us, because it didn't recognized him either.*c*

[2]Dear friends, we are now God's children, but what we will be like hasn't been revealed yet. We know that when Christ*c* is revealed we will be like him, because we will see him as he is.*d* [3]Everyone who has this hope based on him keeps himself pure, just as he is pure.*e*

[4]Everyone who keeps living in sin also practices disobedience. In fact, sin is disobedience.*f* [5]You know that he was revealed to take away sins,*d* and there isn't any sin in him.*g* [6]No one who remains in him goes on sinning. The one who goes on sinning hasn't seen him or known him.*h*

[7]Little children, don't let anyone deceive you. The person who practices righteousness is righteous, just as he is righteous.*i* [8]The person who practices sin belongs to the evil one, because the devil has been sinning since the beginning. The reason that the Son of God was revealed was to destroy the works of the devil.*j* [9]No one who has been born from God practices sin, because God's*e* seed remains in him. Indeed, he cannot go on sinning, because he has been born from God.*k* [10]This is how God's children and the devil's children are distinguished.*f* No person who fails to practice righteousness and to love his brother is from God.*l*

Love One Another

[11]This is the message that you have heard from the beginning: We should love one another.*m* [12]Don't be like Cain,*g* who was from the evil one and murdered his brother. And why did he murder him? Because his own deeds were evil

---

a *2:29* Lit. *from him*   **b** *3:1* Other mss. lack *Yet that is what we are.*
c *3:2* Lit. *he*   **d** *3:5* Other mss. read *our sins*   **e** *3:9* Lit. *his*   **f** *3:10* Lit. *are revealed*   **g** *3:12* Lit. *Not like Cain*

and his brother's were righteous.[a] [13]So don't be surprised, brothers, if the world hates you.[b]

[14]We know that we have passed from death to life, because we love one another. The person who doesn't love[a] remains in death.[c] [15]Everyone who hates his brother is a murderer, and you know that no murderer has eternal life remaining in him.[d] [16]This is how we have come to know love: Christ[b] gave his life for us. We, too, must give our lives for our brothers.[e] [17]Whoever has earthly possessions and notices a brother in need and yet withholds his compassion from him, how can the love of God remain in him?[f] [18]Little children, we must stop loving in word and in tongue, but instead love[c] in action[d] and in truth.[g]

[19]This is how we will know that we belong to the truth and how we will be able to establish our hearts in his presence.[h] [20]If our hearts condemn us, God is greater than our hearts and knows everything.[i] [21]Dear friends, if our hearts do not condemn us, we have confidence in the presence of God.[j] [22]Whatever we request we receive from him, because we keep his commandments and do what pleases him.[k] [23]This is his commandment: to believe in the name of his Son, Jesus Christ, and to love one another as he commanded us.[l] [24]The person who keeps his commandments remains in God,[e] and God remains in him.[f] This is how we can be sure that he remains in us: he has given us his Spirit.[m]

Test What People Say

4 [1]Dear friends, stop believing[g] every spirit. Instead, test the spirits to see whether they are from God, because many false prophets have gone out into the world.[n] [2]This is how you can recognize God's Spirit: Every spirit who acknowledges that Jesus Christ has come in the flesh is from God.[o] [3]But every spirit who doesn't acknowledge Jesus is not from God. This is the spirit of the antichrist. You have

---

2Peter 2:1; 1John 2:18; 2John 1:7; Rev 2:2 **4:2** [o]1Cor 12:3; 1John 5:1

---

a3:14 Other mss. read *doesn't love his brother*   **b**3:16 Lit. *he*   **c**3:18 The Gk. lacks *love*   **d**3:18 Or *work*   **e**3:24 Lit. *in him*   **f**3:24 Lit. *and he in him*   **g**4:1 Or *don't believe*

3:12
[a]Gen 4:4,8;
Heb 11:4;
Jude 1:11
3:13
[b]John 15:18-19;
17:14; 2Tim 3:12
3:14
[c]1John 2:9-11
3:15
[d]Matt 5:21-22;
Gal 5:21;
1John 4:20;
Rev 21:8
3:16
[e]John 3:16; 15:13;
Rom 5:8; Eph 5:2,
25; 1John 4:9,11
3:17
[f]Deut 15:7;
Lk 3:11;
1John 4:20
3:18
[g]Ezek 33:31;
Rom 12:9;
Eph 4:15;
James 2:15;
1Peter 1:22
3:19
[h]John 18:37;
1John 1:8
3:20
[i]1Cor 4:4
3:21
[j]Job 22:26;
Heb 10:22;
1John 2:28; 4:17
3:22
[k]Ps 34:15;
145:18-19;
Prov 15:20;
Jer 29:12;
Matt 7:8; 21:22;
Mark 11:24;
John 8:29; 9:31;
14:13; 15:7;
16:23-24;
James 5:16;
1John 5:14
3:23
[l]Matt 22:39;
John 6:29; 13:34;
15:12; 17:3;
Eph 5:2;
1Thes 4:9;
1Peter 4:8;
1John 2:8,10;
4:11,21
3:24
[m]John 14:23;
15:10; 17:21;
Rom 8:9;
1John 4:12-13
4:1
[n]Jer 29:8;
Matt 24:4-5,24;
Acts 20:30;
1Cor 14:29;
1Thes 5:21;
1Tim 4:1;

4:3
a 2Thes 2:7;
1John 2:18,22;
2John 1:7

4:4
b John 12:31;
14:30; 16:11;
1Cor 2:12;
Eph 2:2; 6:12;
1John 5:4

4:5
c John 3:31; 15:19;
17:14

4:6
d Isa 8:20;
John 8:47; 10:27;
14:17;
1Cor 14:37;
2Cor 10:7

4:7
e 1John 3:10-11,22

4:8
f 1John 2:4; 3:6,16

4:9
g John 3:16;
Rom 5:8; 8:32;
1John 3:16; 5:11

4:10
h John 15:16;
Rom 5:8,10;
Titus 3:4;
1John 2:2

4:11
i Matt 18:33;
John 15:12-13;
1John 3:16

4:12
j John 1:18;
1Tim 6:16;
1John 2:5,18; 4:20

4:13
k John 14:20;
1John 3:24

4:14
l John 1:14; 3:17;
1John 1:1-2

4:15
m Rom 10:9;
1John 5:1,5

4:16
n 1John 3:24; 4:8,
12

4:17
o James 2:13;
1John 2:28; 3:3,
19,21

4:18
p 1John 4:12

heard that he is coming, and now he is already in the world.*ᵃ*

⁴Little children, you belong to God and have overcome them, because the one who is in you is greater than the one who is in the world.*ᵇ* ⁵These people belong to the world. That's why they speak from the world's perspective,*ᵃ* and the world listens to them.*ᶜ* ⁶We belong to God. The person who knows God listens to us. Whoever does not belong to God does not listen to us. This is how we know the Spirit of truth and the spirit of deceit.*ᵈ*

God's Love Lives in Us

⁷Dear friends, let us continually love one another, because love comes from God. Everyone who loves has been born from God and knows God.*ᵉ* ⁸The person who does not love does not know God, because God is love.*ᶠ* ⁹This is how God's love was revealed among us: God sent his only*ᵇ* Son into the world so that we might live through him.*ᵍ* ¹⁰This is love: not that we have loved*ᶜ* God, but that he loved us and sent his Son to be the atoning sacrifice for our sins.*ʰ* ¹¹Dear friends, if this is the way God loved us, we must also love one another.*ⁱ* ¹²No one has ever seen God. If we love one another, God lives in us, and his love is perfected in us.*ʲ* ¹³This is how we know that we remain in him and he in us: he has given us his Spirit.*ᵏ*

¹⁴We have seen for ourselves and can testify that the Father has sent his Son to be the Savior of the world.*ˡ* ¹⁵God remains in the one who acknowledges that Jesus is the Son of God, and he remains in God.*ᵐ* ¹⁶We have come to know and believe in the love that God has for us. God is love, and the person who remains in love remains in God, and God remains in him.*ⁿ* ¹⁷This is how love has been perfected among us: we will have confidence on the day of judgment because, while we are in this world, we are just like him.*ᵒ* ¹⁸There is no fear where love exists.*ᵈ* Rather, perfect love banishes fear. For fear involves punishment, and the person who lives in fear has not been perfected in love.*ᵖ*

---

a 4:5 Lit. *from the world*   b 4:9 Or *unique*   c 4:10 Other mss. read *we loved*   d 4:18 Lit. *in love*

¹⁹We love[a] because he first loved us. ²⁰Whoever says, "I love God," but hates his brother is a liar. The one who doesn't love the brother whom he has seen can't love a God whom he hasn't seen.[a] ²¹This is the commandment that we have from him: the person who loves God must also love his brother.[b]

Faith Overcomes the World

5 ¹Everyone who believes that Jesus is the Christ[b] has been born from God, and everyone who loves the parent also loves the child.[c] ²This is how we know that we love God's children: we love God and keep his commandments.

³For this is the love of God: that we keep his commandments, and his commandments are not difficult,[d] ⁴because everyone who is born from God has overcome the world. Our faith is the victory that overcomes the world.[e] ⁵Who overcomes the world? Isn't it the person who believes that Jesus is the Son of God?[f]

⁶This man, Jesus Christ, is the one who came by water and blood—not with water only, but with water and with blood. The Spirit is the one who verifies this, because the Spirit is the truth.[g] ⁷For there are three witnesses[c][h]—⁸the Spirit, the water, and the blood—and these three are one. ⁹If we accept human testimony, God's testimony is greater, because it is the testimony of God and because he has testified about his Son.[i] ¹⁰The person who believes in the Son of God has this testimony in himself. The person who does not believe God[d] has made him a liar by not believing the testimony that God has given about his Son.[j]

¹¹This is the testimony: God has given us eternal life, and this life is found in his Son.[k] ¹²The person who has the Son has this life. The person who does not have the Son of God does not have this life.[l]

a4:19 Other mss. read *love him*; still other mss. read *love God*   b5:1 I.e. the Messiah   c5:7 Other mss. read *witnesses in heaven—the Father, the Word, and the Holy Spirit, and these three are one.* ⁸*And there are three witnesses on earth—*   d5:10 Other mss. read *the Son*

Cross references:
4:20 a1John 2:4; 3:12,17
4:21 bMatt 22:37,39; John 13:34; 15:12; 1John 3:23
5:1 cJohn 1:12-13; 15:23; 1John 2:22-23; 4:2,15
5:3 dMic 6:8; Matt 11:30; John 14:15,21,23; 15:10; 2John 1:6
5:4 eJohn 16:33; 1John 3:9; 4:4
5:5 f1Cor 15:57; 1John 4:15
5:6 gJohn 14:17; 15:26; 16:13; 19:34; 1Tim 3:16
5:7 hJohn 1:1; 10:30; Rev 19:13
5:9 iMatt 3:16-17; 17:5; John 8:17-18
5:10 jJohn 3:33; 5:38; Rom 8:16; Gal 4:5
5:11 kJohn 1:4; 1John 2:25; 4:9
5:12 lJohn 3:36; 5:24

5:13
a John 20:31;
1 John 1:1-2

5:14
b 1 John 3:22

5:16
c Job 42:8;
Jer 7:16; 14:11;
Matt 12:31-32;
Mark 3:29;
Lk 12:10;
John 17:9;
Heb 6:4,6; 10:26;
James 5:14-15

5:17
d 1 John 3:4

5:18
e James 1:27;
1 Peter 1:23;
1 John 3:9

5:19
f Gal 1:4

5:20
g Isa 9:6; 44:6;
54:5; Lk 24:45;
John 17:3; 20:28;
Acts 20:28;
Rom 9:5;
1 Tim 3:16;
Titus 2:13;
Heb 1:8;
1 John 5:11-13

5:21
h 1 Cor 10:14

Conclusion

13I've written these things to you who believe in the name of the Son of God so that you may know that you have eternal life.*a* 14This is the confidence that we have in him: if we ask for anything according to his will, he listens to us.*b* 15And if we know that he listens to our requests, we can be sure that we have what we ask him for.

16If anyone sees his brother committing a sin that does not lead to death, he should pray that God*a* would give him life. This applies to those who commit sins that do not lead to death. There is a sin that leads to death. I'm not telling you to pray about that.*c* 17Every kind of wrongdoing is sin, yet there are sins that do not lead to death.*d*

18We know that the person who has been born from God does not go on sinning. Rather, the Son**b** of God protects them, and the evil one cannot harm them.*e* 19We know that we are from God and that the whole world lies under the control of the evil one.*f* 20We also know that the Son of God has come and has given us understanding so that we may know the true God.**c** We are in union with the one who is true, his Son Jesus Christ. He is the true God and eternal life.*g*

21Little children, guard yourselves from idols.**d***h*

---

a *5:16* Lit. *he*   **b** *5:18* Lit. *the one who has been born*   **c** *5:20* Other mss. read *the true one*   **d** *5:21* Other mss. read *idols. Amen*

THE LETTER OF
SECOND JOHN

Greetings from John

¹From[a] the elder to the chosen lady and her children, whom I love in the truth, and not only I but also all who know the truth.[a] ²We love you because of[b] the truth that remains in us and will be with us forever. ³Grace, mercy, and peace will be with us from God the Father and from Jesus[c] Christ, the Father's Son, in truth and love.[b]

Living in the Truth

⁴I was overjoyed to find some of your children living in the truth, just as the Father has commanded us.[c] ⁵Dear lady, I am now requesting[d] that we continue to love each other. It is not as though I am writing to give you a new commandment, but one that we have had from the beginning.[d] ⁶This is love: that we live according to his commandments. This is his commandment, just as you have heard it from the beginning. You must live by it.[e]

We Must Reject False Teachers

⁷Many deceivers have gone out into the world. They refuse to acknowledge Jesus Christ as coming in the flesh. Any such person is a deceiver and an antichrist.[f] ⁸See to it that you don't destroy what we have[e] worked for, but that you receive your full reward.[g] ⁹Everyone who does not remain rooted in the teaching of Christ but goes beyond it does not have God. The person who remains rooted in the teaching of Christ has both the Father and the Son.[h] ¹⁰If anyone comes to you and does not bring this teaching, don't take him into your home or even greet him.[i] ¹¹The one who greets him shares in his evil deeds.

Final Greeting

¹²Although I have a lot to write to you, I would prefer

1:1
a John 8:32;
Gal 2:5,14; 3:1;
5:7; Col 1:5;
2Thes 2:13;
1Tim 2:4;
Heb 10:26;
1John 3:18;
2John 1:3;
3John 1:1

1:3
b 1Tim 1:2;
2John 1:1

1:4
c 3John 1:3

1:5
d John 13:34;
15:12; Eph 5:2;
1Peter 4:8;
1John 2:7-8; 3:11,
23

1:6
e John 14:15,21;
15:10; 1John 2:5,
24; 5:3

1:7
f 1John 2:22; 4:1-3

1:8
g Mark 13:9;
Gal 3:4;
Heb 10:32,35

1:9
h 1John 2:23

1:10
i Rom 16:17;
1Cor 5:11; 16:22;
Gal 1:8-9;
2Tim 3:5;
Titus 3:10

a 1:1 The Gk. lacks From   b 1:2 Lit. Because of   c 1:3 Other mss. read the Lord Jesus   d 1:5 Lit. requesting you   e 1:8 Other mss. read you have

1:12
a John 17:13;
1 John 1:4;
3 John 1:13

not to use paper and ink. Instead, I hope to come to you and talk with you face to face, so that our joy may be complete.*a*

[13]The children of your chosen sister greet you.*ab*

1:13
b 1 Peter 5:13

a *1:13* Other mss. read *you. Amen*

THE LETTER OF
THIRD JOHN

Greetings from John

¹From[a] the elder to my dear friend Gaius, whom I love in truth.[a]

Encouragement for Gaius

²Dear friend, I pray that you are doing well in every way and that you are healthy, just as your soul is healthy. ³I was overjoyed when some brothers arrived and testified about your faithfulness[b] and how you live according to the truth.[b] ⁴I have no greater joy than to hear that my children are living according to the truth.[c]

⁵Dear friend, you are faithful in whatever you do for the brothers, especially when they are strangers. ⁶They have testified before the church about your love. You will do well to send them on their way in a manner worthy of God. ⁷After all, they went on their trip for the sake of Christ's name,[c] accepting no support from the Gentiles.[d] ⁸Therefore, we ought to support such people so that we can become their helpers in spreading[d] the truth.

Criticism of Diotrephes

⁹I wrote a letter[e] to the church, but Diotrephes, who loves to be in charge, won't accept us. ¹⁰For this reason, when I come I will call attention to what he is doing in spreading false charges against us. And not content with that, he refuses to accept the brothers. He even tries to stop those who want to accept them and throws them out of the church.

Praise for Demetrius

¹¹Dear friend, don't imitate what is evil, but what is good. The person who does what is good is from God. The person who does what is evil has never seen God.[e]

---

a *1:1 The* Gk. lacks *From* **b** *1:3* Lit. *about your truth* **c** *1:7* Lit. *for the sake of the name* **d** *1:8 The* Gk. lacks *spreading* **e** *1:9* Lit. *wrote something*

1:1
a 2John 1:1

1:3
b 2John 1:4

1:4
c 1Cor 4:15

1:7
d 1Cor 9:12,15

1:11
e Ps 37:27;
Isa 1:16-17;
1Peter 3:11;
1John 2:29; 3:6,9

1:12
a John 21:24;
1 Tim 3:7

[12]Demetrius has received a good report from everyone, including the truth itself. We, too, can testify to this, and you know that our testimony is true.[a]

Final Greeting

[13]Although I have a lot to write to you, I would rather not write with pen and ink.[b] [14]Instead, I hope to see you soon and talk face to face.

1:13
b 2 John 1:12

[15]May peace be with you! Your friends greet you. Greet each of our friends by name.

THE LETTER OF
JUDE

Greetings from Jude

¹From[a] Jude, a servant[b] of Jesus Christ but a brother of James, to those who have been called, who are loved[c] by God the Father and kept safe by Jesus Christ.[a] ²May mercy, peace, and love be yours in abundance![b]

Warning about False Teachers

³Dear friends, although I was eager to write to you about the salvation we share, I found it necessary to write to you and urge you to continue your vigorous defense of the faith that was passed down to the saints once and for all.[c] ⁴For some people have slipped in among you unnoticed. They were written about long ago as being deserving of this condemnation because they are ungodly. They turn the grace of our God into uncontrollable lust and deny our only Master and Lord, Jesus Christ.[d]

⁵Now I want to remind you, even though you are fully aware of these things, that the Lord who once saved his people from the land of Egypt later destroyed those who did not believe.[e] ⁶He has also held in eternal chains those angels who did not keep their own position but abandoned their assigned place. They are held in deepest darkness for judgment on the great day.[d][f] ⁷Likewise, Sodom and Gomorrah and the cities near them, which like them committed sexual sins and engaged in homosexual activities,[e] serve as an example of the punishment of eternal fire.[g]

⁸In a similar way, these dreamers also defile their flesh, reject the Lord's authority,[f] and slander his angels.[g][h] ⁹Even the archangel Michael, when he argued with the devil and fought over the body of Moses, did not dare to bring a slanderous accusation against him. Instead, he said, "May

1:1
[a] Lk 6:16;
John 17:11-12,15;
Acts 1:13;
Rom 1:7;
1 Peter 1:5

1:2
[b] 1 Peter 1:2;
2 Peter 1:2

1:3
[c] Phil 1:27;
1 Tim 1:18; 6:12;
2 Tim 1:13; 4:7;
Titus 1:4

1:4
[d] Rom 9:21-22;
Gal 2:4;
Titus 1:16; 2:11;
Heb 12:15;
1 Peter 2:8;
2 Peter 2:1,10;
1 John 2:22

1:5
[e] Num 14:29,37;
26:64; Ps 106:26;
1 Cor 10:9;
Heb 3:17,19

1:6
[f] John 8:44;
2 Peter 2:4;
Rev 20:10

1:7
[g] Gen 19:24;
Deut 29:23;
2 Peter 2:6

1:8
[h] Exod 22:28;
2 Peter 2:10

---

a 1:1 The Gk. lacks *From*   **b** 1:1 Or *slave*   **c** 1:1 Other mss. read *sanctified*
d 1:6 I.e. the day of judgment   **e** 1:7 Lit. *went after other flesh*   **f** 1:8 Lit. *reject dominions*   **g** 1:8 Lit. *glories*

1:9
a Dan 10:13; 12:1;
Zech 3:2;
2Peter 2:11;
Rev 12:7

1:10
b 2Peter 2:12

1:11
c Gen 4:5;
Num 16:1; 22:7,
21; 2Peter 2:15;
1John 3:12

1:12
d Prov 25:14;
Matt 15:13;
1Cor 11:21;
Eph 4:14;
2Peter 2:13,17

1:13
e Isa 57:20;
Phil 3:19;
2Peter 2:17

1:14
f Gen 5:18;
Deut 33:2;
Dan 7:10;
Zech 14:5;
Matt 25:31;
2Thes 1:7; Rev 1:7

1:15
g 1Sam 2:3;
Ps 31:18; 94:4;
Mal 3:13

1:16
h Prov 28:21;
James 2:1,9;
2Peter 2:18

1:17
i 2Peter 3:2

1:18
j 1Tim 4:1;
2Tim 3:1; 4:3;
2Peter 2:1; 3:3

1:19
k Prov 18:1;
Ezek 14:7;
Hos 4:14; 9:10;
1Cor 2:14;
Heb 10:25;
James 3:15

the Lord reprimand you!"[a][a] [10]Whatever these people don't understand, they slander. Like irrational animals, they are destroyed by the very things they know by instinct.[b] [11]How terrible it will be for them! For they followed the path of Cain, rushed headlong into Balaam's error to make a profit, and destroyed themselves in Korah's rebellion.[c] [12]These people are stains on your love feasts.[b] They feast with you without any sense of awe.[c] They are shepherds who care only for themselves. They are waterless clouds blown about by the winds. They are autumn trees that are fruitless, twice dead, and uprooted.[d] [13]They are wild waves of the sea, churning up the foam of their own shame. They are wandering stars for whom the deepest darkness has been reserved forever.[e]

[14]Enoch, in the seventh generation from Adam, prophesied about these people when he said,[f]

> "Look! The Lord has come with countless
> thousands of his holy ones. [15]He will execute
> judgment on all people and convict everyone
> of all the ungodly things that they have done
> in such an ungodly way, including all the
> harsh things that these ungodly sinners have
> said about him."[d][g]

[16]These people are complainers and faultfinders, following their own desires. Their mouths speak arrogant things, and they flatter people in order to take advantage of them.[h]

Advice to the Readers

[17]But you, dear friends, must remember the statements and predictions of the apostles of our Lord Jesus Christ.[i] [18]They kept telling you, "In the last times skeptics[e] will appear, following their own ungodly desires."[j] [19]These are the people who cause divisions. They are worldly, devoid of the Spirit.[k]

---

a *1:9* This incident is possibly based on *The Assumption of Moses,* an apocryphal Jewish writing.   **b** *1:12 Some* early Christians had a meal along with the Lord's Supper.   **c** *1:12* Or *without fear*   **d** *1:15* 1 Enoch 1:9 (*The Apocrypha*)   **e** *1:18* Or *scoffers*

²⁰But you, dear friends, must continue to build your-selves up on your most holy faith. Pray in the Holy Spirit,[a] ²¹and remain in God's love as you look for the mercy of our Lord Jesus Christ that brings eternal life.[b] ²²Show mercy to those who have doubts. ²³Save others by snatching them from the fire. To others, show mercy, but with fear, hating even the clothes stained by their sinful lives.[a][c]

Final Prayer

²⁴Now to the one who is able to keep you from falling and to make you stand faultless in his glorious presence with rejoicing,[d] ²⁵to the only God, our Savior, through Jesus Christ our Lord, be glory, majesty, power, and authority before all time and for all eternity! Amen.[e]

---

[a]1:23 Lit. *by their flesh*

1:20
[a]Rom 8:26;
Eph 6:18; Col 2:7;
1Tim 1:4

1:21
[b]Titus 2:13;
2Peter 3:12

1:23
[c]Amos 4:11;
Zech 3:2,4-5;
Rom 11:14;
1Cor 3:15;
1Tim 4:16;
Rev 3:4

1:24
[d]Rom 16:25;
Eph 3:20;
Col 1:22

1:25
[e]Rom 16:27;
1Tim 1:17; 2:3

THE BOOK OF
REVELATION

1:1
a John 3:32; 8:26;
12:49; Rev 4:1,3;
22:16

1:2
b 1Cor 1:6;
1John 1:1;
Rev 6:9; 12:9,17

1:3
c Lk 11:28;
Rom 13:11;
James 5:8;
1Peter 4:7;
Rev 22:7,10

1:4
d Exod 3:14;
Zech 3:9; 4:10;
John 1:1; Rev 3:1,
8; 4:5; 5:6

1:5
e John 8:14; 13:34;
15:9; 1Cor 15:20;
Gal 2:20;
Eph 1:20;
Col 1:18;
1Tim 6:13;
Heb 9:14;
1John 1:7;
Rev 3:14; 17:14;
19:16

1:6
f 1Tim 6:16;
Heb 13:21;
1Peter 2:5,9; 4:11;
5:11; Rev 5:10;
20:6

1:7
g Dan 7:13;
Zech 12:10;
Matt 24:30; 26:64;
John 19:37;
Acts 1:11

1:8
h Isa 41:4; 44:6;
48:12; Rev 2:8;
4:8; 5:17; 11:17;
16:5; 21:6;
22:4,11,13

1:9
i Rom 8:17;
Phil 1:7; 4:14;
2Tim 1:8; 2:12;
Rev 6:2,9

The Revelation of Jesus Christ to the Seven Churches

1 ¹This is the revelation of Jesus Christ, which God gave to him to show his servants the things that must happen soon. He made it known by sending his angel to his servant John,*a* ²who testified to what he saw: the word of God and the testimony about Jesus Christ.*b* ³How blessed is the one who reads aloud and those who hear the words of this prophecy and keep what is written in it, for the time is near!*c*

⁴From*a* John to the seven churches in Asia. May grace and peace be yours from the one who is, the one who was, and the one who is coming, from the seven spirits who are in front of his throne,*d* ⁵and from Jesus Christ, the witness, the faithful one,*b* the firstborn from the dead, and the ruler over the kings of the earth. To the one who loves us and has freed*c* us from our sins by his blood*e* ⁶and has made us a kingdom, priests for his God and Father, be glory and power forever and ever! Amen.*f*

> ⁷*Look! He is coming in the clouds.*g*
> *Every eye will see him, even those who*
> *pierced him,*
> *and all the tribes of the earth will mourn*
> *because of him.*

So be it! Amen.

⁸"I am the Alpha and the Omega," says the Lord God, the one who is, the one who was, and the one who is coming, the Almighty.*h*

⁹I am John, your brother and partner in suffering, ruling, and enduring because of Jesus. I was on the island called Patmos because of the word of God and the testimony about Jesus.*i* ¹⁰I was in the Spirit on the Lord's day when I heard

---

a 1:4 The Gk. lacks *From*　**b** 1:5 Or *Jesus Christ, the faithful witness*
c 1:5 Other mss. read *has washed*

a loud voice behind me like a trumpet.[a] [11]It was saying, "Write on a scroll what you see, and send it to the seven churches: Ephesus, Smyrna, Pergamum, Thyatira, Sardis, Philadelphia, and Laodicea."[b]

[12]Then I turned to see the voice that was talking to me, and when I turned I saw seven gold lampstands.[c] [13]Among the lampstands there was someone like the Son of Man. He was wearing a long robe and a gold belt around his waist.[d] [14]His head and his hair were white like wool, in fact, as white as snow. His eyes were like flames of fire,[e] [15]his feet were like glowing bronze refined in a furnace, and his voice was like the sound of raging waters.[f] [16]In his right hand he held seven stars, and out of his mouth came a sharp, two-edged sword. His face was like the sun when it shines with full force.[g]

[17]When I saw him, I fell down at his feet like a dead man. But he placed his right hand on me and said, "Stop being afraid! I am the first and the last,[h] [18]the living one. I was dead, but look—I am alive forever and ever! I have the keys of Death and Hades.[a][i] [19]Therefore, write down what you have seen, what is, and what is going to happen after this.[j] [20]The secret meaning of the seven stars that you saw in my right hand and the seven gold lampstands is this: the seven stars are the messengers[b] of the seven churches, and the seven lampstands are the seven churches."[k]

The Letter to the Church in Ephesus

2 [1]"To the messenger[c] of the church in Ephesus, write:[l]

'The one who holds the seven stars in his right hand, the one who walks among the seven gold lampstands, says:

[2]'I know your works, your toil, and your endurance. I also know that you cannot tolerate evil people. You have tested those who call themselves apostles, but are not, and have found them to be false.[m] [3]You have endured and suffered because of my name, yet

---

a1:18 I.e. the realm of the dead   b1:20 Or angels   c2:1 Or angel

1:10
a John 20:26;
Acts 10:10; 20:7;
1Cor 16:2;
2Cor 12:2;
Rev 4:1-2; 10:8;
17:3; 21:10

1:11
b Rev 1:8,17

1:12
c Exod 25:37;
Zech 4:2;
Rev 1:20

1:13
d Ezek 1:26;
Dan 7:13; 10:5.
16; Rev 2:1;
14:14; 15:6

1:14
e Dan 7:9; 10:6;
Rev 2:18; 19:12

1:15
f Ezek 1:7; 43:2;
Dan 10:6;
Rev 2:18; 14:2;
19:6

1:16
g Isa 49:2;
Acts 26:13;
Eph 6:17;
Heb 4:12;
Rev 1:20; 2:1,12.
16; 3:1; 10:1;
19:15,21

1:17
h Isa 41:4; 44:6;
48:12; Ezek 1:28;
Dan 8:18; 10:10;
Rev 2:8; 22:11,13

1:18
i Ps 68:20;
Rom 6:9; Rev 4:9;
5:14; 20:1

1:19
j Rev 1:12; 2:1;
4:1

1:20
k Zech 4:2;
Mal 2:7;
Matt 5:15;
Phil 2:15;
Rev 1:12,16; 2:1

2:1
l Rev 1:13,16,20

2:2
m Ps 1:6;
2Cor 11:13;
2Peter 2:1;
1John 4:1;
Rev 1:9,13,19;
3:1,8,15

2:3
a Gal 6:9;
Heb 12:3,5

2:5
b Matt 21:41,43

2:6
c Rev 2:15

2:7
d Gen 2:9;
Matt 11:15; 13:9,
43; Rev 2:9,11,
17,29; 3:6,13,22;
22:2,14

2:8
e Rev 1:8,17-18

2:9
f Lk 12:21;
Rom 2:17,28-29;
9:6; 1Tim 6:18;
James 2:5;
Rev 2:2; 3:9

2:10
g Matt 10:22;
24:13 James 1:12;
Rev 3:11

2:11
h Rev 2:7; 13:9;
20:14; 21:8

2:12
i Rev 1:16

you have not grown weary.*a* ⁴However, I have this against you: You have abandoned the love you had at first. ⁵Therefore, remember how far you have fallen. Repent, and do the works you did at first. If you don't, I will come to you and remove your lampstand from its place, unless you repent.*b* ⁶But this is to your credit: You hate the works of the Nicolaitans, which I also hate.*c*

⁷'Let the person who has an ear listen to what the Spirit says to the churches. To everyone who conquers I will give the privilege of eating from the tree of life that is in the paradise of God.'*d*

The Letter to the Church in Smyrna

⁸"To the messenger*a* of the church in Smyrna, write:*e*

'The first and the last, who was dead and became alive, says this: ⁹I know your suffering, your poverty—though you are rich—and the slander on the part of those who claim to be Jews but aren't. They are the synagogue of Satan.*f* ¹⁰Don't be afraid of what you are going to suffer. Look! The devil is going to throw some of you into prison so that you may be tested. For ten days you will undergo suffering. Be faithful until death, and I will give you the crown of life.*g*

¹¹'Let the person who has an ear listen to what the Spirit says to the churches. The one who conquers will never be hurt by the second death.'*h*

The Letter to the Church in Pergamum

¹²"To the messenger*a* of the church in Pergamum, write:*i*

'The one who holds the sharp, two-edged sword, says this: ¹³I know where you

a 2:8,2:12 Or *angel*

live. Satan's throne is there. Yet you hold on to my name and have not denied your faith in me,[a] even in the days of Antipas, my faithful witness. He was killed in your presence, where Satan lives.[a] 14But I have a few things against you: You have there some who hold to the teaching of Balaam, the one who taught Balak to put a stumbling block before the people of Israel so that they would eat food sacrificed to idols and practice immorality.[b] 15You also have some who hold to the teaching of the Nicolaitans.[c] 16So repent. If you don't, I will come to you quickly and wage war against them with the sword of my mouth.[d]

17'Let the person who has an ear listen to what the Spirit says to the churches. To the one who conquers I will give some of the hidden manna. I will also give him a white stone. On the white stone is written a new name that no one knows except the person who receives it.'[e]

The Letter to the Church in Thyatira

18"To the messenger[b] of the church in Thyatira, write:[f]

'The Son of God, whose eyes are like flaming fire and whose feet are like glowing bronze, says this: 19I know your works—your love, faithfulness,[c] service, and endurance—and that your last works are greater than the first.[g] 20But I have this against you: You tolerate that woman Jezebel, who calls herself a prophet and who teaches and leads my servants to practice immorality and to eat food sacrificed to idols.[h] 21I gave her time to repent, but she refused to repent of her immorality.[i] 22Look! I'm going to throw her into a

---

a 2:13 Or *my faith* b 2:18 Or *angel* c 2:19 Or *faith*

2:13
a Rev 2:2,9

2:14
b Num 24:14;
25:1; 31:16;
Acts 15:29;
1Cor 6:13; 8:9-10:
10:19-20;
2Peter 2:15;
Jude 1:11;
Rev 1:20

2:15
c Rev 2:6

2:16
d Isa 11:4;
2Thes 2:8;
Rev 1:16; 19:15,
21

2:17
e Rev 2:7,11; 3:12;
19:12

2:18
f Rev 1:14-15

2:19
g Rev 2:2

2:20
h Exod 34:15;
1Kings 16:31;
21:25; 2Kings 9:7;
Acts 15:20,29;
1Cor 10:19-20;
Rev 2:14

2:21
i Rom 2:4;
Rev 9:20

2:23
a 1Sam 16:7;
1Chr 28:9; 29:17;
2Chr 6:30; Ps 7:9;
62:12; Jer 11:20;
17:10; 20:12;
Matt 16:27;
John 2:24-25;
Acts 1:24;
Rom 2:6; 8:27;
14:12; 2Cor 5:10;
Gal 6:5;
Rev 20:12

2:24
b Acts 15:28

2:25
c Rev 3:11

2:26
d Matt 19:28;
Lk 22:29-30;
John 6:29;
1Cor 6:3;
1John 3:23;
Rev 3:21; 20:4

2:27
e Ps 2:8-9; 49:14;
Dan 7:22;
Rev 12:5; 19:15

2:28
f 2Peter 1:19;
Rev 22:16

2:29
g Rev 2:7

3:1
h Eph 2:1,5;
1Tim 5:6; Rev 1:4,
16; 2:2; 4:5; 5:6

3:3
i Matt 24:42-43;
25:13;
Mark 13:33;
Lk 12:39-40;
1Thes 5:2,6;
1Tim 6:20;
2Tim 1:13;
2Peter 3:10;
Rev 1:11,19;
16:15

sickbed. Those who commit adultery with her will also have great suffering, unless they repent of her works. 23I will strike her children dead. Then all the churches will know that I am the one who searches minds and hearts. I will reward each of you as your works deserve.*a*

24'But as for the rest of you in Thyatira— you who don't hold on to this teaching and who haven't learned what some people call the deep things of Satan—I won't lay on you any other burden.*b* 25Just hold on to what you have until I come.*c* 26To the person who conquers and continues to do my works to the end I will give authority over the nations.*d* 27He will rule them with an iron scepter, as when clay pots are shattered.*e* 28Just as I have received authority from my Father, I will also give him the morning star.*f*

29'Let the person who has an ear listen to what the Spirit says to the churches.'*g*

The Letter to the Church in Sardis

3 1"To the messenger*a* of the church in Sardis, write:*h*

'The one who has the seven spirits of God and the seven stars says this: I know your works. You are known for being alive, but you are dead. 2Be alert, and strengthen the things that are left, which are about to die. I have not found your works to be completed in the sight of my God. 3So remember what you received and heard. Obey it, and repent. If you're not alert, I will come like a thief, and you won't know the time when I will come to you.*i* 4But you have a few people in Sardis who haven't soiled their clothes. They will walk with me in white clothes because they

---

a *3:1* Or *angel*

are worthy.*a* 5The person who conquers in this way will wear white clothes, and I will never erase his name from the Book of Life. I will acknowledge his name in the presence of my Father and his angels.*b*

6'Let the person who has an ear listen to what the Spirit says to the churches.'*c*

The Letter to the Church in Philadelphia

7"To the messenger*a* of the church in Philadelphia, write:*d*

'The one who is holy, who is true,
    who has the key of David,
who opens a door that*b* no one can shut,
    and who shuts a door that*c* no one can open,

says this:

8'I know your works. Look! I have put in front of you an open door that no one can shut. You have only a little strength, but you have kept my word and have not denied my name.*e* 9I will make those who belong to the synagogue of Satan—those who claim to be Jews and aren't, but are lying—come and bow down at your feet. Then they will realize that I have loved you.*f* 10Because you have kept my command to endure,*d* I will keep you from the hour of testing that is coming to the whole world to test those living on the earth.*g* 11I am coming soon! Hold on to what you have so that no one takes your crown.*h* 12I will make the one who conquers a pillar in the sanctuary of my God, and he will never go out of it again. I will write on him the name of my God, the name of the city of my God (the new Jerusalem coming down out of heaven from God), and my own new name.*i*

---

a 3:7 Or *angel*   **b** 3:7 Lit. *who opens and*   **c** 3:7 Lit. *who shuts and*
d 3:10 Lit. *my word of endurance*

3:4
a Acts 1:15;
Jude 1:23;
Rev 4:4; 6:11; 7:9,
13

3:5
b Exod 32:32;
Ps 69:28;
Matt 10:32;
Lk 12:8; Phil 4:3;
Rev 13:8; 17:8;
19:8; 20:12; 21:27

3:6
c Rev 2:7

3:7
d Job 12:14;
Isa 22:22;
Matt 16:19;
Lk 1:32;
Acts 3:14;
1John 5:20;
Rev 1:5,18; 5:14;
6:10; 19:11

3:8
e 1Cor 16:9;
2Cor 2:12;
Rev 3:1

3:9
f Isa 49:23; 60:14;
Rev 2:9

3:10
g Isa 24:17; Lk 2:1;
2Peter 2:9

3:11
h Phil 4:5; Rev 1:3;
2:10,25; 22:3,7,
12,20

3:12
i 1Kings 7:21;
Gal 2:9; 4:26;
Heb 12:22;
Rev 2:17; 14:1;
21:2,10; 22:4

3:13
a Rev 2:7

3:14
b Isa 65:16;
Col 1:15; Rev 1:5;
19:11; 22:6-7

3:15
c Rev 3:1

3:17
d Hos 12:8;
1 Cor 4:8

3:18
e Isa 55:1;
Matt 13:44; 25:9;
2 Cor 5:3;
Rev 7:13; 16:15;
19:8

3:19
f Job 5:17;
Prov 3:11-12;
Heb 12:5-6;
James 1:12

3:20
g Song 5:2;
Lk 12:37;
John 14:23

3:21
h Matt 19:28;
Lk 22:30;
1 Cor 6:2;
2 Tim 2:12;
Rev 2:26-27

3:22
i Rev 2:7

4:1
j Rev 1:10,19;
11:12; 22:6

[13]'Let the person who has an ear listen to what the Spirit says to the churches.'[a]

The Letter to the Church in Laodicea

[14]"To the messenger[a] of the church in Laodicea, write:[b] 'The Amen, the witness who is faithful and true, the beginning[b] of God's creation, says this: [15]I know your works, that you are neither cold nor hot. I wish you were cold or hot.[c] [16]Since you are lukewarm and neither hot nor cold, I'm going to spit you out of my mouth. [17]You say, "I'm rich. I have become wealthy. I don't need anything." Yet you don't realize that you are miserable, pitiful, poor, blind, and naked.[d] [18]Therefore, I advise you to buy from me gold purified in fire so that you may be rich, white clothes to wear so that you may keep the shame of your nakedness from showing, and ointment to put on your eyes so that you may see.[e] [19]I correct and discipline those whom I love. So be serious and repent![f] [20]Look! I'm standing at the door and knocking. If anyone listens to my voice and opens the door, I will come in to him and eat with him, and he will eat[c] with me.[g] [21]To the one who conquers I will give a place to sit with me on my throne, just as I have conquered and have sat down with my Father on his throne.[h]

[22]'Let the person who has an ear listen to what the Spirit says to the churches.'[i]

A Vision of God's Throne

[1]After these things I saw a door standing open in heaven. The first voice, which I had heard speaking to me like a trumpet, said, "Come up here, and I will show what must happen after this."[j] [2]Instantly I was in the Spirit, and I saw a throne in heaven with a person seated on

---

a 3:14 Or *angel*   b 3:14 Or *source*   c 3:20 The Gk. lacks *will eat*

the throne.[a] [3]The person sitting there looked like jasper and carnelian, and there was a rainbow around the throne that looked like an emerald.[b] [4]Around the throne were twenty-four other thrones, and on these thrones sat twenty-four elders wearing white robes and gold crowns on their heads.[c] [5]Flashes of lightning, noises, and peals of thunder came from the throne. Burning in front of the throne were seven flaming torches, which are the seven spirits of God.[d]

[6]In front of the throne there was something like a sea of glass as clear as crystal. In the center of the throne and on each side of the throne were four living creatures full of eyes in front and in back.[e] [7]The first living creature was like a lion, the second living creature was like an ox, the third living creature had a face like a human, and the fourth living creature was like a flying eagle.[f] [8]Each of the four living creatures had six wings and were full of eyes inside and out. Without stopping day or night they were singing,[g]

> "Holy, holy, holy
> 　　is the Lord God Almighty,
> 　　　　who was, who is, and who is coming."

[9]Whenever the living creatures give glory, honor, and thanks to the one who sits on the throne, to the one who lives forever and ever,[h] [10]the twenty-four elders bow down in front of the one who sits on the throne and worship the one who lives forever and ever. They throw their crowns in front of the throne and say,[i]

> [11]"You are worthy, our Lord and God,[j]
> 　　to receive glory, honor, and power,
> 　　because you created all things,
> 　　　　and they came into existence
> 　　　　　　and were created because of your will."

The Lamb Takes the Scroll with Seven Seals

5 [1]Then I saw in the right hand of the one who sits on the throne a scroll written on the inside and on the outside. It was sealed with seven seals.[k] [2]I saw a powerful angel proclaiming with a loud voice, "Who is worthy to open the scroll and break its seals?" [3]No one in heaven, on

4:2
[a]Isa 6:1;
Jer 17:12;
Ezek 1:26; 10:1;
Dan 7:9;
Rev 1:10; 17:3;
21:10

4:3
[b]Ezek 1:28

4:4
[c]Rev 3:4-5; 6:11;
7:9,13-14; 11:16;
19:10,14

4:5
[d]Exod 37:23;
2Chr 4:20;
Ezek 1:13;
Zech 4:2; Rev 1:4;
3:1; 5:6; 8:5;
16:18

4:6
[e]Exod 38:8;
Ezek 1:5; Rev 1:8;
15:2

4:7
[f]Num 2:2;
Ezek 1:10; 10:14

4:8
[g]Isa 6:2-3;
Rev 1:4,8; 6:6

4:9
[h]Rev 1:18; 5:14;
15:7

4:10
[i]Rev 5:4,8-9,14

4:11
[j]Gen 1:1;
Acts 17:24;
Eph 3:9; Col 1:16;
Rev 5:12; 10:6

5:1
[k]Isa 29:11;
Ezek 2:9-10;
Dan 12:4

5:3
a Rev 5:13

5:5
b Gen 49:9-10;
Isa 11:1,10;
Rom 15:12;
Heb 7:14;
Rev 6:1; 22:1,16

5:6
c Isa 53:7;
Zech 3:9; 4:10;
John 1:29,36;
1Peter 1:19;
Rev 4:5; 13:8-9,12

5:7
d Rev 4:2

5:8
e Ps 141:2;
Rev 4:8,10; 8:3-4;
14:2; 15:2

5:9
f Ps 40:3; Dan 4:1;
6:25; Acts 20:28;
Rom 3:24;
1Cor 6:20; 7:23;
Eph 1:7; Col 1:14;
Heb 9:12;
1Peter 1:18-19;
2Peter 2:1;
1John 1:7;
Rev 4:6,11; 7:9;
11:9; 14:3-4,6

5:10
g Exod 19:6;
1Peter 2:5,9;
Rev 1:6; 20:6;
22:5

5:11
h Ps 68:17;
Dan 7:10;
Heb 12:22;
Rev 4:4,6

5:12
i Rev 4:11

5:13
j 1Chr 29:11;
Rom 9:5; 16:27;
Phil 2:10;
1Tim 6:16;
1Peter 4:11; 5:11;
Rev 1:6; 2:3; 6:16;
7:10

earth, or under the earth could open the scroll or look inside it.*a* ⁴I began to cry bitterly because no one was found worthy to open the scroll or look inside it.

⁵Then one of the elders said to me, "Stop crying. Look! The Lion from the tribe of Judah, the Root of David, has conquered. He can open the scroll and its seven seals."*b* ⁶Then I saw a lamb standing in the middle of the throne, the four living creatures, and the elders. He looked like*a* he had been slaughtered. He had seven horns and seven eyes, which are the seven spirits of God sent into all the earth.*c* ⁷He went and took the scroll from the right hand of the one who sits on the throne.*d*

⁸When the lamb had taken the scroll, the four living creatures and the twenty-four elders bowed down in front of him. Each held a harp and a gold bowl full of incense, the prayers of the saints.*e* ⁹They sang a new song:*f*

> "You are worthy to take the scroll and open its seals,
>> because you were slaughtered.
> With your blood you purchased people**b** for God.
>> They are from every tribe, language, people, and nation.
> ¹⁰You made them a kingdom and priests for our God,*g*
>> and they will reign on the earth."

¹¹Then I looked, and I heard the voices of many angels, the living creatures, and the elders surrounding the throne. They numbered ten thousands times ten thousand and thousands times thousands.*h* ¹²They sang with a loud voice,*i*

> "Worthy is the lamb who was slaughtered
>> to receive power, wealth, wisdom, strength,
>> honor, glory, and praise!"

¹³I heard every creature in heaven, on earth, under the earth, and on the sea, and everything that is in them, saying,*j*

> "To the one who sits on the throne and to the lamb
>> be praise, honor, glory, and power
>> forever and ever!"

---

a 5:6 Lit. *the elders, like*　**b** 5:9 The Gk. lacks *people*

[14]The four living creatures said, "Amen!" Then the elders bowed down and worshiped.[a]

The Lamb Opens the First Six Seals

6 [1]Then I saw the lamb open the first of the seven seals. I heard one of the four living creatures say with a voice like thunder, "Go!"[b] [2]Then I looked, and there was a white horse! Its rider had a bow, and a crown had been given to him. He went out as a conqueror to conquer.[c]

[3]When the lamb[a] opened the second seal, I heard the second living creature say, "Go!"[d] [4]A second horse went out. It was fiery red, and its rider was given permission to take peace away from the earth and to make people slaughter one another. So he was given a large sword.[e]

[5]When the lamb[a] opened the third seal, I heard the third living creature say, "Go!" I looked, and there was black horse! Its rider held a scale in his hand.[f] [6]I heard what sounded like a voice from among the four living creatures, saying, "A quart of wheat for a denarius, or three quarts of barley for a denarius.[b] But don't damage the olive oil or the wine!"[g]

[7]When the lamb[a] opened the fourth seal, I heard the voice of the fourth living creature say, "Go!"[h] [8]I looked, and there was a pale horse! Its rider's name was Death, and Hades[c] followed him. They were given authority over one-fourth of the earth to kill people using wars, famines, plagues, and the wild animals of the earth.[i]

[9]When the lamb[a] opened the fifth seal, I saw under the altar the souls of those who had been slaughtered because of the word of God and the testimony they had given.[j] [10]They cried out in a loud voice, "Holy and true Sovereign, how long will it be before you judge and take revenge on those living on the earth who shed our blood?"[k] [11]Each of them was given a white robe. They were told to rest a little longer until the number of their fellow servants and their brothers was completed, who would be killed as they had been killed.[l]

---

a *6:3,6:5,6:7,6:9* Lit. *he*   **b** *6:6* A denarius was equivalent to a day's wage for a laborer.   **c** *6:8* I.e. the realm of the dead

---

Marginal cross-references:

5:14
a Rev 4:9-10; 19:4

6:1
b Rev 4:7; 5:5-7

6:2
c Ps 45:4-5; Zech 6:3,11; Rev 14:14; 19:11

6:3
d Rev 4:7

6:4
e Zech 6:2

6:5
f Zech 6:2; Rev 4:7

6:6
g Rev 9:4

6:7
h Rev 4:7

6:8
i Lev 26:22; Ezek 14:21; Zech 6:3

6:9
j 2Tim 1:8; Rev 1:9; 8:3; 9:13; 12:17; 14:18; 19:10; 20:4

6:10
k Zech 1:12; Rev 3:7; 11:18; 19:2

6:11
l Heb 11:40; Rev 3:4-5; 7:9,14; 14:13

6:12
*a*Joel 2:10,31;
3:15; Matt 24:29;
Acts 2:20;
Rev 16:18

¹²Then I saw the lamb^a open the sixth seal. There was a powerful earthquake. The sun turned as black as sackcloth made of hair, and the full moon turned as red as blood.^{ba} ¹³The stars in the sky fell to the earth like a fig tree drops its fruit when it is shaken by a strong wind.^b ¹⁴The sky vanished like a scroll being rolling up, and every mountain and island was moved from its place.^c ¹⁵Then the kings of the earth, the important people, the generals, the rich, the powerful, and all the slaves and free people hid themselves in caves and among the rocks in the mountains.^d ¹⁶They said to the mountains and rocks, "Fall on us and hide us from the face of the one who sits on the throne and from the wrath of the lamb.^e ¹⁷For the great day of their wrath has come, and who is able to endure it?"^f

6:13
*b*Rev 8:10; 9:1

6:14
*c*Ps 102:26;
Isa 34:4; Jer 3:23;
4:24;
Heb 1:12-13;
Rev 16:20

144,000 People Are Sealed

¹After this I saw four angels standing at the four corners of the earth. They were holding back the four winds of the earth so that no wind could blow on the land, the sea, or any tree.^g ²I saw another angel coming from the east having the seal of the living God. He cried out in a loud voice to the four angels who had been permitted to harm the land and sea, ³"Don't harm the land, the sea, or the trees until we have marked the servants of our God with a seal on their foreheads."^h

6:15
*d*Isa 2:19

6:16
*e*Hos 10:8;
Lk 23:30; Rev 9:6

⁴I heard the number of those who were sealed: 144,000. Those who were sealed were from every tribe of Israel:ⁱ ⁵12,000 from the tribe of Judah were sealed, 12,000 from the tribe of Reuben, 12,000 from the tribe of Gad, ⁶12,000 from the tribe of Asher, 12,000 from the tribe of Naphtali, 12,000 from the tribe of Manasseh, ⁷12,000 from the tribe of Simeon, 12,000 from the tribe of Levi, 12,000 from the tribe of Issachar, ⁸12,000 from the tribe of Zebulun, 12,000 from the tribe of Joseph, and 12,000 from the tribe of Benjamin were sealed.

6:17
*f*Ps 76:7; Isa 13:6;
Zeph 1:14;
Rev 16:14

7:1
*g*Dan 7:2; Rev 9:4

7:3
*h*Ezek 9:4;
Rev 6:6; 9:4; 14:1;
22:4

7:4
*i*Rev 9:16; 14:1

---

a 6:12 Lit. *him*   **b** 6:12 Lit. *became like blood*

God's People Worship Him

⁹After these things I looked, and there was a large crowd that no one was able to count! They were from every nation, tribe, people, and language. They were standing in front of the throne and the lamb and were wearing white robes, with palm branches n their hands.ᵃ ¹⁰They cried out in a loud voice,ᵇ

> "Salvation belongs to our God,
>> who sits on the throne,
>>> and to the lamb!"

¹¹All the angels stood around the throne and around the elders and the four living creatures. They fell on their faces in front of the throne and worshiped God,ᶜ ¹²saying,ᵈ

> "Amen! Praise, glory, wisdom,
>> thanks, honor, power, and strength
>>> be to our God forever and ever! Amen!"

¹³Then one of the elders said to me, "Who are these people wearing white robes, and where did they come from?"ᵉ ¹⁴I said to him, "Sir, you know." Then he told me, "These are the people who are coming out of the terrible suffering.ᵃ They have washed their robes and made them white in the blood of the lamb.ᶠ ¹⁵That's why:ᵍ

> "They are in front of the throne of God
>> and worshipᵇ him night and day in his temple.
>> The one who sits on the throne will shelter them.
> ¹⁶They will never be hungry or thirsty again.ʰ
>> Neither the sun nor any burning heat
>>> will ever strike them.
> ¹⁷For the lamb in the center of the throne will be their
>>> shepherd.ⁱ
>> He will lead them to springs filled with the water
>>> of life,
>> and God will wipe every tear from their
>>> eyes."ᶜ

---

a 7:14 Or *great tribulation*　　b 7:15 Or *serve*　　c 7:17 Isa 25:8

7:9
ᵃRom 11:25;
Rev 3:5,18; 4:4;
5:9; 6:11,14

7:10
ᵇPs 3:8; Isa 43:11;
Jer 3:23;
Hos 13:4;
Rev 5:13; 19:1

7:11
ᶜRev 4:6

7:12
ᵈRev 5:13-14

7:13
ᵉRev 7:9

7:14
ᶠIsa 1:18;
Zech 3:3-5;
Heb 9:14;
1John 1:7;
Rev 1:5; 6:9; 17:6

7:15
ᵍIsa 4:5-6;
Rev 21:3

7:16
ʰPs 121:6;
Isa 49:10;
Rev 21:4

7:17
ⁱPs 23:1; 36:8;
Isa 25:8;
John 10:11,14;
Rev 21:4

8:1
a Rev 6:1

8:2
b 2Chr 29:25-28;
Matt 18:10;
Lk 1:19

8:3
c Exod 30:1;
Rev 5:8; 6:9

8:4
d Ps 141:2;
Lk 1:10

8:5
e 2Sam 22:8;
1Kings 19:11;
Acts 4:31;
Rev 16:18

8:7
f Isa 2:13;
Ezek 38:22;
Rev 9:4; 16:2

8:8
g Jer 51:25;
Ezek 14:19;
Amos 7:4;
Rev 16:3

8:9
h Rev 16:3

8:10
i Isa 14:12;
Rev 9:1; 16:4

8:11
j Exod 15:23;
Ruth 1:20;
Jer 9:15; 23:15

The Lamb Opens the Seventh Seal

8 ¹When the lamb[a] opened the seventh seal, there was silence in heaven for about half an hour.[a]

Seven Angels Are Given Seven Trumpets

²Then I saw the seven angels who stand in God's presence, and seven trumpets were given to them.[b] ³Another angel came with a gold censer and stood at the altar. He was given a large quantity of incense to offer on the gold altar before the throne, along with the prayers of all the saints.[c] ⁴The smoke from the incense and the prayers of the saints went up from angel's hand to God.[d] ⁵The angel took the censer, filled it with fire from the altar, and threw it on the earth. Then there were peals of thunder, noises, flashes of lightening, and an earthquake.[e] ⁶The seven angels who had the seven trumpets got ready to blow them.

The First Four Angels Blow Their Trumpets

⁷When the first angel blew his trumpet, hail and fire were mixed with blood and thrown on the earth. One-third of the earth was burned up, one-third of the trees was burned up, and all the green grass was burned up.[f]

⁸When the second angel blew his trumpet, something like a huge mountain burning with fire was thrown into the sea. One-third of the sea turned into blood,[g] ⁹one-third of the creatures that were living in the sea died, and one-third of the ships were destroyed.[h]

¹⁰When the third angel blew his trumpet, a huge star blazing like a torch fell from heaven. It fell on one-third of the rivers and on the springs of water.[i] ¹¹The name of the star is Wormwood. One-third of the water turned into wormwood, and many people died from the water because it had turned bitter.[j]

¹²When the fourth angel blew his trumpet, one-third of the sun, one-third of the moon, and one-third of the stars were struck so that one-third of them turned dark.

---

a *8:1* Lit. *he*

One-third of the day and one-third of the night were kept from shining.[a]

[13]Then I looked, and I heard an eagle flying overhead say in a loud voice, "How terrible, how terrible, how terrible for those living on the earth, because of the blasts of the remaining trumpets that the three angels are about to blow!"[b]

The Fifth and Sixth Angels Blow Their Trumpets

9 [1]When the fifth angel blew his trumpet, I saw a star that had fallen to earth from the sky.[a] The star[b] was given the key to the shaft of the bottomless pit.[c] [2]It opened the shaft of the bottomless pit, and smoke came out of the shaft like the smoke from a large furnace. The sun and the air were darkened with the smoke from the shaft.[d] [3]Locusts came out of the smoke onto the earth, and they were given power like the power of earthly scorpions.[e] [4]They were told not to harm the grass on the earth, any green plant, or any tree. They could harm only[c] the people who do not have the seal of God on their foreheads.[f] [5]They were not allowed to kill them but were only allowed[d] to torture them for five months. Their torture was like the pain of a scorpion when it stings someone.[g] [6]In those days people will look for death and never find it. They will long to die, but death will escape them.[h]

[7]The locusts looked like horses prepared for battle. On their heads were crowns that looked like gold, and their faces were like human faces.[i] [8]They had hair like women's hair and teeth like lions' teeth.[j] [9]They had breastplates like iron, and the noise of their wings was like the roar of chariots with many horses rushing into battle.[k] [10]They had tails and stingers like scorpions, and they had the power to hurt people with their tails for five months.[l] [11]They had the angel of the bottomless pit ruling over them as king. In Hebrew he is called Abaddon,[e] and in Greek he is called Apollyon.[f][m]

[12]The first catastrophe is over. After these things there are still two more catastrophes to come.[n]

---

a[9:1] Or *from heaven*   b[9:1] Lit. *It*   c[9:4] Lit. *any tree, except*   d[9:5] The Gk. lacks *were only allowed*   e[9:11] I.e. Destruction   f[9:11] I.e. Destroyer

---

8:12
a Isa 13:10; Amos 8:9

8:13
b Rev 9:12; 11:14; 14:6; 19:17

9:1
c Lk 8:31; 10:18; Rev 8:10; 17:8; 20:1-2,11

9:2
d Joel 2:2,10

9:3
e Exod 10:4; Jdg 7:12; Rev 7:10

9:4
f Exod 12:23; Ezek 9:4; Rev 6:6; 7:3; 8:7

9:5
g Rev 11:7,10

9:6
h Job 3:21; Isa 2:19; Jer 8:3; Rev 6:16

9:7
i Dan 7:8; Joel 2:4; Nah 3:17

9:8
j Joel 1:6

9:9
k Joel 2:5-7

9:10
l Rev 9:5

9:11
m Eph 2:2; Rev 2:1

9:12
n Rev 8:13

9:14
a Rev 16:12

9:16
b Ps 68:17;
Ezek 38:4;
Dan 7:10; Rev 7:4

9:17
c 1Chr 12:8;
Isa 5:28-29

9:19
d Isa 9:15

9:20
e Lev 17:7;
Deut 31:29;
32:17; Ps 106:37;
115:4; 135:15;
Dan 5:23;
1Cor 10:20

9:21
f Rev 22:15

10:1
g Ezek 1:28;
Matt 17:2;
Rev 1:15-16

10:2
h Matt 28:18

10:3
i Rev 8:5

10:4
j Dan 8:26; 12:4,9

10:5
k Exod 6:8;
Dan 12:7

¹³When the sixth angel blew his trumpet, I heard a voice from the four[a] horns of the gold altar in front of God. ¹⁴It said to the sixth angel who had the trumpet, "Release the four angels who are held at the great Euphrates River."[a] ¹⁵So the four angels who were ready for that hour, day, month, and year were released to kill one-third of humanity. ¹⁶The number of cavalry troops was 200,000,000. I heard how many there were.[b][b]

¹⁷This was how I saw the horses in my vision: The riders wore breastplates that had the color of fire, sapphire, and sulfur. The heads of the horses were like lions' heads. Fire, smoke, and sulfur came out of their mouths.[c] ¹⁸By these three plagues—the fire, the smoke, and the sulfur that came out of their mouths—one-third of humanity was killed. ¹⁹For the power of these horses is in their mouths and their tails. Their tails have heads like snakes, which they use to inflict pain.[d]

²⁰The rest of the people who survived these plagues did not repent of the works of their hands or stop worshiping demons and idols made of gold, silver, bronze, stone, and wood, which cannot see, hear, or walk.[e] ²¹They did not repent of their murders, their deeds of witchcraft, their acts of sexual immorality, or their thefts.[f]

John Eats a Small Scroll

10 ¹Then I saw another powerful angel come down from heaven. He was dressed in a cloud, and there was a rainbow over his head. His face was like the sun, and his legs were like columns of fire.[g] ²He held a small, opened scroll in his hand. Setting his right foot on the sea and his left foot on the land,[h] ³he shouted in a loud voice as a lion roars. When he shouted, the seven thunders spoke with voices of their own.[i] ⁴When the seven thunders spoke, I was going to write, but I heard a voice from heaven say, "Seal up what the seven thunders have said, and don't write it down."[j]

⁵Then the angel whom I saw standing on the sea and on the land raised his right hand to heaven.[k] ⁶He swore an oath

---

a *9:13* Other mss. lack *four*   **b** *9:16* Lit. *heard their number* by the one who lives forever and ever, who created heaven and everything in it, the earth and everything in it, and the sea and everything in it: "There will be no more delay.^{a} ^{7}In the days when the seventh angel is ready to blow his trumpet, the secret of God will be fulfilled, as he had announced to his servants, the prophets."^{b} ^{8}Then the voice that I had heard from heaven spoke to me again, saying, "Go and take the opened scroll from the hand of the angel who is standing on the sea and on the land."^{c} ^{9}So I went to the angel and asked him to give me the small scroll. He said to me, "Take it and eat it. It will be bitter in your stomach, but it will be as sweet as honey in your mouth."^{d}

^{10}So I took the small scroll from the angel's hand and ate it. It was as sweet as honey in my mouth, but when I had eaten it, my stomach was bitter.^{e} ^{11}Then the seven thunders^a told me, "Again you must prophesy about many peoples, nations, languages, and kings."

The Two Witnesses

11 ^{1}Then I was given a stick like a measuring rod. I was told, "Stand up and measure the temple of God and the altar, and count^b those who worship there.^{f} ^{2}But don't measure the courtyard outside the temple. Leave that out, because it is given to the nations, and they will trample the Holy City^c for forty-two months.^{g} ^{3}I will give my two witnesses who wear sackcloth the authority to prophesy for 1,260 days."^{h}

^{4}These witnesses^d are the two olive trees and the two lampstands standing in the presence of the Lord of the earth.^{i} ^{5}If anyone wants to hurt them, fire comes out of their mouth and burns up their enemies. If anyone wants to hurt them, he must be killed in the same way.^{j} ^{6}These witnesses^e have authority to shut the sky in order to keep rain from falling during the days of their prophesying. They also have authority over the waters to turn them into blood and to strike the earth with any plague as often as they desire.^{k}

^{7}When they have finished their testimony, the beast that

---

a *10:11* Lit. *they*　b *11:1* The Gk. lacks *count*　c *11:2* I.e. Jerusalem
d *11:4* Lit. *These ones*　e *11:6* Lit. *They*

10:6
a Neh 9:6;
Dan 12:7;
Rev 4:11; 14:7;
16:17

10:7
b Rev 11:15

10:8
c Rev 10:4

10:9
d Jer 15:16;
Ezek 2:8; 3:1-3

10:10
e Ezek 2:10; 3:3

11:1
f Num 23:18;
Ezek 40:3;
Zech 2:1;
Rev 21:15

11:2
g Ps 79:1;
Ezek 40:17,20;
Dan 8:10;
Lk 21:24;
Rev 13:5

11:3
h Rev 12:6; 19:10;
20:4

11:4
i Ps 52:8;
Jer 11:16;
Zech 4:3,11,14

11:5
j Num 16:29;
2Kings 1:10,12;
Jer 1:10; 5:14;
Ezek 43:3;
Hos 6:5

11:6
k Exod 7:19;
1Kings 17:1;
James 5:16-17

11:7
a Dan 7:21;
Zech 14:2;
Lk 13:32; Rev 9:2;
13:1,11; 17:8

11:8
b Heb 13:12;
Rev 14:8; 17:1,5;
18:10,24

11:9
c Ps 79:2-3;
Rev 17:15

11:10
d Esth 9:19,22;
Rev 12:12; 13:8;
16:10

11:11
e Ezek 37:5,9-10,
14; Rev 11:9

11:12
f 2Kings 2:1,5,7;
Isa 14:13; 60:8;
Acts 1:9; Rev 12:5

11:13
g Josh 7:19;
Rev 6:12; 14:7;
15:4; 16:19

11:14
h Rev 8:13; 9:12;
15:1

11:15
i Isa 27:13;
Dan 2:44; 7:14,
18,27; Rev 10:7;
12:10; 16:17; 19:6

11:16
j Rev 4:4; 5:8;
19:4

11:17
k Rev 1:4,8; 4:8;
16:5; 19:6

11:18
l Dan 7:9-10;
Rev 6:10; 11:2,9;
13:10; 18:6; 19:5

comes up from the bottomless pit will wage war against them, conquer them, and kill them.[a] 8Their dead bodies will lie in the street of the great city that is spiritually called Sodom and Egypt, where their Lord was crucified.[b] 9For three and a half days some members of the peoples, tribes, languages, and nations will look at their dead bodies and will not allow them to be placed in a tomb.[c] 10Those living on earth will gloat over them, celebrate, and send gifts to each other, because these two prophets had tormented those living on earth.[d]

11But after the three and a half days, the breath of life from God entered them, and they stood on their feet. Those who watched them were terrified.[e] 12Then the witnesses[a] heard a loud voice from heaven calling to them, "Come up here!" So they went up to heaven in a cloud, and their enemies watched them.[f] 13At that moment a powerful earthquake struck. One-tenth of the city collapsed, 7,000 people were killed by the earthquake, and the rest were terrified and gave glory to the God of heaven.[g]

14The second catastrophe is over. The third catastrophe is coming very soon.[h]

The Seventh Angel Blows His Trumpet

15When the seventh angel blew his trumpet, there were loud voices in heaven, saying,[i]

> *"The kingdom of the world has become*
> *the kingdom of our Lord and of his Christ,[b]*
> *and he will rule forever and ever."*

16Then the twenty-four elders who were sitting on their thrones in God's presence fell on their faces and worshiped God.[j] 17They said,[k]

> *"We give thanks to you, Lord God Almighty,*
> *who is and who was,*
> *because you have taken your great power*
> *and have begun to rule.*
> 18*The nations were angry,[l]*

a 11:12 Lit. *they;* other mss. read *I*   b 11:15 I.e. Messiah

559

> but your wrath has come.
> It is time for the dead to be judged—
>   to reward your servants, the prophets, the saints,
> and all who fear your name,
>   both unimportant and important,
>   and to destroy those who destroy the earth."

¹⁹Then God's temple in heaven was opened, and the ark of his covenant was seen inside his temple. There were flashes of lightning, noises, peals of thunder, an earthquake, and heavy hail.ᵃ

Two Signs in the Sky

12 ¹A spectacular sign appeared in the sky: a woman dressed with the sun, who had the moon under her feet and a crown of twelve stars on her head. ²She was pregnant and was crying out from labor pains and the agony of giving birth.ᵇ

³Then another sign appeared in the sky: a huge red dragon with seven heads, ten horns, and seven crowns on its heads.ᶜ ⁴Its tail swept away one-third of the stars in the sky and threw them down to the earth. Then the dragon stood in front of the woman who was about to give birth so that it could devour her child when it was born.ᵈ ⁵She gave birth to a son, a boy, who is to ruleᵃ all the nations with an iron scepter. But her child was snatched away and taken to God and to his throne.ᵉ ⁶Then the woman fled into the wilderness, where a place had been prepared for her by God so that she might be taken care of for 1,260 days.ᶠ

War in Heaven

⁷Then a war broke out in heaven. Michael and his angels fought with the dragon, and the dragon and its angels fought back.ᵍ ⁸But it was not strong enough, and there was no longer any place for them in heaven. ⁹The huge dragon was thrown down. That ancient serpent, called devil and

---

ᵃ12:5 Or shepherd

Marginal cross-references:

11:19
ᵃRev 8:5; 15:5,8; 16:18,21

12:2
ᵇIsa 66:7; Gal 4:19

12:3
ᶜRev 13:1; 17:3, 9-10

12:4
ᵈExod 1:16; Dan 8:10; Rev 8:2; 9:10,19; 17:18

12:5
ᵉPs 2:9; Rev 2:27; 19:15

12:6
ᶠRev 11:3; 12:4

12:7
ᵍDan 10:13,21; 12:1; Rev 12:3; 20:2

12:9
*ª*Gen 3:1,4;
Lk 10:18;
John 12:31;
Rev 9:1; 20:2-3

Satan, the deceiver of the whole world, was thrown down to the earth, and its angels were thrown down with it.*ª*

¹⁰Then I heard a loud voice in heaven say,*ᵇ*

12:10
*ᵇ*Job 1:9; 2:5;
Zech 3:1;
Rev 11:15; 19:1

> "Now the salvation, the power,
>   the kingdom of our God,
>   and the authority of his Christ*ᵃ* have come.
> For the one accusing our brothers,
>   the one who accuses them day and night
>   in the presence of our God, has been thrown out.
> ¹¹They conquered him by the blood of the lamb*ᶜ*
>   and by the word of their testimony,
>   for they did not love their life even in the face
>   of death.

12:11
*ᶜ*Lk 14:26;
Rom 8:33-34,37;
16:20

> ¹²So be glad, heavens, and those who live in them!*ᵈ*
> How terrible it is for the earth and the sea,
>   because the devil has come down to you with
>   great wrath,
>   knowing that his time is short!"

12:12
*ᵈ*Ps 96:11;
Isa 49:13;
Rev 8:13; 10:6;
11:10; 18:20

¹³When the dragon saw that it had been thrown down to the earth, it persecuted*ᵇ* the woman who had given birth to the boy.*ᵉ* ¹⁴However, the woman was given the two wings of a large eagle so that she could fly away from the serpent to her place in the wilderness, where she could be taken care of for a time, times, and half a time.*ᶠ* ¹⁵From its mouth the serpent poured water like a river behind the woman in order to sweep her away with the flood.*ᵍ* ¹⁶But the earth helped the woman by opening its mouth and swallowing the river that the dragon had poured from its mouth. ¹⁷Then the dragon became angry with the woman and went away to do battle against the rest of her children, the ones who keep God's commandments and hold on to the testimony about Jesus.*ʰ* ¹⁸Then the dragon*ᶜ* stood on the sand of the seashore.

12:13
*ᵉ*Rev 12:5

12:14
*ᶠ*Exod 19:4;
Dan 7:25; 12:7;
Rev 17:3; 19:6

12:15
*ᵍ*Isa 59:19

12:17
*ʰ*Gen 3:15;
1Cor 2:1;
1John 5:10;
Rev 1:2,9; 6:9;
11:7; 13:7; 14:13;
20:4

---

a 12:10 I.e. Messiah   **b** 12:13 Or *pursued*   **c** 12:18 Lit. *it*; other mss. read *I*

The Beast from the Sea

13 [1]I saw a beast coming out of the sea. It had ten horns, seven heads, and ten crowns on its horns. On its heads were blasphemous names.[a] [2]The beast that I saw was like a leopard. Its feet were like bear's feet, and its mouth was like a lion's mouth. The dragon gave it his power, his throne, and complete authority.[b] [3]One of the beast's[a] heads looked like it had a fatal wound, but its fatal wound was healed. In amazement the whole world followed the beast.[c] [4]They worshiped the dragon because it had given authority to the beast. They also worshiped the beast, saying, "Who is like the beast, and who can fight a war with it?"[d] [5]The beast was allowed[b] to speak arrogant and blasphemous things, and it was given authority for forty-two months.[e] [6]It opened its mouth to utter blasphemies against God and to blaspheme his name and his residence,[c] that is, those who are living in heaven.[f] [7]It was allowed to wage war against the saints and to conquer them.[d] It was also given authority over every tribe, people, language, and nation.[g] [8]All those living on earth will worship it, everyone whose name is not written in the Book of Life belonging to the lamb that was slaughtered from the foundation of the world.[h]

> [9]Let anyone who has an ear listen:[i]
> [10]If anyone is to be taken captive,[j]
> he must go into captivity.
> If anyone is to be killed with a sword,
> he must be killed with a sword.

This is what the endurance and faith of the saints means.

The Beast from the Earth

[11]Then I saw another beast coming up out of the earth. It had two horns like a lamb and it talked like a dragon.[k] [12]It uses all the authority of the first beast on its behalf,[e] and it makes the earth and those living on it worship the first

---

a 13:3 Lit. *its*   **b** 13:5 Lit. *was given a mouth*   **c** 13:6 Lit. *tent*
d 13:7 Other mss. lack *It was allowed to wage war against the saints and to conquer them.*   **e** 13:12 Or *in its presence*

13:1
a Dan 7:2,7;
Rev 12:3; 17:3,9,
12

13:2
b Dan 7:4-6;
Rev 12:4,9; 16:10

13:3
c Rev 13:12,14;
17:8

13:4
d Rev 18:18

13:5
e Dan 7:8,11,25;
11:36; Rev 11:2;
12:6

13:6
f John 1:14;
Col 2:9

13:7
g Dan 7:21;
Rev 11:7,18;
12:17; 17:15

13:8
h Exod 32:32;
Dan 12:1;
Phil 4:3; Rev 3:5;
17:8; 20:12,15;
21:27

13:9
i Rev 2:7

13:10
j Gen 9:6;
Isa 33:1;
Matt 26:52;
Rev 14:12

13:11
k Rev 11:7

13:12
*a*Rev 13:3

13:13
*b*Deut 13:1-3;
1Kings 18:38;
2Kings 1:10,12;
Matt 24:24;
2Thes 2:9;
Rev 16:14

13:14
*c*2Kings 20:7;
2Thes 2:9-10;
Rev 12:9; 19:20

13:15
*d*Rev 16:2; 19:20;
20:4

13:16
*e*Rev 14:9; 19:20;
20:4

13:17
*f*Rev 14:11; 15:2

13:18
*g*Rev 15:2; 17:9;
21:17

14:1
*h*Rev 5:5; 7:3-4;
13:16

14:2
*i*Rev 1:15; 5:8;
19:6

14:3
*j*Rev 5:9; 15:1,3

14:4
*k*2Cor 11:2;
James 1:18;
Rev 3:4; 5:9; 7:15,
17; 17:14

14:5
*l*Ps 32:2;
Zeph 3:13;
Eph 5:27;
Jude 1:24

beast, whose fatal wound was healed.*a* [13]It performs spectacular signs, even making fire come down from heaven to earth in front of people.*b* [14]It deceives those living on earth with the signs that it is allowed to do on behalf of*a* the first*b* beast, telling them to make an image for the beast who was wounded by a sword and yet lived.*c*

[15]The second beast*c* was allowed to give breath to the image of the first*b* beast so that the image of the beast could talk and put to death those who would not worship the image of the beast.*d* [16]The second beast*d* forces all people— important and unimportant, rich and poor, free and slaves— to be marked on their right hands or on their foreheads.*e* [17]It does this so that*e* no one may buy or sell unless he has the mark, which is the beast's name or the number of its name.*f*

[18]This calls for wisdom: Let the person who has understanding figure out the number of the beast, because it is the number of a person.*f* Its number is 666.*g*

The New Song on Mount Zion

14 [1]Then I looked, and there was the lamb standing on Mount Zion! With him were 144,000 people who had his name and his Father's name written on their foreheads.*h* [2]Then I heard a voice from heaven like the sound of many waters and like the sound of loud thunder. The voice I heard was like the sound of harpists playing on their harps.*i* [3]They were singing a new song in front of the throne, the four living creatures, and the elders. No one could learn the song except the 144,000 who had been redeemed from the earth.*j* [4]They have not defiled themselves with women, for they are virgins. They follow the lamb wherever he goes. They have been redeemed from among humanity as the first fruits for God and the lamb.*k* [5]In their mouth no lie was found. They are blameless.*l*

The Angels Sound a Warning

[6]Then I saw another angel flying overhead with the

---

a *13:14* Or *in the presence of*   b *13:14,13:15* The Gk. lacks *first*
c *13:15* Lit *It*   d *13:16* Lit. *It*   e *13:17* Lit. *So that*   f *13:18* Or *it is a human number*   g *13:18* Other mss. read *616*

eternal gospel to proclaim to those who live[a] on earth—to every nation, tribe, language, and people.[a] [7]He said in a loud voice, "Fear God and give him glory, because the hour of his judgment has come. Worship the one who made heaven and earth, the sea and springs of water."[b]

[8]Then another angel, a second one, followed him, saying, "Fallen! Babylon the Great has fallen! She has made all the nations drink the wine of the wrath of her sexual sins."[c]

[9]Then another angel, a third one, followed them, saying in a loud voice, "Whoever worships the beast and its image and receives a mark on his forehead or his hand[d] [10]will drink the wine of God's wrath, which has been poured unmixed into the cup of his anger. He will be tortured with fire and sulfur in the presence of the holy angels and the lamb.[e] [11]The smoke from their torture goes up forever and ever. There is no rest day or night for those who worship the beast and its image or for anyone who receives the mark of its name."[f] [12]Here is a call for the[b] endurance of the saints, who keep the commandments of God and hold on to the faith of Jesus.[c][g]

[13]I heard a voice from heaven say, "Write this: How blessed are the dead who die in the Lord from now on!" "Yes," says the Spirit. "Let them rest from their labors, for their deeds follow them."[h]

The Earth is Harvested

[14]Then I looked, and there was a white cloud! On the cloud sat someone who was like the Son of Man, with a gold crown on his head and a sharp sickle in his hand.[i] [15]Another angel came out of the temple, crying out in a loud voice to the one who sat on the cloud, "Swing your sickle, and gather the harvest, for the hour has come to gather it, because the harvest on the earth is fully ripe."[j] [16]The one who sat on the cloud swung his sickle over the earth, and the earth was harvested.

[17]Then another angel came out of the temple in heaven. He, too, had a sharp sickle. [18]From the altar came another angel who had authority over fire. He called out in a loud

---

a 14:6 Lit. *sit*   b 14:12 Lit. *Here is the*   c 14:12 Or *to their faith in Jesus*

14:6
a Eph 3:9-11;
Titus 1:2;
Rev 8:13; 13:7

14:7
b Neh 9:6; Ps 33:6;
124:8; 146:5-6;
Acts 14:15; 17:24;
Rev 11:18; 15:4

14:8
c Isa 21:9;
Jer 51:7-8;
Rev 11:8; 16:19;
17:2,5; 18:2-3,10.
18,21; 19:2

14:9
d Rev 13:14-16

14:10
e Ps 75:8;
Isa 51:17;
Jer 25:15;
Rev 16:19; 18:6;
19:20; 20:10

14:11
f Isa 34:10;
Rev 19:3

14:12
g Rev 12:17; 13:10

14:13
h Eccl 4:1-2;
1Cor 15:18;
1Thes 4:16;
2Thes 1:7;
Heb 4:9-10;
Rev 6:11; 20:6

14:14
i Ezek 1:26;
Dan 7:13;
Rev 1:13; 6:2

14:15
j Jer 51:33;
Joel 3:13;
Matt 13:39;
Rev 6:17; 13:12

14:18
ᵃJoel 3:13;
Rev 16:8

14:19
ᵇRev 19:15

14:20
ᶜIsa 63:3;
Lam 1:15;
Heb 13:12;
Rev 11:8; 19:14

15:1
ᵈRev 12:1,3;
14:10; 16:1; 21:9

15:2
ᵉMatt 3:11;
Rev 4:6; 5:8;
13:15-17; 14:2;
21:18

15:3
ᶠExod 15:1;
Deut 31:30; 32:4;
Ps 111:2; 139:14;
145:17; Hos 14:9;
Rev 14:3; 16:7

15:4
ᵍExod 15:14-16;
Isa 66:22; Jer 10:7

15:5
ʰNum 1:50;
Rev 11:19

15:6
ⁱExod 28:6,8;
Ezek 44:17-18;
Rev 1:13; 15:1

15:7
ʲ1Thes 1:9;
Rev 4:6,9; 10:6

15:8
ᵏExod 40:34;
1Kings 8:10;
2Chr 5:14; Isa 6:4;
2Thes 1:9

voice to the angelᵃ who had the sharp sickle, "Swing your sharp sickle, and gather the bunches of grapes from the vine of the earth, because those grapes are ripe."ᵃ ¹⁹So the angel swung his sickle on the earth and gathered the grapes from the earth and threw them into the great winepress of God's wrath.ᵇ ²⁰The wine press was trampled outside the city, and blood flowed out of the wine press as high as a horse's bridle for 200 miles.ᵇᶜ

Seven Angels with Seven Plagues

15 ¹I saw another sign in heaven. It was spectacular and amazing. There were seven angels with the seven last plagues. With them God's wrath has come to an end.ᵈ

²Then I saw what looked like a sea of glass mixed with fire. Those who had conquered the beast, its image, and the number of its name were standing on the sea of glass holding God's harps in their hands.ᵉ ³They sang the song of God's servant Moses and the song of the lamb:ᶠ

> "Your deeds are spectacular and amazing, Lord God Almighty.
> Your ways are just and true, King of the nations.ᶜ
> 4   Lord, who won't fear and praise your name?ᵍ
> For you alone are holy,
>   and all the nations will come and worship you
>   because your judgments have been revealed."

⁵After these things I looked, and the temple of the tent of witness in heaven was open!ʰ ⁶The seven angels with the seven plagues came out of the temple wearing clean, shining linen with gold belts around their waists.ⁱ ⁷One of the four living creatures gave to the seven angels seven gold bowls full of the wrath of God, who lives forever and ever.ʲ ⁸The temple was filled with smoke from the glory of God and his power, and no one could enter the temple until the seven plagues of the seven angels came to an end.ᵏ

---

a14:18 Lit. *to the one*   **b**14:20 Lit. *1,600 stadia*   **c**15:3 Other mss. read *of the ages*

The Seven Angels Pour Out Their Bowls

16 [1]Then I heard a loud voice from the temple saying to the seven angels, "Go and pour the seven bowls of God's wrath on the earth."[a]

[2]So the first angel went and poured his bowl on the earth. A horrible, painful sore appeared on the people who had the mark of the beast and worshiped the image.[b]

[3]The second angel poured his bowl into the sea. It became like the blood of a dead body, and every living thing in the sea died.[c]

[4]The third angel poured his bowl into the rivers and the springs of water, and they turned into blood.[d] [5]Then I heard the angel of the water say,[e]

> "You are just. You are the one who is
>   and the one who was, the Holy One,
>   because you have judged these things.
> [6]You have given them blood to drink[f]
>   because they have poured out the blood of saints
>   and prophets.
> This is what they deserve."

[7]Then I heard the altar reply,[g]

> "Yes, Lord God Almighty,
>   your judgments are true and just."

[8]The fourth angel poured his bowl on the sun. It was allowed to burn people with fire,[h] [9]and they were burned by the fierce heat. They cursed the name of God, who has the authority over these plagues. They didn't repent and give him glory.[i]

[10]The fifth angel poured his bowl on the throne of the beast. Its kingdom was plunged into darkness. People[a] gnawed on their tongues in anguish[j] [11]and cursed the God of heaven because of their pains and sores. But they didn't repent of their deeds.[k]

[12]The sixth angel poured his bowl on the great Euphrates River. Its water was dried up to prepare the way for the

---

a 16:10 Lit. *They*

16:1
a Rev 14:10; 15:1, 7

16:2
b Exod 9:9-11; Rev 8:7; 13:14, 16-17

16:3
c Exod 7:17,20; Rev 8:8-9

16:4
d Exod 7:20; Rev 8:10

16:5
e Rev 1:4,8; 4:8; 11:17; 15:3

16:6
f Isa 49:26; Matt 23:34-35; Rev 3:15; 11:18; 18:20

16:7
g Rev 13:10; 14:10; 15:3; 19:2

16:8
h Rev 8:12; 9:17-18; 14:18

16:9
i Dan 5:22-23; Rev 9:20; 11:13; 14:7; 16:11,21

16:10
j Rev 9:2; 11:10; 13:2

16:11
k Rev 16:2,9,21

16:12
a Isa 41:2,25;
Jer 50:38; 51:36;
Rev 9:14

16:13
b 1John 4:1-3;
Rev 12:3,9; 19:20;
20:10

16:14
c Lk 2:1;
2Thes 2:9;
1Tim 4:1;
James 3:15;
Rev 13:13-14;
17:14; 19:19-20;
20:8

16:15
d Matt 24:43;
2Cor 5:3;
1Thes 5:2;
2Peter 3:10;
Rev 3:3-4,18

16:16
e Rev 19:19

16:17
f Rev 21:6

16:18
g Dan 12:1;
Rev 4:5; 8:5;
11:13,19

16:19
h Isa 51:17,23;
Jer 25:15-16;
Rev 14:8,10;
17:18; 18:5

16:20
i Rev 6:14

16:21
j Exod 9:23-25;
Rev 11:9,11,19

17:1
k Jer 51:13;
Nah 3:4;
Rev 16:19; 17:15;
18:16-17,19;
19:2; 21:9

17:2
l Jer 51:7;
Rev 14:8; 18:3

17:3
m Rev 12:3,6,14;
13:1,9,12

kings from the east.*a* [13]Then I saw three disgusting spirits like frogs come out of the mouth of the dragon, out of the mouth of the beast, and out of the mouth of the false prophet.*b* [14]They are demonic spirits that perform signs. They go to the kings of the whole earth and gather them for the war on the great day of God Almighty.*c*

[15]"See, I'm coming like a thief. How blessed is the person who remains alert and keeps his clothes on! He won't have to go naked and let others see his shame."*d*

Armageddon and the Seventh Angel

[16]The spirits*a* gathered the kings*b* at the place that is called Armageddon in Hebrew.*e*

[17]The seventh angel poured his bowl into the air. A loud voice came from the throne in the temple and said, "It has happened!"*f* [18]There were flashes of lightning, noises, peals of thunder, and a powerful earthquake. There has never been such a powerful earthquake since people have been on the earth.*g* [19]The great city was split into three parts, and the cities of the nations fell. God remembered to give Babylon the Great the cup of wine filled with the fury of his wrath.*h* [20]Every island vanished,*c* and the mountains could no longer be found.*i* [21]Huge hailstones, each weighing about 100 pounds,*d* fell from the sky on people. They cursed God because the plague of hail was such a terrible plague.*j*

Babylon the Great

17 [1]Then one of the seven angels who held the seven bowls came and said to me, "Come, I will show you the judgment of the notorious prostitute who sits on many waters.*k* [2]The kings of the earth committed sexual immorality with her, and those living on earth became drunk with the wine of her immorality."*l*

[3]Then the angel*e* carried me away in the Spirit into a wilderness. I saw a woman sitting on a scarlet beast that was filled with blasphemous names. It had seven heads and ten horns.*m* [4]The woman wore purple and scarlet clothes and

---

a 16:16 Lit. *They*   **b** 16:16 Lit. *them*   **c** 16:20 Or *fled*   **d** 16:21 Lit. *Huge hailstones about a talent*   **e** 17:3 Lit. *he*

was adorned with gold, gems, and pearls. In her hand she was holding a gold cup filled with detestable things and the impurities of her immorality.[a] 5On her forehead was written a secret name:[b]

> "Babylon the Great,
> the Mother of Prostitutes
> and Detestable Things of the Earth."

6I saw that the woman was drunk with the blood of the saints and the blood of the witnesses to Jesus. I was very surprised when I saw her.[c]

7The angel said to me, "Why are you surprised? I will tell you the secret of the woman and the beast with the seven heads and the ten horns that carries her. 8The beast that you saw once was, is no longer, and is going to come from the bottomless pit and go to its destruction. Those living on earth, whose names were not written in the Book of Life from the foundation of the world, will be surprised when they see the beast because it was, is no longer, and will come again.[d] 9This calls for a mind that has wisdom. The seven heads are seven mountains on which the woman is sitting. They are also seven kings.[e] 10Five of them have fallen, one is living, and the other has not yet come. When he comes, he must remain for a little while. 11The beast that was and is no longer is the eighth king,[a] but it belongs with the seven kings[b] and goes to its destruction.[f] 12The ten horns that you saw are ten kings who have not yet received a kingdom. They will receive authority to rule as[c] kings with the beast for one hour.[g] 13They have one purpose: to give their power and authority to the beast. 14They will wage war against the lamb, but the lamb will conquer them because he is Lord of lords and King of kings. Those are called, chosen, and faithful are with him."[h]

15The angel[d] also said to me, "The waters you saw, on which the prostitute is sitting, are peoples, multitudes, nations, and languages.[i] 16The ten horns and the beast you saw will hate the prostitute. They will leave her abandoned

---

a 17:11 *The* Gk. lacks *king*   b 17:11 *The* Gk. lacks *kings*   c 17:12 *The* Gk. lacks *to rule*   d 17:15 Lit. *He*

17:4
a Jer 51:7;
Dan 11:38;
Rev 14:8; 18:6,12,
16

17:5
b 2Thes 2:7;
Rev 11:8; 14:8;
16:19; 18:2,9-10,
21; 19:2

17:6
c Rev 6:9-10;
12:11; 13:15;
16:6; 18:24

17:8
d Rev 11:7; 13:1,3,
8,10-11

17:9
e Rev 13:1,18

17:11
f Rev 17:8

17:12
g Dan 7:20;
Zech 1:18-19,21;
Rev 13:1

17:14
h Deut 10:17;
Jer 50:44-45;
1Tim 6:15;
Rev 14:3; 16:14;
19:16,19

17:15
i Isa 8:7; Rev 8:1;
13:7

17:16
a Jer 50:41-42;
Ezek 16:37-44;
Rev 16:12; 18:8,
16

17:17
b 2Thes 2:11;
Rev 10:7

17:18
c Rev 12:4; 16:19

18:1
d Ezek 43:2;
Rev 17:1

18:2
e Isa 13:19,21;
14:23; 21:8-9;
34:11,14;
Jer 50:39; 51:8,37;
Mark 5:2-3;
Rev 14:8

18:3
f Isa 47:15;
Rev 14:8; 17:2,11,
15

18:4
g Isa 48:20;
52:11 Jer 50:8;
51:6,45;
2Cor 6:17

18:5
h Gen 18:20-21;
Jer 51:9;
Jonah 1:2;
Rev 16:19

18:6
i Ps 137:8;
Jer 50:15,29;
51:24,49;
2Tim 4:14;
Rev 13:10; 14:10;
16:19

18:7
j Isa 47:7-8;
Ezek 28:2;
Zeph 2:15

and naked. They will eat her flesh and burn her up with fire.*a* [17]For God has put it into their hearts to carry out his purpose. So they will give their kingdom to the beast until God's words are fulfilled.*b* [18]The woman you saw is the great city that rules over the kings of the earth."*c*

The Fall of Babylon

18 [1]After these things I saw another angel coming down from heaven. He had great authority,*a* and the earth was made bright by his splendor.*d* [2]He cried out in a powerful voice,*e*

> "Fallen! Babylon the Great has fallen!
> She has become a home for demons.
> She is a prison for every unclean spirit,
> a prison for every unclean bird,
> and a prison for every unclean
> and hated beast.
> [3]For all the nations have drunk*f*
> from the wine of her sexual immorality,
> and the kings of the earth have committed
> sexual immorality with her.
> The merchants of the earth have become rich
> from the power of her luxury."

[4]Then I heard another voice from heaven saying,*g*

> "Come out of her, my people,
> so that you don't participate in her sins
> and suffer from her plagues.
> [5]For her sins are piled as high as heaven,*h*
> and God has remembered her crimes.
> [6]Do to her as she herself has done.*i*
> Give her double for her deeds.
> Mix a double drink for her in the cup she mixed.
> [7]   Just as she glorified herself and lived in luxury,*j*
> so give her just as much torture and misery.
> In her heart she says,
> 'I'm a queen on a throne, not a widow.

---

a 18:1 Or *tremendous power*

I will never see misery.'
⁸For this reason her plagues of death,ᵃ
misery, and famine will come
in a single day.
She will be burned up in a fire,
because the Lord God who judges her is
powerful."

⁹The kings of the earth, who committed sexual immorality with her and lived in luxury with her, will cry and mourn over her when they see the smoke rising from her fire.ᵇ ¹⁰Frightened by her torture, they will stand far away and say,ᶜ

"How terrible, how terrible it is for that great city,
the powerful city Babylon!
For in one hour your judgment has come!"

¹¹The merchants of the earth cry and mourn over her, because no one buys their cargo anymoreᵈ—¹²cargo of gold, silver, gems, pearls, fine linen, purple cloth, silk, scarlet cloth, all kinds of scented wood, all articles made of ivory, all articles made of very costly wood, bronze, iron, marble,ᵉ ¹³cinnamon, spice, incense, myrrh, frankincense, wine, olive oil, flour, wheat, cattle, sheep, horses, chariots, slaves (that is, human souls).ᶠ ¹⁴"The fruit for which your soul craved has left you. All your dainties and your splendor are lost to you. No one will ever find them again." ¹⁵Frightened by her torture, the merchants of these wares who had become rich from her will stand far away. They will cry and mourn,ᵍ ¹⁶saying,ʰ

"How terrible, how terrible it is for the great city
that was clothed in fine linen, purple, and scarlet
and was adorned with gold, gems, and pearls!
¹⁷For in one hour all this wealth has been destroyed!"ⁱ

Every ship's captain, everyone who traveled by ship, sailors, and everyone who made a living by the sea stood far away. ¹⁸When they saw the smoke from her fire, they began to cry out, "What city was like the great city?"ʲ ¹⁹Then they

18:8
ᵃ Isa 47:9;
Jer 50:34;
Rev 11:17; 17:16;
18:10

18:9
ᵇ Jer 50:46;
Ezek 26:16-17;
Rev 17:2-3; 18:13;
19:3

18:10
ᶜ Isa 21:9;
Rev 14:8,17,19

18:11
ᵈ Ezek 27:27-36;
Rev 18:3

18:12
ᵉ Rev 17:4

18:13
ᶠ Ezek 27:13

18:15
ᵍ Rev 18:3,11

18:16
ʰ Rev 17:4

18:17
ⁱ Isa 23:14;
Ezek 27:29;
Rev 18:10

18:18
ʲ Ezek 27:30-31;
Rev 13:4; 18:9

18:19
a Josh 7:6;
1Sam 4:12;
Job 2:12;
Ezek 27:30;
Rev 18:8

threw dust on their heads and shouted while crying and mourning,*a*

> *"How terrible, how terrible it is for the great city,*
> *where all who had ships at sea became rich*
> *because of her wealth!*
> *For in one hour she has been destroyed!*
> [20]*Gloat over her, heaven, saints, apostles, and prophets!*
> *For God has condemned her for you."*

18:21
b Jer 51:64;
Rev 12:8; 16:20

[21]Then a powerful angel picked up a stone that was like a large millstone and threw it into the sea, saying,*b*

18:22
c Isa 24:8; Jer 7:34;
16:9; 25:10;
Ezek 26:13

> *"The great city Babylon will be thrown down*
> *with such force and will never be found again.*
> [22]*The sound of harpists, musicians, flutists, and*
> *trumpeters*c
> *will never be heard in you again.*
> *No artisan of any trade*
> *will ever be found in you again.*
> *The sound of a millstone*
> *will never be heard in you again.*
> [23]*The light from a lamp*d
> *will never shine in you again.*
> *The voice of a bridegroom and bride*
> *will never be heard in you again.*
> *For your merchants were the important people of the world,*
> *and all the nations were deceived by your*
> *witchcraft.*
> [24]*The blood of prophets, saints, and all who had been*
> *murdered*e
> *on earth was found in her."*

18:23
d 2Kings 9:22;
Isa 23:8; Jer 7:34;
16:9; 25:10;
33:11; Nah 3:4;
Rev 17:2,5

18:24
e Jer 51:49;
Rev 17:6

19:1
f Rev 4:11; 7:10,
12; 11:15; 12:10

The Marriage Supper of the Lamb

19

[1]After these things I heard what sounded like the loud voice of a large crowd in heaven, saying,*f*

> *"Hallelujah!*
> *Salvation, glory, and power belong to our God.*
> 2   *His judgments are true and just.*g

19:2
g Deut 32:43;
Rev 6:10; 15:3;
16:7; 18:20

> He has condemned the notorious prostitute
>> who corrupted the world with her immorality.
> He has taken revenge on her
>> for the blood of his servants."

19:3
[a] Isa 34:10;
Rev 14:11; 18:9, 18

³A second time they said,[a]

> "Hallelujah!
> The smoke goes up from her forever and ever."

19:4
[b] 1Chr 16:36;
Neh 5:13; 8:6;
Rev 4:4,6,10; 5:14

⁴The twenty-four elders and the four living creatures bowed down and worshiped God, who was sitting on the throne. They said, "Amen! Hallelujah!"[b] ⁵A voice came from the throne, saying,[c]

19:5
[c] Ps 134:1; 135:1;
Rev 11:18; 20:12

> "Praise our God,
>> all who serve and fear him,
> from the least important
>> to the most important."

19:6
[d] Ezek 1:24; 43:2;
Rev 11:15,17;
12:10; 14:2; 21:22

⁶Then I heard what sounded like the voice of a large crowd, like the sound of raging waters, and like the sound of powerful thunderclaps, saying,[d]

> "Hallelujah!
>> The Lord our God, the Almighty, is reigning.
> ⁷Let us rejoice, be glad, and give him glory,[e]
>> because the marriage of the lamb has come
>> and his bride has made herself ready.
> ⁸She has been given the privilege of wearing fine linen,[f]
>> dazzling and pure."

19:7
[e] Matt 22:2; 25:10;
2Cor 11:2;
Eph 5:32;
Rev 21:2,9

(The fine linen represents the righteous deeds of the saints.) ⁹Then the angel[a] said to me, "Write this: 'How blessed are those who are invited to the marriage supper of the lamb!' " He also told me, "These are the true words of God."[g] ¹⁰I bowed down at his feet to worship him, but he told me, "Don't do that! I am a fellow servant with you and with your brothers who hold on to the testimony of Jesus. Worship

19:8
[f] Ps 45:13-14;
132:9;
Ezek 16:10;
Rev 3:18

---

a 19:9 Lit. he

19:9
[g] Matt 22:2-3;
Lk 14:15-16;
Rev 21:5; 22:6

19:10
a Acts 10:26;
14:14-15;
1 John 5:10;
Rev 12:17; 22:8-9

God, because the testimony of Jesus is the spirit of prophecy!"[a]

The Rider on the White Horse

19:11
b Isa 11:4;
Rev 3:14; 6:2;
15:5

[11]Then I saw heaven standing open, and there was a white horse! Its rider is named Faithful and True, and in righteousness he judges and wages war.[b] [12]His eyes are like a flame of fire, and on his head are many crowns. He has a name written on him that nobody knows except himself.[c] [13]He is dressed in a robe dipped in[a] blood, and his name is called the Word of God.[d]

19:12
c Rev 1:14;
2:16-18; 6:2

19:13
d Isa 63:2-3;
John 1:1;
1 John 5:7

[14]The armies of heaven, wearing fine linen, white and pure, follow him on white horses.[e] [15]A sharp sword comes out of his mouth to strike down the nations. He will rule[b] them with an iron rod and tread the winepress of the fury of the wrath of God Almighty.[f] [16]On his robe and his thigh he has a name written:[g]

19:14
e Matt 28:3;
Rev 4:4; 7:9;
14:20

19:15
f Ps 2:1-12;
Isa 11:4; 63:3;
2 Thes 2:8;
Rev 2:27; 12:5;
14:19-20; 19:16,27

"King of Kings and Lord of Lords."

[17]Then I saw an angel standing in the sun. He cried out in a loud voice to all the birds flying overhead, "Come! Gather for the great supper of God.[h] [18]Eat the flesh of kings, the flesh of commanders, the flesh of warriors,[c] the flesh of horses and their riders, and the flesh of all people, both free and slaves, both unimportant and important."[i]

19:16
g Dan 2:47;
1 Tim 6:15;
Rev 17:14; 19:12

19:17
h Ezek 39:17;
Rev 19:21

[19]Then I saw the beast, the kings of the earth, and their armies gathered to wage war against the rider on the horse and his army.[j] [20]The beast was captured, along with the false prophet who had performed signs on its behalf.[d] By these signs[e] the false prophet[f] had deceived those who had received the mark of the beast and worshiped its image. Both of them were thrown alive into the lake of fire that burns with sulfur.[k] [21]The rest were killed by the sword that belonged to the rider on the horse and that came from his mouth. And all the birds gorged themselves on their flesh.[l]

19:18
i Ezek 39:18,20

19:19
j Rev 16:16;
17:13-14

19:20
k Dan 7:11;
Rev 13:12,15;
14:10; 16:13-14;
20:10; 21:8

19:21
l Rev 17:16;
19:15,17-18

---

a 19:13 Other mss. read *sprinkled with*   b 19:15 Or *will shepherd*
c 19:18 Lit. *the powerful*   d 19:20 Or *in its presence*   e 19:20 Lit. *By which*
f 19:20 Lit. *he*

The Millennial Reign

20 ¹Then I saw an angel coming down from heaven, holding the key to the bottomless pit and a large chain in his hand.ᵃ ²He captured the dragon, that ancient serpent, who is the devil and Satan, and tied him up for a thousand years.ᵇ ³He threw him into the bottomless pit, locked it, and sealed it over him to keep him from deceiving the nations anymore until the thousand years were over. After that he must be set free for a little while.ᶜ

⁴Then I saw thrones, and those who sat on them were given authority to judge. I also saw the souls of those who had been beheaded because of their testimony about Jesus and because of the word of God. They had not worshiped the beast or its image and had not received its mark on their foreheads or hands. They came back to life and ruled with Christ for a thousand years.ᵈ ⁵The rest of the dead did not come back to life until the thousand years were over. This is the first resurrection. ⁶How blessed and holy are those who participate in the first resurrection! The second death has no power over them. They will be priests of God and Christ, and will rule with him for a thousand years.ᵉ

The Final Judgment

⁷When the thousand years are over, Satan will be freed from his prison.ᶠ ⁸He will go out to deceive Gog and Magog, the nations at the four corners of the earth, and gather them for war. They are as numerous as the sands of the seashore.ᵍ ⁹They marched over the broad expanse of the earth and surrounded the camp of the saints and the beloved city. Fire came from Godᵃ out of heaven and burned them up.ʰ ¹⁰The devil, who deceived them, was thrown into the lake of fire and sulfur, where the beast and the false prophet were. They will be tortured day and night forever and ever.ⁱ

The White Throne Judgment

¹¹Then I saw a large, white throne and the one who was sitting on it. The earth and the heaven fled from his

---

a *20:9* Other mss. lack *from God*

20:1
ᵃRev 1:18; 9:1

20:2
ᵇ2Peter 2:4;
Jude 1:6; Rev 12:9

20:3
ᶜDan 6:17;
Rev 16:8,14,16

20:4
ᵈDan 7:9,22,27;
Matt 19:28;
Lk 22:30;
Rom 8:17;
1Cor 6:2-3;
2Tim 2:12;
Rev 5:10; 6:9;
13:12,15-16

20:6
ᵉIsa 61:6;
1Peter 2:9;
Rev 1:6; 2:11; 5:4,
10; 21:8

20:7
ᶠRev 20:2

20:8
ᵍEzek 38:2; 39:1;
Rev 16:14; 20:3,
10

20:9
ʰIsa 8:8;
Ezek 38:9,16

20:10
ⁱRev 14:10-11;
19:20; 20:8

20:11
a Dan 2:35;
2Peter 3:7,10-11;
Rev 21:1

20:12
b Ps 69:28;
Jer 17:10; 32:19;
Dan 7:10; 12:1;
Matt 16:27;
Rom 2:6; Phil 4:3;
Rev 2:23; 3:5;
13:8; 19:5; 21:27;
22:12-13

20:13
c Rev 6:8,12

20:14
d 1Cor 15:26,
54-55; Rev 15:6;
21:8

20:15
e Rev 19:20

21:1
f Isa 65:17; 66:22;
2Peter 3:13;
Rev 20:11

21:2
g Isa 52:1; 54:5;
61:10; 2Cor 11:2;
Gal 4:26;
Heb 11:10; 12:22;
13:14; Rev 3:10,
12

21:3
h Lev 26:11-12;
Ezek 43:7;
2Cor 6:16;
Rev 7:15

21:4
i Isa 25:8; 35:10;
61:3; 65:19;
1Cor 15:26,54;
Rev 7:17; 20:14

21:5
j Isa 43:19;
2Cor 5:17;
Rev 4:2,9; 5:1;
19:9; 20:11

21:6
k Isa 12:3;
55:1 John 4:10,14;
7:37; Rev 1:8;
16:17; 22:13,17

21:7
l Zech 8:8;
Heb 8:10

21:8
m 1Cor 6:9-10;
Gal 5:19-21;
Eph 5:5; 1Tim 1:9;
Heb 12:14;
Rev 20:14-15;
22:15

presence, but no place was found for them.*a* ¹²I saw the dead, both unimportant and important, standing in front of the throne, and books were open. Another book was opened—the Book of Life. The dead were judged according to their works, as recorded in the books.*b* ¹³The sea gave up the dead that were in it, and Death and Hades gave up the dead that were in them. All were judged according to their works.*c* ¹⁴Death and Hades were thrown into the lake of fire. (This is the second death—the lake of fire.)*d* ¹⁵Anyone whose name was not found written in the Book of Life was thrown into the lake of fire.*e*

The New Heaven and the New Earth

21 ¹Then I saw a new heaven and a new earth, because the first heaven and the first earth had disappeared, and the sea was gone.*f* ²I also saw the holy city, New Jerusalem, coming down from God out of heaven, prepared like a bride adorned for her husband.*g* ³I heard a loud voice from the throne say, "See, the tabernacle of God is among humans! He will make his home with them, and they will be his people. God himself will be with them, and he will be their God.*ah* ⁴He will wipe every tear from their eyes. There won't be anymore death. There won't be any grief, crying, or pain, because the first things have disappeared."*i*

⁵The one sitting on the throne said, "See, I am making all things new!" He said, "Write this: 'These words are trustworthy and true.' "*j* ⁶Then he said to me, "It has happened! I am the Alpha and the Omega, the beginning and the end. I will freely give a drink from the spring of the water of life to the one who is thirsty.*k* ⁷The person who conquers will inherit these things. I will be his God, and he will be my son.*l* ⁸But people who are cowardly, unfaithful, detestable, murderers, sexually immoral, sorcerers, idolaters, and all liars will find themselves in*b* the lake that burns with fire and sulfur. This is the second death."*m*

---

a 21:3 Other mss. lack *and he will be their God*   **b** 21:8 Lit. *will have their part in*

The New Jerusalem

⁹Then one of the seven angels who had the seven bowls full of the seven last plagues came to me and said, "Come! I will show you the bride, the wife of the lamb."*ᵃ* ¹⁰He carried me away in the Spirit to a large, high mountain and showed me the holy city, Jerusalem, coming down from God out of heaven.*ᵇ* ¹¹It had the glory of God. Its light was like a valuable gem, like jasper, as clear as crystal.*ᶜ* ¹²It had a large, high wall with twelve gates. Twelve angels were at the gates, and the names of the twelve tribes of Israel were written on the gates.*ᵈ* ¹³There were three gates on the east, three gates on the north, three gates on the south, and three gates on the west.*ᵉ* ¹⁴The wall of the city had twelve foundations, and the twelve names of the twelve apostles of the lamb were written on them.*ᶠ*

¹⁵The angel whoᵃ was talking to me had a gold measuring rod to measure the city, its gates, and its walls.*ᵍ* ¹⁶The city was square: its length was the same as its width. He measured the city with his rod. It was 12,000 stadia long.ᵇ Its length, width, and height were the same. ¹⁷He also measured its wall. According to the human measurement that the angel was using it was 144 cubits.ᶜ ¹⁸Its wall was made of jasper. The city was made of pure gold, as clear as glass. ¹⁹The foundations of the city wall were decorated with all kinds of gems: The first foundationᵈ was jasper, the second sapphire, the third agate, the fourth emerald,*ʰ* ²⁰the fifth onyx, the sixth carnelian, the seventh chrysolite, the eighth beryl, the ninth topaz, the tenth chrysoprase, the eleventh jacinth, and the twelfth amethyst. ²¹The twelve gates were twelve pearls, and each gate was made of a single pearl. The street of the city was made of pure gold, as clear as glass.*ⁱ*

²²I saw no Temple in it, because the Lord God Almighty and the lamb are its temple.*ʲ* ²³The city doesn't need any sun or moon to give it light, because the glory of God gave it light. The lamb was its lamp.*ᵏ* ²⁴The nations will walk in its light, and the kings of the earth will bring their glory into it.*ˡ*

---

a21:15 Lit. *The one who*   b21:16 One stadion is equivalent to 607 feet.
c21:17 One cubit is equivalent to 21 inches.   d21:19 T e Gk. lacks *foundation*

21:9
ᵃRev 15:1,6-7; 19:2,7

21:10
ᵇEzek 48:1-35; Rev 1:10; 17:3; 21:2

21:11
ᶜRev 21:5,23

21:12
ᵈEzek 48:31-34

21:13
ᵉEzek 48:31-34

21:14
ᶠMatt 16:18; Gal 2:9; Eph 2:20

21:15
ᵍEzek 40:3; Zech 2:1; Rev 11:1

21:19
ʰIsa 54:11

21:21
ⁱRev 22:2

21:22
ʲJohn 4:23

21:23
ᵏIsa 24:23; 60:19-20; Rev 22:5,11

21:24
ˡIsa 60:3,5,11; 66:12

21:25
a Isa 60:11,20;
Zech 14:7;
Rev 22:5

21:26
b Rev 21:24

21:27
c Isa 35:8; 52:1;
60:21 Joel 3:17;
Phil 4:3; Rev 3:5;
13:8; 20:12;
22:14-15

22:1
d Ezek 47:1;
Zech 14:8

22:2
e Gen 2:9;
Ezek 47:12;
Rev 2:7; 21:21,24

22:3
f Ezek 48:35;
Zech 14:11

22:4
g Matt 5:8;
1Cor 13:12;
1John 3:2;
Rev 3:12; 14:1

22:5
h Ps 36:9; 84:11;
Dan 7:27;
Rom 5:17;
2Tim 2:12;
Rev 3:21; 21:23,
25

22:6
i Rev 1:1; 19:9;
21:5

22:7
j Rev 1:3; 3:10-12,
20

22:8
k Rev 19:10

22:9
l Rev 19:10

22:10
m Dan 8:26; 12:4,
9; Rev 1:3; 10:4

²⁵Its gates will never be shut by day, because there won't be any night there.*ᵃ* ²⁶People*ᵃ* will bring the glory and wealth*ᵇ* of the nations into it.*ᵇ* ²⁷Nothing unclean, or anyone who does anything detestable, and no one who tells lies will ever enter it. Only those who names are*ᶜ* written in the lamb's Book of Life will enter it.*ᵈᶜ*

The Second Coming of Christ

22 ¹Then the angel*ᵉ* showed me the river of the water of life, as clear as crystal. It was flowing from the throne of God and the lamb.*ᵈ* ²Between the street of the city and the river there was the tree of life visible from both sides. It produced twelve kinds of fruit, each month having its own fruit. The leaves of the tree are for the healing of the nations.*ᵉ* ³There will no longer be any curse. The throne of God and the lamb will be in the city.*ᶠ* His servants will worship him*ᶠ* ⁴and see his face, and his name will be on their foreheads.*ᵍ* ⁵There will be no more night, and they will not need any light from lamps or the sun because the Lord God will shine on them. They will rule forever and ever.*ʰ*

⁶He said to me, "These words are trustworthy and true. The Lord God of the spirits and of the prophets has sent his angel to show his servants the things that must happen soon."*ⁱ* ⁷"See! I am coming soon! How blessed is the person who keeps the words of the prophecy in this book!"*ʲ*

Epilogue and Benediction

⁸I, John, heard and saw these things. When I had heard and seen them, I bowed down to worship at the feet of the angel who had been showing me these things.*ᵏ* ⁹But he told me, "Don't do that! I am a fellow servant with you, your brothers the prophets, and those who keep the words in this book. Worship God!"*ˡ*

¹⁰Then he said to me, "Don't seal up the words of the prophecy in this book, because the time is near.*ᵐ* ¹¹Let the one who does what is evil continue to do evil, and let the

---

a 21:26 Lit. *They*   b 21:26 Or *honor*   c 21:27 Lit. *those who are*
d 21:27 The Gk. lacks *will enter it*   e 22:1 Lit. *he*   f 22:3 Lit. *in it*

filthy person continue to be filthy, and the righteous person continue to do what is right, and the holy person continue to be holy."*a*

12"See! I am coming soon! My reward is with me to repay everyone according to his work.*b* 13I am the Alpha and the Omega, the first and the last, the beginning and the end."*c*

14How blessed are those who wash their robes**a** so that they may have the right to the tree of life and may go through the gates into the city!*d* 15Outside are dogs, sorcerers, immoral people, murderers, idolaters, and everyone who loves and practices falsehood.*e*

16"I, Jesus, have sent my angel to give this testimony to you for the churches. I am the root and descendent of David, the bright morning star."*f*

17The Spirit and the bride say, "Come!" Let everyone who hears this say, "Come!" Let everyone who is thirsty come! Let anyone who wants the water of life take it as a gift!*g* 18I warn everyone who hears the words of the prophecy in this book: If anyone adds anything to them, God will strike him with the plagues that are written in this book.*h* 19If anyone takes away any words from the book of this prophecy, God will take away his portion of the tree of life and the holy city that are described in this book.*i*

20The one who is testifying to these things says, "Yes, I am coming soon!" Amen! Come, Lord Jesus!*j*

21May the grace of the Lord Jesus be with all the saints. Amen.**b***k*

---

a22:14 Other mss. read *who do his commandments*   **b**22:21 Other mss. lack *Amen*

22:11
*a*Ezek 3:27;
Dan 12:10;
2Tim 3:13

22:12
*b*Isa 40:10; 62:11;
Rom 2:6; 14:12;
Rev 20:12; 22:7

22:13
*c*Isa 41:4; 44:6;
48:12; Rev 1:8,11;
21:6

22:14
*d*Dan 12:12;
1John 3:24;
Rev 2:7; 3:2;
21:27

22:15
*e*1Cor 6:9-10;
Gal 5:19-21;
Phil 3:2; Col 3:6;
Rev 9:20-21; 21:8

22:16
*f*Num 24:17;
Zech 6:12;
2Peter 1:19;
Rev 1:1; 2:28; 5:5

22:17
*g*Isa 55:1;
John 7:37;
Rev 21:2,6,9

22:18
*h*Deut 4:2;
12:32 Prov 30:6

22:19
*i*Exod 32:33;
Ps 69:28; Rev 3:5;
13:8; 21:2

22:20
*j*John 21:25;
2Tim 4:8;
Rev 22:12

22:21
*k*Rom 16:20,24;
2Thes 3:18

Appendix

The Value of a Talent as a Monetary Unit
The Parable of the Talents Illustrated in U.S. Dollars

If...	1	day's wages	=	1	drachma[1]
and	1	shekel	=	4	drachma
and	1	mina	=	60	shekels
and	1	talent	=	60	mina
then	1	talent	=	14,400	drachma[2]
and	1	talent	=	14,400	days' wages
If	1	year	=	250	days of work[3]
then	14,400	days	=	57.6	years of work
If	1	year's wages	=	\$45,922[4]	
then	1	talent	=	\$2,645,107[5]	
and	10,000	talents	=	\$26,451,070,000	

[1]One drachma was equal to one Greek denarius.
[2]60 mina x 60 shekels x 4 drachma = 14,400 drachma.
[3]Assumes 52 weeks per year, with 5 work days per week, less 2 weeks' vacation.
[4]Orange County, California, median family income, 1990 census.
[5]\$45,922 per year x 57.6 years.

Weights and Values

1	gerah	=	.6	grams
1	shekel[1]	=	12	grams
1	mina	=	600	grams
1	talent[2]	=	36,000	grams

[1]One shekel equals 20 gerahs.
[2]The weight of a talent varied from 50 shekels (1 Kings 10:17) to 60 shekels (Ezek 45:12) depending on monetary inflation.

The Parables of Jesus

Parable	Matthew	Mark	Luke
A Light under a Basket	5:14	4:21	8:16
The Two Foundations	7:24		6:47
The Unshrunk Cloth	9:16	2:21	5:36
New Wine in Old Wineskins	9:17	2:22	5:37
The Parable about a Sower	13:3	4:3	8:5
The Parable about the Weeds among the Wheat	13:24		
The Parables about a Mustard Seed and Yeast	13:31	4:30	13:18
The Parable about a Hidden Treasure	13:44		
The Parable about a Valuable Pearl	13:45		

Parable	Matthew	Mark	Luke
The Parable about a Net	13:47		
New and Old Treasures	13:52		
The Parable about a Lost Sheep	18:12		15:4
The Parable about an Unforgiving Servant	18:23		
The Workers in the Vineyard	20:1		
The Parable about Two Sons	21:28		
The Parable about the Tenant Farmers	21:33	12:1	20:9
The Parable about a Wedding Banquet	22:2		
The Lesson from the Fig Tree	24:32	13:28	21:29
The Faithful or the Wicked Servant	24:45		12:42
The Parable about the Ten Bridesmaids	25:1		
The Parable about the Talents	25:14		19:12
The Sheep and Goats	25:31		
The Parable about a Growing Seed		4:26	
The Watchful Servants		13:35	12:35
The Creditor			7:41
The Good Samaritan			10:30
A Friend in Need			11:5
The Parable of the Rich Fool			12:16
The Parable about an Unfruitful Fig Tree			13:6
A Lesson about Guests			14:7
The Parable about a Large Banquet			14:16
The Cost of Discipleship			14:28
The Story of the Diligent Housewife			15:8
The Story of the Loving Father and the Prodigal son			15:11
The Parable about a Dishonest Manager			16:1
The Rich Man and Lazarus			16:19
A Master and His Servant			17:7
The Parable about the Judge and the Widow			18:2
The Parable about the Pharisee and the Tax Collector			18:10

The Miracles of Jesus

Miracle	Matthew	Mark	Luke	John
Jesus Cleanses a Leper	8:2	1:40	5:12	
Jesus Heals a Centurion's Servant	8:5		7:1	
Jesus Heals Peter's Mother-in-law	8:14	1:30	4:38	
Jesus Heals Two Demon-Possessed Men	8:28	5:1	8:27	
Jesus Heals a Paralyzed Man	9:2	2:3	5:18	
Jesus Heals Jairus' Daughter and a Woman with Chronic Bleeding	9:20	5:25	8:43	

Miracle	Matthew	Mark	Luke	John
Jesus Heals Two Blind Men	9:27			
Jesus Heals a Man Who Couldn't Talk	9:32			
Jesus Heals a Man with a Paralyzed Hand	12:10	3:1	6:6	
Jesus Heals a Blind and Mute Man	12:22		11:14	
The Faith of a Woman from Syria	15:21	7:24		
Jesus Heals a Boy with a Demon	17:14	9:17	9:38	
Jesus Heals Two Blind Men	20:29	10:46	18:35	
Jesus Heals a Man with an Unclean Spirit		1:23	4:33	
Jesus Heals a Deaf Man with a Speech Impediment		8:22		
Jesus Heals a Woman on the Sabbath			13:11	
Jesus Heals a Man on the Sabbath			14:1	
Jesus Cleanses Ten Lepers			17:11	
Jesus Heals the Ear of the High Priest's Servant			22:50	
Jesus Heals an Official's Son				4:46
The Healing at the Pool				5:1
Jesus Heals a Blind Man				9:1
Jesus Calms the Sea	8:23	4:37	8:22	
Jesus Walks on the Sea	14:25	6:48		6:19
Jesus Feeds More Than Five Thousand People	14:15	6:35	9:12	6:5
Jesus Feeds More Than Four Thousand People	15:32	8:1		
The Coin in the Fish	17:24			
Jesus Curses a Fig Tree	21:18	11:12		
The Large Catch of Fish			5:4	21:1
Jesus Changes Water into Wine				2:1
Jesus Raises a Widow's Son			7:11	
Jesus Brings Lazarus Back to Life				11:1

The Miracles of the Apostles

Miracle	Acts
A Crippled Man Is Healed	3:6-9
Ananias and Sapphira Are Punished	5:1-10
Saul's Sight Is Restored	9:17-18
Aeneas Is Healed	9:33-35
Tabitha Is Healed	9:36-41
Elymas Is Blinded	13:8-11
A Crippled Man Is Healed	14:8-10

Miracle	*Acts*
A Demon Is Driven out of a Girl	16:16-18
The Raising of Eutychus	20:9-10
Paul Is Unharmed by a Viper	28:3-5
Healing of Publius' Father	28:7-9

What the New Testament Says About...

Adultery
| Matt 5:27-32 | Galatians 5:13 | Eph 4:17-5:3 | |

Ambition
| Matt 16:21-27 | Mark 9:33-37 | Mark 10:35-45 | Phil 2:1-4 |

Anger
| Matt 5:21-26 | Eph 4:25-5:2 | James 1:19-27 | |

Anxiety
| Luke 12:22-34 | Phil 4:4-9 | Heb 13:5-6 | |

Atonement
| Romans 3:21-26 | 2 Cor 5:14-21 | Heb 9 | 1 Peter 2:22-25 |

Baptism
| Matt 3:1-12 | Matt 28:16-20 | Romans 6:1-5 | |

Bible Reading
| 2 Tim 3:14-17 | Heb 4:12 | James 1:19-27 | |

Blood of Christ
| Matt 26:27-29 | Heb 9:11-28 | | |

Body of Christ
| Mark 14:22-24 | 1 Cor 12:12-31 | Heb 2:14-18 | |

Celibacy
| Matt 19:4-12 | 1 Cor 7:32-40 | 1 Tim 4:1-5 | |

Children
| Matt 18:1-9 | Mark 10:13-16 | Eph 6:1-4 | |

Compassion
| John 11:17-44 | 2 Cor 1:3-7 | 1 John 3:11-24 | |

Conversion
| John 3:1-21 | 2 Cor 5:17-19 | Eph 2:1-10 | |

Creation
| Rom 1:18-23 | Rom 8:18-27 | Col 1:15-17 | |

Cross
| Mark 8:31-9:1 | Luke 23:26-49 | | |

Death
| John 12:23-26 | Rom 6:1-23 | 1 Cor 15 | |

Discipleship
| Luke 14:25-34 | John 15:1-17 | John 21:15-19 | |

Discipline
| 1 Cor 11:27-32 | Heb 12:1-13 | Rev 3:19 | |

What the New Testament Says About...

Divorce
    Matt 19:1-12   Mark 10:2-12   1 Cor 7:10-16

Eternal Life
    Matt 19:16-30   John 3:1-21   Rom 6:15-23

Faith
    Matt 6:25-34   Rom 3:21-5:11   Heb 11

Freedom
    John 8:31-41   Rom 8:1-17   Gal 4:21-5:26

Friendship
    John 14:23-15:17   Col 3:12-17   1 John 1:1-7

Giving
    Matt 6:1-4   2 Cor 8-9

Grace
    Luke 15:11-31   Rom 5   Eph 2

Greed
    Luke 12:13-21   1 Tim 6:3-10   James 5:1-6

Happiness
    Matt 5:1-12   John 13:1-17   Phil 4:4-9

Heaven
    Matt 6:19-24   Matt 25:31-46   Phil 3:12-4:1

Holy Spirit
    John 14:15-31   John 16:5-16   Acts 2   Rom 8:1-17

Homosexuality
    Rom 1:18-32   1 Cor 6:9-11   1 Tim 1:9-11

Hope
    Rom 5:1-11   Col 1:3-27   1 Peter 1:3-9

Hospitality
    Luke 14:12-14   Rom 12:13   1 Peter 4:9

Hypocrisy
    Matt 6:1-24   Matt 23   James 1:22-27

Joy
    Luke 15   James 1:2-18   1 Peter 4:12-19

Justification
    Rom 3:21-31   Rom 4:1-5:11   Gal 2:15-21

Loneliness
    Matt 26:36-46   2 Tim 4:16-18

Lord's Supper
    Luke 22:7-23   John 13:1   1 Cor 11:17-34

Love
    Mark 12:28-34   1 Cor 13   1 John 4:7-21

Marriage
    Matt 19:1-12   1 Cor 7   Eph 5:22-33

What the New Testament Says About...

Peace

John 14:25-27	Rom 5:1-11	Eph 2:14-18	Phil 4:4-9

Poor

Matt 25:31-46	Luke 1:39-56	James 2:1-13

Profanity

Eph 4:29-32	James 3:1-12

Reconciliation

Matt 5:23-26	2 Cor 5:11-6:2	Eph 2:11-12

Repentance

Matt 4:12-17	Luke 18:9-14	Acts 2:38-41

Resurrection

Matt 27:57-28:20	1 Cor 15

Revenge

Matt 5:38-47	Rom 12:17-21

Reward

Matt 5:3-12	Mark 10:29-31	1 Cor 3:10-15

Salvation

Luke 19:1-10	Acts 16:16-34	Eph 2:1-10

Sanctification

2 Cor 7:1	1 Thes 5:23	2 Peter 1:3-11

Second Coming

Matt 24	John 14:1-4	1 Cor 15:12-28	1 Thes 4:13-5:11

Stewardship

Matt 25:14-30	Luke 12:35-48

Suffering

Rom 8:12-17	1 Peter 3:8-22	1 Peter 4:12-19

Unity

John 17	Eph 4:1-16

What to Do When...

The future seems hopeless

1 Cor 15:20-28	1 Peter 1:1-9	1 Peter 5:10-11	Rev 11:15-19

Seeking God's direction

Rom 12:1-3	Eph 5:15-17	Col 1:9-14	James 1:5-8

You need comfort

John 14	2 Cor 1:3-7	2 Cor 7:6-13

Others disagree with you

Matt 7:1-5	Rom 12:9-21	Rom 14:1-15:7	2 Cor 5:11-21

The world seems enticing

2 Cor 6:14-7:1	James 1:26-27	James 4:4-10	1 John 2:15-17

You need assurance of salvation

John 3:14-21	John 11:25-26	Acts 16:31-34	1 John 5:9-13

What to Do When...

Others have sinned against you
Matt 6:14-15   Matt 18:21-35   Col 3:12-14

You are tempted to be bitter
1 Cor 13   Eph 4:29-5:2   Heb 12:14-15

You are tempted to neglect public worship
Acts 2:42-47   Heb 10:19-25

Your faith needs strengthening
Rom 5:1-11   1 Cor 9:24-27   Heb 10:19-39   Heb 11:1-12:13

You need to control your tongue
Matt 15:1-20   James 3:1-12

You want to judge others
Matt 7:1-5   1 Cor 4:1-5   James 2:1-13   James 4:11-12

You have been cheated
Matt 18:15-17   1 Cor 6:1-8   James 5:1-8   1 Peter 3:8-17

Things are going well
Luke 12:13-21   1 Tim 6:3-19   Heb 13:5   James 2:1-17

You wonder about your spiritual gifts
Rom 12:3-8   1 Cor 1:4-9   1 Cor 12:1-14   1 Peter 4:7-11

You are starting a new job
Matt 5:13-16   Rom 12:1-2   Gal 5:13-26   Eph 1:3-14

You are in a position of responsibility
Mark 10:35-45   Luke 7:1-10   1 Cor 16:13-14   Gal 6:9-10

You are establishing a new home
Eph 5:22-6:4   Col 3:18-21   1 Peter 3:1-7

You have been arguing with someone
1 Cor 3   Eph 4:1-6   2 Tim 2:14-26   James 4:1-12

You are in spiritual warfare
Rom 8:38-39   2 Cor 4:7-18   Eph 6:10-18   2 Tim 4:6-7

You are jealous
Gal 5:13-15   Gal 5:19-21   James 3:13-18

You struggle with laziness
Eph 5:15-16   Phil 2:12-13   1 Thes 4:1-12   2 Thes 3:6-15

You struggle with lust
Matt 5:27-30   Rom 7:7-25   Rom 13:8-14   James 1:13-18

You are angry
Matt 5:21-22   Matt 18:21-26   Eph 4:25-5:2   James 1:19-21

You want revenge
Matt 5:38-42   Rom 12:17-21   1 Thes 5:12-15   1 Peter 3:8-14

You are proud
Matt 25:34-40   Mark 10:35-45   Rom 12:3   Phil 2:1-11

You are addicted to drugs or alcohol
Rom 6:1-23   Rom 12:1-2   1 Cor 6:12-20   Phil 3:17-4:1

What to Do When...

You are greedy
   Luke 12:13-21   2 Cor 9:6-15   Eph 5:3-7   1 John 3:16-18

You want to learn to pray
   Matt 6:5-15   Mark 11:22-25   Luke 18:9-14   Phil 4:4-7

You struggle with apathy
   Matt 25:1-13   Luke 12:35-48   1 Thes 5:1-11   Rev 3:1-6,14-22

Literary Sources Quoted in the New Testament

Reference	*Source*
Acts 17:28	Aratus, *Phainomena* (5)
Acts 17:28	Cleanthese the Stoic
1 Corinthians 15:33	Menander, *Thais* (218)
Titus 1:12	Epimenides
Jude 1:9	The Assumption of Moses
Jude 1:15	Enoch 1:9 (The Apocrypha)

Using the CD-ROM

Your International Standard Version New Testament includes a CD-ROM containing the entire text of the ISV New Testament. It is designed to run under the Windows 95™ or Windows 98™ operating system.

Technical support for the software is provided by the software publisher. If you have questions about installing or using the software on the CD-ROM, or for technical assistance with the software, refer to the information on the label of the CD-ROM. *Please note that Davidson Press does not provide any technical support for the software; please do not contact Davidson Press with questions about installing or using the software.*

It is the policy of Davidson Press to provide free updates to the text of the International Standard Version Bible to all users via the Internet. Please visit the Davidson Press website at http://davidsonpress.com on a regular basis. From our website, you can review our exclusive Change Tables, which document all of the changes made in the ISV text as new version numbers are released. Whenever a new version number of the ISV text is released, you will be able to download it at no charge from the Davidson Press website and from a limited number of mirror sites all around the world.

Read Through the ISV New Testament in One Year

	January	February	March
1	Matt 1:1-25	Matt 20:17-34	Mark 7:24-8:10
2	Matt 2:1-23	Matt 21:1-22	Mark 8:11-30
3	Matt 3:1-17	Matt 21:23-46	Mark 8:31-9:13
4	Matt 4:1-17	Matt 22:1-22	Mark 9:14-32
5	Matt 4:18-5:16	Matt 22:23-46	Mark 9:33-10:12
6	Matt 5:17-5:37	Matt 23:1-36	Mark 10:13-31
7	Matt 5:38-6:18	Matt 23:37-24:14	Mark 10:32-52
8	Matt 6:19-34	Matt 24:15-31	Mark 11:1-26
9	Matt 7:1-23	Matt 24:32-51	Mark 11:27-12:17
10	Matt 7:24-8:17	Matt 25:1-30	Mark 12:18-37
11	Matt 8:18-9:8	Matt 25:31-26:5	Mark 12:38-13:13
12	Matt 9:9-34	Matt 26:6-35	Mark 13:14-37
13	Matt 9:35-10:15	Matt 26:36-56	Mark 14:1-26
14	Matt 10:16-42	Matt 26:57-75	Mark 14:27-52
15	Matt 11:1-24	Matt 27:1-26	Mark 14:53-72
16	Matt 11:25-12:21	Matt 27:27-56	Mark 15:1-20
17	Matt 12:22-37	Matt 27:57-28:20	Mark 15:21-47
18	Matt 12:38-50	Mark 1:1-20	Mark 16:1-20
19	Matt 13:1-23	Mark 1:21-45	John 1:1-34
20	Matt 13:24-35	Mark 2:1-22	John 1:35-51
21	Matt 13:36-58	Mark 2:23-3:19	John 2:1-25
22	Matt 14:1-21	Mark 3:20-4:9	John 3:1-21
23	Matt 14:22-15:20	Mark 4:10-34	John 3:22-36
24	Matt 15:21-39	Mark 4:35-5:20	John 4:1-42
25	Matt 16:1-20	Mark 5:21-43	John 4:43-54
26	Matt 16:21-17:13	Mark 6:1-29	John 5:1-30
27	Matt 17:14-27	Mark 6:30-56	John 5:31-6:15
28	Matt 18:1-20	Mark 7:1-23	John 6:16-59
29	Matt 18:21-19:12		John 6:60-7:9
30	Matt 19:13-30		John 7:10-31
31	Matt 20:1-20:16		John 7:32-53

When you visit the Davidson Press internet site at **http://davidsonpress.com,** you can register to receive each of these daily readings free every day via email. You can also link to Davidson Press from Learn Foundation's site at **http://isv.org.**

Read Through the ISV New Testament in One Year

	April	May	June
1	John 8:1-20	Luke 2:21-52	Luke 16:19-17:10
2	John 8:21-36	Luke 3:1-20	Luke 17:11-37
3	John 8:37-59	Luke 3:21-4:13	Luke 18:1-30
4	John 9:1-12	Luke 4:14-30	Luke 18:31-19:10
5	John 9:13-41	Luke 4:31-5:11	Luke 19:11-27
6	John 10:1-21	Luke 5:12-26	Luke 19:28-48
7	John 10:22-42	Luke 5:27-6:11	Luke 20:1-26
8	John 11:1-16	Luke 6:12-36	Luke 20:27-21:4
9	John 11:17-44	Luke 6:37-7:10	Luke 21:5-38
10	John 11:45-12:8	Luke 7:11-35	Luke 22:1-23
11	John 12:9-36	Luke 7:36-50	Luke 22:24-46
12	John 12:37-50	Luke 8:1-18	Luke 22:47-71
13	John 13:1-30	Luke 8:19-39	Luke 23:1-25
14	John 13:31-14:14	Luke 8:40-56	Luke 23:26-56
15	John 14:15-31	Luke 9:1-17	Luke 24:1-35
16	John 15:1-16:4	Luke 9:18-36	Luke 24:36-53
17	John 16:5-33	Luke 9:37-56	Acts 1:1-26
18	John 17:1-26	Luke 9:57-10:16	Acts 2:1-13
19	John 18:1-18	Luke 10:17-37	Acts 2:14-41
20	John 18:19-40	Luke 10:38-11:13	Acts 2:42-3:10
21	John 19:1-16	Luke 11:14-36	Acts 3:11-26
22	John 19:17-27	Luke 11:37-54	Acts 4:1-22
23	John 19:28-42	Luke 12:1-21	Acts 4:23-5:11
24	John 20:1-23	Luke 12:22-34	Acts 5:12-42
25	John 20:24-21:14	Luke 12:35-53	Acts 6:1-15
26	John 21:15-25	Luke 12:54-13:17	Acts 7:1-23
27	Luke 1:1-25	Luke 13:18-35	Acts 7:24-53
28	Luke 1:26-56	Luke 14:1-24	Acts 7:54-8:3
29	Luke 1:57-80	Luke 14:25-15:10	Acts 8:4-25
30	Luke 2:1-20	Luke 15:11-32	Acts 8:26-40
31		Luke 16:1-18	

When you visit the Davidson Press internet site at **http://davidsonpress.com,** you can register to receive each of these daily readings free every day via email. You can also link to Davidson Press from Learn Foundation's site at **http://isv.org.**

Read Through the ISV New Testament in One Year

	July	August	September
1	Acts 9:1-31	Acts 27:27-44	1 Cor 9:1-27
2	Acts 9:32-10:8	Acts 28:1-16	1 Cor 10:1-22
3	Acts 10:9-23	Acts 28:17-31	1 Cor 10:23-23
4	Acts 10:24-48	Romans 1:1-17	1 Cor 11:1-34
5	Acts 11:1-30	Romans 1:18-32	1 Cor 12:1-31
6	Acts 12:1-25	Romans 2:1-16	1 Cor 13:1-13
7	Acts 13:1-12	Romans 2:17-29	1 Cor 14:1-25
8	Acts 13:13-52	Romans 3:1-20	1 Cor 14:26-15:11
9	Acts 14:1-18	Romans 3:21-4:12	1 Cor 15:12-58
10	Acts 14:19-28	Romans 4:13-5:11	1 Cor 16:1-24
11	Acts 15:1-21	Romans 5:12-6:23	2 Cor 1:1-24
12	Acts 15:22-16:10	Romans 7:1-25	2 Cor 2:1-17
13	Acts 16:11-40	Romans 8:1-30	2 Cor 3:1-18
14	Acts 17:1-14	Romans 8:30-39	2 Cor 4:1-18
15	Acts 17:15-34	Romans 9:1-33	2 Cor 5:1-21
16	Acts 18:1-17	Romans 10:1-21	2 Cor 6:1-7:1
17	Acts 18:18-28	Romans 11:1-36	2 Cor 7:2-8:15
18	Acts 19:1-22	Romans 12:1-21	2 Cor 8:16-9:15
19	Acts 19:23-40	Romans 13:1-14	2 Cor 10:1-18
20	Acts 20:1-16	Romans 14:1-23	2 Cor 11:1-15
21	Acts 20:17-38	Romans 15:1-13	2 Cor 11:16-12:10
22	Acts 21:1-14	Romans 15:14-33	2 Cor 12:11-13:13
23	Acts 21:15-36	Romans 16:1-27	Galatians 1:1-24
24	Acts 21:37-22:29	1 Cor 1:1-31	Galatians 2:1-21
25	Acts 22:30-23:11	1 Cor 2:1-16	Galatians 3:1-29
26	Acts 23:12-35	1 Cor 3:1-23	Galatians 4:1-31
27	Acts 24:1-27	1 Cor 4:1-21	Galatians 5:1-26
28	Acts 25:1-12	1 Cor 5:1-6:11	Galatians 6:1-18
29	Acts 25:13-27	1 Cor 6:12-7:16	Eph 1:1-14
30	Acts 26:1-32	1 Cor 7:17-40	Eph 1:15-2:10
31	Acts 27:1-26	1 Cor 8:1-13	

When you visit the Davidson Press internet site at **http://davidsonpress.com,** you can register to receive each of these daily readings free every day via email. You can also link to Davidson Press from Learn Foundation's site at **http://isv.org.**

Read Through the ISV New Testament in One Year

	October	November	December
1	Eph 2:11-3:21	Heb 1:1-2:4	1 John 2:28-3:24
2	Eph 4:1-24	Heb 2:5-18	1 John 4:1-21
3	Eph 4:25-5:14	Heb 3:1-19	1 John 5:1-21
4	Eph 5:15-6:9	Heb 4:1-16	2 John 1-13
5	Eph 6:10-24	Heb 5:1-6:8	3 John 1-14
6	Phil 1:1-30	Heb 6:9-20	Jude 1-13
7	Phil 2:1-30	Heb 7:1-28	Jude 14-25
8	Phil 3:1-21	Heb 8:1-13	Rev 1:1-20
9	Phil 4:1-23	Heb 9:1-22	Rev 2:1-17
10	Col 1:1-23	Heb 9:23-10:18	Rev 2:18-3:6
11	Col 1:24-2:19	Heb 10:19-39	Rev 3:7-22
12	Col 2:20-3:17	Heb 11:1-40	Rev 4:1-11
13	Col 3:18-4:18	Heb 12:1-11	Rev 5:1-14
14	1 Thes 1:1-2:12	Heb 12:12-29	Rev 6:1-17
15	1 Thes 2:13-3:13	Heb 13:1-25	Rev 7:1-17
16	1 Thes 4:1-18	James 1:1-27	Rev 8:1-13
17	1 Thes 5:1-28	James 2:1-26	Rev 9:1-21
18	2 Thes 1:1-12	James 3:1-18	Rev 10:1-11
19	2 Thes 2:1-3:18	James 4:1-5:6	Rev 11:1-19
20	1 Timothy 1:1-20	James 5:7-20	Rev 12:1-18
21	1 Timothy 2:1-3:16	1 Peter 1:1-21	Rev 13:1-18
22	1 Timothy 4:1-16	1 Peter 1:22-2:10	Rev 14:1-21
23	1 Timothy 5:1-6:2	1 Peter 2:11-25	Rev 15:1-8
24	1 Timothy 6:3-21	1 Peter 3:1-22	Rev 16:1-21
25	2 Timothy 1:1-18	1 Peter 4:1-5:14	Rev 17:1-18
26	2 Timothy 2:1-26	2 Peter 1:1-21	Rev 18:1-24
27	2 Timothy 3:1-4:8	2 Peter 2:1-22	Rev 19:1-21
28	2 Timothy 4:9-22	2 Peter 3:1-18	Rev 20:1-15
29	Titus 1:1-16	1 John 1:1-2:6	Rev 21:1-8
30	Titus 2:1-3:15	1 John 2:7-27	Rev 21:9-22:5
31	Philemon 1-25		Rev 22:6-21

When you visit the Davidson Press internet site at **http://davidsonpress.com,** you can register to receive each of these daily readings free every day via email. You can also link to Davidson Press from Learn Foundation's site at **http://isv.org.**

Index to Maps

1. The Biblical World
2. New Testament Palestine
3. Paul's First Missionary Journey
4. Paul's Second Missionary Journey
5. Paul's Third Missionary Journey
6. Paul's Journey to Rome

City	Map	City	Map	City	Map
Adramyttium	6	Cos	4-5	Phasaelis	2
Aleppo	1	Cyrene	1, 3-6	Philadelphia	2
Alexandria	3-6	Damascus	1-2, 6	Philippi	4-5
Amphipolis	4	Derbe	3-5	Ptolemais	2, 5
Antioch (Pisidian)	2-6	Ecbetana	1	Puteoli	6
Antioch (Syrian)	3-5	Elath	1-2	Qumran	2
Antipatris	2	Emmaus	2	Ramoth-gilead	1
Apollonia (Greece)	4	Ephesus	1, 3-6	Rhegium	6
Apollonia (Palestine)	2	Fair Havens	6	Rhodes	3-5
Ashkelon	2	Gaza	1-2	Rome	6
Asshur	1	Gerasa	2	Salamis	1-6
Athens	1, 3-6	Gozan	1	Salmone	2
Attalia	3-5	Hebron	2	Samaria	2
Azotus	2	Hippus	2	Samothrace	4-5
Babylon	1	Iconium	3-5	Sardis	1, 3-5
Beersheba	2	Jericho	2	Seleucia	3-6
Beroea	4-5	Jerusalem	1-6	Sepphoris	2
Berytus	2	Lasea	6	Sidon	2, 6
Bethany	2	Lystra	3-5	Smyrna	4-5
Bethany (By the Jordan)	2	Machaerus	2	Sparta	1
Bethlehem	2	Masada	2	Susa	1
Bethsaida	2	Memphis	1	Syracuse	6
Caesarea	2-6	Miletus	3-5	Tarsus	1, 3-6
Calah	1	Myra	6	Thebes	1
Cana	2	Nain	2	Thessalonica	3-6
Capernaum	2	Nazareth	2	Three Taverns	6
Carchemish	1	Neapolis	4	Thyatira	4
Cauda	6	Nineveh	1	Tiberias	2
Cenchrea	4-5	Nippur	1	Troas	4-5
Caesarea Philippi	2	Paphos	2-6	Tyre	1, 2, 5
Chorazin	2	Pasargadae	1	Ur	1
Cnidus	6	Perga	3-5		
Corinth	3-6	Pergamum	3-5		

Country or Region	Map	Sea	Map	Mountain	Map
Achea	3-6	Adriatic Sea	6	Mt. Ararat	1
Arabia	2	Aegean Sea	3-6	Mt. Carmel	2
Asia	3-6	Aqaba, Gulf of	2	Mt. Gerazim	2
Bithynia and Pontus	3-6	Aral Sea	1	Mt. Gilboa	2
Cilicia	3-6	Black Sea	1	Mt. Hermon	2
Crete	3-6	Caspian Sea	1	Mt. Hor	2
Cyprus	2-6	Dead Sea	2	Mt. Lebanon	2
Cyrenacia	3-6	Erythracan Sea	1	Mt. Nebo	2
Decapolis	2	Galilee, Sea of	2	Mt. Seir	2
Galatia	3-6	Mediterranean Sea	1-6	Mt. Tabor	2
Galilee	2	Persian Gulf	1		
Egypt	3-6	Red Sea	1-2		
Idumea	2				
Italia	6	River or Well	Map		
Judea	2				
Lycaonia	3-6	Euphrates	1		
Macedonia	3-6	Indus	1		
Malta	6	Jacob's Well	2		
Mysia	3-6	Jaxartes	1		
Nabatea	2	Jordan River	2		
Pamphylia	3-6	Nile	1		
Perea	2	Oxus	1		
Phrygia	3-6	Tigris	1		
Phoenicia	2				
Pisidia	3-6				
Samaria	2				
Sicilia	6				
Sinai	2				
Syria	2-6				
Trachonitis	2				

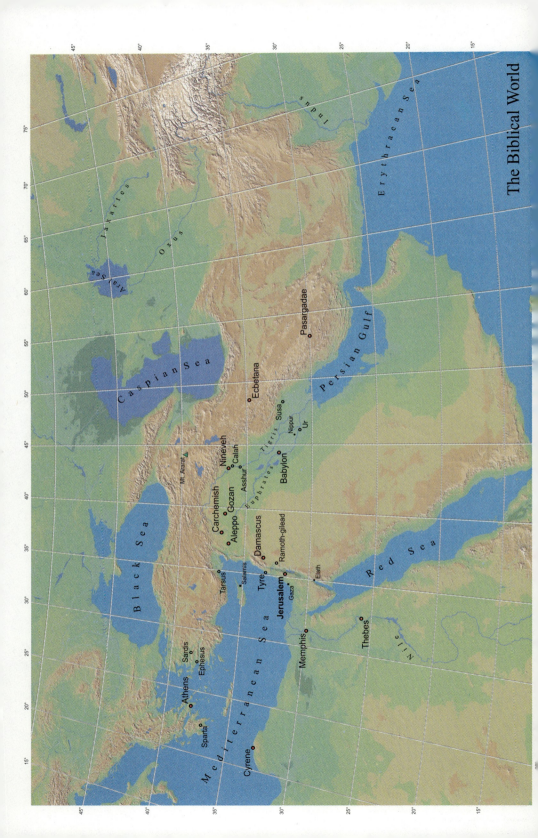

The Biblical World

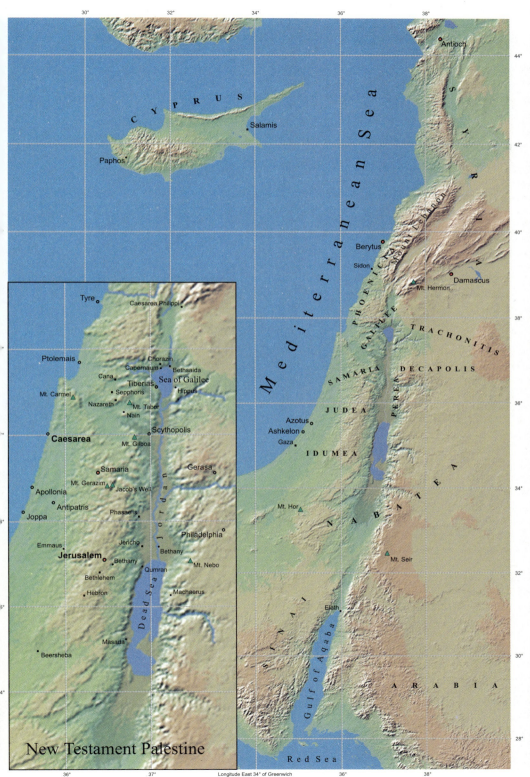

New Testament Palestine

Mercator Projection • Map Copyright © 1999 • Logos Research Systems, Inc. • www.logos.com

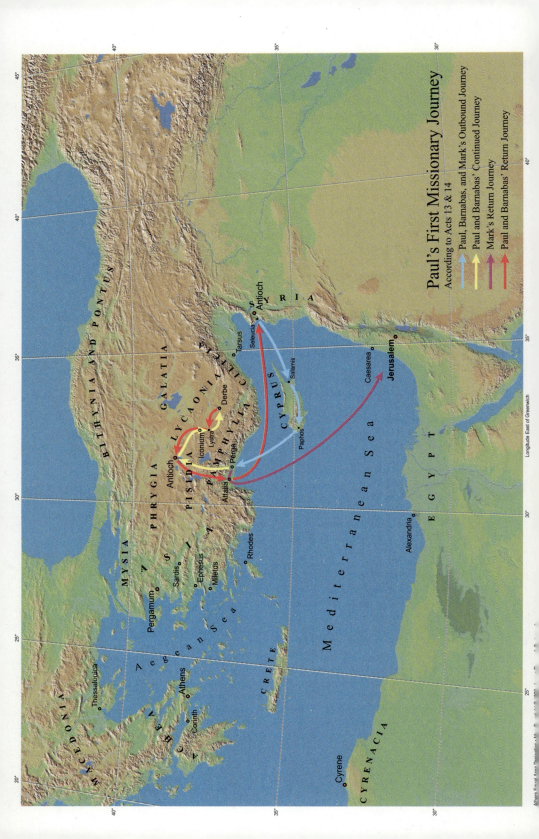

Paul's First Missionary Journey

According to Acts 13 & 14

Paul, Barnabas, and Mark's Outbound Journey

Paul and Barnabas' Continued Journey

Mark's Return Journey

Paul and Barnabas' Return Journey

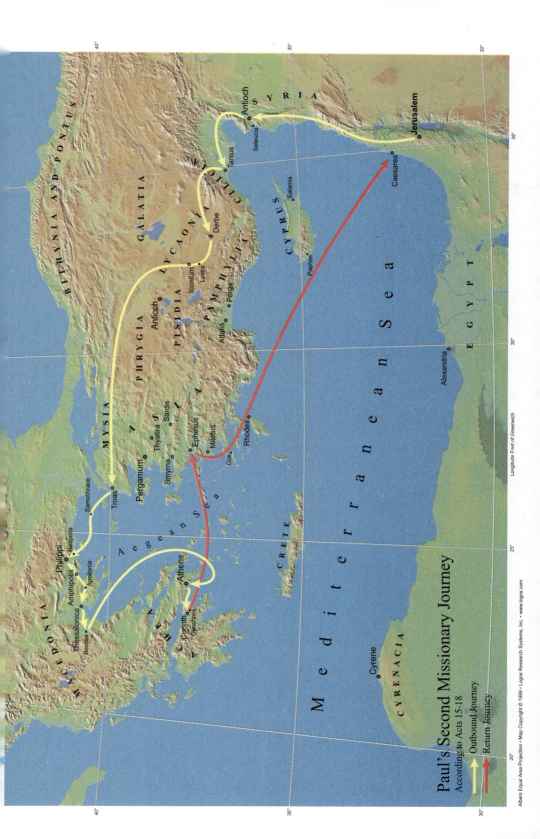

Paul's Second Missionary Journey

According to Acts 15–18

Outbound Journey

Return Journey

Albers Equal Area Projection • Map Copyright © 1999 - Logos Research Systems, Inc. • www.logos.com

Longitude East of Greenwich

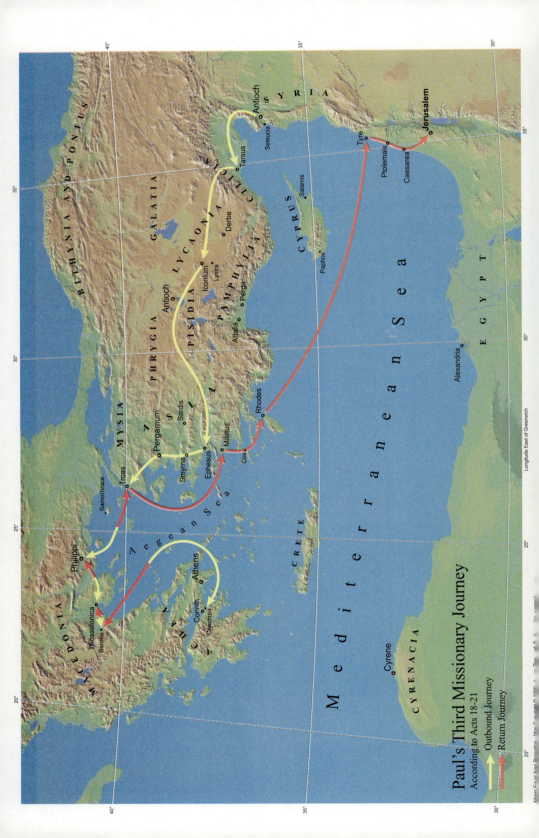

Paul's Third Missionary Journey
According to Acts 18–21

Outbound Journey

Return Journey

Mediterranean Sea

Aegean Sea

BITHYNIA AND PONTUS

GALATIA

MYSIA

PHRYGIA

PISIDIA

LYCAONIA

A

PAMPHYLIA

CILICIA

SYRIA

CYPRUS

CRETE

EGYPT

MACEDONIA

ACHAEA

CYRENAICA

Antioch

Seleucia

Tarsus

Derbe

Iconium

Lystra

Antioch

Attalia

Perga

Miletus

Cos

Rhodes

Ephesus

Smyrna

Sardis

Pergamum

Troas

Samothrace

Philippi

Thessalonica

Beroea

Corinth

Cenchrea

Athens

Salamis

Paphos

Tyre

Ptolemais

Caesarea

Jerusalem

Alexandria

Cyrene

Longitude East of Greenwich

Albers Equal Area Projection

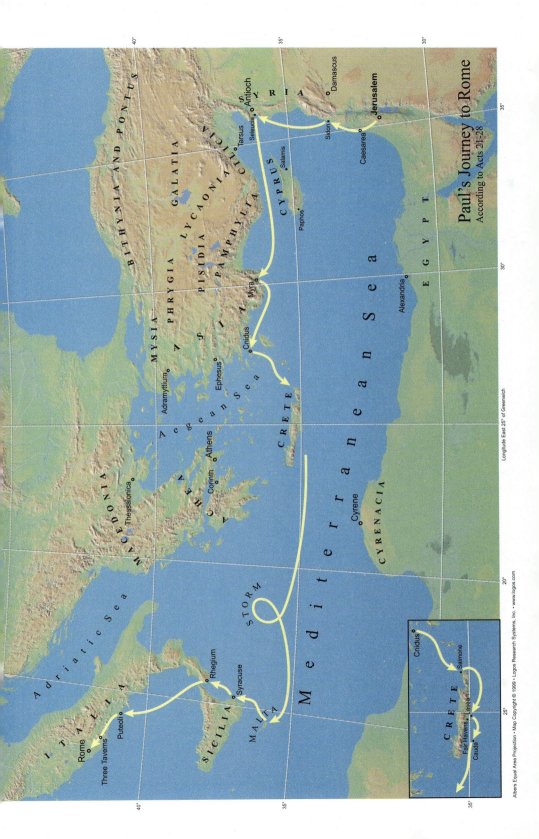

Paul's Journey to Rome
According to Acts 21–28